SUNDERLAND COLLEGE

0015837

EL
428
THO

FOR
REFERENCE ONLY

D0247859

MASTERING

Advanced English Language

Second edition

Sara Thorne

CITY OF
LEARNING
CENTRE
SUNDERLAND COLLEGE

palgrave
macmillan

© Sara Thorne 1997, 2008

All rights reserved. No reproduction, copy or transmission of this publication may be made without written permission.

No paragraph of this publication may be reproduced, copied or transmitted save with written permission or in accordance with the provisions of the Copyright, Designs and Patents Act 1988, or under the terms of any licence permitting limited copying issued by the Copyright Licensing Agency, 90 Tottenham Court Road, London W1T 4LP.

Any person who does any unauthorized act in relation to this publication may be liable to criminal prosecution and civil claims for damages.

The author has asserted her right to be identified as the author of this work in accordance with the Copyright, Designs and Patents Act 1988.

First published 1997 by
PALGRAVE MACMILLAN
Houndmills, Basingstoke, Hampshire RG21 6XS and
175 Fifth Avenue, New York, N.Y. 10010
Companies and representatives throughout the world

PALGRAVE MACMILLAN is the global academic imprint of the Palgrave Macmillan division of St. Martin's Press, LLC and of Palgrave Macmillan Ltd. Macmillan® is a registered trademark in the United States, United Kingdom and other countries. Palgrave is a registered trademark in the European Union and other countries.

ISBN-13: 978–1–4039–9483–7
ISBN-10: 1–4039–9483–8

This book is printed on paper suitable for recycling and made from fully managed and sustained forest sources. Logging, pulping and manufacturing processes are expected to conform to the environmental regulations of the country of origin.

A catalogue record for this book is available from the British Library.

10   9   8   7   6   5   4   3
17   16   15   14   13   12   11

Printed and bound in Great Britain by
Thomson Litho, East Kilbride

CITY OF SUNDERLAND COLLEGE
LEARNING CENTRE E18 4A

	LB 001063
	03/12
ACCESS NUMBER	0015837
RECOMMENDED BY	CLO SM

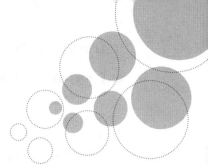

Contents

Preface		x
Abbreviations		xii
Acknowledgements		xiv

I REFERENCE – THE STRUCTURE OF ENGLISH

1 The structure of English — 3

1.1	What is grammar?	3
1.2	Word classes	4
1.3	The structure of words: morphology	21
1.4	Function and form	25
1.5	Phrases	26
1.6	Clauses	32
1.7	Sentences	36
1.8	Mood	42
1.9	Cohesion	43

2 Phonetics and phonology — 47

2.1	The reason for studying phonetics and phonology	47
2.2	Phonetics	48
2.3	Phonology	61

3 Style — 72

3.1	Sentence organisation	72
3.2	Literary and rhetorical devices	77

4 How to use your knowledge — 90

4.1	Grammar	90
4.2	Phonetics and phonology	92
4.3	Style	94
4.4	What to aim for	94

II LANGUAGE ISSUES – ASPECTS OF ENGLISH

5 Some basic concepts 97

5.1 A starting point 97
5.2 Standard English and Received Pronunciation 97
5.3 Attitudes to language 98
5.4 Audience, purpose and context 99
5.5 Register 101
5.6 Spoken and written English 104
5.7 Using the basic concepts 108

6 English: a living language 109

6.1 English: a living language 109
6.2 What changes language? 110
6.3 The changing faces of English 111
6.4 The democratic nature of language change 129

7 Historical change 130

7.1 The reason for studying historical change 130
7.2 The importance of text analysis 130
7.3 The Old English period 131
7.4 The Middle English period 135
7.5 The Early Modern English period 140
7.6 The Modern English period 143
7.7 What to look for when dating a text 147

8 Language variation: regional and social 152

8.1 Regional and social variation 152
8.2 Accent 154
8.3 Dialect 171
8.4 Accent and dialect levelling 177
8.5 What to look for in British accents and dialects 178

9 Child language – learning to talk 181

9.1 The nature of child language acquisition 181
9.2 The theories of language acquisition 182
9.3 The function of communication 184
9.4 Features of child language 185
9.5 Types of child language 193
9.6 What to look for in examples of child language 204

III VARIETIES – ENGLISH IN USE

10 Spoken English   213

10.1 The nature of spoken language   213
10.2 The function of spoken language   214
10.3 Features of spoken language   215
10.4 Types of spoken language   225
10.5 What to look for in spoken language   252

11 The language of newspapers   256

11.1 The nature of newspaper language   256
11.2 The function of newspaper language   262
11.3 Features of newspaper language   263
11.4 Types of newspaper reports   274
11.5 What to look for in newspapers   290

12 The language of advertising   293

12.1 The nature of advertising   293
12.2 The function of advertising   297
12.3 Features of advertising language   298
12.4 Types of advertising   304
12.5 What to look for in the language of advertising   322

13 The language of literature – narrative prose   325

13.1 The nature of narrative prose   325
13.2 The function of narrative prose   325
13.3 Features of narrative prose   325
13.4 Types of authorial intention   329
13.5 What to look for in the language of narrative prose   348

14 The language of literature – poetry   351

14.1 The nature of poetry   351
14.2 The function of poetry   351
14.3 Features of poetry   351
14.4 Types of poetic intention   357
14.5 What to look for in the language of poetry   369

15 The language of law   372

15.1 The nature of legal language   372
15.2 The function of legal language   373
15.3 Features of written legal language   373
15.4 Types of legal language   377
15.5 What to look for in the language of law   391

16 The language of religion 394

16.1 The nature of religious language 394
16.2 The function of religious language 395
16.3 Features of religious language 395
16.4 Types of religious language 401
16.5 What to look for in the language of religion 416

17 The language of politics 419

17.1 The nature of political language 419
17.2 The function of political language 420
17.3 Features of political language 420
17.4 Types of political language 426
17.5 What to look for in the language of politics 453

18 The language of broadcasting 456

18.1 The nature of broadcasting language 456
18.2 The function of broadcasting 458
18.3 Features of broadcasting language 458
18.4 Types of broadcasting language 463
18.5 What to look for in the language of broadcasting 497

19 The language of humour 501

19.1 The nature of the language of humour 501
19.2 The function of humour 502
19.3 Features of the language of humour 504
19.4 Types of humour 516
19.5 What to look for in the language of humour 553

20 Other varieties 557

20.1 How to classify other varieties 557
20.2 Instruction texts 557
20.3 Information texts 561
20.4 Personal texts 566
20.5 Narrative texts 571
20.6 What to look for in an unfamiliar variety of English 574

21 Preparing for a language examination 579

21.1 Coursework 579
21.2 The examination 584
21.3 Examination-style questions 588
21.4 Conclusion 602

IV APPENDICES

A **Answers to activities**   605

B **Glossary**   612

C **Wider reading**   625

   Index   628

Preface

The focus of this book is on the practical. It aims to help you understand how language changes according to its audience, purpose and context; how lexical and grammatical patterns are directly related to content and style; how writers and speakers communicate their attitudes and opinions; and how contextual factors affect the production and reception of speech and writing.

To help you do this, the book is divided into four parts. Part I provides a basic linguistic toolkit – it introduces you to the grammatical, phonetic, phonological and stylistic terminology and frameworks that you will need to analyse spoken and written texts. Part II focuses on general topics that introduce the concepts of language change and variation. It establishes a background against which all kinds of language can be considered. Part III brings together the terminology and approaches of Part I and the concepts of Part II, suggesting ways in which we can talk about the distinctive features of different varieties. Part IV summarises key terms in a glossary and offers suggestions for wider reading in the key areas of language study.

Each part is divided into logical subsections which focus on one element at a time. Starting with general information, each section also includes activities to test your understanding, real examples of English in use, and commentaries to suggest possible responses to the tasks set. The book is designed to encourage you to look closely at everyday examples of spoken and written English, seeing beyond the polished end product to the linguistic elements and frameworks that have been used to construct them.

Language study is all about the application of linguistic knowledge and linguistic frameworks. The key to success, whether you are studying for an examination or from personal interest, lies in close reading and knowing what questions to ask. Close reading skills can help us to identify important linguistic features; asking the right questions can help us to understand why certain features have been chosen and how they affect the meaning. There is no substitute for practice – the worked examples and the 'What to look for' sections offer you guidance, and the more spoken and written texts you explore, the more skilled you will become in recognising significant features and the effects they create.

Writing about the texts you analyse requires additional skills: planning; establishing a coherent and accurate writing style; using appropriate terminology; selecting examples; developing a coherent argument. The commentaries and the advice on how to use your knowledge will demonstrate ways in which you can communicate your findings most effectively.

It is difficult for a book exploring the nature of language and language use to keep pace with linguistic change. This second edition attempts to address some of the changes that have taken place in the last ten years, with new examples to take account of English in the twenty-first century. Finding the texts and exploring them is always fascinating – the more you look and listen, the more there is to discover. I hope that this book will offer you a way into the field of linguistic analysis – the knowledge and skills you gain will make you a more effective language user in your speech, your writing and your reading.

SARA THORNE

Abbreviations

A	adverbial		**l., ll.**	line, lines
ACl	adverbial clause		**L**	Latin
Adj	adjective		**LAD**	language acquisition device
AdjP	adjective phrase		**lex**	lexical verb
Adv	adverb		**LME**	Late Modern English
AdvP	adverb phrase			
AFr	Anglo-French		**m**	pre-modifier
art	article		**MCl**	main clause
aux	auxiliary verb		**ME**	Middle English
AV	Authorised Version		**mod**	modal verb
			ModE	Modern English
BAE	Black American English		**MRP**	Modified Received Pronunciation
BCP	Book of Common Prayer			
BEV	Black English Vernacular		**N**	noun
			NCl	noun clause
C	complement		**neg**	negative
CD-Rom	compact disk – read-only memory		**NFCl**	non-finite clause
Cl	clause		**NP**	noun phrase
Co	complement – object		**N-SE**	non-standard English
ComCl	comment clause		**nuc**	nucleus
CompCl	comparative clause		**num**	number
CompP	comparative phrase			
conj	conjunction		**O**	object
Cs	complement – subject		**Od**	object – direct
			OE	Old English
det	determiner		**OFr**	Old French
dumS	dummy subject		**Oi**	object – indirect
			ON	Old Norse
EME	Early Modern English			
			P	predicator
Fr	French		**(P)**	delayed main clause predicator
			past part	past participle
h	head word		**PH**	pre-head
H	head		**pre-det**	pre-determiner
			prep	preposition
IPA	International Phonetic Alphabet		**PrepP**	prepositional phrase
It	Italian		**pres part**	present participle

prim	primary verb	**T**	tail
pron	pronoun	**thatCl**	*that* clause
		TS	tonic syllable
q	qualifier or post-modifier		
		V	verb
RelCl	relative clause	**VlessCl**	verbless clause
rel pron	relative pronoun	**V/N**	verbal noun
RP	Received Pronunciation	**voc**	vocative
		VP	verb phrase
S	subject		
(S)	delayed subject	**whCl**	*wh*-clause
SAE	Standard American English		
SCl	subordinate clause	**ø**	omitted word(s) or clause
sconj	subordinating conjunction		element(s)
SE	Standard English		
Sp	Spanish		

Acknowledgements

The author and publishers wish to thank the following for permission to use copyright material:

Mitch Benn © 2007 IMWP; Bongo Entertainment, Inc. for an extract from 'Slobberwacky' from *Simpsons Comics*, Issue 42 (April 1999). Copyright © 1999 Bongo Entertainment, Inc. All Rights Reserved. The Simpsons © and ™ Twentieth Century Fox Film Corporation. All Rights Reserved; British Broadcasting Corporation for 'Front Row', BBC Radio 4, 31.5.05; Mona Siddiqui, 'Thought for the Day', BBC Radio 4, 10.10.06; the Uefa cup football match commentary by Ian Browne and Craig Hignet, BBC Radio 5 Live, 15.3.07; and extracts from 'Should I Fight Back?', *Panorama*, televised 5.2.07; Carcanet Press Ltd for Robert Graves, 'The Face in the Mirror' from *Collected Poems* by Robert Graves (2000); Conservative Central Office for an extract from a Welsh Conservative Party leaflet in support of Quentin Gwynne Edwards; The Controller of Her Majesty's Stationery Office for material from a Central Criminal Court judgment; Express Newspapers for extracts from various editions of the *Daily Express* and the *Daily Star*; Cheryl Gillan for an extract from a speech given by her to the Centre for Policy Studies; Guardian News and Media Ltd for extracts from various issues of *The Guardian*. Copyright © date as stated Guardian News & Media Ltd; Faber & Faber Ltd for an extract from T. S. Eliot, 'Prelude 1' from *Collected Poems 1909–1962* by T. S. Eliot (1963); A. M. Heath & Co. Ltd on behalf of Bill Hamilton as the Literary Executor of the Estate of the late Sonia Brownell Orwell and Secker & Warburg Ltd and Harcourt Inc. for an extract from George Orwell, 'A Hanging' in *Shooting an Elephant and Other Essays* by George Orwell. Copyright © 1950 by Sonia Brownell Orwell, renewed © 1978 by Sonia Pitt-Rivers; David Higham Associates on behalf of the Estate of the author for an extract from Louis MacNeice, 'Prayer Before Birth' from *Collected Poems* by Louis MacNeice, Faber & Faber (1979); Michael Howard for an extract from his speech, 'Political Correctness Gone Mad', 26.8.04; Alex Hughes Cartoons and Caricatures and New Internationalist Magazine; Independent News & Media Ltd for extracts from various editions of *The Independent*; ITV for an extract from a *Coronation Street* episode, televised 2.4.07; ITV Sport for the televised Uefa cup football match commentary by John Champion and Jim Beglin, ITV, 15.3.07; Kerber Ltd for 'Cost of Living' cartoon by Neil Kerber included in *The Independent*, 29.7.06; Mirrorpix for extracts from various editions of the *Daily Mirror*; Austin Mitchell for an extract from his book *Teach Thissen Tyke*, Dalesman (1989), p.6; NI Syndication Ltd for Peter Riddell, 'First Casualty of the Non-election', *The Times*, 16.10.07 and 'The Sun Says ... Potty cop', *The Sun*, 16.10.07; direct mailshot © NI Syndication Ltd 2007; Laurence Pollinger Ltd on behalf of the Estate of Frieda Lawrence Ravagli and Viking Penguin, a division of Penguin Books USA, for an extract from D. H. Lawrence, 'Discord in Childhood', from *The Complete Poems of D. H. Lawrence*, eds. V. de Sola Pinto & F. W. Roberts. Copyright © 1964, 1971 by Angelo Ravagli and C. M. Weekley, Executors of the Estate of Frieda Lawrence Ravagli; Oxfam/John French; Solo Syndication for extracts from various editions of the *Daily Mail*; Telegraph Media Group Ltd for extracts from various editions of the *Daily Telegraph*.

Every effort has been made to trace the copyright holders but if any have been inadvertently overlooked the publishers will be pleased to make the necessary arrangement at the first opportunity.

The author would like to thank Andrew Nash for his attention to detail; the people who have read and commented on sections of this book in its revised form; and everyone who has so kindly contributed source material.

Part I

Reference – the structure of English

Chapter 1

The structure of English

1.1 What is grammar?

To focus your study of language, you need to learn about **grammar**. You already **know** instinctively about the grammar of English: you read, speak and write English, only occasionally making mistakes. This section will move beyond your intuitive knowledge so that you can begin to **talk about** grammar in context.

Whether we speak or write, we must arrange our words in certain patterns if we are to be understood. An explicit knowledge of the patterns we use instinctively will help you to recognise usage that conforms to our expectations and usage that does not. By analysing the structure of words and sentences, linguists can begin to discuss **what** speakers or writers are trying to communicate and **how** they do so.

For linguists, GRAMMAR is a study of the **organisation of language**. It involves taking language structures apart in order to see the ways in which we can communicate effectively in a range of situations and for a range of purposes. Linguists look closely at the ways in which words and sentences are made up of different units. They break words down into their smallest component parts so that they can describe the ways in which they are constructed (MORPHOLOGY), and they look at the ways in which words are combined to create sentences (SYNTAX). Both speakers and writers use grammatical patterns to organise what they wish to say or write. Although speech and writing are characterised by different grammatical structures, the basic process of analysis is the same. Linguists are interested in the structures of words and sentences in both spoken and written DISCOURSE (any continuous use of language which is longer than one sentence).

By studying grammar, you will learn to evaluate the flexibility and variety of both written and spoken language use. Grammatical knowledge can also make you a more effective writer because you will be more aware of what you can do in order to achieve certain effects.

For analysis, language is usually divided into different levels. Within each of these levels, there are certain rules and patterns describing how the elements can be combined and how they relate to the elements of other levels. Language is said to have a RANK SCALE because the levels can be arranged hierarchically: a **word** is made up of groups of letters; a **phrase** is made up of groups of words; a **clause** is made up of groups of phrases; and a **sentence** is made up of groups of clauses.

1.2 Word classes

In order to be able to discuss the way words work together in a sentence, it is useful to be able to **classify** them. You are probably familiar with names like *nouns*, *adjectives*, *verbs* and *adverbs* and this section will aim to help you develop a more detailed knowledge of each of these WORD CLASSES. A knowledge of word classes is useful because it allows linguists to look closely at the kinds of words speakers and writers choose and the effects they create.

There are two types of word class: **open** and **closed**.

- OPEN-CLASS WORDS New words can be added to nouns, verbs, adjectives and adverbs as they become necessary, developing language to match changes in the society around us. The computer age, for example, has introduced words like *hardware, software, CD-Rom* and *spreadsheet*; the 1980s introduced words like *Rambo, kissogram* and *wimp*; the 1990s introduced words like *babelicious, alcopop* and *e-verdict*; and the twenty-first century words like *bling, chav, sudoko, bluetooth, chuggers* ('charity muggers'), *mediatrics* ('media dramatics' i.e. a story created from nothing), and *doorstepping* (journalists catching celebrities on their doorsteps to question them about incidents they would prefer not to discuss). Open-class words are often called **lexical words** and have a clearly definable meaning.

- CLOSED-CLASS WORDS New words are rarely added because pronouns (e.g. *I, you, she, he, it, his, hers, ours*), prepositions (e.g. *up, down, over, under, round, of, at, in*), determiners (e.g. *the, a, this, some, many*) and conjunctions (e.g. *and, or, but, if, because*) have a fixed, limited number of words. Closed-class words are often called STRUCTURAL WORDS, FUNCTION WORDS or GRAMMATICAL WORDS because they enable us to build up language grammatically.

Open-class words

Nouns

NOUNS (**N**) are traditionally known as **naming words**; they name people, places and things. You can test a word to see whether it is a noun:

- by trying to place '*the*' in front of it ('the ____')
- by seeing whether it will fit into the structure 'do you know about ____ ?'

Although some words will not fit into these structures even though they are nouns, these tests provide a starting point.

Nouns can be divided in several ways.

Common and proper nouns

COMMON NOUNS classify things into types or general categories:

car   dog   flower   chair

PROPER NOUNS refer to specific people and places and are usually written with an initial capital letter. They do not often appear after the determiners *a* or *the*.

Steven Spielberg   England   Wales   Robin Hood

Concrete and abstract nouns

CONCRETE NOUNS refer to physical things like people, objects and places, things that can be observed and measured:

▌ guitar   table   clothes

ABSTRACT NOUNS refer to ideas, processes, occasions, times and qualities; they cannot be touched or seen:

▌ happiness   week   birth   confinement

Count and non-count nouns

COUNT NOUNS can be counted and therefore have a plural form; they cannot be used after the determiner *much:*

▌ one lorry → two lorries   one pen → two pens   one cup → two cups

NON-COUNT NOUNS refer to substances and qualities that cannot be counted. They have no plural form and cannot follow the determiner *a*; many of them can be used after quantity words such as *some, any, all* or *much*:

▌ silver   information   hockey   traffic

Some nouns are both count and non-count:

▌ joy (non-count)   the joys of spring (count)
▌ water (non-count)   still waters run deep (count)

Plurals

In written language, regular nouns add *-s* to mark the PLURAL. Many nouns, however, are irregular and therefore follow alternative patterns.

› Nouns ending in *-y* form their plurals by changing the *-y* into *-ies*:

▌ story → stories   penny → pennies

› Nouns ending in *-o, -s, -sh, -ss, -tch* and *-x* often form plurals by adding *-es*:

▌ mistress → mistresses   box → boxes   flash → flashes

› Nouns ending in *-f* (except *-ff*) or *-fe* change to *-ves* in the plural:

▌ hoof → hooves (or sometimes hoofs)   life → lives

› Some nouns form a plural by changing a vowel or using a suffix other than *-s*:

▌ mouse → mice   tooth → teeth   ox → oxen   child → children

› Some nouns are the same in the singular and the plural:

▌ sheep   fish (or sometimes fishes)

COLLECTIVE NOUNS, although singular in form, refer to groups of people, animals and things:

▌ crowd   family   committee

Possessives

In written language, *'s* or *'* is added to the noun to mark possession. The following rules govern use of the POSSESSIVE ENDING in written English.

- Add an apostrophe and an -s to singular nouns to form the possessive:

  a *baby* → a *baby's* bottle   an *engine* → an *engine's* design

- Add an apostrophe to regular plurals:

  the *cars* → the *cars'* colours   the *pictures* → the *pictures'* frames

- Add an apostrophe and an -s to irregular plurals:

  the *children* → the *children's* games   the *oxen* → the *oxen's* strength

- Singular nouns ending in -s usually add an apostrophe and an -s:

  Dylan *Thomas's* poetry   King *Louis's* throne

The overall classification

For purposes of analysis, it is useful to see the relationship between these sub-categories of the open word class 'nouns'. The diagram in Figure 1.1 summarises the ways in which nouns can be classified.

Figure 1.1 **The classification of nouns**

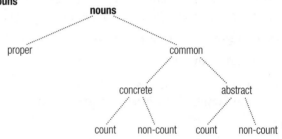

ACTIVITY 1.1

1 Read through the extract below and list all the nouns.

December 1984

Monday December 24th

CHRISTMAS EVE

Something dead strange has happened to Christmas. It's just not the same as it used to be when I was a kid. In fact I've never really got over the trauma of finding out that my parents had been lying to me annually about the existence of Santa Claus.

To me then, at the age of eleven, Santa Claus was a bit like God, all-seeing, all-knowing, but without the lousy things that God allows to happen: earthquakes, famines, motorway crashes. I would lie in bed under the blankets (how crude the word blankets sounds today when we are all conversant with the Tog rating of continental quilts), my heart pounding and palms sweaty in anticipation of the virgin Beano album.

Sue Townsend, *True Confessions of Adrian Albert Mole*

2 Classify the following nouns, deciding whether they are proper or common nouns, concrete or abstract.

a parents	e Beano	i bed
b Christmas	f heart	j anticipation
c existence	g Santa Claus	
d quilt	h trauma	

Answers on page 605

Adjectives

ADJECTIVES (**Adj**) are traditionally known as **describing words**. They provide extra information about nouns by giving details of physical qualities like colour and shape, and of psychological qualities like emotions; and by providing evaluative judgements:

▌ some *green* leaves   a *heavy* sack   a *funny* film   a *good* story   a *foolish* excuse

Adjectives specify a noun's **FIELD OF REFERENCE**: that is, they narrow the range of meaning by providing us with specific detail. You can test a word to see whether it is an adjective:

- by placing it between *the* and a noun
- by placing *very* before it

▌ the *old* tree   very *sad*

Adjectives have the following characteristics.

Position in relation to nouns

Adjectives can be used in two positions: before a noun (**ATTRIBUTIVE ADJECTIVES**), and after the verb *to be* and other **COPULA VERBS** (or **COPULAR VERBS**) or **LINKING VERBS** such as *to become* and *to seem* (**PREDICATIVE ADJECTIVES**):

- **Attributive**   the *large* balloon   a *pure white* stallion
- **Predicative**   the balloon is *large*   the essay was *very good*

Grading

Adjectives can be **GRADED** so that nouns can be compared:

▌ a *big* car   a *bigger* car   the *biggest* car

Monosyllabic and disyllabic adjectives form the **COMPARATIVE** by adding *-er* and the **SUPERLATIVE** by adding *-est*:

▌ long → *longer* → *longest*   sad → *sadder* → *saddest*
  happy → *happier* → *happiest*   clever → *cleverer* → *cleverest*

Polysyllabic and some disyllabic adjectives form the **comparative** by using *more* and the **superlative** by using *most* before the adjective:

▌ *more* fortunate → *most* fortunate   *more* grateful → *most* grateful

Irregularity

Some adjectives are **irregular**, as the following patterns show:

▌ bad → *worse* → *worst*   good → *better* → *best*

Words from other word classes

Sometimes words from other word classes do the job of an adjective:

▌ the *running* boy (V)   the *garden* wall (N)

In these examples, a noun and a verb give extra details about the nouns *boy* and *wall*. The verb *running* and the noun *garden* are not adjectives, even though they occur in the same position as an adjective and are describing the *boy* and the *wall*. Linguists call any word that describes a noun a **MODIFIER**: this takes account of the fact that not all words used will be from the adjective word class.

ACTIVITY 1.2

1 Read the following extract and underline all the modifiers.

> The gloomy day became a glorious evening as the ancient crimson sun dropped to the far horizon. As it began to sink lower and lower, the sea became redder and redder. It was calm, the calmest sea I'd seen for a long time, and the tiny waves rolled to the seaweed-edged shoreline. I walked to the glowing dunes and sat and watched the flying gulls dip and glide as they searched for food left by the careless tourists, both young and old. I closed my eyes and listened to the harsh sounds of the gulls as they fought for rotting scraps. The beauty of the evening contrasted with my solemn mood. I was lonely, sad and despairing because my customary companion, my large golden dog, had disappeared and there now seemed little hope of his return.

2 Try to categorise the modifiers under the following headings:
   a descriptive adjectives
   b size or distance adjectives
   c age adjectives
   d colour adjectives
   e comparative and superlative adjectives
   f noun or verb modifiers.

Answers on page 605

Verbs

VERBS (V) are traditionally known as **doing words**, but this does not cover all their possible meanings. A more accurate definition would be that verbs can express **actions** and **states**. **STATIVE VERBS** express states of being or processes in which there is no obvious action; they are not often used as commands and do not usually occur after the verb *to be* with an *-ing* ending:

  to know   to believe   to remember   to realise   to suppose   to appear

DYNAMIC VERBS express a wide range of actions which may be physical, like *jump*; mental, like *think*; or perceptual, like *see*. They can be used as commands and occur after the verb *to be* with an *-ing* ending:

  to buy → buy! → buying

TRANSITIVE VERBS must be followed by an **OBJECT** (the person or thing to which the action of the verb is done) to complete their meaning:

  I *carried* the baby.   They *found* the lost ring.   We can *make* a Christmas cake.

INTRANSITIVE VERBS do not need to be followed by an object to make sense. Many verbs describing position (*to sit*; *to lie*) and motion (*to run*; *to go*) are intransitive – the verb will often be followed by a description of place or destination:

  It *happened*.   The children *laughed*.   The girl *went* to the cinema.

It is important to realise that many verbs can be both transitive and intransitive:

I was *eating*. I was *eating* cake.   He is *writing*. He is *writing* a story.

You can test to see whether a word is a verb:

- by adding an *-ing* ending
- by placing it after *I* or *we*.

Verbs have the following characteristics.

Regular verbs

Regular verbs have four forms:

Example (base form)	Infinitive (*to* + base form)	Third person singular present tense	Past tense and past participle (*past part*)	Present participle (*pres part*)
walk	to walk	walks	walked	walking

Irregular verbs

Irregular verbs often have five forms:

Example (base form)	Infinitive (*to* + base form)	Third person singular present tense	Past tense	Past participle (*past part*)	Present participle (*pres part*)
show	to show	shows	showed	have shown	showing
write	to write	writes	wrote	have written	writing
give	to give	gives	gave	have given	giving
put	to put	puts	put	have put	putting

Types of verbs

There are two main types of verbs: lexical and auxiliary. **LEXICAL VERBS (lex)** express the **meaning** in a verb phrase:

the boy *ran* to school   the dog *jumped* and *frisked*

AUXILIARY VERBS (aux) can be used to construct different timescales, questions and negatives, to add emphasis or to give information about the mood or attitude of a speaker or writer. The **PRIMARY VERBS (PRIM)** *to be*, *to have*, and *to do* can act as auxiliaries:

I *have* gone.   The girl *has* swum.   *Do* you want to go to the cinema?
I *did* not watch television.   The baby *does* want food.

The **MODAL VERBS (mod)** *can/could, may/might, must/shall/should* and *will/ would* convey a range of attitudes and moods about the likelihood of an event taking place:

- **Ability**   I *can* swim.
- **Intention**   You *will* do as you are told.
- **Necessity/obligation**   You *must* go at once. You *should* do as you are told.
- **Permission**   *Can* I leave the classroom, please? *May* I leave the room?
- **Prediction**   He *will* come today, I'm sure. I *shall* finish tonight.
- **Possibility**   I *can* go. I *may* go.

Past and present tenses

There are two **TENSES** in English: the present and the past. The **PRESENT TENSE** has two forms: the **BASE FORM** (a verb which has no ending or vowel change) is used with *I, you, we* and *they*; while for *he, she* and *it*, an *-s/-es* ending is added to the base form.

> I *live* at home.　　They *enjoy* going to the cinema.
> He *lives* in town.　　She *enjoys* going to the theatre.

The present tense can be used to describe states of affairs and events that occur on a regular basis. It is also used in spontaneous sports commentaries, proverbs and sayings.

> I *know* about dinosaurs.　　He *goes* to work by bus.
>
> And he *takes* the ball and *runs* down the wing towards the goal. He *cuts* infield, *shoots* and *scores* – the game *is* over, the champions *win* the day!
>
> A bird in the hand *is* worth two in the bush.　　A stitch in time *saves* nine.

The **PAST TENSE** for regular verbs has only one form: in most cases, *-ed* is added to the base form of the verb. It refers to actions and states that took place in the past; it is sometimes used to record indirect or reported speech; and it can be used to refer to something that is supposed to be happening.

> I *loved* my primary school.　　　　We *missed* the bus for school.
>
> He said that the girl *stayed* for tea.　　She *replied* that they *played* happily.
>
> If I *walked* faster, perhaps I could win.　　It is time you all *went* home.

Many verbs are **irregular** and do not form the past tense by adding *-ed*. You use these irregular verbs in your speech and writing automatically, but you now need to become more conscious of their forms.

> *be* → I *was*; we *were*　　　　*become* → *became*
> *freeze* → *froze*　　　　　　　*hear* → *heard*
> *catch* → *caught*　　　　　　　*swim* → *swam*
> *hit* → *hit*　　　　　　　　　　*spell* → *spelt* (or *spelled*)

Future time

In order to create a sense of **FUTURE TIME**, English can use a range of structures.

1 The **simple present**:

> I *leave* tomorrow.　　She *starts* next week.

2 The **modal verbs *shall*** or ***will* + *base form verb***:

> I *shall* go to town later.　　They *will* go on holiday soon.

3 ***Be going* + *infinitive***:

> I *am going* to visit France next year.　　We *are going* to travel by train.

4 ***To be* + *present participle***:

> My friend *is coming* to tea tomorrow night.
> They *are moving* to Australia next year.

5 ***Will*** or ***shall* + *be* + *present participle***:

> I *shall be writing* again next week.　　We *will be waiting* for you.

Aspect

ASPECT describes the timescale of a verb – it establishes whether the action or state of a verb is complete or in progress. There are two types of aspect: the perfect (or perfective) and the progressive. The PERFECT ASPECT is constructed using the auxiliary *have + past participle*. The PRESENT PERFECT (*has* or *have + past participle*) is used for any action continuing in the present or having relevance in the present.

> We *have eaten* in this restaurant for years. [We still do.]

The PAST PERFECT (*had + past participle*) describes a previous time in the past.

> The building *had decayed* years ago.

The PROGRESSIVE ASPECT is constructed using the auxiliary *be + present participle* or the auxiliaries *have + be + present participle*. The progressive aspect implies that an activity is ongoing and is probably not complete.

- **Present progressive** The boys *are playing* football.
- **Past progressive** The ladies *were playing* tennis.
- **Present perfect progressive** The lions *have been roaring* wildly all day.
- **Past perfect progressive** The weeds *had been growing* throughout the summer.

Voice

The action of a verb and the person(s) or thing(s) responsible for it can be conveyed in two ways using VOICE: the active voice and the passive voice.

The ACTIVE VOICE is more common: it expresses the action of the verb, directly linking it to the person or thing carrying out the action.

> The car stopped suddenly.　　The girl picked up a book.

The PASSIVE VOICE changes the focus of the sentence by reordering the elements. The basic structure of the passive is as follows:

1 the **subject** or actor of the active sentence (the person or thing **doing** the verb) is moved to the end of the passive sentence and becomes the optional passive **agent** (i.e. *by + subject* of active sentence)

2 the **object** of the active sentence (the person or thing **receiving the action** of the verb) is moved to the front of the passive sentence and becomes the **subject**

3 the active verb is replaced by a verb in the passive form: *to be + past participle* or *have + to be + past participle*.

> Active:　The police hit the rioter.
> Passive:　The rioter *was hit* [by the police].

> Active:　The young child threw the ball and broke the window.
> Passive:　The ball *was thrown* and the window *was broken* [by the child].

Because the passive voice allows us to take the subject from the front of the sentence and replace it with something that is not the actor, we are able to change the focus of the active sentence. The passive is used for a variety of reasons:

1 Using *by* + *actor*, the subject can be delayed to the end of the sentence; this can create suspense:

The murder *was committed* by the infamous Mr Smith.

2 If the actor is a long phrase that seems awkward at the start of the sentence, it can be placed at the end for fluency:

A tremendous meal *was prepared* and [*was*] *served* by the cooks and waiters from the local hotel who trained at the college.

3 By omitting the *by* + *actor*, it is possible to exclude the person or thing responsible for the action of the verb:

Despite the explosion, nuclear power *was reported* [by the government] to be quite safe.

Finite and non-finite verbs

Verbs can be classified into two main types: finite and non-finite. **FINITE VERBS** change their form to show contrasts of number, tense and person. **NON-FINITE VERBS** never change their form.

▸ **Finite verbs**	she *lives* in Europe; she previously *lived* in America	(contrast of tense)
	he *eats*; they *eat*; I *am*; you are	(contrast of number/person)
▸ **Non-finite verbs**	(*is*) *living*	(*-ing* participles)
	(*has*) *lived*	(*-ed* past participles)
	live	(base form of the verb)
	to live	(the infinitive)

It is important to recognise the difference between the **PAST TENSE** and the **PAST PARTICIPLE** of regular verbs since both have an *-ed* ending. The past tense is finite because it is showing a change of tense; usually **the past participle follows an auxiliary** and does not change its form.

ACTIVITY 1.3

Complete the following exercises to test your knowledge of verbs.

1 Underline the verbs and decide whether each is a lexical or an auxiliary verb.
   a She had gone to town.
   b They had a picnic in the country.
   c I can do the work.
   d Did you like the concert?

2 List the verbs in the following sentences and decide whether each is finite or non-finite. Then use the diagram in Figure 1.2 to describe their forms exactly.

The boy *runs* to school.
   runs: finite; present tense; third person; singular.

   a The eagles flapped their wings.
   b She laughs at herself.
   c You have gone mad.
   d I carried the child away.

Figure 1.2 **The classification of verbs**

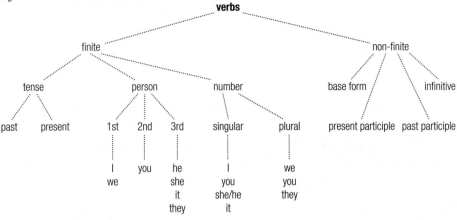

e The frog was croaking loudly.

f We chased the intruder.

g You have been silly.

h What has been happening?

i Does he know?

3 Rewrite the following active sentences in the passive voice, including the passive agent.

a The strong waves lifted the boat above the dangerous sandbank.

b The monks rang the bells to warn the surrounding villagers of the impending danger.

c After the disturbance, the police shut the pub.

4 Rewrite the following active sentences in the passive, omitting the passive agent. Comment on the effect created in each case.

a The guards beat the prisoners.

b The bully left the child face down in the playground.

c The scientists discovered the way to split the atom and created the first atom bomb.

Answers on page 605

ACTIVITY 1.4

Read the passage below and answer the questions that follow it.

Wednesday December 26th

BOXING DAY

I was woken at dawn by the sound of Grandad Sugden's rusty Ford Escort refusing to start. I know I should have gone down into the street and helped to push it but Grandma Sugden seemed to be doing all right on her own. It must be all those years of flinging sacks of potatoes about. My parents were wisely pretending to be asleep …

Went back to sleep but the dog licked me awake at 9.30, so I took it for a walk past Pandora's house. Her dad's Volvo wasn't in the drive so they must still be staying with their rich relations. On the way I passed Barry Kent, who was kicking a football up against the wall of the old people's home. He seemed full of seasonal goodwill for once and I stopped to talk with him. He asked what I'd had for Christmas …

Sue Townsend, *True Confessions of Adrian Albert Mole*

1 Underline all the verbs in the extract.

2 Find examples of the following:
   a two lexical verbs
   b two stative verbs
   c two dynamic verbs
   d two primary auxiliary verbs
   e two modal auxiliary verbs.

3 Find an example of the passive voice and rewrite the sentence in the active voice.

4 Find one example of the progressive aspect and one of the perfective aspect.

5 Find one example of the present tense and one of the past tense.

6 Find two examples of a finite verb and two examples of a non-finite verb.

Answers on page 606

Adverbs

ADVERBS (Adv) are modifying words. They give information about time, place and manner, and can express a speaker's attitude to or evaluation of what is being said. They can modify:

- **verbs**   The car drove *slowly*.
- **adjectives**   The house was *very* pretty.
- **other adverbs**   The mural was painted particularly *carefully*.
- **sentences**   *Certainly*, the work will be completed on time.
       I went home; my friend, *meanwhile*, stayed to chat.

CIRCUMSTANCE ADVERBS (or ADJUNCTS) modify verbs, giving details of circumstances such as time, manner and place:

- **manner**   He was sleeping *well*; the cat was fighting *furiously*.
- **time**   You must go to school *now*; *afterwards*, you can go swimming.
- **frequency**   I *always* visit my grandmother on Sundays; I *never* stay at home.
- **place**   Go *there* to get a coat; *upstairs* they have shirts too.

  - To test for an *adverb of manner*, ask yourself the question '*how?*'
  - To test for an *adverb of time*, ask yourself the question '*when?*'
  - To test for an *adverb of frequency*, ask yourself the question '*how often?*'
  - To test for an *adverb of place*, ask yourself the question '*where?*'

DEGREE ADVERBS (or MODIFIERS) modify adjectives or adverbs:

- **Degree**   It is *very* good to see you; I *really* missed you; I'm *so* glad to be back.

  - To test for an *adverb of degree*, ask yourself the question '*to what degree?*'

SENTENCE ADVERBS (**disjuncts** and **conjuncts**) modify a whole sentence. DISJUNCTS express speakers' or writers' attitudes, allowing them to comment on what is being said or written; CONJUNCTS can be used to link sentences.

- **Linking**   *Firstly*, I intend to go away; *however*, I will write postcards.
- **Attitude**   I could *perhaps* do the work, but *surely* you could get someone else.

Adverbs have the following characteristics.

Forming adverbs

Many adverbs are formed by adding *-ly* to adjectives:

> calm (Adj) → calm<u>ly</u> (Adv)   shabby (Adj) → shabb<u>ily</u> (Adv)
> gentle (Adj) → gent<u>ly</u> (Adv)

Comparatives and superlatives

Like adjectives, adverbs can have **COMPARATIVE** and **SUPERLATIVE** forms. Although some can take the *-er* and *-est* endings, most require the use of *more* and *most*:

> early → earl<u>ier</u> → earl<u>iest</u>
> loudly → <u>more</u> loudly → <u>most</u> loudly
> crucially → <u>more</u> crucially → <u>most</u> crucially

Irregular adverbs

Some adverbs are **irregular**:

> badly → *worse* → *worst*   little → *less* → *least*
> much → *more* → *most*   well → *better* → *best*

Position

There are three main **positions** for adverbs.

1 The front of the sentence:

> *Actually*, I have loved this place for a long time.

2 The middle of a sentence – after the first auxiliary, after the verb *to be* as a lexical verb, or before the lexical verb:

> I have *actually* loved this place for a long time.
> I am *actually* in love with this place.
> I *actually* loved the place.

3 The end of the sentence:

> I loved the place *actually*.

Distinguishing between adjectives and adverbs

Sometimes the same word can be both an **adjective** and an **adverb**. In order to distinguish between them, it is important to look at the **context** of the word and its **function** in a sentence.

> The *fast* train from London to Cardiff leaves at three o'clock.
> The sprinter took the bend *fast*.

> The bed was *hard* and gave me a bad night's sleep.
> After faltering, the horse hit the fence *hard*.

In the first and third sentences, the words *fast* and *hard* modify nouns. The first is an attributive adjective, coming before the noun it modifies; the second is a predicative adjective, coming after the verb *to be*. In the second and fourth sentences, the words *fast* and *hard* modify verbs. These are both circumstance adverbs which are in the end position.

Underline the adverbs in the following passage and identify them as:

1 circumstance adverbs
2 degree adverbs
3 sentence adverbs.

> The sun shone brightly there on that crisp December morning. Nevertheless, I could not help feeling that the day would not go well. Again and again, I was aware of the completely isolated nature of the spot here and anxiously I waited for the others to arrive. I knew I was being really silly, but generally my intuitions were correct. I had found recently that things happened as I knew they would. It made me very suspicious and often I would look around warily. Sometimes, however, I was wrong and I hoped desperately that I was being over-sensitive this time. I tried to relax and to think about something else. What would take my mind off my premonitions? Perhaps the beauty of the day could make me forget. Actually, I was here on holiday and I had to make sure that I enjoyed my stay properly.

Answers on page 606

Closed-class words

Pronouns

PRONOUNS (pron) are used instead of nouns, noun phrases or noun clauses. There are seven main types of pronouns.

Personal pronouns

SUBJECT PRONOUNS are used for the **actor** of the sentence:

▶ first person singular	*I*		▶ first person plural	*we*
▶ second person singular	*you*		▶ second person plural	*you*
▶ third person singular	*he/she/it*		▶ third person plural	*they*

> The next-door neighbour visited today. *She* was in a good mood.
> Children should always be seen and not heard. *You* should be seen and not heard.

When a pronoun replaces the noun that receives the action of the verb (**object**), an **OBJECT PRONOUN** is used:

▶ first person singular	*me*		▶ first person plural	*us*
▶ second person singular	*you*		▶ second person plural	*you*
▶ third person singular	*him/her/it*		▶ third person plural	*them*

> The people carried their parcels indoors. The people carried *them* indoors.
> Give your brother the book. Give *him* the book.

Possessive pronouns

POSSESSIVE PRONOUNS are used when you need to show possession of something:

▶ first person singular	*mine*		▶ first person plural	*ours*
▶ second person singular	*yours*		▶ second person plural	*yours*
▶ third person singular	*his/hers*		▶ third person plural	*theirs*

It is my book. It is *mine*.
We think it is our choice. We think it is *ours*.
They told us that it was their taxi. They told us it was *theirs*.

Reflexive pronouns

REFLEXIVE PRONOUNS are used when the *same* person is the **actor** (subject) and **receiver** of the action (object) in a sentence. They can also be used to create emphasis:

- first person singular   *myself*
- second person singular   *yourself*
- third person singular   *himself/ herself/itself*

- first person plural   *ourselves*
- second person plural   *yourselves*
- third person plural   *themselves*

You should wash *yourself* carefully.
You *yourself* know how dangerous it is.
He said he saw her worry *herself* unnecessarily.

Demonstrative pronouns

DEMONSTRATIVE PRONOUNS are used to 'point' to the relationship between the speaker and a person or a thing. They are said to have a **'deictic' function**. There are four demonstrative pronouns:

- *this* and *these* point to something that is close to the speaker
- *that* and *those* point to something that is distant from the speaker.

I like the apples. I like *these*.   The lady over there is my aunt. *That* is my aunt.

Interrogative or question pronouns

INTERROGATIVE or QUESTION PRONOUNS are used to ask questions. There are five types: *what, which, who, whom* and *whose.*

Who can come?
What do you think the time is?
To *whom* did you address your letter?

Relative pronouns

RELATIVE PRONOUNS follow directly the nouns they describe. They introduce relative clauses, although sometimes the pronoun itself is omitted. There are five forms: *that, which, who, whom* and *whose.*

The man *who* has white hair lives close to me.
I went to the library to return the book *that* you got out for me.
I saw a car *which* drove the wrong way down a one-way street.

Indefinite pronouns

INDEFINITE PRONOUNS have a less certain reference point than the other pronouns listed here. There are two types:

- *of* PRONOUNS: *all of, both of, each of, either of, neither of* and *some of* are followed by a noun, an object pronoun, or a relative pronoun:

I want *all of* the books. I want *all of* them.
I will buy a shirt and a jacket, *both of* which must be very colourful.

- **COMPOUND PRONOUNS** *every-*, *some-*, *any-* and *no-* + *-thing*, *-one* and *-body*:

> They don't want dinner. They don't want *anything*.
> We live near no other people. We live near *nobody*.

ACTIVITY 1.6

List the pronouns in the following passage and identify them as:

1 personal pronouns
2 possessive pronouns
3 reflexive pronouns
4 demonstrative pronouns
5 interrogative pronouns
6 relative pronouns
7 indefinite pronouns.

> We enjoyed our days at the beach that summer. It had been glorious weather and everyone had relished the warmth and light after the harshness of a long winter which had seemed endless. Some ran the length of the sand to the sea; some lay peacefully on their towels. I decided to paddle, and covered myself in suntan lotion before walking lazily to the sea which shimmered before me. Why was it not like this all the time? Everything seemed perfect. The day was ours to do with as we wished. As I turned back to the beach, a small boy sat on my towel.
>
> 'Get off,' I shouted. 'That is mine.' He stood up suddenly and shouted something. Who could he be talking to? Then I saw the girl a short distance away. He had clearly thought the towel was hers.
>
> I lay back down and closed my eyes to think of the girl that I had met earlier in the day. What was she doing now, I wondered? I still had her book and I would have to return it to her.

Answers on page 607

Determiners

DETERMINERS (**det**) precede nouns. There are five main types.

Articles

ARTICLES can be definite (*the*) or indefinite (*a* or *an*). The former specifies something particular, while the latter does not:

> *the* dog   *a* dog   *the* house   *a* house

Possessive determiners

POSSESSIVE DETERMINERS are used to suggest ownership of a noun. There are seven forms: *my, your, his, her, its, our* and *their*.

> *my* book   *our* suitcases   *their* motives

Demonstrative determiners

DEMONSTRATIVE DETERMINERS express a contrast, establishing either a close or a more distant relationship.

> *This* week is going slowly.
> The shop assistant said that she wanted *these* things kept aside for her.

Indefinite determiners

INDEFINITE DETERMINERS convey a range of meanings. The most common ones are: *all, some, any* and *no*; *every, each, either, neither, one* and *another*; *both, several* and *enough*; *many, more, most, few, little, fewer, less, fewest* and *least*.

> *Some* grapes would be nice. *Every* adult must take some responsibility.
> *Several* children are expected today. *More* chocolate, anybody?

Numbers

When **NUMBERS** precede nouns, they are functioning as determiners. Both **cardinal numbers** (*one, two, three,* and so on) and **ordinal numbers** (*first, second, third,* and so on) can be used as determiners.

> *First* place goes to Jack. *Six* sheep have escaped from the farm.

Distinguishing between pronouns and determiners

Because there is a considerable overlap between pronouns and determiners, it is important to look closely at the context to distinguish between the two. A **determiner** *precedes* a noun, while a **pronoun** *replaces* a noun, noun phrase or noun clause.

> *That* book is worth reading. *That* is worth reading.
> det   pron
>
> *Both* children are really hard workers. *Both* are really hard workers.
> det   pron

ACTIVITY 1.7 ─────────────────────────────────────

List the determiners in the following passage and try to classify them under the headings below:

1 articles: definite and indefinite
2 possessive determiners
3 demonstrative determiners
4 indefinite determiners
5 numbers.

> The old lady reached the doorstep of her home and put her bag down to search for a key in her pocket. This search was always the worst part of any trip out. However hard she tried, she could never find either key – she always carried one key for the front door and one key for the back door in case of emergencies. On many occasions she had been sure that both keys were lost. But this time was an exception.
>
> She skilfully slotted one key into the lock and turned it carefully. In two minutes she was indoors, but for the second time that day, she drew her breath sharply. Every day recently she had had some visitors, but enough was enough. There was more mess than even she could bear and for the rest of that day, she concentrated on making her home her own again.

Answers on page 607

Prepositions

PREPOSITIONS (prep) describe relationships that exist between elements in sentences. They convey the following relationships:

- **Place**   *at, on, by, opposite*
- **Direction**   *towards, past, out of, to, through*
- **Time**   *at, before, in, on*
- **Comparison**   *as... as, like*
- **Source**   *from, out of*
- **Purpose**   *for*

It is important to be aware that some words that have the **form** of a preposition do not have the same **function**.

> The girl read *in* the library.   The rioters kicked *in* the door.

The form of the preposition *in* is identical in each case, but the function is different. In the first sentence, *in* describes where the girl is reading – it is therefore a preposition of place. In the second sentence, however, *in* is directly related to the verb *kicked* – in this case, it is called a **PARTICLE**.

ACTIVITY 1.8

Decide whether the words <u>underlined</u> below are prepositions or particles.

1 Steven threw <u>out</u> the rubbish.
2 Judith ran <u>into</u> the bedroom.
3 The pilot flew <u>out of</u> the local airport.
4 Will you carry <u>on</u> preparing the meal?
5 The warring factions gave <u>in</u> to the demands of the United Nations.
6 The sea rolled inexorably <u>towards</u> the defensive wall.
7 The car broke <u>down</u> at the traffic lights.
8 The plane rose high <u>above</u> me, but I could still remember the moment of take-off.
9 It's difficult to be a single-parent family and to bring <u>up</u> two children alone.
10 I turned to my companion and we went <u>down</u> the stairs.
11 They cleared <u>out</u> the attic ready for moving-day.

Answers on page 607

Conjunctions

CONJUNCTIONS (conj) are joining words, and there are two types.

Co-ordinating conjunctions

CO-ORDINATING CONJUNCTIONS (*and, but, or, neither... nor* and *either... or*) link lexical units of equal value.

> The girl *and* the boy.   They saw *and* understood.
>   N   N   V   V
>
> The dog was gentle *and* friendly.   The day was wet *and* the trip was ruined.
>   Adj   Adj   sentence   sentence

Subordinating conjunctions

SUBORDINATING CONJUNCTIONS join a subordinate clause to a main clause. They often give information on *when, where, why, if* or *how* an action takes place. A clause introduced by a subordinating conjunction cannot stand alone.

The list below contains some of the main subordinating conjunctions:

- **Time**   *when(ever), while, as, before, until, after, since, once, when*
- **Place**   *where, wherever*
- **Purpose**   *so that, in order that*
- **Reason**   *because, as, since*
- **Condition**   *if, unless, whether*
- **Contrast**   *although, while, whereas*
- **Comparison**   *as, than, like, as if, as though*

> I love going to the theatre *because* it makes texts studied in college come alive.
> *Whenever* we visit France, I remember that first holiday.
> I want to study at the moment, *so that* I can go to university.
> I go to restaurants *where* I can get a good vegetarian meal.
> *If* they travel at a reasonable speed, they should be here by evening.
> The woman looked *as if* she were going to shout.
> *While* she loved her new home, she still yearned for her old cottage.

ACTIVITY 1.9

Read through the passage below and choose an appropriate conjunction to fill each of the gaps in the text. Identify the type of conjunction used in each case.

> _____(1) the doctor hurried from one bed to another, the nurses went about their tasks calmly. They had beds to make _____(2) medicine to allocate, _____(3) it was all part of the daily routine. _____(4) they were accustomed to being shorthanded, they found ways to divide the tasks. _____(5) they were really busy, things went quite smoothly.
>
> The ward was full at the moment _____(6) they all knew that there were at least two patients waiting for admission. It always seemed to happen these days – _____(7) a bed was vacated, it was stripped and filled within half an hour. _____(8) the nurses looked, they saw the need for more beds, more facilities and above all, more nurses. _____(9) they had to cope with the cuts, they had to think only of the job in hand. It was not worth wasting energy on bewailing the conditions in which they had to work, _____(10) they needed all their strength to cope with their long shifts. It was better _____(11) working on a production line, surely!

Answers on page 607

1.3 The structure of words: morphology

A knowledge of morphology will be useful when you study the history of language, **ETYMOLOGY** (the study of the origin of words) and **PHONOLOGY** (the study of the sounds of a language). **MORPHOLOGY** is the study of **MORPHEMES**, the smallest units of grammar.

Free and bound morphemes

There are two kinds of morphemes: free morphemes and bound morphemes. A **FREE MORPHEME** can stand alone and is understandable in isolation:

> boy (N)   happy (Adj)   run (V)

A **BOUND MORPHEME** cannot occur alone:

▌ -ly   un-   -ish

These bound morphemes are also called **AFFIXES**, and can occur at the beginning or at the end of a free morpheme.

Prefixes

A **PREFIX precedes** a free morpheme:

▌ <u>un</u>kind   <u>dis</u>like

Suffixes

A **SUFFIX follows** a free morpheme:

▌ kind<u>ness</u>   lean<u>ing</u>

Words can have multiple affixes (<u>un</u> + *like* + <u>li</u> + <u>hood</u>).

ACTIVITY 1.10 ━━━━━━━━━━━━━━━━━━━━━━━━━━━━━━━

Divide the words below into bound and free morphemes, bearing in mind that the addition of suffixes sometimes changes the spelling of free morphemes.

1 unjustifiable
2 summative
3 midnight
4 daily

5 negativity
6 unlikely
7 pitiful.

━━━━━━━━━━━━━━━━━━━━━━━━━━━━━━━━━━━━━ *Answers on page 607*

Derivational and inflectional morphology

Bound morphemes are used in two distinctive ways: they can be used to create new words (**DERIVATIONAL MORPHOLOGY**) or to change the form of words (**INFLECTIONAL MORPHOLOGY**).

Derivational morphology

Words can be created by using prefixes, suffixes, or both:

▌ <u>un</u>real, <u>re</u>draft (prefixes)
▌ sad<u>ly</u>, boy<u>ish</u> (suffixes)
▌ <u>un</u>accept<u>able</u>, <u>sub</u>consciousl<u>y</u> (affixes)

Although it is always important to look closely at words in context, it is still possible to make some generalisations about the words created by prefixation, suffixation and affixation.

Prefixes

Prefixes alter the **meaning** of a word, but they do not always change the word **class**:

Prefix	Word class of free morpheme	Word class of created word
hyper-	tension (N)	hypertension (N)
be-	devil (N)	bedevil (V)
re-	style (V)	restyle (V)

Suffixes

Suffixes usually, but not always, change the *class* of the free morpheme to which they are attached:

Word class of free morpheme	Suffix	Word class of created word
exploit (V)	-ation	exploitation (N)
joy (N)	-ful	joyful (Adj)
friend (N)	-ship	friendship (N)

Suffixes associated with nouns

Words ending with the bound morphemes *-acy, -ation, -er/-or, -ess, -ity, -ment, -ness* and *-ship* are usually nouns:

diplomacy	similarity	jubilation	compartment	writer
sadness	conductor	relationship	poetess	

Suffixes associated with adjectives

Words with suffixes like *-able, -ful, -ical, -less, -like, -ous* and *-y* are usually adjectives:

a *profitable* account	an *animal-like* noise	a *gloomy* day
a *courageous* child	a *theatrical* show	a *godless* society

Suffixes associated with verbs

Words with the suffixes *-ise* or *-ize* are usually verbs:

dramatise   democratise

Suffixes associated with adverbs

Words with the suffix *-ly* are usually adverbs:

the bus moved off *slowly*   the dog ate *eagerly*

Words formed from two free morphemes

Words can also be formed by the **compounding** (adding together) of two free morphemes:

duty + free → duty-free   sign + post → signpost

ACTIVITY 1.11

Add appropriate bound morphemes to the underlined words in order to derive new words.

1 Add a prefix to the verb <u>present</u>.
2 Add a suffix to the noun <u>hospital</u>.
3 Make an adverb by adding the appropriate suffix to the adjective <u>calm</u>.
4 Add an appropriate suffix to the noun <u>child</u> to create an adjective.
5 Make a noun by adding an appropriate ending to the following: <u>glorify</u>, <u>audit</u> and <u>act</u>.

Answers on page 608

Inflectional morphology

Open-class words can be altered by adding a suffix. However, while derivational morphology often involves a change in word class, inflectional morphology *never* does.

In written English, inflection can mark the following.

Plurals

The **plural** of nouns:

Free morpheme	Bound morpheme	Inflected word
cat	-<u>s</u>	cat<u>s</u>
book	-<u>s</u>	book<u>s</u>
gas	-<u>es</u>	gas<u>es</u>
penny	-<u>ies</u>	penn<u>ies</u>

Possessives

The **possessive** of all nouns:

Free morpheme	Bound morpheme	Inflected word
girl	-<u>'s</u>	the girl<u>'s</u> jumper
children	-<u>'s</u>	the children<u>'s</u> toys
adults	-<u>'</u>	the adults<u>'</u> books

Present tense

The **present tense** of regular third person singular verbs:

Free morpheme	Bound morpheme	Inflected word
run	-<u>s</u>	he run<u>s</u>
cry	-<u>ies</u>	the baby cr<u>ies</u>

Present participle

The **present participle** form of verbs:

Free morpheme	Bound morpheme	Inflected word
do	-<u>ing</u>	do<u>ing</u>
justify	-<u>ing</u>	justify<u>ing</u>

Past tense and past participle

The **past tense** and **past participle** of regular verbs:

Free morpheme	Bound morpheme	Inflected word
walk	-ed	walk<u>ed</u>
dress	-ed	dress<u>ed</u>

ACTIVITY 1.12

List the suffixes in the examples below and try to identify the kind of inflection used in each case:

1 sailors   3 the girls' bags   5 the dog's bone
2 viewed   4 dreaming   6 the tiger snarls

Answers on page 608

ACTIVITY 1.13

For each of the examples below, list the free and bound morphemes and then identify:

a the word class of each example
b the word class of each free morpheme
c whether derivational or inflectional morphemes have been used.

morality (N)
 Free morpheme = *moral* (Adj); bound morpheme = *-ity*; derivational morphology (change of word class: words ending with the suffix *-ity* are nouns).

lives (V)
 Free morpheme = *live* (V); bound morpheme = *-s*; inflectional morphology (inflection marking a third person singular present tense verb).

1 greatness   5 inter-rivalry   9 institutionalise
2 multigym   6 illogical   10 reassesses
3 declaration   7 predetermination
4 delimited   8 horrifying

Answers on page 608

1.4 Function and form

It is important to look at more than just the word class of a word, because the same word can perform quite different jobs in a sentence.

(a) At seven o'clock, the man will *light* the bonfire.
(b) When I was cleaning, the *light* fell on the floor and broke.
(c) This room is very *light*.

In each of these sentences, the appearance of the word *light* is identical, but the job the word does is different. In example (a), *light* is a lexical verb preceded by a modal auxiliary *will*; in example (b), it is a noun preceded by the determiner *the*; in example (c), it is a predicative adjective following the copula verb *is*.

Linguists analyse words in terms of both their FORM (the word class) and their FUNCTION (the job they fulfil). By describing words in this way, linguistic analysis can be very precise – it allows linguists to focus specifically on the words chosen and the results created by different writers and speakers.

> (a) a *costumed* concert performance
> (b) the *award-winning* dramatisation of the novel by Roald Dahl
> (c) one of the biggest *floating* book shops in the world

Each of the words in italic print is a verb in form, although each is functioning as a modifier. In examples (a) and (b) the verb modifiers *costumed* and *award-winning* help the promoters to convey the nature of the event concisely. In example (c), the verb modifier *floating* is dramatic because it is followed by the nouns *book shops*. It makes an effective advertisement for the ship's book shop because these are not words we are accustomed to seeing together – they attract attention because of the novelty of their juxtaposition.

When linguists analyse **phrases** (groups of words), an awareness of function and form is important because it enables them to describe exactly what words are doing and how particular effects are created. **Generative** or **phrase structure grammar** is based on the principle that there is a series of structural rules that govern grammatical sequences of language. These rules dictate the **transformations** or movements of syntactic components that can be made within a grammatically well formed sentence. They establish the general principles and relationships that exist in language. While this book describes the processes underpinning transformational-generative grammar, it adopts a slightly different approach to phrase analysis. It focuses on both the identification of each different phrase as a discrete linguistic unit (**form**) and on the recognition of the job each phrase fulfils in the sentence as a whole (**function**).

There are three key terms that describe the function of words in a phrase: the **HEAD WORD** (**h**) is the main word; words that come before the head word and that modify or change it in some way are called **PRE-MODIFIERS** (**m**); and words that provide extra information after the head word are called **POST-MODIFIERS** or **QUALIFIERS** (**q**). Using these terms, it is possible to describe the function of individual words in a phrase exactly.

1.5 Phrases

A **PHRASE** is a single word or a group of words that act together as a unit but that do not usually contain a finite verb.

Noun phrases

A **NOUN PHRASE** (**NP**) usually begins with a determiner and normally has a **noun** as its most important word. It can act as a **subject**, and as an **object** or a **complement** in a clause (see Section 1.6). Noun phrases have the following characteristics.

Nouns and pronouns as head words

The **HEAD WORD** or main word of a noun phrase is usually a **noun**, but it can be a **pronoun**.

> *The baby* is crawling over *the grass.*   *He* is crawling over *it.*
>   NP   NP   NP   NP
> det   N   det   N   pron   pron

Adjectives as head words

Sometimes an **adjective** can function as the head word of a noun phrase.

> *The old* often get a raw deal.
>   NP
> det   Adj

Constituents of a noun phrase

A noun phrase can be made up of either a **single noun** or a **noun** with one or more **pre-modifiers** and **post-modifiers** or **qualifiers**:

> h   h   m   h   m   h   FUNCTION
> *Dogs* eat *bones.*   *The girls* are picking *the flowers.*
> NP   NP   NP   NP   FORM
> N   N   det N   det   N

> m   m   h   q   m   m   h   q   FUNCTION
> *The beautiful sky of blue* rose above *the glimmering sea of green.*
> NP   NP   FORM
> det   Adj   N prep Adj   det   V   N prep Adj

Pre-modification

Pre-modification can take the following forms:

pre-determiners	determiners	pre-modifiers	head
(*all, all of,* *each of*)	(numerals (**num**), adjectives, noun or verb modifiers)		

> m   m   m   m   m   h   FUNCTION
> *all the first long distance* runners
> NP   FORM
> pre-det det num Adj   N   N

> m   m   m   m   m   h   FUNCTION
> *some of those four young school* girls
> NP   FORM
> pre-det   det   num   Adj   N   N

Post-modification

Post-modification or **qualification** can take the following forms.

Prepositional phrases

A **PREPOSITIONAL PHRASE** (**PrepP**) will always begin with a **preposition**.

> m   h   q   FUNCTION
> the baby *on the floor*
> NP   FORM
> det   N   PrepP

Non-finite clauses

A NON-FINITE CLAUSE (NFCl) will always begin with a non-finite verb (see Section 1.6).

m h q	h q	FUNCTION
the baby *chewing his rattle*	time *to go home*	
NP	NP	FORM
det N NFCl	N NFCl	

m h q	FUNCTION
a man *called Jack*	
NP	FORM
det N NFCl	

Relative clauses

A RELATIVE CLAUSE (RelCl) will usually begin with a relative pronoun (see Section 1.6).

m h q	FUNCTION
the baby *who was chewing his rattle*	
NP	FORM
det N RelCl	

ACTIVITY 1.14

Read the following passage, then list all the noun phrases and try to identify:

1 the head word of each noun phrase
2 the kind of modification (pre- or post-) used.

> The first summer's day burst through my curtains unexpectedly. The new dawn's sun-light highlighted the paths of dust which lay on the ancient sea chest. The scratches paid tribute to a life of hardship and I couldn't help wondering about the interesting stories which were linked to the marks. The drowned men who had owned this chest could tell their own versions of events, but I would never know them.
>
> I turned lazily towards the wall, but I was merely met by another withered mark of the past. This time, I was confronted by the faded rose wallpaper. The memory of another place slowly filtered through my hazy mind, forcing me to make connections. I remembered that first disturbing visit to the ruined cottage and its ongoing effects. This second historical link waiting for me, unexpectedly, stirred me at last.

Answers on page 608

ACTIVITY 1.15

Analyse the following noun phrases from the extract in terms of function and form:

1 the interesting stories which were linked to the marks
2 their own versions of events
3 the wall
4 the faded rose wallpaper
5 This second historical link waiting for me.

Answers on page 609

Adjective phrases

An ADJECTIVE PHRASE (AdjP) has an adjective as its main word. Adjective phrases have the following characteristics.

Adjectives as head words

The **head word** of an adjective phrase is an **adjective**. While attributive adjectives precede nouns as pre-modifiers in a noun phrase, predicative adjectives follow nouns (often after a copula verb) and are the head words of adjective phrases.

h	FUNCTION
The sky grew *black*.	
AdjP	FORM

h	FUNCTION
The horse was *black* and stood out against the whiteness of the snow.	
AdjP	FORM

Pre-modification

Adverbs and some **adjectives** can pre-modify an adjective:

m h	m h	m h	FUNCTION
very bold	*extremely* dangerous	*pure* white	
AdjP	AdjP	AdjP	FORM
Adv Adj	Adv Adj	Adj Adj	

Post-modification

Post-modification of adjective phrases can take the following forms.

Prepositional phrases

A **prepositional phrase** will always begin with a **preposition**:

h q	FUNCTION
afraid *of ghosts*	
AdjP	FORM
Adj PrepP	

Non-finite infinitive clauses

A **non-finite infinitive clause** will always begin with an **infinitive**:

h q	FUNCTION
anxious *to please*	
AdjP	FORM
Adj NFCl	

Noun clauses

A **NOUN CLAUSE** (**NCl**) will always start with the **subordinating conjunction** *that*, although this may be **omitted** (marked in analysis by the symbol ø).

h q	FUNCTION
sure *that he'll get lost*	
AdjP	FORM
Adj NCl	

h q	FUNCTION
sure *(ø) he'll get lost*	
AdjP	FORM
Adj NCl	

ACTIVITY 1.16

Read the following passage and then list the adjective phrases and analyse them in terms of function and form. The first example is completed for you.

```
     m     h    q
very glad to meet him
              AdjP
 Adv   Adj   NFCl
```

I was <u>very glad to meet him</u> on that winter's day. The snow, deep and white, fell quickly, covering the ground like a blanket. He seemed rather sad, but quite sure of his need for company. He was very sincere about the purpose of his journey – he wanted to visit the place, isolated and very bleak though it was, to remind himself of everything that had happened. Surprisingly fierce, he justified his arrival, quite certain that he had made the right decision. As we walked, however, he became so unbelievably withdrawn that I could not agree with his interpretation of events. He was unsure and rather quiet, and I was certain he wished he had not come.

Answers on page 609

Verb phrases

A **VERB PHRASE** (**VP**) generally has a **lexical verb** as its main verb. It can be made up of one lexical verb, or one or more auxiliary verbs and a lexical verb. Verb phrases have the following characteristics.

Lexical verbs as head words

A verb phrase may consist of one **lexical verb** as a head word:

```
              h
The girl saw some horses.
             VP
             V
```

Generative grammar would describe the verb phrase in a different way: the noun phrase following the verb would be seen as an integral part of the verb phrase. In the example given above, for instance, *some horses* would be embedded in the larger phrase of which the verb *saw* is the key word. This could be recorded on a tree diagram as follows:

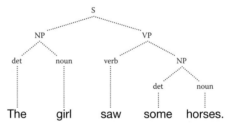

Adopting the **functional approach** which will be used in this book, the example would be represented in a different way in order to distinguish between the contrasting roles of the constituent phrases:

Auxiliary verbs

A verb phrase may have up to four **auxiliary verbs** – the lexical verb will always be the last element in a verb phrase:

		FUNCTION
h	h	

      h   h   FUNCTION

I *have seen* the horses.   I *may see* the horses.
   VP   VP   FORM
aux   lex   aux   lex
(prim)   (mod)

         h   h   FUNCTION

I *may have seen* the horses.   I *should have been seeing* the horses.
   VP   VP   FORM
aux   aux   lex   aux   aux   aux   lex
(mod) (prim)   (mod) (prim) (prim)

                        h   FUNCTION

She *must have been being helped at* the time.
                 VP   FORM
   aux   aux   aux   aux   lex
  (mod) (prim) (prim) (prim)

Phrasal verbs

Some verb phrases, called **PHRASAL VERBS**, are made up of a verb and an adverb:

I *gave away* my tickets.   The manager *looked up* the prices.
  VP   VP
  V   Adv   V   Adv

Many phrasal verbs can stand alone: they do not need anything to follow them (*grow up*, *break down*).

Prepositional verbs

Some verb phrases are made up of a verb and a preposition or particle. They are called **PREPOSITIONAL VERBS**.

I *looked at* the pictures.   He *stood against* his opponent.
  VP   VP
  V   prep   V   prep

Prepositional verbs cannot stand alone: they must be followed by a **noun phrase**.

Phrasal and prepositional verbs are common in informal speech and writing. They can often be replaced by one lexical item.

Prepositional phrases

A **PREPOSITIONAL PHRASE** (**PrepP**) has a **preposition** as its main word. It is normally followed by a noun phrase. Prepositional phrases add extra information and are therefore optional – they can be omitted without affecting the meaning. They have the following characteristics.

Post-modification

Prepositional phrases are used to **post-modify** other phrases.

  m   h   q   m   h   q   FUNCTION
the boys *from the town*   rather unhappy *about the prospect*
   NP   AdjP   FORM
det   N   PrepP   Adv   Adj   PrepP

Adverbials

Prepositional phrases can function as **adverbials** in a sentence, providing information about time, manner and place (see Section 1.6).

	A		A		A	FUNCTION
We went	*to town*		*in the afternoon.*	The girls sat	*in the shade.*	
	PrepP		PrepP		PrepP	FORM
	prep NP	prep	NP		prep NP	

Adverb phrases

An **ADVERB PHRASE** (**AdvP**) has an **adverb** as its main word. Adverb phrases have the following general characteristics.

Adverbs as head words

The **head word** of an adverb phrase is an adverb:

	h		m	h	FUNCTION
the child laughed	*loudly*	the crowd jostled	*very*	*impatiently*	
	AdvP		AdvP		FORM
	Adv		Adv	Adv	

Extra information

Adverb phrases provide **extra information** – if omitted, the sentence will still make sense:

	h	FUNCTION
The choir sing	*gloriously.* The choir sing.	
	AdvP	FORM
	Adv	

Adverbials

Adverb phrases can function as **adverbials** in a sentence, providing information about time, manner and place:

	A		A	FUNCTION
We visited France	*recently.*	They go to the cinema	*quite regularly.*	
	AdvP		AdvP	FORM
	Adv		Adv Adv	

1.6 Clauses

CLAUSES (**Cl**) are the main structures used to compose sentences. A sentence will be made up of at least one **MAIN CLAUSE** (a clause that makes sense on its own and that is not dependent on or part of another clause); it may also contain one or more **SUBORDINATE CLAUSES** (a clause that cannot stand on its own and that is dependent on the main clause). Clauses may be **finite** (containing a verb marked for tense, number and person); **non-finite** (containing a present participle, a past participle or an infinitive); or **verbless** (containing no verb).

- **Finite clause**   (The guests *arrived* late).
- **Non-finite clause**   (*Arriving* late), the guests crowded around the door noisily.
- **Verbless clause**   (Well I never)!

There are five types of CLAUSE ELEMENT and each has a different **function** and **site** (position within the clause).

Subject

The SUBJECT (S) normally describes the person who or the thing which does the action of the verb. It is also called the **actor** of a sentence. You can check which part of the clause is a subject by asking *who?* or *what?* is responsible for the action or process of the verb.

Kinds of subject

The subject is usually a **noun phrase** or a **pronoun**, but it can also be a **clause**:

> S   S   FUNCTION
> (*The girl*) was a good swimmer. (*She*) was a good swimmer.
> NP   NP   FORM
> det   N   pron

> S   FUNCTION
> (*What I look forward to*) is a restful Christmas.
> Cl   FORM

Position in the clause

In a statement, the subject usually **precedes** the verb:

> S
> (*The whole family*) went to town.

Position in a question

In a question, the subject usually **follows** the auxiliary verb:

> S
> Did (*the girl*) go to town?

Effect on the verb

The subject dictates the form of the verb:

> S   S
> (I) *go* to town. (The old lady) *goes* to town.

Effect on the object or complement

The subject sometimes controls the form of the **object** or **complement** in a sentence:

> S   S
> (She) cut *herself*. (They) cut *themselves*.

Verb

VERBS or PREDICATORS (P) can express a range of meanings – actions, processes, states and so on. They are the most important clause element: they cannot be omitted, except in a MINOR SENTENCE:

> *Like father, like son.*

Only a **verb phrase** can fill the verb site of a clause:

> I *should go* to town.

Object

The **OBJECT** (**O**) describes something that is **directly affected** by the verb. You can check which part of a clause is in the **DIRECT OBJECT** (**Od**) site by asking *who?* or *what?* is affected by the action or process of the verb:

Od
The dog ate (*the bone*).

Indirect objects

The object can also be something that is **indirectly affected** by the verb. Usually an **INDIRECT OBJECT** (**Oi**) will **precede** the direct object, but it may instead **follow** the direct object. You can check whether an object is indirect by placing it after the direct object and putting *to* before it:

Oi Od   Od   Oi
The child gave (*her friend*) (a present). The child gave (a present) (*to her friend*).

Kinds of object

The object is usually a **noun phrase** or a **pronoun**. If the object is a pronoun, it may have a distinctive form:

Od   Od
The rain soaked (*the boy*). The rain soaked (*him*).

Oi   Oi
He gave (*the visitors*) a cup of tea. He gave (*them*) a cup of tea.

Position in the clause

Normally, the object **follows** the verb.

Complement

The **COMPLEMENT** (**C**) gives **extra information** about the **subject** (**Cs**) or about the **object** (**Co**):

Cs   Co
The sun was (*bright*). The teacher considered his pupil (*a genius*).

Kinds of complement

The complement can be an **adjective phrase**, a **noun phrase**, a **pronoun**, a **numeral** or a **clause**:

Cs	Co	FUNCTION
The musician was (*excellent*).	The man thought the wine (*a bargain*).	
AdjP	NP	FORM

Cs	Cs	FUNCTION
The book is (*his*).	The old lady was (*ninety*).	
pron	num	FORM

Cs	FUNCTION
This field is (*where the battle took place*).	
Cl	FORM

Position in the clause

Usually, the complement **follows** a verb (*appear, seem, become, be*):

Cs   Cs
The man felt (*gloomy*). The garden had become (*overgrown*).

Adverbials

ADVERBIALS (A) give information about time, manner and place. You can check which part of a clause is an adverbial by asking questions like *how?, when?, where?* and *how often?*

Kinds of adverbial

Adverbials can be **adverb phrases, prepositional phrases, noun phrases** or **clauses**:

| | | | | FUNCTION |

A	A	A	A	FUNCTION
They went (*to town*) (*yesterday*).		They went (*to town*) (*on Saturdays*).		
PrepP	AdvP	PrepP	PrepP	FORM

A	A	A	A	FUNCTION
They went (*to town*) (*last week*).		They went (*to town*) (*when it rained*).		
PrepP	NP	PrepP	Cl	FORM

Number of adverbials

More than one adverbial can be added to a clause:

A	A	A	FUNCTION
(*Twice a week*) the boy ran (*to his grandmother's house*) (*for tea*).			
NP	PrepP	PrepP	FORM

Position in the clause

An adverbial can change its **position** in order to create different kinds of emphasis:

| A | A | A |
| (*Actually*), we went (*to the library*) (*on Mondays*). | | |

| A | A | A |
| (*On Mondays*), we (*actually*) went (*to the library*). | | |

Clause structure

Most clauses will have a **subject** and a **verb**. Other clause elements are **optional** and will be used depending upon the information and the kind of verb selected.

It is useful to distinguish between the **form** or **word class** of a verb (**V**) and the **grammatical role** or **function** of a verb phrase in a clause. To do this, linguists call the verb site the **PREDICATOR** (**P**) in clause analysis:

S	P	S	P	Od	FUNCTION
(I) (run).		(The children) (will need) (some food).			
NP	VP	NP	VP	NP	FORM
pron	V	det N	aux lex	det N	

Clause types

There are seven types of clause, in which the elements are combined in different ways.

1 Subject + verb:

| S | P |
| (They) (voted). | |

2 Subject + verb + direct object:

| S | P | Od |
| (They) (ate) (dinner). | | |

3 Subject + verb + indirect object + direct object:

      S   P   Oi   Od

(Father Christmas) (gave) (each child) (a present).

4 Subject + verb + subject complement:

     S   P   Cs

(Snow) (is) (disruptive).

5 Subject + verb + direct object + object complement:

       S   P   Od   Co

(The government) (considered) (its election promises) (inappropriate).

6 Subject + verb + adverbial:

    S   P   A

(You) (must not go) (near the derelict house).

7 Subject + verb + direct object + adverbial:

   S   P   Od   A

(They) (packed) (their bags) (for school).

ACTIVITY 1.17

Try to identify the clause elements in the following passage. The first sentence is completed for you. Use the following abbreviations:

s subject	**c** complement
P predicator or verb	**A** adverbial
Od direct object	**conj** coordinating conjunction
Oi indirect object	**neg** negative

          A   S   P   C

(After William the Conqueror), (the next King of England) (was) (his son William). He was a very strong and good-looking man, but he had a red face and rather reddish hair. He was not a good man and was cruel to his people. Like his father, he enjoyed hunting animals. One day the Red King's arrow just missed a big deer. William was very excited and called out to his friend, Walter. Walter fired an arrow, but by accident it stuck in the King's eye and he fell dead. Walter was very frightened and he rode away. The King's body lay in the forest all day. In the evening it was carried away in a workman's cart and buried in the big church at a town called Winchester.

Answers on page 609

1.7 Sentences

A **SENTENCE** is a grammatical construction that makes sense on its own. In writing, it begins with a capital letter and ends with a **full stop** or an **exclamation** or **question mark**. This section will help you to recognise and describe the different kinds of sentences. Before beginning work on sentence structure, it would be useful to look back over word classes, phrases, clause elements and clause types.

Simple sentences

A **SIMPLE SENTENCE** contains just **one clause**. It has only **one finite verb** and is described as a **MAIN CLAUSE** (**MCl**).

```
              S       P
(The cook) (ate).
              S       P        Od
(The cook) (ate) (dinner).
              S        P        Oi            Od
(The cook) (made) (the guests) (dinner).
              S         P        Cs
(The cook) (became) (hot).
              S         P           Od          Co
(The cook) (thought) (the guests) (rude).
              S         P         A
(The cook) (worked) (quickly).
              S        P        Od                    A
(The cook) (made) (a large stew) (for the evening meal).
```

Compound sentences

A **COMPOUND SENTENCE** contains **two or more simple sentences** linked by
CO-ORDINATING CONJUNCTIONS (*and, or, but*). Each clause in a compound sentence carries equal weight and makes sense on its own, so each can therefore be
described as a **main clause**. Sentences will often be linked like this because they
share content in some way.

```
MCl  S        P         Od        MCl  P         Od              A
(The girl) (weeded) (borders) and (removed) (dead flowers) (from the roses).
                                   conj
MCl    S      A        P       Od       MCl  S        P          Od
(The children) (often) (watched) (television) but (they) (preferred) (the cinema).
                                              conj
MCl    S      P        A        MCl  S        P          Od
  (We) (could go) (to the park) or (we) (could visit) (the museum).
                                conj
```

When two sentences are linked, it is usually better to avoid repetition. This can be
achieved by using substitution or ellipsis.

Substitution

In **SUBSTITUTION**, a pronoun replaces a noun or a noun phrase:

```
MCl     S        P        Od      MCl  S   P       A
(The tearful boy) (took) (his coat) and (he) (left) (immediately).
MCl  S      P        Od          A        MCl  S  P   A    C
(Dickens) (wrote) (many stories) (in his lifetime) and (he) (is) (still) (popular).
```

Ellipsis

ELLIPSIS is the omission of an element of language. As long as the reader can easily recognise exactly what has been deleted, part of a sentence can be omitted to
avoid repetition.

```
MCl    A          S      P       A              MCl  (ø)       P        A
(In autumn), (the leaves) (fall) (to the ground) (and) [the leaves] (blow) (around the
                                                  conj
        A
garden) (untidily).

MCl          S                  P         A          MCl      (ø)
(The latest film releases) (are publicised) (extensively) (but) [the latest film
                                                          conj
```

```
                    P               C
releases] (are not) (always successful).
                    neg
```

You can usually recognise a subordinate clause by identifying the **word class** of the first word in the clause. It may be a **SUBORDINATING CONJUNCTION (sconj)**, a *wh-* **word** or a **non-finite verb**. It is important to remember that subordinate clauses can be used in all the clause sites except the verb. In other words, a subordinate clause can be used as a subject, an object, a complement or an adverbial.

```
MCl                              S                        P          C
(That the emergency services work very hard) (is) (a well-known fact).
SCl–NCl
 (sconj)
```

```
MCl S    P              Od
(I) (know) (who sent me the Valentine card).
            SCl–RelCl
            (rel pron)
```

```
MCl         S              P          C
(The prospective candidates) (were) (what we had hoped for).
                                      SCl–NCl
                                      (wh- word)
```

```
MCl  S       P        Od                    A
(We) (will discuss) (the new house) (when we know if we've sold this one).
                                      SCl–ACl        SCl–ACl
                                      (sconj)        (sconj)
```

In assessing the **role** of the subordinate clause, always check whether it functions as the **whole** of a clause element or just as **part** of the clause element.

```
MCl S    P              Od
(I) (know) (the boy who sent me the Valentine card).
                       SCl–RelCl
```

```
MCl S    P        Od
(I) (know) (what to do next).
           SCl–NCl
```

In the first example, the subordinate clause could be omitted and part of the object would still remain: *the boy*. The function of the relative clause is to **post-modify** the head noun. In the second example, the subordinate clause stands as the **object** on its own. If it were omitted, the sentence would have no object.

Clauses in **COMPLEX SENTENCES** do not have equal value. One is a **main clause** and the one or more other clauses are called **subordinate** or **dependent clauses**. A subordinate clause does not make sense standing on its own.

There are six types of subordinate clause.

Noun clauses

A **NOUN CLAUSE** (**NCl**) can fill the subject or object site of a clause. There are two main kinds of noun clause.

That-clauses

A **THAT-CLAUSE** (**thatCl**) will begin with *that* (**sconj**), but it may be elided.

```
MCl S     P                    O
     (I) (decided) (that the essay was too long).
                    SCl–NCl
```

Wh-clauses

A **WH-CLAUSE** (**whCl**) will begin with a *wh-* word.

```
MCl S     P          O
     (I) (wonder) (what I can do).
                   SCl–NCl
```

Adverbial clauses

An **ADVERBIAL CLAUSE** (**ACl**) functions as an adverbial within the main clause. It answers questions such as *when?*, *why?* and *what for?* An adverbial clause can be recognised by the **subordinating conjunction** that marks its beginning (*if, because, unless, where,* etc.).

```
MCl S    P            A                 MCl     A           S    P       O
     (I) (went) (when I saw the time).      (Because I left late), (I) (missed) (the train).
                 SCl–ACl                     SCl–ACl
```

Relative clauses

A **RELATIVE CLAUSE** (**RelCl**) adds extra information about one of the nouns in the main clause. The beginning of a relative clause is usually marked by a **relative pronoun** (*who, whose, which* and *that*), although it can be omitted. Relative clauses follow the nouns they post-modify or qualify:

```
MCl   S                       P    C
(The man who lives next door) (is) (deaf).
          SCl–RelCl
```

```
MCl   S        P              O
(Our friend) (likes) (stories that come from other countries).
                                 SCl–RelCl
```

Comparative clauses

A **COMPARATIVE CLAUSE** (**CompCl**) starts with *as* (**equal comparison**) or contains *than* (**unequal comparison**).

```
MCl S   P       C              MCl S    P            O
     (I) (am) (faster than he is).   (We) (took) (as many pictures as he did).
             SCl–CompCl                           SCl–CompCl
```

Non-finite clauses

A **NON-FINITE CLAUSE** (**NFCl**) can be recognised by an **infinitive**, a **present participle** or a **past participle** at the beginning of the clause.

```
MCl S   P        O    MCl         A              S   P      C     A
     (I) (wanted) (to go).   (Leaving it all behind), (I) (was) (happy) (at last).
                  SCl–NFCl   SCl–NFCl
```

Verbless clauses

While **VERBLESS MAIN CLAUSES** (**VlessCl**) like *What about a cup of tea?*, *Good thing too!* and *Lovely weather!* are more likely to be used in informal speech, a **VERBLESS SUBORDINATE CLAUSE** is more common in formal written English.

```
     MCl   A        S    P            A          P              O
    (Once alone), (I) (cried).    (If in doubt), (call) (the freephone number).
     SCl–VlessCl                   SCl–VlessCl
```

Compound–complex sentences

In making a **COMPOUND–COMPLEX SENTENCE**, **co-ordination** and **subordination** are used together:

```
     MCl  S        P                        Od            MCl  A     P        Od
    (The police) (needed) (to discover who had been seen) (and) (then) (hoped) (to make
                           SCl–NFCl      SCl–RelCl         conj              SCl–NFCl
     an arrest).
```

The first main clause here has two subordinate clauses in the object site. It is co-ordinated with another main clause of equal value which has one subordinate clause in the object site.

```
     MCl  S      P             A              MCl    P              A
    (The lorry) (left) (when it had been loaded) (and) (returned) (after it had delivered its
                        SCl–ACl                   conj             SCl–ACl
     its load).
```

Each main clause in the sentence above contains a subordinate clause functioning as an adverbial. Each subordinate clause starts with a subordinating conjunction, *when* or *after*; the two main clauses are joined by a co-ordinating conjunction, *and*.

Major and minor sentences

All the sentences considered so far can be described as **REGULAR** or **MAJOR SENTENCES** because they are constructed using regular patterns.

Some sentences, however, do not follow expected patterns and these are called **IRREGULAR** or **MINOR SENTENCES**. Minor sentences lack some of the essential clause elements considered so far. They use unusual patterns which cannot easily be analysed. Minor sentences are often used in everyday conversation, on posters, in headlines, in advertisements and in slogans. You can check to see whether a sentence is minor by trying to change the verb into the past tense. If you can do so and the sentence still makes sense, it is probably a major rather than a minor sentence.

Minor sentences can be:

- **formulae** used in social situations: *hello, thanks, bye*
- **interjections** used to express some kind of emotion: *ah!, tut tut!*
- **abbreviated forms** often used on postcards or in spoken commentaries: *wish you were here, nearly there*
- words or phrases used as **exclamations**, **questions** or **commands**: *what a day!, congratulations, never!, taxi!*

Analysing a sentence

In order to analyse a sentence, use the following process.

1 Underline the **verbs** in the sentence – if there are none, it is an example of a minor sentence.
2 Identify the main **lexical verb(s)** and mark the **main clause(s)**.
3 Label the **clause elements**.
4 Identify any **subordinate clauses** and decide whether they function as a whole or as a part of the clause element.
5 Identify the **type** of subordinate clause by identifying the word class of the first word. Table 1.1 summarises the kinds of words that appear in the initial position of a subordinate clause and the clause types in each case.

Table 1.1 **The classification of subordinate clauses**

Word in initial position	Clause type	Function
who, whose, which, that	Relative	Post-modify noun phrases.
that, wh- words	Noun	Fill subject or object site.
subordinating conjunctions	Adverbial	Answers questions such as *why?, when?, how?* and *where?*
as, than	Comparative	Making comparisons.
to + verb, present participle, past participle	Non-finite	Can be used in subject, object or complement clause sites. More succinct than finite clauses as they use fewer words.

ACTIVITY 1.18

Underline the subordinate clauses in the following passage and try to identify their type. Remember that a subordinate clause can:

1 replace a whole clause site: subject, object, complement or adverbial
2 post-modify a noun phrase
3 add extra information to a complement, etc.

I shall always remember the day when we arrived at the new house. It was perfect. The weather was good and our spirits were high. Things did not remain the same for long because things were not quite what they seemed. Looking back, I now regret many things.

The first problem was the key which did not fit. Then the removal van did not arrive, leaving us stranded. With no furniture and no boxes, there was nothing for us to do. The fact that we were helpless was not too disturbing, but the sudden change in the weather was since we were stuck outside. The estate agent was sent for and the removal company phoned. Although we could do nothing for the moment, I felt obliged to act, rushing around like a headless chicken while the rain fell steadily.

The time passed slowly. Eventually, someone did bring a new key, so that we could go into the house and wait for the removal van in the dry. We had been assured that it was on its way at last!

The unpredictable day became a peaceful night as we settled into a bare and disorganised house. Our immediate problems were over, but we had not anticipated what was to come next …

Answers on page 610

1.8 Mood

The **MOOD** of a sentence shows the attitude of the speaker to the action or event referred to in the verb phrase: we can **tell** someone something, or **ask** them or **command** them to do something. There are three moods.

Declarative mood

The **DECLARATIVE MOOD** is used for making statements. You can recognise the declarative by checking whether the **subject** comes first in the clause and is followed by the **verb**. If the sentence is complex, the mood is determined by the main clause, so always look at that first.

> S   P   C   A
> (The old man) (was) (content) (in the park).

> S   P   A   A
> (The symphony orchestra) (played) (resoundingly) (in the new concert hall).

Interrogative mood

The **INTERROGATIVE MOOD** is used for addressing questions. You can recognise the interrogative by checking whether the **subject** follows the **auxiliary verbs** *do*, *have* or *be*:

> P S   P A   A
> (Did) (the old man) (sit) (in the park) (contentedly)?
> aux   lex

> P   S   P A   A
> (Was) (the symphony orchestra) (playing) (well) (in the new concert hall)?
> aux   lex

In speech, if the word order is unchanged and **INTONATION PATTERNS** (the way the voice moves up and down) are used to indicate a question, the mood is said to be **declarative**. The only examples of the **interrogative** mood in which words are not inverted are in sentences in which *wh-* **words** fill the subject site.

> S   P   A   S P O
> (What) (happens) (next)?   (Who) (wants) (tea)?

Imperative mood

The **IMPERATIVE MOOD** is used for addressing commands or orders. You can recognise the imperative by checking that there is **no subject** and that the **verb** is in the **base form** (the unmarked form).

> P A   P   A   A
> (Sit) (in the park). (Vote) (in the European elections) (today)!

Sometimes the person addressed is named but not in the traditional subject site of the clause; instead, a **VOCATIVE** (**voc**) is used. This refers to the person to whom the sentence is addressed. A vocative has two functions:

- to call someone, in order to gain her or his attention;

> *Joseph*, it's tea-time. It's your turn on the computer now, *Julie*.

- to address someone, expressing a particular social relationship or a personal attitude.

> *Waiter*, there's a fly in my soup! *You fool*, what are you trying to do?

Vocatives are optional and can occur at the beginning, middle or end of the sentence. They can be:

- **names**: *Andrew, Sharon*
- **family titles**: *Mummy, Dad, Aunt*
- **labels** that reflect **status** or **respect**: *sir, madam, ladies and gentlemen*
- **professional titles**: *nurse, doctor, councillor*
- words reflecting **evaluative judgements**: *pig, darling, sweetheart*
- *you* as an **impolite term of address**.

1.9 Cohesion

Language has a hierarchical structure. So far, you have studied words, phrases, clauses and sentences: these are divided in terms of their **RANK**. **Words** are described as having a **lower rank** and **sentences** as having a **higher rank**. This is because a sentence may be made up of more than one clause; clauses may be made up of more than one phrase; and phrases may be made up of more than one word.

You now need to think about the ways in which sentences are combined into larger units or **DISCOURSE** – the linguistic term used to describe spoken or written language that is longer than a sentence in length. In any study of **COHESION**, you will need to consider the ways in which sentences are linked to create text.

There are five forms of cohesion which it is useful to be able to recognise: lexical cohesion, substitution, ellipsis, referencing, and linking adverbs and conjunctions.

Lexical cohesion

LEXICAL COHESION is a kind of textual linking dependent on a writer or speaker's choice of words. A number of cohesive techniques can be used.

Collocations

In **COLLOCATIONS**, words are associated within **phrases**. Because they are often well known, they are predictable. Many can be described as **IDIOMS** and **CLICHÉS**.

> *home and dry*   *safe and sound*   *free and easy*

Repetition

In **REPETITION** either words or phrases are directly repeated or **SYNONYMS** (related words with a similar meaning) are used.

> *This little pig* went to market,
> *This little pig* stayed at home,
> *This little pig* had roast beef …

Superordinates and hyponyms

SUPERORDINATES are **general words**; **HYPONYMS** are **subdivisions** of the general categorisation. Both these types of words can be used to provide cohesion.

- Superordinate: *dog*   Hyponyms: *alsatian, poodle, spaniel*
- Superordinate: *crockery*   Hyponyms: *plate, cup, bowl*

Many written or spoken texts have a clear content focus and could therefore be described as **SUBJECT-SPECIFIC**.

> I saw a *ship* a-sailing,
>   A-sailing on the sea,
>   And oh, but it was laden
> With pretty things for thee.
>   There were comfits in the *cabin*,
>   And apples in the *hold*.
>   The *sails* were made of silk,
> And the *masts* were all of gold.

Traditional nursery rhyme

Substitution

In linking by **SUBSTITUTION**, one linguistic item is replaced by a shorter one. The substitution will usually occur in the second clause so that the meaning is clear. Several parts of a sentence can be replaced.

Noun phrases

Personal pronouns can be substitutes for noun phrases in the subject or object clause sites. They should only be used if the identity of the person or thing is clear.

>   S   P   O   S   P   O
> (Joseph) (loves) (toy trains) (and) (Joseph) (has) (two toy trains).
>   conj

>   S   P   O   S   P   O
> (Joseph) (loves) (toy trains) (and) (*he*) (has) (two *of them*).
>   conj

Either the head or the whole of a noun phrase can also be replaced by the **indefinite pronouns** *one* or *some* or by the **noun phrase** *the same*:

> 'Would you like *a coffee?*' 'I'd love *one*.'
> 'I'd like *the vegetarian lasagne and salad*, please.' 'And I'll have *the same*.'

Equally, **superordinates** and **hyponyms** can be substitutes:

> *The alsatian* was large and the child was obviously afraid of *the dog*.
> *The flowers* were in abundance and people came from miles around to see *the newly blooming roses*.

Verb phrases

A verb phrase or a verb phrase plus object can be replaced by the **auxiliary verb** *do*:

>   S   P   O   A   S   P   A
> (I) (saw) (*Pirates of the Caribbean 3*) (last week). (I) (did) (yesterday).

>   S   P   O   S   P   A
> (Julie) (*likes*) (*swimming*) (and) (Mark) (*does*) (too).

Clauses

Clauses can be replaced using *so* as a substitute for a **positive clause** and *not* as a substitute for a **negative clause**:

'It's going to be sunny today?' 'They say *so*.'
'I wonder if *I need to buy a new ticket?*' 'The driver said *not*.'

Ellipsis

In **ELLIPSIS**, part of a sentence is left out. If the sentence is to remain meaningful, it must be clear what the omitted words are.

Noun phrases

The head of a simple noun phrase and the head and any modifiers or qualifiers in a complex noun phrase can be omitted:

        S   P   C   (ø)   P   A
(*The buttercups*) (were) (bright yellow) (and) [*the buttercups*] (stretched) (for miles).
                          conj

              S   P   A   (ø)
(*The black clouds of the impending storm*) (rose) (above us) (and) [*the black clouds of*
                                    conj
           P   A
the impending storm] (loomed) (threateningly).

Verb phrases

Repeated lexical and auxiliary verbs can be omitted from a verb phrase:

The children *ate* jelly and ice-cream and the adults [*ate*] bread and cheese.
We were *shopping* in Cardiff and Lucy was [*shopping*] in Swansea.
We *had* visited the cinema and [*had*] looked around the museum.
They *have been* riding and [*have been*] surfing this week.

Clauses

Whole clauses can be omitted, usually within sentence boundaries rather than outside:

'Who was *playing the clarinet last night?*' 'Susan was [*playing the clarinet last night*].'

Referencing

REFERENCES cannot be interpreted alone because they **point** to something else in a discourse. **Pronouns** (also called **SUBSTITUTE WORDS**) are often used to make these references, but **comparative structures** expressing particular similarities or differences can also be used.

The girl loved reading, so *she* often visited the library.
The black horse ran fast, but *the white one* was faster.

There are three main kinds of reference.

Anaphoric references

ANAPHORIC REFERENCES point **backwards** in a text. In other words, the reader or listener must look back to a previous noun phrase to make sense of the pronoun or comparative structure used:

The boy broke the window and then *he* ran away.

Cataphoric references

CATAPHORIC REFERENCES point **forwards** in a text. In other words, the reader or listener must look ahead to a subsequent noun phrase in order to understand the structure used:

> *This* was *the life* – lying in the sun with the waves roaring in the background.
> *These* are *the words* he used: 'I cannot stand it any longer and I'm leaving.'

Exophoric references

EXOPHORIC REFERENCES point **beyond** a text. In other words, the reader or listener must make a connection with something **outside** the discourse.

> 'I was *this* high then.'   '*That* boat over there is mine.'

A gesture or a context is needed to accompany each of these statements if it is to make sense.

Linking adverbs and conjunctions

LINKING ADVERBS and CONJUNCTIONS are joining words that provide links either within a sentence or within the larger context of discourse. There are four main types.

Additive adverbs and conjunctions

ADDITIVE ADVERBS and CONJUNCTIONS add on information, possibly as an afterthought: *and, furthermore, besides, incidentally.*

Adversative adverbs and conjunctions

ADVERSATIVE ADVERBS and CONJUNCTIONS help to create a contrast between the sentence they introduce and the preceding sentence: *yet, however, nevertheless, on the contrary.*

Causal adverbs and conjunctions

CAUSAL ADVERBS and CONJUNCTIONS link two clauses or sentences by suggesting that one has been the result of the other: *because, since, therefore, as a result, thus.*

Temporal adverbs and conjunctions

TEMPORAL ADVERBS and CONJUNCTIONS create a time link between one clause or sentence and another: *before, while, then, after that, at once, meanwhile.*

Chapter 2

Phonetics and phonology

2.1 The reason for studying phonetics and phonology

Spoken language is a very important part of any linguistic study because it is so central to our everyday lives. A knowledge of grammar helps linguists to explain some distinctive features of each spoken variety, but it is also necessary to be able to describe the **sounds** of language. **PHONETICS** is the study of **spoken sounds**, and it focuses on the way in which sounds are produced. Instead of considering sound production in general, **PHONOLOGY** focuses on sounds in a particular language. It focuses on the ways in which sounds are combined to produce meaning.

The study of phonetics and phonology gives linguists the means to discuss a range of key areas in spoken language. It helps them focus their analysis in a wide range of contexts by providing an appropriate analytical framework. When studying spoken varieties, language students also need to be able to use appropriate terminology and analytical approaches. A knowledge of phonetics and phonology will help you to study:

- **accent** – social and regional variations in pronunciation can be transcribed exactly
- **the history of English** – changes in pronunciation can be identified and described accurately
- **child language** – immature pronunciation can be recorded as children experiment with new words
- **informal conversation** – changes in speech linked to audience, purpose and context can be discussed precisely
- **scripted speech** – the realism of speech on television and the radio can be analysed and compared with 'real' speech
- **other spoken varieties** – key linguistic features of television advertisements, commentaries and public speeches can be identified.

The information here will help you to tackle these areas of your course. It is not necessary to learn the material systematically, but you should be able to use it as it will help you to discuss the sounds and characteristics of spoken English concisely.

Phonetics is the scientific study of the ways in which humans make sounds. It can be used to analyse any language and it attempts to describe, classify and transcribe **all** possible sounds.

There are three key areas:

▸ the **way** sounds are made by the vocal organs – ARTICULATION
▸ the **physical properties** of sounds as they travel from the mouth to the ear – TRANSMISSION
▸ the way in which the ear and the brain **receive** and **respond** to sounds – RECEPTION.

The main focus in this section will be on **articulation**, since it is useful to understand the way in which the speech organs create sound.

In **Received Pronunciation** (RP – see Section 5.2), there are 44 recognisable sounds: 24 consonant sounds and 20 vowel sounds. Because the ROMAN ALPHABET used for recording written English does not reflect this range, linguists use a specially designed PHONETIC ALPHABET which tries to classify each variation. The idea of creating a phonetic alphabet was first proposed by Otto Jespersen (1860–1943) in 1886, and the first version of the INTERNATIONAL PHONETIC ALPHABET (IPA) was published in 1888. The aim of the system was to create a separate symbol for each sound which could then be used in any language in which the sound appeared. In order to make it accessible, the symbols of the Roman alphabet were used as often as possible. DIACRITICS – marks or points that slightly alter the sound quality of the original symbol – were added to some symbols to give a greater range of sounds. Alongside these, some new symbols were created. The IPA has been altered and extended several times (most recently in 1989), but is still used by linguists throughout the world.

Table 2.1 records all the IPA symbols: it classifies each sound according to the way in which it is physically produced. The list of diacritics and other symbols provides linguists with the means to record all kinds of variations in the sound quality. In your study of language, you are unlikely to need such a wide range of symbols: this section will therefore introduce you to the basic sounds and symbols that will be useful in recording the sounds of English.

The symbols of the International Phonetic Alphabet record the 'sound' of words exactly. They allow linguists to distinguish between words that **look** similar in traditional orthography, but that **sound** quite different. Words transcribed phonetically are enclosed in square brackets to show that the focus is on the **way** that sounds are made.

cough	[kɒf]	enough	[ɪnʌf]
dough	[dəʊ]	through	[θruː]

The articulators – the organs of speech

To understand **how** we speak, linguists need to know something about the organs involved in the production of sound and the way in which these move. When we make sounds, we alter the flow of breath through the mouth and nose

CONSONANTS

(pulmonic air-stream mechanism)

	Bilabial	Labio-dental	Dental, Alveolar, or Post-alveolar	Retroflex	Palato-alveolar	Palatal	Velar	Uvular	Labial-Palatal	Labial-Velar	Pharyngeal	Glottal
Nasal	m	ɱ	n	ɳ		ɲ	ŋ	ɴ				
Plosive	p b		t d	ʈ ɖ		c ɟ	k g	q ɢ		k͡p g͡b		ʔ
(Median) Fricative	ɸ β	f v	θ ð s z	ʂ ʐ	ʃ ʒ	ç ʝ	x ɣ	χ ʁ		ʍ w	ħ ʕ	h ɦ
(Median) Approximant		ʋ	ɹ	ɻ		j	ɰ		ɥ	w		
Lateral Fricative			ɬ ɮ									
Lateral (Approximant)			l	ɭ		ʎ	ʟ					
Trill			r					ʀ				
Tap or Flap			ɾ	ɽ				ʀ				

(non-pulmonic air-stream)

	Bilabial	Labio-dental	Dental, Alveolar, or Post-alveolar	Retroflex	Palato-alveolar	Palatal	Velar	Uvular
Ejective	p'		t'				k'	
Implosive	ɓ		ɗ			ʄ	ɠ	ʛ
(Median) Click	ʘ		ʇ	ʗ				
Lateral Click			ʖ					

DIACRITICS

- ○ Voiceless n̥ d̥
- ˏ Voiced s̬ t̬
- ʰ Aspirated tʰ
- ¨ Breathy-voiced b̤ a̤
- ː Dental t̪
- ˛ Labialised t̫
- ˎ Palatalised t̡
- ˤ Velarised or pharyngealised ɫ ɫ̵
- ̩ Syllabic n̩ l̩
- ‿ or ⁀ Simultaneous (but see also under the heading 'AFFRICATES')

- ˎ or ˔ Raised e̝, e̝ ᶷ
- ˏ or ˕ Lowered e̞, e̞ ᶩ
- - or ˖ Advanced u̟+ u̟
- ∷ Retracted i̠ i- t̠
- ¨ Centralised ë
- ~ Nasalised ã
- ˞ r-coloured aʴ
- ː Long aː
- ˑ Half long aˑ
- ˘ Non-syllabic ŭ
- ˒ More rounded ɔ˒
- ˓ Less rounded y˓

OTHER SYMBOLS

- ɕ ʑ Alveolo-palatal fricatives
- ʓ Palatalised ʃ
- ɿ Alveolar fricative trill
- ɺ Alveolar lateral flap
- ɧ Simultaneous ʃ and x
- ʆ Variety of ʃ resembling s, etc.
- ɪ = i
- ʊ = u
- ɜ = Variety of ə
- ɚ = r-coloured ə

VOWELS

	Front	Back	Front	Back
	Unrounded		Rounded	
Close	i ɨ	ɯ u	y ʉ	u
Half-close	e ɘ	ɤ o	ø ɵ	o
Half-open	ɛ ɜ	ʌ ɔ	œ ɞ	ɔ
Open	æ a	a ɑ	ɶ	ɒ

STRESS, TONE (PITCH)

ˈ stress, placed at beginning of stressed syllable; ˌ secondary stress; ˉ high level pitch, high tone; ˍ low level; ˊ high rising; ˏ low rising; ˋ high falling; ˎ low falling; ˆ rise-fall; ˇ fall-rise.

AFFRICATES can be written as digraphs, as ligatures, or with slur marks: thus ts tʃ dʒ; t͡s t͡ʃ d͡ʒ; ʦ ʧ ʤ; c, ɟ may occasionally be used for tʃ, dʒ.

Table 2.1 **The International Phonetic Alphabet**

by moving the tongue and other organs related to the production of sound. By describing the process involved in creating each sound, linguists can classify and analyse the particular sounds making up a language. Figure 2.1 identifies the main ARTICULATORS.

Air passes from the LUNGS through the LARYNX and into the VOCAL TRACT. Here the VOCAL CORDS produce two kinds of sounds. When spread apart, the air can pass between them without obstruction to make sounds which are described as VOICELESS. If you place your fingers on your larynx and say *pick* and *fish* you will feel no vibrations. When the vocal cords are drawn together, however, the air from the lungs has to push them apart, creating a vibration. This produces a VOICED sound – try saying *big* and *visit*. The opening between the vocal cords is called the GLOTTIS – when the cords are apart, the glottis is said to be **open**; when they are pressed together, the glottis is said to be **closed**.

Having passed through the vocal cords, the air is then affected by the **speech organs**. The TONGUE, the SOFT PALATE and the LIPS, for instance, move to produce a range of sounds. The resonance of these sounds is influenced by the shape of the ORAL and NASAL SPACES through which the air passes.

Some of the articulators, like the UPPER TEETH, the ALVEOLAR RIDGE and the HARD PALATE, are described as **passive** because they do not move. Other articulators are described as **active** because they move to change the spaces through which the air passes. The **soft palate** in normal breathing is lowered so that air can pass through the nasal cavity easily. In speech, however, it can be raised to force air through the mouth; lowered to allow air to escape through the mouth and nose; or lowered with the mouth closed so that air is forced through the nose. The LIPS may be closed or held open in a range of positions. The JAW controls the size of the gap between the teeth and the position of the lips. The TONGUE is the most important vocal organ: because it is so flexible, it helps to create a wide range of sounds.

ACTIVITY 2.1

In English, many consonants (all the letters of the alphabet except *a*, *e*, *i*, *o* and *u*) form pairs of sounds in which one is *voiced* and the other *voiceless*. The distinction between voiced and voiceless sounds is important because it enables us to distinguish between words that would otherwise be phonetically the same.

Read through the list of consonantal sounds (IPA symbols are enclosed in square brackets) and accompanying words. Try singing each one aloud and compile a list of those that can be sung and those that cannot. Then create pairs by deciding which voiceless sounds can be made into voiced sounds by doing nothing but opening the vocal cords.

1 thth [θ] – <u>th</u>ank
2 ssss [s] – <u>s</u>nake
3 vvvv [v] – <u>v</u>ase
4 zzzz [z] – <u>z</u>oo
5 shsh [ʃ] – <u>sh</u>oe

6 nnnn [n] – <u>n</u>eck
7 mmmm [m] – <u>m</u>onkey
8 zhzh [ʒ]- trea<u>s</u>ure
9 ffff [f] – <u>f</u>ast
10 thth [ð] – <u>th</u>ere.

Figure 2.1 **The organs of speech**

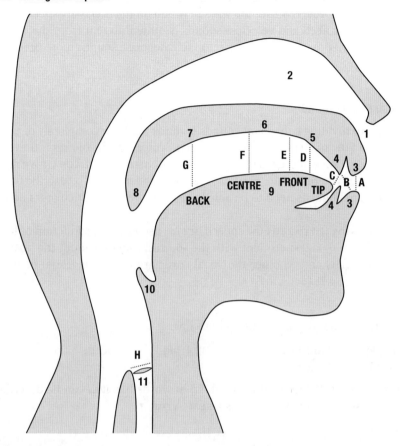

KEY	**Organs of speech**		
1	nostril	7	soft palate (velum)
2	nasal cavity	8	uvula
3	lips	9	tongue
4	teeth	10	epiglottis
5	alveolar ridge	11	vocal cords
6	hard palate		

KEY	**Places of articulation**		
A	bilabial	E	palato-alveolar
B	labio-dental	F	palatal
C	dental	G	velar
D	alveolar	H	glottal

COMMENTARY

To sing aloud, the vocal cords must vibrate. Any consonant that can be sung is therefore likely to be a voiced sound. From your experimentation, you should have found that the following consonants are voiced: [v], [z], [n], [m], [ʒ], [ð]. The sounds in your other list are all voiceless consonants: [ʃ], [s], [f] and [θ]. By changing the voiceless sounds into voiced sounds, it is possible to recognise pairs: [ʃ] → [ʒ]; [s] → [z]; [f] → [v]; and [θ] → [ð]. In some examples, the sound of two words may be almost identical except for the fact that a particular consonant is voiced or voiceless. The distinction in sound can help us to recognise semantic differences.

sue (voiceless) → zoo (voiced)   wreath (voiceless) → wreathe (voiced)
fast (voiceless) → vast (voiced)

The basic division of sounds into voiced and voiceless, depending on the position of the vocal cords, is one of the ways in which linguists classify speech sounds. But each of the voiced and voiceless sounds is quite different from the others, so linguists use other methods of description to categorise sounds more precisely.

Consonants

The place of articulation

In addition to dividing consonant sounds (sounds made by completely or partially blocking the flow of air) into the categories of 'voiced' and 'voiceless', they can be classified by the speech organs used to articulate them. The **PLACE OF ARTICULATION** describes where the airstream is stopped in the mouth. To describe the place of articulation, linguists need to be able to refer to the main articulators named in Figure 2.1.

The following list records the speech organs used in the production of RP consonants. As you read, experiment with the sounds, thinking about the position of the speech organs and whether the vocal cords are apart (voiceless) or together (voiced).

Bilabials

BILABIALS are sounds formed using both lips.

[p] pig   (voiceless)   [b] big   (voiced)
[m] milk   (voiced)

The place of articulation for the sound [w] in words like *well* can be described as bilabial, but some linguists class it as a **SEMI-VOWEL**.

Labiodentals

LABIODENTALS are sounds formed using the lower lip and upper teeth.

[f] four   (voiceless)   [v] vase   (voiced)

Dentals

DENTALS are sounds formed by placing the tip of the tongue behind the upper front teeth or between the teeth.

[θ] thin   (voiceless)   [ð] there   (voiced)
    teeth   teethe

Alveolars

ALVEOLARS are sounds formed by placing the tip of the tongue on the alveolar ridge just behind the upper teeth.

[t] tin   (voiceless)   [d] din   (voiced)
[s] sin   (voiceless)   [z] zip   (voiced)
[n] nip   (voiced)   [l] lip   (voiced)

Because the tongue is curled back when the consonant [r] is articulated, it does not actually touch the alveolar ridge. Linguists sometimes therefore describe [r] as a **POST-ALVEOLAR SOUND**.

[r] rip   (voiced)

Palato-alveolars

PALATO-ALVEOLARS are sounds formed by placing the tongue at the front of the hard palate near the alveolar ridge.

[ʃ] shin   (voiceless)   [tʃ] chips   (voiceless)
    sugar   chin
[ʒ] pleasure (voiced)   [dʒ] trudge   (voiced)
                                         gem

Palatal

A **PALATAL** is a sound formed by putting the tongue against the middle of the palate.

[j] you   (voiced)
    yet

Velars

VELARS are sounds formed using the soft palate and the tongue.

[k] kick   (voiceless)   [g] get   (voiced)
    car
[ŋ] sing   (voiced)
    tongue

Glottals

GLOTTALS are two sounds that can be produced without using the tongue or other articulators. The glottis can be opened so that there is no obstruction to the air in the mouth.

[h] high   (voiceless glottal)
    horse

Alternatively, the glottis can be briefly closed completely and then released.

[ʔ] bottle   (as pronounced with a Cockney accent and in Estuary English)
    bitter

The manner of articulation

Having classified sounds as 'voiced' or 'voiceless' and by the place of articulation, linguists also refer to the **MANNER OF ARTICULATION** or the **way** in which consonants are produced. This enables them to distinguish between sounds that although quite different may be produced in the same part of the mouth and that may both be voiced or voiceless.

[d] and [z] are both voiced alveolars
[b] and [m] are both voiced bilabials

To describe the manner of articulation, linguists focus on what happens to the airstream after it has passed through the vocal cords. It may be stopped, partly blocked or allowed to move freely. Sounds that are completely blocked in the mouth are called **STOPS**; sounds in which the airstream is uninterrupted or only partly interrupted in the mouth are called **CONTINUANTS**. All sounds are either stops or continuants.

The following list records what happens to the airstream once it has entered the mouth. As you read, experiment with the sounds, thinking about the passage of air, the position of the speech organs, and whether the vocal cords are together or apart.

Plosives

PLOSIVES are sounds produced by stopping the airstream. A blockage may be created by the movement of one articulator against another, or by the movement of two articulators against each other. The air trapped by the blockage is then released suddenly, making a noise loud enough to be heard.

▸ [p] [b] [t] [d] [k] [g]

The consonants [p], [t] and [k] are always voiceless; the others are usually voiced, but may be only partly voiced when they occur in initial or final position (the beginning and end of words). The glottal stop [ʔ] is also a plosive, but it is less important than the others because it is usually just an alternative pronunciation for [p], [t] and [k].

Fricatives

FRICATIVES are sounds produced by a partial blockage of the airstream resulting in friction as the air is forced through the small gap. Fricatives are continuants: it is possible to continue making each sound until all the air in the lungs has been exhausted.

▸ [f] [v] [θ] (thing) [ð] (this) [s] [z] [ʃ] [ʒ] (pleasure) [h]

Other than the glottal [h], the fricatives in the English language are paired according to their place of articulation. For each type, there is one voiced and one voiceless consonant: the labiodental [f] is voiceless, whereas [v] is voiced; the dental [θ] is voiceless, whereas [ð] is voiced; the alveolar [s] is voiceless, whereas [z] is voiced; and the palato-alveolar [ʃ] is voiceless, whereas [ʒ] is voiced.

The consonant [h] alters depending upon the vowel it precedes: h*i*t; h*a*t; h*o*t. Some linguists therefore describe it phonetically as a **VOICELESS VOWEL**. Nevertheless, it behaves like a consonant because it almost always precedes a vowel. When it appears between voiced sounds, it too is voiced.

Affricates

AFFRICATES are sounds produced by combining a brief blockage of the airstream with an obstructed release which causes some friction. Like the plosives, these are called **stops**.

▸ [tʃ] (church) [dʒ] (judge)

Nasals

NASALS are sounds produced when the soft palate is lowered and the airstream is forced into the nasal cavity. Although the airstream continues to flow in the production of these sounds, they are called **stops** because a blockage in the mouth prevents air escaping orally.

 ▸ [m] [n] [ŋ]

While [m] and [n] frequently occur in the word-initial position, [ŋ] cannot. In RP, if [ŋ] is at the end of a morpheme, it usually occurs without a following [g].

 ▌ banger (bang + er) = [bæŋə]

If it is in the middle of a morpheme, it is usually pronounced.

 ▌ bingo = [bɪŋgəʊ]

In the word-final position, it is rarely followed by [g] except in some regional accents.

 ▌ bring = [brɪŋ] RP; [brɪŋg] regional

Laterals

[l] can be described as a **LATERAL** consonant because the passage of air through the mouth is along the sides of the tongue rather than along the centre. This is caused by a blockage created where the centre or front of the tongue makes contact with the front of the alveolar ridge behind the upper front teeth.

The consonant [l] sounds different depending upon its position in a word: [l] before a vowel sounds quite different from [l] in other positions.

 ▌ leg, log, lag (clear *l*)   meal, till, betrayal (dark *l*)

Varying pronunciations of a consonant are called **ALLOPHONES**. Another allophone occurs when [l] follows [p] or [k] at the beginning of a stressed syllable – in words like *place* or *klaxon* the consonant is not voiced as it is in other words.

Approximants or frictionless consonants

The sounds [r], [w] and [j] are described as **APPROXIMANTS** or **FRICTIONLESS CONTINUANTS** because although they are consonants they do not adopt the articulator positions of the plosives, nasals or fricatives.

The consonant [r] is articulated with the tip of the tongue near the alveolar area, but the tip never actually touches the ridge as it would in the production of [t] or [d]. The tongue is usually curled backwards, and this positions it slightly further back than in the alveolar sounds – [r] is therefore often described as a **POST-ALVEOLAR APPROXIMANT**. If [r] is preceded by [p], [t] or [k], it becomes voiceless.

 ▌ tray [treɪ]   print [prɪnt]

If it is in the initial position or is preceded by anything other than [p], [t] or [k], it is voiced.

 ▌ read [riːd]   abrasive [əbreɪsɪv]

If a word is spelt with a final *r* or if the letter *r* is followed by a consonant, the *r* is not pronounced.

 ▌ car [kɑː]   bears [beəs]

Some dialects pronounce [r] in the final position and before a final consonant – these are called **RHOTIC ACCENTS**. RP, however, is a **NON-RHOTIC ACCENT**.

The consonants [w] and [j] are sometimes described as **SEMI-VOWELS**. Although phonetically they may sound like a vowel, phonologically they are consonants, only occurring before vowels. They are produced when the tongue moves from one position to another, and are therefore sometimes called **GLIDES**.

Describing consonants

By using these three kinds of classification, it is possible to define the nature of a consonant very precisely. Linguists can record the exact production of a sound by describing:

1 the **positions of the vocal cords** – together or open
2 the **place of articulation** – bilabial, labiodental, dental, alveolar, post-alveolar, palato-alveolar, palatal, velar or glottal
3 the **manner of articulation** – plosive, fricative, affricate, nasal, lateral, approximant.

| [d] voiced alveolar plosive | [v] voiceless labiodental fricative |
| [w] voiceless bilabial approximant | |

ACTIVITY 2.2

Use the following exercises to check your understanding of the phonetic nature of consonants.

1 Say the following words and work out the place of articulation for the initial sound in each word:

a fox   c music   e shop
b night   d thing   f king

2 Say the following words and try to decide whether the final sound is voiced or voiceless:

a ship   c lid   e fall
b ditch   d teething   f nudge

3 Define the following consonants by describing the position of the vocal cords and the place and manner of articulation. Use Table 2.2 to check your description.

[k] *voiceless velar plosive*

a [g]   c [v]   e [m]
b [ʃ]   d [p]   f [h]

Answers on page 610

Vowels

Pure vowels

Vowel sounds are produced by the **free flow of air** and the position of the **tongue**, which influences the shape of the space the air has to pass through. The method of description used for consonants needs to be adapted – it is not appropriate

Table 2.2 **The classification of consonants**

Place of articulation	Plosives VL	Plosives V	Fricatives VL	Fricatives V	Affricates VL	Affricates V	Nasals VL	Nasals V	Laterals VL	Laterals V	Approximants VL	Approximants V
Bilabial	p	b						m				w
Labiodental			f	v								
Dental			θ	ð								
Alveolar	t	d	s	z				n		l		
Post-alveolar												r
Palato-alveolar			ʃ	ʒ	tʃ	dʒ						
Palatal												j
Velar	k	g						ŋ				
Glottal	ʔ			h								

to talk about the place and manner of articulation. Instead linguists have to ask themselves three key questions about a vowel sound.

How high is the tongue?

The tongue's height may be described as CLOSE (**high**), HALF-CLOSE, OPEN (**low**) or HALF-OPEN – these relate to the closeness of the tongue to the roof of the mouth.

   [iː] close vowel   [æ] open vowel
   [ʊ] half-close   [ɜː] half-open

Which part of the tongue is raised or lowered?

By raising or lowering different parts of the tongue, different sounds are made. The parts of the tongue involved in making vowel sounds are the FRONT, CENTRE and BACK.

   [æ] front   [ʌ] centre
   [ɑː] back

What is the position of the lips?

As well as defining vowels in terms of tongue height and the part of the tongue involved, linguists have to consider the shape of the lips. There are three main positions involved – ROUNDED LIPS, such that the corners of the lips come together and the lips are pushed forward; SPREAD LIPS, such that the corners of the lips move away from each other, as they do for a smile; NEUTRAL, in which the lips are not noticeably rounded or spread.

   [uː] rounded   [ɜː] neutral
   [iː] spread

Vowels that are not marked with diacritics are described as SHORT VOWELS: [ɪ], [e], [æ], [ʌ], [ɒ], [ə] and [ʊ]. The LONG VOWELS are marked with diacritics /ː/, which

Figure 2.2 **The eight primary cardinal vowels**

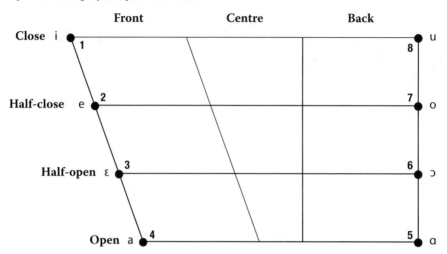

denote length: [iː], [ɑː], [ɔː], [ɜː] and [uː]. It is important to remember, however, that the length of all vowels in English varies according to the context.

Describing pure vowels

By using these three areas of classification, it is possible to define the nature of a pure vowel sound precisely. Linguists can record the exact production of a sound by describing:

1 the **height of the tongue**
2 the **part of the tongue**
3 the **shape of the lips**.

> [e] p<u>e</u>t
> The **front** of the tongue is between **half-open** and **half-close** position with the lips **neutral**.
>
> [ɔː] r<u>oa</u>r
> The **back** of the tongue is between **half-open** and **half-close** position with the lips **rounded**.
>
> [iː] sl<u>ee</u>p
> The **front** of the tongue is raised in a **high** or **close** position with the lips **spread**.

Because vowel sounds are so variable, linguists need some points of reference. The **CARDINAL VOWELS** are not 'real' vowels, but are inflexible standards against which the vowel sounds of everyday usage are set. These eight sounds are formed using clearly contrasting tongue heights and parts of the tongue, and are therefore often called **REFERENCE VOWELS**. Figure 2.2 records the way in which these eight key vowels are produced – linguists learn to make and recognise these vowels so that they can use them as a norm. By starting from the clearly defined positions of the cardinal vowels, they are then able to describe other vowels, comparing their production with those already marked on the chart.

Figure 2.3 **Tongue positions for the pure vowels in English**

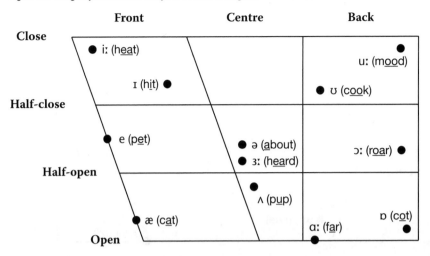

The cardinal vowels have been chosen as reference points because they occur at clear intervals around the chart, but many vowels do not fall so neatly into categories. In regional accents, for instance, it is usually the vowels that are noticeably different from RP, rather than the consonants. The same chart allows linguists to define the exact nature of an individual's vowel sounds by placing them at **any** appropriate point. For instance, a vowel sound may lie between half-close and close or between centre and back rather than at an exact intersection (see Figure 2.3).

ACTIVITY 2.3

Define the following cardinal vowels by describing:

a the height of the tongue
b the part of the tongue raised or lowered
c the shape of the lips.

  1 [i]   2 [ɔ]   3 [a]   4 [o]   5 [u]

Answers on page 610

ACTIVITY 2.4

Define the following IPA vowels by describing:

a the height of the tongue
b the section involved in production of the sound
c the shape of the lips.

Use Table 2.3 to check your description.

> [ɜː] he<u>ar</u>d [hɜːd]
> The centre of the tongue is between half-open and half-close position with the lips in a neutral position; it is different from the eight cardinal vowels because the centre of the tongue rather than the front or back is raised.

  1 [ʌ] abr<u>u</u>pt   2 [iː] tr<u>ee</u>   3 [uː] b<u>eau</u>ty   4 [æ] c<u>a</u>mp

Answers on page 610

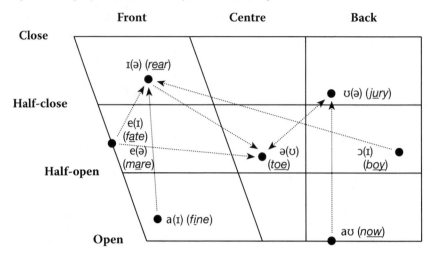

Figure 2.4 **Tongue positions for the compound vowels in English**

Compound vowels

Some vowels are described as **COMPOUND VOWELS** or **DIPHTHONGS**. These glide from one vowel sound to another and involve a change in the position of the tongue – the first part of the sound is always stronger than the second. Linguists describe these vowels as either closing or centring, and this process can also be summarised in a chart (see Figure 2.4). **CENTRING DIPHTHONGS** end in a [ə]:

▌ ear   [ɪə]   air   [eə]   cure   [ʊə]

CLOSING DIPHTHONGS end in either [ɪ] or [ʊ]:

▌ late   [eɪ]   time   [aɪ]   voice [ɔɪ]   home [əʊ]   cow   [aʊ]

Using Figure 2.4, linguists can describe the ways in which these sounds are made:

▌ [aɪ] high
   The **front** of the tongue is just above **open** position, moving towards a **close** position.

▌ [ʊə] tour
   The **back** of the tongue is just above **half-close** position, moving towards the **centre**.

ACTIVITY 2.5

By referring to Table 2.4, describe the following diphthongs in more detail.

▌ [ɪə] fear
   The front and then centre of the tongue move from just above half-close to between half-open and half-close position with the lips in a neutral position; it is a centring diphthong.

    1 [eɪ] great   2 [əʊ] mode   3 [ʊə] cure   4 [aʊ] brow

Answers on page 610

Table 2.3 **The classification of pure vowels**

Vowel sound	Height of tongue	Part of tongue	Lip shape	Length
iː	Close	Front	Spread	Long
ɪ	Just above half-close	Front	Loosely spread	Short
e	Between half-open and half-close	Front	Neutral	Short
æ	Just above open	Front	Neutral	Short
ʌ	Just below half-open	Centre	Neutral	Short
ɑː	Open	Back	Neutral	Long
ɒ	Open	Back	Slightly rounded	Short
ɔː	Between half-open and half-close	Back	Moderately rounded	Long
ə	Between half-open and half-close	Centre	Neutral	Short
ɜː	Between half-open and half-close	Centre	Neutral	Long
ʊ	Just above half-close	Back	Rounded	Short
uː	Close	Back	Closely rounded	Long

Table 2.4 **The classification of compound vowels**

Vowel sound	Height of tongue	Part of tongue	Lip shape	Type
eɪ	Between half-open and half-close to just above half-close	Front	Neutral to loosely spread	Closing
aɪ	Just above open to just above half-close	Front	Neutral to loosely spread	Closing
ɔɪ	Between half-open and half-close to just above half-close	Back to front	Moderately rounded to loosely spread	Closing
aʊ	Open to just above half-close	Back	Neutral to rounded	Closing
əʊ	Between half-open and half-close to just above half-close	Centre to back	Neutral to rounded	Closing
ɪə	Just above half-close to between half-open and half-close	Front to centre	Loosely spread to neutral	Centring
eə	Between half-open and half-close and then lowered slightly	Front to centre	Neutral	Centring
ʊə	Just above half-close to between half-open and half-close	Back to centre	Rounded to neutral	Centring

2.3 Phonology

Ultimately, **phonetics** deals only with the **physical properties** of speech sounds – what sounds are. Linguists, however, also need to consider the meaningful combinations of sounds in spoken language. **PHONOLOGY** is the study of the **sound system** of a particular language and its specific organisation. It considers distinctive patterns of sound so that general statements can be made about a language system. Its focus is on the **function** of sounds – that is, their role in expressing meaning. Because of this it is sometimes called **functional phonetics**.

In a study of phonetics, the focus is on the pronunciation of sounds and on the way each sound is produced. Phonology is more interested in the way in which different sounds or PHONEMES change **meaning**.

The International Phonetic Alphabet includes a wide range of symbols because it aims to convey **all** sound. A phonetic transcription using IPA symbols indicates the physical details of pronunciation – it is not interested in the role of sounds in conveying meaning. Linguists use square brackets to distinguish between traditional orthography and phonetic symbols:

> [t] a voiceless alveolar plosive   [d] a voiced alveolar plosive

A phonemic transcription, on the other hand, would use fewer IPA symbols and diacritics because it focuses on speech sounds that create meaning in a particular language. This kind of transcription is often described as **broad** – it focuses only on phonemes that convey different meanings, not on the physical process involved in the production of sounds.

> /t/ and /d/ are phonemes that change **meaning** – /ten/ can be contrasted in meaning with /den/

Phonemic transcriptions use slant brackets, to distinguish them from traditional orthography. They are not meant to be a faithful representation of pronunciation. The transcriptions in this book are **phonemic** and therefore use **slant brackets**. **Square brackets** are used only where the focus is on details of **articulation**.

The phonemic symbols needed to transcribe the **sounds** of English are as shown in Table 2.5. These symbols allow linguists to distinguish between the spoken and the written word. They are a useful means of transcribing things like the immature pronunciation of a child or the regional pronunciation of a particular dialect. They will be used in the rest of this section to describe the sounds that make up the English language.

Segmental phonology

The focus so far has been on individual sounds, but in spoken language sounds rarely occur on their own. In continuous speech, some sounds are elided, others merge into each other, and some are modified by the sounds that come before and after them – the boundaries are not distinct.

SEGMENTAL PHONOLOGY involves analysing the distinctive units or PHONEMES of speech – it is a means of reducing the large number of possible sounds to a set which have a clear function in a particular language. It is possible to find out which sound units or phonemes have a distinct function in English by considering the ways in which the substitution of certain phonemes in words changes the meaning. MINIMAL PAIRS are pairs of words, such as *big* and *bag*, which are identical in form except for one phoneme that occurs in the same position – they are words that differ in meaning when only one sound is changed.

> tar/bar/far/car   hike/hide/hire/hive   bit/beat/bought/bat

Table 2.5 **Phonemic symbols**

Consonants					
/p/	pit, top	/f/	fan, rough	/m/	mat, small
/b/	ban, rub	/v/	van, love	/n/	net, snow
/t/	ten, step	/θ/	thin, athlete	/ŋ/	bring, singer
/d/	din, bad	/ð/	this, either	/h/	hit, behind
/k/	cave, scar	/ʃ/	shin, bush	/w/	wit, one
/g/	gave, big	/ʒ/	beige, treasure	/j/	yet, cure
/s/	sit, loss	/tʃ/	cheap, latch	/r/	rat, bran
/z/	zoo, easy	/dʒ/	jeep, judge	/l/	lot, pill
Vowels I – pure vowels					
/æ/	cat, sat	/e/	bet, many	/uː/	boot, rude
/ɑː/	bar, heart	/ɒ/	pot, want	/ʌ/	but, blood
/iː/	beat, key	/ɔː/	port, talk	/ɜː/	bird, word
/ɪ/	bit, busy	/ʊ/	put, wood	/ə/	about
Vowels II – diphthongs					
/eɪ/	bay, late	/aʊ/	pout, cow	/eə/	bare, pear
/aɪ/	buy, die	/əʊ/	boat, know	/ʊə/	jury, cure
/ɔɪ/	boy, noise	/ɪə/	beer, here		

In the first example, the phonemes /t/, /b/, /f/ and /k/ are used to change the meaning; in the second /k/, /d/, /r/ and /v/ and in the third /ɪ/, /iː/, /ɔː/ and /æ/ perform the same function. The words in each list make up a **MINIMAL SET**.

Analysis of minimal pairs and sets enables linguists to establish patterns of the types of sound combinations possible in English. When a change in the pronunciation of a word results in a change of meaning, the two different segments can be described as two distinct phonemes. A change in the phonetic form, however, does not always result in a change in meaning. The substitution of a **GLOTTAL STOP** for a medial position /t/, for example, does not create a new word:

▌ bottle [bɒʔl]

The glottal stop in English is therefore a **FREE VARIANT**: it is an alternative phonetic realisation of certain phonemes, and is said to have **phonemic status** when used in positions where RP has a voiceless plosive.

ACTIVITY 2.6

The words below are minimal pairs which show that the phonemes /d/ and /t/ in English contrast in initial, medial and final positions.

- ▸ Initial: dot/tot
- ▸ Medial: medal/metal
- ▸ Final: cad/cat

Find similar minimal pairs for the following phonemes in initial, medial and final positions.

1 /k/ and /g/
2 /m/ and /n/
3 /s/ and /ʃ/
4 /b/ and /v/

Answers on page 611

Assimilation

In studying the phonological properties of continuous speech, linguists have established certain distinctive features.

ASSIMILATION describes the process in which two phonemes occurring together are influenced by each other, making the sounds more alike. For example, a vowel preceding a nasal sound like [m] or [n] will become more nasal itself (indicated on a transcription with the diacritic ˜).

p[ĩ]n pin   p[æ̃]n pan

Assimilation may alter the place of articulation, so an alveolar /t/ may become more like a dental when followed by a dental fricative /θ/:

that theatre

The position of the vocal cords can also be assimilated: a voiced plosive like /d/ can be devoiced (losing its voiced qualities) before a voiceless sound like /s/:

cold soup

Assimilation is particularly noticeable in conversational speech where utterances are unplanned and exchanges tend to be fast:

I can go /aɪ kæn gəʊ/ → [aɪkæŋgəʊ]

In the example here, the pronunciation of the alveolar [n] and that of the velar [g] move closer together and the resulting sound is more like the velar [ŋ] + [g] rather than [n] + [g].

Some assimilations are inevitable and they should not automatically be seen as examples of lazy pronunciation. In segments where **all** speakers assimilate the sounds of particular phonemes, there is usually a physical reason for doing so. In other cases, individual speakers may modify sounds without a valid practical reason. While linguists see such modification as evidence that English is a living language, changing according to user, use and context, some people find such assimilation unacceptable.

ACTIVITY 2.7

Read the following utterances and mark the points at which assimilation might occur. Try to record the changed sounds using a broad phonemic transcription.

behind you [bɪhaɪndʒ u:]
The word-final /d/ becomes palato-alveolar affricate /dʒ/ before palatal approximant /j/, which disappears.

1 is the train coming?   2 he sails ships   3 what do you want?

Answers on page 611

Elision

In deliberate and controlled pronunciation the speaker will articulate all the sounds in a word, but in conversational speech many are often omitted. Just as assimilation changes the pronunciation of words at boundaries, so too does ELISION (the complete disappearance of a sound).

> me and you /miː ænd juː/ → [miːənjuː]
> The final /d/ phoneme has been lost and the stressed vowel phoneme /æ/ has been reduced to /ə/, the unstressed vowel sound called **schwa**.

One can summarise the main kinds of elision in English spoken with an RP accent.

Initial-position /h/

An initial-position /h/ is often elided in informal speech:

> what's the height? [wɒtsðiaɪt]

Alveolar plosive followed by continuant consonant

Words ending with an alveolar plosive preceded by a continuant consonant (one which can be sung, like /s/, /f/, /ʃ/, /n/, /l/, /z/, /ð/, /v/) followed by a word with a consonant in the initial position will often elide the final /t/ or /d/:

> next day [neksdeɪ]   last week [laːswiːk]

Plosive or affricate followed by /t/ or /d/

Words ending with a plosive or an affricate followed by a /t/ or /d/ will also often elide the final phoneme:

> pub door [pʌdɔː]   tick-tock [tɪtɒk]

/t/ or /d/ followed by /t/ or /d/

If one word ends with /t/ or /d/ and the next starts with /t/ or /d/, one consonant is elided to simplify pronunciation:

> you've got to [gɒtə]   sat down [sædaʊn]

Verbal negative contractions

In verbal negative contractions, the final /t/ is elided if the next word begins with another consonant:

> I can't come [kaːnkʌm]

Liaison

This process also changes the pronunciation of words at boundary points, a change called **LIAISON**. A linking /r/ is inserted between words in continuous speech that end with a vowel or semi-vowel like the letter *w* and that are followed by another word with a vowel in the initial position:

> law and order /lɔː ænd ɔːdə/ → [lɔːrənɔːdə]

In some examples of liaison, the written form of an utterance does contain an *r*:

> here and there [hɪərənðeə]   the far east [ðəfaːriːst]

In most, however, the inserted /r/ is no more than a vocalised link.

Reduction

REDUCTION tends to occur in monosyllabic function words or in unstressed syllables of words with more than one syllable. Pronunciation is again changed, but no longer at the boundaries of words – front and back vowels are replaced by weak central vowels like /ə/:

▌ of /ɒv/ → /əv/   have /hæv/ → /(h)əv/

ACTIVITY 2.8 ───────────────────────────────

Identify any examples of assimilation, elision, liaison or reduction in the following utterances, and record the effects created in a broad phonemic transcription.

▌ I can't wait
 Elision of alveolar plosive /t/ in a negative contraction preceding the consonant /w/ [kɑːnweɪt]

1 she should have gone home   3 the train came in late
2 she'll be here in an hour or two

Answers on page 611

All these segmental features are common in connected speech – without them our spoken language would seem artificial in any but the most formal contexts. Broad transcriptions usually identify only the most significant examples of assimilation, elision, liaison and reduction at word boundaries where pronunciation changes.

Non-segmental phonology – prosodics and paralinguistics

While segmental phonology focuses on segments (consonants and vowels) of spoken language, **PROSODICS** is interested in larger units – the form and function of connected utterances of speech. It is a study of the ways in which speakers:

▸ organise utterances into meaningful units, just as paragraphing and punctuation do in written language
▸ make words more striking and memorable
▸ use varying intonation patterns to convey different attitudes
▸ change rhythm, pitch, pace and volume to express different moods and levels of interest in a subject
▸ draw attention to key sections of an utterance by ordering clause elements in a certain way and by keeping new information distinct from things that are already known
▸ interact – signalling the ends of turns, latching on, overlapping and so on.

Non-segmental phonology also includes a study of **PARALINGUISTICS**. This focuses on the way in which facial expressions and body language can be used alongside spoken utterances. Linguists are interested in the way smiles, frowns or gestures can either support or challenge the meaning conveyed by language. Vocalisations like giggles, sighs and coughs can also contribute to the meaning system.

In studying non-segmental phonology, linguists have established certain distinctive features.

Intonation

INTONATION describes variations in the sound quality of a speaker's voice. Because speakers rarely stay at one level, linguists listen to the **changes** in TONE. Tone can be described as LEVEL or MOVING, and moving tones can be identified as RISING (´) or FALLING (`). In transcription or a written record of spoken language, these variations can be marked with the appropriate symbols either over the main vowel or at the beginning of the word:

> **Level tone**   yes or –yes
> **Falling tone** yès or `yes
> **Rising tone**   yés or ´yes

Each variation performs a certain linguistic function: if you mark moving tones on a transcription, it is important to comment on their purpose. A level tone tends to be used in more restricted situations, and often conveys a feeling of routine – for example, calling out names from a list. Often a falling tone implies a sense of finality, while a rising tone suggests that something more is to follow. The mood of a sentence also affects the tone – interrogatives tend to use a rising tone, while declaratives adopt a falling tone:

> **Statement** you want an àpple   **Question** you want an ápple

Rising and falling tones can be combined to create more subtle effects too: a fall–rise pattern (ˇ) can suggest limited agreement of some kind, or can express surprise or disbelief; a rise–fall (ˆ) pattern can convey strong feelings of approval, disapproval or surprise:

> **Fall–rise** pŏssibly or ˇpossibly   **Rise–fall** wêll or ˆwell

Intonation patterns can also mark GRAMMATICAL BOUNDARIES at the end of a phrase or clause. They help listeners to recognise the end of an utterance, just as punctuation in written discourse divides language into meaningful units. By drawing attention to key words, intonation can **distinguish between new and old information** in a speech encounter.

> wé saw a good film yesterday   Focus: the people involved
> we saw a góod film yesterday   Focus: the nature of the film

Intonation changes can structure a discourse by marking the **end** of a story on the television news or by hinting at scores in the football results. (Pauses (.) are discussed on page 70.)

> And fìnally …
> Cardiff City 2 (.) Bristol Rovers 1

Intonation contributes to the RHYTHM of utterances:

> Humpty Dúmpty sat on the wàll,
> Humpty Dúmpty had a great fàll

Distinctive intonation patterns can make the spoken language of particular kinds of speakers easily identifiable. Preachers, 'rag and bone' men and auctioneers, for instance, each have a distinctive spoken style by which they can be immediately recognised:

Evening Pòst (street newspaper vendor)   lèt us pray ... (preacher)
góing (.) góing (.) gòne (auctioneer)

The **PITCH** of an utterance is closely related to intonation. It may be high, low or anywhere in between. Transcriptions use a variety of methods to record significant **pitch changes**.

- Solid lines at low, mid and high points mark the pitch, and dotted lines mark transition points:

You know I don't like going there

- The symbols for different tones (falling, rising, and so on) are used at various heights to mark low, mid and high pitches:

–you ´know I don't like going ˌthere

- Arrows are placed before and after the word in which movements up or down occur:

You ↑know↑ I don't like going ↓there↓

The **VOLUME** of an utterance will often change in conjunction with variations in intonation and pitch. Usually, the louder the utterance, the more important the speaker considers the meaning to be. On a transcription, details about volume are recorded in marginal notes, with the start and end of the feature marked by inverted commas (*I 'will finish' on time*): **'forte'** (loud), **'piano'** (quiet); **'cresc'** (getting louder), **'dimin'** (getting quieter).

'cresc'   if I can't go 'now I'll scream'

To summarise, intonation enables speakers to express emotions and attitudes, thereby adding another layer of meaning to spoken language. It does this by emphasising particular parts of the utterance through variations in pitch and volume. Such variations help the listener to recognise key grammatical points in what is being said: the mood of a sentence, the relative importance of particular phrases, clauses or sentences, and so on. Semantically, it prepares the listener for contrasts or links in material and can signal what kind of a response is expected.

Rhythm

The English language has quite a regular pattern of stressed and unstressed syllables – in other words, the **RHYTHM** is regular. However, speakers often vary the **beat** of their language depending upon their audience, purpose and context. A formal debate, for instance, may require a very regular and conscious rhythmic pattern; a situation in which a speaker is ill at ease may cause hesitant and arrhythmic speech; and an informal conversation will probably fall between these two extremes.

Conversational features

Conversational features like **assimilation** and **elision** may alter the rhythm of speech. Equally, **liaison**, in which words are slurred rather than pronounced as distinct sound units, can change the pattern.

Elision: police /pəliːs/ → /pliːs/

Stress

STRESS can be used for emphasis both within an individual word and within larger units of spoken discourse. It is not usually produced by greater force of articulation, but by changing pitch on a syllable. To study stress in individual lexical items, it is important to be able to recognise SYLLABLES and SYLLABIC STRESS. Some syllables are described as WEAK because they are **unstressed**; others are described as STRONG because they are **stressed**.

There are four kinds of weak syllables in English, and these are indicated in transcription by specific IPA symbols: the vowel schwa [ə]; a close front unrounded vowel [i], which is shorter than [iː]; a close back unrounded vowel [u], which is shorter than [uː]; and a syllabic consonant (a syllable with no vowel) like [l] or [n].

> trader /treɪdə/   lovely /lʌvli/   to /tu/   muscle /mʌsl/   often /ɒfn/

In informal conversation, unstressed pronunciations are common since few people articulate each syllable distinctly.

A stressed syllable can be marked in transcription by placing a small vertical line (') just before the syllable it relates to. Stressed syllables are said to have PROMINENCE because they are usually louder and longer and have a noticeably different pitch from that of unstressed syllables. The primary stress in English may fall on any syllable.

> 'mo ther   First syllable stressed
> e 'la tion   Middle syllable stressed
> per 'haps   Final syllable stressed

A SECONDARY STRESS is marked by a small vertical line (ˌ) just before the syllable it relates to.

> ˌun 'sure (Adj)   First syllable carries secondary stress; second syllable carries primary stress
> 'pro ˌgress (N)   First syllable carries primary stress; second syllable carries secondary stress
> 'mon u ˌment (N)   First syllable carries primary stress; final syllable carries secondary stress

Some linguists, however, use other typographical means to highlight stress: capitalisation, bold print or underlining.

English is basically a free-stress language – it is possible for some words to differ only in their internal stress patterns:

> ˌex 'port (V)   'ex ˌport (N)

It is not easy to predict which syllable will be stressed, but in continuous utterances stresses tend to be patterned quite regularly.

Tone units

Having established the stress points in individual words, linguists can divide the UTTERANCES into tone units. A TONE UNIT is a segment of information consisting of one or more syllables with a series of rises or falls in tone where there is one particularly marked syllable. This is called the TONIC SYLLABLE (**TS**) or NUCLEUS (**nuc**): it is stressed and carries a tone.

you've had enough haven't you

STRESS (y<u>es</u>)   TS   ` FALLING TONE

As well as a tonic syllable, a tone unit consists of other key elements.

1 The **HEAD** (**H**) describes the section of an utterance from the first stressed syllable up to but not including the last stressed syllable:

H   TS
(<u>you</u> must be) (<u>right</u>)

2 The **PRE-HEAD** (**PH**) describes any unstressed syllables preceding the head:

PH   H   TS   PH   H   TS
(in a) (little more than three) (w<u>ee</u>ks)   (oh) (<u>what</u> can I) (d<u>o</u>)

3 The **TAIL** (**T**) describes any part of an utterance that follows the tonic syllable:

TS   T
(wh<u>é</u>re) (did you go)

By changing the tonic syllable, it is possible to change the focus of an utterance:

PH   H   TS   T
(I) (<u>want</u> to visit the) (p<u>à</u>rk) (now)   Focus: the park rather than anywhere else

PH   H   TS   T
(I) (<u>want</u> to) (<u>visit</u>) (the park now)   Focus: visit the park rather than drive past

STRESS PATTERNS are usually directly linked to the syntactic structure of a sentence. By understanding the nature of the stresses used in connected utterances, it is possible to understand the semantic intentions of the speaker.

4 Changes in **PACE** also affect the rhythm of spoken discourse. The speed of utterances is directly related to meaning and to the speaker's relationship with the topic – an **increase** in speed may indicate excitement or anticipation; a decrease in speed may mark a change in mood or a dramatic emphasis of some kind. Significant changes in pace are marked in the margin of a transcript using the following abbreviations based on musical annotations: **'alleg'** (fast), **'lento'** (slow); **'accel'** (getting faster), **'rall'** (getting slower).

'accel'   I want to 'go out n<u>ò</u>w'

Similarly, an abrupt irregular delivery can be described as **'stacc'** and a drawled elongation of words can be marked **'leg'**.

5 In almost all spoken contexts, **PAUSES** are acceptable, although particularly long pauses can cause embarrassment. The frequency of their occurrence means that the rhythm of spoken language is often uneven. Very brief pauses, or **MICRO-PAUSES**, are marked on a transcription by the symbol (.); longer pauses can be timed in seconds and marked in figures – for example, (6). A pause may mark the grammatical end of an utterance or indicate hesitation on the part of a speaker.

well (.) I (.) I know I was (.) <u>meant</u> to do it (2) I just (.) forgot

Formal spoken discourse can use pauses to dramatise and stylise utterances: they will be exaggerated for effect. In informal speech encounters, however, pauses at the ends of utterances are often omitted – the audience is usually known, and the participants can therefore take up cues rapidly.

Other kinds of pauses are also used frequently: **VOICELESS HESITATIONS** (silences); **VOICED HESITATIONS** like *um* and *er*, and **WORD SEARCHING**. These are called **NORMAL NON-FLUENCY FEATURES** and are distinctive characteristics of spontaneous speech. They are found in both formal and informal spoken contexts, but are more acceptable in the latter. Because such pauses are irregular, they tend to make spoken language arrhythmic.

To comment on the **rhythm** of spoken utterances, linguists focus on segmental features like assimilation, elision and liaison, and on prosodic features like stress patterns within single words, the structure of tone units, the pace, the delivery, and the kinds of pauses used. These are all directly linked to meaning and work alongside the actual words uttered to make communication effective.

Paralinguistics

PARALINGUISTICS or **BODY LANGUAGE** can also reinforce the semantics of spoken discourse. Comments on such features are always directly related to the intentions of the speaker. Vocalisations like **giggling** may express nervousness, enjoyment or amusement; **sighs** may express sadness, agitation or annoyance. **Gesture** can reinforce or challenge the apparent meaning of words. Paralinguistic features are usually marked on a transcription in square brackets in italic print.

> SPEAKER A   I (.) well I hardly dare to say it [*giggling*] (.) I actually spŏke to him today (.)
> can you believe it
> SPEAKER B   whŏ (.) him [*pointing*] (.) wonders will never cease

By considering both language and paralinguistic features, linguists can analyse not only what is said, but the speaker's intentions too. They can identify any underlying tensions between what the actual words convey and what the paralinguistic features imply.

Chapter 3

Style

So far you have considered the basic building blocks of spoken and written English and the ways in which these are **normally** used. However, language can be manipulated, and writers and speakers can draw our attention to key features of their discourse by using slightly different language patterns. There are two important stylistic areas you need to consider: **sentence organisation** and **literary and rhetorical devices**.

3.1 Sentence organisation

Grammatical patterns are used to add variety to a discourse, to emphasise particular features and to engage the reader or listener. There is a range of syntactical elements that a writer or speaker can manipulate.

Sentence types

In a traditional simple declarative sentence, the subject will come first, followed by the predicator and any other appropriate clause elements. **SIMPLE SENTENCES**, for example, can suggest an innocence and naivety of style.

> S   P   A   S   P   O
> (The Vances) (lived) (in number seven). (They) (had) (a different father and mother).
> S   P   C
> (They) (were) (Eileen's father and mother).
>
> James Joyce (1882–1941), *A Portrait of the Artist as a Young Man*

The simple sentences here portray a style that is reminiscent of a child. Joyce, in a book that is charting the path of Stephen Daedalus' growth from childhood to adulthood, varies his style to suit the age of his main character at each stage of his development.

Writers use **COMPLEX SENTENCES**, on the other hand, to deal with more intricate ideas. These can be designed to withhold information until a certain point in the sentence, or to subordinate some ideas to others that seem more important.

> MCl
> (That was the work of devils, *to scatter* his thoughts and *overcloud* his conscience,
>   SCl–NFCl   SCl–NFCl

> *assailing* him at the gates of the cowardly and sinful corrupted flesh); *(and)* *(praying*
> SCl–NFCl   conj   SCl–NFCl
>
> MCl
> God timidly *to forgive* him his weakness, <u>he crawled up on to the bed</u>), *(and)*
>   SCl–NFCl   conj
>
> MCl
> *(wrapping* the blankets closely about him, <u>covered his face again with his hands</u>).
> SCl–NFCl

This is an extract from *A Portrait of the Artist as a Young Man* when Stephen Daedalus is older. Having listened to a sermon about sin and the horrors of hell, he feels that every word has been directed at him. He returns to his room in a state of inner turmoil and the complexity of the sentence here reflects his emotional mood. The underlined sections mark out the simple main clauses in the compound–complex sentence; the additional clauses create an intensity, a sense of entrapment. While most of the italicised non-finite verbs function as adverbials, the opening pronoun *That* is a cataphoric reference to the infinitives *to scatter... overcloud*, the main subject of the clause. By placing them after the predicator and object, Joyce gives them additional weight, emphasising Daedalus' personal horror at his supposed sinfulness. Joyce is dealing with a character who is overwhelmed by a sense of guilt and his sentence structure is designed to reflect this.

Marked theme

Some elements of the clause can be moved to the front of a sentence, replacing the usual thematic subject. **Adverbials** are the most flexible clause elements and therefore thematic adverbials are most common. The device of placing a clause element other than the subject at the front of a sentence is called **FRONTING** or **FOREGROUNDING**. The clause element that has replaced the subject in the **initial position** is called a **MARKED THEME**.

>   S   P   A   A
> Unmarked theme: (The train) (departed) (on time) (that morning).
>
>   A   S   P   A
> Marked theme: (That morning), (the train) (departed) (on time).
>
>   S   P   A   A
> Unmarked theme: (He) (came) (into the room) (at last).
>
>   A   S   P   A
> Marked theme: (At last), (he) (came) (into the room).

Objects and **complements** can also function as marked themes. This is more common in spoken than in written English, where stress and intonation help to emphasise the theme. However, in literary language, writers can also change the expected order of objects and complements in order to create dramatic effects.

>   S   P   C   A
> Unmarked theme: (The garden) (was) (uncontrolled) (after years of neglect).
>
>   C   P   S   A
> Marked theme: (Uncontrolled) (was) (the garden) (after years of neglect).
>
>   S   P   O   A   A
> Unmarked theme: (Lynne) (brought) (five kittens) (home) (last night).
>
>   O   S   P   A   A
> Marked theme: (Five kittens), (Lynne) (brought) (home) (last night).

End focus

New information can be put towards the **end** of a sentence, thus emphasising the end rather than the beginning. This is described as **END FOCUS**.

> S   P   Oi   Od   S   P   Od   Oi
> (I) (gave) (John) (*a brand new pen*).   (I) (gave) (a brand new pen) (*to John*).

Sometimes the longest clause element is placed at the end of a sentence, for stylistic reasons or to make comprehension easier for the reader or listener:

> S   A   P   O
> (I) (quickly) (opened) (the door of the unnamed, unknown and secret chamber).

> S   P   Od   Oi
> (I) (gave) (directions) (to the tall, elegant and undoubtedly striking blonde woman).

Existential 'there'

It is also possible to create an end focus by using the existential *there*. Such sentences often **point** to the general existence of some state of affairs and they are therefore called **EXISTENTIAL SENTENCES**. By using *there* as a dummy subject, the writer or speaker can delay introducing the real subject of the sentence. *There* is called a **DUMMY SUBJECT, dumS**, because it has no meaning in itself – its function is to put the real subject in a more prominent position.

Existential sentences have the following pattern: *There + to be + (S)*. *There* becomes the dummy subject at the front of the sentence; and the true subject of the statement, though syntactically a complement, becomes a **DELAYED SUBJECT**, **(S)**, which is given added emphasis because of its position.

> S   P   C   dumS P   (S)
> (A great many people) (are) (worried).   (There) (are) (a great many worried people).

> S   P   A   dumS   P   (S)   A
> (The guard) (was) (on the train).   (There) (was) (a guard) (on the train).

The verb *to be* is not the only verb that can be used in this way. Others, such as *to arise* and *to occur*, can also follow the dummy subject *there*, but these are less common and are more likely to be found in literary language.

> S   A   P   dumS   A   P   (S)
> (A strange event) (then) (occurred).   (There) (then) (occurred) (a strange event).

Similar structures can be found in sentences where *it* is the dummy subject. There are two main patterns:

1 *It + be + (S/O/A) + relative pronoun that + Cl:*

> dumS   P   (S)   (P)   Oi   Od
> (It) (was) (Lucy) (that) (told) (me) (the news).
>   rel pron + Cl

2 *It + P + (C/Oi/Od) + NCl:*

> dumS P   C   (S)
> (It) (is) (no concern of yours) (what I really want).
>   SCl–NCl

These rearrangements of clause elements refocus the information, allowing writers and speakers to place emphasis on selected parts of sentences. The sentences from which these examples derive present the information in a less emphatic way.

```
         S       P     Oi        Od
(Lucy) (told) (me) (the news).
                   S            P            C
(What I really want) (is) (no concern of yours).
  SCl–NCl
```

Passive voice

Another way to alter the focus of a sentence is to use the **passive voice** instead of the active. In an active sentence, the clause elements follow the usual pattern, but by using the passive, the writer can change the focus.

```
                            S            P              O            A
Active              (The bank-tellers) (counted up) (the change) (at closing
                    time).
```

```
                            S            P            A          A
Passive             (The change) (was counted up) (at closing time) (by the
                    bank-tellers).
```

The inclusion of the adverbial *by + agent* is not compulsory, and omitting it can also change the focus.

```
                            S        P        O                          A
Active              (The boys) (made) (the beds), (while the girls collected
                                                       SCl–ACl
                    water and started the fire).
```

```
                            S          P          A                      A
Passive with agent  (The beds) (were made) (by the boys), (while the water
                                                               SCl–ACl
                                            A
                    was collected and the fire started) (by the girls).
```

In the passive sentence here, the focus is on the boys and girls because the position of the *by + agent* always creates end focus. By omitting the adverbial, emphasis is placed not on the people but on the events:

```
                            S          P                         A
Passive without agent  (The beds) (were made), (while the water was collected
                                                       SCl–ACl
                       and the fire started).
```

ACTIVITY 3.1

Discuss the organisation of the information in the following pairs of sentences. Comment on the effects created in each case.

1 a The tree creaked and groaned, swaying dangerously in the blustery weather.
   b In the blustery weather, swaying dangerously, the tree creaked and groaned.

2 a Park safely near schools.
   b Near schools, park safely.

3 a The old cinema building was knocked down so that a modern development of luxury flats could bring new life to the area.
   b A private company knocked down the old cinema building so that a modern development of luxury flats could bring new life to the area.

4 a A spring was in her step because she'd just heard good news.
   b There was a spring in her step because she'd just heard good news.

5 a The playground was busy. I waited. I waited for a long time. I was by myself and no-one played with me. I was sad. When would the bell ring?

   b The playground was busy as I stood alone and frightened, waiting and waiting for someone to say or do something. I was sad, suddenly struck by my difference, my isolation from the moving throng. Disconcerted and afraid, I stood fearfully, longing for the ringing of the bell that would free me from my misery.

COMMENTARY

The organisation of the grammatical elements in a sentence can affect our response to a spoken or written text. By using stylistic devices, a writer or speaker can control the order in which we receive information, alter the importance given to different parts of a sentence, or change the pace and voice. While each pair of sentences above communicates the same basic information, the emphasis is slightly different in each case because of the stylistic choices made by the writer.

In the first pair of sentences, changes are made in the order of the information we are given. The first has an **unmarked theme** – the grammatical elements appear in the traditional order for a declarative sentence:

>   S   P   A   A
> (The tree) (creaked and groaned) (swaying dangerously) (in the blustery weather).
>   conj

The emphasis is on the subject (*the tree*), which is the theme of the sentence. In the second version, however, there is a **marked theme**: the subject has been moved away from the front of the sentence, allowing greater emphasis to be placed on the adverbials which give us information about the weather and the condition of the tree. The effect is more dramatic both because of the descriptive nature of the fronted adverbials and because we have to wait for the main clause. It is a stylistic device common in fiction because of the dramatic potential created by the change of emphasis: by first drawing attention to the weather and the movement of the tree, the writer can build the tension before something happens.

A similar reordering of information is used in the second pair of sentences. Appearing on roadside information boards, the unmarked imperative *Park safely near schools* is meant to be a reminder about the need for care when in the proximity of a school. The emphasis on the information at the front of the sentence, however, could be seen to suggest that schools offer motorists a safe place to park their cars. In the second version, on the other hand, the **foregrounding** of the adverbial *Near schools* draws attention to the location and thus emphasises the importance of vigilance when trying to park a car near a school.

The third pair of examples demonstrates how the use of the **passive** or **active voice** can alter the effect of a sentence. Using the passive voice brings the object to the front of the sentence, allowing the writer to draw attention to the old building and to the future of the site. It also enables the subject to be omitted so that there is no reference to the party responsible for the actions. The second version, which uses the active voice, begins with the subject (*A private company*) and thus immediately establishes responsibility for what is taking place. Newspapers often use the passive voice when reporting sentences passed on defendants: the issue of which specific judge allocated the punishment is usually of no significance to the story. Similarly, science textbooks use the passive because the focus is on the result of experiments rather than on the scientists who carry them out. The passive voice gives an air of authority to a text: it can suggest that the content is beyond debate and give weight to what may in fact be spurious claims.

New information in a sentence may also be placed towards the end of a clause for dramatic effect. In the first version of the fourth pair of examples, the grammatical elements of the sentence occur in the traditional order, so there is no emphasis on the noun phrase *A spring* which fills the subject site. The **existential 'there'** at the beginning of the second version, however, allows the writer to draw attention to the girl's mood by delaying the subject and filling the subject site at the front of the sentence with a dummy subject. By focusing on the noun phrase as the topic of the clause, this version suggests that some change has taken place and that this new mood is significant.

The two versions of the fifth example establish the same context and communicate the same mood, but create a sense of two very different speakers. The effect is achieved by varying the language and the **sentence types**. The first example uses simple and compound sentences to convey the speaker's experience.

> S P C S P A
> (The playground) (was) (busy). (I) (waited) (for a long time).
>
> S P A S P O
> (I) (was) (by myself) and (no-one) (played with) (me).
> conj

We are presented with a sequence of observations that reflect both what is happening and what the speaker feels. The fact that the sentences are short and simple gives the extract a dramatic immediacy and suggests that the narrator is a child. The movement from declarative to interrogative mirrors the child's desperation.

The second version replaces the six simple and compound sentences with three complex ones made up of sequences of clauses.

> S P C A A
> (The playground) (was) (busy) (as I stood alone and frightened), (waiting and waiting
> SCl–ACl SCl–NFCl
>
> for someone to say or do something).
> SCl–NFCl SCl–NFCl

The mood is reflective rather than dramatic, suggesting an older narrator who is more aware of the context. The complexity of the sentences, the patterning of the repetition, the use of a marked theme and the sophistication of the language together make this seem like a retrospective account in which an adult recalls a childhood experience from a position of understanding and maturity. There is less emphasis on the immediacy of the experience than on the feelings of the narrator. By altering the type of sentences used, the writer is able to portray two very different accounts of the same experience.

3.2 Literary and rhetorical devices

LITERARY AND RHETORICAL DEVICES are used by speakers and writers to heighten and intensify the power of the texts they create. Conscious patterns in the lexical choice, the sound, the imagery and the structure draw attention to the content, allowing speakers and writers to move beyond the literal and to focus attention on what is most important to them.

RHETORIC is the art of persuasive discourse. It is used in everyday life to persuade people to do or believe things and in literature to help readers engage with and believe in the fictional world with which they are presented. The Greek philosopher Aristotle (384–322 BC) was perhaps one of the first people to define rhetoric, and he established three key types of persuasion.

> **ETHOS** is a form of persuasion that is dependent upon the individual **character of the speaker or writer** as it is this which will determine the viewpoint and the tone chosen for the discourse.

> **PATHOS** is a form of persuasion that works on the **emotions of the audience**, directly appealing to their sensitivities.

> **LOGOS** is a form of persuasion that is based on **reasoned argument**; the structure is important since it will help convince the audience of the logic of what is being said or written.

FIGURATIVE LANGUAGE enables writers and speakers to intensify the effect of the words they use – it allows them to say one thing in terms of something else. The words therefore mean something in addition to their literal meaning and this enhances the semantic possibilities of a text. It is an important part of successful persuasive discourse because it allows a speaker or writer to combine everyday language with literary devices that create special semantic effects.

Literary and rhetorical devices are examples of a strategic use of language and structure where the aim is to influence the intended audience. It is useful to identify the techniques used to achieve certain effects, and these can be categorised into four key areas.

Lexical choice

Always consider a writer's or speaker's **LEXICAL CHOICE**. The **choice of words** may be influenced by the viewpoint and tone adopted for a particular subject or situation (**ethos**); it may be dictated by the particular emotive response a writer or speaker wishes to evoke in the audience (**pathos**); or it may be governed by the subject-specific nature of a topic which requires technical lexis (**logos**). Look closely at the kinds of words selected and be prepared to assess the approaches used. Always discuss the **effects** created by the features you identify.

The grammatical function of words

The **GRAMMATICAL FUNCTION** of words can be changed.

> Young girls lie *bedded soft* or glide in their dreams, with rings and trousseaux, *bridesmaided* by glow-worms ... The boys are dreaming *wicked* of *the bucking ranches* of the night and *the jolly rodgered sea.*
>
> Dylan Thomas (1914–53), *Under Milk Wood*

Thomas uses the highlighted words in unusual contexts. He takes the nouns *bed* and *bridesmaid* and turns them into verbs in order to create a sense of movement in the dreams of the girls. Equally, by using the adjectives *soft* and *wicked* where we would expect adverbs, he draws the audience's attention to the nature of these dreams. In the noun phrases *the bucking ranches* and *the jolly rodgered sea*, Thomas has taken attributes associated with horses and the sea and used them as verb modifiers. This also creates a sense of movement and characterises the boys who are dreaming of stereotypical boys' things – cowboys and pirates.

Literary devices

LITERARY DEVICES can be used to clarify a point, to add colour and intensity, or for their emotive impact. They have a **figurative** function, enabling writers to say one thing in terms of something else. Aim to be able to recognise and evaluate the function and impact of the following.

Irony

IRONY is the use of a word, phrase or paragraph turned from its usual meaning to a contradictory or opposing one, usually to satirise or deflate the person or issue:

> I do therefore humbly offer it to public consideration, that of the hundred and twenty thousand children already computed, twenty thousand may be reserved for breed … That the remaining hundred thousand may at a year old be offered in sale to the persons of quality, and fortune, through the kingdom, always advising the mother to let them suck plentifully in the last month, so as to render them plump, and fat for a good table. A child will make two dishes at an entertainment for friends, and when the family dines alone, the fore or hind quarters will make a reasonable dish, and seasoned with a little pepper or salt will be very good boiled on the fourth day, especially in winter.
>
> Jonathan Swift (1667–1745), 'A Modest Proposal for preventing the children of poor people in Ireland from being a burden to their parents or country, and for making them beneficial to the public'

In this text, Swift adopts an ironic stance, suggesting that eating babies is the only way to tackle Ireland's problems of poverty and overpopulation. By making such a shocking and emotive proposal, Swift aims to draw attention to the failures of both England and Ireland in governing and providing for the people.

Metaphor

A **METAPHOR** describes one thing in terms of another, creating an implicit comparison:

> I remember sharing the last of my moist buns with *a boy* and *a lion*. *Tawny* and *savage*, with *cruel nails* and *capacious mouth*, the *little* boy *tore* and *devoured*.
>
> Dylan Thomas, 'Holiday Memory'

Metonymy

METONYMY is the term used when the name of an attribute or thing is substituted for the thing itself:

> the Stage   the theatrical profession   the Crown   the monarchy

Overstatement

OVERSTATEMENT or **HYPERBOLE** is a form of persuasive exaggeration:

> Prettier musings of *high-wrought love* and *eternal constancy* could never have passed along the streets of Bath, than Anne was sporting from Camden-place to Westgate-buildings. It was almost enough to *spread purification and perfume all the way*.
>
> Jane Austen (1775–1817), *Persuasion*

Austen's use of hyperbole here results in a **PARODY** (a comic imitation) of contemporary romantic novels. **Exaggeration** of this kind will often be adopted to create a comical or less than serious tone.

Oxymoron

An **OXYMORON** puts two apparently contradictory words together to create a special effect:

> *delicious poison*   Robin Hood was an *honest thief*

Paradox

A **PARADOX** consists of an apparently self-contradictory statement that contains some kind of deeper meaning below the surface:

> War is peace. Freedom is slavery.   George Orwell (1903–50), *Nineteen Eighty-Four*

Personification

PERSONIFICATION is the term used when an object or idea is given human qualities:

> On the *parade ground* of language accidence, morphology, phonology, and semantics are *drills* the words perform individually, like *new recruits* being made to *march*, *halt* ... the *squad drilled* by *Sergeant Major Grammar*.
>
> Philip Howard, *The State of Language*

> The *winter evening settles down*.   T.S. Eliot (1888–1965), 'Preludes'

Puns

A **PUN** is a play upon words. **HOMONYMS** have the same sound and spelling but a different meaning, and **HOMOPHONES** have the same sound but a different spelling and meaning:

> Thief is court out   *Daily Mirror* (6 May 2005)

This headline uses a homophone (*court/caught*) to head an article about a thief who slipped out of court and was arrested for shoplifting while waiting for his sentence hearing for an earlier shoplifting offence. Through a play on sound and meaning, the pun emphasises the irony of the event by linking the court case and the arrest.

> Flight of fancy to drive you bats   *The Daily Telegraph* (10 September 2004)

This headline plays on language by combining two sayings ('flight of fancy' and 'drive you bats') through the cohesion created by the verb *flight* and the noun *bats*. In their context they have a literal meaning beyond cliché, as the related article reviews *Bat Boy: The Musical*, a stage show based on a report of a 'bat boy' living in a cave in West Virginia. The reviewer's attitude is clearly conveyed by the negative connotations of the sayings.

Newspaper headlines often play with words in a more generalised way to attract attention. The following headline was designed to sensationalise an article about a GP who continues to practise after undergoing a sex change operation:

I've been doctored. *Daily Star* (11 October 2005)

By punning on the professional occupation of the individual and the informal verb 'to doctor' (to castrate), the journalist has created a hook to encourage us to read on. Ironically, however, the article is about a woman who became a man and thus the central concept of 'doctoring' is sensational rather than scientifically accurate.

Simile

In a SIMILE two things are explicitly compared by using a marker such as the prepositions *like* or *as*:

And the cold postman ... tingled down the tea-tray-slithered run of the chilly glinting hill. He went in his ice-bound boots *like a man on fishmonger's slabs*. He wagged his bag *like a frozen camel's hump* ...

Dylan Thomas, 'A Child's Christmas in Wales'

Symbolism

SYMBOLISM is the use of an object to represent or stand for something else – *scales*, for instance, symbolise *justice*; a *dove* symbolises *peace*.

S.O.S. – is there a *lifeboat*? Thankfully God has a *rescue plan*: Jesus Christ, God's Son, died on the cross to throw us a *life-line* and bridge the gap between man and God.

Logos, promotional leaflet

Synecdoche

SYNECDOCHE is a figurative device in which the part stands for the whole, and something wider than the thing actually mentioned is intended.

The prisoner was placed behind bars [in prison].

Understatement

UNDERSTATEMENT or LITOTES leaves the audience to recognise that the writer or speaker could have put the point more strongly.

I have, myself, full confidence that if all do their duty, if nothing is neglected, and if the best arrangements are made ... we shall prove ourselves once again able to defend our island home, to ride out the storm of the war, and to outlive the menace of tyranny ... *At any rate*, that is what we are going to *try* to do ...

Winston Churchill (1874–1965)

All of these literary devices allow writers and speakers to influence their audience's perceptions of the subject. By encouraging readers and listeners to make wider associations, writers and speakers can work on their emotions (pathos), and can also convey their own viewpoint (ethos) in a more personal way.

Writers and speakers can also use a range of devices that play on the patterns and sounds of words to create certain stylistic effects. These are chosen to enhance the meaning and to focus audience attention. You should be able to recognise and evaluate the effect of the following **SOUND PATTERNS**.

Alliteration

ALLITERATION is the repetition of a consonant, often in the initial position:

> Help Labour <u>B</u>uild a <u>B</u>etter <u>B</u>ritain   <u>P</u>ick up a <u>P</u>enguin   Persil <u>W</u>ashes <u>W</u>hiter

In advertisements, captions and headlines, this device can be used to make the text more eye-catching and memorable.

Assonance

ASSONANCE is the repetition of a vowel in a medial position (an element that does not occur in the initial or final position):

> The pallor of girls' br<u>ow</u>s shall be their pall;
> Their fl<u>ow</u>ers the tenderness of s<u>i</u>lent m<u>i</u>nds,
> And each slow dusk a drawing-d<u>ow</u>n of bl<u>i</u>nds.
>> Wilfred Owen (1893–1918), 'Anthem for Doomed Youth'

This poetic device makes words sound sonorous and musical, and is often used to create a grave or pensive tone.

Consonance

CONSONANCE is the repetition of a consonant in the medial or final position:

> Bea<u>nz</u> Mea<u>nz</u> Hei<u>nz</u>

This device can draw attention to a product name in advertising or enhance the meaning of literary language by creating a hard sound.

Onomatopoeia

ONOMATOPOEIA is the term used when the sound of a word directly links to its meaning:

> … at night when the wind rose, the *lash* of the tree
> *Shrieked* and *slashed* the wind …
>> D. H. Lawrence (1885–1930), 'Discord in Childhood'

The emphasis on the sound quality of words focuses the reader's or listener's attention on the aural aspects of the discourse, thereby creating another dimension to the meaning.

Rhyme

RHYME or **HALF-RHYME** are the exact or partial repetition of a sound, usually at the end of a poetic line:

> And you, my father, there on the sad *height*,
> Curse, bless, me now with your fierce tears, I pray.

> Do not go gentle into that good *night*.
> Rage, rage against the dying of the *light*.
>
> Dylan Thomas, 'Do Not Go Gentle Into That Good Night'

This kind of sound patterning can be used to draw attention to certain words. It creates a kind of end focus and can be used to signal the conclusion of a poem or a speech in verse drama.

Rhetorical devices

In order to be successful in persuading an audience, a writer or speaker not only uses devices to enhance the meaning, but also makes conscious decisions about the structural patterns of discourse. You should be able to comment on the following **RHETORICAL TECHNIQUES** and the effects they create.

Antithesis

ANTITHESIS is the technique of placing two words or ideas in opposition to bring out a contrast:

> Leeds was *working class*, was built on work; Watermouth was *bourgeois*, built on tourism, property, retirement, pensions, French chefs … you could be anything here. *Radical philosophy* approved this, but here it was *bourgeois indulgence*.
>
> Malcolm Bradbury (1932–), The History Man

The opposition here is used to create a contrast between two places and two ways of life. The author undermines Watermouth by choosing words with connotations of superficiality and unnecessary luxury. He draws the reader's attention to this through the juxtaposition of antithetical words and phrases.

Branching

BRANCHING is the arrangement and order of subordinate and main clauses in a discourse. The **order** determines whether left or right branching has been used. **LEFT BRANCHING** forces the reader or listener to **wait** for the main clause by using subordination at the beginning of a sentence. The results can often be dramatic because the reader or listener has to wait for all the information. This device is better suited to writing than to speech because of the demands it makes on the memory.

> Every body has their taste in noises as well as in other matters … When Lady Russell, not long afterwards, was entering Bath on a wet afternoon and driving through the long course of streets from the Old Bridge to Camden-place, amidst the dash of other carriages, the heavy rumble of carts and drays, the bawling of newsmen, muffin-men and milkmen, and the ceaseless clink of pattens, *she made no complaint*.
>
> Jane Austen, Persuasion

Austen uses left branching to convey a sense of the hustle and bustle of town life in Bath. The description leading up to the main clause creates a negative view of Bath and the reader does not anticipate that Lady Russell will relish the atmosphere. By forcing the reader to wait for the main clause at the end of a very long sentence, Austen suggests that she herself does not see Bath in the same way that Lady Russell does.

RIGHT BRANCHING gives the important information **first** and then supplies a commentary on it or additional information. It can often seem more natural because it deals with information cumulatively and in what seems to be a more logical order: it provides the main clause first, before any embedded subordinate clauses.

> *There is in the Midlands a single-line tramway system* which boldly leaves the country-town and plunges off into the black, industrial countryside, up hill and down dale, through the long ugly villages of workmen's houses, over canals and railways, past churches perched high and nobly over the smoke and shadows …
>
> D. H. Lawrence, 'Tickets, Please'

Lawrence's use of right branching creates a different kind of effect from Austen's use of left branching. The reader is immediately presented with the main information and what follows is an elaboration. The very pattern of the subordinate clauses reflects the nature of the journey on which the reader is taken, while the connotations of the verb *plunges* reinforce the sense of isolation as the reader journeys through the bleak industrial landscape.

From these examples we can see that the way a writer chooses to order the information in a sentence affects the reader's response to the content. The sentences below contain the same information, but it is presented to us differently.

> With the shirts washed and hung, the beds made below, the decks scrubbed clean, the cabin boy stitched a torn sail.

> The cabin boy stitched a torn sail, with the shirts washed and hung, the beds made below, the decks scrubbed clean.

The first version uses left branching, forcing us to wait for the main clause by foregrounding a sequence of non-finite clauses. The emphasis is on all the tasks that the cabin boy has already completed, suggesting the urgency and pace with which he has had to work. By positioning the main clause at the end of the sentence, the writer creates a sense of pity for the character – there is no sense of finality in the stitching of the sail, which is just one more of the endless tasks to be completed. With right branching, the main clause is at the beginning of the sentence and the tone is quite different – there is almost a sense of relief, contentment even. The emphasis here is on what would appear to be the final task; the subordinate clauses are rendered less significant by their position at the end of the sentence. Where the pace of the first version is frenetic, the second seems controlled.

Listing

LISTING has an accumulative effect and enables a writer or speaker to create a range of impressions. A list can convey confusion and chaos or logic and reason, depending on its context. Equally, a writer or speaker can build towards a climax or defy expectations by concluding in an anti-climax.

If conjunctions are used to co-ordinate groups of words, a list is said to be **syndetic**; if commas are used instead with no co-ordinating conjunction, the list is described as **asyndetic**.

> [1] Only you can see, in the blinded bedrooms, the coms and petticoats over chairs, the jugs and basins, the glasses of teeth, Thou Shalt Not on the wall, and the yellowing

dickybird-watching pictures of the dead. [2] Only you can hear and see, behind the eyes of the sleepers, the movements and countries and mazes and colours and dismays and rainbows and tunes and wishes and flight and fall and despairs and big seas of their dreams.

Dylan Thomas, Under Milk Wood

In this example, Thomas uses listing in both sentences, but the effects achieved are different. In sentence 1, the accumulation of objects creates a claustrophobic atmosphere which epitomises the everyday lives of the inhabitants of Llareggub. In sentence 2, however, the use of syndetic co-ordination and the repetition of the co-ordinating conjunction *and* conveys a sense of freedom that they find in the limitless nature of their dreams.

Repetition

REPETITION of words, phrases, clauses or sentences draws attention to the key ideas.

Kids, aren't they just the cutest?

I must scribble on the walls
I must draw on my shoes
I must write on doors
I must doodle on the tiles

From now on they can be as creative as they like, thanks to Flash Mark & Stain Eraser

Flash advert in Tesco 'Kids Club' leaflet for parents (July 2004, extract)

The repetition of the first person subject pronoun *I* and the modal verb *must* are reminiscent of the traditional school 'lines' given as punishment. Here, however, the repetition is ironic: by omitting the negative the child is given permission to do what would normally be deemed wrong, since the new product from Flash can easily eliminate all signs of such 'creativity'. The repetition is persuasive because it is humorous, both in its inversion of a recognised tradition and in its use of childlike handwriting.

Patterning

Where **PATTERNING** is used, phrase, clause and sentence structures are repeated to give to a discourse a sense of balance and reason. **PARALLELISM** is a common device in which language structures of similar construction and meaning are placed side by side so that they create a sense of balance. **TRIPLING** is the use of three similar words, phrases or clauses for dramatic effect. **JUXTAPOSITION** brings words or ideas together in order to develop a relationship between them – it may be used to emphasise a contrast or to suggest similarities.

As a society, we have begun to be intolerant of things we should tolerate, and tolerant of things we should not tolerate. We have become illiberal in our desire to curb what was once normal behaviour. And we have become too liberal when it comes to tolerating and excusing behaviour which undermines society itself. All around us we see a lack of respect, discipline and decent values – but we just put up with it. We put up with the rowdy teenagers on the bus. We accept that people are afraid to venture out for a meal or a quiet drink in their town centre on a Friday or Saturday night.

Michael Howard, Leader of the Conservative Party (26 August 2004)
Speech on 'Political correctness gone mad'

The patterning in this extract from Michael Howard's speech revolves around the opposition created between antithetical concepts (*intolerant/tolerant*; *illiberal/liberal*). The first three sentences establish the argument, building to a climax in the fourth where the tripling of the abstract nouns *respect, discipline* and *values*, framed with the negative *a lack of*, emphasises the current state of affairs as Howard perceives it. He aims to take his audience with him, however, by creating unity through his recurrent use of the inclusive first person plural pronoun *we*. The repetition of the informal phrasal verb *put up with* suggests that a change of attitude is, essentially, what we all desire. The patterning is rhetorical, aiming to unite speaker and audience in a common cause.

ACTIVITY 3.2

The extract that follows is taken from an article called 'A Hanging' written by George Orwell and published in *Adelphi* in 1931. Its content, as the title suggests, is based on the execution of a Hindu man in Burma. It is written emotively and clearly conveys Orwell's own attitude to the whole process. It is not, however, a typical 'opinion' piece in which the author explicitly debates the arguments for and against, and comes to personal conclusions. Instead, Orwell uses a range of literary and rhetorical devices to influence his reader implicitly.

Read the extract and answer the following question:

Explore the literary and rhetorical devices Orwell uses to influence his reader.

You may like to think about:

▶ the lexical choice
▶ the literary devices
▶ the sound patterning
▶ the rhetorical devices.

1 It was in Burma, a sodden morning of the rains. A sickly light, like yellow tinfoil, was slanting over the high walls into the jail yard. We were waiting outside the condemned cells, a row of sheds fronted with double bars, like small animal cages. Each cell measured about ten feet by ten and was quite bare within except for a plank bed
5 and a pot of drinking water [...]
    We set out for the gallows. Two warders marched on either side of the prisoner, with their rifles at the slope; two others marched close against him, gripping him by arm and shoulder, as though at once pushing and supporting him [...] Suddenly, when we had gone ten yards, the procession stopped short without any order or war-
10 ning. A dreadful thing had happened – a dog, come goodness knows whence, had appeared in the yard. It came bounding among us with a loud volley of barks, and leapt round us wagging its whole body, wild with glee at finding so many human beings together [...] For a moment it pranced round us, and then, before anyone could stop it, it had made a dash for the prisoner, and jumping up tried to lick his face [...]
15 It was about forty yards to the gallows. I watched the bare brown back of the prisoner marching in front of me [...] At each step his muscles slid neatly into place, the lock of hair on his scalp danced up and down, his feet printed themselves on the wet

gravel. And once, in spite of the men who gripped him by each shoulder, he stepped slightly aside to avoid a puddle on the path.

20   It is curious, but till that moment I had never realised what it means to destroy a healthy, conscious man. When I saw the prisoner step aside to avoid the puddle, I saw the mystery, the unspeakable wrongness, of cutting a life short when it is in full tide. This man was not dying, he was alive just as we were alive. All the organs of his body were working – bowels digesting food, skin renewing itself, nails growing,
25   tissues forming – all toiling away in solemn foolery … He and we were a party of men walking together, seeing, hearing, feeling, understanding the same world; and in two minutes, with a sudden snap, one of us would be gone – one mind less, one world less […]

The Collected Essays, Journalism and Letters of George Orwell,
Volume 1: An Age Like This 1920–40 (Penguin, 1968)

COMMENTARY

Orwell adopts an unusual approach to an issue that is still topical in the twenty-first century: he takes a personal experience and uses it as a vehicle to reveal his own point of view about hanging.

He uses all three types of persuasion defined by Aristotle to guide our response. The lexis and tone (ethos) are, at first sight, surprisingly neutral. On closer reading, however, Orwell's attention to detail is clearly important: the cell's measurements and contents; observations of the dog and the prisoner. These become fundamental to our understanding of this experience. The emotive subject matter and Orwell's narrative approach lure us into the Burmese world he re-creates, leading us to the argument by working on our emotions (pathos). The dominant tone may be narrative, but Orwell makes us aware of his argument (logos), albeit implicitly. The different strands of his persuasive techniques work together both to convey his own stance and to force the reader to agree with his logic – by implication we are left with the impression that anyone who does not agree is guilty of *unspeakable wrongness* (l. 22).

The **lexical choice** communicates Orwell's personal experience in an emotive and compelling way. The subject matter itself, with its lexical field of *warders, prisoners, gallows* and *cells*, is dramatic, and to reinforce this Orwell uses verb modifiers like *condemned* (l. 2), intensifying the mood and appealing to our emotions. A noun like *procession* (l. 9), with its formal and often funereal connotations, adds to the tone of despair. There is, however, an alternative to this in the dynamic verbs (*bounding* l. 11, *leapt* l. 12, *pranced* l. 13, *jumping* l. 14) associated with the dog. These suggest a sense of life, which initially seems absurdly out of place at this time of death.

The concrete nouns in the first half of the extract help to create the physical setting. In the final paragraph, however, Orwell replaces them with abstract nouns like *mystery* and *wrongness* (l. 22). Inversely, the negative modifiers of the opening (*sodden* and *sickly* l. 1, *condemned* l. 2) are replaced by more positive ones like *healthy* and *conscious* (l. 21). This marks the turning point at which Orwell moves beyond his immediate experience to the ethics of hanging, turning from narrative to reflection.

Antithesis is central to the tone. The contrast of life and death is conveyed by the introduction of the dog, but equally by the present participles *pushing* and *supporting* (l. 8) describing the warders' treatment of the prisoner. It highlights the tragic absurdity of the situation even before Orwell makes it explicit.

The **literary devices** perhaps play the most important part in influencing the reader. The *sodden morning* (l. 1) is immediately symbolic, representative of the atmosphere of despair and disillusionment. It is a mood reinforced by the oxymoron *sickly light* (l. 1), where the modifier disrupts readers' expectations. Similes make an unknown experience more familiar and by comparing the quality of the light with *yellow tinfoil* (l. 1), Orwell gives the abstract mood a concrete presence. The link established between the cells and *small animal cages* (l. 3) also prepares us for the way in which the condemned prisoners are treated.

The introduction of the dog is ironic since its exuberance is in opposition to everything that has been described so far. Orwell draws further attention to this discrepancy through his use of metaphor. The dog's *volley of barks* (l. 11), with its connotations of something continuous, provides the disruption which changes Orwell's focus – it makes him see the prisoner in a new light. The *lock of hair* (l. 17) becomes symbolic of the man's life and Orwell uses the dynamic verb *danced* to represent the change in tone. Similarly, concrete nouns (*muscles* l. 16, *feet* l. 17, *shoulder* l. 18) are used to establish a sense of the man's unique life: his body parts seem to exist and function in a way that belies the finality of the moment.

Building to a climax, Orwell uses the metaphor of the *full tide* (ll. 22–3), with its connotations of perpetual motion, to emphasise how wrong this hanging will be. It is reinforced by the oxymoron *solemn foolery* (l. 25), which suggests the pointlessness of the body's mechanical perfection in such an absurd and, as Orwell wishes us to see it, reprehensible situation.

Sound patterning in prose tends to be less obvious than that used in genres like poetry or advertising, but Orwell does intensify the effect of his writing by drawing on the sound quality of particular words. The sibilance of the opening lines establishes a sonorous and resonant tone that reinforces the gravity of the specific experience he describes as well as the wider concept of hanging. Alliterative patterns like *bare brown back* (l. 15) and the similar sounds of *sudden snap* (l. 27) with its harsh final plosive use strong consonants to reflect the cold reality of Orwell's observations. The soft assonance of *seeing, hearing, feeling* (l. 26), on the other hand, marks the poignancy of Orwell's understanding of what is about to be done.

The use of **rhetorical devices** is also designed to influence the reader. Orwell uses lexical repetition to draw the reader's attention to key elements. Inevitably, nouns such as *cells/cell* (l. 3) and verbs such as *gripping/gripped* (ll. 7, 18) and *marched* (ll. 6, 7) recur because these are associated with the lexical field. Perhaps the most important repetition, however, is that of the clauses. In the following example, repetition of the clause forces the reader to recognise the moment of epiphany: the first is a main clause (narration) and the second is a fronted adverbial subordinate clause (reflection).

```
      S       P        A         A            A
... (he) (stepped) (slightly) (aside) (to avoid a puddle)                (ll. 18–19)
                                          SCl–NFCl
```

```
                           A                                 S    P
(When I saw the prisoner step aside to avoid the puddle), (I) (saw) ...    (ll. 21–2)
   SCl–ACl                                              SCl–NFCl
```

It is the second turning point in the extract, and the repetition of the clause marks the point at which Orwell understands the symbolic significance of an apparently minor observation.

Listing is another means of highlighting something of significance and Orwell, through his use of dynamic present participles (ll. 24–5), builds to an anti-climax. By ending with the present participle *toiling*, with its connotations of serious and purposeful work, he seeks to persuade the reader of the *unspeakable wrongness, of cutting a life short*. This is reinforced with the asyndetic co-ordination of the present participles *walking... seeing, hearing, feeling, understanding* (l. 26), which suggest the discrepancy between the apparent unity of the group and what is about to happen, between life and death.

The patterning that runs throughout the last paragraph of the extract shows Orwell trying to give a sense of balance and reason to his argument. The juxta-position of

```
     S        P          C      S    P      C
(This man) (was) (not) (dying), (he) (was) (alive)                          (l. 23)
                  neg
```

emphasises the central opposition of the whole extract. The poignancy of the situ-ation is further enhanced by the tension created between the compound phrase *He and we* and the post-modified noun phrase *a party of men walking together*. While the collective noun *party* is inclusive, the pronouns clearly distinguish between the prisoner and his captives – Orwell wants us to see that, while united by a common experience of the world, an *unspeakable wrongness* divides them.

The complexity of the sentences in the last paragraph is quite unlike the simple and compound narrative sentences of the opening. The left branching of the final clause (ll. 27–8) creates a poignant end. The prepositional phrases (*in two minutes; with a sudden snap*) delay the main clause with its emotive verb phrase *would be gone*, and the parallel noun phrases (*one mind less, one world less*) make explicit all that Orwell has implicitly encouraged us to feel.

Just as Orwell moves from personal experience to a wider and more general consideration of the ethics of hanging, so too his style moves away from descrip-tive narrative to philosophical debate. It is the subtlety of the changes in tone and the range of literary and rhetorical devices he uses that make this extract so evoca-tive and so persuasive.

Chapter 4

How to use your knowledge

The information covered in Part I should be used as a reference point – be prepared to dip into it to build up a technical **knowledge** base. The exercises that accompany each section are drills to test your understanding of the key concepts, but your study of language will require you to do more than just recognise grammatical, phonetic, phonological and stylistic features. You will instead need to learn how to **use** the knowledge you have gained. The suggestions below should prepare you for the sections of the book that follow, showing you how a knowledge of grammar, phonetics, phonology and style can be used in a variety of contexts.

4.1 Grammar

Words and phrases

Sometimes it is useful to consider the ways in which words and phrases are used. You will not, however, be required merely to identify all the nouns, adjectives and so on. Instead, you will have to think about why a writer or speaker has made certain **lexical choices**. Your first step should be to text mark any words or lexical sets that seem to be particularly effective: comment on their **connotations**, **context** and **register**. In your analysis of phrases, you need to discuss the **function** and **form** of key examples, considering the importance and effect of modifiers and qualifiers. At all times, try to comment on the **effects** created, focusing on the **purpose**, **audience** and **context** of the variety you are analysing.

Table 4.1 records the abbreviations you should be able to use in your analysis at the level of words and phrases.

Clauses and sentences

Within any discourse analysis, a consideration of clauses and sentences or utterances is central. You need to understand how **clause elements** and **main** and **subordinate clauses** are used, and the ways in which writers and speakers can manipulate these to create certain effects. You will not have to identify the type of every clause or sentence or utterance, but you should be able to discuss key

Table 4.1 **Abbreviations**

Word classes			
N	noun	prim	primary verb
Adj	adjective	mod	modal verb
V	verb	lex	lexical verb
Adv	adverb	aux	auxiliary verb
pron	pronoun	pres pa	present participle
det	determiner	past pa	past participle
prep	preposition	conj	conjunction
Phrases			
NP	noun phrase	PrepP	prepositional phrase
AdjP	adjective phrase	m	modifier
VP	verb phrase	h	head word
AdvP	adverb phrase	q	post-modifier or qualifier

examples. Writers and speakers use clauses and sentences or utterances in different ways; as you focus on a range of spoken and written varieties in the following chapters, practise selecting appropriate examples for analysis. It is useful to identify examples of simple, compound, complex and compound–complex sentences or utterances, because the choices writers or speakers make are often directly linked to their **purpose**, **audience** and **context**. You should always link the structures you describe to the **meaning** by considering both the **effects** created and the ways in which these relate to a writer's or speaker's **intentions**.

Table 4.2 records the abbreviations you should use in your analysis.

Table 4.2 **Abbreviations**

Clauses and sentences			
S	subject	MCl	main clause
P	predicator	SCl	subordinate clause
C	complement	NCl	noun clause
Cs	subject complement	ACl	adverbial clause
Co	object complement	RelCl	relative clause
Od	direct object	CompCl	comparative clause
Oi	indirect object	NFCl	non-finite clause
A	adverbial	VlessCl	verbless clause

Cohesion

When analysing cohesion in a discourse, it is necessary to look for examples of all types of linking devices. For instance, writers and speakers inevitably use **pronoun referencing**, substituting pronouns for noun phrases to avoid repetition, and usually there is nothing out of the ordinary in this process. However, you should be prepared to identify and comment on examples where cohesion has been used to achieve distinctive effects. **Lexical sets** may be linked to a specific field or register which will help you to identify the subject matter or focus of a text. A writer's or speaker's **use of pronouns** instead of proper nouns may leave the identity of a character intentionally vague, so that a dramatic revelation can be made at a significant moment. Examples of **repetition, referencing** or **ellipsis** may be used to draw attention to some key element of the discourse. In any discussion, you must remember to link your comments to the writer's or speaker's **intentions**.

4.2 Phonetics and phonology

Phonetics

Phonetics focuses on the ways in which sounds are produced. It deals specifically with **the physical properties of sounds** and it does not look at the way sounds are combined to create meaning. It is useful to be able to describe **the place and the manner of articulation of consonants** and **the ways in which different vowel sounds are formed**. You should be able to use appropriate **IPA symbols** to record immature sounds used by children or characteristic regional variations. Equally, your knowledge of phonetics should enable you to discuss topics like the advantages and disadvantages of **traditional orthography** and **phonetic spelling**.

Phonetics is a complex area of language study and your course will only require you to show an understanding of some basic concepts. Try not to be daunted by the material contained in Chapter 2 – instead, aim to acquire a working knowledge so that you can describe the production of sounds in spoken English.

Phonology

Because you are studying sounds within a particular sound system – RP English – most of your work will be on areas associated with phonology. It is useful to be able to analyse the **phonological units** or **segments** of English: you should know about **minimal pairs** and the way these are used to convey meaning; you should be able to discuss the effects created by **elision, assimilation, liaison** and **reduction** in continuous speech; and you should have a basic knowledge of the **rhythm** and **intonation patterns** in spoken English. Identifying and commenting on features like these will help you to show how spoken language is quite different from written language. In addition, analysis of **vocalisations** and **gesture** will show how speakers either support or challenge the actual words they utter. By discussing segmental and non-segmental features and by considering speakers' attitudes and opinions, you will be able to demonstrate the complexity of spoken interaction.

Transcription

A **phonetic transcription** is marked by **square brackets**. It aims to reflect the nature of sounds exactly and uses the **International Phonetic Alphabet** to do so. Although many symbols are directly related to the Roman alphabet we use

Table 4.3 **Annotations used in transcriptions**

/ /	slant brackets indicate that the transcription is more interested in the phonemic structure of an utterance than in the exact nature of the sounds articulated		
gó	rising tone	gò	falling tone
gô	rising–falling tone	gǒ	falling–rising tone
'alleg'	fast	'lento'	slow
'accel'	getting faster	'rall'	getting slower
'forte'	loud	'piano'	quiet
'cresc'	getting louder	'dimin'	getting quieter
'stacc'	clipped pronunciation	'leg'	drawled pronunciation
'alleg' 'stacc'	Gascoigne gets the ball and beats the defender (.) 'runs down the wing' 'inside to Ince (.) on to Shearer (.) back (.) to Ince' (.) who shoots		
↑go↑	raised pitch	↓go↓	lowered pitch
g̲o̲	word stress	a'bout	syllabic stress
d.	incomplete word	(.)	micro-pause
(2)	timed pause	[pointing]	gesture
ₒh	in breath	h°	out breath
ʰ	heavy aspiration		
[coughing]	non-verbal vocalisation	cho͞o cho͞o	held word or syllables
(indistinct)	indistinct sound or word	g.go	stutters, false start
I'll come over later (.) give me a ring ‖ if you decide to go out ‖ yeah (.) great		overlapping speech	
I'll come over later (.) give me a ring if you decide to go out = = yeah great		smooth latching of turns	

for written discourse, other symbols have been created or drawn from other alphabets to take account of the wide range of sounds that make up languages in general. In order to record exactly the kind of sounds heard, linguists have a range of **diacritics** and other symbols to describe any variations from the norm.

A **phonemic transcription** is less detailed – it focuses on the relationships between sounds rather than on a description of their exact quality. Because it analyses sounds in context, this kind of transcription considers the structure and meaning of sounds. A phonemic transcription is marked by **slant brackets** and uses a limited selection of the IPA symbols relating specifically to one particular language.

For your course, you will need to produce broad transcriptions which record the main phonological features of spoken discourse. You are unlikely to have to use complex systems of diacritics to mark things like aspiration, the nasalisation of vowels, or voiceless and voiced syllables. However, if you have a personal interest in this area of spoken language, this can be developed in project work.

Linguists use a range of symbols to mark phonological features on their transcriptions: you need to decide on the ones that will suit you best. Table 4.3 records the annotations used to mark prosodic features on transcriptions in this book.

4.3 Style

You will not find examples of all the stylistic techniques in a passage for analysis, but it is worth being able to recognise them when they do appear. Both spoken and written varieties of English use **sentence organisation**, distinctive **lexical choices**, **literary devices**, **sound patterning** and **rhetorical devices** to influence their respective audiences. By analysing the stylistic techniques used, you can draw conclusions about the distinctive features of different varieties. Equally, you will be able to assess and evaluate exactly **what a writer or speaker is trying to achieve**. It is important to **comment** on the **semantic effects** of the devices you find: you will gain little credit for merely recognising them. Instead, once you have identified certain stylistic techniques, consider **why** the writer or speaker has chosen them and the ways in which these will **influence the reader or listener**.

4.4 What to aim for

You should refer to Part I of this book regularly, using the contents list, the index and the glossary to help you find your way around. The definitions, examples and exercises will provide you with a starting point since they introduce you to important linguistic terminology. As you read the following chapters, you will gain confidence in your technical knowledge – the source material and commentaries will provide you with concrete examples of the way to use theoretical information in practice. The analytical approaches to each variety will show you how to annotate and discuss unseen material, and how to use appropriate terminology in context.

Ultimately, you must aim to bring together your grammatical, phonetic, phonological and stylistic knowledge so that you can comment on the distinctive characteristics of spoken and written English in an informed way. As a linguist, you must aim to identify the techniques different speakers and writers use to convey their message, and to discuss these linguistically. The section of 'Examination-style questions' at the end of the book will give you the opportunity to experiment with a range of materials. Use your knowledge to text mark the examples and collect the kind of information required to answer the questions in each case.

Part II

Language issues
– aspects of English

Chapter 5

Some basic concepts

5.1 A starting point

As well as a general knowledge of the structure of spoken and written English, linguists use certain core concepts to classify language. The key terms introduced in this section will provide you with the necessary basis for linguistic analysis since they establish a background against which all kinds of language change and variety can be considered.

5.2 Standard English and Received Pronunciation

STANDARD ENGLISH (SE) is a form of English which has been accepted as a norm. It is the variety with which other forms of English are compared. Sometimes it is called a *dialect*, although it is not linked to a specific region and has no regionally distinctive words or grammatical structures.

All language users adapt the form of their language according to where they are, what they are trying to communicate, and the audience to whom they are speaking or writing. Even Standard English, therefore, exists in a variety of forms – spoken and written; formal and informal; personal and impersonal. Although most people speak either a regional variety of English or a mixture of Standard English and regional forms, Standard English provides the country with a unified means of communication. It is what we usually hear on the television and radio news, for instance, because it is a form that cuts across regional differences. In its written form, Standard English is found in print and in formal written varieties like essays and business letters. It is also called **BBC ENGLISH** or **THE QUEEN'S ENGLISH**, and for some people it is the symbol of 'good English'. It is a prestigious language form because it is associated with government, the law, education, the Church and the financial world. It is the form taught to second-language speakers because it is universally understood and this perpetuates its cultural value.

Linguists are interested in the varieties of English we use and in order to describe them they use Standard English as a point of comparison. Any variety which does not use the same vocabulary or grammar as Standard English is called **NON-STANDARD ENGLISH**. By using this term, linguists can avoid value judgements – non-standard varieties of English are not wrong, but different.

Just as Standard English provides linguists with a convenient norm for describing variations in vocabulary and grammar, **Received Pronunciation** (**RP**) provides a standard form of pronunciation. It is an accent often associated with the South-East, where most RP speakers live, but unlike regional accents it is not confined by regional boundaries. In fact, RP tells you more about speakers' social and cultural backgrounds than about the region from which they come.

There are no linguistic reasons for describing RP as the 'best' accent, but socially it is associated with respectability, good education and high social status. It is prestigious because it is linked to the law, public schools and the Church. Second-language learners are often taught an RP accent, and it has been linked to the BBC since the early days of broadcasting.

Today, although RP still exists, only 2–3 per cent of the British population speak it in its original pure form. Now it most commonly exists as **Modified Received Pronunciation** (**MRP**), educated speakers having mixed characteristics of RP with regional forms. Speakers equally modify regional accents by moving towards a spoken form that they see as more prestigious, a form that they believe will improve their social status. The **Estuary English** at the end of the twentieth century, for example, shows the way some regional speakers adapted their accent by using features of RP. Although it originated in the South-East, young people as far north as Hull now adopt Estuary English as a 'trendy' accent.

Because language change is constant, some people argue that RP will not survive in its original form. Social judgements about regional varieties have to some extent become less dogmatic and this inevitably affects the way that users view different accents. The use of RP is no longer a prerequisite to social status – television and radio presenters, academics and politicians may now retain their regional accents, although often in a modified form. Ultimately, the use of Standard English is socially more important than the use of Received Pronunciation.

5.3 Attitudes to language

There are two distinct approaches to language: **prescriptivism** and **descriptivism**. The **prescriptivists** believe that English is governed by a set of rules that dictate a 'proper' and 'correct' use of language. They believe that if the 'rules' are not obeyed, the speaker or writer is 'wrong'. The form of English they see as 'correct' has a high social prestige – it is associated with formal written and spoken language and is used in dictionaries, grammar books and language handbooks. Because prescriptivists regard one particular form of English as the 'best', they dislike linguistic change. They see it as a process of decay which erodes standards and leads to a debased form of English.

The **descriptivists**, on the other hand, observe language as it is spoken or written in different situations. They aim to describe the ways in which language varies according to the user, the use and the context. While prescriptivists dislike language change, descriptivists accept it as inevitable. They recognise that a living language cannot be fixed, but will adapt to meet the demands of its users.

Despite this, descriptivists recognise the need for a standard form of language as a point of comparison. Although they believe that some usage is 'wrong' (*I in live town the*), they are more interested in describing variations from the standard as 'non-standard' than as 'incorrect'. In other words, they do make judgements, but these are based on a knowledge of audience, purpose and context.

5.4 Audience, purpose and context

All speakers and writers make decisions about the kinds of language they use – often subconsciously. They think about whom they will be addressing (**audience**) and the kind of relationship they need to create. They assess the formality or informality of the occasion (**context**) and the reason for the speech or writing (**purpose**). Lexical choices are then a reflection of their assessment of the linguistic situation.

Each individual has a wide range of language forms: a **PERSONAL REPERTOIRE**. We draw on these, speaking and writing in different ways according to the impression we want to make – with friends we are informal and familiar; with employers or teachers we are polite and formal. By assessing what is expected of us according to our audience, purpose and context, we regularly make decisions about what is **appropriate** or suitable. The term **APPROPRIATENESS** offers linguists an alternative to the right/wrong approach of the prescriptivists. It encourages a recognition of the variety and flexibility of language, and recognises that there are different linguistic expectations for different situations.

Language can also be assessed for its **ACCEPTABILITY** – whether it is considered permissible or normal by ordinary users. Linguists use **acceptability tests** to assess what is and what is not acceptable and their results show that language users do not always agree. Variations in opinions are caused by geographical, cultural, social and personal factors. To a linguist, however, any form of language that is regularly in use in speech or writing is acceptable in an appropriate context.

ACTIVITY 5.1

Read through the following examples of informal spoken English and then answer the questions below.

- a Are these utterances acceptable or unacceptable to you?
- b If they are unacceptable, can you identify what does not seem normal?
- c To what extent would the acceptability of these utterances depend upon the formality or informality of the context?

Examples:

1 I never do nothing on a Friday night.
2 I'm going to town now, me.
3 Don't forget to get off of the bus at the right stop.
4 Who did you speak to?
5 They always start *Star Trek* by saying 'To boldly go where no man has gone before'.
6 I was badder than my brother when I was little.
7 I met up with Julie when I went to town.
8 Tom forgot to pick me up and I was sat there for more than half an hour.
9 You'm all right now. You just need a good rest.
10 We was going shopping for mum when it happened.

11 The little boy fed hisself quite well for a toddler.

12 The temperature today will be 19° through 21°.

13 I can't make an appointment with the doctor while 5 o'clock.

14 The mouses were running everywhere last night.

15 The chairperson picked up her brief for the meeting.

16 I'm betterer than he is at writing stories.

17 I likes it better when my friend comes to play.

COMMENTARY

You may or may not have found examples that seemed unusual to you. Although many of these utterances differ from the norm or standard, descriptivist linguists would say that they are all **acceptable** because they are real examples of everyday usage in British regional dialects. However, it is important to realise that they would not be **appropriate** in all contexts. The comments below summarise some of the grammatical and linguistic features to which you may have responded.

Verb forms will often be different from the standard in regional dialects. In utterance 8, the verb phrase *was sat* would be replaced in Standard English by the progressive *was sitting.* The use of the verb *to be + past participle* is associated with the passive voice and linguistic purists would argue that in this example the *by + agent* has been omitted from a passive construction – that is, *I was sat there… by someone.* In utterance 10, there is evidence of a dialectal standardising process in which the first person plural past tense of the verb *to be* is replaced by the singular *was.* A similar process of standardisation occurs in utterance 17 – the verb *likes* has the *-s* inflection we would expect to see with the third person singular present tense. *You'm* in utterance 9 also standardises an irregular pattern: it is a dialectal contraction of *you are* in which the first person singular *am* is contracted to *-m* and applied to all parts of the verb. These are all common processes of regularisation, since dialects often simplify irregular patterns.

Other **non-standard features** linked to verbs can be seen in the use of a multiple negative in utterance 1. In Late Modern Standard English, the use of *never* and *nothing* together cancel each other out, although in earlier forms of English, listing of negatives was used for emphasis. The phrasal-prepositional verb *to meet up with* used in utterance 7 is a new combination and its meaning is still not yet stable. While some speakers use it to denote an accidental meeting, others would interpret it as an arranged meeting. This ambiguity is evidence of the way in which language change takes place – during the process of change, several variants often exist alongside each other. Finally, utterance 5 may or may not have seemed non-standard to you. Prescriptivists argue that an infinitive like *to go* is a lexical item and should not be split by a word placed in between. They would say that *to go boldly* is the 'correct' form, while descriptivists would argue that language is flexible and that *to boldly go* is far more dramatic in this context.

Pronouns are also often non-standard in regional dialects. In utterance 2, the object pronoun *me* is semantically redundant, but it is used in some dialects for emphasis. The reflexive pronoun *hisself* in utterance 11 also simplifies a pattern. Most reflexive pronouns are formed by adding *-self* or *-selves* to a possessive determiner: *my* + *self*; *your* + *self/selves*; *our* + *selves*. For the third person singular, however, *-self* is added to the object pronoun *him*. The dialectal form regularises the pattern by using the possessive determiner *his* + *self*.

Several examples here show how **prepositions** can be flexible in dialects. In utterance 3, the preposition *of* is not needed in Standard English to describe the direction of the movement since *off* denotes this itself. In utterances 12 and 13, Standard English would use a different preposition – *through* would be replaced by '*from* ___ *to* ___' (SE) and *while* by *until* (SE). This kind of dialectal substitution can cause problems in communication since speakers not familiar with the dialect could fail to understand the meaning. The utterance in example 4 may not have seemed unusual, but prescriptivists would argue that sentences should not end with a preposition. They would see *To whom did you speak?* as the 'correct' form, with the preposition moved to the initial position and an object pronoun form of the relative pronoun *who* following it. This structure is more common in writing than in speech.

Some **adjectival** use is also non-standard. Example 16 highlights the process of grading adjectives. In Standard English, mono- and many disyllabic adjectives add the inflection *-er* (*slow* + *er*, *easy* + (*i*)*er*); some disyllabic and all polysyllabic adjectives add *more* (*more* + *recent*; *more* + *intelligent*). Irregular adjectives do not follow this pattern, but instead have distinctive forms. The example here uses *better*, the irregular comparative form of *good*, adding the regular *-er* inflection as well. In utterance 6, an irregular comparative *worse* is standardised in the form of *badder*. This kind of simplification can be found in child language where a child recognises a language pattern and then overuses it by applying 'the rule' to irregular as well as regular words.

Some **nouns** may also be different in non-standard forms of English. In utterance 14 an irregular noun plural *mice* has been standardised as *mouses*. The regular *-s* inflection has been added where in Standard English the plural is marked by a change in the vowel. (In written language the consonant also changes, from *s* to *c*, but it is important to remember that these sound the same phonologically, and in speech would both be realised as /s/.) This is another instance of overextension in which a child assimilates a 'rule' and then overuses it. Finally, the use of *chairperson* in utterance 15 may or may not have attracted your attention. Purists may argue that the use of *chairperson* is unnecessary and awkward, but most people would prefer it since there is no need to distinguish between the sexes in this role.

The dialectal forms here may be **inappropriate** in some contexts, but in others they are **appropriate**. If they were used in informal contexts within regional boundaries where the audience was familiar with such variations, they would not cause problems in understanding. Modern linguists would not automatically describe them as 'wrong', therefore, but would assess the appropriateness of each utterance by considering the audience, purpose and context.

5.5 Register

REGISTER is a term used to describe variations in language according to use – lawyers use a legal register, doctors a medical register, and priests a religious register. When analysing an example of spoken or written language, linguists ask questions about three key areas of register. The **MODE** can either be spoken or written, although subdivisions can be identified where a formal speech is written to be read aloud or a written record is made of spoken language. A letter to the Prime Minister and an informal conversation with a friend, for instance, would use different registers: one a written mode and the other a spoken one. The **MANNER** describes the relationship between the participants and the formality or informality of the context in which communication takes place. A written examination essay does not aim to create a personal relationship with an unknown examiner because it is a formal task, while a postcard to a friend is both informal and personal. The **FIELD** is linked to the subject matter – by looking at the kind of words used, linguists can come to conclusions about the topic or focus of communication. A medical field, for example, may use words like *medicine, patient, asthma* and *inhalant,* while a legal field may use *judge, fixed penalty, sentence* and *witness.*

By considering mode, manner and field, linguists can draw conclusions about the role and form of language in different contexts. Different varieties of English are characterised by distinctive features and 'register' is a logical starting point for analysis.

ACTIVITY 5.2

Some writers adopt different registers in order to create particular effects. The following extract, from *Ulysses* (1922), an experimental novel by James Joyce, describes a June day in Dublin in 1904, mainly from the viewpoint of Leopold Bloom whose thoughts and activities are in some ways a parallel to the epic adventures of Homer's Ulysses.

The extract focuses on a conversation between friends in a pub. Read it through and try to identify changes in register. To help you, think about Joyce's use of:

1 direct speech and description
2 religious language
3 legal language
4 informal and colloquial language.

1   – I know that fellow, says Joe, from bitter experience.
    – Cockburn. Dimsey, wife of David Dimsey, late of the admiralty: Miller, Tottenham, aged eightyfive: Welsh, June 12, at 35 Canning Street, Liverpool, Isabella Helen. How's that for a national press, eh, my brown son? How's that for Martin Murphy the
5 the Bantry jobber?
    – Ah, well, says Joe, handing round the boose. Thanks be to God they had the start of us. Drink that, citizen.
    – I will, says he, honourable person.
    – Health, Joe, says I. And all down the form.
10   Ah! Ow! Don't be talking! I was blue mouldy for the want of that pint. Declare to God I could hear it hit the pit of my stomach with a click.
    And lo, as they quaffed their cup of joy, a godlike messenger came swiftly in, radiant as the eye of heaven, a comely youth, and behind him there passed an elder of noble gait and countenance, bearing the sacred scrolls of law, and with him his lady
15 wife, a dame of peerless lineage, fairest of her race.
    Little Alf Bergan popped in round the door and hid behind Barney's snug, squeezed up with the laughing, and who was sitting up there in the corner that I hadn't seen

snoring drunk, blind to the world, only Bob Doran. I didn't know what was up and Alf
kept making signs out of the door. And begob what was it only that bloody old panta-
20 loon Denis Breen in his bath slippers with two bloody big books tucked under his
oxter and the wife hotfoot after him, unfortunate wretched woman trotting like a
poodle. I thought Alf would split.

– Look at him, says he. Breen. He's traipsing all round Dublin with a postcard someone sent him with u.p.: up on it to take a li …
25 And he doubled up.

– Take a what? says I.

– Libel action, says he, for ten thousand pounds.

– O hell! says I.

The bloody mongrel began to growl that'd put the fear of God in you seeing some-
30 thing was up but the citizen gave him a kick in the ribs.

James Joyce, Ulysses

COMMENTARY

Changes in **mode** are noticeable where direct speech (spoken mode) becomes
description (written mode) at lines 12, 25 and 29. The extract opens with spoken
language and the **manner** is informal because these are friends drinking socially.
The informality is marked by exclamations like *Ah!* (l. 10), *eh* (l. 4) and *Ow!* (l. 10).
The use of shortened forms (contractions) like *How's* (l. 4), colloquial language like
boose (l. 6) and dialect like *oxter* (l. 21: Irish and Scots dialect for *armpit*) also reflect
the informality of the manner. In the second line, however, one of the characters
reads aloud from the births and deaths column of a newspaper. Information is provided in the almost note-like written form associated with obituaries placed in a
newspaper personal column. The register changes again when Joyce uses another
written style, drawing on the **field** of religion: *And lo* (l. 12), *the sacred scrolls of law*
(l. 14). Contrasting with this is the **field** of myth, which talks of a *godlike messenger*
(l. 12) and *a dame of peerless lineage* (l. 15).

The result here is comic because Joyce's choice of **register** contrasts with the
reality of his characters. By juxtaposing (setting one thing against another) *boose*
(l. 6) with *quaffed their cup of joy* (l. 12), and *an elder of noble gait and countenance*
(ll. 13–14) with Denis Breen *in his bath slippers with two bloody big books tucked
under his oxter* (ll. 20–1), Joyce encourages his reader to see both the comedy
and the grandeur of ordinary life. This effect can also be seen in the contrasting
descriptions of *Little Alf Bergan* (l. 16) as a *godlike messenger* (l. 12) and a *comely
youth* (l. 13) and Denis Breen's wife, an *unfortunate wretched woman* (l. 21), as the
fairest of her race (l. 15).

The **field** of law is briefly used to establish another contrast. The references to
libel action (l. 27) are juxtaposed with the informality of the context and the insignificant reason for the libel case. Finally, Joyce's repeated use of *bloody* (ll. 20, 29),
establishing a realistic informal context, can be juxtaposed with his use of a literary **register** in describing Denis Breen's wife *trotting like a poodle* (ll. 21–2). This is
not a traditional simile, but nevertheless creates a vivid image for the reader.

By identifying register changes, the reader can see links between the grand
world of myth and the ordinary world of Dublin. This enables Joyce to elevate the

city of Dublin and its inhabitants through his mythological references, but also to satirise them because of the difference between myth and reality.

5.6 Spoken and written English

There are significant differences between speech and writing. For instance, a lawyer summing up in court uses language in a different way from a legal document like a will; the language of an estate agent discussing a valuation with a client wishing to sell property differs from that of an estate agent's written selling details; the language of a live television news interview differs from that of a tabloid newspaper report; the language of a television cookery programme differs from that of a cake recipe in a cookery book; and a child's explanation to her mother about why she wishes to miss gym at school will be different from the note the mother writes to the teacher. In each case, the register is different: the **mode** for some is spoken, while for others it is written; the **manner** for some is more formal than others, which affects the kind of relationship created between participants; and the **field** varies depending on the subject matter. Just as we can write in a variety of ways, so we vary our speech according to our audience, purpose and context.

Many people believe that written language is more prestigious than spoken language – its form is likely to be closer to Standard English, it dominates education and is used as the language of public administration. In linguistic terms, however, neither speech nor writing can be seen as superior. Linguists are more interested in observing and describing all forms of language in use than in making social and cultural judgements with no linguistic basis.

Linguists' analysis of speech and writing has highlighted key differences between spoken and written language.

The nature of speech and writing

Spoken	Written
Speech is spontaneous and often transient. Most forms of everyday speech are not recorded for repeated listening, although in the age of the mass media much of what we hear on radio and television can be bought on cassette, DVD or video, downloaded from the internet, or recorded for repeated home use.	Writing is permanent: the same text may be read repeatedly or by several different readers (e.g. a recipe; a newspaper).

Audience

Spoken	Written
Spoken encounters (conversations) usually take place **face-to-face** with a particular person or persons. A telephone conversation is a notable exception.	Written language may be intended for a particular reader (e.g. a postcard; a letter), but often it will be addressed to an **unknown audience** (e.g. a coursework essay; an anthology of poetry).

Speakers can use **paralinguistic features** as well as words to check that communication is meaningful.	There is usually **no immediate feedback** for a piece of written text – texting and messaging services online have, to some extent, changed this since an ongoing 'written' conversation can take place between two mobile phone or computer users. Equally, the time difference between the writing and reading of the text means that writers must make sure that there is no unintentional ambiguity.
Deictic expressions like *this one, over there* and *just now*, referring to the present situation, are common.	All **references** need to be built into the written text because the reading context will be different for each reader (e.g. a novel; DIY instructions).
Interruptions and **overlaps** allowing the addressee to participate are common (e.g. informal conversation; BBC Television's *Question Time*).	Communication is **one-way**. Although the reader may respond in a written or spoken form, the response is rarely immediate (e.g. the reply to a letter; an examiner's comments on an essay).

Style

Spoken	Written
Speech is not usually **planned** in advance and speakers tend to think ahead as they speak (e.g. informal conversation; 'Question Time' in Parliament).	Writing is often **pre-planned** and ideas can therefore be carefully organised (e.g. a poem; an opinion essay).
Speech often has a **loose structure**, marked by repetitions, rephrasing of ideas, and comment clauses. Errors once uttered cannot be withdrawn.	Interruptions during the process of writing are not visible in a final copy. **Drafting** also means that errors can be corrected.
Lexis is often informal and there may be examples of a personal lexicon developed between familiar speakers (e.g. family conversation). In more formal contexts, vocabulary may be subject-specific (e.g. a political speech), but speech is still likely to be marked by contractions and comment clauses.	In many contexts informal **lexical** features like contractions will be unacceptable (e.g. a job application; an essay). Some lexical items will rarely be used in spoken language (e.g. chemical and mathematical equations).
Intonation and pauses are used to mark the **grammatical boundaries** of utterances. They are often long, with **multiple co-ordination**. **Subordination** is used but speakers have to make sure that embedded subordinate clauses do not place too many demands upon listeners, who cannot easily reconsider an utterance.	Punctuation and layout are used to mark the **grammatical boundaries** of sentences. In more formal kinds of writing, sentences are often marked by **multiple subordination** and balanced **syntactical structures**.

Prosodic features like volume, pace, rhythm, tone and stress patterns, as well as words, communicate meaning.	Writers use **paragraphing** and **page** layout to organise their text. **Capitalisation** and **underlining** can be used for stress, while **question marks** and **exclamation marks** can be used to convey attitude.

Function

Spoken	Written
Speech is a useful **social tool** which can develop relationships, convey attitudes and opinions directly, and so on.	Written texts can be used to record **facts** and **ideas**, make **notes**, develop large-scale **fiction**, and so on. They are more permanent than speech, and can be longer without causing communication problems.

Inevitably, a summary like this generalises the **differences** between speech and writing, but the distinctions here are a useful starting point. It is important, however, to be aware of the **overlap** between spoken and written forms. Written texts, for instance, can imitate spoken words so that when spoken they sound spontaneous; and similarly, spoken texts can be transcribed. An informal conversation and a formal essay can be seen as two extremes – between these, there will be varying degrees of difference. In assessing the differences between spoken and written examples, linguists first establish the audience, purpose and context of the discourse. Having done this, they can consider the extent to which a text or an utterance is typical of speech or writing.

Society is invariably judgemental about language – people write to papers like *The Times* bewailing the poor standards of English; well-known public figures such as Prince Charles have spoken of what they describe as a deterioration in standards, resulting from a supposedly sloppy attitude towards language and a lack of knowledge about it. At the centre of complaints like these lies the debate about the relative worth of spoken and written language.

Recently, emphasis has moved away from written language as the only mode of value. Traditionally written language was seen as most significant because it was the medium for education and literature and was therefore prestigious: now, however, schools both use and assess spoken language alongside written language. Our society is dependent upon the telephone, the television and the radio, all of which use spoken language in a variety of forms. Often politicians no longer deliver their speeches as formal written texts that are read aloud, but 'speak' them directly from notes or from the autocue.

While prescriptivists see speech as inferior because of its errors and hesitations, descriptivists use speech as the basis for much of their research because it reflects how language is used in society. It is important to remember that language is first and foremost a spoken phenomenon – written language is a by-product.

Copy and complete Table 5.1 with appropriate examples (1–5), considering the general features of spoken and written language.

Table 5.1 **Features of spoken and written language**

Features	Spoken	Written
Level of formality ▸ Formal ▸ Informal	Politician's speech *(1)*	Examination essay Shopping list
Level of permanence ▸ Permanent ▸ Short-lived	*(2)* Conversation with a neigh-bour over a garden wall	Novel *(3)*
Use of Standard English ▸ Standard English ▸ Non-standard English	BBC News *(5)*	*(4)* Use of non-standard language in literature

COMMENTARY

The table shows that spoken and written language do not always appear at extreme ends of the scale – in many instances **formal speech**, for instance, will be marked by features of written language, and **informal writing** will have similarities with speech. The choices you made in each case will have been dictated by your instinctive knowledge of language and the way it is used.

As an example of informal speech (1), you could have chosen 'friends chatting in a nightclub'. The **context** is informal, the **participants** are familiar and the **purpose** is social. Permanent speech (2) is not typical of spoken language, but a taped police confession, for instance, will be listened to by different people in different contexts. The **context** is formal, and although some **participants** may be known (other police officers), others may be unknown (a jury). The **purpose** is official.

Written lists like shopping lists and reminders of tasks to be completed are short-lived (3) because they are usually destroyed once the job has been done. The **context** tends to be informal and personal; the **audience** is often the writer alone and the **purpose** is informative. Most writing, because it tends to be formal, will use Standard English (4). Students will choose Standard English for A-level work, for instance, because the **context** is formal and the **audience** is unknown. The **purpose** is to reveal academic knowledge and to demonstrate written skills.

Non-standard speech (5) is common in any informal **context** in which participants feel no pressure to conform to the standard. Often the **purpose** of communication will be social and the **audience** will be known. Equally, a television soap opera that aims to imitate life will use the regional accent and dialect appropriate to the area in which it is set. In BBC1's *EastEnders*, for instance, the young people speak to one another informally in an East End, London, accent.

5.7 Using the basic concepts

All the terms used here play a central part in the study of English because they provide a means for linguists to classify different attitudes and varieties.

Different attitudes to language determine the way usage is classified – while a **prescriptivist** may say a particular usage is 'wrong', a **descriptivist** will describe it as **appropriate** or **inappropriate**. When faced with a range of spoken and written varieties of English, linguists need to establish the **register** (mode, manner and field) and to assess whether the language use is **standard** or **non-standard**. This kind of information enables linguists to avoid uninformed evaluative judgements, ensuring instead that analysis is based on **linguistic evidence**.

Because the terms highlighted here will be used frequently throughout the rest of this book, it is important that you understand them before moving on.

Chapter 6

English: a living language

6.1 English: a living language

Perhaps one of the first things to understand as you begin a study of the English language is that it is constantly changing. It is a **living language**, adapting to an ever-changing world which, in its turn, requires new and varied means of communication. The English language has embraced industrial, technological and social changes, and we as its users decide what will and what will not survive.

There are always people who yearn for the English language of the past. They believe that English now exists in a corrupted form, simplified and less subtle than its sophisticated antecedent. Their argument suggests that change is a new phenomenon running parallel to the breakdown of society. Taking this to its logical conclusion, we must therefore expect the English language to continue to deteriorate until it exists in a form no longer recognisable or comprehensible. The linguistic pessimists who view the English language in this way are concerned about several factors: supposedly decreasing standards of literacy marked by poor spelling and grammatically incomplete or 'incorrect' sentences; the use of informal spoken language in written contexts; allegedly inaccurate pronunciation; and the way in which international forms of English may affect British English in the future. The list of their complaints could be endless.

However, the debate is two-sided: while the critics bewail the lost glory of English, others see in the adaptability of the English language a flexibility and vitality. The people who believe in language as a democratic process see current linguistic developments as broadening our world view: new words reflect new experiences, more liberal attitudes and a greater understanding of the world. Language cannot exist on its own since it is a product of the people who speak and write it daily, and therefore it develops to meet their **needs**. Certainly the English language is changing and certainly the rate of change is rapid, but that is merely a reflection of the society we live in. It does not automatically imply a downward spiral towards an impure and ineffective form of English.

A study of the English language should be based on an awareness of these two crucial attitudes. In linguistic terms, the two views can be summarised as the **prescriptive** and the **descriptive** approaches to language.

Language change can be considered in either of two ways. If viewed from a historical perspective, the focus is on language as a constantly changing form. Linguists study the ways in which English has evolved from its early form (Old English) to its current form (Late Modern). This is called a **DIACHRONIC APPROACH**. If instead change is considered at a particular moment in time, a 'snapshot' is taken of English during a specific stage of its development. Linguists analyse a clearly defined period in order to identify characteristic features of English at that time. This is called a **SYNCHRONIC APPROACH**.

6.2 What changes language?

Because the sound of words and their order in sentences seems to vary very little, language appears to be quite static. Linguists have now demonstrated, however, that lexis, syntax and semantics are constantly in flux, changing from person to person and from place to place. Until quite recently, it was considered almost impossible to identify and record language changes because they were so gradual that they could easily go unnoticed. Now it is known that although the early stages of change are slow, once they have caught on and are used more regularly, change can be rapid.

Because language **patterns** remain constant, we can assume that change is not random. If change were arbitrary, the English language would eventually be made up of disjointed sequences that language users could not connect into sensible and meaningful patterns. If this were the case, people who see all linguistic change as cause for concern would be justified in their gloomy predictions for the future of the English language. However, linguistic research has shown that language users have a tendency to readjust patterns that have been disturbed. Because the basic function of language is to communicate, its users subconsciously protect its expressive capabilities.

Language change therefore can be seen as **systematic**. Social, historical, cultural or geographical influences can alter the words and structures that we use. These determinants can be described as 'triggers' because they stimulate change in distinctive ways:

- **Historical factors** Wars, invasions, industrial and technological changes all provide the context for the creation of new words.
- **Cultural transmission** Although each generation uses the form of language handed down by the previous generation, language is usually adapted and altered to suit the personal requirements of the next generation. Equally, a distinctive form of language can give a cultural group a sense of identity, uniting 'insiders' and alienating 'outsiders'.
- **Social factors** Education, social class, age, gender, ethnic background, occupation and personal identity will influence the words and grammar that individual speakers use.
- **Geographical location** The pronunciation of words (**accent**) and the kinds of words and grammatical structures used (**dialect**) will vary and change according to the region from which a speaker comes.

- **The use of different registers** The words, grammatical structures and formats chosen will vary according to use. Different fields – such as law, advertising and religion – each have distinctive characteristic features.
- **The development of English as a world language** The power of the mass media, international trade, the blurring of international boundaries and easily accessible travel all mean that English is affected by change both within the United Kingdom and beyond.

Linguists analysing the changing faces of English can categorise their findings by grouping together similar changes. A diachronic study of English will isolate the **historical changes** that have taken place over time. A society-based study of English will analyse **social changes**, such as new technological development, changing attitudes, and other social determinants affecting the kind of English we use. A cultural study of English will identify **cultural changes**, whereby groups of people with a distinctive heritage adapt a form of English to draw attention to their common background. A dialectal study of English will map out the **geographical changes** that result in regional variations. An international study of English will focus on **worldwide changes** to English as it is adapted to meet the needs of new first- and second-language speakers. A study of different varieties of English will concentrate on **register changes** which alter the words, structures and formats of spoken and written English.

6.3 The changing faces of English

As a living language, English is constantly changing to meet the needs of its users. As soon as new forms are observed, described and recorded, other newer forms appear. Discussion of linguistic change can therefore never be complete: the summaries provided here merely outline some of the characteristic features in each case. Since historical (Chapter 7), geographical (Chapter 8) and register changes (Chapters 10–20) are considered later in this book, this section will try to pin down some of the social, cultural and worldwide changes that have resulted in distinctive forms of English.

Social changes: gender and language

While SEX describes the biological distinction between men and women, GENDER describes a cultural system by which society constructs different identities for men and women. Feminists believe that images of gender have developed in such a way that the masculine perspective has been given a dominant position. They believe that society instils certain codes of behaviour in boys and girls from a young age: men are seen as logical, rational and objective, and women as emotional, intuitive and subjective; masculinity is associated with power and strength, and femininity with passivity and domesticity. Many people now believe that such stereotypical representations of gender should be challenged – individuals should not necessarily be expected to learn the behaviours and attitudes that society sees as appropriate to their sex.

The nature of language is at the very heart of this debate: it is language that teaches individuals to act in a certain way; it is language that reinforces society's expectations; and it is language that makes people powerful. SEXIST LANGUAGE reinforces stereotypical attitudes and expectations – it often implies male superiority. While men are *masterful*, women are *domineering*; while men *discuss*, women *chat* and *gossip*; and while men are *forceful*, women are *bossy*. Often words associated with men have positive connotations: they are *virile*, *manly* and *sporty*; words like *strength*, *independence* and *courage* are commonly linked to them. Women, on the other hand, are associated with *weakness* and with *emotional* and *erratic* behaviour; words like *frailty*, *dependence* and *vulnerability* are traditionally linked to them. Language use like this builds on a stereotypical view of women and men – it implies that differences between women and men are wholly based on gender rather than on individual personalities. Such language can suggest that women are inferior.

It is difficult to change these ingrained habits, but in an age of **political correctness** this kind of divisive language is often seen as quite unacceptable. Many workplaces now have 'equal opportunities' policies in which anti-sexist alternatives are promoted as substitutes for the traditional male-dominated language of the office or shop floor. The *chairman* becomes a *chairperson*; *man-hours* become *work-hours*; a *master copy* becomes a *top copy*. For all the outdated terms marked by the generic term *man*, there are viable alternatives.

Some people argue that language change must be actively promoted if the status quo is to be altered – that laws should define new acceptable terms of address, and that positive discrimination should be used. Others believe that language will change automatically to reflect the new roles women have in society – because language is democratic, its users will dictate what is acceptable and what is not, and changes will follow naturally. The problem seems to be that although equal opportunity policies can suggest new lexical items to replace the older, more sexist alternatives, it is very difficult to change habits. While employers may insist on certain words being used in the workplace, society's underlying attitudes and expectations are far more difficult to challenge.

Research carried out by linguists suggests not only that language use is sexist, but also that the very roles men and women take in informal conversation are different. On a level of **discourse**:

▸ men are more likely to interrupt
▸ men will often reject topics introduced by women, while women will talk about topics raised by men
▸ women are more likely to use supportive minimal vocalisations like *mm* and *yeah*
▸ while women are more likely to initiate conversations, they succeed less often because males are less willing to co-operate
▸ men are more likely to use familiar terms of address, even where the relative status and background of the speakers would seem to suggest that a formal, impersonal tone is more appropriate.

The **grammatical structures** used by women and men are also different:

- women use tag questions more frequently
- modal verbs, modal adverbs like *probably* and *possibly*, and tentative verbs like *think* and *suppose* occur more often in women's utterances
- men are more likely to use commands – where women do use them, they are often framed as interrogatives like *Would you mind passing me that book?* or as hypothetical statements like *I wonder if you could pass me that book*.

Similarly, **lexical choices** often seem to be related to a speaker's gender:

- women are more likely to use evaluative adjectives like *wonderful*, *brilliant* and *great*
- adverbs of degree like *so* and *very* are more common in women's speech
- adjectives describing approximate amounts like *about* and *around* seem to be more common in women's utterances
- reduplicated forms like *teeny-weeny* and *itsy-bitsy* are associated with women rather than men – because they are linked to baby talk, men see them as inappropriate
- men are thought to use slang and swearing more frequently
- women's speech is characterised by the frequency of politeness markers like *please* and *thanks*.

Phonological differences are seen in the fact that women are far more likely to use high-prestige forms and to adjust their accents to match other participants in a formal speech encounter. They are less likely to drop final consonants and to speak with a broad accent if they feel that they need to make a good impression.

Inevitably all the features outlined here are stereotypical – they imply that all women and all men speak in the same way. However, they are interesting to linguists because they illustrate that society's gender expectations influence far more than just the words we choose.

It is easy to see why sexist language is often seen as no more than a matter of lexical choice – it is an area in which linguistic inequality is more obvious than the gender biases that linguists identify in discourse and grammar. It is also the area in which change could be promoted most easily. For the people who wish to accelerate the process of change, it is possible to introduce lexical items as substitutes for the traditional sexist terms. Although lexis is the most accessible part of a language, unless lexical alternatives are set within the context of grammatical and discourse changes, attitudes will change only slowly.

Terms of address can provide a starting point for changing attitudes. Nameplates on office doors need no longer distinguish between *Dr D. B. King* and *Dr Dorothy B. King*; newspapers could standardise their references to males and females, avoiding descriptions of *bubbly blonde Debs* as opposed to *Mr Jackson*. In many contexts, there is no need to distinguish the gender of workers: *firefighter* can replace *fireman*; *conductor* can replace *conductress*; *officer* can be used for *policeman*; *businessperson* for *businessman*. Such changes in lexis reflect **social changes** – women are now part of the workforce at all levels and language needs to reflect this. Descriptions of the *working mother* or *working wife* are outdated: many women now combine domestic and occupational roles, and the concept of a woman outside the home environment is no longer unusual.

Many words belittle women, making them seem no more than **sexual objects**. Although often meant to be friendly, in a formal context terms like *love* and *dear* can be offensive since they suggest that women do not have equal status with men. Other informal terms of address like *chick*, *doll* and *bird* also equate women with sexual objects. Where the words *master* and *mistress* were originally equivalents, the male term has gained far greater prestige. It is now used in a much wider sense – its connotations are positive, suggesting competence, authority and skill. Those associated with *mistress* on the other hand, are now negative – its field of reference has become narrower until it is now primarily associated with sexuality and illicit affairs.

The **generic *man*** is perhaps the word that causes most upset and for which many people have offered non-sexist alternatives. In Old English, *mann* meant *person*. This term was then accompanied by other distinct forms which marked differences in gender: *wer* (adult man); *wif* (adult woman); *wæpman* (adult male person); and *wifman* (adult female person). By 1850, an Act of Parliament had ruled that 'words importing the masculine gender shall be deemed and taken to include females'. However, many people feel that collocations like *political man* cannot possibly conjure up an image of political females as well as males. Similarly, in a historical context, people who wish to actively promote language change believe that it is necessary to substitute phrases like *prehistoric people* for *prehistoric man*, *ancestors* for *forefathers*, and *humankind* for *mankind*.

Many other **collocations** use the generic *man*: *the man in the street*; *the common man*; *no-man's-land*; *an Englishman's home is his castle*. Although these are all meant to be inclusive, it is difficult to believe that speakers clearly visualise both men and women. Where *woman* is used in collocations, the connotations tend to be negative – phrases like *women of the night* and *woman driver* are pejorative. The **order of words** in compound phrases also presents a male-dominated view of the world: *husband and wife*; *boys and girls*; *Mr and Mrs*; *man and wife*. Some people would argue that the order of words does not matter, but in the sixteenth century the structure of these phrases was directly linked to the belief that men came before women in the natural order.

The use of the **third person singular pronoun *he*** also causes a lot of controversy. Sixteenth-century grammar books established its use – grammar books were written by men for schoolboys in a male-dominated society. In this context, the use of *he* was therefore logical: it reflected a literal reality. In the twenty-first century it no longer reflects a society in which girls have equal access to free education and in which women are supposed to have equal employment opportunities. Although it is meant to be an inclusive reference, linguistic research suggests that in informal conversation, *he* is always a gender-specific reference.

Because English does not have an indefinite pronoun which could replace the supposedly inclusive *he*, many new **pronominal forms** have been suggested. The third person plural *they* which does not distinguish between genders is sometimes used, but purists complain that it is grammatically inaccurate to use it after a singular noun reference: *each person must now collect their ticket*. Another straightforward alternative is to use both the feminine and the masculine singular pronouns: *s/he*, *he/she*. More drastic measures have been suggested by some people, who propose new pronoun forms: *hesh* for *he/she*; *hirm* for *him/her*; *gen* for the generic *man*; *bod* for *anybody*. If these were to become realistic alternatives and not just gimmicks, it would be necessary to dictate their usage. Schools and government institutions would have to establish a new awareness of these as the 'standard' forms – they would have to enforce usage until it became the norm.

Gender and language are closely linked because it is through language that we communicate and construct models which help us to understand society. Sexist language can disparage and trivialise women and many people believe that the words we use should be carefully chosen to promote sexual equality – women can feel invisible because the English language defines everyone as male. Language does change as society places different demands upon it, and it seems likely that it will come to encompass changes in women's roles. Inevitably this kind of evolution takes time, however, and in the meantime political correctness and equal-opportunities policies will endeavour to provide lexical alternatives. Behaviour that is more deeply engrained, like female and male roles in discourse, will take longer to alter – legislation cannot tackle this because it requires people to have linguistic knowledge and to develop different attitudes and expectations. Despite this, as social attitudes do change, language changes too.

ACTIVITY 6.1

The following examples are all marked by words or structures that reinforce a male-dominated perspective of society. Try to find alternatives that are gender-neutral, and decide whether or not gender bias in language matters.

Examples:

1 man-made
2 as a mammal, early man breastfed his young
3 manpower
4 Mr Legg runs a company in partnership with his wife
5 lady doctor
6 cameraman
7 the local Girl Guides were manning the sideshows
8 I'll have my girl type that immediately
9 the old masters are well represented in this gallery
10 a one-man show
11 statesman

COMMENTARY

Gender-biased language does not present women and men as equal. Instead, it implicitly suggests that men are superior and therefore reinforces the gender roles that society assigns to males and females. The examples in this activity can be divided into three distinct categories: sexist language in the workplace; gender-biased terms of address; and uses of the generic *man*.

The language here associated with the **workplace** (examples 1, 3, 5 and 6) fails to take account of changing employment patterns – many such words and phrases do not recognise that women are now likely to work alongside men in almost all occupations and at all levels. Nouns like *manpower* (3) can be replaced by a gender-neutral term such as *staff* or *workforce* in order to reflect social changes in women's roles. Equally, a product labelled with an adjective like *man-made* (1) can more accurately be described as *synthetic* or *artificial.* Two other examples highlight the need for gender-neutral job titles: in most cases, there is no need to label male or female workers, so terms like *lady doctor* (5) and *cameraman* (6) should be replaced by *doctor* and *camera operator.* The alternatives offered are not cumbersome and substitution would cause no problems of understanding.

Another key area of gender bias can be seen in the **terms of address** (examples 4, 8 and 9) used to define people. These words limit our perceptions because of the connotations they carry. If a (male) boss refers to his personal secretary as *my girl* (8), for instance, he is reducing her role to something insignificant. She is diminished and becomes little more than an object owned by her employer. Similarly, the utterance in which one business partner is named as the *wife* (4) of the other may suggest that she is of minimal importance to the company. While her husband is formally named as *Mr Legg*, she is no more than an attribute of him. In both cases, the gender bias of the noun is underpinned by the use of a possessive determiner which defines the female as a possession of the male. The description of famous artists of the past as *old masters* (9) suggests that there were no women amongst them – the connotations of *master* are linked directly to our concept of successful men. Although many people would not agree that the use of *masters* in this context is as serious as some of the other examples of gender-biased language here, it is easy to replace it with a neutral description like *major artists.*

The use of the **generic *man*** (examples 2, 7, 10 and 11) is more controversial: many people feel that a male reference cannot possibly be all-inclusive. In collocations like a *one-man show* (10) and nouns like *statesman* (11), the generic *man* can be replaced by the general reference *person*: a *one-person show*; *statesperson.* Many people find this kind of substitution awkward, preferring alternatives like *leader* and *politician* to the compound created with *person.* In other cases, verbs derived from the generic *man* can be replaced quite easily: *manning* (7) becomes *staffing* or *running.* In some historical contexts, references to *man* can be contradictory – the example here (2) can easily be made meaningful. The noun phrase can be made gender-specific since it was the women who fed the babies, thus *early man* becomes *early woman*, and *his* becomes *her*; or it can be made neutral by changing the word order and using the passive voice – *as mammals, the babies of early people were breastfed.*

In some contexts it is possible to promote change by actively encouraging the use of alternatives: in the workplace, in textbooks and in the way that we name each other in everyday encounters. Inevitably, such change takes time and many people will continue to use more traditional forms. Despite this, because language does influence the way we see others, it is important that people are encouraged to recognise that there are alternatives. Language will continue to change to meet the needs of its users and will slowly reflect changing attitudes to gender roles, but positive action to enhance this natural change could help to challenge outdated, preconceived outlooks.

Cultural changes – Black English

Because of technological developments, increased travel opportunities and international multimedia links, it is possible that different languages and variants of the same language will in time become increasingly uniform. Despite this possibility, however, there are still many examples of linguistic diversity. In some instances, changes to a standard form of language are linked directly to social class or to the promotion and preservation of a particular cultural background or ethnic identity.

BLACK AMERICAN ENGLISH (**BAE**), for instance, is the language used by lower-class Blacks in urban communities. Probably 80 per cent of Black Americans can speak this variety, but as Blacks have become more integrated and as a Black middle class has developed, the language form used by the other 20 per cent has moved closer to Standard American English. **BLACK ENGLISH VERNACULAR** (**BEV**) is not a regional dialect because it is difficult to link it directly to a specific geographical area. Instead, it tends to be classified as a **CULTURAL** or **SOCIAL VARIANT** from the standard form. It is often described as a **'political' non-standard form** because as a distinct and separate variety of spoken English it is in direct conflict with **STANDARD AMERICAN ENGLISH** (**SAE**).

The history of Black English in America can be linked to the slave trade in the seventeenth, eighteenth and nineteenth centuries, when Africans were taken from their native lands to American plantations. There are different theories about the way in which Black English developed. Some people believe that because the slaves learned English from their masters as a second language, they passed on to their children a form of American English that was grammatically different from American Standard English. Because of racial segregation, the dialect features of this variety persisted and are still to be found in Late Modern Black English. Another view of the development of Black English suggests that many of its features are directly linked to West African languages. In the seventeenth and eighteenth centuries, African slaves who spoke the same languages were always kept apart, to prevent slave revolts. This meant that English was often the slaves' only common language. Rather than SAE, the slaves used a language made up of English and West African linguistic features: the vocabulary was dominated by English words and the grammatical structures were simplified.

To allow English-speaking whites to communicate with Africans, a **CONTACT** or **PIDGIN LANGUAGE** was developed. Pidgins are marginal languages created by people who need to communicate but have no common language. They are marked by a **simplified grammar** and a **small vocabulary** (about 700–2000 words), and they have a **smaller range of functions** than either of the source languages from which they are formed. They can be distinguished from dialects because they are clearly made up from two source languages – parts of them will not be understandable to speakers who know only one of the source languages. Most pidgins are based on European languages (**English, French, Spanish, Dutch and Portuguese**), reflecting Europe's history of colonisation. Often when the original need for communication is no longer important, pidgin languages die – in Vietnam, for example **French Pidgin** no longer served any purpose when the

French left and was therefore no longer used. Some, however, become so useful that they develop a more formal role, gaining official status and expanding to meet the needs of users. A language that develops in this way is called an **EXPANDED PIDGIN** or a **LINGUA FRANCA**. In Papua New Guinea, for instance, **Tok Pisin** is now recognised both as a primary language in urban centres and as a lingua franca in more remote areas.

When a pidgin becomes the main language of a community, it has to become more complex and to be able to fulfil a wider range of functions. When later generations learn it as a first language, it is called a **CREOLE**. Creoles can develop in a variety of ways – if pidgin speakers can no longer use their first language, the pidgin will become a primary rather than an auxiliary language; in a community of mixed races, if the pidgin language is used in private contexts like the home as well as in public contexts, children will begin to learn it as a first language. For a pidgin language to become a creole, certain criteria must be met: the **vocabulary** has to be expanded; **grammatical structures** have to be able to communicate more complicated meanings; and **style** has to be adaptable.

There are two kinds of creole Englishes: **Atlantic** and **Pacific creoles**. Because Portuguese explorers had been trading in gold and people from the coast of West Africa since the early fifteenth century, later European traders found that many Africans used a simplified version of Portuguese. This formed the basis for a new pidgin, and English creoles are marked by the number of Portuguese words they still contain. The Atlantic varieties are connected to the languages of the West African coast.

The **grammatical structures** of creole languages tend to be marked by the following features:

‣ The absence of plural forms – creoles usually rely on the context to indicate whether or not a noun is plural. In Atlantic varieties, *dem* is often placed immediately after the noun.
‣ Third person singular pronouns are not marked for gender – *i* is used for *he*, *she* and *it*.
‣ Nouns can be marked for gender by adding *man* (man) or *meri* (woman).
‣ Verbs are not marked for person or tense – all verbs are used in the base form. Different timescales are indicated by the addition of auxiliary verbs like *did* or *been*, or by creole words like *baimbai* (by and by) for future time or *pinish* (finish) for past time.
‣ Multiple negatives are common.
‣ Some varieties distinguish between two kinds of *we*: *yumi* (you and me); *mipela* (me and other people, not including you).

Certain **lexical patterns** are distinctive:

‣ **REDUPLICATION** of words is used to extend a limited vocabulary: *ile* (hilly) → *ileile* (choppy sea).
‣ Reduplication can also distinguish between two words that sound similar: *sun* and *sand* would both be articulated as *san*, so *sand* is realised as *sansan*.
‣ Reiterated words are also used to intensify meanings, to mark continuity and to create emphasis: *smal* (small) → *smalsmal* (very small).

- Many nautical words were introduced in the first contact languages that evolved as a means of communication between the native language speakers and traders. In the creole varieties, these have modified their original terms of reference: *galley* (ship's kitchen) → *gali* (any kitchen).

In America, the pidgin English used on the slave plantations became a first-language creole. It was no longer just used for basic communication, but evolved so that it was central to the community. It was used in practical contexts for every-day communication; in ritual contexts for developing community worship; in cele-brations and in oral storytelling traditions. Perhaps most importantly, it became a language of resistance since it was markedly different from the standard form of English used by the plantation owners. Creoles are often regarded as inferior by speakers who use a standard form of language.

In social terms, creole languages have no educational status and little social prestige, and are usually spoken by people in the poorer social classes. Because they are linked to slavery and subjection, users are under pressure to adopt standard forms of language instead. The process by which creoles are modified by standard usage is called **DECREOLISATION**. As speakers adapt their language use, the origi-nal creole then exists in a variety of forms, all varying in different degrees from the standard. This range of creole forms is called the **POST-CREOLE CONTINUUM**. In some cases, speakers will automatically reassert the value of their first-language creole to challenge the superiority of the standard language that society wishes them to speak. This results in **HYPERCREOLISATION** – speakers use pure creole forms to emphasise their ethnic and cultural background.

Black English is not a creole, but its source lies in the pidgin and creole lan-guages spoken by the African slaves on the plantations. Just as the history of the slave trade resulted in the development of social and cultural creole language forms, so too the social and cultural background of American Blacks resulted in the creation of Black English. Like the earlier creole languages, Black English dif-fers from Standard American English in its vocabulary and grammatical patterns; it is an **ANTI-LANGUAGE** which is used as a challenge to the authority of society's accepted channels of communication.

An anti-language is an extreme version of a social dialect which is used by speakers who are on the edges of society – legally, financially, or culturally. The use of an alternative to the accepted standard reinforces **group identity** and empha-sises that the users are outsiders. The use of Black English in America confirms Black solidarity and self-value in the face of segregation and white opposition. It creates links with the ancestral and cultural past of the speakers, while distancing them from mainstream society. Its distinctive grammatical patterns set it apart from American Standard English, challenging the accepted and ordered vision of life that the traditional language affirms. Its use can therefore be described as a **political statement** since it aims to challenge the status quo. Although commonly associated with Blacks in the lower social classes, educated people use Black English to convey political or cultural messages.

The **grammatical variations** from the standard that occur in Black English are rule-governed – that is, they are not haphazard, but follow distinctive patterns. The following features are typical of Black English.

- The copula verb (a linking verb) *to be* is omitted (*he good*).
- The base form of the verb *to be* is used as an auxiliary to express habitual action in the progressive aspect (*she be thinking*).
- Verbs in the present tense third person singular are not inflected with *-s* (*she eat*).
- The past participle of the verb *to be* is used to convey past activity when it still has a current relevance (*we been going there for years*).
- The auxiliary verb *do* is used with the past participle to imply a finished activity (*he done painted the room*).
- Plural nouns are uninflected (*two apple*).
- Multiple negation is common (*we don't go no more*).
- Pronoun usage differs from Standard English (*me take it to dem later*).

Pronunciations are also distinctive, and this affects the spelling of Black English when in a written form.

- Consonant clusters are simplified at the end of words, particularly where one of the consonants is an alveolar /t/, /d/, /s/ or /z/ (*ast* for *asked*).
- /θ/ is realised as /f/ or /t/, and /ð/ as /v/ or /d/ (*tink* for *think*; *de* for *the*).
- Vowel sounds reflect pronunciation (*git* for *get*; *mek* for *make*; *kus* for *curse*; *ketch* for *catch*).
- /r/ is deleted in intervocalic and final positions (*duing* /duːiŋ/ for *during*).

There are other differences between Black English and Standard American English, but the features listed here demonstrate that changes to the standard language form are systematic and similar to other dialectal variations. This highlights the fact that Black English is not linguistically substandard. When described as primitive and illogical, the judgements being made are social, not linguistic.

By using Black English alongside the American standard, Black speakers can switch between two viable linguistic systems. The choice of language system becomes as important as the words uttered in conveying a political, social or cultural message.

ACTIVITY 6.2

Read the text below and comment on the following:

1 the different registers used
2 features typical of Black English
3 the message the writer is trying to convey.

1   White English in Blackface, or Who Do I Be?
                                GENEVA SMITHERMAN

Ain nothin in a long time lit up the English teaching profession like the current hassle over Black English. One finds beaucoup sociolinguistic research studies and language
5 projects for the 'disadvantaged' on the scene in nearly every sizable black community in the country. And educators from K-Grad. School bees debating whether: (1) blacks should learn and use only standard white English (hereafter referred to as WE); (2) blacks should command both dialects, i.e., be bi-dialectal (hereafter BD); (3) blacks should be allowed (??????) to use standard Black English (hereafter BE or BI). The
10 appropriate choice having everything to do with American political reality, which is

usually ignored, and nothing to do with the educational process, which is usually claimed. I say without qualification that we cannot talk about the Black Idiom apart from Black Culture and the Black Experience. Nor can we specify educational goals for blacks apart from considerations about the structure of (white) American society.

15 And we black folks is not gon take all that weight, for no one has empirically demonstrated that linguistic/stylistic features of BE impede educational progress in communication skills, or any other area of cognitive learning. Take reading. It's don been charged, but not actually verified, that BE interferes with mastery of reading skills. Yet beyond pointing out the gap between the young brother/sistuh's phonological and

20 syntactical patterns and those of the usually-middle-class-WE-speaking-teacher, this claim has not been validated. The distance between the two systems is, after all, short and is illuminated only by the fact that reading is taught *orally*. (Also get to the fact that preceding generations of BE-speaking folks learned to read, despite the many classrooms in which the teacher spoke a dialect different from that of her stu-

25 dents.)

For example, a student who reads *den* for *then* probably pronounces initial /th/ as /d/ in most words. Or the one who reads *duing* for *during* probably deletes intervocalic and final /r/ in most words. So it is not that such students can't read, they is simply employing the black phonological system. In the reading classrooms of today,

30 what we bees needin is teachers with the proper attitudinal orientation who thus can distinguish actual reading problems from mere dialect differences. Or take the writing of an essay. The only percentage in writing a paper in WE spelling, punctuation, and usage is in maybe eliciting a positive *attitudinal* response from a prescriptivist middle-class-aspirant-teacher. Dig on the fact that sheer 'correctness' does not a good writer

35 make. And is it any point in dealing with the charge of BE speakers being 'non-verbal' or 'linguistically deficient' in oral communication skills – behind our many Raps who done disproved that in living, vibrant color?

What linguists and educators need to do at this juncture is to take serious cognizance of the Oral Tradition in Black Culture. The uniqueness of this verbal style

40 requires a language competence/performance model to fit the black scheme of things. Clearly BI speakers possess rich communication skills (i.e., are highly *competent* in using language), but as yet there bees no criteria (evaluative, testing, or other instrument of measurement), based on black communication patterns, wherein BI speakers can demonstrate they competence (i.e., *performance*). Hence brothers

45 and sisters fail on language performance tests and in English classrooms. Like, to amplify on what Nikki said, that's why we always lose, not only cause we don't know the rules, but it ain't even our game.

Leonard Michaels and Christopher Ricks (eds), *The State of the Language*

COMMENTARY

The **field** of the essay focuses on the issue of language and education. **Lexical sets** based on each of these key areas are wide-ranging. Subject-specific linguistic terminology is used frequently: *dialects, bi-dialectal* (l. 8), *prescriptivist* (l. 33), *intervocalic* (ll. 27–8), *phonological system* (l. 29) and *phonological and syntactical patterns* (ll. 19–20). The educational terminology is linked directly to speaking, reading and the assessment of skills: *cognitive learning* (l. 17), *oral communication skills* (l. 36), *language performance tests* (l. 45), *actual reading problems* (l. 31), *educational process* (l.11), *educational progress* (l.16), *educational goals* (l.13) and *empirically demonstrated* (ll.15–16). All these examples highlight the formal **mode** of the piece – it is written by an expert for other experts. Formal words are chosen where everyday alternatives would be equally acceptable: *employing* (l.29) for 'using', *cognizance* for 'notice' (ll.38–9), *hereafter* (l.7), *wherein* (l.43) and *juncture* (l.38). However, this tone is not used throughout and an informal conversational register is juxtaposed with it on several occasions. The informal mode can be recognised in a variety of ways: words like *hassle* (l.3), *ain't* (l.47), *cause* (l.46); phrases like *Also get to the fact...* (ll.22–3) and *Dig on the fact that...* (l.34); ellipses like *(there) Ain nothing* (l.3); and words like *And...* (l.15) and *Like...* (l.45) in the initial position.

This juxtaposition of tones forces the reader to respond actively to the content. It encourages an intellectual focus on the issues being discussed. At first sight it would appear to be no more than an academic essay on the importance of *Black Culture* (l.13) and the strengths of *Black English* (l.4) or the *Black Idiom* (l.12). The issues are brought to life, however, because the style as well as the content challenges preconceived attitudes towards 'standard white English' and Black English. A theoretical discussion of the way in which politics affects educational matters is made both personal and emotive.

The **noun phrases** are long and complex, providing a lot of information in a short space:

m	m	m	h	q
a positive	attitudinal	response	from a prescriptivist middle-class-aspirant-teacher
det	Adj	Adj	N	PrepP

(ll.33–4)

This approach adds to the formality of the tone. Many of the verbs are also not associated with everyday conversation: *impede* (l.16), *validated* (l.21), *eliciting* (l.33) and *illuminated* (l.22). Other examples suggest, however, that the writer is not wholly serious, that she is challenging society's easy acceptance of white dominance. By using the French *beaucoup* (l.4) alongside subject-specific lexis like *sociolinguistic research studies* (l.4), the writer seems to mock Standard American English.

There are certain features that mark this essay as **American English**: the spelling of *sizable* (l.5) and *color* (l.37); and a collocation like *The only percentage in...* (l.32). The **Black English** features, however, do more than identify this as American English – they provide concrete evidence of the writer's argument. Some lexis is commonly associated with Black speakers: *brother/sistuh's* (l.19), *brothers and sisters* (ll.44–5) and *Raps* (l.36). Certain **spellings** can be linked directly to Black English phonological features: *gon* (l.15), *don* (l.17), *nothin* (l.3) and *sistuh* (l.19). The **grammar** is also distinctive. Many of the verbs are marked in a distinctive way: non-agreement between subject and verb – *we black folks is not gon...* (l.15) and *they is* (l.28); the copula verb *to be* is used in non-standard forms – *School bees debating* (l.6), *we bees needin* (l.30), *there bees no criteria* (l.42); the dummy auxiliary *to do* is used to convey a sense of something that has been finished in the past – *It's don been charged* (ll.17–18) and *Raps who done disproved* (ll.36–7). In one instance, the pronoun system is simplified so that the personal pronoun *they* is used instead of the possessive determiner 'their' (l.44).

The writer's approach draws attention to the **message** underlying the stylistic variations. She clearly lists the three possible linguistic alternatives: Blacks should only use standard white English; they should be able to use both dialects; or society should 'allow' them to use Black English. Smitherman makes her views plain by enclosing six question marks in brackets after using the verb *allowed* (l. 9) in the passive voice with its connotations of a superior authority granting permission to an inferior group. Having established her attitude implicitly in the beginning, she then develops her argument in a more concrete way. She emphasises that the battle over white and Black English has more to do with politics than education – because their language is directly linked to *Black Culture and the Black Experience* (l. 13), its use is a challenge to the white status quo. She points out that there is no evidence to suggest that Black English hinders educational progress – spoken language and reading are not adversely affected. Apparent reading problems are a result of a different phonological system, not an inability to learn. Smitherman suggests that Blacks fail on language performance tests because these are all designed for white speaking students and are not designed to show the Black students' skills. She concludes her argument by reminding readers of two things: the power of white English lies only in the social and educational attitudes to it; and the power of the *Oral Tradition in Black Culture* (l. 39) lies in its rich and vibrant communication skills.

The essay ends with the **metaphor** of a game in which Black English speakers are expected to compete without knowing the rules. This is an effective and dramatic end to an unusual and thought-provoking piece.

International changes – English as a world language

In the sixteenth century, there were under 5 million English speakers in the world; at the end of the twentieth century, there were 300–400 million first-language speakers and probably 1.5 billion English speakers worldwide. In the twenty-first century, English is spoken in all five continents and is the recognised language of trade and international affairs.

Various **criteria** must be met if a language is to become a 'world' language: the number of first-language speakers must be high; users must be spread over a wide geographical area; and political and economic affairs must be stable so that the language can spread without large-scale opposition. Inevitably the source language changes as it comes into contact with new geographical and cultural environments. Although pessimists believe that this process of change will ultimately make English no more than a series of overlapping dialects which will eventually become mutually incomprehensible, multimedia technology and the printed word can help to prevent such dramatic linguistic change. The Live 8 concert in London, for instance, took place in cities across the world and was watched by worldwide television audiences; international pop stars like Elton John, Madonna and Robbie Williams were joined by popular contemporary bands such as Coldplay and the Stereophonics, Snoop Dogg and Snow Patrol. These kinds of influences are stabilising forces which limit the changes taking place.

The worldwide status of English is linked to the growth of the **British Empire** and the **colonisation** of places like India and Southern Africa from the seventeenth century onwards. In the military and commercial contacts that followed, native languages were often suppressed by the British rulers. The arrival of British settlers in North America in the early seventeenth century was also a significant stage in the development of English as a world language – by the end of the eighteenth century, English was the dominant language in North America.

The recognition of **English's role as a world language** has continued to grow. Far from breaking away into mutually incomprehensible dialects, **world English** is developing a distinctive form of its own. This particular form of the language has no geographical markers and has been described as **standard international English**. It is used by international organisations like the European Free Trade Association (EFTA); by pilots and air traffic controllers at airports ('airspeak'); by international traders; and by police involved with international investigations ('police-speak'). Although each of these varieties has its own distinctive characteristics, linguists see the many common features as evidence that a 'standard world English' is emerging.

By looking at examples of world English it is possible to see the ways in which each variation changes the standard English that is spoken in the United Kingdom. In new environments, English acquires local nuances, particularly in its lexis. English, for instance, came to Australia with the first settlers in the eighteenth century and **AUSTRALIAN ENGLISH** emerged as the language evolved to fit its new historical, cultural and geographical circumstances. Many of the early settlers were convicts from the lower social classes who were more likely to use distinctive regional dialects, and it is therefore sometimes thought that the distinctive Australian accent resulted from the mix of UK regional accents handed down to descendants of the first English speakers. Australian English is marked by the number of Aboriginal words that have been assimilated into the language: *kangaroo, koala, billabong* (stagnant pool). These words filled gaps where there were no English equivalents for previously unknown plants, animals or geographical features. Television has made us familiar with examples of Australian English like *sheila* for a girl and *Pom* for someone from the UK.

AMERICAN ENGLISH is another distinct variety. Noah Webster's dictionary of American English in 1828 formalised the difference between UK English and American English spellings. It established American English as a separate form with its own spelling patterns: *color, theater, center* and *traveling*; and distinctive pronunciations: *missile* in American English rhymes with 'bristle' in UK English, and *momentary* has its stress on the third syllable (*mo men 'ta ry*, rather than *'mo men ta ry* as used traditionally in UK English – though the American version is now becoming more common in Britain too). Idioms like *have a nice day*, prepositions like *from…through*, and lexis assimilated from America's immigrant population like *pastrami* and *bagel* are now often heard and sometimes used by UK English speakers. As with other versions of world English, much of our knowledge of American English comes from television and cinema.

Multimedia technology has also made mass audiences familiar with other forms of English. Websites that explore the linguistic features of **JEWISH ENGLISH** and sites that collect and categorise Jewish jokes draw attention to the ways in which Yiddish pronunciations, vocabulary and syntax modify Standard English to create a distinctive variety. Recognisable features include hardened consonants at the end of words (/hænd/ → /hændt/); the replacement of the voiceless bilabial approximant /w/ with the voiced labiodental fricative /v/; the use of Yiddish words (*schlemiel*, a fool; *schlep*, to drag or carry; *gelt*, money; *mitsve*, good deed); and the inversion of sentence elements to create a mock emphasis of disbelief (*That you call a meal!*) or to express amazement (*She dances beautifully, that girl!*). While many Yiddish words are used as slang (*goyim*, *schmuck*), others such as *chutzpah* and *schmaltz* have become a part of the English lexicon in their own right since they communicate a particular shade of meaning that is not reflected in any English word.

Other forms of world English are only just beginning to appear on British television screens, but are equally significant in terms of the international growth of the language. In India, there are about fifteen official languages and thousands of dialect variations. Often, the only common language will be **INDIAN ENGLISH**. This too has developed distinctive features since it is usually learnt from books which rarely keep up to date with the subtleties of linguistic change; Indian English is often considered to be very formal and rather dated. Words are sometimes used in a slightly unusual way. For example, analogies are used to make new forms that have no parallel in UK English: knowing the word *backside*, for instance, Indian English also uses *frontside*, *rightside* and *leftside*. Contracted phrases are also common, resulting in a kind of telegraphic talk: *key bunch* (bunch of keys) and *Godlove* (love of God). On British television, BBC 2's *The Kumars at Number 42* and the one-off ITV comedy *Mumbai Calling* provide a sense of the distinctive intonation patterns and pronunciation of Indian English.

In countries where English is a second language, new formations are more common. Some words used may seem amusing to those for whom English is their first language, simply because they are almost but not quite what listeners are accustomed to. **JAPANESE ENGLISH**, for instance, is known for minor 'misinterpretations' in translation – sandwiches are *sand witches*, the orchestra pit is an *orchestra box*, pedestrians are *passengers of foot*, and motorists *tootle* their horns. Such variations from the source language, however, seldom cause real problems in understanding.

Not all countries welcome the spread of English, and indeed English has been described by some linguists as a **virus** because it seems possible that it will eventually replace the first languages of many ethnic groups. At the height of European colonisation there were approximately 1500 languages in the 'New World', but the majority have already died out. Despite attempts to revive and regenerate some of these languages, the pressure of ethnic minorities to learn English makes their ultimate survival doubtful.

In **France**, the Académie Française is an official body which protects and regulates the French language. Speakers commonly use terms like *le weekend, le fast food* and *le sandwich*, and objections have been raised by some about the way in which English words are infiltrating French. The Académie has banned the use of blended words like *un Walkman* and *un disc-jockey* on the radio – instead, the

French equivalents *un baladeur* and *un animateur* must be used, and failure to do so results in a fine. Many of these words reflect the fact that the concept or product is not a part of French cultural tradition. French purists believe that whenever a new product appears on the international market, a new French word should be created to name it. The safety airbag now fitted in many cars, for instance, is called *l'airbag* in French, and many people believe that this blended word should be replaced by a distinctive French word, arguing that the process of creation would enrich French vocabulary, allowing the language to reflect changes in lifestyle as they occur.

Electronic English

As we move into the twenty-first century, perhaps the most dramatic change of English can be seen in our use of electronic forms of communication: **web pages** and **emails** sent via the internet and **texts** sent to and from mobile phones. Bridging the gap between spoken and written language, ELECTRONIC ENGLISH often adopts the **informality** and **spontaneity** of speech in a written mode.

Technical inaccuracies or inconsistencies of spelling, punctuation and typography are common because the immediacy of communication is seen to be of more importance than producing an edited and polished written text. The tone is usually informal and the recognised codes of social formulae (such as greeting one another, talking about the weather or health, and signing off) used in more traditional channels of communication, such as letters or phonecalls, are omitted. The emphasis is on time- and space-saving devices like abbreviations and ellipses. Sentences are often loosely structured with the dash replacing conjunctives. Minor sentences are common.

Electronic English alters the relationship between writer and reader. Traditionally writing has not been seen as an interactive medium because of the delay between the writer's initial process of recording words and the reader's response to them. With the development of electronic mail, however, receipt and response can be immediate – interaction can take place internationally at the press of a button. Although the interaction may not have the face-to-face immediacy of speech, this new medium of communication creates a context for interaction that is typical of spoken English.

Electronic communications are economical and efficient. They can be sent and read at a time that suits each participant; they are not bound by 'office hours'; and delivery is immediate, even when large documents are sent as attachments. Hyperlinks from emails and web pages to other documents enable users to access information, compare prices, place orders, download files or run applications.

Blogs

WEB LOGS or BLOGS are online journals in which both the professional and the personal can provide a source of material. They allow individuals to interact: issues may be discussed with other individuals or with thousands or even tens of thousands of people. Bloggers offer personal perspectives, reporting on new stories or adding their own commentaries to existing stories. Some blogs focus on culture, others on technology; some aim to reveal misrepresentations or omissions they see in the established news channels, others challenge particular companies; some give an account of the day-to-day life of a politician, while others focus on niche concerns such as the risk of developing leukaemia from living near phone masts or the dangers of genetic modification in agriculture.

Advocates believe that blogging gives a voice to the ordinary person, bringing politics back to the grass roots. Its critics, on the other hand, believe that blogs can blur the dividing line between fact and opinion, and that the overwhelming emphasis on the personal voice can hinder the development of sophisticated arguments. Critics see blogging as a medium which can too easily be hijacked by pressure groups that do not necessarily represent the majority view – not every household has access to the internet, so blogs cannot possibly represent all view-points. While recognising the effectiveness of blogs in tackling local issues, their critics do not believe that these can convert heartfelt principles into practical means of government.

As with emailing and e-messages, the style of blogs tends to be informal, with linguistic features indicative of conversation. Debate often focuses on **opinion** and what may be **limited perspectives**, so readers must be prepared to make objective judgements about the relative subjectivity of what they read. Because anyone can create a site or post a message, things may not always be as they seem: the electronic age has opened the way for new kinds of fraud and deception. Contributors' sources and motives may be dubious, and users need to be aware of this. When reading a blog for the first time, it is therefore important to consider the **status** of the blogger. Ask yourself some simple questions:

- What is the blogger's **purpose**? – to inform? to entertain? to persuade? to argue a case? to expose a 'wrong'? to find like-minded people?
- What is the **relationship between the blogger and the material** on the site? – personal or impersonal? professional or amateur?
- What kind of material is included in the **content**? – subject-specific or general? academic research? statistics? practical or technical experiences? personal experiences? subjective opinions? reflections? criticisms?
- What **tone** is adopted? – formal and detached? personal and subjective?
- What is distinctive about the **style**? – standard or non-standard grammar? spoken or written features? formal or informal? conversational or academic?

By asking yourself these questions, you will be better able to assess the value of a particular blog. You may be reading for entertainment, for information, or in order to shape your opinions on a particular issue: thinking about the purpose, content, tone and style will ensure that you understand the ways in which blogs try to influence their readers.

Texting

TEXT MESSAGING or **SMS** (**SHORT MESSAGE SERVICE**) allows mobile-phone users to send and receive text messages via their phone server. This means of communication has grown at a phenomenal rate, some 20 billion text messages being sent in the UK in 2003. With over 49 million mobile phones and 70 per cent of these users sending and receiving messages, it is hardly surprising that a new variety of English has evolved to suit the medium.

There are many advantages for users. **TEXTING** is available 24 hours a day and 95 per cent of messages are delivered within 10 seconds. Because connection time is minimal, it is a cheap means of communication. Texts do not get lost – they are stored until the mobile phone can receive the message. The process of texting is time-consuming, however, and, as phones become ever smaller, typing letters individually according to the number of presses made on the keys of the phone pad can be increasingly fiddly.

Like e-messaging and emailing, texting narrows the differences between written and spoken modes: the manner is conversational and informal and the style is elliptical. What makes this particular variety of English distinctive, however, is its approach to spelling. Words are often contracted (e.g. *wd* – 'would'; *spk* – 'speak'; *pls* – 'please'); individual letters are used to represent whole words (e.g. *u* – 'you'; *b* – 'be'; *c* – 'see'; *r* – 'are'); acronyms represent longer phrases (e.g. *BBL* – 'be back later'; *GBH&K* – 'great big hugs and kisses'); number symbols are used in conjunction with letters (e.g. *B4* – 'before'; *L8r* – 'later'; *F2T* – 'free to talk?'). Spelling becomes a matter of individual choice, with the only principle being 'the shorter and simpler the better' (e.g. *luv* – 'love'; *neva* – 'never'; *sum1* – 'someone').

PREDICTIVE TEXT is an inbuilt system that aims to 'predict' the word as you begin to key it, reducing the necessity of keying each word in full. This too is affecting the kind of English we use. Its sometimes apparently random association of words can be quite bizarre: while keying in *h* may correctly predict *Hi*, keying in *co* for 'come' may yield *canon*. Stephen Fry tells an anecdote in which the informal term of approval *cool* has been replaced by *book* amongst teenagers because it is what some predictive text systems predict when you start to type *cool*. Since speed is of the essence, the predicted word *book* is not corrected manually but has instead gained credence as a 'code' word with street-credibility.

SMILEYS or **EMOTICONS** are another distinctive linguistic feature of texting. These use punctuation marks alongside letters and numbers to create sideways faces that are symbolic of a mood:

amazement	8-]	fury	[>ō<]
laughter	:D	devilry	>;->

Smileys can also represent a particular reaction:

asleep	I-I	oh oh!	:-O
wow man!	8-]	ouch	:@

Or a statement:

lips are sealed	:-X	you talk a lot	:-[ ]
you're a big big liar	:- - - - -]		

While texting is a cheap, efficient and popular means of communication, evidence of its potential for misuse is becoming apparent. In a study of eight hundred 11–19 year olds, one in five had received insulting and threatening messages and pictures – a high-tech form of **bullying**. Another worrying trend can be seen in the use of mobile phone cameras to film attacks on individuals – known unofficially as 'happy-slapping'. It is in fact illegal to send threatening pictures and messages, and operating companies such as Vodaphone are looking for ways to tackle such problems.

GCSE English examiners' reports published in September 2005 were critical of the repeated use of street and text language in candidates' work. Abbreviations like *m8*, *i* and *u*, *gonna*, *aint* and *wanna* were used across the ability range. Examiners expressed concern about the inability of some candidates to distinguish between language appropriate to informal contexts (emails and text messages) and that required by a more formal context (examinations).

6.4 The democratic nature of language change

Ultimately, as the history of language shows, it is very difficult to artificially control any language – language growth is organic, evolving to meet the demands users place upon it. Whatever linguists feel about the effects that social, cultural and worldwide changes have on language, therefore, if the changes are found to be useful they will probably survive. Those which have no real function, on the other hand, may be fashionable for a period before disappearing without trace. History also suggests that English and its 'world' variations are highly unlikely to become mutually incomprehensible as the political and cultural developments of the twenty-first century are bringing nations together rather than separating them.

Change is at the heart of a living language: by embracing it rather than fearing it, language users can benefit from the diversity that linguistic flexibility offers. The national and international dialects of English do not threaten but enrich the UK standard.

Chapter 7

Historical change

7.1 The reason for studying historical change

In order to see how English has developed, it is important to think about the language both **synchronically** (as a snapshot of a particular moment) and **diachronically** (as part of a historical process). By concentrating on key periods and by analysing textual examples it is possible to establish the characteristics of the English language at different times in its history, and thus to see how older forms differ from the English we speak and write today. To focus your attention appropriately, for each period you will need to think about the changes in **semantics**, **lexis**, **syntax**, **phonology** and **graphology**.

To understand how and why the English language has become what it is, linguists study both the **causes** of change and the **characteristics** of English at key stages. For convenience, they refer to five distinct periods in the history of the English language: OLD ENGLISH (OE), 450–1150; MIDDLE ENGLISH (ME), 1150–1500; EARLY MODERN ENGLISH (EME), 1500–1700; MODERN ENGLISH (ModE), 1700–1900; and LATE MODERN ENGLISH (LME), 1900–. These dates give a general indication of the different stages, but are only approximate since linguistic change does not take place neatly within boundaries. Linguists draw attention to the most significant linguistic features in each key period, and looking back it is easy to recognise the points at which each change occurs. However, it is important to remember that the process is gradual, often taking place over hundreds of years.

As the aim of this book is to give you practice in handling source material, this chapter will not cover the historical background of each period. This information can be found in many language textbooks, some of which are listed in Appendix C. Use the summaries following each extract to help you structure your reading and note-making.

7.2 The importance of text analysis

All that remains of earlier forms of English is to be found in surviving written documents. Linguists use these to build up a sense of what English was like. By analysing lexis, syntax and graphology, it is possible to chart how and why English changed. Some assumptions can also be made about the phonological structure of English, but until the age of recording, this can only be informed guesswork.

The Old English to Modern English periods will be represented here by prose texts. Close analysis of the examples highlights characteristic features of each key period, providing concrete evidence of the ways in which English was used. Inevitably, written examples can only hint at the nature of the language of everyday communication, and literary language in particular is more likely to be manipulated and crafted to achieve certain effects. The constraints of poetic structure, for instance, can mean that word order is changed to achieve the right number of syllables in a line or to create a rhyme. Although poetic language has all the characteristic features of the period in which it was written, additional alterations may be linked to **prosody** (distinctive features of verse) rather than the nature of English at the time. By concentrating on **prose**, therefore, it is possible to understand more precisely the characteristic features of the language.

Surviving Old English poems like 'Beowulf' and 'The Seafarer' are marked by distinctive poetic features like half-line divisions and alliterative patterns. These features make Old English poetic language quite different from the English used in prose and speech. Non-fiction prose like *The Anglo-Saxon Chronicle* is not so consciously crafted. It recorded events in the form of a year-to-year diary. Early entries are list-like and are more likely to resemble everyday usage.

Middle English poems like Chaucer's *Canterbury Tales* and the anonymous *Gawain and the Green Knight* and Early Modern English plays by Shakespeare provide linguists with crucial information about literary language. It is prose texts, however, that highlight linguistic features of English at each stage of its development. *The Paston Letters*, for instance, were written by individuals during the Middle English and Early Modern English periods. Because they are examples of private correspondence, they provide linguists with evidence of the way in which ordinary people used English.

As a contrast, the Modern English texts cited here are examples of fictional prose. Since both are first person narratives (stories told from the point of view of a particular character), the writers are to some extent imitating individual style. Written language will usually be more formal than spoken language, but the narrative texts highlight some of the distinctive features of the period in real contexts.

By this stage in the history of English, there are few differences between the style and structure of Modern English and Late Modern English. No Late Modern English text is discussed here since the rest of the book will provide a range of examples for analysis.

7.3 The Old English period

It is by reading the surviving manuscripts of the Old English period that linguists have been able to ascertain so much about the lexis and grammar of Old English. The surviving alliterative poetry, the documentation of charters and wills, and the religious homilies all provide linguistic evidence for analysis.

Alfred the Great saw the need for a compilation of important events, and towards the end of the ninth century he ordered that *The Anglo-Saxon Chronicle* should be written. This key historical document was continued for two centuries after his death. The fact that it was written in English helped to give the English people a sense of their own identity.

ACTIVITY 7.1

Read the extract below, from *Cunewulf and Cyneheard*, and answer the questions that follow it.

1 755 Hēr Cynewulf benam Sigebryht his rīces ond Westseaxna wiotan for unryhtum dǣdum, būton Hamtūnscīre; ond hē hæfde þa oþ hē ofslog þone aldormon þe him lengest wunode. Ond hiene þā Cynewulf on Andred ādrǣfde; ond hē þǣr wunade oþ þæt hiene ān swān ofstang æt Pryfetes flōdan – ond hē wræc þone aldormon
5 Cumbran.

Sweet's Anglo-Saxon Reader in Prose and Verse

1 Identify any unusual letter forms.
2 Make a list of all the Old English words that you think look familiar, and their Contemporary English equivalents. Record any changes in spelling.
3 List any words that appear to be inflected.
4 Using the Old English word list below, make a word-for-word translation of the extract.

Because Old English is an inflected language and because irregular patterns often change vowels, words in the text may appear in a slightly different form in the list.

ædrǣfan; ādrǣfde (past tense)	to drive
benǣman; benam (past tense)	to deprive
būton	except for
dǣd	deed/act
(e)aldor-man	prince/leader
habban; hæfde (past tense)	to have/to possess
Hamtūnscīre	Hampshire
hēr	in this year
hiene/hine	him
ofslēan; ofslog (past tense)	to slay
ofstingan; ofstang (past tense)	to stab to death
oþ þæt	until
Pryfetes flōde	the stream at Privett
rīce	kingdom
swān	swineherd
þa (adv)	then
þa (det)	the/that
þær (adv)	there
þe (pron)	who
þone	that

unryht	wrong/wicked
wiote	councillors
wrecan; wræc (past tense)	to take revenge
wunian; wunode/wunade (past tense)	to remain

5 Compare your version with the Contemporary English translation below and comment on any differences in lexis or syntax (word order).

1 **757** In this year Cynewulf and the councillors of the West Saxons deprived Sigebryht of his kingdom because of his unjust acts, except for Hampshire; and he retained that until he killed the prince who stood by him longest; and then Cynewulf drove him into the Weald, and he lived there until a swineherd stabbed him to death by the stream
5 at Privett. He was taking revenge for Prince Cumbran.

COMMENTARY

Although some vowels are marked for length, most of this extract uses the letters of the **ROMAN ALPHABET**. It also, however, uses two of the Anglo-Saxon **RUNES**: þ and æ. It is these and the unfamiliar words that make Old English seem so alien to modern readers. The words that are recognisable are all **closed-class words** with a grammatical function:

- determiners: *ān* (l. 4), *his* (l. 1)
- pronouns: *hē* (l. 4), *him* (l. 2)
- prepositions: *for* (l. 1), *on* (l. 3), *æt* (l. 4)
- conjunctions: *ond* (l. 2).

Some **open-class words**, like the noun *dǣdum* (l. 2), the superlative adjective *lengest* (l. 3) and the adverb *þǣr* (l. 3), are also recognisable. Most of these words survive in an identical form in Late Modern English, but some have undergone minor changes in spelling: *deed* has replaced *dǣd* (l. 2); *at* has replaced *æt* (l. 4); *and* has replaced *ond* (l. 2); *longest* has replaced *lengest* (l. 3); and *there* has replaced *þǣr* (l. 3).

To produce a fluent Late Modern English version, **lexical and syntactical changes** have to be made to the original Old English text. The Old English preposition *for* (l. 1), for instance, can be replaced by the phrase *because of*, while the Old English adjective *unryhtum* (l. 1) is best conveyed by the Late Modern English *unjust*. While these alterations create greater fluency, other lexical changes **clarify meanings**. Old English *ofslog* (l. 2) is now archaic, so it needs to be replaced by a more general term *kill* to reflect changes in warfare. The Old English verb *wunian* (l. 3) is given a wider variety of meanings – the Late Modern English idiom *to stand by* is used with a distinctive meaning quite separate from *to live*, whereas Old English uses the same verb.

Because Late Modern English is dependent on **word order** to convey meaning, it is necessary to alter some of the Old English constructions. In the original text, the plural noun phrase *Westseaxna wiotan* (l. 1) has a nominative (subject) case inflection, so despite the fact that it is separated from the rest of the subject, *Cynewulf* (l. 1), it is possible to recognise its function. In Late Modern English, however, it is necessary to put the two phrases together. Similarly, to a modern reader the pronoun *hiene* (l. 3) may appear to be the subject of the sentence because of its position – *hiene ba Cynewulf* (l. 3) and *hiene ān swān ofstang* (l. 4) – yet because of its accusative (object) form, it must be translated as *him*.

Such changes emphasise both the development of the WORD STOCK and the simplification of **inflections** since the Old English period.

Summary

Examples of surviving Old English texts tell linguists something about the nature of English at the time.

Semantics

A modern reader cannot rely on understanding words in context since so many are alien to us: *būton* (l. 2) and *þone* (l. 2). Much of the writing seems to focus on battle and conflict: *ofslog* (l. 2), *ofstang* (l. 4) and *wræc* (l. 5).

Lexis

A few words have remained unchanged (particularly the closed-class words) while others can be recognised even though the spelling may be unfamiliar. The majority of the Old English word stock, however, has now disappeared in a process that started as words were borrowed from Latin and Old Norse: *benæman/benam* (l. 1) was displaced by *deprivāre* (L); *ofslean/ofslog* (l. 2) by *slā* (ON).

Grammar

The **word order** is reasonably close to that of Late Modern English, but because Old English was an inflected language, the order is more flexible. Modern readers therefore have to consider inflections carefully to work out the function of a particular word. For example, *his rīces* (l. 1) is marked by the genitive (possessive) singular neuter noun declension *-es* to indicate the possessive of *his kingdom*.

The system of Old English **declension** to mark **case** disappeared as the language was simplified – prepositions now imply relationships within a sentence. There were considerably more **strong** or **irregular verbs** in Old English than in Late Modern English and this too is evidence of the way in which language evolves. Language often simplifies usage, and irregular Old English past tense verbs that took a vowel change are often regular in Late Modern English: the irregular *ofstang* (l. 4) has been replaced by the regular *stabbed* and the irregular *benam* (l. 1) has been replaced by the regular *deprived*.

Phonology

Linguists can only make assumptions about the pronunciations of Old English, but from a study of surviving texts it is possible to identify a range of **dialectal differences** just as we have in Late Modern English. The **stress** was always on the first syllable of each word and contemporary versions of surviving manuscripts mark long vowels with ¯ to distinguish between the different sounds. There were no silent letters in Old English, so an *-e* in the word-final position was pronounced. The OE *flōde* for LME *stream*, for instance, would have been pronounced phonetically as [fləʊdə] rather than as the LME *flood* [flʌd]. Old English was very much part of the **oral tradition** in which literature was handed down from generation to generation in a spoken form. It used techniques such as **alliteration** to emphasise the sound of the language.

Graphology

The Roman alphabet was used to record Old English in written forms, but additional runic symbols were added to mark sounds that were not represented. In contemporary versions, þ (**thorn**) and ð (**eth**) are still used to reflect a *th* sound, while the runic Ρ (**wynn** or **wyn**) and ȝ (**yogh**; also ȝ) are usually replaced by *w* and *g* or *j*. The æ symbol is used to convey a short *a* as in LME *cat* [kæt].

This brief summary highlights some key features of Old English. It is a synchronic study of English during the Old English period. To understand the way in which language changes over time, however, linguists consider Old English's relationship with other periods, undertaking a diachronic study of the historical process.

7.4 The Middle English period

Because French was the prestige language in the years after the Norman Conquest, most patronage of the arts focused on the production of French texts. However, the incentives were different in religious contexts and any literature recorded in English in the years 1150–1250 was almost exclusively religious: paraphrases of the Bible, interpretations of the Gospels, and so on. There was inevitably a range of popular literature in English, but because this will have been part of the oral culture little remains of the ballads of the time. After 1250, there is evidence that English was used to write romances, but our main experience of Middle English written texts comes from a period which is now often called 'the age of the great individual writers' and the text that you will now consider falls into this period (1350–1400).

Middle English text

Private letters still exist in quite large numbers from the fifteenth century onwards. The example you are about to read is taken from one of many letters saved by the Paston family over several generations. They are mostly personal records of everyday events, but perhaps the most interesting feature is in the actual form of English used to record these. Although by the mid-fourteenth century a standard form of the language was beginning to emerge from the London area, private correspondence like the letters of the Paston family did not yet reflect this. They therefore provide evidence of the extent to which official language policy filtered down to the people using English in less formal contexts.

ACTIVITY 7.2 ─────────────

Read the letter written by Margaret Paston to her husband John in 1442 or 1443 and answer the questions that follow it.

1 *To my ryght worchepful husbond, John Paston, dwellyng in the Inner Temple at London, in hast*

Ryth worchipful hosbon, I recomande me to yow, desyryng hertely to her of yowr wilfar, thanckyng God of yowr a mendyng of the grete dysese that ye have hade; and
5 I thancke yow for the letter that ye sent me, for be my trowthe my moder and I wer nowth in hertys es fro the tyme that we woste of yowr sekenesse, tyl we woste verely of your a mendyng.

James Gairdner (ed.), The Paston Letters

1 Comment on the content of the letter and what it tells you about the relationship between the writer and the addressee and the historical or social context.

2 Using the headings below, comment on the lexis:
   a the register and the lexical field
   b the spelling and source of words
   c the formal set phrases and collocation
   d any idiosyncrasies.

3 Using the headings below, comment on the grammar:
   a the use of inflections
   b pronoun forms
   c verb forms.

COMMENTARY

The letter's **tone** conveys a strange mixture of the formal and the informal. Despite the fact that a wife is addressing her husband, the opening greeting is very formal: *To my ryght worchepful husbond, John Paston* (l. 1). Not only is Paston's full name used, but he is given his role of husband before he is named. This immediately suggests something about the respective social status of man and wife at this time – in the tone she uses, Margaret Paston clearly adopts a subservient position.

The comments on John Paston's illness and on Margaret's and her mother's response to it suggest a time when health care was less developed and less widely available. The underlying suggestion is that any sickness can cause death, and this indicates a quite different life expectancy from that of modern readers. The reference to God implies a society in which the Church has considerable influence and in which many people try to understand the inexplicable through religion and God's divine intentions.

The **register** too is an unusual mixture of formal and informal features. It is a written document, which means that it is not a transitory means of communication and is therefore associated with a more accurate and considered use of language than speech. Yet in its style and inconsistency it seems more like a record of something that is being spoken. The **lexical field** is fairly narrow, concentrating on the relationship of a husband and wife and the illness from which he has just recovered.

The **sources** of words in this extract are typical of the Middle English period. Many, like *sekenesse* ('sickness', l. 6), *hertely* ('heartily', l. 3) and *trowthe* ('truth', l. 5), can be traced back to the Old English word stock: *sēoc* or *sick*, *heorte* and *trēowth*. Others, like *hosbon* ('husband', l. 3) and *tyme* ('time', l. 6), derive from Old Norse:

hūsbōndi and *tīmī*. The significant difference between texts of the Old English and Middle English periods are the words like *desyryng* ('desire', l. 3), *dysese* ('disease', l. 4) and *letter* (l. 5) with their source in French: *desirer, desaise* and *lettre*.

The **spelling** in the letter seems quite unfamiliar to modern readers. The introduction of the printing press in 1476 began to fix English spelling, but this letter is the work of a private individual at a time when even the professional copyists did not always spell words in a standard way. The inconsistencies here could also be seen as the result of social attitudes towards the education of women, who were far less likely to be instructed in a formal way at this time.

Many of the distinctive features of Middle English spelling are highlighted in this letter. The remains of the Old English **inflection** of nouns and adjectives can be seen in words like *grete* (l. 4) and *trowthe* (l. 5). In other examples, Late Modern usage of vowels like *i* and *u* is not yet settled: *ryght* (l. 1), *dwellyng* (l. 1) and *dysese* (l. 4); *yow* (l. 3) and *yowr* (l. 4). Other Late Modern English vowel patterns have also not yet emerged: some groups are simplified in words like *hertely* ('heartily', l. 3) and *grete* (l. 4); others use a different vowel in words like *husbond* or *hosbon* (ll. 1, 3), *wilfar* ('welfare', l. 4) and *dysese* (l. 4); and sometimes the final silent *-e* is omitted in words like *hast* ('haste', l. 2), *wilfar* (l. 4) and *wer* ('were', l. 5). Consonant patterns have changed less dramatically and are therefore closer to Late Modern English usage. Variations can be seen, however, in a word like *recomande* (l. 3), where Middle English has single consonants and Late Modern English has double.

The Middle English spelling used here is not only different from Late Modern English, but is inconsistent within the letter itself. Both the Late Modern English *husband* and *worshipful* are spelt in two ways: *husbond* (l. 1) and *hosbon* (l. 3); *worchepful* (l. 1) and *worchipful* (l. 3). Despite the emergence of a standard form of English, therefore, the spelling patterns of ordinary people do not always conform to it.

Although there are irregularities, few words remain completely incomprehensible: those that do should be commented upon. Probably one of the least recognisable words is *woste* (l. 6) which is the past tense form of the Middle English verb *witen*, 'to know'. This is derived from the Old English *witan*, now obsolete and replaced by 'to know', derived from the Old English *cnawan*. Another word unfamiliar to modern readers is *nowth* (l. 6) which is representative of Late Modern English *mouth*. The spelling here perhaps reflects the confusion that sometimes occurred in the formation of *m* and *n*. Nevertheless the word can be understood from the collocation or set phrase 'my heart in my mouth', which is still used in Late Modern English. Equally, *es* (l. 6) can be deduced from its context as the Late Modern English 'as'.

Although idiosyncratic – that is, reflective of the individual who has written the letter – there is no longer the great barrier of unfamiliarity that modern readers encounter when they face Old English texts. Spelling has begun to resemble the Late Modern English with which we are familiar.

Just as spelling has begun to move closer to Late Modern English patterns, so too has the **grammar**. Certain significant features, however, are still distinctive. Middle English is not a highly inflected language and this is evident here. The complex patterns used for Old English nouns and adjectives have been dramatically simplified. The plural of the Middle English noun *herte*, for instance, is formed by the addition of the suffix *-s*, although it would seem here (l. 6) that Margaret Paston has substituted *-ys* in order to mark the plural. The use of inflections on adjectives is also far less complex than in Old English. Within this letter, *worchipful* (l. 3) is an example of the simplified Middle English inflections. Where Old English would have used an adjectival inflection on the modifier in the opening noun phrase, Middle English has dropped it. This suggests that final vowels were beginning to lose their pronunciation.

There is still evidence of a variety of pronoun forms because it was necessary to distinguish between the different kinds of reference. In this letter, Margaret Paston uses *ye* (l. 5) for the subject pronoun in the second person, *yow* (l. 3) for the object, and *yowr* (l. 4) for the possessive determiner. A similar distinction can be seen in her use of *I* (l. 3) in the subject site, *me* (l. 3) in the object site, and *my* (l. 5) as a possessive determiner.

The verb forms cause few problems for the modern reader since they follow recognisable Late Modern English forms even though the spelling may be different. The present tense in the first person singular can be seen in the reflexive verb *I recomande me...* (l. 3) and in *I thancke* (l. 5). The past tense of the verb 'to be' in the first person plural *wer* (l. 5) uses the same pattern as Late Modern English and the present participle adopts an *-yng* suffix which is a parallel to Late Modern English *-ing*. The perfect aspect is used in *have hade* (l. 4) and the infinitive form of *to her* (l. 3) uses the same Late Modern English structure of the preposition 'to' + base form verb.

Summary

Examples of Middle English texts tell linguists something about the nature of English at the time.

Semantics

A modern reader can now rely on context to a large extent to understand any **words** that seem unfamiliar: *nowth in hertys* (l. 6) and *dysese* (l. 4). The number of texts surviving from this period is greater, so the registers and lexical fields linguists can study are more wide-ranging. Since much of the literary work was dominated by the idea of courtly love and romance, epic adventure and religious thought, the lexis tended to reflect this. Private correspondence, on the other hand, offers the modern reader an insight into life and everyday affairs in the Middle English period.

Lexis

Most words are now recognisable although the **spelling** may be unfamiliar: *wer* (l. 5) and *thanckyng* (l. 4). In poems from the early part of the period, variations in the **dialectal form** can cause problems. The Northern forms of Middle English contained far more Old Norse and Old French words than the Midland dialect that formed the basis for Standard English: since many of these words are now obsolete, they can be a barrier to understanding.

Many of the words that have remained unchanged are closed-class words handed down directly from Old English: prepositions like *to* and *of*; determiners like *the* and *a*; and pronouns like *I* and *we*. The **word stock** was significantly different from Old English, however, because of the borrowings made from French: *desyryng* (l. 3) from the French *désirer*.

Grammar

During this period of levelled inflections, Middle English grammar was dominated by word order and this makes it far easier for modern readers to understand. **Plural nouns** were still marked by a suffix, but the system had been simplified. Adjectives were inflected with -*e* in all cases until the final syllable was no longer pronounced and the -*e* was eventually dropped from the spelling too. During the process of change, usage was inconsistent – some adjectives, like *grete* (l. 4), would be marked with an inflection while others, like *worchipful* (l. 3), were not. **Pronouns**, however, retained distinctive forms because it was still grammatically useful to distinguish between subject and object functions: *he* and *him*. Many **verbs** lost their strong forms and adopted the **weak patterns**, partly because English had for so long been a spoken language rather than a written one.

However, all these changes slowed down as the Midlands dialect was adopted as a **standard form** and as **printing** began to disseminate this standard to a far wider audience.

Phonology

The diversity of **dialects** at the beginning of the period was reflected in the range of pronunciations. If you listen to Middle English poems like *Gawain* and Chaucer's *Canterbury Tales* read aloud, they sound almost like two distinct languages rather than two forms of Middle English. Linguists believe that the spelling in each case is a very rough phonetic guide to the pronunciation of each dialect. Literary texts used distinctive **sound patterning** like **rhyme** and **alliteration**, following the oral traditions of Old English.

Graphology

Although the **Roman alphabet** was used predominantly, two **runic symbols** survived into the Middle English period: þ and ȝ. The 'thorn' (þ) survived longest in the initial position, while 'yogh' (ȝ) was retained after *g* had become established in vernacular texts. Most modern typesetters now substitute *th* and *g*.

There were two distinct forms of **handwriting** in use: the CURSIVE STYLE was common in charters, records and memoranda; the other form, in which the letters were separately written, was regularly used for literary texts and is often called the BOOK HAND. In handwritten manuscripts, letter forms were not as precise as they are in print and this meant that copyists sometimes mistook one letter for another. This led to some of the inconsistencies that the modern reader observes in Middle English spelling.

7.5 The Early Modern English period

The range of surviving texts from this period is vast: poetry, prose and drama exist alongside both public records and private correspondence. There is no longer any great linguistic barrier preventing a modern reader from understanding these. Linguists focus on the expanded vocabulary and the few grammatical features surviving which have since disappeared or been standardised.

Early Modern English text

This next private letter is taken from the same collection as the letter in the Middle English section, but it was written sixty years after that of Margaret Paston. Archbishop Warham is writing in 1503 to his cousin William Paston about the death of his father.

ACTIVITY 7.3

Read the letter and jot down notes to answer the questions that follow it.

1

Archbishop Warham to William Paston
To my cousyn Master William Paston
September 6 1503

Cousyn Paston, I recommaunde me unto you, and have received your letter, by
5 the which I undrestand of the deth of my cousyn your fadre, whose soule Jesu assoile. I wol counsaile and exhorte you to take it as wel and as paciently as ye can, seeyng that we al be mortal and borne to dey.

James Gairdner (ed.), The Paston Letters

1 Comment on the content of the letter and what it tells you about the relationship between the writer and the addressee.

2 Using the headings below, comment on the lexis:
- a the register and the lexical field
- b the spelling
- c word sources
- d formal set phrases.

3 Using the headings below, comment on the grammar:
- a the use of inflections
- b pronoun forms
- c verb forms
- d the order of sentence elements.

COMMENTARY

Because the **content** of the letter deals with death, the **tone** clearly needs to be formal. Archbishop Warham is offering both personal and professional sympathy since he is writing as a cousin and in his role as a religious adviser. He does not use his cousin's first name in the opening address, but begins the letter with *Cousyn Paston* (l. 4), which may suggest that they are not on close terms. Equally, he uses his official title, reinforcing his role rather than his family relationship.

The **register** is written and formal. However, since much of the advice offered is very personal, there is also a somewhat less official tone. The **lexical fields** can easily be divided: the religious field is marked by nouns like *soule* (l. 5), *Jesu* (l. 5) and *Archbishop* (l. 1) and the adjective *mortal* (l. 7); the field of death is conveyed by the noun *deth* (l. 5), the adjective *mortal* (l. 7) and the verb *dey* (l. 7). Inevitably the two fields overlap.

The **spelling** is more uniform than in Margaret Paston's letter of 1442, but some words have not yet adopted Late Modern spelling. The use of *i* and *y* is still different, but the writer is consistent: *cousyn* (ll. 2, 4, 5) and *seeyng* (l. 6). Certain vowel groups also continue to be different from those used in Late Modern English. The simplification of *deth* (l. 5) is perhaps idiosyncratic, but the *au* in *recommaunde* (l. 4), the *ai* in *counsaile* (l. 6) and the *re* in *undrestand* (l. 5) could be related to French pronunciation and spelling. The use of the final -*e* is no longer inflectional as it is not pronounced: its use here in words like *soule* (l. 5), *borne* (l. 7) and *assoile* (l. 5) may reflect the fact that private individuals were slower to adopt the standard form. Since the letter is from an Archbishop, however, it is clearly an example of the writing of an educated man who is more likely to have had experience of the written standard. Other spelling irregularities are minor: single consonants where we would use double, in *wel* (l. 6); different consonants with the same sound, in *paciently* (l. 6); and some vowel variations, in *wol* (l. 6).

There is evidence here of Latinate words which have been Anglicised by dropping the ending: *recommaunde* (l. 4) has its source in the Latin *commendāre*; *counsaile* (l. 6) was adopted via the French *counseil* but has a Latin root, *consilium*; and *exhorte* (l. 6) derives from the Latin infinitive *exhortārī*. There are French words that also have Latin links: the archaic *assoile* (l. 5) meaning 'to absolve' (AFr *assoiler*, from the Latin *absolvēre*); and *paciently* (l. 6); from the French, which was adopted from the Latin *patientia*. Nevertheless, the majority of the vocabulary here still derives from Old English: *fadre* (l. 5, OE *fæder*); *soule* (l. 5, OE *sāwol*); and *wol* (l. 6, OE *willa*). The word *dey* (l. 7) is interesting because it is assumed to have come from an OE word *dēgan* of the Anglian dialect which has since been lost. Its other possible source would be in the Old Norse word *deyja*.

Set phrases are apparent both in the context of the letter and in the religious nature of the correspondence. The formulaic phrase *I recommaunde me unto you* (l. 4) was also used in the earlier Paston letter, and it would seem to be an example of written etiquette. The phrases *we al be mortal* and *borne to dey* (l. 7) can be linked to the teachings of the Church and the content of the letter.

The **grammar** is similar to that of Late Modern English and there are now only a few noteworthy features. Other than the final -*e* used at the end of some verbs and the noun *soule* (l. 5), inflections are not apparent. The examples already cited have no grammatical function and therefore cannot be described as inflections. Pronouns are now more or less standard, and both subject and object pronouns are used as in Late Modern English. There is, however, one use of the now archaic *ye* (l. 6) in the subject site. By the fifteenth century, it could be used as both subject and object and remained interchangeable until it disappeared from usage. Verb endings are standard and they are used in a variety of forms: perfect aspect (*have received*, l. 4); modal followed by the base form of a verb (*wol counsaile*, l. 6); the infinitive (*to take*, l. 6); and the present participle (*seeyng*, l. 6). The only nonstandard example can be found in the use of *be* (l. 7) rather than the first person plural *are* which we would use in Late Modern English.

Sentence elements follow patterns we recognise from Late Modern English:

```
S          P          Od         Oi                    P                  Od
(I) (recommaunde) (me) (unto you) (and) (have received) (your letter…)
```

Each sentence has a structure in which several subclauses are embedded: *which…* (l.5) and *whose…* (l.5), relative clauses; *to take…* (l.6), a non-finite clause; and *seeyng that…* (ll.6–7), an adverbial clause.

Summary

From looking at examples of early Modern English texts, linguists can draw certain conclusions about the nature of English at the time.

Semantics

There should now be few problems for modern readers, who will understand Early Modern English texts except for a limited number of words that have not survived into the Late Modern English word stock, the occasional archaic word, or words that have changed their meaning.

Lexis

Lexis is probably the most important area of development at this time since the vocabulary was expanding significantly. It is important to be aware of the range of **sources** from which words were drawn: *explain* from *explānāre* (*L*), *chocolate* from *chocolate* (*Sp*) from the Nahuatl language of the Aztecs *chocólatl*; *detail* from *détailler* (*Fr*), and *violin* from *viola* (*It*).

There was wide-ranging debate about the quality of language, and this led to the production of spelling texts that attempted to **standardise** the spelling of 'hard' words. Those which attempted to reform spelling failed because it proved impossible to impose an artificially created system on language. Other spelling books focused on current usage, which proved a far more logical approach to standardisation. It was these latter texts which recorded many of the spelling patterns that we now use. Purists objected to the wide-scale borrowing that was taking place and described the new foreign words as INKHORN TERMS. Nevertheless, many of these have survived into Late Modern English since they were introduced to fill gaps in the English language as it stood.

The most important thing to remember about English at this time was that it had now been accepted as an appropriate language for academia and learning.

Grammar

Almost nothing remained of the earlier complexities of English **inflections** – the only ones left were those used to mark plurals and possessives on nouns and some verb endings. In the third person singular present tense, most verbs now used the *-s* inflection, although the archaic *-(e)th* was still in evidence in a few verbs. **Double comparatives** and **superlatives** were acceptable to create emphasis, as were **multiple negatives**. **Pronouns** were now used more or less as in Late Modern English.

Phonology

There was a dramatic change in the pronunciation of **long vowels**, which linguists still cannot fully explain. However, it meant that by the end of the period the pronunciation of Early Modern English had moved closer to that of Late Modern English.

Typographical features

The use of **printing** largely eliminated the need for handwritten manuscripts since now numerous identical copies of a single text could be distributed easily. In fact, PUBLISHING became a commercial venture, and this helped to reinforce the use of a standard written form across the country. The **Roman alphabet** was now used exclusively, so the surviving texts from this period are typographically very similar to those from our own.

7.6 The Modern English period

The texts of the Modern English period will cause few problems for the contemporary reader. There is a wide variety of poetry, prose and drama from which to draw examples. The biggest changes to English during the period were once again in the vocabulary. The only grammatical differences between Modern English and Late Modern English are the occasional change in word order or an unusual verb structure.

Modern English texts

The following extracts are taken from first person narratives in which the fictional 'I' character tells her or his own story. Inevitably, the prose is literary rather than spoken, but the author in each case creates a distinctive contemporary voice for the central character. The versions here have been modernised so that the spelling conforms to Late Modern patterns.

ACTIVITY 7.4

Read the texts carefully and identify the linguistic features that mark the texts as non-standard in any way. Try to explain these features in relation to their historical context. You should refer to the word form, vocabulary and grammar where appropriate.

TEXT 1 (1722)

1 I went out now by daylight, and wandered about I knew not whither, and in search of
    I knew not what, when the devil put a snare in my way of a dreadful nature indeed,
    and such a one as I have never had before or since. Going through Aldersgate Street,
    there was a pretty little child had been at a dancing-school, and was agoing home
5 all alone; and my prompter, like a true devil, set me upon this innocent creature. I
    talked to it, and it prattled to me again, and I took it by the hand and led it along till
    I came to a paved alley that goes into Bartholomew Close, and I led it in there. The
    child said, that was not its way home. I said, 'Yes, my dear, it is; I'll show you the way
    home.' The child had a little necklace on of gold beads, and I had my eye upon that,
10 and in the dark of the alley I stooped, pretending to mend the child's clog that was

loose, and took off her necklace, and the child never felt it, and so led the child on again.

Daniel Defoe (?1660–1731), Moll Flanders

TEXT 2 (1860–1) ··

1 My father's family name being Pirrip, and my Christian name Philip, my infant tongue could make of both names nothing longer or more explicit than Pip. So, I called myself, Pip, and came to be called Pip.

I give Pirrip as my father's family name, on the authority of his tombstone and my
5 sister – Mrs. Joe Gargery, who married the blacksmith. As I never saw my father or my mother, and never saw any likeness of either of them for their days were long before the days of photographs, my first fancies regarding what they were like, were unreasonably derived from their tombstones. The shape of the letters on my father's, gave me an odd idea that he was a square, stout, dark man, with curly black hair. From
10 the character and turn of the inscription, '*Also Georgiana Wife of the Above*', I drew a childish conclusion that my mother was freckled and sickly. To five little stone lozenges, each about a foot and a half long, which were arranged in a neat row beside their grave, and were sacred to the memory of five little brothers of mine – who gave up trying to get a living exceedingly early in that universal struggle – I am indebted
15 for a belief I religiously entertained that they had all been born on their backs with their hands in their trousers-pockets, and had never taken them out in this state of existence.

Charles Dickens (1812–70), Great Expectations

COMMENTARY

Both the extracts are written in the **first person**, using the personal pronoun *I* to convey a personal experience. In *Moll Flanders* the reader is introduced to an uneducated character who is writing about life as a pickpocket, while in *Great Expectations* the reader learns about Pip's background in a far more detailed way. Dickens uses a retrospective account in which his central character is looking back at his life and writing from a point at which he has gained maturity. This means that the extract from *Great Expectations* is far more complex than the straightforward recollection of events in Defoe's narrative.

The **word forms** and the **word classes** now vary very little from Late Modern usage. Both Dickens and Defoe use proper nouns to establish the credibility of their story: the *Moll Flanders* extract draws on real London place names to create a sense of reality: *Aldersgate Street* (l. 3), and *Bartholomew Close* (l. 7). Dickens is more interested in presenting character in this extract, and therefore frequently uses names: *Pirrip* (l. 1), *Pip* (l. 2), *Mrs. Joe Gargery* (l. 5), and *Georgiana* (l. 10). The majority of nouns in *Moll Flanders* are concrete: *child* (l. 4), *hand* (l. 6) and *necklace* (l. 9). These reflect the ordinary nature of Moll's life, which is governed by the need to survive. By contrast, Dickens's text uses more abstract nouns: *existence* (l. 17), *conclusion* (l. 11) and *memory* (l. 13). This is indicative of the reflective nature of the main character who is at a time in his life when he wants to reconsider what has made him who he is.

These extracts are taken from novels, and their authors use a range of modifiers to create atmosphere. Adjectival inflections are no longer used in either text:

m	m	h	m	m	h		m	m	h	
a	dreadful	nature	a	dancing-school	(COMPOUND)		a	paved	alley	(DEFOE)
det	Adj	N	det	V	N		det	V	N	

m	m	h		m	m	h	h	
My father's	family	name		my	first	fancies	my mother was freckled	(DICKENS)
det	N	N	N	det	num	N	V (predicative)	

Other word forms used now closely resemble Late Modern English usage. Pronouns are varied in both the eighteenth and nineteenth centuries: *I* and *it*, personal pronouns; *mine* and *its*, possessive pronouns. The third person *its* was established in the Early Modern English period and is clearly now used standardly.

The **vocabulary** used by Defoe may seem slightly dated to a modern reader. Lexis like the adverb *whither* (l. 1) and the preposition *upon* in the verb phrase *set me upon* (l. 5) are unlikely to be used in the same context now. Lexical sets also reflect the time: *devil* and *prompter* (l. 5) suggest the moral outlook, while *Street* (l. 3) and *alley* (l. 10) set the urban scene. Many of the words are of Old English origin: *snare* (l. 2: OE *sneare*); and inevitably many derive from French and Latin sources: *prompter* (l. 5: L *prōmptus*) and *alley* (l. 10: OF *alee*). However, reflecting the increasingly cosmopolitan nature of the English word stock, *prattled* (l. 6) derives from the Low German *praten*.

Dickens's vocabulary moves even closer to that with which we are familiar in Late Modern English. The use of *photographs* (l. 7) is interesting because we can precisely date its introduction into English in 1839. The word's derivation is typically classical, reflecting the technical nature of the processes involved: Greek *phōs/phōtos* (*light*) + *graphein* (*to draw*). The lexical sets centre on the key areas of the content: *family name* (l. 4) and *Christian name* (l. 1) focus on the issue of personal identity; *tombstones* (l. 8), *grave* (l. 13) and *existence* (l. 17) remind us of the fact that Pip is an orphan and that life expectancy at the time was often short.

Defoe's **grammar** is also close to our own, but there are specific examples that mark it as typical of the beginning of the Modern English period. In clauses like *I knew not* (l. 1) the author does not use the dummy auxiliary *do* with which we construct negatives in Late Modern English: *I did not know*. The use of the archaic *agoing* (l. 4) also dates the text. It was not until the nineteenth century that this form of the progressive was consistently shortened to *going*. The loosely co-ordinated sentences with embedded subordinate clauses reflect the way in which Defoe tries to imitate spoken language.

S	P	O	S	P	O	A	S	P	O	A
(I)	(talked to)	(it),	(and)	(it)	(prattled to)	(me) (again),	(and)	(I)	(took)	(it) (by the hand)
				conj				conj		

	P	O	A		A
(and)	(led)	(it)	(along)	(till I came to a paved alley that goes into Bartholomew Close),	
conj			SCl–ACl	SCl–RelCl	

	S	P	O	A
(and)	(I)	(led)	(it)	(in there).
conj				

The relative pronoun *that* (l. 7) is used to post-modify the noun *alley*, while the subordinating conjunction *till* (l. 6) is used to introduce an adverbial clause of time. The Early Modern English period saw the introduction of the relative pronoun *who*, and although Defoe omits it in the clause *a pretty little child* [*who*] *had been...* (l. 4), the structure suggests that *who* is now used standardly. Finally, it is worth commenting on the range of verb forms in the extract: simple present (*it is*, l. 8); simple past (*I went*, l. 1); use of modals (*I'll show*, l. 8); the progressive (*was agoing*, l. 4); and the perfect aspect (*I have never had*, l. 3).

The grammar of *Great Expectations* is very similar to that of Late Modern English. There are only three features worth commenting on in order to establish development from the 1722 extract. The relative pronoun *who* is used several times; the passive form of verbs also recurs: *were arranged* (l. 12), *had ... been born* (l. 15); and the present participle now resembles Late Modern English usage: *being* (l. 1) and *regarding* (l. 7).

Summary

Examples of Modern English texts mean that linguists can draw certain conclusions about the nature of English between the years 1700 and 1900.

Semantics

Modern readers can rely on understanding the **meaning** of words because of the similarities between Modern and Late Modern English.

Lexis

The **word stock** of English became increasingly cosmopolitan during the period as words were borrowed from a wider range of **sources**. Equally, technical, social and political developments were reflected in the **lexis**. Scholars continued to object to certain features of the language and many desired to perfect and fix English in order to prevent it becoming 'more corrupt'. Rules governing the language were stated and the beginning of 'prescriptive' grammar can be seen at this time.

Grammar

Few features of **grammar** are different from that in Late Modern English. Use of the **progressive** and the **progressive passive** became more common towards the end of the period. The changes that took place were dictated by a semantic need – writers and speakers adapted structures that enabled them to convey more subtle shades of meaning.

Phonology

Pronunciation was remarkably similar to that in the present day. In some of the later literature of the period, writers tried to convey **accent** through the spelling, but this was confined to dialogue in novels and to some regional poetry.

Graphology

No differences in **graphology** can be recorded here, but it is useful to remember the interest during the period in **spelling reform**. Many of the early schemes required either new **phonetic alphabets** or **additional symbols** in order to convey the phonetic sounds of English. None of the schemes had a lasting effect because the scale of the changes they required was too dramatic.

7.7 What to look for when dating a text

The following checklist can be used to identify characteristic features of English at each key stage of its development. You will not find all of the features in every textual extract, but the list can be used as a guide. For instance, you will only be able to discuss the sources of words if you have access to an appropriate dictionary or if an examination question provides you with etymological information. The points made here are general, so discussion of specific examples will need to be adapted to take account of the specific context, style and purpose. Remember that you need to evaluate the effect of the features you identify, exploring what they tell you about the historical and social contexts.

The following are helpful questions to ask.

Register

1 What is the **mode**?
   - written.
2 What is the **manner**?
   - formal or informal relationship between the writer and the reader?
   - personal or impersonal?
   - public or private communication?
3 What is the **field**?
   - subject matter?
   - linked to the audience, purpose, and context?

Old English texts

Graphological features

1 Are any **runes** from the Anglo-Saxon alphabet used?
   - æ, þ, ð, ρ, ʒ (or ꞩ)?

Lexis

1 What **sources** of words can be identified?
   - Germanic? Celtic? Latin? Old Norse?
2 Are there any examples of **word creation**?
   - compounding?
   - affixation?
3 Is there any evidence of **assimilation**?
   - Old English inflections such as -*ian* (infinitive)?
   - loan words, indicated by suffixes such as -*dom*?
4 Are there any words that have remained **unchanged** or **nearly unchanged** since the Old English period?

Grammar

1 Are there any noticeable **word endings**?
   - open-class words (nouns, adjectives)?
   - closed-class words (determiners, pronouns)?
2 Are there any **strong verbs** that are regular in Late Modern English?
3 Is the **word order** noticeably different from Late Modern English?

Graphology/orthography

1 Is there any evidence of surviving Anglo-Saxon **runes**?
   - þ, ð, ʒ, þ?
2 Have Old English **spellings** been changed?
   - *sc* to *ss*, *sch* or *sh*? *cw* to *qu*?
3 Are any **letters** still interchangeable?
   - *u* and *v* and *i* and *y*?
4 Have Old English **marked long vowels** been replaced by **double vowels**?

Lexis

1 What new **sources** of words can be identified?
   - French? Latin?
2 Do the loan words appear in distinctive **lexical fields**?
   - administration? Church? law? military? social? art and learning? general?
3 Are any Old English words replaced by a **French equivalent**?
4 Is there any evidence of **word creation**?
   - affixation?

Grammar

1 Is there any evidence of **simplified inflections**?
   - open-class words (nouns, adjectives)?
   - closed-class words (determiners, pronouns)?
2 How are **plural nouns** marked?
   - *-s? -es? -en*?
3 Are there any differences in the **verbs**?
   - Old English strong verbs that are regular in Late Modern English?
   - weak or strong past participle forms?

Emergence of a standard form

1 Has the **standard form** of English influenced the spelling?
2 Are there still examples of **inconsistencies**?

Orthography

1 Are any words **unfamiliar**?
2 Are some words **recognisable** but with a different spelling from the Late Modern English version?
3 Is spelling still **inconsistent** or is there any evidence of **standardisation**?

Lexis

1 What **sources** of words can be identified?
   - Latin? French? Italian? Spanish? Portuguese?
2 Have any **archaic words** been revived from earlier periods?
3 Are there any examples of **new coinages**?

Grammar

1 How is the **possessive** marked?
  - -es? -ys? -'s?

2 Are **comparatives** and **superlatives** used in a more flexible way than in Late Modern English?

3 Are **pronouns** noticeably different from Late Modern English or have they adopted the patterns still used today?
  - *ye* (subject), *you* (object)?
  - *thou, thee* and *thy* (informal, familiar)?
  - *you, ye* and *your* (respectful, unfamiliar)?

4 Have the **possessive pronoun** *its* and the **relative pronoun** *who* been introduced?

5 Are **third person singular present tense verbs** inflected with *-s* or *-(e)th*?

6 Are there any **reflexive verbs**?

7 Is the **interrogative mood** constructed without the dummy auxiliary *do*?

8 Is the **dummy auxiliary *do* + *base form verb*** used where Late Modern English would use a progressive?

9 Are the **negatives** distinctive?
  - *not* placed before the verb?
  - omitting the dummy auxiliary *do*?
  - using multiple negatives?

Modern English texts

Orthography

1 Is **spelling** becoming more consistent?

2 Are there any **differences** between Modern English and Late Modern English spelling?

Lexis

1 In what areas is **new vocabulary** introduced?
  - general word stock?
  - British Empire? trade? changes in society?

Grammar

1 Is there evidence that **verbs** are now used in a wider variety of forms?
  - use of the auxiliary *do* for emphasis?
  - progressive? progressive passive?

2 Are there any examples of the **subjunctive**?

Late Modern English texts

Orthography

1 Is there any evidence of changes to standardised **spelling**?
  - American English?
  - simplified spelling?
  - artificial systems to match spelling to pronunciation?

Lexis

1 In what areas is **new vocabulary** introduced?
   * military or political?
   * social, cultural or the media?
   * technological or scientific?

2 What are the **sources** of new words?

3 Are there any examples of **word creation**?
   * affixation or coinages?
   * proper nouns?
   * old words with new meanings or first usages?

4 Is there any evidence of **doublespeak** (language that is seen as confusing and obscuring rather than clarifying)?
   * official language?
   * advertising?

5 Are there any examples of **ephemeral language** (language that continually changes to mirror social attitudes and groups), which mark the text as typical of its time?
   * slang? euphemisms? idioms?

Grammar

1 Does the **prepositional usage** differ from earlier periods?

2 Are any **transitive verbs** used intransitively?

3 Are there any other examples of **distinctive usage**?
   * split infinitives?
   * phrasal verbs?

Summary

Language change can be identified in three main areas: lexis, pronunciation and grammar. The changes taking place are gradual and go almost unnoticed by speakers and writers using the language from day to day. This gradual spread of change is called **LEXICAL DIFFUSION**. Because of the pace of change, it is very difficult to identify new forms as they emerge. Retrospectively, however, points of change can be seen quite distinctively. **LEXICAL CHANGE** is perhaps the most straightforward way in which a language can be altered: words are adapted, borrowed or created to meet new demands. Often additions to the existing word stock are linked directly to new objects, ideas, experiences or attitudes. The emergence of **sound changes** is more difficult to pinpoint because the spread of alternative pronunciations is very gradual. Some sound changes are adopted for physiological reasons – the new version is easier to say. Others may be due to the adoption of non-standard regional pronunciations beyond local boundaries as people move from area to area. At first a sound change will probably affect only a few words, but as the new pronunciation spreads, the old form will be replaced by the new. **Grammatical changes** usually involve regularisation or simplification which reduces the number of irregular forms. Since so much grammatical simplification has already taken place, any further grammatical change is unlikely to be dramatic.

There are many **underlying tendencies** that cause language change – historical, social, cultural, political and economic forces have influenced English and made it what it is today. Language, however, has an inbuilt tendency to make **readjustments**, restoring disrupted patterns when change is too dramatic. It creates a balance between new and old forms to prevent problems in communication.

Change can be **conscious** or **subconscious**. New forms can spread through intentional imitation when certain pronunciations or words are **purposefully** adopted. Other changes **infiltrate** language – users are unaware of the new forms they adopt. While the change is in progress, several parallel forms will exist, until eventually one form will replace the existing variant forms.

Modern linguists recognise that English is always in FLUX and that it is almost impossible to fix it. Changes are inevitable, but because they take place slowly we hardly notice them in our everyday use of the language. It is only by looking back at written records that we can identify points of change. The new forms that appear do not always survive, but if they do they are consolidated as new generations of children learn them. Because language is changed by the people who use it, it is highly unlikely to break down into mutually incomprehensible dialects as the linguistic pessimists fear. In fact, where changes do occur, there will usually be valid linguistic reasons for them.

Chapter 8

Language variation: regional and social

8.1 Regional and social variation

Not only does language change over time, it also has different forms that exist simultaneously. As children grow up in different communities and acquire language, for instance, they do not all learn one identical form of communication: instead, each learns a version that is distinctive to her or his particular **social**, **regional**, and **cultural background**. Children who acquire English as a first language in Britain will begin to speak in a variety that is used by the people around them – they will sound similar to these people, and they will use similar words and grammatical structures.

Language is constantly changing, not only from region to region and from social group to social group, but also from person to person. Even within one region, the words, grammatical structures and pronunciations of each individual may be different – and one individual may adopt slightly different kinds of pronunciations, words and grammatical structures depending upon the purpose of the communication, the audience and the context. In research, linguists must also take note of IDIOSYNCRATIC **linguistic features**, since although regional, social and cultural variants affect language usage, ultimately each member of the speech community will adopt a form of English that is in many ways personally distinctive.

As well as regional, social and personal characteristics, linguists also have to take into account a person's **age**, **gender**, **occupation** and **educational background**. The older speakers are, the more likely they are to use traditional forms of language, whereas younger speakers are more likely to be influenced by current trends. Women are often thought to be more sensitive to 'standard' forms of language in formal contexts than men and tend therefore to be more likely to use SE and standard pronunciations. Not only do certain jobs have subject-specific lexis associated with them, but people with professional and non-professional jobs will tend to use language very differently: professional people are more likely to use the 'prestige' forms associated with SE and to some extent with RP; non-professional workers are more likely to use non-standard versions. Educational experience is directly linked to this occupational variation in language use – the longer individuals spend in education, the more likely they are to adopt standard lexis and grammar and the less likely they are to speak with a strong or broad regional accent.

The study of language variation is therefore very complex, and analysis of particular forms of English must include consideration of both general and personal variants. The variety people use may or may not be Standard English and linguists are interested both in the kinds of variants that change Standard English and in the changes themselves.

Having recognised that personal identity, social, cultural and educational background affect the kind of language an individual uses, linguists analyse the changes that these variants cause. By using **STANDARD ENGLISH** and **RECEIVED PRONUNCIATION** as norms, they can discuss variations in lexis, grammar and pronunciation. Rather than seeing any differences as examples of 'bad' English, however, they recognise all forms as equally valid in appropriate contexts.

In the nineteenth century, the phrase 'Standard English' was used to describe a form of English that was 'common' or 'universal' because it was a recognised system of writing. By the 1930s, however, it had become associated with **social class** and was seen by many as the language of the educated. In the 1933 'Supplement' to the *Oxford English Dictionary*, it was defined as a form of language with cultural and social status which many users considered to be the 'best' form. The introduction of social judgements in the early part of the twentieth century made the concept of SE very emotive. By linking it to social class, feelings of social superiority and inferiority were reinforced in the very language that different people used. Describing SE as the 'best' implied that all other varieties were substandard, and suddenly implicit judgements were made not only about the different versions of English but also about the people who used them.

Most modern linguists try to avoid the political and class associations of SE. Instead, they see it as a form of national communication and treat it as a benchmark. Because it is not limited to any particular region, SE can act as a point of comparison for all other varieties of English, whether they are marked by personal, social or geographical variations.

Just as SE establishes a norm for the lexis and syntax of spoken and written language, so Received Pronunciation fulfils a similar function. It is a regionally neutral accent which is closely associated with public school education and high social class. Linguists can describe and classify the sounds heard in different versions of spoken English by comparing pronunciations of vowels and consonants in regional accents with the list of RP phonemes (Chapter 2).

As well as language forms changing, so too do **attitudes** to the different forms of English. Because young people tend to be most influenced by and involved in language changes, the role of education in maintaining 'standards' is much debated. Newspapers regularly report on falling standards of literacy, poor general knowledge and on the increase in 'lazy' and 'careless' speech – particularly among the young. Such coverage sensationalises issues by focusing on judgemental social perceptions while failing to take account of linguistic factors. Individual cases are presented as evidence for a general picture of linguistic doom and gloom.

In the wake of all the changes in education during the 1980s and 1990s, the Conservative government focused attention on the nature of 'correct' English and on what should be taught in schools. The 1990s National Curriculum highlighted what children had to be taught about SE: it was the language of wide social communication and was generally required in formal contexts. Many people objected, fearing that non-standard varieties of English would be undermined on the basis of social rather than linguistic judgements. If this happened, they believed, children themselves would be made to feel worthless since language and **identity** are so closely interwoven. A revised version of the document in 1993 altered the focus slightly by stating that all children should be taught to use SE – implicitly suggesting that children were being offered choice rather than being forced to adopt only one form of language. A document drawn up by government advisers in 1994 went one step further by establishing non-standard varieties of English in a position of respectability. When used in the right context, non-standard versions of spoken and written language were seen to be beneficial as they demonstrated to school pupils the richness of English. The original declaration that SE should be taught as a requirement for formal settings was rephrased: although young people should be able to use SE when appropriate, they should also be free to adapt their language to suit any situation in which they found themselves. The 1994 document therefore recognised that there are many kinds of English which can be acceptable and that children already come to school as language experts, able to adopt one form of language for the home environment, another for their interaction with friends, and another for the classroom. This allowed teachers to encourage young people to have the confidence to move between their different **REPERTOIRES** rather than just dictating the exclusive use of one form which is socially, not linguistically, seen as the 'best'.

Inevitably, however, social judgements are still made on the way in which people speak and write – communication is all about imparting information and a limited repertoire will be reflected in limited self-expression. A knowledge of SE is therefore crucial – it is the language of the media, of education, of the law courts and the Church, and in many contexts it is necessary to be able to use the universally recognised form of English. Nevertheless, in more personal situations it is often more appropriate to adapt language so that regional, social or cultural group identities can be developed. Rather than insisting that there is only one acceptable form of English, an education system needs to develop students' linguistic awareness of the different varieties of English and of the importance of audience, purpose and context. If young people are actively involved in finding out about both standard and non-standard varieties they will be able to make informed choices about the kinds of language they wish to use.

If the education system teaches young people to be language experts then it will have succeeded. If people can make conscious decisions about the appropriate kind of language for a particular situation, they will be proficient speakers and writers. If they can use regional, social and personal varieties alongside SE, then they will be active and effective participants in the language community.

8.2 Accent

ACCENT refers only to pronunciation that indicates where a person is from, geographically or socially. A **REGIONAL ACCENT** links a speaker to a specific area in which certain kinds of pronunciations are heard; a **SOCIAL ACCENT** relates to the cultural and educational background of a speaker. Speakers of RP are often described as having no accent, but in the field of linguistics everyone has some kind of accent: RP is therefore just one of many English accents, despite the fact that it is not linked to a specific region. When pronunciation differs dramatically from RP, speakers are said to have a **BROAD ACCENT**.

Change occurs far more quickly in spoken language than in written. Pronunciation is therefore extremely variable. Research has shown that one speaker rarely says the same words in precisely the same way twice and pronunciation is altered constantly to suit the context. Even RP speakers do not all pronounce words identically. For instance, in RP a word like *poor* used to be pronounced as a **DIPHTHONG**, /pʊə/; in modified RP, it is pronounced as a **MONOPHTHONG** (a simple vowel sound), /pɔː/.

When linguists analyse accents, they consider three key areas: **personal accent**, **social accent**, and **regional accent**. By focusing on relevant features under these headings, they can come to conclusions about the kind of pronunciations an individual or a group uses. The regional elements of an accent are usually dominant, but a particular regional variety can be modified by an individual speaker's personal style or cultural background.

Personal accents

Individual pronunciation changes may be linked to different contexts or moods, or to physical reasons like a sore throat or a mouth full of food. Whether consciously or subconsciously, speakers make decisions each time they participate in a speech encounter. In a formal context, speakers are far more likely to articulate words carefully – elision, assimilation, liaison and reduction (see Chapter 2) will be less prominent. In informal interaction, speech will often be quicker and the articulation will be less precise – some sounds will disappear or will be modified.

Formal context	Informal context	
green gate	/griːŋɡeɪt/	(assimilation)
here and now	/hɪərənaʊ/	(liaison)
first stop	/fɜːstɒp/	(elision)
I could have done it	I could /həv/ done it	(reduction)

All of these segmental phonological features affect a speaker's accent to a greater or lesser degree. Such changes will be more apparent and more frequent in conversation than in an interview, for instance, but there will be examples of these features in almost every speaker's utterances in some context or another.

Linguists are interested in the ways individual speakers alter their language according to their situation. Some speakers are very aware of changing contexts and their accent may alter significantly depending upon the relationship between participants. **CONVERGENCE** describes the process of accent change in which two speakers modify their accents in order to become more similar. Usually a speaker with a non-standard accent will standardise pronunciation in order to sound more like an RP speaker, but equally the existence of modified RP is evidence that RP can also be altered by regional and social influences. **DIVERGENCE** reflects an opposite movement in which accents become further apart – this will usually only happen in a situation where a community is isolated from the influence of other communities. On a small scale, it can occur where two speakers take part in a hostile speech encounter, both exaggerating their different accents in order to emphasise their opposing positions – an RP speaker may exaggerate 'standard' sounds, while a speaker with marked regional pronunciation may adopt a 'broad' accent.

The most important thing about a personal accent is that it will rarely impede understanding. Most people at some point will adopt the characteristics of informal speech and linguists study both the reasons for this and the kinds of modifications that take place.

Social accents

When linguists consider the 'social' elements of an individual's accent, they are interested in aspects such as the speaker's class, educational background, occupation and gender. Traditionally, speakers in lower social classes tended to have left formal education earlier and to have non-professional rather than professional jobs. They were far more likely to have a regional accent and to have speech marked by informal segmental features like elision and assimilation. Speakers from higher social classes were more likely to have stayed in education and to have professional jobs, so they were more likely to speak RP or modified RP. The New Labour government elected in 1997 and led by Tony Blair promised a classless society for the twenty-first century. In 2007, however, as Blair left office, some commentators argued that society was actually less open to social mobility than ever before – changes in the labour market and in access to higher education might have altered the balance of the traditional class system, but inequalities of wealth and power continued to divide Britain and social background still influenced the way people spoke.

People who wish to be upwardly mobile tend to modify their accent in order to resemble RP more closely, and this inevitably reinforces the prestige of RP. Speakers who are trying to emulate RP often **OVERCOMPENSATE**: in making sure that the phoneme /h/ is pronounced in the initial position, for instance, a speaker may also pronounce it where it is not needed. This process is called **HYPERCORRECTION**.

Attitudes in society change and in the twenty-first century it is common to hear both modified RP and regional accents on radio and television. Many politicians have regional accents: the Labour MP Kim Howells has a Welsh accent, for example, and the Conservative MP Liam Fox has a Scottish accent. Comedians like Paul Merton (South), Peter Kay (North-West) and Johnny Vegas (North-West) do not use RP; while some celebrities, such as the singer Charlotte Church (Wales), purposely reject RP in favour of a non-standard accent. Despite this, many people still modify their regional pronunciation in order to acquire social prestige.

Figure 8.1 **The main accent and dialect regions of the United Kingdom**

Regional accents

In order to deal with accents in a practical way, linguists often divide the country into several very broad areas. The map in Figure 8.1 shows the broad regions that will be used here. Each line, or ISOGLOSS, marks the boundary of an area in which a particular accent or dialect is used. When you cross an isogloss, you pass from one accent or dialect type to another. Although the boundaries in Figure 8.1 are general, differences across each isogloss are more significant than variations within each area.

The following list summarises the **main pronunciation differences** which can be identified between RP and other British accents. It provides a starting point for analysis of regional accents in Britain and shows how they contrast with RP.

Consonants

The phoneme /h/

While RP pronounces the phoneme /h/ in the initial position, most regional dialects do not. This means that some minimal pairs sound the same: /eə/ might be *air* or *hair*; /iːt/ might be *eat* or *heat*; /ɪə/ might be *ear* or *hear/here*.

The phoneme /ŋ/

The phoneme /ŋ/ may vary in one of two ways in regional accents. In almost all informal spoken discourse, accents other than RP will pronounce /ŋ/ as /n/ in the final position: /kraɪɪn/ *crying*, /siːɪn/ *seeing*, /rʌnɪn/ *running*. In some parts of the Midlands and the North, speakers pronounce a final /g/ phoneme, thus articulating /ŋg/ at the end of words: /kraɪɪŋg/ *crying*, /siːɪŋg/ *seeing*, /rʌnɪŋg/, *running*.

Consonant followed by /uː/

In RP, certain words beginning with a consonant followed by the pure vowel /uː/ are pronounced with a /j/: /njuːz/ *news*, /mjuːzɪk/ *music*, /fjuːz/ *fuse*. This pronunciation is a remnant of earlier forms of English in which far more words were pronounced with the /j/. Nowadays even RP pronunciation does not include the /j/ in words beginning with /r/, and it is dying out in words beginning with /s/. Some RP speakers, however, will still articulate *suit* as /sjuːt/. In some regional accents, the loss of the phoneme /j/ is common in many more words: /buːtɪfʊl/ for the RP /bjuːtɪfʊl/ *beautiful*, and /tuːb/ for the RP /tjuːb/ *tube*.

The post-vocalic /r/

In Chapter 2, the process of liaison described the way in which speakers insert a linking /r/ between words that end with a vowel sound and are followed by another word with a vowel in the initial position: /heərɔɪl/ *hair oil*. All accents including RP pronounce the **post-vocalic** /r/ after a vowel, but RP would only pronounce it at word boundaries: while RP would pronounce *sawing* as /sɔːɪŋ/, a regional variant would be /sɔːrɪŋ/. In the speech of older regional speakers, the post-vocalic /r/ still occurs in words ending with a vowel sound: *tar* would be pronounced /tɑː/ in RP and /tɑːr/ by an older speaker in a rural community.

The glottal stop

In RP, the **glottal stop** is used on very few occasions, but in regional dialects it is common, particularly amongst young people in urban areas. It frequently occurs as an **ALLOPHONE** (a variation in the articulation of a particular phoneme) of /t/ in the medial and final position: *water* would be pronounced /wɔːtə/ in RP and /wɔːʔ/ in a non-standard accent.

Vowels

The phoneme /iː/

In RP, words ending with *-y* or *-ey*, and some words ending with *-ee*, are pronounced with the phoneme /ɪ/: /pɪtɪ/ *pity*, /hʌnɪ/ *honey*, /kɒfɪ/ *coffee*. Northern accents also use /ɪ/: /tʃærɪtɪ/ *charity*, /nɔːrməlɪ/ *normally*; while Southern accents tend to use /iː/: /rɪəliː/ *really*.

Vowel a

In RP, the vowel *a* is pronounced as /ɑː/ rather than /æ/ when it precedes a voiceless fricative (/f/, /θ/ or /s/) or a consonant cluster with the phonemes /m/ or /n/ in the initial position: /ɡrɑːs/ *grass*, /bɑːθ/ *bath*, /trɑːns/ *trance*, /sɑːmpl/ *sample*. Most Northern accents, however, will use the short /æ/: /ɡræs/, /bæθ/, /træns/, /sæmpl/.

Phoneme inventory

Some vowels that occur in RP are absent from regional dialects. It is therefore possible to distinguish between dialects by creating a **PHONEME INVENTORY** – a list of the phonemes that are or are not used. The phonemes /ʌ/ and /ʊ/ both occur in RP; in many regional dialects, however, only /ʊ/ is used: /ʃʊt/ and /bʊt/ for RP /ʃʌt/ *shut* and /bʌt/ *but*. Some older regional dialect speakers use /uː/ to distinguish between pairs of words that would otherwise sound the same: RP /tʊk/ *took* may be pronounced as /tʊk/ or /tuːk/ in a regional accent; RP /tʌk/ *tuck* may be pronounced as /tʊk/ in regional accents.

By studying **transcripts of speakers** from different parts of Britain, it is possible to see accent variations in context. The following examples will help you to identify the differences between RP and regional accents and to build up an awareness of some distinctive accent characteristics. Each transcript represents a specific accent, but in a general sense they can be seen as illustrative of the broader areas represented on the map in Figure 8.1.

The transcriptions are broad and do not aim to describe the exact articulation of sounds. Instead, they aim to give an overall sense of the speakers' accents in a simplified form. **PHONEMIC SYMBOLS** are used to record pronunciations that differ significantly from RP. To show where vowels are either more open or closed than RP, the following IPA **DIACRITICS** will be used: ˔ tongue raised; ˕ tongue lowered; /ː/ long vowel.

To help you read the transcriptions easily, a written version using traditional orthography and conventional punctuation will precede each monologue (Activities 8.2–8.5). In the dialogue, the written version will record only the non-standard accent of the second speaker (Activity 8.1). A key to the prosodic symbols can be found on page 93.

A key to the prosodic symbols can be found on page 93.

ACTIVITY 8.1 ────────────────────────────

The following transcript records a conversation between two speakers who grew up in Yorkshire. Although both speakers have lived away from Yorkshire for a number of years, Speaker 2 has largely retained his accent, while Speaker 1 has consciously modified his pronunciation.

Read through the script and rewrite the words transcribed phonemically in SE. Then comment on:

1 distinctive pronunciations of consonants
2 distinctive pronunciations of vowels
3 the main differences between the accents of the two speakers.

As we remember it. As we remember it. What, thirty-eight years ago. It was a very busy town, full of steel works. Now, to my knowledge, most of the steel works have gone. Shopping centres have. Covered shopping centres have taken their place and a large sports area. Also all the houses have gone. Where the people have gone, I've no idea. They've gone somewhere, but where I don't know. It used to be a nice. It's a large town, but it used to be a nice safe place to be in because as a child, well not as as a child but a young fellow, I used to do a lot of cycling into Derbyshire and camping on the weekends. No problem. Used to get spuds off the farmer for little jobs around the farm or whatever. Yes. Just a mass of smoke. Lots of smoke. Actually it was a dirty, sooty place. Yes. Through Sheffield. Oh yes, yes. I worked there. Um I know the place. That's. That was called then, when I when I left school, The English Steel Corporation. The full length of the railway. No there was two. There was one. There was two businesses, but one ran the full length of the railway, from what we used to call the Wicker Arches right out to the other side of Sheffield into Rotherham. There I first started in the building trade there.

SPOKEN VERSION

```
 1 SPEAKER 1  we'll talk about Sheffield =
   SPEAKER 2  = /əz/ we remember it =
   SPEAKER 1  = as we ‖ remember it
   SPEAKER 2          ‖ /əz/ we remember it (.) what /θɜːtɪ e̝ːt/ years /əgɔː/ (.) it was a
 5            ‖ very busy ↑tőwn↑ (.) full of steel wőrks (.) now (.) to my knowlĕdge (.)
   SPEAKER 1  ‖ yes umm
   SPEAKER 2  /mɔːst/ of the steel works have ↑gone↑ (.) /ʃɒpɪn/ centres have (.) /kʊvəd/
              ʃɒpɪn/ centres have /te̝kən/ their ↑/ple̝ːs/↑ and a large sports ↓area↓
              (.) /ɒlsɒ/ all the /aʊzəz əv/ gone (.) where the people /əv/ ‖ gone I've no
10 SPEAKER 1                                                               ‖ yeah
   SPEAKER 2  idea =
   SPEAKER 1  = have they gone sőmewhere =
   SPEAKER 2  = they've gone /sʊmweər/ (.) but where I don't knŏw (.) it used to be /ə/
              nice (1) it's a large town (.) but it used to be a nice /se̝ːf ple̝ːs/ (.) to be̝
15            in (.) /kɒs əz/ a child (1) well not /əz/ as a child but a /jʊŋ felə/ (.) I used
              to do a /lɒtə saɛklɪn/ into /daːbɪʃə/ and /kæmpɪn/ on the weekends (.)
              ‖ no pròblem (.) used to get spuds off ‖ the /faːmə/ (laughs) (.) for little jobs
   SPEAKER 1  ‖ mm                                   ‖ yes
   SPEAKER 2  round the /fáːrm/ or /wɒ'tevə/ =
20 SPEAKER 1  = and when you went into Derbyshire did you look down on Shéffield =
   SPEAKER 2  = yes =
   SPEAKER 1  = what did you see thére =
   SPEAKER 2  = just a mass of ↑/smɔːk/↑ (.) lots of ‖ ↓/smɔːk/↓ (.) actually it was a dirty,
   SPEAKER 1                                         ‖ yeah mm
25 SPEAKER 2  /sʊtɪ/‖/plè̝s/
   SPEAKER 1         ‖um (.) I remember (.) the train to Scar‖borough (.) every now and
   SPEAKER 2                                                 ‖ yeah
   SPEAKER 1  again it would be diverted thro‖ugh Sheffield and along the side of the
   SPEAKER 2                                  ‖through Sheffield
30 SPEAKER 1  railway track (.) there'd be sort of these arched (1) buildings (.) with fur-
              naces inside ‖ all the way along it ‖ looked like ‖ hell
   SPEAKER 2               ‖ oh yeah              ‖ yeah        ‖ I worked there (.) um I
```

/nɔː/ the /plɛːs/ that's (.) that was called <u>then</u> (.) when I when I left school
(.) The English Steel /kɔ̰ːpəreːʃən/ =
35 SPEAKER 1   = it was /wɒn wɒn/ (.) I remember it on the right hand ‖side of the /rɛːl-
    SPEAKER 2   ‖the full length
    SPEAKER 1   weː/ (.) oh so it was just /wɒn/ business (.) =
    SPEAKER 2   = no there was two (.) there was /wʊn/ (.) there was two búsinesses (.)
                 but ‖/wʊn/ ran the full length of the ‖/rɛːlweː/ (.) from what we used to
40 SPEAKER 1   ‖yeah   ‖um
    SPEAKER 2   call the Wicker Arches ‖right out to the other side of ‖Sheffield (1) into
    SPEAKER 1   ‖yeah   ‖um
    SPEAKER 2   /'rɒð̰ˌrəm/ ‖ <u>thère</u> (.) I first /staːtɪd/ in the building /trɛːd/ there
    SPEAKER 1   ‖ yeah

COMMENTARY

The two speakers talk about Sheffield as they remember it. The **context** is informal
and friendly and the interaction reflects this – the speakers are clearly known to
one another and there is a lot of supportive affirmation (see Chapter 10 for discussion of the terms used in conversation analysis): *mm, yeah*. **Turn-taking** is
relaxed: although Speaker 2 is dominant and takes longer turns, Speaker 1 initiates
the topic and adds new information where appropriate.

It is in the pronunciation of **vowels** that regional variations are most likely
to differ from RP, but in Yorkshire accents some **consonantal features** are also
characteristic. The dropping of /h/ in /aʊzəz/ *houses* and /əv/ *have* (l. 9) and the
pronunciation of the *-ing* inflection as /ɪn/ in /ʃɒpɪn/ *shopping* (l. 8) and /kæmpɪn/
camping (l. 16) are common in many accents and typical of a Yorkshire accent.

Many of the RP **pure vowels** are realised in a slightly different way – usually they are closer than in RP. In words like /daːbɪʃə/ *Derbyshire* (l. 16), /faːmə/
farmer (l. 17) and /staːtɪd/ *started* (l. 43), the pure vowel /ɑː/ is articulated with the
tongue raised, creating a harder and shorter sound. Another distinctive feature
of Yorkshire accents appears in the absence of /ʌ/ in the phoneme inventory. In
words like /kʊvəd/ *covered* (l. 7), /sʊmweər/ *somewhere* (l. 13) and /jʊŋ/ *young* (l. 15),
/ʌ/ is articulated as the closer /ʊ/. The following pure vowels are also realised with
the tongue raised: /ɜː/ in words like /θɜːtɪ/ *thirty* (l. 4); /æ/ becomes the unstressed
vowel /ə/ in /əz/ *as* (l. 4); and /ɔː/ in words like /kɔːpəreːʃən/ *Corporation* (l. 34). The
-y at the end of words is pronounced as /ɪ/ in /sʊtɪ/ *sooty* (l. 25).

Yorkshire accents articulate **RP diphthongs** in distinctive ways. In some cases,
they become narrower so that the two sounds of the diphthong are less distinct or
become a monophthong. For instance, /eɪ/ RP is realised as a long pure vowel /ɛː/
in words like /teːkən/ *taken* (l. 8), /plɛːs/ *place* (l. 8), /ɛːt/ *eight* (l. 4), /seːf/ *safe* (l. 14),
/rɛːlweː/ *railway* (ll. 35–7) and /trɛːd/ *trade* (l. 43); /əʊ/ is realised as /ɔː/ in /əgɔː/
ago (l. 4), /mɔːst/ *most* (l. 7), /smɔːk/ *smoke* (l. 23), and /nɔː/ *know* (l. 33).

Speaker 2 no longer has a broad Yorkshire accent, but his pronunciations are
characteristic – the narrow diphthongs; the close pure vowels; and the realisation
of *-ing* as /ɪn/. Other non-standard pronunciations are linked to the stress patterns
of Yorkshire accents: /wɒˈtevə/ *whatever* (l. 19) and /'rɒð̰ˌrəm/ *Rotherham* (l. 43).

Although both speakers will have had the same accent in the past, Speaker 1 has consciously altered his pronunciation. He uses a modified RP and so his regional accent is more difficult to pinpoint. However, occasionally his realisation of a sound falls between the two accents. This is an example of **hypercorrection** – in aiming to pronounce a word in RP, the speaker produces a form that differs from the norm. For instance, the typically Yorkshire pronunciation of *nothing* would be replaced by a form that does not exist in RP. The RP /nʌθɪŋ/ would become /nʊθɪŋ/ in a Yorkshire accent: the half-close back vowel /ʊ/ would be replaced by an open back vowel /ɒ/ in the process of realising the RP half-open central vowel /ʌ/. A similar process of hypercorrection occurs when Speaker 1 says /wɒn/ *one* (l. 37), which in RP is realised as /wʌn/.

While the transcript reflects the speech patterns of one individual, the pronunciation features discussed here are **characteristic** of a YORKSHIRE ACCENT:

1 The phoneme /h/ is dropped in the initial position.
2 The *-ing* inflection is articulated as /ɪn/.
3 The pure vowel /ɑː/ is articulated with the tongue raised /aː/, so that it is closer than in RP.
4 The phoneme /ʌ/ is absent from the phoneme inventory – it is articulated as /ʊ/.
5 Words ending in *-y*, *-ey* or *-ee* are pronounced with /ɪ/.
6 Diphthongs are often narrower than in RP: /eɪ/ becomes /e̞ː/; /əʊ/ becomes /ɔː/; /aɪ/ becomes /aɛ/.

Although each accent within the 'Northern' area will be different, many will display the kinds of pronunciation features highlighted here.

ACTIVITY 8.2

This next recording was made in an informal context – the participants were known to one another and topics emerged spontaneously as the conversation developed. The extract here focuses on a speaker who moved from the Midlands four years ago, but lived in Birmingham up to that point. Although she does not have a broad accent and most pronunciations are close to RP, there is still evidence of a Birmingham accent, particularly in the realisation of vowels.

Read through the transcript and try to identify characteristic features of Midlands accents. Try to suggest reasons why the speaker may have lost a strong accent.

WRITTEN VERSION

I queued from three in the morning for Bob Dylan and mother thought I was crazy, but I ended up a few rows back. Mother said 'if it was Joan Baez I could understand'. So I queued from four o'clock the previous afternoon for Joan Baez. I was at the front of the queue. Queued for seventeen hours and I got her a ticket as well. But I met Bob Dylan. Fifth of May 1965. Yeh. Although I was a few rows back, I went back stage and I held his jacket there while he did an encore.

SPOKEN VERSION

1 I /kjaʊd/ from three in the morning for Bob Dylan and /mʊðə/ thought I was /kræɪzaɪ/ but I ended up a few /raʊs/ back (.) /mʊðə/ said if it was Joan Baez I could /ʊndəstænd/ (.) so I /kjaʊd/ from four o'clock the previous /æftənaʊn/ for Joan Baez

(.) I was at the /frʊnt/ of the /kjaʊ/ (.) /kjaʊd/ for /sevəntəin/ hours (.) and I got her a
5 /tikit/ as well (.) but I met Bob Dylan (.) fifth of /mæɪ nɔɪntəin sɪxti-fɔɪv/ (.) yeh (.)
although I was a few /rʌʊs/ back I went back /stæɪdʒ/ and I held his jacket /ð̞ɜ:/ while
he did an encore

COMMENTARY

There are examples here where **RP pure vowels** sound closer: the RP /ɪ/ is realised
closer to /i/ in /tikit/ *ticket* (l.5); the RP /ʌ/ becomes /ʊ/ in /mʊðə/ *mother* (l.1) and
/frʊnt/ *front* (l.4), and the RP /ɑ:/ becomes /æ/ in /æftənaʊn/ *afternoon* (l.3). Many
of the sounds are wider than in RP: /u:/ becomes /aʊ/ in /kjaʊ/ *queue* (l.4) and
/æftənaʊn/ (l.3); /i:/ becomes /əi/ in /sevəntəin/ *seventeen* (l.4). A similar widening
is seen in the diphthongs: /aɪ/ RP becomes /fɔɪv/ *five* (l.5); /əʊ/ RP becomes /rʌʊs/
rows (l.2); /eɪ/ RP becomes /stæɪdʒ/ *stage* (l.6), /mæɪ/ *May* (l.5) and /kræɪzəi/ *crazy*
(l.2); and /eə/ RP becomes /ð̞ɜ:/ *there* (l.6).

The speaker is a professional, so despite the fact that she has lived almost all
her life in Birmingham, her accent has been modified. Her educational and occupational background means that most sounds are similar to those of RP; even
where pronunciations are different, the accent is not broad.

While the transcript reflects the speech patterns of one individual, the pronunciation features discussed here are **characteristic** of a BIRMINGHAM ACCENT:

1 The phonemes /æ/ and /ɑ:/ are both articulated as /æ/.
2 The phoneme /ʌ/ is absent from the phoneme inventory – it is instead articulated as /ʊ/.
3 Some pure vowels become diphthongs: /u:/ becomes /aʊ/; and /i:/ becomes
   /əi/.
4 Many diphthongs are wide (the movement between the two vowels is greater
   than in RP): /eɪ/ becomes /æɪ/; /əʊ/ becomes /ʌʊ/; and /aɪ/ becomes /ɔɪ/.
5 Other vowels are also distinctive: /ɪ/ becomes /i/ and /eə/ becomes /ɜ:/.

In a broad Birmingham accent, you could also expect to find the following
pronunciations:

1 /h/ is usually absent
2 *-ing* is realised as /ɪn/ and sometimes as /ŋg/
3 /ɔ:/ becomes /ʌʊə/.

Although each accent within the 'Midlands' area will be different, many will display the kinds of pronunciation features highlighted here.

ACTIVITY 8.3

The speaker in the next transcript is an old man who has lived in Norfolk all his life.
His accent is broad and there are quite marked differences between his pronunciations
and those of RP. The phonemic transcriptions pick out the words that illustrate his
accent most effectively.

The extract takes the form of a spontaneous oral narrative in which the speaker
recalls a walk with his great-nieces when they were younger. The context is informal

and the speaker is in the dominant position – he chooses the topics and dictates the length of turns.

Read through the written version which follows and try to rewrite the phonemic transcriptions in SE. Then comment on:

1 consonantal features that are typical of this Eastern accent
2 vowel variations that are typical of this Eastern accent.

Finally, try to suggest some reasons why the speaker may have such a broad accent.

WRITTEN VERSION

Well, one day my great-nieces they came over there with their mother and course they wanted me to show them round the village. Well there wasn't much to show them. I show them round the church, round the mission room and the village green and then I I said, 'Well, we'll go and have a look round the crematorium. They've got some really nice gardens round there.' So off we went and they weren't very old. I suppose one was about three, another was about six and another about nine. Anyway, we they were lovely gardens. We enjoyed it and they had little bridges to go over the dykes with. But Charlotte there, the middle one, she thought she was cleverer than the others. She tried jumping the dyke and when I looked, she'd jumped into it. Course she come out of there with all her socks, her boots wet so I had to take her socks off and she had to walk home like that and then when we got home, well I hunted some more socks out for her and she'd got them on when her ma saw her or I wouldn't have been popular. Anyway, everything went all right and they jolly well enjoyed theirselves.

SPOKEN VERSION

1 wèll one /dæɪ/ my great /neəsəs/ they came over there with their /mɑːðə/ (.) and /kɔːs/ they wanted me to /ʃʊ əm/ round the vìllage (.) well there /wɔːnt/ much to /ʃʊ əm/ (.) I /ʃʊ əm/ round the /tʃʌtʃ/ (.) round the /mɪʃən rʊm/ and the village /greən/ (.) and ↑then↑ I I (.) I said well we'll go and have a look round the /krémə'tɔːrəm/ they've
5 got some really nice /gɑːdəns/ round ↓thére↓ (.) so /ɔːf/ we wènt (.) and they /wɔːnt veəriː/ old (.) I /spʊ/ one was bout thrée (.) /nʌðə/ was about síx (.) and /nʌðə/ one bout /nɔɪn/ (.) anyway we they were lovely /gɑːdəns/ we enjóyed it and they had little bridges to go over the /dɔɪks/ with (.) but Chárlotte there (.) the middle óne (.) she thought she was /klevrə/ than the others she tried /dʒʌmpən/ the /dɔɪk/ (1) and
10 when I looked (.) she'd jumped ↑/ɪntɪt/↑ (.) course she come out of there with all her /sáːks/ her boots wet so I /æd/ to /tæɪk/ her /saːks ɔːf/ (.) and she had to walk /əʊm/ like /æt/ (.) and then when we got /hʊm/ well I hunted some more /saːks/ out for her and she'd got them on when her /maː sɔːrə/ or I /wɔːnt əv bɪn pɒpələ/ (.) anyway /evriːθən/ went /ɔːrɔɪt/ and they jolly well enjoyed theirselves

COMMENTARY

Many of the **consonants** illustrate distinctive features of a Norfolk accent. The pronunciation of the -ing inflection as /ən/ is common and can be illustrated by examples like /dʒʌmpən/ jumping (l. 9) and /evriːθən/ everything (l. 14). Norfolk accents do not always elide the initial position /h/, and this can be seen in the speaker's inconsistent pronunciations of one word: /əʊm/ and /hʊm/ home (ll. 11, 12). He also elides the phoneme /j/ preceding the /uː/ in popular (l. 13): /pɒpjʊlə/ RP becomes /pɒpələ/ in a Norfolk accent. On several occasions the phoneme /ð/ in the initial position is elided: /æt/ *that* (l. 12) and /əm/ *them* (l. 2).

The vowels are more significantly different from RP. Many of the RP **pure vowels** are realised as longer sounds or as diphthongs: /ɒ/ becomes /ɔː/ in /wɔːnt/ *wasn't* (l. 2) and /ɔːf/ *off* (l. 11); /ʌ/ becomes /ɑː/ in /mɑːðə/ *mother* (l. 1); /ʊ/ becomes /ɔː/ in /wɔːnt/ *wouldn't* (l. 13); /iː/ becomes /eə/ in /neəsəs/ *nieces* (l. 1) and /greən/ *green* (l. 3); and /e/ becomes /eə/ in /veəriː/ (l. 6). Other variations can be identified in /tʃʌtʃ/ *church* (l. 3) where RP would use the phoneme /ɜː/ and /rʊm/ *room* (l. 3) where RP would use /uː/. Words ending with -*y* are pronounced as /iː/ in /veəriː/ *very* (l. 6).

Diphthongs are also modified: /eɪ/ becomes /æɪ/ in /dæɪ/ *day* (l. 1) and /tæɪk/ *take* (l. 11) and /aɪ/ becomes /ɔi/ in /dɔik/ *dyke* (l. 9) and /ɔːrɔɪt/ *all right* (l. 14). Some diphthongs are realised as monophthongs: /əʊ/ becomes /u/ in /ʃu/ *show* (l. 2) and /ʊ/ in /hʊm/ *home* (l. 12). Many of the vowel sounds are made with the back of the tongue raised or lowered rather than the centre or front used to articulate them in RP.

Phonological features like elision and reduction are also characteristic of Norfolk accents. Unstressed syllables at word boundaries are dropped and words are merged as in /ɪntɪt/ for *into it* (l. 10) and /wɔːnt əv/ for *wouldn't have* (l. 13). Liaison can be seen in the merging of word boundaries like /sɔːrə/ *saw her* (l. 13). Within words, unstressed syllables are elided: /kreməˈtɔːrəm/ *crematorium* (l. 4) and /klevrə/ *cleverer* (l. 9). The stress patterns within longer utterances are also distinctive in Norfolk accents – stressed syllables tend to be held (marked by double underlining on the transcript) while unstressed syllables are very short: /g̲ɑːdəns/ *gardens* (l. 5) and /nʌðə/ *another* (l. 6).

The speaker's educational and occupational background have not taken him outside the isogloss boundaries for the Eastern accent for any significant length of time, so his accent has not been modified by contact with speakers who have different pronunciation systems. The words transcribed phonemically here therefore illustrate both regional and social characteristics of his accent. Some pronunciations are idosyncratic, illustrating personal features of the speaker's accent.

While the transcript reflects the speech patterns of one individual, the pronunciation features discussed here are **characteristic** of a NORFOLK ACCENT:

1 The phoneme /h/ is sometimes dropped in the initial position.
2 The -*ing* inflection is realised as /ən/.
3 The semi-vowel or approximant /j/ is lost after consonants.
4 Words ending with -*y*, -*ey* or -*ee* are pronounced with the phoneme /iː/.
5 RP /uː/ is sometimes realised as /ʊ/.
6 Some pure vowels are longer than in RP: /ɒ/ becomes /ɔː/ and /ʌ/ becomes /ɑː/.
7 Some pure vowels are realised as diphthongs: /iː/ and /e/ become /eə/.
8 Some diphthongs are also modified: /eɪ/ becomes /æɪ/; /aɪ/ becomes /ɔɪ/; and /əʊ/ becomes /ʊ/.

Although each accent within the 'Eastern' area will be different, many will display the kinds of pronunciation features highlighted here.

The following monologue is taken from an informal conversation between two people who are well known to each other. Having been born within the sound of Bow Bells, the speaker is a true Cockney and although he has lived away from London for a number of years, his accent is still broad.

Read through the transcript below and identify the pronunciations that mark the speaker as a Cockney. The transcription is broad and phonemic symbols are used only to highlight the pronunciations that are most obviously characteristic of Cockney accents.

WRITTEN VERSION ··

I was born in Bow, you know, London. That's the East End. Er, I worked in the market as a barrow boy. That was my first job. I went to school till I was fifteen like and that was boys, a boys' school. Boxing and football and that was it and the education was er terrible, you know. I tried to join the army when I was sixteen and er left the Smoke and er joined the Welsh Regiment and they sent me up to, you know, Shrewsbury. I was up there for a bit and then I went to the Gulf. I fought there for a bit and I went to Ireland. We was the first Regiment to go into Ireland. That was sixty-eight. I had one tour in Ireland and that turned me right off. I applied to join the Air Force then. Cor, I've got a lovely history I have. In the Air Force for five years. I see a bit of the world. I went to Singapore and I went to Alaska. Absolutely superb. I mean, I'd go back there tomorrow if I could live there. Lovely place. Ah, then after my five years, I come out and believe it or not, I joined the Police Force and I was a copper for twelve years and um as I say, I enjoyed some of it. You know, it's all right, but where I come from in London, there is a thing between coppers and people. There is more of a gel, do you know. Down here, when I joined, they were trying to do away with the gelling and putting them in cars to get them away from the people. I can't hack that lark. I always still like to be hands on. I still like to see people and talk to people. So I come out in eighty-four and since then I've been trying to find some form of employment. I've done silly jobs in between, but nothing constructive.

SPOKEN VERSION ··

1   I was /bəʊn/ in /bæʊ/ (.) /jə næʊ/ (.) /lændən/ (.) that's the East /éɪnd/ (.) er I worked
    in the ma̋rket as a /bærə bóy/ (.) that was my first job (.) I /wen/ to /skuːʊ/ til I was
    fifteen /lɔɪk/ and that was boys (.) /əʊ bɔɪskuːʊ/ (.) /boksɪn/ and /fʊtbəʊ/ and that
    was it (.) and the education was er /terɪbʊ/ (.) /jə næʊ/ (.) I tried to join the army when
5   I was síxteen (.) and er left the /smæʊk/ and er joined the /weʊʃ/ Regiment and they
    sent /mɪ/ up to /jə næʊ/ Shrewsbury (.) I was up there for a /bɪ/ and then I went
    to the /gæʊf/ (.) I /fəʊt/ there for a /bɪ/ and I /wen/ to Ireland (.) we was the first
    Regiment to go into Ireland (.) that was ooo /síxtiː æɪʔ/ (.) I had one tour in Ireland and
    that turned me right /ɔːf/ (.) I applied to join the /eə fəʊs/ thén (.) cor I've got a /lævliː
10 ɪstriː/ I /əv/ (.) in the /eə fəʊs/ for /fɒɪv jɜːs/ (.) I see a bit /əvə/ world (.) I /wen/ to
    Singapore and I /wen/ to Aláska (.) absolutely superb (.) I mean (.) I'd go back there
    /təmɒrə/ if I could live there (.) /lævliː/ place (.) ahh (.) then after /mɪ fɒɪv jɜːs/ I come
    /aːt/ and believe it or not I joined the police /fəʊs/ and I was a /kɒpə/ for twelve /jɜːs/
    and um as I say I enjoyed ↑some↑ of it (.) /jə næʊ/ it's /əʊrɒɪt/ but where I come from
15 in /lændən/ (.) there is /ə/ thing between /kɒpəs/ and /pʰiːpʊ/ (.) there is more of a
    /dʒəʊ dʒənæʊ/ (.) down /ɪə/ when I joined they were /trɒɪɪn/ to do /əwæɪ/ with the
    /dʒelɪn/ and /pʊtɪn əm/ in cars to get them /əwæɪ/ from the /pʰiːpʊ/ (.) I can't /ek̪/

that lark (.) I /əʊwæɪs/ still /lɒɪk/ to be /ɛ̠nds/ on (.) I still /lɔɪk/ to see /pʰiːpʊ/ and talk to /pʰiːpʊ/ (.) so I come /aːʔ/ in /æɪʔi: fʊə/ (.) and since then I've been /trɒɪɪn/
20 to find some form of employment (.) I've done silly jobs in between but /nʌfɪŋk/ constructive

---

COMMENTARY

The **consonant** variations are distinctive. The phoneme /h/ in the initial position is elided on almost all occasions: /ɪstriː/ *history* (l. 10), /əv/ *have* (l. 10), /ɛ̠k/ *hack* (l. 17) and /ɛ̠nds/ *hands* (l. 18). The realisation of the *-ing* inflection as /ɪn/ is also common: /bɒksɪn/ *boxing* (l. 3), /dʒelɪn/ *gelling* (l. 17) and /pʊtɪn/ *putting* (l. 17). The pronunciation of the suffix at the end of *nothing* is also typical of a Cockney accent: /nʌfɪŋk/ (l. 20). Glottal stops can be seen in /æɪʔ/ *eight* (l. 8) and /aːʔ/ *out* (l. 19) and the lack of distinction between /θ/ and /f/ is illustrated in /nʌfɪŋk/ (l. 20). The heavy aspiration of /p/ associated with Cockney accents occurs in the words /pʰiːpʊ/ *people* (l. 15). There are also many examples of the ways in which Cockney accents pronounce /l/ in different positions within a word. It is realised as a vowel: after a vowel – /skuːʊ/ *school* (l. 2), /əʊwæɪs/ *always* (l. 18) and /dʒəʊ/ *gel* (l. 16); before a consonant – /weʊʃ/ *Welsh* (l. 5); and when it occurs in a syllable on its own – /terɪbʊ/ *terrible* (l. 4). After /ɔː/ in the final position, however, /l/ is elided: /fʊtbəʊ/ *football* (l. 3), /əʊ/ *all* (l. 3) and /əʊrɒɪt/ *all right* (l. 14).

As in many other regional accents, Cockney accents pronounce *-y, -ey* and *-ee* at the end of words as /iː/: /sɪktiː/ *sixty* (l. 8) and /æɪʔiː/ *eighty* (l. 19). Other vowels, however, are more distinctive. The **pure vowels** of RP are significantly different: /æ/ is realised as /ɛ̠/ in /ɛ̠nds/ *hands* (l. 18) and /ɛ̠k/ *hack* (l. 17); /ʌ/ is realised as /æ/ in /lævliː/ *lovely* (l. 9), /lændən/ *London* (l. 1) and /gæʊf/ *Gulf* (l. 7). Some pure vowels are articulated as diphthongs: /e/ as /eɪ/ in /eɪnd/ *end* (l. 1); /ɔː/ as /əʊ/ in /bəʊn/ *born* (l. 1), /fəʊs/ *Force* (l. 10) and /fəʊt/ *fought* (l. 7), and /ɔː/ in the final position as /ʊə/ in /fʊə/ *four* (l. 19).

Diphthongs also change their sounds – they tend to be wider than in RP. In Cockney accents, /eɪ/ becomes /æɪ/ in /əwæɪ/ *away* (l. 16); /əʊ/ becomes /æʊ/ in /bæʊ/ *Bow* (l. 1), /næʊ/ *know* (l. 6) and /smæʊk/ *Smoke* (l. 5); /aɪ/ becomes /ɒɪ/ in /fɒɪv/ *five* (l. 12) and /trɒɪɪn/ *trying* (l. 19); and /aʊ/ becomes /aː/ in /aːt/ *out* (l. 13). Two other distinctive vowel sounds here occur in /jɜːs/ *years* (l. 13) for RP /jɪəs/ and /ɔːf/ *off* (l. 9) for RP /ɒf/.

Many other variations occur in the pronunciation patterns illustrated by this speaker. These can often be linked to features of **informal spoken language**. The replacement of unstressed vowels with a schwa is common: /bærə/ *barrow* (l. 2), /əvə/ *of the* (l. 10), /təmɒrə/ *tomorrow* (l. 12) and /kɒpə/ *copper* (l. 13). Equally, the elision of final consonants is typical of conversation: /bɪ/ *bit* (l. 7) and /wen/ *went* (l. 11). In informal speech, /ð/ is sometimes elided when it appears in the initial position: /əm/ *them* (l. 17). Vowels are often shortened in grammatical function words like /mɪ/ *me* (l. 12) and /jə/ *you* (l. 1). Finally, word boundaries are sometimes blurred: /bɔɪskuːʊ/ *boys' school* (l. 3) and /dʒənæʊ/ *do you know* (l. 16).

While the transcript reflects the speech patterns of one individual, the pronunciation features discussed here are **characteristic** of a Cockney accent:

1 The phoneme /h/ is often elided.
2 The -*ing* inflection is realised as /ɪn/, while words ending with the suffix -*thing* are pronounced /ɪŋk/.
3 Glottal stops are common.
4 The distinction between /θ/ and /f/ is often lost. (A similar process occurs with /ð/ and /v/.)
5 The phoneme /ð/ in the initial position is elided or may be pronounced as /d/.
6 The phoneme /p/ is heavily aspirated in the initial position.
7 The phoneme /l/ is replaced in a distinctive way: in the final position, after a vowel, before a consonant in the same syllable or in a discrete syllable, it is realised as a vowel, /ʊ/; when /l/ follows /ɔː/, it is elided.
8 Words ending in -*y*, -*ey*, -*ee* tend to be realised with /iː/.
9 Some pure vowels sound slightly different to RP: /æ/ becomes /ę/; /e/ becomes /eɪ/; /ʌ/ becomes /æ/.
10 Some diphthongs are wider: /eɪ/ becomes /æɪ/; /əʊ/ becomes /æʊ/; /aɪ/ becomes /ɒɪ/; /aʊ/ becomes /aː/.
11 When /ɔː/ is in the final position, it is realised as /ʊə/; in a non-final position, it becomes /əʊ/.

Although the Cockney accent is distinctive and other Southern accents differ in many ways, some of the pronunciation features highlighted here are found in other 'Southern' accents.

ACTIVITY 8.5

Read the following oral narrative about a local gardening competition which is held just outside Cardiff. The speaker has lived in the area all his life and his accent, although not broad, displays many of the accent features associated with South Wales. The transcription is broad and marks only the pronunciations that differ significantly from RP.

Having read the transcription, rewrite the words transcribed phonemically and try to assess the ways in which they differ from RP. Then comment on:

1 the distinctive consonantal features of this Welsh accent
2 the distinctive vowel sounds of this Welsh accent

WRITTEN VERSION

Who started the garden competition? I'm not sure. It may have been requested via the Taffs Well Horticultural Society, I'm not sure, and then run by the Taff Ely Council, broken up into various areas: Taffs Well, Nantgarw, Ty Rhiw. The judges. In total, I'd say there's about ten judges who er try to er judge an area that they don't actually come from. Me and er myself and Dave judge Taffs Well because we're from Gwaelod-y-Garth, you see and er various people from Taffs Well will judge Nantgarw and so forth and you're judging gardens against hanging baskets. It's a difficult one that. I always maintain that particularly if you've got a corner plot, nicely set, you're way in front of something that's got a small frontage or even no frontage. So that the wording of the actual schedule regarding garden or sort of hanging baskets, you know, must be really a separate thing. We have had trouble with this. It's a er er. It's difficult to define um and put down in words erm. For a judge to judge a garden when you go along and see a so-called garden is very limited to the fact that it's just er out on the pavement with no garden at all with a few containers and hanging and climbing plants which is really unfair to that to them people who have put a lot of effort in but are very limited at the end of the day.

1 who /staːtɪd/ the /gaːdən/ cómpetition (.) I'm not /ʃʊwə/ (.) it /mę æv/ been /rəkwęstɪd/
   via the Taffs Well /hɔːtɪkəltrəl/ Society (.) I'm not /ʃʊwə/ (.) and then run by the Taff
   Ely Council (.) /brɔːkən/ up into /vęərɪəs ęərɪəs/ (.) Taffs Wéll (.) Nantgárw (.) Ty Rȟíw
   (3) the judges (.) in /tɔːtəl/ I'd say there's about (3) could be about °h tén judges (1)
5 who er /traɪ/ to er judge an /ęərɪə/ that they /dɔːnt/ actually come fróm (.) me and
   er (.) myself and (.) Dave judge Taffs Well because we're from Gwaelod-y-Garth you
   sée (2) and er /vęərɪəs/ people from Taffs Well will judge (.) Nantgárw and /sɔː/ forth
   (2) and you're judging /gaːdəns/ against /æŋgɪn baːskɪts/ (.) /ɪs/ a difficult one /æt/
   (.) I always main<u>tain</u> that (.) /paːtɪkuliː/ if you've got a <u>corner plot</u> (.) /naɪsliː/ <u>set</u> (.)
10 you're way in <u>front</u> of /sʌmθɪn/ that's got a small frontage (1) or even /nɔː/ fróntage
   (.) so that the /wȝːdɪn/ of the actual /ʃeduːl/ (.) /regaːdɪn gaːdən/ or sort of (.) /æŋgɪn
   baːskɪts/ (.) you /nɔː/ (.) must be /riːliː/ (.) a separate thing (2) we have /æd/ trouble
   with /ɪs/ (.) /ɪs/ a er er (.) /ɪs/ difficult to de<u>fine</u> (.) um and put down in /wȝːdz/ erm (.)
   for a judge to judge (.) a /gaːdən/ (.) and when you /gɔː/ along and see a /sɔː/ called
15 /gaːdən/ (.) is very <u>lim</u>ited (1) to the fact that it's just er out (.) <u>on</u> the /pęvmənt/ with
   /nɔː gaːdən/ at all (.) with a few containers and /æŋgɪn/ and climbing ↑/plænts/↑ (.)
   which is /riːliː/ unfair to that (.) to them people (.) who've put a /lɒrə/ effort in but are
   very limited at the end of the day

COMMENTARY

Because the discourse takes place in a relaxed environment, many of the features associated with informal conversation are present. The liaison that occurs in the phrase /lɒrə/ *lot of* (l. 17) is an example of a **segmental phonological feature** which alters the pronunciation of words at boundary points. This kind of word linkage is common to many accents and does not illustrate a characteristic of a Welsh accent. Similarly, the elided /ð/ in /ɪs/ *this* (l. 13) and /æt/ *that* (l. 8) and the elided /t/ in /ɪs/ *it's* (l. 8) are common to many accents.

Other **consonantal** features can, however, be described as typically Welsh. The dropped /h/, for instance, is common: /æv/ *have* (l. 1), /æd/ *had* (l. 12) and /æŋgɪn/ *hanging* (l. 8). The speaker does not elide /h/ consistently – it is usually only elided when it occurs in an unstressed position. The pronunciation of the inflection *-ing* is consistently /ɪn/: /sʌmθɪn/ *something* (l. 10), /æŋgɪn/ *hanging* (l. 8) and /wȝːdɪn/ *wording* (l. 11). The /j/ phoneme that RP realises in front of /uː/ is absent: /paːtɪkuliː/ *particularly* (l. 9).

As would be expected, the most significant variations from RP come in the **vowels**. Words ending with *-y* are pronounced as /iː/: /riːliː/ *really* (l. 17) and /naɪsliː/ *nicely* (l. 9). Many of the RP **pure vowels** are produced with the tongue raised so that the sound is closer: /ɑː/ becomes /aː/ in /staːtɪd/ *started* (l. 1), /gaːdən/ *garden* (l. 1), /baːskɪts/ *baskets* (l. 8) and /regaːdɪn/ *regarding* (l. 11); /e/ in /rəkwęstɪd/ *requested* (l. 1); and /ȝː/ in /wȝːdz/ *words* (l. 13). The long RP /ɑː/ is shortened to /æ/ in words like /plænts/ *plants* (l. 16) and /ʌ/ is pronounced as /ə/ in words like /hɔːtɪkəltrəl/ *Horticultural* (l. 2).

Diphthongs are usually either narrow or are realised as monophthongs. Sounds like /eɪ/ in /me̝/ *may* (l. 1) and /pe̝vmənt/ *pavement* (l. 15), /eə/ in /ve̝ərɪəs/ *various* (l. 3) and /e̝ərɪəs/ *areas* (l. 3) and /aɪ/ in /tra̝ɪ/ *try* (l. 5) and /na̝ɪsliː/ *nicely* (l. 9) are all closer than the equivalent RP vowel sounds. The RP diphthong /əʊ/ becomes a monopthong /ɔː/ in words like /brɔːkən/ *broken* (l. 3), /tɔːtəl/ *total* (l. 4), /dɔːnt/ *don't* (l. 5), /sɔː/ *so* (l. 7), /nɔː/ *no* (l. 10) and *know* (l. 12), and /gɔː/ *go* (l. 14). Another distinctive feature of a Welsh accent is the broadening of diphthongs so that the two sounds are quite distinct: /ʃʊwə/ for RP /ʃʊə/ *sure* (l. 1).

The most distinctive features of the speaker's accent can be seen in the close pure vowel sounds, the narrow diphthongs, the dropped /h/ in unstressed positions and the pronunciation of *-ing* and /juː/. The frequency with which utterances end with a rising tone is also characteristic of Welsh accents. Although not illustrated in this transcript, the plosives /d/, /b/ and /g/ are aspirated in the initial position, while /p/, /t/ and /k/ are aspirated in all positions /pʰɒpʰ/ *pop*).

While the transcript reflects the speech patterns of one individual, the pronunciation features discussed here are **characteristic** of a **CARDIFF ACCENT**:

1 The phoneme /h/ is dropped.
2 The *-ing* inflection is realised as /ɪn/.
3 The semi-vowel or approximant /j/ is dropped before /uː/; in some words it is replaced by /ɪu/.
4 Words ending in *-y*, *-ey* and *-ee* are realised with /iː/.
5 The phoneme /ʌ/ is pronounced as /ə/.
6 The phonemes /æ/ and /ɑː/ are distinguished by length rather than height; /ɑː/ is less open than in RP, and is realised as /aː/.
7 The phonemes /ɜː/ and /e/ are closer than in RP.
8 Many diphthongs like /eɪ/, /eə/ and /aɪ/ are narrow (marked ̝ on the transcript); others are realised as monopthongs: /əʊ/ becomes /ɔː/ and /eɪ/ becomes /e/.
9 Some diphthongs are broadened so that the two sounds of the RP glide are quite distinct: /ʊə/ becomes /ʊwə/ and /ɪə/ becomes /ɪjə/.

Although the Cardiff accent is quite different both from the South Wales valleys and from North Wales accents, some of the pronunciation features highlighted here will be found in other Welsh accents.

Summary

Although the guidelines in this section cover the distinctive accent features of particular accents, many speakers will not exhibit all the characteristics. When assessing **why a speaker does not conform to expected accentual patterns**, linguists have to consider the following possibilities:

1 speakers may have lost a broad accent by moving away from the area in which they grew up
2 the speakers' educational experience may have made their accent more like RP (modified RP)
3 the context in which the speech is taking place may be formal and speakers may be consciously or subconsciously modifying their speech (convergence)

4 the speakers' occupations may have required them to move into a new regional or social context, and they may therefore be adopting the speech behaviour associated with their new speech community

5 travel and listening to the media may have modified strong accentual features.

If an accent is very **broad**, linguists need to consider the following possibilities:

1 speakers may have lived in one particular area for a long time with little contact with other speech communities

2 speakers may be old and their accents may retain features that are not as common among the younger people of the speech community

3 speakers may be purposefully adopting broad accentual features either to identify themselves with a particular group or to consciously alienate other speakers who do not speak in the same way (divergence)

4 speakers may belong to a social group that is characterised by a broad accent or may have chosen to leave education early.

The **study of accents** is very complex. Whole books have been written on individual accents and linguists spend years researching single areas. The summaries here deal only with very basic differences between the main accents of the United Kingdom, acting as an introduction to characteristic features of regional pronunciation.

8.3 Dialect

A **DIALECT** is a subdivision of a language that is identified by variations in **lexis** and **grammar**. The different dialects of English may vary **socially** or **regionally**, just as accents do, but despite variations they will remain largely comprehensible to other English speakers.

English is made up of a number of regional dialects that correspond more or less to the broad regions established in Figure 8.1. Linguists can identify the main characteristics of different regions, and the isoglosses establish boundaries which group together non-standard dialect forms with similar distinctive linguistic features. Inevitably, there are some overlaps – although non-standard lexis tends to be located in specific regions, non-standard grammatical features are similar across boundaries.

Regional variation can be seen in the dialectal differences between town and country. In rural areas, non-standard dialects are often stronger because the arrival of newcomers who use different dialects is less common. Urban areas, on the other hand, are far more likely to contain a linguistic mix. When people move round the country for employment, they introduce new dialects into the local speech community. Equally, **age** can affect the kind of dialect used. The broadest non-standard dialects tend to be spoken by older members of a community who have had little prolonged contact with other dialect users. Younger people, however, are exposed to a wider range of language forms, particularly Standard English. They are therefore less likely to speak the broad non-standard dialects of their grandparents. Instead they will use a dialect form which is modified in the direction of Standard English.

Some linguists believe that non-standard dialects are dying out. This may be the case with some of the older rural forms of English, but many new forms of English are appearing to replace them. This is particularly true of urban areas. The linguistic diversity of cities provides the right conditions for the emergence of new dialects, clearly illustrating that language is always in flux and that change is inevitable.

As urban centres grow and as educational and occupational opportunities increase the possibility of social mobility, non-standard dialects can be defined on a **social** rather than a regional basis. The use of particular words and grammatical structures can be linked directly to specific social groups or classes. For instance, people with broad accents are more likely to use the third person singular present tense inflection in all parts of the verb: *I goes* and *we goes*; while people with modified accents are more likely to use a standard agreement of subject and verb: *I go* and *we go*. This kind of differentiation in use is clearly linked to educational and occupational background – the longer people stay in formal education, the more likely they are to use Standard English.

Although non-standard dialects are most commonly associated with spoken language, non-standard usage of words and grammatical structures can also be seen in **written work**. In formal writing most people use Standard English rather than a non-standard dialect because it is the language form used and taught in education. Informal writing may contain non-standard dialect features because it is the written variety that most closely approximates the spoken word. Novelists or poets may also choose to write in non-standard English in order to create certain effects.

It is important to remember that Standard English is one of the many dialectal forms of English. As the dominant variety it is used for writing, but its choice as the prestige form is based on social rather than linguistic judgements.

Lexical variation

Within different geographical regions, words often develop that are unique to a certain community. These may be incomprehensible to people from another area, although when heard in context other English speakers will probably be able to work out an approximate meaning:

nobby	smart, brilliant, really good	cutch	cuddle	(South Wales dialect)
loke	path leading up to a house	dyke	ditch	(Norfolk dialect)

Some words, like *borrow/lend* and *teach/learn*, are used non-standardly in more than one dialect. Because non-standard dialects are predominantly spoken, colloquial words and collocations are common: *and all, like I said, and that, and everything, cos*.

It is useful to distinguish between non-standard dialect words and informal conversational words and phrases: the latter tend to be used across isogloss boundaries, while the former can usually be quite clearly linked to a particular region.

Grammatical variation

Many of the non-standard grammar features that can be identified occur across boundaries – verbs and pronouns are particularly likely to vary from the standard. The following list summarises the main variations that occur in non-standard English dialects (N-SE). Where appropriate, reference is made to the specific regions associated with a feature.

Nouns

The plural of a noun is usually formed by adding the inflection -s. However, in many phrases that contain a noun of measurement and a cardinal number, no plural inflection is used. This occurs in many regional dialects: *three mile* and *six pound*. In some dialects, a few plurals are still formed using the archaic inflection /n/: *housen*. The /n/ inflection used in this dialectal form accounts for the plural *children*, which is one of the few remaining irregular plurals in SE. In Middle English the singular noun was *childre*, which was made plural with the addition of the /n/ inflection. In some regional non-standard dialect forms, the archaic *childer* is still used.

Adjectives

Some adjectives in SE end in -*en* (*golden, silken, wooden* and *olden*) – these are all that remain of the OE system of case inflections. A few regional dialects in the South-West, however, still use archaic inflections on some adjectives: *papern*. In SE, the comparative and superlative are formed either by adding the suffixes -*er*/-*est* to an adjective, or by using *more/most* before an adjective. In many non-standard regional dialects, both forms are used simultaneously: *the more fiercer dog* and *the most coldest wind*.

Adverbs

In many non-standard dialects, the adverb -*ly* inflection is not used. This means that regular adverbs and adjectives have exactly the same form – they can, however, still be distinguished by their position and function.

		FUNCTION
^m the *slow* bus <small>Adj</small>	^A the bus drove *slow* [*slowly* SE] <small>Adv</small>	 FORM

Prepositions

Prepositions of place tend to vary from the standard forms in many of the regional dialects: *I went up town* (*to* SE); *It's along of a mile away* (*about* SE). In some cases, usage is so widespread that the non-standard versions are now often described as informal SE: *We got off of the bus* (*off* SE); *I got it off Julie* (*from* SE). In Northern dialects, *till* is used for SE *to* – for example, *she's going till the theatre*. In the South-West, the preposition *to* which accompanies verbs in the infinitive form often appears as *for to* – for example, *tell me how for to do it*. In some areas, the *to* is elided – for example, *tell me how for do it*. There are a few phrases in which the *for ... to* structure is still used in SE: for example, *for me to understand* and *the idea is for us all to get involved*. In dialects, this construction occurs more extensively in places where it is no longer used in SE.

Conjunctions

In Northern dialects *while* is used for SE *until* (*I'm going while dinnertime*) and *without* is used for SE *unless* (*you can't go without you tidy up*).

Pronouns

Pronominal forms vary significantly in non-standard dialects. **Subject** and **object personal pronouns** are often interchangeable, particularly in the dialects of the South-West: *she went out, didn't her; have you seen she?* This usage seems to be governed by rules: the object pronoun tends to be used in the subject site only when there is no emphasis; the subject pronoun is used in the object site when emphasis is needed. The pronouns that occur in unstressed positions often take the following weak forms: *ee* (*you*), *er* (*he* in the subject site), *n* (*he* in the object site), *er* (*she*), *us* (*we*) and *m* (*they*). In Northern dialects, the first person plural object pronoun is used for both singular and plural references: *give it us*. This usage occurs in colloquial Standard English in some collocations like *give us a kiss* or *do us a favour*. Informal (*thou, thee*) and formal (*you*) second person pronouns are widespread. The possessive pronouns *hisn, hern, ourn, yourn* and *theirn* are also common except in the North.

In SE, **reflexive pronouns** are formed by adding *-self* or *-selves* to either the personal object pronouns or to possessive determiners.

Object pronouns	Possessive determiners	Reflexive pronouns
me	my	*my*self
you	your	*your*self *your*selves
him	his	*him*self
her	her	*her*self
it	its	*it*self
us	our	*our*selves
them	their	*them*selves

SE itself is not consistent and many dialects use non-standard forms that actually standardise the system – they base all the forms on the **possessive determiner** + *-self/-selves* structure: *hisself, itsself* and *theirselves*.

Relative pronouns are frequently non-standard in regional dialects. Where SE uses *who* or *that* for people and *which* or *that* for non-human things, non-standard dialects will often use *which* for people and *what* for both human and non-human things: *the man which I described is here* and *the house what I live in is big*.

Demonstrative pronouns are also frequently non-standard: where SE uses *those*, many regional dialects will use *them* or *they* – for instance, *them horses are wild* or *they horses are wild*. In Northern dialects, the demonstrative *yon* is added to the SE *this, that, these* and *those*. It is used to refer to things that are more distant than *that* – for example, *yon field used to be full of horses*.

Verbs

Verbs are the most complicated part of a language system, and in non-standard dialects they are frequently different from the standard forms. In the **present tense** many regional dialects standardise the patterns of SE. Eastern dialects tend to drop the third person singular -s inflection: *he walk*. Dialects of the North, South-West and Wales, however, tend to add the -s inflection throughout: *I walks, you walks, we walks* and *they walks*.

The simple present tense can be used to refer to events in the past – this is called the HISTORIC PRESENT:

> Well, they're in the room before you know it and he looks round and laughs. They just turn and leave – he's not sure what to do, so he carries on as though it's all fine.

This form of the present tense is not common, although it can be used to make a story more exciting. In Scottish and Irish dialects, the present historic can be recognised by the -s inflection used in the first and second persons and the third person plural: *they thinks hard and decides to go*.

Past tense verbs are even more likely to be non-standard in dialects. Many verbs are irregular in SE and dialects often try to standardise the patterns. The verb *to be* in the past tense, for instance, may be conjugated with *was* or *were* for all persons. The regular past tense inflection -ed is often added to irregular verbs: *seed*; *doed*. Where verbs have two separate forms for the **simple past tense** and the **past participle**, regional dialects often use only one form:

Base form	Simple past (SE)	Past participle	Dialect form
see	saw	seen	*seen* (simple past)
come	came	come	*come* (simple past)
fall	fell	fallen	*fell* (past participle)
swim	swam	swum	*swam* (past participle)

Sometimes, the vowel change occurring in the past participle of an irregular verb in SE is used alongside the regular past tense suffix in the simple past: *swolled* for *swelled* (past participle *swollen*).

Present participles are often used in an archaic form in which the prefix *a-* is added, particularly in the Midlands and in Eastern dialects: *a-going, a-running, a-sewing*. Where SE uses the **present** and **past progressive**, Northern dialects often replace the present participle with the past participle: *I was sat there like an idiot*. In SE, the verb *to do* can be used as a lexical verb or as a dummy auxiliary in interrogatives, negatives and emphatic utterances. In South-Western and Welsh dialects, it is often used with another verb in wider contexts: *I do go every night* or *we d'see him regular*.

Negatives

MULTIPLE NEGATIVES are used in many dialects. Although now considered non-standard, in older forms of English, multiple negatives were used to create emphasis. The most commonly occurring form is the double negative: *I haven't done nothing* or *you didn't bring no presents*. Forms of the negative vary from dialect to dialect. The negative verb *ain't*, however, is very common. It can be used for the negative of the first person singular and plural and the third person singular of the verb *to be*, and as the negative of the auxiliary *to have*: *I ain't happy* for SE *am not*; *he ain't buying a shirt* for SE *is not*; *you ain't got an apple* for SE *have not*. Another common dialect feature can be seen in the use of *never* to refer to a single occasion, where SE would use *didn't*: *she never came last night*. Other variations are more closely linked to specific regions – for example, *amn't* is the Midlands dialect for *am not*. The use of *no* or *nae* instead of *not* to construct the negative is a distinctive feature of Scottish dialects: *he's no coming*.

ACTIVITY 8.6

Reread the transcripts in Activities 8.1–8.5 and identify any examples of non-standard grammar. Group similar features together and try to categorise the grammatical variations you find.

COMMENTARY

The following non-standard grammatical features are illustrated in the transcripts:

1 non-standard use of **prepositions**: *spuds off the farmer* (Activity 8.1: l. 17) for SE *from*
2 non-standard use of **pronouns**: *theirselves* (Activity 8.3: l. 14) for SE *themselves*; *them people* (Activity 8.5: l. 17) for SE *those*
3 non-standard **agreement of subject and verb**: *there was* (Activity 8.1: l. 38) for SE *were*; *we was* (Activity 8.4: l. 7) for SE *were*
4 non-standard **past tense verbs**: *she come* (Activity 8.3: l. 10) for SE *came*; *I see* (Activity 8.4: l. 10) for SE *saw*.

All the examples here are typical dialect features which occur frequently in many regional dialects. The non-standard usage can be classified by focusing on variations from SE in the following areas: prepositions, pronouns and verbs.

ACTIVITY 8.7

Read through the transcript of a Cockney accent below and identify any non-standard usage.

1 I done all that (.) I build it (.) that cost me one hundred and fifty-eight pound (.) well when we first come here (.) it was a rock garden come say about six foot to the window (.) just all a mass of rocks and rubble so what we done (.) I dug it back and (.) we done the plans here (.) we looked out the window and thought do this do that (.) you
5 know (.) and as I dug it it just formed itself (.) you know (.) it's er (.) it holds it back (.) and them two beds here are full of rocks (.) there's about sort of a foot of earth in there but (.) the rest of it's all unbelievable (.) I mean I didn't put no foundations down under them stones because it's so solid (.) I just put sand down and put other things down on top of them (.) and it's just stayed there (.) it's been done what four or five
10 years (.) hasn't moved

Once again the most significantly non-standard forms are the **verbs**. The **simple past tense** forms of the irregular verbs *do* (l. 1), *build* (l. 1) and *come* (l. 2) are simplified.

Infinitive	Past tense (SE)	Past participle (SE)
do	did	done
build	built	built
come	came	come

In the first and third examples, the speaker uses the irregular past participle form for the simple past tense, thereby reducing three verb forms to two. In the second example, he uses the verb in its base form rather than using the irregular SE *built* – the two forms, however, are very close and the speaker is merely replacing the voiceless /t/ with a voiced /d/.

Other typical non-standard grammar can be seen in:

▸ the use of a **double negative**: *didn't put no foundations* (l. 7)
▸ the **absence of a plural on a noun following a cardinal number**: *one hundred and fifty-eight pound* (l. 1) and *six foot* (l. 2)
▸ the use of an **object pronoun** where SE would use a demonstrative determiner *those*: *them two beds* (l. 6) and *them stones* (l. 8)
▸ the replacement of the **prepositional phrase** *out of* with an adverb: *looked out the window* (l. 4).

8.4 Accent and dialect levelling

A diachronic study of the English language shows its changes over time, but it is also possible to identify changes that are taking place now. As society changes to mirror developments in technology, politics, morals and culture, so language is adapted to meet the new demands placed upon it. Some people dislike the idea of linguistic change – they see new forms of English as lazy and inaccurate. Others, however, see them as part of an inevitable process in which only the useful modifications will survive.

Because people are now far more likely to move around the country, some linguists believe that the traditional regional accents and dialects are dying out. They believe that older forms of English are modified by contact with the language of newcomers – different accents and dialects then emerge within the local speech community. At first, old and new forms will exist alongside each other, but as the young people who use the new forms themselves have children, the more traditional accents and dialects will slowly disappear. Because of contact with other forms of English, regional accents and dialects lose their distinctive features and become more similar. Linguists call this process LEVELLING.

Some people change their social status as well as their regional base, and this too affects the nature of English. The appearance of 'social' rather than regional accents and dialects is a sign of the way in which people see themselves in terms of their language. By choosing a social rather than a regional form of English, speakers are making a statement about their cultural and political identity rather than their regional background.

The emergence of new or adapted forms of English is linguistically important because of the social changes the process reflects. People are making choices consciously or subconsciously and the results of this are seen in the accents and dialects they use.

An example of the natural evolution of accents and dialects can be seen in the emergence of **ESTUARY ENGLISH**, also called the **NEW LONDON VOICE**. It has a high profile because of the number of radio and television personalities who use it – for instance, Ben Elton, Paul Merton and Jonathan Ross. Some people even noted features characteristic of Estuary English in the speech of Tony Blair, Prime Minister of the Labour government, 1997–2007. It was first associated with speakers on the banks of the Thames in Essex and in North Kent, but because of the influence of the media it has now spread much further afield. The following characteristic features can be identified:

- /t/ in the medial position is elided: /gæwɪk/ *Gatwick*
- as in the Southern accent, /l/ is often pronounced as /ʊ/: /bɪʊd/ *build*
- /p/ and /k/ sounds in the final position are elided: /pɒ/ *pop* and /stɪ/ *stick*
- it has a distinctive vocabulary with many Americanisms: *cheers, basically, guesstimate.*

It is sometimes described as **HIGH COCKNEY**: although both non-standard dialects are similar, many of the traditional 'low prestige' features associated with a Cockney accent have been dropped – the glottal stop for the medial position /t/ is rare; /f/ does not replace /θ/; and /v/ does not replace /ð/.

Estuary English is a social rather than a regional dialect, mirroring the supposed reduction in differences between social classes. It is used by young people who feel that it is a form of English with street credibility. The middle classes use it to avoid being marked out as 'posh'; Southerners who are upwardly mobile adopt it, losing the harshest features of Southern accents in order to move closer to 'prestige' forms of English; and it is used in the City instead of RP which is seen as alienating many people. It is often called a **CLASSLESS DIALECT** because its appeal seems to be so wide.

Although some linguists do not believe that Estuary English is a new phenomenon, others see its emergence as an important development in the history of the English language. They believe that this form of the language could replace RP as the dominant accent and dialect for the middle classes around London, changing the language map of Southern England quite dramatically.

8.5 What to look for in British accents and dialects

The following checklist can be used to identify key features in examples of different accents and dialects. You will not find all of the features in every transcript, but the list can be used as a guide. The points made are general so discussion of specific examples will need to be adapted to take account of the specific context, the participants and the purpose of the communication. Remember that you need to evaluate the effect of the features you identify, exploring what they tell you about the personal, social and geographical contexts.

The following are helpful questions to ask.

Register

1 What is the **mode**?
   - written or spoken?
2 What is the **manner**?
   - formal or informal relationship between participants?
   - socially equal or unequal participants?
   - familiar or unfamiliar participants?
3 What is the **field**?
   - linked to subject matter?
   - linked to social standing and educational background of the participants?
   - linked to the region?

Accent

1 Are any of the **consonants** different from RP?
   - dropped phoneme /h/ in the initial position?
   - pronunciation of the phoneme /ŋ/?
   - articulation of the phoneme /j/ before the pure vowel /uː/?
   - post-vocalic /r/?
   - glottal stops?
   - distinctive realisation of the phoneme /l/?
   - aspirated consonants?
   - consonants replaced with other phonemes?
2 Are any of the **vowels** different from RP?
   - -y, -ey and -ee realised as /iː/ or /ɪ/?
   - /æ/ and /ɑː/ distributed as in RP?
   - both /ʌ/ and /ʊ/ used in the phoneme inventory?
   - pure vowels closer than in RP?
   - diphthongs narrower or wider than in RP?
   - distinctive features associated with a particular region?
3 Do the consonant and vowel variants suggest the speaker has an **accent**?
   - regional, social or personal?
   - broad or modified?
4 Is there any evidence of **convergence** or **divergence**?
5 Are there any examples of **hypercorrection**?

Lexis

1 Are there any words that are unique to a **particular region**?
2 Are any of the words **archaic**?
3 Are any words **idiosyncratic**, reflecting an individual view of the world rather than one influenced by a particular region or social group?
4 Are there any examples of **colloquial** words and phrases that cross **isogloss** boundaries?

Grammar

1 Are any **open-class words** other than the verbs non-standard?
- noun plurals with no -s inflection after a cardinal number or with an archaic -n suffix?
- adjectives marked by archaic inflections or double comparatives and super-latives?
- adverb inflections dropped?

2 Are the **verbs** non-standard?
- third person singular -s inflection?
- simple past tense regular and irregular forms?
- present and past participles?
- dummy auxiliary *do*?

3 Are any **closed-class words** other than the pronouns non-standard?
- prepositions or conjunctions?

4 Are the **pronouns** non-standard?
- archaic forms like *thee* and *thou*?
- interchangeable subject and object pronouns?
- reflexive pronouns?
- relative pronouns?
- demonstrative pronouns?

5 Are the **negatives** non-standard?
- multiple negatives?
- use of *ain't*?
- references to a single occasion using *never*?
- distinctive regional forms?

Summary

Accents and **dialects** reveal something about a speaker's **social, regional** and **personal identity**. They may be consciously or subconsciously modified and most speakers will STYLE-SHIFT in order to meet the requirements of each speech encounter.

Speakers need to make linguistic choices about the most appropriate kind of English for each speech encounter. If they have a **wide repertoire** they will be more able to move between standard and non-standard accents and dialects.

Variations from the norms of SE and RP should not automatically be seen as 'bad' or 'incorrect'. Accents and dialects are not a lazy way of speaking, but are varieties in their own right with **distinctive rules** and **structural systems**.

Few people now remain in one speech community all their lives and we all hear a wide range of accents and dialects on the radio and television. This means that most speech communities show evidence of **dialect contact** – the result of this is **dialect levelling**, and a reduction in the differences between non-standard and standard forms of English.

Chapter 9

Child language –
learning to talk

9.1 The nature of child language acquisition

Just as children develop physically at more or less the same rate, so all normal children develop language at about the same time. Because of this parallel between physical and mental growth, it could be suggested that **LANGUAGE ACQUISITION** is a biologically determined process. This cannot provide the complete explanation, however, because children deprived of normal social contact do not acquire language. This has been seen in cases where children have apparently been reared by wild animals away from a human environment. Equally, where children have been isolated and have received only minimal human contact, their language skills are non-existent. Even when reintroduced to society, children deprived of language during their early years fail to acquire much more than a very basic linguistic knowledge.

If language acquisition was innate (natural to the mind) and linked only to biological factors, then once the appropriate triggers were provided such children should have been able to acquire language in the usual way. Recorded cases of children who have experienced extreme social isolation have therefore led linguists to believe both that language acquisition is dependent on an appropriate linguistic input and that this language experience must be gained before a certain age.

In very general terms, it seems that language acquisition is linked to:

- **physical growth**: the body has to be mature enough for the child to produce recognisable words by manipulating the speech organs effectively and consciously
- **social factors**: the environment and culture in which a child grows up influences the kind of language input experienced and this, in turn, affects the child's linguistic abilities
- **a critical age**: if input and language experience occur before a certain point in the child's physical and mental development, learning is easy, quick, effortless and complete.

Because so many children acquire language effortlessly, it is easy to underestimate the complexity of the process taking place. Research in this field is comparatively new, however, and linguists still have much to learn about language acquisition.

9.2 The theories of language acquisition

There are four key linguistic approaches that try to explain the ways in which children acquire language.

Behaviourist approach

The **BEHAVIOURISTS** believe that children learn to speak by **imitating** the language structures they hear. Parents automatically **reinforce** and correct children's utterances, and this forms the basis for a child's knowledge of language.

There are, however, significant problems with this theory of language development. Although imitation is obviously important in learning pronunciation and in acquiring new vocabulary, children do not seem to automatically pick up 'correct' forms from imitation. With irregular verbs, for instance, children do not necessarily use the standard form because they hear adults use it. Instead, they over-extend the language patterns they already know:

> steal → *stealed* (stole)   grow → *growed* (grew)

Equally, children seem unable to imitate adult 'corrections':

CHILD	my train is /beə/
MOTHER	no (.) not 'by there' (.) just 'there'
CHILD	my train is /beə/
MOTHER	no just 'there'
CHILD	óh (.) my train is just /beə/

Such evidence suggests that child language acquisition cannot be based on imitation and reinforcement alone. Although children may add new words to their repertoire by using **LABELS** (words with a naming function) an adult has just introduced, they rarely imitate speech that is not directed at them. Equally, they do not appear to assimilate syntactical structures by imitation. Above all, this approach fails to explain how children are able to produce structures that they have not heard before.

Cognitive approach

The **COGNITIVE** approach links language acquisition directly to intellectual development. The research of Jean Piaget (1896–1980), a Swiss psychologist who did much work on the intellectual development of children, suggested that children can only use a certain linguistic structure when they understand the **concept** involved. For instance, children will only understand the past tense when they understand the concept of past time; they must have learnt to recognise and conceptualise visual and physical differences before they can talk about size and colour. This approach to language acquisition seems to be most effective in describing linguistic progress during the first one and a half years. Even at this stage, however, it is difficult to make precise connections between cognitive and linguistic developmental stages.

Nativist approach

The **NATIVISTS** believe that children are born with an **innate capacity** for language development. When the brain is exposed to speech, it automatically begins to receive and make sense of utterances because it has been 'programmed' to do so. Noam Chomsky, an American linguist (1928–), suggests that the human brain has a **language acquisition device (LAD)** which enables children to use the language around them to work out what is and what is not linguistically acceptable. This device also provides young children with an innate understanding of the underlying grammatical rules that govern language usage. The programmed patterns are general, and the child then has to learn exact rules through trial and error. The nativists believe the presence of the LAD explains the facts that:

▶ all normal children acquire language skills in the same kind of order and at the same kind of speed
▶ children are able to understand new sentences and constructions without having had any previous experience of them.

The nativists, however, do not appear to pay sufficient attention to the importance of input, the critical age aspect, and the role of imitation and reinforcement.

Interactive approach

Recent studies have shown the importance of **INTERACTION**. Adults alter the way they talk to children, giving them specific opportunities to take part in the discourse. For instance, utterances are simplified; intonation patterns are distinctive; extra information is given for clarification; and questions invite direct participation. Often adults also often expand on a child's speech, and research suggests that this can be one of the most positive ways to increase a child's awareness of grammatical structures. This kind of interaction is called '**MOTHERESE**' or '**CARETAKER SPEECH**', and it differs quite markedly from speech between two adults. Key features can be summarised as follows:

▶ **Vocabulary** is simplified so that concrete objects are named in broad categories: *dog* rather than *spaniel* or *labrador*; *ball* rather than *football, cricket ball* or *tennis ball*. '**Baby words**' like *doggie* or *moo-cow* do not help a child to learn language more efficiently. The reduplication of sounds in words like *baba* and *dada*, on the other hand, does enable babies to communicate because the words are easy to say.
▶ **Conversations** tend to be based on concrete things that relate directly to the child's environment.
▶ **Sentence structures** tend to be short and often use pauses to stress the end of grammatical units. Certain sentence patterns recur regularly: *where is _____ ?*; *do you want a _____ ?*; *that's* (pointing) *a _____.*
▶ **Commands** occur frequently and young children assimilate and use them in their own speech.
▶ **Tag questions** – questions added to the end of a statement inviting a response from the listener: *isn't it?, aren't we?* – are used to invite direct participation and

to encourage a child to ask for clarification if necessary. The high percentage of questions makes 'caretaker speech' distinctive.

- **Repetition** reinforces new words or structures and clarifies meaning.
- Parents often use a higher and wider **pitch range** when talking to small children, possibly because it keeps the child's attention. The singsong intonation and exaggerated stress on key words also make 'caretaker speech' distinctive.
- The **pace** is often slower than in conversations with other adults.

Because the baby or young child receives attention as a direct result of any attempts to communicate, the process is rewarding. 'Caretaker speech' is therefore an important means of creating a positive relationship with the parent which will form the basis for future meaningful communication.

Although the benefits of 'caretaker speech' are clear, it is not possible to identify precisely the links between the language structures parents use and their appearance in the child's language.

The basic principles

Each of the four theoretical approaches highlights a particular element of child language acquisition, but none can provide a complete explanation on its own. More research is needed before linguists can be completely sure about the processes that take place, but it is possible to summarise the basic principles:

- To acquire language, children must be part of a **social and linguistic community**.
- **Physical development** plays a part in children's ability to articulate the particular phonemes making up a language.
- Children have some kind of **instinctive awareness** of language patterns that enables them to experiment with structures they have not previously heard.
- In order to use language structures (like the comparative, for example), children must be able to **intellectually conceptualise** the world around them – language acquisition is therefore linked in some way to intellectual development.
- Through **imitation**, children can acquire new vocabulary and may be introduced to new grammatical structures.
- **Parental reinforcement** highlights non-standard usage and draws attention to 'correct' versions – although children often do not accept adult correction.
- **Especially adapted forms of speech** create a positive speech environment in which children are encouraged to participate in a meaningful way.

9.3 The function of communication

Interaction with other language users gives children a purpose – if they too can acquire language, they will be able to participate in the communication processes that are taking place around them. They may begin by using different kinds of cries to attract attention to their needs, but as they become more adept at using language, their range of communication can become more complex. Through their use of language, they can:

- establish relationships with the people around them
- express their feelings and opinions
- get others to do as they wish
- find out new information by asking questions
- get what they need by explaining exactly what they want
- communicate their ideas to other people
- tell stories and use language expressively.

As children acquire language, they become active participants in society. They can suddenly communicate purposefully in a way that others can interpret easily and so can express their own individuality.

9.4 Features of child language

Children acquire language skills rapidly during the first three years of their life. Even before birth, babies have become accustomed to the sound of the human voice; at one day old, they can distinguish their mother's voice from others; and by their second week, they can distinguish between human voices and non-human sounds. This prepares the ground for the communication that will take place before recognisable words are uttered.

Parents and other adult carers tend instinctively to encourage interaction from very early on by establishing the pattern for conversation. They:

- leave pauses where responses could be made
- use question structures frequently
- include the baby's own 'sounds' in a running dialogue.

This intuitive behaviour prepares babies for language acquisition. It immerses them directly in a simplified version of the linguistic patterns of the adult world by establishing basic turn-taking structures.

The process of language acquisition can be broken down into five main stages and linguists consider certain key areas within each one: **pronunciation**; **prosodic features**; **lexis**; **grammar**; and **PRAGMATICS** (an understanding of the social factors affecting spoken interaction).

0–12 months

In the first two months, the sounds babies make are linked to their **physical conditions**. They cry if they are hungry or wet; they gulp, burp and cough noisily; and they grizzle if they want to be held. They have to control the flow of air to make these noises and this same control will be used in a more refined way as their ability to communicate becomes more sophisticated.

Between 2 and 5 months, babies begin to experiment more and start to respond directly to parental smiles. At 6–8 weeks, babies often begin to **coo**. This is a softer sound than crying, made up of velar sounds like [k] and [g] and high vowels like [i] and [uː]. As the baby realises that cooing will elicit a response, the first interactive dialogues begin. Although cooing sounds like [gæ] and [guː] are sometimes strung together, there are no recognisable patterns yet. Between 2 and 4 months, the baby begins to **respond to the 'meaning'** of different tones of voice – anger, pleasure, humour. At around 16 weeks, the first **laugh** encourages even more varied responses from the parents, and this widens the scope of possible interaction.

Physical developments at this stage also prepare the baby for greater communication:

- as the child starts to look around and sit up, parents begin to point to things and their intonation becomes more exaggerated
- simple games like peekaboo make interaction fun
- the tongue starts to move horizontally and vertically, enabling the baby to produce a wider range of sounds
- the vocal cords are used in conjunction with the movements of the tongue
- the lips and the tongue play a greater part in sound production, helping the baby to make new sounds – it is possible that at this stage babies are beginning to imitate the mouth movements of adult speech.

Parents respond instinctively to these physiological developments and interaction becomes more like a two-way communication.

From 6 months, babies begin to **relate their utterances to specific contexts**. They seem to **recognise some words**, particularly names of family members. By the end of the first year, most are able to **point to things in answer to a question**; to **respond** in some way to situations requiring predictable feedback (*say bye-bye; say night-night*); and to **understand several words** even though they cannot yet say any recognisable words. Because the parents respond more to utterances that appear to be meaningful than to random sounds, the baby's communication begins to be more deliberate. Utterances in the 6–12 month period become **more varied**. Segments are longer and consist of frequently **repeated consonant and vowel-like patterns**. The **pitch level** is usually high, but also marked by GLIDES from high to low as the baby experiments.

From the baby's experimentation with a large range of sounds, a smaller, more frequently occurring set emerges. This stage is known as BABBLING. The sounds are now less randomly selected and begin to adopt rhythms that are closer to that of adult speech. **Reduplication of patterns**, like [bæbæbæ], and sequences in which the consonants and vowels change in each segment, like [dæbæ], are common. As the baby reaches 9 months, **recognisable intonation patterns** will be used for these consonant-vowel combinations. By 10–11 months, when babies can pull themselves into a standing position, they will use **vocalisations to express emotions**. The utterances at this stage are important because they will form the basis for the sounds of early speech.

IMITATIONS and SOUND PLAY at this point in their linguistic development give babies a much wider experience of the social role of speech. Equally, by **observing adults** they learn a great deal about conversation even though they cannot yet take a full part in it. Although many of the sounds of babbling, particularly in the earlier part of this period, do not appear to have meaning, babies do seem to consciously use them to communicate with the people around them. This kind of language use is called JARGON.

Towards the end of the first year, children become able to indicate their intentions more specifically. **INTONATION** is used to mark different kinds of purpose: the meaning of particular utterances may be unclear, but intonation patterns enable parents to interpret them. At this stage, the first real steps towards language acquisition are made as the **first words** are formed, often with the same intonation patterns each time. Language used at this stage does not really resemble adult speech, but parents familiar with the context in which **PROTO-WORDS** appear will be able to understand many of the utterances. Up to this stage, almost all children develop in the same way and at more or less the same speed, but after this children's language becomes much more individual.

From 12 to 18 months onwards, children begin to produce a **variety of recognisable single-word utterances** based on everyday objects. These utterances are **HOLOPHRASTIC** – they are grammatically unstructured and each consists of a single word. At this stage, pronunciation is often idiosyncratic. In general, children tend to choose and avoid the same kinds of sounds, but each child has marked preferences for some sounds rather than others. Equally, the same child might pronounce one word in different ways at different times: *cheese* might be articulated as /giː/, /kiːs/ and /iːs/.

Children at this stage acquire between ten and twenty new words a month. The vast majority of these are words with a **naming function**, focusing on people, food, body parts, toys, clothing and household things. During the holophrastic stage, children use a **limited vocabulary** to refer to a wide range of unrelated things. **OVER-EXTENSION** is therefore common – children use the same word to refer to different objects because they see a similarity in size, shape, sound or movement. *Baby*, for instance, may refer to all children, or *flower* to anything with leaves. It is common for the middle term of a set of **HYPONYMS** to be used: for instance, *dog* instead of *animal* or *spaniel*.

As the child gains linguistic experience, over-extension is replaced by a **narrowing of the field of reference** – more words have been learnt, so references can be more precise. Other examples of a lack of linguistic sophistication at this stage can be seen in:

▶ **UNDER-EXTENSION**, in which words are given a narrower range of reference than is usual – *car*, for instance, may be used to refer only to a family car
▶ **MISMATCH**, in which words are used to label objects with no apparent logic – *doll*, for instance, may be used to label a child's trousers.

Between 12 and 18 months, the first **modifiers** are used to describe things; **action utterances** (one word accompanied by gestures) like *gosleep* or *allgone* form the basis for the first verbs; and **social expressions** like *bye-bye* mark a growing awareness of cultural expectations. Although the utterances are holophrastic, intonation and gesture help the single word to convey the meaning and mood of a sentence.

The **conversational skills** of a child at this stage are still limited. Adults continue to do most of the talking and much of the child's communication takes the form of a **monologue**.

By the age of 2, a child's **vocabulary** has probably reached two hundred or more words. **Pronunciation** continues to be erratic, but certain commonly occurring pronunciations can be identified:

- words are often shortened, with unstressed syllables dropped: /teɪtəʊ/ *potato* and /mɑːtəʊ/ *tomato*
- consonant clusters are avoided: /gaɪ/ *sky* and /deɪ/ *stay*
- consonants at the end of words are dropped: /be/ *bed* and /je/ *yes*
- many words are simplified using reduplication of sounds: /dəʊdəʊ/ *Joseph* and /biːbiː/ *baby*
- vowels often differ from adult pronunciation: /diːdiː/ *daddy* and /nuː/ *no*
- initial-position consonants, particularly velars and fricatives, are often replaced: /dɒp/ *shop* or *stop*, /duːlz/ *tools* and /det/ *get*.

The standardisation of pronunciation takes place over a long period. Some consonants will not be produced accurately until after the age of 4. Between the ages of 1½ and 2, for instance, children begin to pronounce the voiced alveolar nasal [n], but it may take another twelve months for accurate pronunciation of:

- the voiceless labiodental fricative [f]
- the voiced bilabial approximant [w]
- the voiced velar nasal [ŋ].

Between 12 and 18 months, although two words may sometimes be used they are spoken as a single unit. From 18 months, words are used as distinct rhythmic units and they can often be analysed as **grammatical sequences**:

S	P	S	A	P	O	S	C
(baby)	(go)	(dummy)	(there)	(eat)	(apple)	(sock)	(red)

These minimal structures mean that the child can describe: a person carrying out an action, the position of something, the effect of a process (verb) on a person or thing (object), and a person's or thing's condition. Adults respond to such utterances even when they are neither grammatical nor complete, and thus the child becomes a part of real communication. The adult can often determine the meaning from the context and from the child's intonation. For example, an utterance like *Jo-Jo cup* may mean:

- this is Jo-Jo's cup (possession)
- give me my cup (command)
- Jo-Jo has got his cup (statement)
- where is Jo-Jo's cup? (question).

During this period, children also begin to use some **inflections**. Around 18 months they begin to experiment with the present participle, although it may not be used correctly for several months. **Questions** appear at this stage, usually marked by a rising intonation: *eat cheese nów?* Sometimes, however, *wh-* question words like *where?* and *what?* are attached to the beginnings of utterances: *where téddy?, what thát?* At the end of this stage, the first **negative words** emerge. *No* and *not* are used as one-word sentences or are tagged onto the beginning of any expression: *no* (in response to a request); *no sit; not car*.

The **feedback** children receive during this period of language acquisition is one of the most important elements in the learning process since it establishes them as participants in 'real' communication. Because parents respond to all utterances even if they do not appear to be meaningful, children are encouraged to experiment and therefore to work out what is and what is not acceptable.

2–3 years

This stage is marked by what is called **TELEGRAPHIC TALK**. Only the most important lexical words are used to express ideas, and grammatical function words (prepositions, determiners, auxiliary verbs and inflections) are often omitted. To understand children's telegraphic speech, it is important to know the **context** – particularly because children tend to talk about the present rather than the past or the future.

Vocabulary expands very quickly; by 2 years 6 months (2;6) children initiate talk rather than just responding to adults. They become inventive, creating new words from patterns they have heard but do not remember accurately:

> buffalosaurus (buffalo + dinosaur)   tipping bronco (bucking bronco)

Pronunciation becomes closer to the standard adult form too:

> tractor: /tæk-tæk/ (2;6) → /tæktə/ (2;8) → /træktə/ (2;9)
> badger: /bæbɪdʒ/ (2;5) → /bædʒə/ (2;6)
> shirt: /sɜːt/ (1;11) → /ʃɜːt/ (2;6)

Immature pronunciations typical of the previous developmental stage often continue during the 24- to 36-month period. Some sounds, however, are standardised:

- the bilabial plosives [p] and [b], the alveolar plosives [t] and [d], and the velar plosives [k] and [g]
- the voiced bilabial nasal [m]
- the voiceless glottal fricative [h]
- the voiced palatal approximant [j].

Three further sounds begin to be pronounced correctly between the ages of 2;8 and 4;0:

- the voiceless alveolar fricative [s]
- the voiced alveolar lateral [l]
- the voiced post-alveolar approximant [r].

The age at which children accurately produce these sounds will vary, but most will be using them correctly by the age of 4.

The pronunciation of many words is still idiosyncratic, but adult correction is ineffective in encouraging children to change their pronunciations. Because they do not seem to hear their own mispronunciations, children do not recognise the mispronounced word the parent tries to change. A child may say /æliːæm/ for *animal* and will not recognise the difference between her own and the standard version. If an adult tries to persuade her to say the word differently, therefore, she will be unable to do so:

CHILD	full /diːm ədɜːn/
MOTHER	is your boat going full /diːm ədɜːn/?
CHILD	no
MOTHER	how is your boat going?
CHILD	full /<u>diːm ədɜːn</u>/
MOTHER	oh (.) full steam astern
CHILD	<u>yes</u>

Utterances become longer. Combinations of three and four words are used in a variety of ways, and **clause elements** are less likely to be deleted:

    P   O
(Need) (potty) (2;4)

      S   P   O
(Mummy) (give) (chair) (2;4)

  S   P   A
(I) (going) (to your house). (2;7)

    S   P   O   A
(Little pigs) (want) (a ride) (in the boat). (2;7)

   S   P   O
(We) ('ve got) (bricks that you can use like heavy boxes to pile up for your presents
                 SCl–RelCl   SCl–NFCl
and things). (2;10)

Utterances are often quite sophisticated because of the embedding of subordinate clauses, and children use structures that are far more complicated than the simple sentences of early reading books. **Inflections** are used more frequently and more accurately during this period. Initially suffixes are overused before standardisation occurs:

- *-s* to mark plural nouns: *sheep → sheeps; information → informations*
- *-ed* to mark regular past tense: *steal → stealed; go → goed; build → builded*

Auxiliary verbs are still often omitted, but usage becomes more accurate towards the age of 3:

Little pigs always *having* fun. (2;7)   It *be chugging* in the tunnel. (2;10)

Modal auxiliaries are used more frequently to convey variations in attitude:

Frog *might* have a swim. (2;7)   We'*ll* need a ladder. (2;10)

Present participles are more likely to be used with the primary verb *be*, although this will still often have an unmarked form. At the age of 2, **wh- question words** are tagged onto the beginning of utterances: *what?* and *where?* are used first, followed by *why?* and later *how?* and *who?*

Where baby? (2;4)
Where's the carriage? (2;10)   *What* the name? (2;10)

Throughout the period, question structures become more complex, although the use of rising intonation to mark a question is still common:

Daddy put it ón. (2;4)   You need a big bóx. (2;6)
Why did Daddy put it on? (2;10)   *Do* you need a big box? (2;10)

Negatives are used with more subtlety too. Additional forms like *can't* and *won't* appear alongside *no* and *not*, which are now placed in front of the appropriate verb rather than at the beginning of the utterance:

No books there. (2;4)	I *not* tell story. (2;6)	I *can't* know. (2;8)
I *don't* know.	I *didn't* say anything.	It's *not* Lixie's. (2;10)

Pronouns are used with more variety during this developmental stage, but children are often inaccurate. Because they hear themselves referred to as *you*, they tend to use the second person pronoun to talk about themselves. Equally, the first person singular *I* is used to refer to other people. This shows that imitation does play a part in language acquisition. Although children may copy the pronoun referencing they hear, they seem instinctively to sense that their meaning is unclear – their words are therefore often accompanied by gestures to clarify the reference. A similar confusion occurs with **possessive determiners**:

CHILD	I mending /maɪs/ chair
MOTHER	are you mending your chair?
CHILD	no (.) I mending /maɪs/ chair *(pointing to mother)*
MOTHER	oh (.) you're mending mummy's chair
CHILD	yes (.) Mummy's chair (2;5)

As they become more familiar with the different pronouns and determiners, however, children learn to correct their own mistakes. By the age of 3;0 they will often **repair a breakdown** in understanding by repeating the utterance with the key word changed:

this toast is for you (1) toast is for me

Children continue to experiment with language patterns and although they do not always get them right, they clearly begin to initiate and practise new structures:

willn't   satting   pavementless (no pavements)   sickless (not ill)

Between the ages of 2 and 3, children develop language skills at a remarkable speed. Grammar and pronunciation become steadily more consistent and standard, conversational skills become more sophisticated, and children actively develop their vocabulary by asking for new names and labels.

From 3 years

After the age of 3, telegraphic speech is replaced by more **fluent** and **sophisticated** language use. **Vocabulary** continues to expand and diversify and **pronunciation** continues to become more standard. The last consonantal sounds to be produced accurately are:

- the voiceless palato-alveolar fricative [ʃ]
- the palato-alveolar affricates [tʃ] (voiceless) and [dʒ] (voiced)
- the voiced labiodental fricative [v]
- the voiced alveolar fricative [z]
- the dental fricatives [ð] (voiced) and [θ] (voiceless).

The first sounds listed above may be standard before the age of 3;6, but others may not be pronounced in a mature way until after the age of 4.

The **structure of utterances** becomes more varied. Co-ordination is common by the age of 3, but now subordination is increasingly used. Conjunctions like *because* (/kɒs/), *so, if, after* and *when* help children to create longer sentences, which are often made up of four or five clause elements. The utterances are not always grammatical and are often marked by **normal non-fluency features**. For a time, regular and irregular **past tense verbs** are confused and a child may use both a standard and a non-standard variant: *broked/breaked* and *broke*; *sitted* and *sat*; *bringed* and *brought*; and *blewed/blowed* and *blew*. By the age of 4, however, most children have worked out the appropriate patterns. It is usually during the early part of this stage that children begin to use the **third person singular inflection -s** more consistently. It appears first with lexical verbs and slightly later with primary auxiliaries: *here it comes*; *the song says she blew*; *he's got a little son*.

Questions are now framed by inverting the subject and verb of a declarative sentence, although in the early part of the period, children do not always use an inversion following a *wh-* word. They still need to learn that questions beginning with a *wh-* word must alter the word order and that where there is no auxiliary verb, the dummy auxiliary *do* must be added: *where is the picture?*; *did I have my milk?* **Other auxiliary forms** like *didn't* and *won't* become part of the repertoire at this stage, and the use of *not* becomes more accurate: *I didn't catch it*; *she won't give it to me*. **Multiple negatives** are used for emphasis: *I didn't get nothing today*. The last negative form to be acquired is usually *isn't*. This means that some inaccurate negative constructions from the previous developmental stage continue to appear alongside standard constructions: *he not going* instead of *he isn't going*; *this not Lixie's* instead of *this isn't Lixie's*. In the early school years children begin to experiment with more complicated negative structures like *any*.

During this last period of dramatic linguistic change, children learn more about the art of **conversation**. They **initiate** dialogue and become skilful in controlling **turn-taking**. They can respond appropriately to other speakers and they start to learn how to **alter their register** for different contexts and audiences. They are able to **anticipate problems** and to **repair simple breakdowns** in communication by repeating things that have not been understood or by asking for clarification.

The 4-year-old begins to sort out any remaining grammatical inaccuracies and language use becomes consistently more adult. By the age of 5, most children have an operating vocabulary of more than two thousand words and they are using more complicated grammatical structures. Over the next few years (6–11), children acquire what is probably their last intuitive grammatical knowledge: **comparative** structures; **comment** and **attitude adverbials**; the ability to recognise the **differences between similar sentences**; and an awareness of the **different ways in which meaning can be conveyed** (such as active or passive sentences). They also begin to recognise **implicit meaning** and **figurative uses** of language. By the ages of 8 or 9 most grammatical structures have been understood, but children are still learning about **semantics** (meaning).

9.5 Types of child language

Monologues

Children involved in imaginative play often speak at length about what they are doing. Their actions are accompanied by a discourse which has no obvious intended audience – they may adopt the role of a character, describe their actions, retell or create stories, issue commands or ask questions. As they become older and more able to play alone, the speech utterances become more like narrative. As their language skills develop, children are able to construct a complete discourse without needing to rely on adult interventions to sustain the speech.

ACTIVITY 9.1a

The following extracts were recorded over a period of three months. In each instance, Joseph is playing and the speech accompanies his activities. His parents are present, but they do not take part in the spoken discourse.

Between the ages of 2 and 3 children acquire new language skills incredibly quickly and the transcriptions here demonstrate linguistic and syntactical features that are typical of the stages of child language acquisition. Within three months, the vocabulary, the grammar and the ability to sustain an extended turn change noticeably. By focusing on Joseph's pronunciation, his lexical choices, his grammar and his ability to create a narrative, it is possible to chart key features of his language development.

Read through the extracts and comment on:

1 the lexical and grammatical features
2 Joseph's ability to sustain an extended turn
3 the developmental differences revealed by each transcript.

Each transcription is preceded by a standard written version using traditional orthography and punctuation to help you follow Joseph's immature speech patterns. The transcriptions mark prosodic features selectively. A key to the symbols used can be found on page 93.

Joseph, aged 2;4, is playing with his ride-along tractor and pretending to be a local beach life guard.

WRITTEN VERSION

> Fall off. Yes. Dirt on my shirt. Mm. Fall off tractor. Dirt on shirt. Yes. Mm. Think. Mm. Dirt from sand. Fall off tractor. Oh yes dirt on me mm oh oh. Move round chair. Move tractor. Vroom, vroom, vroom, vroom, vroom, vroom, vroom. Cold. Blooming cold. Blooming, blooming cold. Life guard brush off dust. Fell off. Sand. Life guard. Dirt. Little little (*indistinct*). Look out. Tractor in sea.

SPOKEN VERSION

> 1 fall off (.) /jeθ/ (.) dirt on my (.) /sɜːt/ (4) mm (5) fall off (.) /træk-træk/ oh dirt on (.) /sɜːt/ /jeθ/ mm /fɪŋk/ (.) mm (.) dirt (1) from sand (.) /fɔːlə/ off (.) /træk-træk/ (1) oh /jeθ/ dirt (.) /æn/ (.) me mm oh oh (.) move /raʊn teə/ (.) move /træk-træk/ (.) /vrúːm vrúːm vrʌ́m vrʌ́m vrʌ́m vrʌ́m vrʌ́m/ (.) /kɒld/ (.) /blʌmɪn kɒld/ (.) /blʌmɪn
> 5 blʌmɪn kɒld/ (2) life guàrd (2) /brʌs/ (.) off (.) /dʌs/ (.) fell off (.) sand (.) life guard (.) dirt (.) /lɪlɪ/ (.) /lɪlɪ/ (*indistinct*) (2) look /aʊ/ (.) /træk-træk/ in sea

The extract here is clearly an example of telegraphic talk. At the age of 2;4, Joseph's utterances are staccato and his intonation is often monotone. Although he is joining words together to form grammatical units, his utterances are incomplete.

The following points can be made about Joseph's language at the age of 2;4.

LEXIS

Joseph's vocabulary is growing quickly and this extract includes examples of the ways in which children learn from the range of experiences to which they are exposed.

Linguistic features	Examples
Words taken from familiar stories (Raymond Briggs, *Father Christmas*)	/blʌmɪn kɒld/ blooming cold (l. 5)
Words taken from personal experience (limited lexical set of the 'seaside')	life guard (l. 5); sand (l. 2); sea (l. 6)
Words taken from the play context	/træk-træk/ tractor (l. 1); /sɜːt/ shirt (l. 2); /teə/ chair (l. 3)
Onomatopoeic words	/vrúːm/ /vrʌ́m/ (l. 4)
Growing range of verbs	fall (l. 1); move (l. 3); look (l. 6); /brʌs/ brush (l. 5); /fɪŋk/ think (l. 2)
First modifiers used	/blʌmɪn/ (l. 4) – euphemism, slang for 'bloody'; life (l. 5) – noun modifier for guard

PRONUNCIATION

Many of the immature pronunciations from the previous developmental stage are still evident in Joseph's speech. Some simplified words continue to be used, although most are now in a recognisably adult form.

Linguistic features	Examples
Immature vocabulary (reduplication)	/træk-træk/ (l. 1); /lɪlɪ/ little (l. 6)
Difficult phonemes are avoided:	
◗ the voiceless palato-alveolar affricate [tʃ] is replaced	/teə/ (l. 3)
Initial-position fricatives are replaced:	
◗ the voiceless palato-alveolar fricative [ʃ]	/sɜːt/ (l. 2)
◗ the voiceless dental fricative [θ]	/fɪŋk/ (l. 2)
Consonants in the final position are dropped or replaced by another phoneme:	
◗ the voiceless alveolar fricative [s]	/jeθ/ yes (l. 1)
◗ the voiceless alveolar plosive [t]	/dʌs/ dust (l. 5)
◗ the voiced alveolar plosive [d]	/raʊn/ round (l. 3)
◗ the voiced velar nasal [ŋ]	/blʌmɪn/ blooming (l. 4)
◗ the voiceless palato-alveolar fricative [ʃ]	/brʌs/ (l. 5)

Vowels differ from adult pronunciation: ▸ [əʊ] → [ɒ] ▸ [uː] → [ʌ] ▸ [ɒ] → [æ]	/kɒld/ (l. 4) /blʌmɪn/ blooming (l. 4) /æn/ (l. 3)
Idiosyncratic pronunciation is used alongside the adult form	fall (l. 1) /fɔːlə/ (l. 2)

GRAMMAR

Utterances are getting longer and combinations of different clause elements make them more varied, but Joseph's clauses are still incomplete. As is typical of telegraphic speech, some clause sites are not filled and determiners are elided. Inflections are not used in this extract and the verb *to be* is omitted. Joseph's meaning is usually clear, but there are points at which an outsider would struggle to understand.

Linguistic features	Examples
Clause elements are now quite varied and are usually in the appropriate position: ▸ (S P) (S) A ▸ (S) P O ▸ (S) P A ▸ (S P) C	(S) A (dirt) (on my /sɜːt/) (l. 1) P O (fall off) (/træk-træk/) (l. 1) P A (move) (/raʊn/) (l. 3) C (/blʌmɪn kɒld/) (l. 4)
There is no evidence of co-ordination yet – the utterances are basically simple. There is one grammatically complete simple utterance, although the third person singular inflection is not used	S P O (life guard) (/brʌs/ off) (/dʌs/) (l. 5)
Most of the extract is in the declarative mood, but Joseph uses two imperatives	/fɪŋk/ (l. 2) look (l. 6)
Most verbs are unmarked for tense, but Joseph uses one irregular past tense form accurately	fell off (l. 5)
No subject pronouns are used but a first person object pronoun and a possessive determiner are used accurately	/æn/ (.) me (l. 3) my (.) /sɜːt/ (l. 1)

SUSTAINING AN EXTENDED TURN

Joseph's speech is all directed towards himself – he shows little awareness of his parents although they are present. His monologue, however, becomes almost a running dialogue with himself. His discourse is marked by **normal non-fluency features** like the repeated *mm* which helps him to sustain the extended turn. Joseph seems immersed in the story he is creating and the **pauses** are all brief. The **rhythm** is still very disjointed and the **lexis** and **syntax** are quite repetitive.

Joseph, aged 2;7, playing with a miniature toy park, the three bears' house and various small figures.

WRITTEN VERSION

Case little pigs want ride in a boat. In a boat. Going in a boat. Always going in a boat. Always going in a boat. Have fun. Always having fun in girl's house. Oh be. Have tea. Beings, beings, beings, beings under there. Not anybody in the park. No anybody in the park. Nobody in the park. Frog playing in it. Frog might have a swim. Swimming. 'We mi. might visit the park' say Mummy Bear, Daddy Bear and Baby Bear and Baby Bear might see little wee wee frog in the pond. Baby Bear might have a look over there. Look over there. Having a swim. Oh Goldilocks peeping and peeping and peeping. Goldilocks. Goldilocks ha. hang on. Somebody in the pool. Peace and quiet. Goldilocks go and cook. I coming going to yours house little while seeing who in the pond and peered and peered and peered and peered over fence and Baby Bear and and the frog went to went to find the pool. Little little fre. Little animals in in the in the pool. Goldilocks, Goldilocks, Goldilocks saying 'hello all'. Somebody else in the pond. Somebody else in the pond. All the trees. All yellow trees. All yellow trees.

SPOKEN VERSION

1   case /lɪlɪ/ pigs want ride in a boat (2) in a boat (.) going in a boat (.) all (.) ways going in a boat (.) all (.) ways going in a boat (3) have fun (.) all (.) ways having fun in girl's house (.) oh be (.) have tea (.) /biːʌŋs biːʌŋs biːʌŋs/ (.) /biːɪŋs/ under /eə/ (.) not anybody in /ə/ park (.) no (.) anybody in /ə/ park (.) no (1) body in /ə/ park (.) frog playing /ɪnɪt/ (.)
5   frog might (.) have a /wɪm/ (.) /wɪmɪŋ/ (2) we mí. (.) mí́ght visit /ə/ park say Mummy Bear and Daddy Bear and /biːbiː/ Bear and /biːbiː/ Bear mí́ght see /lɪlɪ/ wee wee frog in /ə/ pond (.) /biːbiː/ Bear might (.) have (.) look over /eə/ (.) look over /eə/ (.) having a /wɪm/ (.) oh (.) /gɒlɒks pi̱ːpɪn/ and /pi̱ːpɪn/ and /pi̱ːpɪn/ (.) /gɒlɒks/ (.) /gɒlɒs/ ha. (.) hang on (1) /sʌmbiː/ in /ə/ pool (.) peace and quiet (1) /gɒlɒks/ go and cook (.) I
10 /kʌmɪn/ (.) going to /ɔːz/ house /lɪlɪ/ while seeing /uː/ in /ə/ pond (.) and pée̯red and pée̯red and pée̯red and pée̯red over fence and /biːbiː/ Bear (.) and and /ə/ frog went to (.) went to find pool (.) /lɪlɪ lɪlɪ fre/ (.) /lɪlɪ æliːæms/ (10) in (2) in /ə/ in /ə/ pool (.) /gɒlɒs/ (.) /gɒlɒs gɒlɒks/ saying he̯llo all (.) somebody else in /ə/ pond (.) somebody else in /ə/ pond (.) all /ə/ trees (.) all /leləʊ/ trees all /leləʊ/ trees

COMMENTARY

The second transcript is longer and Joseph is more able to sustain his discourse. He is becoming more standard in both his pronunciation and grammar, and uses a more varied range of prosodic features. His monologue is now much closer to a recognisable form of narrative which most listeners could understand.

Focusing more closely, it is possible to list the following points about Joseph's developmental stage.

LEXIS

The vocabulary used in this example is far more diverse. Although it is still dominated by concrete nouns like *trees* (l. 14) and *house* (l. 2), abstract nouns like *peace and quiet* (l. 9) are beginning to appear. Dynamic verbs like *playing* (l. 4) and *going*

(l. 1) occur more frequently, but stative verbs like *want* (l. 1) and *have* (l. 2) are now more common than in the earlier extract. Equally, having understood the concept of position, a range of prepositions like *under* (l. 3), *over* (l. 7) and *in* (l. 1) are used to describe 'place' precisely.

Linguistic features	Examples
Words are still often linked to familiar stories	/lɪlɪ/ pigs (l. 1), Mummy Bear and Daddy Bear and /biːbiː/ Bear (ll. 5–6), /gɒlɒks/ (l. 9)
As Joseph's vocabulary widens, he begins to use synonyms	pool (l. 9), pond (l. 10) /piːpɪn/ (l. 8), peered (l. 11)
By listening to adults, Joseph is able to identify and later use collocations	peace and quiet (l. 9)
Modifiers are used more often and are more varied	*wee wee* frog – Adj (l. 6); *girl's* house – possessive NP (l. 2); /lelə ʊ/ trees – Adj (l. 14)
Inevitably much of the vocabulary is still linked to Joseph's own experiences	park (l. 4), trees (l. 14), house (l. 2)
The verbs are far more varied	want (l. 1), have (l. 2), playing (l. 4), /wɪmɪŋ/ (l. 5)

PRONUNCIATION

In just three months, there is a noticeable difference in Joseph's pronunciation: most words are now pronounced standardly; words that are still pronounced in an immature way are usually close enough to the adult form to be quite easily recognisable.

Linguistic features	Examples
Immature vocabulary (reduplication)	/lɪlɪ/ (l. 1)
Consonant clusters are still avoided: ‣ [sw] is simplified	/wɪm/ (ll. 5, 8), /wɪmɪŋ/ (l. 5)
Initial-position fricatives are absent: ‣ the voiced dental fricative [ð] ‣ the voiceless glottal fricative [h]	/eə/ there (l. 3); /ə/ the (l. 4) /uː/ who (l. 10)
Vowels differ from the 'caretaker speech' (Modified RP), but self-correction eventually results in a standard pronunciation of the vowel: ‣ [iːʌ] instead of [iːɪ] ‣ [iː] instead of [eɪ], adult = /beɪbiː/ The diphthong in the first syllable is simplified and Joseph reduplicates a pure vowel instead: ‣ [ɒ] instead of [əʊ], adult = /gəʊldiːlɒks/	/biːʌŋs/, /biːɪŋs/ beings (l. 3) /biːbiː/ baby (l. 7) /gɒlɒs/ (l. 8)
The voiced palatal approximant [j] is absent	/ɔːz/ yours (l. 10)
Some pronunciations are still idiosyncratic	/æliːæms/ animals (l. 12)

Certain words are pronounced inconsistently – sometimes they will have an adult form and sometimes not	/gɒlɒs/, /gɒlɒks/, /gɒlɒks/ Goldilocks (ll. 8–9, 13) /sʌmbiː/ somebody (l. 9)

GRAMMAR

Joseph's language is now more grammatically complete. Determiners are usually included; inflections appear more consistently; and sentences include both co-ordination and subordination. Co-ordination:

$$\underset{}{\text{(/gɒlɒks/)}} \; \overset{P}{\text{(go)}} \; \underset{\text{conj}}{\text{(and)}} \; \overset{P}{\text{(cook)}} \qquad\qquad\qquad (l. 9)$$

S P P
(/gɒlɒks/) (go) (and) (cook)   (l. 9)
                    conj

Subordination:

S   P   A   A   A
(I) (/kʌmɪn/ going) (to /ɔːz/ house) (/lɪlɪ/ while) (seeing /uː/ in /ə/ pond) (and)
                                                        SCl–NFCl

P   A   S   P   A
(peered …) (over fence) (and) (/biːbiː/ …) (went) (to find pool)   (ll. 10–12)
                                      SCl–NFCl

Linguistic features	Examples
Clause elements are used in a variety of ways to make the narrative interesting. Clause sites are rarely left empty now: ▸ S P O ▸ S P A ▸ S P O A	S P O (frog) (might have) (a /wɪm/) (l. 5) S P A (/gɒlɒs/) (hang) (on) (ll. 8–9) S P O A (/biːbiː/ Bear) (might have) (look) (over /eə/) (l. 7)
The narrative uses the declarative mood	frog might have a /wɪm/ (l. 5)
The verb *to be* is still elided	somebody else in /ə/ pond (ll. 13–14) frog playing /ɪnɪt/ (l. 4)
Quoting and quoted clauses are used, adding to the effective creation of a narrative atmosphere	QUOTED QUOTING ('We might visit…', (say MB and DB and /biːbiː/ B) (ll. 5–6)
There are still many unmarked verbs, but some verb forms are marked for tense	hang (l. 9), cook (l. 9) – unmarked verb forms went (l. 11) – irregular simple past tense
Inflections are used more standardly: ▸ present participle inflection -*ing* ▸ regular past tense inflection -*ed* ▸ possessive noun suffix inflection '*s* ▸ plural noun suffix -*s*	having (l. 2), playing (l. 4), going (l. 1) peered (l. 10) girl's house (l. 2) /biːʌŋs/ (l. 3)
There is still no evidence of third person singular -*s* inflection	/gɒlɒks/ go[es] and cook[s] (l. 9)
Modal auxiliaries are used correctly	might visit (l. 5)

Pronouns are now more accurate:	
▸ first person subject pronouns ▸ compound indefinite pronouns ▸ second person possessive pronoun used as a possessive determiner	I /kʌmɪn/ (ll. 9–10), *we might visit* (l. 5) anybody (l. 4), nobody (l. 4), somebody (l. 13) /ɔːz/ house (l. 10)
Negatives are used here – Joseph consciously works through a pattern until he finds the structure he believes is right	not anybody … (.) no (.) anybody … (.) no (1) body (ll. 3–4)

SUSTAINING AN EXTENDED TURN

In this example, telegraphic speech is being replaced by discourse that is closer to the patterns of adult speech. Although Joseph's monologue is still marked by many micro-pauses, the overall **rhythm** is far less disjointed than in the transcript made at the age of 2;4. Longer **pauses** reflect Joseph's ability to concentrate for longer on his play activity and this increased concentration results in the creation of a more sophisticated narrative. Utterances are still sometimes **grammatically incomplete** but the meaning of each is now usually clear. For instance, Joseph uses the compound noun phrase *peace and quiet* as a grammatical utterance – although this is grammatically incomplete, a listener can more or less understand the meaning from the context.

Prosodic features are now used with more sophistication. **Stress** is used to highlight important words and the **pitch range** is quite varied. Joseph often adopts the singsong intonation patterns that are common in the speech of young children. **Normal non-fluency features** like repetition of words (*and and*) and false starts (*mi. might*; *ha. hang*) are typical of all spoken language. Another interesting development can be seen in the way Joseph is starting to **correct himself**. Often he uses repetition to work through a range of alternatives until he finds what he thinks is the correct pronunciation or grammatical form.

The extract here is far more developed than the previous example – Joseph can now **sustain an extended turn** quite successfully. The narrative is linked directly to his play and although it is often repetitive, there is a sense that he is telling a chronological story.

SUMMARY

The extracts clearly show the ways in which Joseph's language has developed within a three-month period. His **lexis** has become more varied; his **grammar** is more accurate; and he uses **prosodic features** more explicitly to highlight key words and to draw attention to important parts of his monologue. At the age of 2;7, he still does not **pronounce** all his words in an adult form and his utterances are still sometimes **grammatically incomplete**. However, it would no longer be difficult for an adult who does not know him to understand what he is saying.

Dialogues

Parents engage children in conversations from very early on. Even before speech acquisition begins, babies are learning about communication from the smiles and sounds which they begin to recognise as responses to their cries and gurgles. After 6 months, mothers tend not to respond to every vocalisation, but pay special attention to utterances that appear to be meaningful. By 8 months, babies will try to attract attention by pointing. It is at this stage that they also become fascinated by adult conversations, watching each speaker and thus learning implicitly about turn-taking.

In the early stages of language acquisition, children rarely initiate dialogue and they cannot easily sustain a conversation. Parents help them by:

▸ asking direct questions
▸ repeating words and phrases spoken by the child
▸ basing dialogue on the immediate activities and context.

ACTIVITY 9.2a

The following extracts were recorded over a period of six months: the first was made when Joseph was 2;4 and the second when he was 2;10. Each transcript reveals the same kinds of lexical and grammatical features discussed in Activity 9.1, but the examples are now dialogues rather than monologues. In each case, Joseph is at home talking to his parents. Read through the transcripts and comment on Joseph's ability to sustain a conversation. A key to the symbols used can be found on page 93.

Joseph (J), aged 2;4, talking to his father (F).

```
 1 J  need potty
   F  okay (8) how many clocks have we got?
   J  Mummy póint (.) Daddy póint (.) one (.) one (.) one
   F  so how many clocks have we got, Joseph?
 5 J  two (5) pointing
   F  point at what (.) what do you want Daddy to point at?
   J  clock
   F  clock (.) where's the other clock (2) over there (.) right
   J  on /self/
10 F  on shelf (.) yes on the shelf
   J  by books
   F  by the books and where's the other clock?
   J  /eə/ (.) no books
   F  no books
15 J  mm
   F  what's it near?
   J  /pɪkpɪks/
   F  the picture and what's underneath the clock?
   J  /niːf/
20 F  underneath (.) what's underneath the clock?
   J  /niːf/ (4) /dɔːdiː/ (.) /dɔːdiː/ (.) Daddy get
   F  you want Georgie
   J  woof woof woof woof (.) furry /dɔːdiː/ (.) woof woof /iːiːiːiː/
   F  what are you doing to Georgie?
25 J  grab
   F  you've grabbed ‖ him
   J              ‖ grab him (.) /drəʊk/ him
```

F	where are you putting him?
J	/bækɪt/
30 F	he's in the <u>basket</u>
J	give /bækɪt/ (2) pl. (5) Daddy Daddy (2) /dɔːdiː/
F	where's Georgie now?
J	on (.) /eə/
F	where?
35 J	/<u>teə</u>/
F	chair (.) on the chair
J	one /eə/ (.) one /teə/
F	one chair
J	/lɪlɪ teə/ (.) give
40 F	little chair (.) so that's a little chair (.) what's this chair?
J	Mummy's
F	Mummy's chair
J	give
F	you want Georgie do you?
45 J	give (.) give (.) give (.)
F	where is Mummy?
J	give Mummy give /deə/
F	Mummy gave you ‖ the chair
J	‖ /teə/

COMMENTARY

There are signs that Joseph is becoming a more active participant in dialogue. The **turn-taking** is quite smooth, although there is one instance in which he starts his utterance before his father's is grammatically complete: *you've grabbed ‖ him* (ll. 26–7). Everything that he says follows on logically from what has gone before, and in each utterance his meaning and intentions are quite clear. The conversation, however, is typical of a child between the ages of 2;0 and 2;6 – Joseph's father **initiates the topics** (ll. 2, 24, 40) and **sustains the dialogue** with a series of questions (ll. 2, 8, 16). Joseph answers the questions appropriately, providing the necessary information: *on /self/* (l. 9). Sometimes, his answer clearly does not give the information his father expects. In the exchange about the size of the chair, the father takes up the idea of a little chair (l. 40), expecting Joseph to describe the 'big' chair. He instead describes it as *Mummy's* (l. 41) – his response is appropriate although unexpected and shows that he has the **vocabulary** and **necessary grammatical knowledge** to construct a range of meaningful answers. In another instance, Joseph actually completes the utterance simultaneously with his father, showing his **intuitive knowledge of grammar** and his ability to use a word from the appropriate word class: *grab him* (l. 27). There are points at which Joseph changes the direction of the conversation by indicating that he wants something: *Daddy get* (l. 21). He uses imperatives to get things done: *Daddy point* (l. 3).

The father tries to correct Joseph's **pronunciation** by reiterating key words: /self/, *on shelf (.) yes on the shelf* (ll. 9–10); /niːf/, *underneath* (ll. 19–20). The father's reiterations also make Joseph's utterances grammatically complete by including the function words that Joseph omits: /pɪkpɪks/, *the picture* (ll. 17–18). Despite the father's attempts to 'educate' him explicitly, Joseph continues to pronounce words idiosyncratically and to omit words such as determiners. He can, however, recognise when understanding has become a problem and he can **repair the dialogue** in a very basic way. For instance, the father fails to understand that Joseph is saying his mother gave him the chair. To clarify the meaning of his utterance, Joseph stresses the lexical verb *give* (l. 45) and repeats it until his father has understood. The father then provides the grammatically standard version, to which Joseph adds the noun /teə/ (l. 49) in the object site. In some places Joseph tries to **correct his own pronunciation** by repeating a word in slightly different forms until it sounds more like the adult version: *one* /eə/ (.) *one* /teə/ (l. 37). The pause marks Joseph's awareness that his first version is not a recognisable word and that there might be a problem in communicating his meaning.

ACTIVITY 9.2b

Joseph (J), aged 2;10, talking to his mother (M).

1 J /ə/ train is taking /ɪm/ to his ‖ wêdding

    M   ‖ watch your knees

    J his wedding (.) /ə/ train taking /ɪm/ to his wêdding (3) where's /ə/ carriages ‖ oh ha.

    M   ‖ watch

5   your knees Joseph (.) that's a good boy

    J /eɪ/ meant to have carriages if /eɪ/ taking Lixie to church

    M mm

    J /eɪ/ meant to have carriages

    M yes they are (.)

10 J meant ‖ to

    M   ‖ careful

    J /məʊk/ (.) /æt/ be near /ə/ track

    M mm (.) smoke

    J /æt/ is /ə/ stătion (.) runaway train went over /ə/ hill (.) /ə/ church is /æt/ way

15 M the church is <u>that</u> way

    J (*indistinct*) /ə/ Lixie's sitting in /ə kəʊwʌl/ carriage

    M not /kəʊwʌl/ (.) can you say cóal

    J in a bit of /kəʊwʌl/

    M coal

20 J bit of /kəʊwʌl/

    M can you say cóal

    J coal (*shouted*)

    M that's it

    J in a bit of coal (*quiet*)

25 M <u>lo</u>vely (.) lovely

    J Lixie don't go (.) and he was slowly (1) and he slept in a béd (2) for ages and ages and he fêll out (.) he fe. (.) wait he says /kɒs/ I not want to have it he says and /ə/ train púffs away (.) and it puffs slowly away to take /ɪm/ home

    M where is he góing

30 J some people call /a/ house homes

    M some people call them homes (.) a house ‖ or

    J   ‖ a home

M   what's Lixie going to call it

J   a <u>cott</u>age (4) /ə/ train is coming out of /ə/ tunnel

35 M   here it comes out of the tunnel

J   mm it (.) it coming out soft of a tunnel

M   it's coming out sóft (.) what does that méan

J   /ə/ <u>track</u> is soft

M   the track is sóft

40 J   mm

M   what does that méan (2) what happens if the track is sòft

J   one bit is bending in the <u>tunnel</u>

M   mm

J   <u>ooo ooo</u> (*train noises*) the runaway train went over the hill (2) and he came onto

45   the track track track (1) he's going into the tunnel now now now (2) where's /ə/ (.)
where's /ə/ tráin (.) it just went into /ə/ tunnel (2) /iː/ it chuffs (*train noises*) out of
/ə/ túnnel Lixie (.) out of /ə/ túnnel (.) well (.) Lixie heard it go slow (7) and then /ə/
signal went dòwn (.) and /ə/ <u>signal</u> banged dòwn (.) and /ə/ signal banged down
(2) clack (4) look out (*indistinct*) for /ə təʊ/ town (.) /təʊ/ ‖town

50 M   ‖look out for whát

J   /təʊ/ town

M   what's thát

J   ‖no

M   ‖what did you sáy

55 J   I didn't say anything

COMMENTARY

Joseph is clearly more in charge in the second transcript and is far more able to sustain a conversation in his own right. He still drifts between monologue and dialogue, but he is now much more aware of his audience. He is able to **question** (l. 3) as well as **respond** (ll. 33–4) and the **rhythms** of his speech are far less disjointed. Both participants are actively involved and Joseph is clearly listening to the utterances in detail. He **initiates the topics** (ll. 1, 6, 30) and his mother merely helps to develop them with her spoken contributions to the game that he is playing (ll. 34–40). He is more aware of **grammatically complete utterances** and there are few examples of overlapping speech – except where his mother is telling Joseph to be more careful with his toys (ll. 1–4). Everything that Joseph says is recognisable except where he talks about /təʊ/ *town* (l. 49). His mother asks him to reiterate the word in order to clarify what he has said. Joseph, however, refuses to explain, instead opting for an escape – *I didn't say anything* (l. 55). Joseph can now also respond to adult correction. When his mother draws his attention to a mature pronunciation of *coal* (l. 17), he is able to replace /kəʊwʌl/ with *coal* (ll. 18–24).

The second transcript shows the speed at which children acquire linguistic skills. Within six months, Joseph has acquired a much more **diverse vocabulary**; he is able to **recognise** and **use complete grammatical structures** and he is able to **control the conversation** and deal with **turn-taking** effectively.

As well as learning about language structures, children have to understand the patterns that underpin spoken communication. They must learn about turn-taking and repairs; they must recognise when a situation demands an apology or when it is necessary to ask for clarification. Children are never taught these skills, but assimilate them both from participating in and observing spoken interaction in different contexts. The study of the things that influence our choice of language in social contexts is called **PRAGMATICS**.

Young children often make mistakes as they learn about the 'rules'. A child answering a telephone might be asked 'Is your mother in?': if she replies 'Yes' and puts the receiver down, she has failed to understand the pragmatics of the inter-action. Pragmatic 'mistakes' do not prevent understanding and cannot be classed as 'wrong', but they are seen as 'socially inappropriate'. Children inevitably make such mistakes, but by school age they have acquired a subconscious knowledge of many of society's expectations.

At the age of 2;10, Joseph is well aware of the pragmatics or social rules of conversation. He has already learnt when to speak and how to use language to get the desired result, and he knows the kinds of utterance that are expected in a range of contexts. He has assimilated the 'rules' that prevent spoken language exchanges being anarchic and he recognises in an unsophisticated way how to choose the appropriate tone. He can repair simple breakdowns, repeat things when required to do so, and respond directly to his mother's utterances.

9.6 What to look for in examples of child language

The following checklist can be used to identify key features in examples of dif-ferent stages of child language acquisition. You will not find all of the features in every transcript, but the list can be used as a guide. The points made are general so discussion of specific examples will need to be adapted to take account of the particular context. Remember that you need to evaluate the effect of the features you identify, exploring what they tell you about the participants, the purpose and the context.

The following are helpful questions to ask.

Register

1 What is the **mode**?
   * spoken
   * monologue or dialogue?
2 What is the **manner**?
   * relationship between the participants?
   * extent of interaction?
   * function of the communication?
3 What is the **field**?
   * linked to subject matter, context or activity?

Lexis

0;6–1;0

1 Does the child use **reduplicated sound patterns** to represent meaningful words?
2 Are there any **proto-words**?

1;0–1;6

1 Are there any recognisable **single-word utterances** used to name things directly related to the child?
   - people, food, body parts, toys, etc.?
2 Are there any examples of **misuse** of words?
   - over-extension? under-extension?
   - narrowing of the field of reference?
   - mismatch?
3 Are there any examples of the first **modifiers**?
4 Are there any **action utterances** accompanied by gestures which will form the basis for the first verbs?
5 Are there any **social expressions** typical of the child's cultural background?

1;6–2;0

1 Are there any examples of a **wider range of vocabulary** reflecting the child's growing understanding of the world?

2;0–3;0

1 Does the lexis relate to **familiar stories** or the child's **personal experience**?

3;0+

1 Is there any evidence of the child's growing **word stock**?

Pronunciation

0;2–1;0

1 Are there any examples of **cooing** using the first recognisable English sounds?
   - high vowels [iː] and [uː]?
   - velar sounds like [k] and [g]?
2 What kinds of **reduplicated sounds** are used in any examples of babbling?

1;0–1;6

1 Is the pronunciation of holophrastic utterances **idiosyncratic**?
2 Are the same words pronounced in a **variety of ways**?

1;6–2;0

1 Are any words shortened by **dropping unstressed syllables**?
2 Are **consonant clusters** avoided?
3 Are **final consonants** dropped?
4 Are any words **simplified** using reduplicated sounds?
5 Do any of the **vowels** differ from the 'caretaker' accent?
6 Are any **initial-position velars** or **fricatives** replaced?

2;0–3;0

1 Are there still instances of **immature pronunciation** from the previous developmental stage?

2 Has the child standardised:
  * the plosives [p] and [b], [t] and [d], [k] and [g]?
  * the voiced bilabial nasal [m]?
  * the voiceless glottal fricative [h]?
  * the voiced palatal approximant [j]?

3 Are some of the **consonantal sounds** still immature?
  * the voiceless alveolar fricative [s] and the voiced alveolar lateral [l]?
  * the voiced post-alveolar approximant [r]?

3;0+

1 Are pronunciations now **closer to adult forms**?

2 Are the last consonantal sounds to be produced accurately now standard?
  * the voiceless palato-alveolar fricative [ʃ]?
  * the palato-alveolar affricates [tʃ] (voiceless) and [dʒ] (voiced)?
  * the voiced labio-dental fricative [v]?
  * the voiced alveolar fricative [z]?
  * the dental fricatives [ð] (voiced) and [θ] (voiceless)?

Grammar

1;0–1;6

1 Are **single words** used to represent a grammatically complete utterance?

1;6–2;0

1 Are there any **grammatical sequences** in the rhythmic units?

2 What different kinds of **meaning** do these minimal structures convey?

3 Are any present participle *-ing* **inflections** used?

4 Are **questions** framed using *wh-* **words** at the beginnings of sentences (usually *where* or *what*)?

5 Are the **negatives** *no* and *not* used in one-word sentences or at the beginning of a variety of expressions?

2;0–3;0

1 Are combinations of three or four words representing different clause elements (usually in standard positions) used to construct a range of **clause types**?

2 Does the discourse exemplify **telegraphic talk**, in which many **grammatical function words** are omitted?

3 Is a wider range of **inflections** used?
  * *-s* to mark plural nouns?
  * *-ed* to mark the past tense of regular verbs?

4 Are any of the inflections **overused** as the child experiments?

5 Are any **auxiliary verbs** (primary or modal) used or are they still omitted?

6 Is the **primary verb** *to be* used with present participles?
  * marked for person/number?
  * still used in the base form?

7 Are **question structures** becoming more complex?
  * *why?* and *how?*
  * *where?* and *when?*

8 Are **negatives** used in a more sophisticated way with *no* and *not* placed before the relevant verb?

9 Are **pronouns** used in a range of contexts, but without a complete understanding of the different forms?
  • second person pronouns used for first person references?

3;0+

1 Has telegraphic speech been replaced with **more sophisticated sentence structures**?

2 Are there examples of **co-ordination** and **subordination**?

3 Are **inflections** now used standardly?
  • regular past tense verbs with *-ed*?
  • third person singular present tense with *-s*?

4 Are the subject and verb inverted in **questions** using *wh-* words?

5 Is the **dummy auxiliary** *do* used to frame questions and negatives?

6 Are there **contractions** like *don't*, *won't* and *isn't*?

Prosodic features

0–1;0

1 Is there any evidence that the baby is responding to the meaning of **different tones of voice**?

2 Does the parent use **exaggerated intonation patterns** to attract and hold the child's attention?

3 Does the baby use a **high pitch level** for repeated consonant and vowel-like segments?

4 Are any **intonation patterns** repeated for consonant-vowel combinations?

1;0–1;6

1 Is the child using **intonation** to mark different kinds of purpose?

2 Does the **variation of intonation** contribute to the meaning of utterances?

1;6–2;0

1 Are questions marked by a **rising intonation**?

2 Are the **rhythms** of two-word grammatical units distinctive?

3 Are **pauses** used frequently in unusual positions?

2;0–3;0

1 Does the child still use **rising intonation** to mark questions?

2 Are any syllables or key words **stressed**?

3 Are **rising–falling** or **falling–rising** intonations used to make utterances more distinctive?

4 Do **pauses** mark the ends of grammatically complete utterances instead of creating the disjointed rhythms of telegraphic speech?

3;0+

1 Is the child now using **pitch, pace, pause, rhythm** and **stress** in more sophisticated ways to enhance the meaning of utterances?

Conversation skills

0;6–1;0

1 Do the utterances seem to be related directly to **specific contexts**?
2 Are there examples in any of the exchanges in which the child and parent(s) take **recognisable turns**?

1;0–1;6

1 Does the adult take the role of **initiating** and **sustaining** conversation?
2 Does the child produce a **monologue-like string of utterances** with no real sense of audience?

1;6–2;0

1 Is there any evidence that the child is **taking part in real conversations** despite the fact that utterances are still grammatically incomplete?
2 Is the **context** crucial to an understanding of any utterances?
3 Does the child seem to be experimenting with **turn-taking** with an adult who makes all utterances meaningful?

2;0–3;0

1 Is it still important to know the **context** of the talk at this telegraphic stage?
2 Is the child **more actively involved in conversations**?
   • asking for names of objects, people and places?
   • relating responses directly to earlier utterances?
   • initiating topics?
3 Are there any examples of **normal non-fluency features**?

3;0+

1 Is the child skilful in controlling **turn-taking**?
2 Are **responses** to other speakers **appropriate**?
3 Is the **register altered** for different contexts, audiences and topics?
4 Are any simple breakdowns in communication **repaired**?
   • repeating key words or phrases?
   • requesting clarification?

Summary

Once children have acquired language, they can become **active participants** in all kinds of communication: they can establish relationships, express their feelings, get others to do things for them, ask for information or explanations, or use language creatively. The more experience they have, the more skilful they will become in adapting their language use to suit their context, audience and purpose.

Apparently effortless **language acquisition** will take place if the child can consciously manipulate the speech organs, if the child lives in a developed social and cultural environment and experiences an appropriate range of language input, and if these language experiences are gained before a critical age. If all these conditions are met, language acquisition will usually take place without any formal language teaching.

There are four main **theories** which try to explain the nature of language acquisition. The behaviourists believe that children learn by imitating the language structures that they hear; the cognitive approach suggests that children must have an intellectual understanding of a concept before they can use linguistic structures; the nativists believe that all children have an innate capacity for language acquisition; and more recent studies suggest that interaction is the key. More research needs to be carried out before language acquisition is really understood, but current thinking suggests that each of these theories throws some light on the complex processes involved.

Part III

Varieties –
English in use

Chapter 10

Spoken English

10.1 The nature of spoken language

Linguists have become increasingly interested in spoken language, crediting it in recent years with far more significance than did the traditionalists of earlier centuries.

In the 1990s, the publishing company Longman initiated a large-scale collection of spoken language. The result was the **BRITISH NATIONAL CORPUS**: a database of ten million words that reflects the nature of spoken English at the end of the twentieth century. Two thousand people were selected according to age, gender, social status and region, and asked to record all their speech encounters for the period of one week. Spontaneous conversation, business meetings, lectures, speeches, chat shows and other everyday situations provided linguists with real sources of current usage.

Based on the more than one hundred million words collected, lexicographers have been able to trace the **current development and disappearance** of words and expressions in a very concrete way. They have analysed **frequency of usage** and the ways in which **gender**, **age** and **social** or **regional differences** affect the language we use. By comparing the results of this Spoken Corpus with those of the Longman/Lancaster Corpus (a collection of thirty million words taken from written sources such as literature, magazines, newspapers, leaflets and packaging), they have also been able to see how differently language is used in speech and writing.

There can be no doubt that this research has resulted in the world's largest database of spoken English, giving prestige to the study of spoken English and encouraging us to recognise the importance of **PHATIC COMMUNICATION** – language used to establish an atmosphere or to create a social contact. The real examples collected in the project have been used as the basis for a new 'learners' dictionary', *The Longman Dictionary of Contemporary English* (4th edition: 2006). Alongside the words and their definitions, this dictionary includes 155,000 example sentences based on the usage recorded in the Longman Corpus study.

Spoken language is the dominant **mode** in our society: most of us use speech to communicate in a variety of **contexts**, for a range of **purposes** and in various

registers. We are all experts, able to adapt to the demands of each speech encounter almost subconsciously. This makes a study of the sounds and features of speech central to an understanding of the English language – spoken language is a variety in its own right, with distinctive **lexical**, **grammatical**, **stylistic** and **structural characteristics**.

The CULTURAL EXPECTATIONS and SHARED VALUES of a society dictate the roles speakers must fill if they are to be accepted, and we begin to learn the necessary skills from a very early age. To enable effective spoken communication to take place, we assimilate ritualistic patterns as the basis for spoken exchanges. Participants are involved in a constant process of evaluation which can be both conscious and subconscious: identifying what is and what is not acceptable; making lexical and grammatical choices which are appropriate for the context; using PARALINGUISTICS (non-verbal communication using gesture, posture, facial expression, and so on) to reinforce and underpin the words spoken; interpreting the meaning of utterances, and so on. Although different kinds of speech encounter display different characteristics, it is possible to establish distinctive features that make spoken and written discourse very different.

10.2 The function of spoken language

For many people, written language is more prestigious than spoken language and yet far more people use speech on a daily basis. **Writing** does have obvious benefits – it is permanent; it makes communication over a physical distance possible; it can be revised and carefully crafted; it can be reread at any time; it can overcome the limits of human memory and therefore encourages intellectual development; and it has made it possible to preserve the canon of literature. SPOKEN LANGUAGE, however, has other strengths that cannot be matched by written language – it enables people to take an active role in social groups; responses are often immediate; and the speech of each user is made distinctive by characteristic sound qualities, mannerisms and accompanying gestures. It is far more difficult to establish a personal style of writing than a personal style of speaking.

Even though participants may not be equal, most forms of spoken language are **interactional**: points can be clarified; questions can be asked; topics can be easily changed; and any number of people can take part. Because most spoken communication takes place in a face-to-face situation, speech does not have to be as explicit as writing. We can rely on **non-verbal signals** like gesture, facial expression and non-verbal sounds as well as the words themselves to understand an exchange. Equally, because the **audience** is more likely to be known, shared knowledge will prevent problems arising from any vagueness.

Just as written varieties can have a wide range of **purposes**, so too can spoken language. It may be informative, as in a lecture (REFERENTIAL); it may be social, as in an informal conversation (PHATIC); it may aim to get something done, as in a telephone call to a plumber (TRANSACTIONAL); or it may convey a speaker's personal state of mind or attitude at a certain time (EXPRESSIVE). In each case, the context, the audience and the speaker's intentions will dictate the linguistic and prosodic choices made.

The key to analysing any spoken discourse is to start by asking yourself the following questions:

- Who are the **participants** and what are their **roles**?
- Do they have equal **status**?
- What is the **purpose** of the exchange?
- How is the discourse affected by the **context**?

Answers to these questions will provide the basis for a closer focus. Having identified the general framework for communication, linguists then consider lexical, grammatical and prosodic choices made by an individual in a specific situation.

10.3 Features of spoken language

Spoken language covers such a wide range of examples that it is difficult to draw up a definitive list of linguistic characteristics. Nevertheless, it is possible to establish a number of distinctive features that mark it out as different from other varieties.

Manner

The **MANNER** will depend upon the relative status of the participants – the inequality at a job interview between interviewers and interviewee means that the tone will be **formal**; the equality between two students having a chat in the common room means that the tone will be **informal**. Lexical, grammatical and prosodic choices will be dictated by the manner – that is, by the relative formality or informality of the encounter. Because of the cultural and social expectations assimilated from an early age, participants in any spoken discourse will often make the same kinds of decision about what is and what is not acceptable. Despite the fact that many speech encounters are informal and spontaneous, therefore, spoken language is quite formulaic.

The speakers

The **RELATIONSHIP** of the speakers or their **RELATIVE STATUS** is the first area of a transcript to address. Aspects such as the educational, social or economic status of the participants are fixed, but other features are not. Speakers may take it in turns to select topics; turn-taking may be co-operative or one speaker may be more dominant than others; and the purpose of the discourse can change, making a different participant the 'expert'.

The topic

The **TOPIC** and the **GOAL** of a spoken encounter are also directly related to the manner and the participants. The more clearly defined the purpose, the more formal the exchange is likely to be. A formal **speech** will often first be written in note form or in full, and will have a predetermined content; the subject matter of spontaneous informal **conversation**, on the other hand, is usually random, with no clear pattern or evidence of conscious planning. In an informal spoken exchange a speaker can introduce a wide range of material and jump from one topic to another; in a formal context, the topic will be less adaptable. For example, a prearranged **lecture** on 'the nature of political language' for a group of A-level students will be far more structured and the content far less flexible than a conversation taking place in the common room.

TOPIC SHIFTS – points at which speakers move from one topic to another – mark key points in spoken discourse. The speaker responsible for initiating a new topic is clearly in charge of the turn-taking, and this role may be taken by different participants during an exchange or one particular person may be dominant throughout. Even though TOPIC PLACEMENT may seem to be random, participants try to introduce topics as though they arise naturally. In informal conversation this may mean that the **main topic** – the reason for the exchange – does not come first.

The **end of a topic** can be identified by linguistic signals: in informal conversation, phrases like *by the way...* and *incidentally...* or clauses like *that reminds me...* and *to change the subject...* may be used to bring one topic to an end and establish a new one; in formal contexts, adverbials like *lastly...* and non-finite clauses like *to conclude...* can be used as indicators that something different will soon be introduced. **New topics** can be found by reintroducing material that cropped up earlier in the exchange but in a **new form** (*as I was saying before...*), by relating a new topic to the old one (*speaking of which...*), by taking a completely new direction (*let's talk about something else...*), and so on. **Interruptions** may be seen to bring a topic to its end before its natural conclusion. After a digression, an attempt may be made to revive the old topic (*where was I?*), or the new topic may be allowed to replace it because it is seen as more interesting. This kind of **topic management**, however, is unlikely to take place in a formal speech context, such as a lecture or interview, where the topic is usually predefined and particular speakers are dominant.

The structure

The **structure** of spoken exchanges is distinct despite the apparent randomness. Formal discourse, where the words spoken may have been planned on paper before being spoken, will often adopt structural devices typical of written language. Informal speech, however, has its own distinctive structural features. Sequences of utterances called ADJACENCY PAIRS create a recognisable structural pattern. They:

- follow one another
- are produced by different speakers
- have a logical connection
- conform to a pattern.

Questions and answers, greetings, and a command followed by a response are all examples of adjacency pairs.

A Can I come in?	A Shut that door now.
B Of course you can.	B I will any minute, just don't nag.

The order of **TURN-TAKING** also structures spoken discourse. Participants are skilful in manipulating turns: usually only one person will speak at a time; despite the fact that turns vary in length, **TRANSITIONS** from one speaker to another occur smoothly, often with no gap; the **order of participation** is not planned in advance, but speakers seem to instinctively identify when turns are coming to an end; and if an **OVERLAP** does occur, it rarely lasts for long. Speakers have to make decisions about turns throughout an exchange, but the knowledge used to do so has not been learnt explicitly. Research into turn-taking suggests that participants build up an awareness of general **frameworks** and then use these as the basis for their decisions. For instance, they 'learn' the pattern of exchanges that will take place in a job interview or a classroom and can therefore contribute effectively to the spoken discourse. Speakers can also rely on their knowledge of structures like adjacency pairs: in a meeting with a new person, participants can confidently introduce themselves using a familiar pattern of statements and questions and answers. Assimilated grammatical knowledge also facilitates smooth turn-taking – speakers know when an utterance is grammatically complete. Non-verbal clues can work alongside the linguistic ones: changes in eye contact, intonation or volume can indicate that a turn is coming to an end; the final syllable of a turn may be lengthened; or a gesture may imply that a speaker has no more to say.

OPENINGS and **CLOSINGS** are marked by distinctive features. Social equals might use a neutral starting point or opening in a conversation by talking about the weather. This may then lead into a **self-related comment** (focusing on the speaker) or an **other-related comment** (focusing on the listener). Vocatives are common as they help to personalise an encounter. Speakers have a wide range of possible openers to draw on: social greetings; **HOSPITALITY TOKENS** (linguistic references to customary social acts that are used to receive and entertain guests) such as *have a drink, can I get you something?* or *do sit down*; neutral topics; or self- or other-related remarks. They can also establish a co-operative atmosphere by selecting a topic that reflects the interests and experiences of all the participants.

Spoken words	Comment
A morning (.) oh (.) Richard (.) I must tell you about the holiday = B = ah (.) I was going to ask about that	The first speaker establishes the topic. He initiates the discourse with a phatic opening, a vocative and a self-related comment. The second speaker adopts a supportive role by creating a link between 'self' and 'other'.
A come in (.) Peter (.) hang on a sec I've got to turn the oven off (4) do you want a drĭnk = B = thought you'd never âsk	The use of the vocative and imperative show that the speaker is focusing on the other participant in the conversation. Speaker B's response is directly related to the last part of the first speaker's utterance, creating an adjacency pair.

CLOSINGS are used to sum up the exchange. Reference is often made to something outside the speech encounter as a reason for ending the discourse. Self- and other-related remarks are common, but neutral tokens like the weather are not.

Closings are often repetitive since the speakers use delaying tactics, referring back to earlier topics and adopting frequently occurring formulae.

Spoken words		Comment
A	better be off now (.) I know you're busy (.) enjoy yourself tomorrow (.)	An other-related remark is used as a reason for ending the speech encounter. This is followed by a return to an earlier topic (reference to an event taking place on the next day). Both of these establish conventional patterns in which Speaker A focuses interest on Speaker B. The exchange is clearly repetitive – social formulae are reiterated.
B	I'll make sure I do (.) thanks for coming =	
A	= have a lovely time =	
B	= I will (.) and thanks again =	
A	= thanks (.) bye (.)	
B	bye =	
A	= bye	

In the main body of a dialogue, SPEAKER MOVES can be used:

‣ to FRAME, by using openings and closings to create an overall structure
‣ to INITIATE, by establishing a topic
‣ to FOCUS, by using comments to clearly specify the direction of a topic and to ensure its development
‣ to SUPPORT or FOLLOW UP, by continuing discussion of a topic
‣ to CHALLENGE, by interrupting a topic or introducing a new one without mutual agreement.

Prosodic features

PROSODIC FEATURES are a means of dividing spoken utterances into smaller units, just as punctuation, capital letters and paragraphing do in a visual way for written language. Whether they are marked or not on a transcript depends upon the purpose of the transcription. A narrow phonetic transcription will contain a lot of information about the quality of sounds used, but most transcriptions you will analyse will be broad – that is, less detailed or phonemic. The list below indicates some of the variations that can be identified and the symbols that may be used to highlight them. (These are discussed in more detail in Chapter 2.) It takes great expertise to identify and mark all the prosodic changes in spoken discourse, but you should be able to recognise the symbols and the sound qualities they represent. The transcripts used here are broad and selective, marking only the most prominent prosodic features.

Intonation

INTONATION PATTERNS can vary dramatically, and each change will usually reinforce the meaning in some way. By varying the intonation, speakers can convey different grammatical moods and attitudes of surprise, excitement, pleasure and so on.

nǒ	I rĕally mean it	nô	I dòn't think so
(indignant)	(certainty)	(doubtful)	(matter-of-fact)

Intonation has functional as well as semantic uses – it marks grammatical boundaries and structures turns.

Pitch

Pitch may be high, low or anywhere in between. Variations (high, mid or low) can be marked on a transcription, but the level, particularly for monosyllabic utterances, will often be quite uniform. Changes in pitch are usually linked to meaning and the speaker's relationship to the topic: a raised pitch often indicates excitement or enthusiasm, whereas a lowered pitch marks a finale or anticlimax of some kind:

> and the most ↑fantastic thing↑ has happened (.) everyone is standing ↑up↑ (.) the concert is almost over but people are ↑still clapping↑ (.) the soloist is ↓smiling↓ (.) the conductor is ↓acknowledging↓ the orchestra (.) and what a concert it's ↓been↓ (.) the last night of the Proms is over for another ↓year↓

Stress

The pattern of **STRESSED** and **UNSTRESSED WORDS** in English is directly linked to the rhythm of utterances. It also marks words of importance – a change of stress can change meaning:

> I <u>ate</u> an icecream   Focus: *ate* rather than bought or made
> <u>I</u> ate an icecream   Focus: *I* rather than someone else
> I ate an <u>icecream</u>   Focus: *icecream* rather than another kind of food

TONE UNITS help to organise the discourse, directing listeners' attention to the syntactic structure of an utterance, the relative prominence of the clause elements, and any new information.

Loudness and pace

The **LOUDNESS** (loud, quiet, increasing or decreasing in volume) and the **PACE** (fast, slow, getting faster or slower) of spoken language can also influence the meaning and reveal attitude. Variations in the volume of utterances, for instance, are used to reflect the relative importance of what speakers say:

> 'forte'   it's important (.) 'I <u>need</u> to have it by' ↓tomorrow↓
>
> 'cresc'   and it's a 'goal (.) Gerrard's scored for England again' (.) and ↑what↑ a
> 'dimin'   'goal it ↓was↓'

Pauses

Pauses are seen to be acceptable in many kinds of spoken discourse, particularly where the manner is informal. This means that the **RHYTHM** is often uneven. Where the manner is formal, however, although pauses may be used for dramatic effect the rhythm is usually more regular and stylised. This kind of rhetorical style is commonly found in speeches written to be spoken:

> Never (.) in the field of human conflict (.) was so much owed (.) by so many (.) to so few.

Winston Churchill (20 August 1940)

VOICELESS HESITATION, VOICED PAUSES and **WORD SEARCHING** also create pauses in spoken language. Sometimes they are used intentionally by speakers to encourage equality of status between participants – they prevent speakers from giving the impression that they are experts by suggesting that information is not spontaneously available but requires thought. A student, for instance, might hesitate in talking about *Hamlet* so that she did not seem too knowledgeable:

> Hamlet is a (.) complex character who (1) uses his madness to (.) conceal his (1) real intentions

It is important to remember that where written language identifies the end of a sentence with a full stop, spoken language uses a pause. Some pauses therefore have a functional role in spoken discourse – these tend to be **MICRO-PAUSES** rather than **TIMED PAUSES**.

Vocal effects

VOCAL EFFECTS (**giggling**, **coughing** and **throat clearing**) and **PARALINGUISTICS** (**gestures** and **posture**) can reinforce or contradict the meaning conveyed by the spoken word.

Lexis

The **lexis** of spoken discourse is often less formal than that associated with written language. If a topic does require formal subject-specific language, unless a speaker is specifically assigned the role of expert, participants will often underplay the importance of key words by introducing clauses like *you know* and phrases like *sort of*. An informal atmosphere can be recognised in the use of **conversational lexis** (*yeah, cos, all right*), **colloquial idiom** (*in a minute, the thing is, as far as I can see*), clichés (*that's life*), **hyperbole** (*on and on and on, really stupid, thousands*), and **phatic communication** and **vocalisations**. **Abbreviations** may be used where the speakers are sufficiently well known to one another to have established a code based on familiarity and a shared view of the world. Equally, in-slang or in-jokes will be mutually intelligible among 'insiders'.

Spoken discourse is often **ambiguous** because speakers use language inexplicitly. Ambiguities usually cause no problems with understanding, however, because participants can rely on the context and non-verbal communication for extra information. Deictic expressions like *this one, over there* or *right now* are common. They are typical of face-to-face interaction where speakers can refer directly to specific characteristics of the context. Their meaning is always relative to the speech situation. Phonologically vague utterances like **MUMBLING** and **TAILING OFF** can also be overcome because there is a permanent possibility for **RECAPITULATION**.

Grammar

The **GRAMMAR** of spoken language tends to be looser and more rambling than that of written language, which can be crafted. Typically, informal spoken discourse is marked by frequent use of minor 'sentences' and co-ordinated clauses, phrasal verbs and informal 'filler' verbs, and contracted forms. In more formal situations, grammar is less erratic and more likely to conform to standard patterns.

In general terms, phrases tend to be relatively straightforward. Noun phrases are often simple; where they are complex, they tend to consist of one pre-modifier rather than a string. Post-modification occurs less frequently. As the topic becomes more serious and the manner more formal, noun phrases are more likely to be complex. Certain adverbial intensifiers like *very* and *a bit* occur frequently. Verb phrases also tend to have a simple structure: they are often made up of a lexical verb standing alone or an auxiliary plus a lexical verb. If the manner is formal, a wider range of tense forms and aspects will be used. In many spoken encounters, contracted verbs are common. Colloquial ellipses occur frequently, but use of the passive voice is limited.

Clauses are often quite uncomplicated, made up of S P O/C A:

```
  S      P       C        A          S     P        A
(it) (was) (great) (yesterday) – (I) (went) (into town)
    P      S       P              O
(can) (you) (bring in) (Mr Jones's letter)
   aux         lex
```

Clause structure is often developed by the addition of strings of adverbials which are normally found in the final position:

```
   S       P     C      A           A            A           A
(the train) (was) (late) (in Swansea) (on Platform 2) (last night) (as usual)
```

If the manner is informal, the relative pronoun that introduces the relative clause is often omitted:

```
                 S                        P        C
(the boys [who go] down the Leisure Centre) (are) (really mad)
```

The structure of utterances is difficult to establish in spoken discourse because it is hard to say exactly where each one begins and ends. Length is more variable in speech than in any other variety and minor 'sentences' are common as responses to questions or in summary statements. Grammatically incomplete utterances tend to be accepted more readily than in many other varieties. Longer utterances tend to be associated with a developing argument or anecdote. Co-ordination of clauses tends to be loose, often using a clause like *you know* as an introductory link. Internal linkage is created through pronoun referencing, cross-referencing of determiners, and ellipsis. Tag questions and examples of phatic communication maintain the pace of spoken discourse. In most forms of spoken language, interrogatives are more common than the imperative mood. Vocatives in the initial position help to create a personal relationship between speakers and encourage interaction.

Spoken language is very versatile – it can use a range of grammatical modes: reported speech, direct quotations, first-person accounts of events, and so on. Changes in modality are also common.

In most spoken contexts, the relationship created between speakers is sympathetic. Even if the speakers are using different kinds of structures (dialect versus Standard English), the discrepancy will not be mentioned. One speaker may, for instance, use the standard form *we were* while someone else may use the dialectal *we was*. Such variations are usually seen as a reflection of the speaker's individuality and background. Even within one conversation, an individual may be inconsistent, using both standard and non-standard grammatical forms alongside one another. The willingness to accept such variation is indicative of the co-operative principles that govern most speech exchanges.

NORMAL NON-FLUENCY FEATURES are common, clearly distinguishing between written and spoken language. The more formal the manner, the less likely there are to be examples of hesitancy, slips of the tongue, simultaneous speech, and the like. However, even in contexts such as an interview on a news programme or a formal debate, transcripts may reveal evidence of non-fluency. The interesting thing is that such 'errors' are taken for granted and often go unnoticed.

Brief **OVERLAPS**, for instance, are quite common in conversation. They may occur where speakers are having to compete for a turn in a speech encounter in which many participants are involved (such as a group of friends chatting in a pub); equally, a speaker may have misjudged the end of a turn (as when the speaker adds extra information having already used closing formulae to signal the end of a turn); or one speaker who is particularly dominant may insist on interrupting (a heckler at a political meeting).

```
A  I would like to speak today about our policy on the National ‖ Health Service on the
B                                                               ‖ you haven't got one
A  National Health Service (.) since we have been in Government ‖ we have spent
B                                                               ‖ oh yeah
A  please let me finish =
B  = if you must =
A  = as I was trying to say …
```

The example here is typical of a negative speech interaction in which the overlaps are caused by Speaker B's desire to challenge and disrupt Speaker A's turn. Most speech encounters are co-operative, however, so overlaps are usually resolved quickly, with one participant ceasing to speak.

Some simultaneous speech is not classed as an interruption because it enhances the collaborative approach of spoken discourse. Where a second speaker utters **MINIMAL RESPONSES** like *mmm* or *yeah*, the function of the utterances is often to support rather than to challenge:

```
A  have you seen the colour of that wall (.) it's horrific (.) it'll have ‖ to be repainted
B                                                                         ‖ mmm
A  we'll have to say something (.) ‖ I just can't be expected to put up with that
B                                  ‖ yeah
```

VOICED HESITATIONS or **FILLED PAUSES** are also examples of non-fluency that are tolerated in spoken language. Speakers can use these to protect themselves from interruption while they think. In formal contexts, speakers use fillers like *um*, *er* or *ah* to prolong their turns. In a co-operative speech encounter it is unacceptable to interrupt halfway through a clause, so by pausing in the middle a speaker can prevent another speaker from taking the turn. Voiced hesitations and false starts can also be used to gain the attention of an audience who have not yet settled. Politicians or public speakers will often repeat the opening of a speech several times during clapping until quiet has again been established: they will move on only when they are sure that everyone is listening.

Normal non-fluency features may therefore be attributed to inaccuracies associated with informal speech encounters, but they may also be used consciously to control turn-taking and to ensure that all participants are listening.

Problems

There can be **PROBLEMS** in spoken language which the participants must solve if the speech encounter is to continue. Temporary interruptions can be dealt with in a variety of ways.

Repairs

REPAIRS involve practical approaches to restore conversation. If a speaker chooses a wrong word, for example, she can correct herself or another speaker can correct her; if a listener mishears a word, he can ask for clarification. Even though a side sequence is created running alongside the main topic, the interruption is only temporary.

Spoken words	Comment
A you know Michelle (.) you know (.) the nurse (.) er (.) no (.) that's it (.) Susan = B = I know who you mean now (.) yeah she's called Susan	Speaker A starts with a formulaic opener. The number of brief pauses indicates hesitancy and suggests that she is unsure of her information. She corrects herself and Speaker B supports her final choice.
A I've got English next lecture = B = English (.) we had English earlier (.) A sorry (.) yeah (.) you're right (.) it's French actually	Speaker B questions Speaker A's statement by reiterating the key word and introducing information which challenges it. Speaker A accepts the challenge and the repair is complete.

Topic loops

TOPIC LOOPS can offer an alternative method of dealing with a problem. These involve reintroducing an earlier topic in order to move away from the disruption. For instance, a speaker may invite an evaluation from the listener; if the response is minimal or negative, then the first speaker may return to an earlier, safer topic of conversation to repair the damage to the co-operative interaction. An example is shown on the next page.

Listener response

A speaker who is **aware of listener response** can make repairs before communication breaks down. Expressions like *you know, you see* or *you understand* are a speaker's way of encouraging the listener to acknowledge that communication is effective. Direct address can also draw listeners into the conversation: *and you know what I said?, can you guess what happened?, if you ask me....* Such expressions require the listeners to show some kind of approval or encouragement to continue. Questions can have a similar function: *are you with me?, do you get what I mean?* or *OK?* If the listener response is negative, the speaker must repair the

Spoken words	Comment
A I went to town this morning to get some felt pens and stuff to make a (.) some party invitations (.) B mmm =	Instead of providing a positive response to Speaker A's opening, Speaker B offers a minimal acknowledgement. This suggests that the interaction may not be co-operative.
A = I couldn't resist getting this too = [*holding up a dinosaur magic painting book*] B = why (.) A well you know he's crazy about them at the moment so ‖ I B ‖ but we've already got his present (.) A I know (.) I (.) but he'll like it = B = yes but you can't keep buying things (.)	Speaker B's question also signals practical trouble since it denies Speaker A the expected positive evaluation. Because of the structure of an adjacency pair, Speaker A is forced to respond. Speaker B is now controlling the turn-taking. The practical trouble is caused by Speaker B's implied criticism of Speaker A's actions. The co-operative nature of the conversation has been lost – the frequency of overlaps and Speaker B's negative evaluations highlight this.
A I know (1) it <u>was</u> in the sale ‖ so I B ‖ that's not an excuse for buying everything =	The speakers continue the topic, making no attempt to repair the damage. The disjointed turn-taking suggests that the conversation is still not collaborative.
A = I (.) well it was only a one off = B = [*laughs*] fine (.)	Speaker B's laugh is significant because the tone of the conversation has not been humorous: instead it implies disbelief. The accompanying utterance is also dismissive.
A I did get all the stuff for the invitations so I can do (.) make those tonight	Speaker A is forced to make a topic loop in order to repair what would otherwise be a complete breakdown in communication.

point of breakdown before moving on. Restating or rephrasing points made can solve the problem: *what I was trying to say was…* or *what I really meant was…* or *in other words…* . By clarifying structures, this kind of monitoring behaviour can prevent spoken discourse from breaking down. It is a form of repair that relies on the speaker being sensitive to listeners.

Silence

SILENCE in a conversation can require repair. Utterances in spoken discourse often come in pairs, and if for some reason an answer is not given quickly to a question or if a greeting is not returned, a speaker must decide whether to ignore the breakdown in cooperation or to tackle it. If the lack of response has been due to mishearing, repeating the utterance may repair the breakdown; if not, it may instead reinforce the conflict.

Pauses can also be responsible for creating a silence, so they are usually kept to a minimum in speech. A long pause may cause embarrassment if it is seen as an indicator of failure. Often several people will then begin to speak at once in an attempt to fill the gap. Once a new topic has been established, the collective embarrassment is replaced with relief that the repair has been accomplished.

Silence must always be considered within the spoken context because it can also be used for dramatic effect, particularly in public speaking. Before deciding whether a repair is necessary, participants will have to assess the role of the silence within the discourse. If it enhances the meaning of utterances, it is probably purposeful; if it makes the participants uneasy, it can probably be seen as a breakdown in co-operative behaviour.

10.4 Types of spoken language

A spoken narrative

The following transcript is an extract from a family conversation in which three young girls listen to their great uncle telling stories from his youth. The dominant speaker is the storyteller, whose turns are extended, and the extract here focuses specifically on one of the narratives.

ACTIVITY 10.1

The transcription is a broad one: it takes no account of regional accent and only the most prominent examples of intonation and stress are marked. A key to the symbols can be found on page 93.

Read through the transcript and respond to the following.

1 Comment on the opening and closing of the narrative and any other distinctive structural features.
2 Describe the effects of the main prosodic features marked on the transcript.
3 Highlight any significant lexical or grammatical features.
4 List and describe the normal non-fluency features.
5 Identify any points at which the speaker tries to ensure that his audience is still paying attention, and comment on the ways in which he does this.

NARRATIVE (1 MINUTE) ···

1 Well (.) you know I was in the bànd (.) St. Faiths bànd you know (.) well we went
  a-carol-pláying there one (.) just before Christmas (2) we went all round St. Faiths
  and Newton St. Faiths (.) and then we went up to the Mànor (3) and there was a lot a
  mud up that old loke and ol' Jack Fisher sáid (.) i.i.i. ah.h o.o.o. w.wor what about the
5 m.mud (.) he said (.) I g.got some w.water boots on b.but they g.got a h.hole in the
  bottom (1) course ol' Jack used to stùtter you see (.) anyway, we kept agóing 'n' they
  called at the King's Head and that got on there 'til past ten and so they said (.) well
  we'd better (.) have one more túne before we go hòme (1) so they played a cárol or
  one or two cárols round there (.) 'til someone said (.) you know what you are doing
10 altogether don't yá (2) what someone said (.) you're playing to an old hàystack (.) huh
  they said (.) that was a wrŏng un (.) so we had to pack that up (.) and of course we
  had to go hóme cos some of them weren't feeling too gòod (.) it was dark you knòw
  (.) and we didn't know where we wère ...

Both the **opening** and the **closing** of the narrative provide a framework for the story: the speaker directly addresses his audience using the comment clause *you know* three times (ll. 1, 12). This is typical of storytelling within a conversation because the speaker has to ensure that the audience have accepted his dominant role in the turn-taking. To be effective, a narrative turn needs to be uninterrupted – by **monitoring audience response**, the speaker can prevent a problem occurring in the conversation. If speakers fail to monitor audience response and a breakdown does occur, the necessary repairs interrupt the smooth development of the story, spoiling the atmosphere and destroying the narrative's momentum.

The narrative starts and finishes with a statement that explains something to the audience. First, the speaker describes his own relationship with the story and events using a **self-related comment** – the use of the first person pronoun clearly establishes the tale as autobiographical. The use of the linking adverb *Well* (l. 1) establishes the informal manner and gives the speaker time to think before he starts the story. The concluding statement explains the narrative to the audience in case they have missed the point – it provides a summary which clearly marks the **end of the speaker's turn**.

The speaker uses several **narrative techniques** to dramatise the incident he is recalling. Much of the turn is taken up describing a sequence of events, but there are also key points at which characterisation becomes the focus of the narrative. Direct speech is used to give a sense of the people involved. Old Jack Fisher is distinctive because of the speaker's imitation of his stuttering – to prevent a breakdown of communication at this point, the storyteller again speaks directly to his audience using the comment clause *you see* (l. 6). This enables him to explain the reason for his non-standard speech. Informal utterances like *don't ya* (l. 10) and vocalisations like *huh* (l. 10) are used to animate the story and give it validity.

The **prosodics** help the storyteller to emphasise certain points in the narrative. **Emphatic stress** is used regularly to highlight key words: <u>band</u> (l. 1), <u>Christmas</u> (l. 2) and <u>haystack</u> (l. 10). It ensures that the audience are focused on the central theme. The **intonation patterns** are typical of the speaker's regional accent (Norfolk). Simple rises or falls are often used to mark the end of grammatical utterances or as a lead-in to direct speech. On one occasion a falling–rising tone (l. 11) is used, stressing the response of the players to what they have just been told. It adds variety after the climax of the story has been reached in the stressed noun phrase *an old haystack* (l. 10). **Pauses** are mostly brief and usually correspond to the end of an utterance, helping the listener to divide the speech into meaningful units.

The **lexis** establishes the narrative in **time** (*Christmas*, l. 2) and **place** (*St. Faiths*, ll. 1, 2; *Newton St. Faiths*, l. 3; *Manor*, l. 3; *King's Head*, l. 7). **Lexical sets** build up a sense of the story's focus: rural (*mud*, l. 4; *haystack*, l. 10; *water boots*, l. 5), musical (*band*, l. 1; *carol playing*, l. 2; *carols*, l. 9; *tune*, l. 8), and at night (*past ten*, l. 7; *dark*, l. 12). Only one character is named, but **direct speech** helps to create a sense of other participants. Spoken narratives are far less descriptive than written narratives, but the speaker does use a few **complex noun phrases** to build up the atmosphere:

	m		m	h		m		m		h
	that	**old**		**loke**		**an**		**old**		**haystack**
	det	Adj		N		det		Adj		N

The noun *loke* (l. 4) is a Norfolk **dialect word** which describes a path leading up to a house – it makes the narrative distinctive because it links the speaker directly to his regional and cultural background. Examples of **abbreviated words** like *'til* (l. 9), *'n'* (l. 6) and *we'd* (l. 8) are typical of all informal speech, not of a particular dialect.

The **grammar** is mostly standard, but it is marked by some dialectal features. While the use of the archaic **present participle** *a-…playing* (l. 2) and *agoing* (l. 6) is typical of dialects in general, the use of the **pronoun** *that* instead of *it* is a variation specifically associated with a Norfolk dialect: *we had to pack that up* (l. 11).

The **sentence structures** are typical of spoken narratives: **co-ordination** is far more common than subordination. It is possible to analyse the clauses using the following model:

CConj	SConj	S	P	O/C/(S)	A
					Well
		you	know		
	(that)	I	was		in the band …
		we	went	a-carol-playing	there
					just before Christmas
		we	went		all round …
and					then
		we	went		up to the Manor
and		there	was	a lot of mud	up that old loke…
					anyway
		we	kept	agoing	
and		they	called		at the King's Head
and		that	got		on there 'til past ten

The columns here indicate clearly the dominance of co-ordinated clauses in the narrative, which is typical of the rambling nature of spoken language. The co-ordination allows the speaker to sustain his turn without interruption. In written language, the structure would seem repetitive, but in speech we accept it. There are examples of **subordinate clauses** like *'til someone said…* (l. 9) and *cos some of them* (l. 12), but these are far less common.

Although the **pronouns** begin in the first person (*I* and *we*), the speaker slips into the third person halfway through the narrative: *they* (l. 6). Inconsistencies like these would be eliminated in a first draft in a written narrative, but the audience here would probably barely notice them.

Normal non-fluency features do not significantly affect the fluency of the story. In fact, the speaker is very controlled in his extended turn. There are some examples of restarts like *one (.) just before Christmas* (l. 2) in which the speaker repairs the breakdown himself, and a few longer pauses in which the speaker organises his thoughts before continuing with his tale, but on the whole the narrative seems effortless. Lexis and clause structures are quite repetitive, but that is typical of much spoken discourse.

The speaker uses the same technique on several occasions to ensure that his audience is still responsive. The comment clauses *you know* (l. 1) and *you see* (l. 6) require some kind of response from the listeners which, in a narrative turn, are more likely to be paralinguistic than vocal. Nods of the head, direct eye contact and minimal vocalisations like *mm* will satisfy the speaker that he still has the audience's consent to continue dominating the turn-taking.

A telephone conversation

The next transcript is an extract from a telephone conversation between a husband (David) and wife (Lucy) in which they discuss everyday events. The speakers are involved in a co-operative exchange in which they take more or less equal turns. Because they cannot rely on clues other than linguistic ones, however, the turns are not so clearly marked as they are in face-to-face informal conversation.

ACTIVITY 10.2

The transcription is a broad one, focusing on only the most significant changes in intonation patterns and stress. A key to the symbols can be found on page 93.

Read through the transcript and respond to the following.

1 Comment on the opening and closing of the conversation and any other distinctive structural features (topic management; turn-taking).
2 Identify and discuss the main prosodic features and their effects.
3 Highlight any significant lexical or grammatical features.
4 List and describe the normal non-fluency features.
5 Comment on the main differences between one speaker telling a story and two speakers contributing to a conversation.

TELEPHONE CONVERSATION (3 MINUTES)

```
 1 L   héllo (.)
   D   Lǔcy =
   L   = yès (.) hiỳa (.) work OḰ=
   D   = mmm (.) same as ever (.) have you found out when (.) where the place ‖ís
 5 L                                                                              ‖ yeah (.) I
       phoned College (.) and Susan didn't knów (.) Mark didn't knów (.) but then Jane did
       knòw (2) that's Jane at work =
   D   = oh ‖ yes
   L        ‖ mm (.) it's the big one =
10 D   = the one on the corner of the road you turn into (.) into for the schòol =
   L   = that's it ‖ yeah
   D              ‖ I don't know where you'll park =
   L   = well no (.) she said something about parking in the car park d. down by the
       Odeon cinema (.) ôh she means the mǔlti-stòrey =
```

15 D　= mm̌ (.) the Odeon um (.) I don't know whether she means the old (.) I think there's
　　an Odeon cinema which is now a Bingo Hall (.) is̀n't it́ (.)
　L　ôh (.) right =
　D　= you know ‖ which is just between that ‖ turning
　L　　　　　‖ I know　　　　　　　　　　　‖ but I don't know where there's a car park
20　there =
　D　= mm =
　L　= anyway (.) she says you probably can park on the road =
　D　= mm (.) you might (.) shǒuld be able to (.) depending on how many people are
　　there (.)
25 L　I'm just wondering whether to go in at half elevenish (.) so I can buy the paper
　　first =
　D　= the páper =
　L　= er (.) typing paper =
　D　= oh (.) oh yeah (.) I for̀got you were (.) going to do that (.) you've got the card 'n'
30　stuff in (.) it didn't mind (.) matter ‖ if you
　L　　　　　　　　　　　　　　　　‖ I think it's er downstairs =
　D　= oh =
　L　= the form says (.) do you think it'd be er bùsiness ‖ úse
　D　　　　　　　　　　　　　　　　　　　　　　　‖ ehh (.)
35 L　it's not actually home use really =
　D　= mm I'm er not mm cônvinced ‖ er
　L　　　　　　　　　　　　　　‖ one of the bits then later oǹ you know (.) it's got
　　what's it for and it's got education ‖ and
　D　　　　　　　　　　　　　　　　‖ well put (.) dò that ‖ then
40 L　　　　　　　　　　　　　　　　　　　　　　　‖ and later ‖ on
　D　　　　　　　　　　　　　　　　　　　　　　　　　　　‖ you can put edu-
　　cation (.) publishing (1) or sómething like that (.) well I ‖ won't be
　L　　　　　　　　　　　　　　　　　　　　　　　　‖ we won't be playing games
　　or ‖ anything
45 D　‖ no (.)
　L　I don't expect it actually makes much difference ‖ I
　D　　　　　　　　　　　　　　　　　　　　　‖ it's probably just for their infor-
　　mation (.) they mìght (.) they might (.) ‖ circular (.) circularise things for ‖ bùsinesses
　L　　　　　　　　　　　　　　　　　‖ yeah　　　　　　　　　　　　　‖ is there any-
50　thing else we need from tówn =
　D　= I can't think of anything (.) er I won't be going for a run er now (.) at lunch ‖ time
　L　　　　　　　　　　　　　　　　　　　　　　　　　　　　　　　　　　‖ you're
　　góing ‖ tó
　D　‖ well I won't be ‖ nòw
55 L　　　　　　　　‖ I was thinking you were being a ‖ bit brave
　D　　　　　　　　　　　　　　　　　　　　　‖ yeah (.)
　L　did you go swimming in the énd =
　D　= yeah (.) I did 60 (.) cos I was doing breaststroke (.) and I interspersed with some
　　crawl (1) crawl being the operative word (.) ‖ I think (.)
60 L　　　　　　　　　　　　　　　　　‖ [laughs]
　D　but ‖ well
　L　　‖ hang on =
　D　= I'd better go ‖ now
　L　　　　　　　‖ right well I'll go and get on with some typing =

D = OK (.) I'll let you get on ‖ so I'll see you later =
       L   ‖OK
       D = bye =
       L = bye

COMMENTARY

The beginning and end of the conversation are marked by **formulaic utterances**: *hello* (l.1), *I'd better go now* (l.64) and *bye* (ll.68–9). These clearly signal the intentions of the speakers in one of the few spoken contexts where the participants cannot see each other. Because they cannot rely on visual feedback from the exchange, they use patterned linguistic structures to prevent any possible ambiguity.

The **introductory section** includes the formulaic opening (ll.1–2) and an other-related comment in which Lucy asks David a question (l.3). Having responded to that, David introduces the first **topic**: finding out about *the place* (l. 4). Because the speakers are familiar, they have a shared knowledge of the topic. This means that they do not make explicit exactly what they are talking about – the participants understand the sequence of exchanges, but for an external listener they are ambiguous. The first **topic shift** occurs when a new topic is introduced by Lucy: buying *the paper* (l.25). It leads naturally into a third related topic: the entrance card and the appropriate form for entry to the stationery shop (l.29). The conversation begins to come towards an end when David introduces a self-related remark: *I won't be going for a run* (l.51). The **closing section** is typical of the end of a conversation – it is repetitive; David shows concern for Lucy in a statement which conclusively marks the end of the exchange (*I'll let you get on*, l.65) and traditional formulae are used. The **topic management** is quite equally divided – both speakers introduce and develop the content.

The **turn-taking** is typical of a telephone conversation: speakers tend to avoid long utterances without introducing brief pauses for listeners to mark their continued interest. On the whole, turns are quite short, with neither participant dominating. Because the turns cannot be clearly marked by paralinguistic features, there are many examples of overlaps. Some of these are supportive minimal vocalisations: *yeah* (l.5), *mm* (l.9) and [*laughs*] (l.60), but others mark points at which both speakers talk at once. Because the context is co-operative, usually one speaker will stop to allow the other participant to complete the utterance:

   L I don't expect it actually makes much difference ‖ I
   D   ‖ it's probably just for their infor-
      mation   (ll.46–8)

   D I'd better go ‖ now
   L   ‖ right well I'll go and get on with some <u>typing</u>   (ll.63–4)

Usually a telephone call has a **specific purpose** – the conversation does not take place by chance. By dialling a specific phone number, a caller expresses a desire to speak to someone in particular. This means that most topics will not be randomly selected.

The **prosodic features** show the typical variations in **intonation patterns** that mark informal conversation. Because the participants cannot see each other, speakers on the telephone often compensate by making their intonation more varied. There are many examples in this extract of falling, rising, rising–falling and falling–rising tones. Their function is varied: rising tones can be used to mark a question: *work OḰ* (l. 3); falling tones can be used to show agreement: *dò that* (l. 39); rising–falling tones can reflect sudden understanding: *ôh she means the <u>multistorey</u>* (l. 14); and falling–rising tones can reflect uncertainty: *Lǔcy* (l. 2). Speakers use variations to maintain the listener's interest and to enhance the meaning.

Emphatic stress is used to highlight key lexical items: <u>work</u> (l. 7) and <u>education</u> (l. 38). It helps to establish a relationship between two participants who cannot see each other. In a telephone conversation, **pauses** are kept to a minimum. Longer pauses could create a breakdown in communication because participants cannot rely on visual clues to know whether the gap is intentional or not – the listener may think the call has been cut off. Equally, long pauses could leave room for unwanted interruptions. To prevent this kind of breakdown, participants tend to use pauses only to mark the end of grammatical utterances or while they momentarily order their thoughts. **Voiced hesitations** are common since these allow speakers to pause without communication breaking down: *mm* (l. 21), *er* (l. 31) or repetitions of words.

The **lexis** is linked directly to the topics: directions to *the place* (l. 4), *paper* (l. 25) and *card* (l. 29). There are few examples of descriptive use of language because the purpose here is far more practical than a narrative. Colloquialisms like *hiya* (l. 3), *yeah* (l. 11), *well* (l. 39) and *won't* (l. 42) and imprecise references like *stuff* (l. 30) are common because the manner of the exchange is informal.

The **grammar** has similarities with casual conversation too. There are many grammatically incomplete utterances that function as complete clauses: *the paper* (l. 27) and *same as ever* (l. 4). Because they are in context, the participants can easily understand them. Such **minor sentences** are often used in answer to a question – as part of an adjacency pair, the response is clearly linked directly to the question that precedes it. There are both compound and subordinate clauses, but there are seldom strings of dependent clauses embedded within a main clause. This would place a large load on the memory of the listener and informal conversation is not usually demanding in that way.

	S	P	O		S	P	S	P		A	S
(I)	(phoned)	(College)	(and)	(Susan)	(didn't know)	(Mark)	(didn't know)	(but)	(then)	(Jane)
			conj		neg		neg		conj	

S	P
(did know)

(COMPOUND: ll. 5–7)

S	P	O
(I)	(was thinking)	(you were being a bit brave)
		SCl–NCl

(COMPLEX: l. 55)

Although the structure of sentences is still often loose, subordination occurs more frequently than it did in the narrative. The telephone conversation has a quicker pace and the alternation of the two speakers seems to add more variety to the clause patterns.

There are many examples of **normal non-fluency features**. The conversation is spontaneous and this means that both speakers make **false starts** (*have you found out when (.) where the place is*, l. 4); **repeat** words or phrases (*you turn into*

(.) into..., l. 10); use **voiced hesitations** (*er*, l. 28; *ehh*, l. 34; *mm*, l. 36); **leave utter-ances incomplete** (*I don't know whether she means the old (.)*, l. 15); and **speak over the top** of the other participant. Because the exchange is co-operative, speak-ers tend to make their own **repairs** – *you might (.) should be able to* (l. 23); *well put (.) do that then* (l. 39). If corrections are made by the other speaker this may cause tension, but here both participants are at ease because they know one another. No judgements are being made based on the way they speak and this allows them to participate without feeling self-conscious. Equally, all the examples of non-fluency features are typical of informal conversation – when we take part in a conversa-tion, we rarely even notice them. The fact that such inaccuracies are accepted is a distinctive trait of this kind of spoken language.

There are obvious **linguistic differences** between the two transcripts. In the earlier example, the narrative monologue is far less varied both in grammatical structures and prosodic features. The story demands an extended turn which the speaker sustains by repetition of the co-ordinating conjunction *and*; the telephone conversation, on the other hand, specifically involves two participants who share the turns. This automatically makes the grammatical structures of the two types of spoken language quite different: the short bursts of speech in the telephone con-versation tend to have a more clearly defined structure in which subordination plays a greater part. Equally, because the storyteller has been granted the right to an extended turn, the prosodic features tend to be less varied; the participants in the telephone conversation cannot see each other and therefore have to use greater variation in intonation patterns and stress in order to keep the conversation alive. Both use formulaic techniques, but the opening and closing of the telephone con-versation use conventional formulae far more rigidly because the participants can-not rely on non-linguistic clues. Despite the differences in grammar and prosodic features, in each case the participants are aware of their audience so they use lan-guage in a way that will ensure effective communication is taking place.

An interview

The third transcript is an extract from the Radio 4 evening arts magazine pro-gramme, *Front Row*, on Tuesday 31 May 2005. It is an interview between the pre-senter, John Wilson (JW), and two members of the band Coldplay – the guitarist Johnny Buckland (JB) and the singer Chris Martin (CM). In the interview, they discuss Coldplay's song-writing process and their latest album, *X&Y*, released on 6 June 2005 on EMI.

In many interview situations, participants do not have equal status – in a job interview, for example, the interviewee clearly does not have any control over the speech encounter. Here, however, the situation is rather different – Johnny Buckland and Chris Martin are representatives of a renowned and highly successful band and have, therefore, equal status with the presenter of the nightly 30-minute programme. Because the speech encounter takes place within a very precise time allocation, the linguistic and prosodic features of the discourse are distinctive.

The transcription is broad and prosodic features are marked selectively. (A key to the symbols can be found on page 93.) Read through the transcript and make notes on the following areas.

1 Comment on the way in which the speech encounter is structured.
2 Identify the main prosodic features and consider their effects.
3 Highlight any significant lexical or grammatical features.
4 List and describe the normal non-fluency features.
5 Comment on the differences between an informal telephone conversation between two speakers and a radio interview.

RADIO INTERVIEW (EXTRACT: 4½ MINUTES)

1	JW	but fírst (.) Bob Geldof announced details of his twentieth anniversary
'accel'		sequel to <u>Live</u> Aid this morning (.) 'a series of concerts' to be called <u>Live</u> 8
'accel'		in reference to the G8 Summit 'hosted by Britain' later this yèar (1) ↑two↑
		decades ago (.) a young band (.) just three albums old (.) tried to steal
5		the show from the superstars 'who were topping the bill' at Wèmbley (.)
		this time round <u>U2</u> will be <u>among</u> the veterans on the bill (.) and their role
		in <u>upstaging</u> the superstars (.) is likely to be taken by <u>Còldplay</u> (.) whose
		own <u>third</u> album (.) X&Y (.) is released next week

[*SOUNDTRACK*] (16)

10		Speed of <u>Sound</u> by Coldplay the single which was (.) kept off the number
		one chart spot this weekend by a (.) <u>mobile phone ringtone</u> the crázy
		frog is unlikely to get in the way of the new album thòugh (.) X&Y (1) is
		the most keenly awaited pop recording of the year not least by EMI (.)
		whose shares plùmmeted at the news that Coldplay had <u>scrapped</u> the
15		first draft (.) and had started again in the studio (.) ↑five↑ years on from
		their <u>sensitive</u> debut album Parachute (.) Coldplay have matured into a
		<u>swaggering stadium band</u> (.) and their famously <u>shy</u> (.) and (.) <u>insecure</u> (.)
		singer Chris Martin is married to a Hollywood actress Gwyneth Paltrow
		X&Y builds on the epic musical elements of the last album (.) the multi-
20		<u>million</u> selling Rush of Blood to the Héad (.) to create a big (.) bold (.)
		unashamed <u>rock</u> àlbum (.) when they came to the Front Row studio (.)
		earlier today (.) ↑I asked↑ Coldplay guitarist Johnny Buckland and singer
		Chris Martin abóut the <u>song</u> writing prócess =
	JB	= it tends to <u>start</u> (1) in the middle of the night (.) when we‖ um um
25	CM	‖I'm not gen-
		erally there then [*laughter*] =
	JB	= unless we've had a <u>crazy</u> evening we don't really sleep together
		it's normally like the <u>kernel</u> of an idea so it's like song lyrics (1) um (.)
		↑sómetimes↑ it's a whole song but (.) often it's just two chords um you
30		know rough sketch (3)
'accel'	JW	'and you talk‖about'
	JB	‖a skeleton really =
	JW	= and that idea in the middle of the night that's <u>one</u> song which is álmost
'rall'		the centrepiece of the album one of the most '<u>bare</u> (.) <u>stripped down</u> (.)
35		songs' The Message which starts on an acoustic guitar (.) is ↑probably
		closer↑ to those songs that you did in the past particularly‖on <u>Párachute</u>
	JB	‖mm mm

JW　that was (.) I think you said one of those um middle of the night =

JB　= that's the song to which we've attached the middle of the night story

40　　　　　　[*laughter*]

'accel'　CM　we've only really got one <u>anecdote</u> and we apply it [*laughter*] (1) 'to various songs'

[*SOUNDTRACK*] (8)

'accel'　JW　well I'll 'give you a few song titles' and then you can apply the right

45　　anecdote to the sóng (1) ↑what about↑ (.) um talking of titles (.) ↑X&Y↑ is there any significance a particular significance in the (.) title =

JB　= it just seemed to fit with everything (.) we were thinking about and everything we were doing at (2) the fact that um everything seemed to have two sides (2) we can be very optimistic about what we're doing but

50　　also very (.) er (.) <u>depressed</u> and (.)‖ <u>pessimistic</u> yeah about about what

CM　　　　　　　　　　　　　　　　　　　　　　　‖insecure

JB　we're doing you know from one day to the next we'll think something's tèrrible or ↑amazing↑ =

'accel'　JW　= I mean Chris chipped in the word <u>insecure</u> there which is 'a word which

55　　<u>has</u> <u>been</u> (.) associated' with‖ you because of the lyrics =

CM　　　　　　　　　　　　　　　　　　　‖yeah

CM　= well with me largely‖ I guess

JW　　　　　　　　　　　‖with y<u>ò</u>u (.) is that that's not a um shared <u>trait</u> amongst the band members =

60　'accel'　CM　'you know I think it' you know I think it's (1) I'm sure we're not the only people in the world to get a bit w<u>ó</u>rried about th<u>í</u>ngs =

'accel'　JW　= 'it's just when you're a song writer' those insecurities are are writ <u>large</u> =

'rall'　CM　= oh they're 'pure g<u>ò</u>ld' [*laughter*] ↑thank goodness↑ [*laughter*] thank

65　　goodness‖ I wake up sweating about the state of things =

JW　　　　‖ and

JB　= we'd be Alice Cooper if it weren't for his ins<u>é</u>curity

[*SOUNDTRACK*] (7)

JW　and the song (.) What If (.) the second track on the album I think is one

70　　of um er (1) y. y. I suppose it's <u>about</u> insecurity <u>isn't</u> <u>it</u> (1) it's a love song but it's about fragility (.) about relationships breaking down or whether

'rall'　　they '<u>will</u> last' (1) er but that is (.) again (.) insecurity writ very <u>large</u> isn't it (1) it's a positive yeah I mean it's an epic ballad and so‖ while

CM　　　　　　　　　　　　　　　　　　　　　　　　　　　　‖y. y. er you're one

75　　of the only people who uses that complimen<u>tar</u>ily [*laughter*] normally those two words are like ehh‖ but ehh

JW　　　　　　　　　　　　　　　‖ what ↑epic ballad↑ you mean =

CM　= yeah yeah =

'accel'　JW　= 'I didn't mean it in the <u>Bryan</u> Adams sense' =

80　CM　= ↑no no↑ I think it's <u>great</u> (.) what I was going to say was that the chorus of that song What If is very positive =

JW　= yeah =

CM　= and so whilst (.) a lot of (.) the album is <u>questioning</u> (.) and is very

'accel'　　<u>simple</u> (.) lyrics really (.) a lot of 'it is also very positive' (1) now (.) 'some

85　'rall'　　people (1) really (.) hate (.) our lyrics (.) because they're (.) the they're' (.)

'accel'　　'not very (1) I don't think they're very poetic (.) and I don't pretend to be a great lyricist but' (1) all I (2) try and do (1) is just write (.) down (.) honestly what I (1) feel about things (1) which can be very (.) I think it (.) some people find it quite em<u>barr</u>assing (2) but that's er that's er just what I feel (.) should be <u>done</u> =

90 'rall' JW = because you 'wear your (.) heart on your <u>sleeve</u>' (.) to use a cliché =

CM = I don't know about yeah if you want ↑to use a cliché↑ that's a good one to <u>u̠se</u>

[*SOUNDTRACK*] (17)

COMMENTARY

The **manner** is formal because the three speakers are participating in a radio broadcast. Despite the formality of the setting, however, they are obviously at ease with each other and also have equal status. This means that their language mixes both formal and informal registers.

An interview does not usually involve a range of topics because it has a clear purpose, but the presenter of *Front Row*, John Wilson, **opens** this interview with a related topic: the Live 8 concerts organised by Bob Geldof to draw attention to world poverty. This allows him to build up a sense of anticipation as he draws a parallel between the role of U2 in the original Live Aid concert and that of Coldplay in the 2005 event. An opening that establishes the theme, albeit indirectly, is typical of this kind of spoken encounter.

After the minute-and-a-half introduction, which includes a sixteen-second sound track and was recorded after the interview had taken place, the rest of the discourse is directly focused on Coldplay's music and their new album. The end of this transcription occurs half way through the complete interview. Although it does not mark the **closing** of the speech encounter as a whole, there is a sense that the discussion of lyrics is coming to an end. Instead of continuing the challenge he has begun, Chris Martin accepts the cliché adopted by John Wilson (l. 92), using an affirmation *yeah* and reiterating the technical term *cliché* (l. 93) to demonstrate that the topic is finished.

The **turn-taking** in an interview is distinctive. The structure is based on **adjacency pairs** in which the presenter asks a question and the interviewee replies. This framework is used throughout the speech encounter. Turns are rarely short: the presenter tends to make a statement that leads into a question and the interviewee's answers are fully developed.

In this interview, while the presenter asks some direct questions (ll. 45–6, 58–9), both of which are false starts, and uses tag questions (ll. 70, 72) to elicit a response, the grammatical mood is dominated by the declarative. John Wilson's statements provide a springboard to Chris Martin and John Buckland, offering them the opportunity to speak at length on particular aspects of their music. Because the participants are co-operative, each giving the others space to develop their responses, the radio listener learns a lot about Coldplay: their status, their musical development, their approach to writing songs, their attitudes and their new album. However, it is important to recognise that in this kind of speech encounter the main body of the interview deals with the subjective rather than the objective – it explores opinions and personal interpretations, allowing us an insight into the way in which the band see themselves and their music.

In a radio interview, the participants have only a limited amount of time to complete their discourse. In most interviews, the turn-taking will therefore be carefully organised. In the extract here, the participants **latch-on** to each other very smoothly: as one speaker finishes, another picks up the cues and starts to speak. This means that many of the turns are marked by = in the transcription. Because there are three participants, the number of **overlaps** is higher than would be seen in a conversation between two people.

On two occasions, the overlaps are caused by minimal responses (*mm*, l. 37; *yeah*, l. 56) that support the speaker. At other times, the interviewer speaks at the same time as the interviewee as he tries to steer the conversation in a new direction (l. 31) or to clarify a point made (l. 58). Other instances reflect the familiarity of the two Coldplay members – as Johnny Buckland hesitates, Chris Martin makes a joke (l. 25); as Johnny Buckland describes changing moods of the band, Chris Martin intercedes with a single utterance *insecure* (l. 51) which is then picked up and developed by the interviewer. On each occasion, the overlap is minimal because the speech encounter is co-operative and the context is formal and public.

The prosodic features seem more prominent than in normal conversation. The participants are 'performing' for their radio audience and they therefore exaggerate the prosodics to animate the conversation for listeners who have no visual clues. Key words are often **stressed**. These are often modifiers revealing particular attitudes of the band (*sensitive*, l. 16; *shy*, l. 17; *depressed ... pessimistic*, l. 50; *insecure*, ll. 17, 54), attributes of the songs (*rock*, l. 21; *bare stripped down*, l. 34; *questioning*, l. 83; *simple*, l. 84), or general responses (*crazy*, l. 27; *pure gold*, l. 64; *great*, l. 80). Other stressed words draw attention to proper nouns (*Live 8*, l. 2; *U2*, l. 6; *Coldplay*, l. 7; *Parachute*, l. 36), and some highlight key words that signpost the topic (*song writing*, l. 23; *kernel*, l. 28; *anecdote*, l. 41).

Intonation patterns enhance the meaning of utterances. Here **rising tones** are used to mark the beginning of the feature on Coldplay (*but first*, l. 1); and to draw attention to the name of their albums: *X & Y* (l. 12), *Rush of Blood to the Head* (l. 20) and *Parachute* (l. 36). **Falling tones** tend to be used at the end of a grammatical utterance (*Wembley*, l. 5; *ringtone*, l. 11) and to give emphasis to an utterance (*pure gold*, l. 64; *something's terrible*, ll. 52–3; *with you*, l. 58).

Pitch changes are used to mark a change of direction: as the interviewer moves from a summary of Coldplay's past to an assessment of their current standing (↑five↑ *years on*, l. 15) ; as he moves from an extended introductory turn to the interview (↑*I asked*↑, l. 22); and to emphasise contrasts (↑*sometimes*↑, l. 29; ↑*amazing*↑, l. 53; ↑*no, no*↑, l. 80). Changes in **pace** add interest and are indicative of both the medium of the speech encounter (radio interview) and the participants. On a number of occasions, the interviewer speeds up (ll. 2, 3, 31, 54, 62) and this is perhaps directly linked to his role – he must keep the conversation going and guide it in directions that he considers will be most profitable. Where the pace becomes slower, the information is given added weight (ll. 34–5, 64, 72). It can also, however, reflect the personal characteristics of a speaker or the personal nature of the content (ll. 84–5).

While many of the **pauses** mark the end of a complete grammatical utterance (ll. 12, 22, 70), others mark hesitancy (ll. 28, 45, 50) or draw attention to key words (ll. 17, 34, 50). They can also be used to direct our attention, focusing the listener on one section of an utterance at a time:

>   A   S   P
> (Two decades ago) PAUSE (a young band PAUSE just three albums old) PAUSE (tried)
>   O
> (to steal the show from the superstars PAUSE who were topping the bill at Wembley).

In Chris Martin's extended turn (ll. 83–90), the number of pauses creates a staccato effect as the singer explores a sensitive subject area: his lyrics and his personal relationship with them.

The **lexis** is all related to music and song-writing, but it is not technical. Although there are some subject-specific terms (*chords*, l. 29; *acoustic guitar*, l. 35; *epic ballad*, l. 73; *lyrics*, l. 84), much of the language is informal (*you know*, ll. 29–30; *I mean*, l. 54; *I guess*, l. 57; *well*, ll. 44, 57). Proper nouns help to establish the musical context: names of famous singers (*Bob Geldof*, l. 1; *Alice Cooper*, l. 67), bands (*U2*, l. 6), concerts (*Live Aid … Live 8*, l. 2) and venues (*Wembley*, l. 5). Other lexis establishes a specific time context: the reference to *Live 8* (l. 2) and to the *crazy frog* ringtone (ll. 11–12) that prevented Coldplay's new single making number one in the charts.

The **grammatical structure** is quite complicated because of the length of the utterances. Although the relationship between the participants is not formal, most utterances are grammatically complete because the context is formal and because there is a clearly defined purpose. Utterances tend to be complex:

>   A   S   P   A   S
> (This time around) (U2) (will be) (among the veterans on the bill) (and) (their role in
>   conj
>   P   A   P   A
> upstaging the superstars) (is) (likely) (to be taken) (by Coldplay whose own third
>   passive verb phrase   SCl–RelCl
> album is released next week).   (COMPOUND–COMPLEX: ll. 6–8)
>   S P   C
> (I) ('m) (sure ø we're not the only people in the world to get a bit worried about
>   SCl–NCl   SCl–NFCl
> things).   (COMPLEX: ll. 60–1)

There is also some evidence of the loosely co-ordinated clauses that are more typical of spoken language (ll. 70–3, 86–90) and of fronted co-ordinating conjunctions (ll. 1, 33, 69, 83).

The **normal non-fluency features** are typical of any spontaneous speech. Here the speakers are under some pressure because they are speaking to a large unseen audience and this means that despite their fluency, they make some mistakes (*they're (.) the they're*, l. 85). **Voiced hesitations** such as *um* (ll. 24, 28, 38, 45) and *er* (ll. 50, 70, 89) are common in the utterances of presenter and interviewees. **Restarts**, however, occur more frequently in the turns of Chris Martin and Johnny Buckland because the presenter of the programme has more experience in the medium. Some of the hesitations are clearly allowing the speaker thinking time while informing the other participants that the turn is not yet complete: *when we um um* (l. 24); *the fact that um everything* (l. 48); *y. y. er. you* (l. 74).

In some places, utterances are **grammatically incomplete**: *I think it…* (l. 88). Even though an utterance is grammatically incomplete, however, intonation patterns ensure that understanding is not affected. John Wilson, for instance, uses the prepositional phrase *with you* (l. 58), which functions on its own as a minor sentence. Its reinforcement of Chris Martin's previous phrase *with me* and its falling intonation ensure that listeners understand its significance.

The speech encounter is co-operative and all **repairs** are self-repairs. For example, the interviewer refines his question, replacing the rather vague *any significance* with a more specific *a particular significance* (l. 46) as he asks Johnny Buckland and Chris Martin about their new album's title. The speakers are **supportive** of each other – turns start with an affirmation *yeah* (ll. 78, 82, 92) or a co-ordinating conjunction marking the continuation of a particular topic. There are two occasions where a challenge is suggested by the use of a negation: *no no* (l. 80) and *I don't know about…* (l. 92). In each case, however, the speaker replaces the negative with a positive (*I think it's great; yeah if you want to use a cliché*), which allows the conversation to continue co-operatively.

It is possible to summarise in a table the main differences between a telephone conversation and a radio interview:

Linguistic features	Informal telephone conversation	Radio interview
Audience	One specific person who is known and whose number has been dialled.	On one level the participants are speaking to each other, but they are also speaking to a wider unknown audience listening to the radio programme.
Topic	Although a telephone conversation will normally have a specific purpose, new topics are likely to emerge as the speech encounter develops. To an outsider, topics may seem to arise randomly, but to the participants with their shared knowledge there may well be a logical progression from one to another.	The participants will normally have a clearly defined reason for their discourse. There will often be no more than one topic as the focus for the speech encounter. Tentatively connected topics are unlikely to be a part of the developing discourse.
Turn-taking	Turns tend to be short so that speakers can be sure that the other participant is still listening. Lack of visual clues means that the end of each turn must be clearly marked to avoid confusion. Overlaps are common because speakers do not always interpret linguistic clues properly. Because the context is co-operative, however, the overlaps do not tend to be long.	Turns tend to be quite long and their organisation is very precise. Adjacency pairs are created by the question/answer framework. Because of time limits, latching on makes the turn-taking smooth – each speaker picks up exactly where the last one finishes. Some overlaps occur, but they are rarely long.

Openings and closings	Because speakers cannot see each other, beginnings and endings are marked by formulaic utterances which are easily recognisable.	To ensure that listeners can follow the different parts of a programme, the start and finish of each section must be clear. An interview therefore opens with a statement that focuses attention on the topic and closes with a summary.
Prosodic features	Participants seem to use stress and varied intonation patterns to sustain listener interest. Pauses are usually short so that turn-taking does not become confused. Voiced hesitations are common.	Speakers often exaggerate stress and intonation patterns to add interest to what is being said. Because utterances are often long, pauses divide them into easily understandable units. Pace and pitch also vary quite dramatically. Voiced hesitations give speakers time to order their thoughts.
Lexis and grammar	The words are often informal and grammatical structures are often incomplete. Participants accept inaccuracies because the speech environment is co-operative and supportive. Co-ordination may be more common than subordination.	Lexis can be formal and subject-specific, informal or a mixture of the two depending upon the participants, their topic and the context. Utterances are usually grammatically complete and subordination is more common.

Unscripted commentary

The most common forms of unscripted commentary are those which accompany sports events broadcast on television or radio. There are, however, other examples that fall into this category: unscripted commentaries may be used when an event like a royal wedding is televised or when a state occasion like the opening of Parliament is covered on the radio.

Sometimes commentators speak from a text, but live coverage requires them to describe and comment on events as they happen. This means that the commentators must speak spontaneously. The purpose of a **television** commentary is clearly different from a **radio** version of the same event. Both radio and television commentators comment on and evaluate what is taking place, but because radio listeners cannot see what is happening, a radio commentator must also use language to convey an exact description of the developing action.

ACTIVITY 10.4

The last transcripts in this section are taken from commentaries accompanying the live Uefa Cup football match between AZ Alkmaar and Newcastle United on 15 March 2007. The first is a commentary for the televised match on ITV, by John Champion (JC) and Jim Beglin (JB); the second is from the Radio 5 Live coverage, by Ian Brown (IB) and Craig Hignet (CH). (A key to the symbols can be found on page 93.)

Read through each transcript and make notes on the following:

1 the turn-taking
2 the main prosodic features and their effects
3 any distinctive lexis or grammatical structures
4 normal non-fluency features
5 the characteristics of unscripted commentary and the differences between radio and television commentaries.

TELEVISION COMMENTARY (4½ MINUTES) ···

1 'accel' JC 'there's ↑Parker↑' (3)
'accel' JB great <u>position</u> (.) and again <u>Sibierski</u> causing problems (.) 'with his size with his head' (3) you know that ther. the. they're always hard to execute it looks easier from here but he should be getting
5 abôve it (2) difficult =
JC = Huntingdon replaced by N'Zogbia (5) no time for caution now (10) Newcastle have been given a frée kìck (2) Given has chárged out to be able to <u>take</u> this and allow his colleagues to get úp fìeld (2) remember in De Kuip (3) in Rotterdam it was Cráig Bèllamy in
10 <u>stoppage</u> <u>time</u> that scored the goal that qualified Newcastle for
'accel' 'the next phase of the Champions League' <u>Solano</u> (2) two players out <u>there</u> tonight the goalkeeper (1) and Kieron Dyer (.) who were part of <u>that</u> team (.) and they need to <u>draw</u> on the same <u>well</u> of in-spiration (4) Tîtus Bràmble (3) Táylor is forward (3) Sîbierski (1) and
15 'accel'/'rall' Dyer 'whistle's ↑gone↑' 'it wón't coùnt' Scott Pàrker turned it in but a second or so <u>after</u> Bertrand Layec had blown his whistle (4)
JB well there was just a <u>slight</u> protest from Kieron Dyer I think he's the one that's committed the offence (3) just hére (2) well I tell you what th. there isn't much wrong with that to <u>me</u> he's put his arms
20 ùp but there's no <u>real</u> púshing gone on <u>there</u> and Scott Parker's done só wèll to follow it up and tuck it away I think that's <u>very</u> <u>very</u> <u>harshly</u> given against him (2)
JC Opdam (3) Démbele <u>Alkmaar</u> can finish it here (1) it's ↑Arveladze↑
'accel' it's '↑still Arveladze↑' Given with a <u>wonderful</u> <u>save</u> helped by the
25 wóodwork tòo (3)
JB that would have settled it (1) he does extremely well to try and let it run across his body gets a little bit of luck when he goes past Taylor ↑whàt↑ a save (.) from Gîven (2) <u>fantastic</u> touch to take it on to the woodwork =
30 JC = Shota Arveladze has Newcastle at his <u>mercy</u> (2) they are <u>still</u> ↑alive↑ (17) <u>Emre</u> (2) those that have followed the Magpies' cáuse
'accel' for (1) <u>many</u> <u>many</u> <u>years</u> (.) will acknowledge that nothing 'ever comes éasily' to Newcastle United (1) it's always associated with
'leg' '<u>drama</u> and <u>concern</u> and <u>worry</u>' (2) and <u>angst</u> (1) and <u>uncèrtainty</u>
35 (5) ás things stand Alkmaar are going through on the <u>away</u> goals rule (5) here though is Stéven Tàylor (2) who a long long time ago (.) in the first hálf (.) could well have been sent óff for an èlbow (1) <u>Martins</u> (2) with a shimmy (.) <u>and</u> then he was drágged dòwn <u>and</u> it's a free kick within range (3)
40 JB ‖ thing is
JC ‖ and it could be a ‖ yellow card =
JB ‖ yeah

JB = deserves it (1) I think he knew what he was doing (.) John (.)
once he was outfoxed with the footwork from Martins (1) he was

45 just happy to pull him dòwn =

JC = Tim de Cler who's not one of the five Alkmaar players (.)
one booking (.) short of a ban =

JB = great feet (4) [indistinct] =

JC = if Newcastle score (4) it would in all probability be enough

50 'leg' to send them into the quarter finals (3) 'down below us the fourth
official preparing the electronic board' (2) to tell us all how much
stoppage time they have to work with (5) Turkish cunning South
American flàir which is it to be (1) Sólano or Emre (2) they need to
produce the free kick of their lives (3) it's Émre (3)

55 JB nah if it had've been low enough the keeper Waterman sees it nice
and early would have dealt with it

RADIO COMMENTARY (4½ MINUTES) ··

57 IB there a high ball (.) into the (.) AZ (.) penalty area (1) it drops for
'cresc'/'accel' '↑Parker↑' and he volleys it on his 'left foot over the top of the bar'
(.) it was headed back by Sibierski he couldn't control the shot (.)

60 it's into the cròwd and here comes a change and Húntingdon (2)
is going óff after a very uncómfortable evening for him here in (1)
North Holland (.) and N'Zogbia is on =

CH = yeah difficult chance for Scottie Parker that one it was in the air
(.) on his left foot er décent connection (.) but it was never threat-

65 ening the goal (2) this will be interesting now cos N'Zogbia 'll. will
play wide left (1) they're er asking Emre Parker and Nicky Butt (1)
to keep the midfield (.) but it looks like Párker's been thrown up as
well (3) so they're playing with four up frónt virtually (3) five if you
count N'Zogbia =

70 IB = yéah (2) wèll (1) they've got to throw ábsolutely everything here
(.) at Alkmaar have Newcastle in these (1) clòsing mìnutes we're
into the fiñal four minutes more or less (.) plus stoppage time

'stacc' here's Solano 'for (.) Newcastle' they néed a goal they néed it now
'accel' it's 'played to the edge of the area headed away by dé Zèeuw'

75 comes back to Émre (.) he slices it out to the near side and
'accel' N'Zógbia (.) the Frenchman (.) 'coming in off the flank' strong run
by him but he's challenged well by (2) Martens (.) Maarten Martens
'accel' it comes to (1) Bramble (.) arcs back into the penalty area 'Táylor's
'accel' up heads it across towards Sibierski ↑will it 'drop for Dyer↑ inside

80 the penalty area ↑or maybe Scott Parker' Scott Parker↑ is in there
'cresc'/'rall/dimin' (1) 'and he's ↓scored↓' or 'has he not' the referee (.) I don't think
'rall' has ↑given the goal↑ it's been disállowed and it's going to bè 'a
free kick for Álkmaar' =

CH = I think there was a (.) slight push in the penalty area but (.) I'm

85 not sure (2) the referee did blow his whistle though before Parker
put the ball into the ‖ net

IB ‖ yeah Newcastle realised that hence the the
‖ lack of celebration which was a big clúe [laugh] to me that it

CH ‖ yeah

90		IB wasn't a gòal [*laugh*] ‖ or else
		CH ‖ they've had a a couple of opportunities like

'accel'   'rall'   'rall' lines appear in left margin.

90   IB wasn't a gòal [*laugh*] ‖ or else

       CH   ‖ they've had a a couple of opportunities like that where the ball just hasn't <u>bóunced</u> for them but (1) there it did and <u>Scottie</u> Parker fînished it (2)

95   'accel' IB at the other end though it's Lens into 'the penalty area drags it

       'rall'   back to (.) Shota ↑Arveladze↑ oh he 'hits the ↓bar↓' and that bounces ↑awây↑ and it should have been <u>three</u> for <u>AZ</u> Alkmaar and gôodnight to Newcastle in Europe but it <u>glánces</u> the <u>bar</u> (.)

       'rall'   '<u>bóunces awày</u>' ‖ they can't believe it on the Alkmaar bénch =

          CH   ‖ ahh

100   CH = well it's fantastic skill from Arveladze again he's he's fóoled Bramble with a a great touch and then left foot (.) did Given get a touch to ît (.) hît the bár =

       IB = uhh wouldn't like to be certain on that (3)

       CH it's a <u>great</u> sáve if he has =

105   IB = yup (2) he's certainly capable of that <u>kind</u> of <u>save</u> (.) is ‖<u>Shay</u>

       CH   ‖yeah

       IB Given (3) either way (1) Newcastle <u>stîll</u> <u>bréathing</u> and just for a ↑<u>splît second</u>↑ Scott Parker (1) had lîfted (1) Newcastle hearts by putting the ball into the net but the whistle <u>had</u> gone (.) it's <u>stîll</u>

110   two <u>nîl</u> Alkmaar (.) 4–4 on aggregate (.) the away goals rule at the moment (.) is <u>doing</u> for Newcastle (2) here's N'Zogbia running the wrong way and being challenged by <u>Dembele</u> and it's out of play for a (.) AZ thrów în (1) two minutes plus stoppage time so the French fourth official Monsieur le [*indistinct*] is going to be (.) an

115   important figure (1) in the next moment or so (2) how much time have Newcastle genuinely got <u>left</u> (2) to get the <u>goal</u> they <u>need</u>

       'accel' '<u>hére's</u> <u>Taylor</u> coming forward (.) up to the half-way <u>line</u>' (1) touches it back to (3) Silano (2) now it's (.) Obafemi Martins good turn by

       'accel' him 'strong running sidesteps away from the defendant' de Cler

120 'accel/cresc' who brings him down and ↑'this is a <u>free</u> kick for Newcastle'↑ it's

       'stacc' going to be a '<u>yellow</u> <u>card</u> <u>as</u> <u>well</u>' for de Cler it was quite cynical

       'stacc' 'frée kick (.) céntral position (.) 3̂0 yards out' (1) now is the tîme (2)

       CH good distance for Emre on Nobby Silano (3) both of them have got <u>really</u> <u>good</u> <u>quality</u> from free kicks (2) just hit the tárget and make

125   the goalkeeper wòrk (2)

       'leg' IB now is most definitely the time if Newcastle 'are going to escape' (.) with a place (.) in the <u>quarter</u> <u>finals</u> they <u>have</u> to <u>score</u> (1)

       'stacc' 'Alkmaar (1) are preparing (1) another substitute (1) Boukhari but not (.) before (.) the free kick' (.) îs taken (1) Émre (2) the Turk is be-

130   hind the ball (.) and Solano (2) the Peruvian (.) Solano on his right fôot (.) Emre on his léft Solano dummies to run up (1) the referee

       'accel' wants the wall back right on 'the edge of the penalty área more or

       'rall'/'accel' less' five in a wall for 'AZ Alkmaar' (2) Solano (1) or Émre 'one of the two' it's ↑Emre↑ over the top of the ↑bár↑ it was <u>always</u> going

135   too hîgh =

       CH = yeah always rising it was a bit of a <u>lazy</u> <u>strike</u> really (.) there was no dip on the ball he's disappointed with it himself you can see on his face

COMMENTARY

The **function** of a commentary is to describe a sequence of actions, to give the listener or viewer background information and to entertain. The **target audience** will usually be people who are interested in the particular activity taking place and who already have a reasonable knowledge of the subject-specific language and structure of the event.

A commentary must be **spontaneous** and **sustained** as it mirrors the process of the activity. This does not mean, however, that the **structure** is random. In fact, unscripted commentary is quite different from the loosely structured nature of informal conversation since the **topic** is predefined and utterances must be orderly. Commentators can use notes to give their utterances structure, but this is really only feasible when they are filling long breaks in the action (such as half-time or injury time). They must therefore be able to describe ongoing actions fluently and develop a more personal level of comment and interpretation when little is happening.

The **structure** of an unscripted commentary will vary depending upon the kind of activity that is taking place: a cricket match will take place over a longer period of time than a football match, for instance, so the commentary for each will have a different pace. When little is happening, commentators might give **background information** summarising the state of the game so far; when significant activity develops, they will describe **what is happening** and will try to **create an appropriate atmosphere** for people watching or listening; where events follow a recognisable pattern, they may use a **formulaic utterance**; if the outcome of a predictable sequence of moves is exciting, they will choose **emotive language**, and if nothing develops from the initial activity, they will choose more **reserved language**. Alongside descriptions of the activity itself, a skilful commentator will provide **interpretative comment** and often **personal asides**. It is this part of a commentary that allows commentators to be idiosyncratic and to develop a personal style.

The **turn-taking** has to be very orderly, just as it is in an interview. Often there are two people to talk about the activity: one in the role of commentator and the other often a sportsman or sportswoman who advises or summarises. The two participants will sometimes directly interact in informal conversation, but usually their turns will be directly related to the event they are watching. In the examples here, the commentators are John Champion (television) and Ian Brown (radio); the advisers are the ex-footballers Jim Beglin (television) and Craig Hignet (radio). The approach of the commentators and advisers is usually quite different.

In the transcripts of the Uefa Cup football match, in almost every example the speakers pick up clues promptly and **latch on** smoothly. The pace of this particular match is quite slow, which means that the commentaries are marked by more frequent **timed pauses** at the end of a turn than is often the case. In the television commentary, the adviser pauses on a number of occasions before commenting on the event that has just taken place (ll. 1, 16, 25, 39, 54); in the radio commentary, the commentator waits until the next sequence of action develops (ll. 93, 125). Similarly, the frequency of **overlaps** is higher because the match is not characterised by dramatic action. Where events take place in quick succession there will be a clear structure to the turn-taking. Here, however, there are occasions where both speakers begin at once, commenting on an event that has taken place while there is no action on the pitch, both in the television (ll. 40–1) and radio transcripts (ll. 86–7, 90–1). Other examples represent the co-operative nature of the discourse: the overlaps, for example, are affirmations (ll. 42, 87, 105). There is no confusion caused by the overlaying of words because the overlaps are minimal. While perhaps less dominant here because of the nature of this specific football match, the use of **latched turns** is an indication of the highly structured nature of unscripted commentary. Although it is a form of spontaneous speech, it is clearly an acquired skill in which certain techniques must be learnt and practised.

Unscripted commentaries are distinctive for the wide range of **prosodic features** on which they draw – even at first sight, the marginal notes are obviously more detailed than the other transcripts considered so far. As the activity on the pitch changes, so too do the intonation patterns, the pitch, the pace and the volume. Radio commentators use these to animate the scene they are creating for their listeners, who cannot see what is happening; and television commentators use them to focus the viewer and to personalise the event for the audience. The **timing** of utterances is crucial and this is another reason why spontaneity and sustained speech are so important.

In both transcripts, the commentators use a far wider range of prosodic features than the advisers. This emphasises the fact that unscripted commentary is a variety for which there are techniques that can be learnt. The **pace** of utterances is directly linked to the speed of the activity taking place. Where exciting developments occur, commentators frequently increase the pace of their utterances (marked on the transcript as 'accel'). These are usually followed by a noticeable decrease in pace as the height of activity falls away (marked 'rall'). To signal the end of a dramatic passage of play and the end of a turn, a commentator might use a distinctively slow delivery (marked 'lento'). Changes in **volume** often accompany changes in pace: as excitement builds, the volume increases (marked 'cresc'); and as a particular period of activity dies away, so too does the volume (marked 'dimin'). Dramatic changes of pitch are also distinctive: a commentator may raise pitch (marked ↑↑) to reflect anticipation and enthusiasm, or lower it (marked ↓↓) to indicate a return to less fevered activity.

Emphatic stress is used to highlight key words, just as it is in other forms of spoken language. What can perhaps be seen as a distinctive feature, however, is the emphatic stringing together of stressed words: *one booking short of a ban* (l. 47); *glances the bar bounces away* (l. 98). Stress patterns like these are often accompanied by a **rhythmic delivery**: short, abrupt vocalisations (marked 'stacc') may be used to describe players' positions as quickly as possible; drawling, prolonged vocalisations (marked 'leg') may add emphasis to important moments.

Intonation patterns are also noticeably exaggerated in unscripted commentary. **Rising tones** mark excitement (*Craig Bellamy*, l. 9; *free kick (.) central position (.) 30 yards out*, l. 122). They are often used repeatedly as the activity builds to a climax. **Falling tones** tend to mark the end of a turn (*happy to pull him down*, l. 44) or the end of a grammatical unit (*Solano or Emre*, l. 53). **Rising–falling** and **falling–rising tones** are used to give emphasis to key words (*Given*, l. 28; *disal-*

lowed, l. 82; *finished*, l. 93). Intonation patterns are also used to give coherence to utterances where clause elements are often deleted to achieve brevity.

Pauses in commentaries are used in a distinctive way. Because sustained speech is so important, there are few examples of the kinds of casual pauses associated with informal conversation. The variety as a whole is noted for its lack of voiced hesitation, so pauses tend to be used consciously: to add emphasis (*Martens (.) Maarten Martens*, l. 77); to reflect lack of specific activity (*they are still ↑alive↑ (17) Emre*, ll. 30–1); to punctuate a sequence of actions (*Titus Bramble (3) Taylor is forward (3) Sibierski (1) and Dyer*, ll. 14–15); and to breathe (*arcs back into the penalty area Taylor's up heads it across towards Sibierski ↑will it drop for Dyer↑ inside the penalty area ↑or maybe Scott Parker Scott Parker↑ is in there (1) and he's scored*, ll. 78–81). It is important to remember that pauses do not always correspond to the end of a grammatical utterance in unscripted commentaries.

The advisers alter the pitch, pace, volume and tone of their utterances less often. Their pace may become fast (marked 'alleg') in order to complete their turn before the next piece of play is described by the commentator, but usually their delivery is far less exaggerated. They imitate the techniques of commentators, but do not always manage to control them as skilfully because they have had less practice. In some stretches of their turns, utterances become very long (ll. 17–22).

The basic function of the **language** of unscripted commentaries is to name things and people (nouns) and to describe actions (verbs). The lexis is **subject-specific** because the focus of attention is inevitably on one particular kind of activity: *free kick* (ll. 39, 83, 122), *stoppage time* (ll. 10, 52, 72, 113) and *yellow card* (ll. 41, 121). Many of the technical terms are used in everyday discourse, but in the sporting context have a more specific meaning: *offence* (l. 18), *sent off* (l. 37), *booking* (l. 47), *bench* (l. 98), *the wall* (l. 132). Alongside the technical terms, colloquialisms are common: contractions (*whistle's gone*, l. 15; *yeah*, l. 42; *nah*, l. 55; *he's*, l. 105); phrasal verbs (*thrown up*, l. 67; *have… got left*, l. 116); the informal use of *well* as a linking adverb (ll. 17, 70); and conversational collocations (*as things stand…*, l. 35; *thing is*, l. 40; *a couple of…*, l. 91; *a bit of a…*, l. 136). There tend to be other **collocations** which are directly linked to a particular context: *up field* (l. 8), *away goals rule* (ll. 35–6, 110), *fourth official* (ll. 50–1, 114) and *inside the penalty area* (ll. 79–80). There is a high proportion of **proper nouns** because the commentators have to describe a sequence of actions carried out by a limited number of participants: *N'Zogbia* (ll. 6, 62, 65, 69, 111), *Parker* (ll. 1, 15, 20, 58, 63, 67, 80, 85, 93, 108), *Sibierski* (ll. 2, 14, 59, 79) and *Arveladze* (ll. 23, 24, 30, 95, 100). **Modification** is used to add detail and often consists of numbers. Positive modifiers (*a wonderful save*, l. 24; *fantastic touch*, l. 28; *a great save*, l. 104) draw attention to the players' skills; adverbial intensifiers (*very very harshly*, ll. 21–2; *a very uncomfortable evening*, l. 61; *really good quality*, l. 124) are emphatic. Often extra detail will be added by placing phrases in apposition: *it was Craig Bellamy… that scored the goal that qualified Newcastle for the next phase of the Champions League* (ll. 9–11). Both pre- and post-modification are used:

m	h	m	h	
Turkish	cunning	(South American)	flair	(ll. 52–3)
Adj	N	Adj	N	

<pre>
 m   m   h   q
</pre>
the free kick of their lives   (ll. 54)
<pre>
det   Adj   N   PrepP
</pre>

<pre>
  h   q
</pre>
those that have followed the Magpies' cause   (l. 31)
<pre>
pron   RelCl
</pre>

Individual commentators develop a **personal approach**. They try to avoid high-frequency clauses like *you see, you know* or *I mean* which are common in informal conversation and instead try to make their choice of words striking. Unusual **descriptive noun phrases** such as *the same well of inspiration* (ll. 13–14), *the woodwork* (ll. 25, 29), *a shimmy* (l. 38) and *quite cynical free kick* (ll. 121–2) make the account of what is happening more distinctive. Unexpected **verbs** can prevent commentaries describing an event in which similar sequences of action recur from becoming repetitive: *outfoxed* (l. 44), *slices* (l. 75), *arcs* (l. 78), *drags* (l. 94), *fooled* (l. 100), *sidesteps* (l. 119) and *dummies* (l. 131). The use of nouns linked semantically to dynamic verbs reflects the emphasis on activity in a sports commentary: *kick* (ll. 7, 120), *pushing* (l. 20), *run* (l. 76), *push* (l. 84), *touch* (ll. 28, 101) and *strike* (l. 136). Because the participants have to interpret events spontaneously, comment clauses such as *I tell you what* (ll. 18–19), *I think* (ll. 17, 21, 84), *I don't think* (l. 81) and *I'm not sure* (ll. 84–5) indicate the potentially subjective nature of a commentary. The professionalism of the commentators means that these clauses are more likely to appear in the turns of the advisers.

The other way in which a commentator can create a distinctive style is to use **metaphors**. A metaphor may be used so often that it loses its figurative impact and becomes a **dead metaphor** or **cliché**, and there are many well-known examples of such sporting clichés: *sick as a parrot, over the moon, the game's not over until the final whistle's blown* and *it's a game of two halves.* When a commentator uses a new image, however, it can animate the scene being described. Metaphorical language is in complete contrast to the factual language used to record what is happening at moments of intense activity – it will most often occur when the speed of the match has slowed down, allowing the commentator to indulge in a more impressionistic kind of comment. In the transcripts here, there are no extended metaphors but there are examples of language that is figurative – it functions at a level that is creative rather than literal. In the television commentary, the image of the *well of inspiration* (ll. 13–14) and the antithetical noun phrases *Turkish cunning* and *South American flair* (ll. 52–3) are vivid expressions. Quite unlike the literal descriptions of the activity taking place on the pitch, their wider connotations enhance the atmosphere of the moment. In the radio commentary, the personification of the Newcastle team (*still breathing*, l. 107) dramatises the tension in a match that will decide Newcastle's fate in the Uefa Cup, while the dead metaphor *lifted… hearts* (l. 108) neatly summarises the crowd's momentary change in mood as it appears that the crucial goal has been scored.

The **grammar** of unscripted commentaries has many distinctive features. Because the discourse is spontaneous, **grammatically incomplete utterances** are common, but in the focused context of a sporting activity these are rarely noticed. Most utterances are in the **declarative**, but **questions** may be asked where two people are involved. These may take the form of tag questions requesting affirmation of a point just made, like *isn't it*, or may momentarily involve the participants in something more like conversation than commentary (ll. 102–5). At moments of tension, commentators may ask rhetorical questions in which they anticipate the outcome. **Clause elements** usually appear in a standard order – inversion may be used for dramatic effect, but **marked themes** are uncommon in unscripted commentary. They are more likely to appear in the turns of the adviser than those of the commentator:

                           A   S   P   C

A   S   P   C

(once he was outfoxed with the footwork from Martins) (he) (was) (just happy to pull
SCl–ACl   NFCl

him down)   (ll. 44–5)

    A   S   P   S   P   O

(there) (it) (did) (and) (Scottie Parker) (finished) (it)   (ll. 92–3)

The **main verb** usually comes early in the clause and the sentence structures are often **simple**:

   S   P   A   S   P   A

(Taylor) (is) (forward) (l. 14)   (it) (comes) (to Bramble) (l. 78)

   S   P   O   A

(the referee) (wants) (the wall) (back right on the edge of the penalty area) (ll. 131–2)

Just as informal conversation is marked by loose co-ordination of utterances, so too is spontaneous unscripted commentary. The use of *and* in the initial position is common since it allows speakers to latch onto the end of the previous turn and to sustain the continuous flow of speech:

    S   P   O

(and) (it) (could be) (a yellow card)   (l. 41)
conj

    S   P   P   S

(and) (he) ('s scored) (or) (has) (he) (not)   (l. 81)
conj   conj   neg

Subordination is more common in evaluative or summative comment than in description of the action, but long, embedded clauses are not common.

S   P   A   A   A

(Given) (has charged) (out) (to be able to take this) (and) (allow his colleagues to get
                               SCl–NFCl   SCl–NFCl   conj   SCl–NFCl   SCl–NFCl

up field)   (ll. 7–8)

    A   P   S   A   P   A

(how much time) (have) (Newcastle) (genuinely) (got left) (to get the goal they need)
                                             SCl–NFCl   SCl–RelCl

                                                            (ll. 115–16)

One of the most distinctive features of the grammar of unscripted commentary is the number of **deletions**. **Minor sentences** are common – often the subject or predicator or both are omitted, leaving only the essential information. This happens most often when activity is at its height. It is appropriate in this variety, because if all the clause elements were included it is likely that the overall structure would be very repetitive. By analysing the clause structure of a particular section of a commentary using a table, it is possible to see which elements are commonly omitted. There is often a marked difference between the deletions in television and in radio commentaries.

Television (ll. 9–16)

Co Conj	Sub Conj	S	P	O/C	A
		∅	remember		in De Kuip
					in Rotterdam
		it	was	Craig Bellamy	in stoppage time
	that		scored	the goal	
	that		qualified	Newcastle	for the next phase of the Champions League
		Solano	∅	∅	
		∅	∅	two players	out there tonight
				the goalkeeper and Kieron Dyer	
	who		were	part of that team	
and		they	need	to draw on that same well of inspiration	
		Titus Bramble	∅	∅	
		Taylor	is	forward	
		Sibierski	∅	∅	
and		Dyer	∅	∅	
		whistle	's gone		
		it	won't count		
		Scott Parker	turned	it	in
but		∅	∅		a second or so
	after	Bertrand Layec	had blown	his whistle	

Commonly deleted elements here are verbs and objects/complements. Since this is a television commentary, viewers would be able to see what was happening and would be able to anticipate the kind of words that could fill each empty slot. The meaning is clear, therefore, in spite of the omissions. Where the clause elements are longer, there tends to be little action on the pitch, allowing the speaker to develop a more complete and complex grammatical structure. This accounts for the number of subordinate clauses in this example. A commentary describes a series of actions that exist: it would therefore be possible to use the *existential there* + *be* structure repeatedly. The use of minor sentences creates a more varied style and reflects the need for precision in a time-bound context in which the pace may be very fast.

Radio (ll. 73–81)

Co Conj	Sub Conj	S	P	O/C	A
					here
			's		
		Solano			for Newcastle
		they	need	a goal	
		they	need	it	now
		it	's played		to the edge of the area
		ø	ø headed		away
					by de Zeeuw
		ø	comes		back to Emre
		he	slices	it	out to the near side
and		N'Zogbia the Frenchman	ø coming		in off the flank
		ø	ø	strong run	by him
but		he	's challenged		well by Martens
					Maarten Martens
		it	comes		to Bramble
		ø	arcs		back into the penalty area
		Taylor	's		up
		ø	heads	it	across
					towards Sibierski
			will		
		it	drop		for Dyer
					inside the penalty area
or					maybe Scott Parker
		Scott Parker	is		in there
and		he	's scored		
or			has		
		he	(not) ø		

The radio commentary is far more complete than that of the televised version of the match. Perhaps because the radio listener is far more reliant on the commentator for details, a radio commentary needs to be more precise. It is also possible that the number of deletions will vary according to the speed of the action at the time and according to the style of the commentator.

The verb tenses in unscripted commentaries are distinctive. The simple present is used to describe actions as they are happening: *goes* (l. 27), *volleys* (l. 58), *hits* (l. 95) and *dummies* (l. 13). The present progressive is used to create a sense of ongoing movement: *[is] causing* (l. 2), *was never threatening* (ll. 64–5), *[are] still breathing* (l. 107) and *are preparing* (l. 128). The simple past tense is used in any reference to events that have just taken place. It is more likely to be found in the summative comments of the advisers: *was* (l. 17), *knew* (l. 43) and *finished* (l. 93). The present or past perfect may also be used in the reflective sections of the commentary: *has charged* (l. 7), *'s gone* (l. 15), *hasn't bounced* (l. 92) and *had lifted* (l. 108). In many cases, **passive** rather than active sentences are used. They can create end focus by repositioning the subject at the end of the sentence as an adverbial (*headed away by de Zeeuw*, l. 74); they can place greater emphasis on the verb by repositioning a long subject at the end of the sentence (*he was outfoxed with the footwork from Martins*, l. 44); or they can omit the subject where it is either unclear who is responsible for a particular act (*he was dragged down*, l. 38), or where it is not yet known who will carry out an event (*not before the free kick is taken*, l. 129).

There are few examples of **normal non-fluency features** in either commentary. **Voiced hesitations** are rarely heard. If they do occur, they are more likely to be in the advisers' summaries: *er* (ll. 64, 66) and *uhh* (l. 103). Other examples of hesitancy are also rare in the official commentators' utterances, but may appear in the advisers' comments: repetition (*with a a great touch*, l. 101); false starts (*ther. the. they're*, l. 3) and unexpected pauses (*a (.) slight push in the penalty area but (.) I'm not sure (2)*, ll. 84–5). The exceptional fluency of unscripted commentary is one of its distinctive features.

The distinctive features of unscripted commentary can be summarised as follows:

- The **audience** have expert knowledge so they are able to fill in the gaps left by the economic nature of the variety as a whole. While television viewers can rely on visual and linguistic clues to decode the event, radio listeners have only language.
- The discourse is **spontaneous** and so it has many of the features of informal conversation. However, there are also marked differences because commentaries have to be **fluent** and **continuous**, unlike the casual, random nature of conversation.
- The **topic** is predefined and apart from asides in which a commentator may make connections with other things, the focus is on the actions taking place.
- The **structure** is very precisely ordered. The commentary must: describe the process (particularly on radio where listeners rely on the commentator's linguistic recreation of actions); create an appropriate background atmosphere; engage the audience's attention; and entertain with interpretation, comment and personal asides.
- **Turn-taking** is co-operative and orderly, as it is in an interview. The professional commentator provides focused description of who is doing what where and the 'player expert' comments and summarises. Most turns end smoothly – each speaker picks up signals marking the end and takes over promptly. Overlaps occur infrequently and are minimal. Some timed pauses occur at the end of an adviser's turn when the commentator waits for the next sequence of events to develop. This is more likely to happen on television

where the audience can watch the action; a complete silence on the radio, even for a few seconds, would cause problems for listeners. Radio commentators must therefore be even more fluent and sustained in their commentaries than television presenters. Turn-taking may be less orderly where the pace of a match is slow because the clearly defined roles of commentator and adviser may begin to overlap – where there are periods of inaction, the commentator may also interpret, make comparisons or summarise.

▸ **Prosodic features** are used extensively to animate the commentary, particularly by the commentator. Pitch, pace, volume and variations in intonation patterns reflect the dynamics of the event. Stress and rhythm are used to enhance meaning – it is common to find strings of words with emphatic stress that is quite different from most other varieties of spoken language. Pauses tend to be used for emphasis, to punctuate utterances, when nothing of significance is happening, and for breathing: they rarely indicate hesitation. Good timing is very important. Advisers tend to be less fluent and less able to manipulate the range of prosodic features to create dramatic effects.

▸ The **lexis** is subject-specific and technical. However, because unscripted commentaries are spontaneous, examples of informal conversational language are also common. Collocations may be technical or conversational. The variety is marked by its prominent use of proper nouns and its personal and idiosyncratic choice of lexis. Figurative language can also make commentaries very characteristic, enabling commentators to develop a recognisable personal style. Modification is common because it adds precise detail – radio commentaries require particularly well-focused descriptions and adverbials of place are common.

▸ The **grammar** is very distinctive. Grammatically incomplete utterances are common, although these will rarely be noticed in the speed and intensity of the action. The mood is usually declarative, but questions may be addressed to other participants. This kind of interaction can make commentaries resemble informal conversation. Utterances rarely have marked themes – the subject and predicator tend to be placed at the front of the clause so that the actors and processes are clear. Passive sentences, however, can be used to refocus the order in which we receive information. Clause structures are often simple or loosely co-ordinated, just as in informal conversation. The co-ordinating conjunction *and* is often used in the initial position as one turn moves smoothly into another – this enhances the audience's sense of a continuous speech turn. Where subordination is used, it rarely involves strings of embedded dependent clauses.

The most noticeable grammatical feature of unscripted commentaries is the number of deletions. Because the focus is on a description of actions which exist, commentators commonly use the *existential there + be* structure. To avoid repetition, the subject and predicator are often omitted, resulting in an unusually large number of minor 'sentences'. This is in line with the need to be economic, using as few words as possible to effectively convey the nature of the event. Radio commentaries often have fewer deletions than televised versions because their listeners cannot rely on visual clues to fill in the gaps.

Simple present tense and the present progressive are used to describe the facts, creating a sense of immediacy; simple past and the present perfective are used to comment and give opinions.

‣ The variety can be recognised by an almost complete absence of **normal non-fluency markers**. The commentaries of less experienced speakers may be marked by voiced hesitations, false starts and repetitions, but professional commentators are exceptionally fluent.

10.5 What to look for in spoken language

The following checklist can be used to identify key features in transcripts of spoken language. You will not find all of the features in every extract, but the list can be used as a guide. The points made are general, so discussion of specific examples will need to be adapted to take account of the particular context, participants and function of the discourse. Remember that you need to evaluate the effect of the features you identify, exploring the ways in which they create meaning.

The following are helpful questions to ask.

Register

1 What is the **mode**?
  • spoken.
2 What is the **manner**?
  • formal or informal relationship between participants?
  • personal or impersonal?
  • participants' status?
  • dominant speaker or co-operative participants?
3 What is the **field**?
  • subject matter?
  • linked to the audience, purpose and context?

Topic management

1 Is there **one clearly focused topic** or are there a number of apparently **random topics**?
2 How are the **topics chosen**?
  • directly related to the context (job interview, lecture, etc.)?
  • related to the interests and experiences of the participants?
3 Are there any **topic shifts**?
  • who introduces new topics?
4 Do new topics emerge **logically** from previous topics or do they appear to be **unconnected**?
5 After an **interruption**, are there any linguistic signals that a speaker is trying to **return to an earlier topic**?
6 How is the **end of a topic** marked?

Structure

1 Are there any examples of **adjacency pairs**?
  • questions and answers? greetings? command and response?

2 What kind of **opening** is used?
- neutral? self-related comment? other-related comment?
- social greetings or hospitality tokens?
- vocatives to personalise the discourse?

3 How is the **turn-taking** organised?
- dominant speaker? equally shared turns?
- latching on? overlaps?
- efficient recognition of linguistic and paralinguistic clues signalling the end of a turn?

4 What kinds of **speaker moves** are used in the main body of the discourse?
- framing? initiating? focusing? supporting? challenging?

5 What kind of **closing** is used?
- reference to something outside the speech encounter?
- repetition? delaying tactics? formulaic utterances?
- self- or other-related remarks?

Prosodic features

1 Do **intonation patterns** vary?
- to convey the speaker's attitude?
- to mark the end of grammatical utterances?
- to distinguish between new and old information?
- to indicate the end of a turn?

2 How do the intonation patterns relate to the **semantics** of an utterance?
- rising? (question)
- falling? (statement or completion)
- rising–falling? (reprimand or denial)
- falling–rising? (surprise or disbelief)

3 Does the **pitch** change to reflect the speaker's involvement in the discourse?
- high? (excitement or enthusiasm)
- low? (formality or seriousness)
- midway? (everyday speech encounters)

4 Is **emphatic stress** used to highlight key words?

5 Does the **volume** change significantly to enhance the meaning of utterances?
- 'forte'? 'piano'? 'cresc'? 'dimin'?

6 Does the **pace** change?
- 'alleg'? 'lento'? 'accel'? 'rall'?

7 Does the **style of delivery** change?
- 'stacc'? 'leg'?

8 What are the functions of the **pauses**?
- to allow the speaker to breathe?
- to mark the grammatical end of an utterance?
- to create emphasis? to dramatise an utterance?
- to mark hesitation? to let the speaker search for a word?
- to make the speech encounter informal?

9 Is the transcript marked with any **vocal effects** or **paralinguistics**?
- how do these relate to the words actually spoken?

Lexis

1 Is the language **formal** or **informal**?

2 Is it **subject-specific** or **general**?

3 Are there examples of **high-frequency** conversational clauses?
   * *you know, I see, I mean*, etc.?

4 Are there any **colloquial idioms** or **collocations**?

5 Is there any evidence of an **abbreviated code**?
   * based on shared knowledge or shared expertise?

6 Are there any **ambiguities**?

7 Is **modification** used to create an atmosphere?

Grammar

1 What **clause structures** are used?
   * simple? compound? complex? a mixture?

2 Are **loosely co-ordinated** clauses more common than **subordinated** ones?

3 Are there any **minor 'sentences'**?
   * which clause elements are omitted?

4 Are **phrases** complex or simple?
   * NPs? AdjPs? VPs? AdvPs?
   * how do they relate to the topic and manner of the speech encounter?

5 Are **different grammatical modes** used to add variety?
   * direct speech? reported speech?
   * quotations?
   * changes in mood? changes in voice?

6 Are there any **grammatically inaccurate** or **incomplete utterances**?
   * do other participants show any awareness of these?

7 Are there any marked themes?

Normal non-fluency features

1 Are there any **overlaps** in the speech turns?
   * for how long do they last? what causes them? how do the participants respond?
   * do the overlaps mark an intentional challenge, a supportive minimal vocalisation, or a misreading of linguistic clues?

2 Are there any **voiced hesitations**?
   * to prevent interruptions?
   * to prolong a turn?
   * to provide thinking time?

3 Are there any **false starts** or **repetitions**?

Dealing with problems

1 Are there any **repairs**?
   * self-corrections? other corrections?

2 Are there any **topic loops**?
   * after a minimal response or a negative evaluation?
   * which topic is reintroduced? why is it considered a safe topic?

3 Is the speaker aware of **listener responses**?
- self-monitoring?
- use of direct address? use of questions requiring some kind of response?
- restating or rephrasing of points made?

4 Are there any **silences**?
- lack of response to a question?
- failure to introduce new topic?
- utterances misheard?

Summary

An **analysis of spoken language** is central to any linguistic study because it is speech rather than writing that is dominant in society – it is at the centre of our daily lives and we deal instinctively with the demands of each spoken encounter as it arises. We all have a range of repertoires on which we can draw; and we are all experts, able to make decisions about the kinds of language appropriate for different people and different contexts.

There are many **varieties** of spoken language, all with their own distinctive features. However, it is possible to pinpoint some features that are common to most forms of spoken discourse. Where speech is spontaneous, even if the context is formal, there will be grammatical inaccuracies and incomplete utterances. In written language, these would be unacceptable – in speech, they often remain unnoticed. Because we all assimilate the 'rules' of spoken language from an early age, most speech encounters take place within a co-operative framework – turns are taken in an orderly way; participants find topics that reflect their shared interests; and a wide range of language is accepted as normal.

The **immediacy** of speech makes it an important social tool – it forms the basis for face-to-face interaction in both formal and informal contexts.

Chapter 11

The language of newspapers

11.1 The nature of newspaper language

In the eighteenth century, newspapers were used by the government as a means of promoting their own interests. The structure and style were therefore formal. By the nineteenth century, however, what can be described as 'modern journalism' began with the appearance of newspapers still popular today: by 1829, *The Times* was very powerful; 1821 marked the first printing of the *Manchester Guardian*; later in the century, this was followed by the *Daily Mail* (1896); and at the beginning of the twentieth century, by the *Daily Express* (1900) and the *Daily Mirror* (1903). Newspaper reporting became more scandalous, and style and form changed to suit the new approaches. The British press became renowned for its distinctive headline styles and its personal and idiosyncratic reporting.

Today, there is much debate about what makes a good news story. Journalists and academics study newspaper reporting and find great variation in what different newspapers will print. Anything **unexpected** or **dramatic** is newsworthy and 'bad news is always good news' for the journalists and editors trying to meet tight deadlines and sell papers. Equally, **élite persons**, whether royalty, pop stars or politicians, make the front pages because many readers like to know about the lifestyles and the scandals of the rich and famous. Editors look for **relevance** in the stories they print – culturally, socially or politically, the content must have some direct bearing on the people of Britain. Certain **élite nations** will receive more coverage, too – we are more likely to read about the United States of America, for instance, than about a smaller country that has fewer political, economic, cultural and historic links with Britain. **Continuity** is important and newspapers like to be able to develop running coverage of an event. To make abstract issues like politics and economics more engaging, journalists try to **personalise** them: 'Gordon Brown' is foregrounded, rather than his role as Prime Minister; on her death the Princess of Wales was portrayed as an individual with ordinary emotions, rather than as a distant princess to whom the ordinary public could not relate. The NEWS VALUES of a newspaper govern the kind of stories which editors print. The choices made are ultimately based on what will sell newspapers, both to readers and advertisers.

Having identified an **audience** that endorses or accepts their attitudes and ideas, journalists can explicitly support a particular political viewpoint or social group. This can lead to **bias** (favouring one viewpoint over another), which is evident in the lexical choice and in the selection or exclusion of particular stories.

Newspaper formats

Newspapers have often been divided into two main categories: **tabloid** and **broadsheet**. This is a very basic distinction and the terms mean different things to different people. In very general terms, a TABLOID paper is printed on A2-size paper, which is folded to A3; this is therefore smaller than the full spread of a BROADSHEET, which is printed on A1 and folded to A2. All the mass-circulation papers are tabloid. The divide between 'big' and 'small' papers goes further, however: broadsheet papers have also been called the **'serious'** or **'quality' press**, while tabloid papers have been called the **'popular'** or **'gutter' press**.

The latter definitions go beyond the factual distinction of size and become judgemental and evaluative. Dealing in very general terms, the broadsheets provide information, while the tabloids provide sensation; the former aim for factual representation of the 'truth', whereas the latter package stories for their entertainment value. More recently, a move to a COMPACT form brought *The Times* and *The Independent* to tabloid size. When the change was made the editors insisted that the quality and style of these publications would not be affected.

Table 11.1 breaks down some of the key linguistic and typographical differences between tabloids and broadsheets/compacts.

Table 11.1 **Tabloids and broadsheets/compact newspapers**

Tabloids	Broadsheets/compacts
Headlines are typed in bold print and may extend across the whole page. They are often capitalised.	**Headlines** usually only extend over two columns; the print tends to be smaller. Front page headlines, however, are sometimes an exception.
Paragraphs are usually only a few lines long.	**Paragraphs** are longer so the reader has to concentrate for longer periods of time.
A shocking 150,000 betting-mad Brits are getting hooked on gambling every year. *Daily Star* (6 May 2005)	Light from the star was analysed for the signatures of two radioactive elements – uranium and thorium – which decay at a fixed rate over billions of years. The ratios of these elements and other metals, such as europium, osmium and iridium, can be used to estimate the star's age at 13.2 billion years, plus or minus two billion years. *The Times* (14 May 2007, compact)
The **typographical features** are very varied: the first paragraph generally uses larger print and is often bold; the second paragraph is slightly smaller; the third paragraph uses standard print size. Initial letters are usually large.	The **typographical features** are more standard. The same size of print is used throughout, except for headlines, straplines and sub-headlines.

Punctuation is used sparingly.

- Commas are often omitted after initial adverbials and between strings of adjectives. This avoids breaking up the text and complicating the reading process.

  > Down on the farm she's dubbed desperate Donna.

- Inverted commas are used to mark direct speech and to highlight key words.

  > Hubby tells of 'bizarre' garden accident
  > *The Sun* (6 May 2005)

- Dashes mark parentheses, which make the style quite informal and chatty.

  > Kelly – who was treated for painkiller addiction last year – recently took on a minder to keep her off the booze.
  > *The Sun* (6 May 2005)

Punctuation is used traditionally and more formally than in tabloids. Dashes are less frequent.

> Vice-chancellors say that although part-time students must pay fees upfront without access to the same generous loans, many will feel unable to raise the money, even though the cost of provision is the same, and will instead cut courses.
> *The Times* (6 May 2005, compact)

Alliterative patterning is used to make the text more memorable.

> IT'S JAZZY JACKO
> *Daily Star* (6 May 2005)

> TWO-TIME SEX SWAPPER SUES
> *The Sun* (16 September 2005)

Rhetorical patterning is more complex. Rhythmical effects are achieved through balanced phrases and antithesis.

> Du vin, du pain, do keep paying our CAP subsidies
> *The Times* (2 July 2005, compact)

Sentence structure is often simple or compound, although the structure of one main clause and one subordinate clause is common.

- Long sentences are kept away from the beginning.

  > The BBC triumphed in the battle of the soaps at the awards ceremony.
  > *The Sun* (5 September 2006)

- Paragraphs are usually composed of one or two sentences.
- Word order can be changed.

  > Said the TV star, 'It's true.'

Sentence structure is varied to sustain the interest of the reader. Few paragraphs are of only one sentence.

> Yesterday was another black day in the "war on terror".
> (Simple sentence: S P C)
> *The Independent*
> (5 September 2006, compact)

> The desk, called a vertical work station, can be positioned over a wheel which employees can turn as though operating an old-fashioned treadle sewing machine or emulating a small furry rodent in a cage.
> (Complex sentence: S P A with an embedded non-finite clause in the subject, and an embedded relative clause and two non-finite adverbial clauses in the adverbial)
> *The Times* (15 May 2007, compact)

Paragraphs may, however, be made up of only two or three sentences.

Co-ordinators in the initial position are common: these act as a bridge and sustain the narrative pace. Loosely co-ordinated sentences reflect speech patterns.

> *And* only those with decent skills and schooling will escape the scrap-heap, says bosses' leader Richard Lambert
> *The Sun* (5 September 2006)

Co-ordinators in the initial position are less common. Cohesion is created through referencing and lexical repetition rather than through conjunctions.

Adverbials at the start of sentences change the focus and keep readers interested.

> *In a revealing black dress*, the star was greeted with gasps of admiration.

Adverbials are used in a variety of positions, depending upon the emphasis most appropriate to the meaning.

Modifiers are common and very few nouns stand alone. Pre-modification is more common than post-modification.

- Modifiers are coined.

> IT'S
> WAXO
> JACKO
> <u>Plastic star's dummy date</u>
> > *The Daily Star* (11 October 2005)

> The *bling* king

> YOU *DESERTY* RAT
> <u>Jailed ex-soldier is six-times wed</u>
> <u>bigamist</u>
> > *The Sun* (5 September 2006)

- Description is often vivid.

> [Steve Irwin's] *excitable* style, *broad* accent and *wild* antics gave him *widespread* appeal. Perhaps one of the *biggest* tributes to his fame and the *higher* profile he brought to the issues of conservation was how often he was *affectionately* parodied by comedians and impressionists.
> > *Daily Express* (5 September 2006)

> *Reject Virgin Trolley* Dollies Take Revenge
> > *Daily Star* (11 October 2005)

(Air hostesses rejected by the Virgin airline won a legal battle after claiming age discrimination.)

Modifiers are used to provide accurate detail. Description is always precise.

> an *RAF C130 Hercules transport* aircraft
> *Food Standards* Agency
> *secondary school healthy eating* initiative

Post-modification is as common as pre-modification.

> lawyers *for up to a dozen suspected foreign terrorists being held in Britain without trial*

> a blizzard *of sub-atomic particles that stream out from the sun*

Lexis is often inventive and emphatic.

- The tone is informal and colloquialisms are common:

> arm candy
> a load of plonkers
> goss (gossip)

- Compounds are created to attract attention:

> snap-happy
> love-rat

- Puns are common:

> Biggest blandside ever
> > *Daily Star* (6 May 2005)

(After a Labour election victory, dubbed *the most boring general election in history* by the *Daily Star*; compound of 'bland' and 'landslide'.)

Lexis is more specific, formal and restrained. Vivid, dramatic lexis is not used merely to sensationalise.

> the North Korean Foreign Minister
> American-style compensation culture

> You doughnut have to say anything, but anything you do say may be used in evidence against you
>
> # GOBCHA!
>
> <u>Cop from apple-nick force caught eating at wheel</u>
>
> A COP from the force that spent £10,000 nailing a woman for eating an apple has been snared – scoffing a doughnut.
>
> *The Sun* (31 January 2005)
>
> (Pun on *doughnut* for 'do not' and *Gobcha* for the colloquial 'gotcha'.)

The **angle** adopted is usually human – news stories (political, economic, etc.) are directly linked to people and the ways in which they are affected by an event or issue. The tone is conversational and the approach is often sensational and dramatic. Individual ideas are not always developed and the order of points can seem illogical.

The **angle** adopted tends to be more factual. There is more likely to be evidence of research and a greater concern with accuracy. The tone is often restrained and controlled. Summaries are provided and topic sentences make the approach seem more precise.

Changes in format

Some newspapers can be easily classified in terms of 'tabloid' and 'broadsheet'. Others, however, although tabloid in size, would object to being ranked as tabloids because of the wider connotations of this term. A third category is therefore useful: the **MIDDLE-MARKET PAPER**. These fall between tabloids and broadsheets: although adopting the A3 format, they would rebut any claims that their content was merely for entertainment or that they were interested only in scandal. It is also important to remember that the stylistic differences between tabloid and broadsheet newspapers are not always clear-cut – broadsheets do sometimes adopt the stylistic features typically associated with the tabloids.

In late 2003, two mainstream broadsheet newspapers launched daily tabloid editions to run alongside their traditional full-size papers in certain regions. It was a move that marked an increasing interest in smaller-format newspapers. Over the past decade, new supplements and sections in a number of broadsheets have been introduced in tabloid-size (broadsheet–tabloid hybrids), but the conversion of *The Independent* and *The Times* to a smaller format, including their Saturday publications, has had significant effects on the market. Because of the pejorative connotations often associated with the tabloids, the new smaller-size broadsheets have been named **COMPACTS**. This name allowed editors to make the change in size while distancing their publications from the traditional tabloid papers.

There is inevitably an effect on the layout and journalism of a paper when it becomes a compact: in general the cover focuses on headlines, while the main reporting is saved for pages two and three. Some argue that *The Independent* and *The Times* are now increasingly dependent on tabloid-style splashes on the front page, focusing on high-drama stories about topics such as the MRSA hospital superbug, bird flu, or the one billion children at risk from poverty and hunger.

Critics of the new format suggest that there is a lower story count with shorter, less complete texts, larger photographs and headlines, and softer journalism that no longer maintains the ground-breaking, opinion-forming style of the broadsheets. They see the change in format as indicative of a move from factual to subjective reporting. Increasing sales figures, however, indicate that the tabloid-sized broadsheets have not lost favour with their readers. Research suggests that *The Independent* sales grew by 35 per cent when it became a compact, with an increase of the market share from 10 per cent to 12 per cent. The newspaper has also benefited from increases in sales to two key demographic groups that appeal to advertisers: ABC1 (professional, managerial, administrative and clerical workers), up by 35 per cent, and younger readers (15–44), up by 40 per cent. Traditional *Times* readers may have expressed dissatisfaction at the removal of the crossword from the back page, but free CDs, large numbers of papers on the shelves, the practical convenience of the format and continued high-quality reportage have persuaded readers to embrace the compact format.

For advertisers, the compacts offer great opportunities: broadsheets are often folded in half vertically or horizontally, thus reducing the area of the paper on view; a compact will usually have both pages open simultaneously. This, together with the increase in sales to the lucrative ABC1 demographic group, ensure that advertising revenues are buoyant.

In a world in which technology prides itself on the ability to make things smaller, the success of the compacts is perhaps not surprising. *The Independent* and *The Times* have combined the practicality of the A2 folded sheet with the principles of broadsheet journalism, following in the footsteps of France's *Le Monde*, a compact with a reputation for quality. While *The Daily Telegraph* and *The Financial Times* have to date refused to join the move to compact form, *The Guardian* has opted for a slightly different format: the Berliner (320 mm × 470 mm).

Important as format is, however, it is not the only defining feature of a newspaper, and adopting a tabloid size need not necessarily lead to 'dumbing down'. In the fast-changing modern environment with its 24-hour news channels and ready internet access, newspapers, like other institutions, must be prepared to adapt.

The latest challenge comes in the form of free newspapers distributed on the city streets. *Metro*, launched in 1999, is a free daily tabloid morning paper available in 15 cities. Its circulation has now reached 1.1 million, making it the fourth largest national daily paper in Britain. It has exclusive rights to distribute at stations until 2010, and a recent ruling means that it will also have access to the afternoon market in the future. In London, two free evening tabloids added to the increasingly competitive battle for readers: since 30 August 2006, Associated Newspapers have been distributing 400000 copies of its new evening paper, *London Lite*, to commuters; and on 19 September 2006, Rupert Murdoch's News International launched *thelondonpaper*. Both companies are trying to secure contracts that will allow them to distribute at mainline stations and the London Underground.

Such changes in the newspaper world give rise to speculation that the age of paid-for newspapers could be nearing its end.

Newspaper ideologies

Whether a newspaper is broadsheet or compact, tabloid or middle-market, the **IDEOLOGY** or **POINT OF VIEW** of its owner and its editor dictates the kinds of stories printed and the political or moral slant transmitted to the reader. The political leanings of a paper, however, may vary in degree according to the kind of story reported.

The style of the tabloid papers is distinctive, with its sensational approach and its dominant front-page headlines. Its power can be seen in the way it has affected even the broadsheets in small ways – they are now more likely to use puns and emotive language than they were in the past, and their style is more like that of ordinary language. Even the regional and evening papers now adopt the style of the popular press for many of their reports.

Linguists are interested in the kinds of language different newspapers choose to attract their intended audience. Tabloids, compacts and broadsheets choose different stories to feature on their front pages; they select different angles in presenting their material; and they use different formats (column lengths, balance of images and text, typefaces, and so on).

11.2 The function of newspaper language

Originally, newspapers were used by governments to promote certain political views; by the nineteenth century, they were used to convey news; and in the twenty-first century newspapers now deal as much with entertainment as they do with information. Many are closer to magazines in the kinds of features and columns they regularly print. Although their function is **referential**, therefore, **entertainment** has become equally important in the battle to win readers.

Nevertheless, national newspapers do convey **information** about everyday events that affect our daily lives. The breadth of the information they cover is very wide, and includes international, national and local news; reviews of film, television, radio, books, music and art; reports of sports events; advice on financial matters; articles on scientific developments; and help with personal problems. Local newspapers act as **community bulletins**, providing information about local events and issues: their focus is far more specific.

Newspapers can be **influential**: they can affect the way we think about international events and British politics by presenting issues in a certain way. The choice of words, the decisions about which facts to include and which to exclude, and the ranking of events on the front page all influence the reader. The editor of a newspaper will seek to present the world in a certain way so that the intended audience identify with the paper's viewpoint.

Different types of people buy different types of papers. Broadsheets tend to be associated with educated professional people, while tabloids are associated with the traditional working class. The middle-market papers fall somewhere between the two. Within these broad categories, people may buy a particular paper because of its ideology, because of a journalist whose style they like, because certain features appear regularly, or because of the front-page news, the cover price, a free gift or a competition. Although such breakdowns are very general and many readers do not fall neatly into a specific category, it is useful to bear these in mind when analysing a report from a particular paper.

11.3 Features of newspaper language

Analysis of newspapers involves a consideration of both **headlines** and **reporting styles** since these will both reveal much about the ideology and aims of an individual paper.

Headlines

There are three kinds of headlines:

- the main **HEADLINE** will be larger than the others and may occasionally be in colour to draw attention
- the **STRAPLINE** or **OVERLINE** is the secondary headline that appears above the main one – it is used to provide extra information or to clarify the main headline
- the **SUB-HEADLINE** follows the main headline, and qualifies or elaborates it.

Just as the selection of news items and the balance of photographs to text differs between broadsheets, compacts and tabloids, so too do the headlines. While the broadsheets may aim for a **factual** interpretation of an event, the tabloids may look for **sensation**.

> ## Ikea blamed for pandemonium as 6,000 turn up for bargains
>
> *The Guardian* (11 February 2004, broadsheet)

> ## 6,000 IN IKEA CHAVALANCHE
> ### Mob turn on manager and beat him senseless as they fight for bargain sofas
>
> *Daily Star* (11 February 2004)

Each of these headlines reports the same event: the midnight opening of a new store in north London for the popular Swedish furniture retailer Ikea. *The Guardian* uses restrained language to convey a sense of the chaos, which it sees as the responsibility of the store – the use of the passive voice brings *Ikea* to the front of the sentence, giving it additional stress. The *Daily Star*, on the other hand, focuses on the violence. The connotations of the words, the initial position of the number and the pun on 'chav' and 'avalanche' suggest that responsibility lies with the people who created the riot. The approach is sensational rather than factual. Such variation typifies the difference between headlines in broadsheets/compacts and in tabloids.

To catch readers' attention, headlines need to be **simple**, **easily readable** and **appropriate** to the kind of newspaper in which they are printed. The choice of words for headlines is affected by the **ideas to be expressed**, the **kind of reader** associated with the paper, and the paper's HOUSE STYLE. Typographically, broadsheets/compacts and tabloids have quite different approaches. Tabloids frequently use capitalisation and colour to draw attention to a front-page report – blue or purple print, or white printed on a blue or purple background, may be used for a royal headline, while the death of a famous person may be headlined in white print on a black background. Broadsheets/compacts, on the other hand, are much more conservative: they rarely capitalise whole headlines, and use colour for the main front-page photographs, for advertisements and for some features.

The **lexis** chosen indicates something about the political persuasion of the newspaper and about the intended audience. By analysing **connotations** of the words chosen and the **point of view** conveyed, it is possible to come to conclusions about the aim of a report. During a murder investigation, for instance, newspapers report events in different ways. The three headlines below, taken from newspapers on the same day, each use a different approach to report the events:

DEAD BABIES: COPS SEARCH HOUSE No3
Dog team in gran's home

John Coles, *The Sun* (6 May 2005)

Grandmother described as pillar of community is murder suspect after
discovery of three bodies
Estate in shock at babies in attic case

Rosie Cowan, *The Guardian* (6 May 2005, broadsheet)

Third home being searched by police after three tiny bodies found in attics
House ripped apart in 'dead babies' probe

Nick Fagge, *Daily Express* (6 May 2005)

The Sun's headline foregrounds the emotive noun phrase *DEAD BABIES*. This, along with the simple sentence that follows, dramatises the report. The use of the dynamic present tense verb *search* and the cardinal number create a sense of immediacy, while the abbreviated familiar *gran's* of the sub-headline enhances the sensational aspect of the case. To attract readers' attention, the comfortable connotations of this possessive noun modifier and the head noun *home* are set against the horrific nature of the supposed crime.

The Guardian adopts a different tone: it deals in fact rather than sensation. The main headline focuses on the response of local people, using *estate* as a collective noun that unites residents in their common experience. The connotations of *shock* suggest disbelief, and this is reinforced by the post-modified noun phrase of the strapline, in which the link between the head word *grandmother* and the noun phrase *pillar of community* draws attention to the suspect's past achievements. The approach is more impersonal than that of *The Sun*: the full word *grandmother* is a more formal term of address; the emotive noun phrase *three bodies* is kept away from the front of the sentence; and the use of the noun *suspect* recognises that the woman has not yet been proven guilty.

The *Daily Express* falls between these two extremes. The emotive dynamic verb *ripped apart*, with its connotations of urgent and unchecked action, and the emotive modifier *tiny* highlight sensational aspects of the case. This appeal to readers' emotions, however, is balanced by a more formal presentation of the facts. In addition, the 'tabloidese' shorthand for investigation (*probe*) reminds us that this case is still under review. By combining a detached tone with the more emotive elements of the report, the middle-market paper can provide its readers with both facts and sensation.

The **style** of headlines is important: they need to be **simple**, but must also create **IMPACT**. Broadsheets/compacts and tabloids aim to fulfil these criteria in very different ways. The headlines accompanying a broadsheet report will usually be informative and straightforward:

'Grim' financial future for graduates

Nigel Morris, Home Affairs Correspondent
The Independent (18 September 2006, compact)

Haig's son attacks pardoning of 306 soldiers shot for cowardice

Stephanie Condron, *The Daily Telegraph* (5 September 2006, broadsheet)

A tabloid, however, will aim for a different kind of simplicity. Puns are common and headlines will often disrupt collocations. This gives the headlines a less formal tone and can suggest that the journalists are not being completely serious about the issue. On the other hand, the tabloids' informal approach and their emphasis on human-interest stories can result in a very personal and emotive appeal to their readers, as illustrated on page 266. In the first example, the newspaper alters the well-known army command 'Attention!' to discuss the creation of a new kind of trainer designed and tested by the army. The repetition of the traditional 'left, right' marching order immediately sets the context and the replacement of /ətenʃən/ with /ətenʃuː/ creates humour. The second headline describes an incident in which police questioned a man who was driving a vehicle in spite of the fact that he was totally blind. It uses patterning for dramatic effect. While the repetition of the negative (*no*) and the subject-specific nouns (*MoT, insurance, licence*) are commonplace in a report on car crime, the final noun phrase is unexpected. The

Left, right, left, right, left, right, left, right

ATTEN-SHOE!

Army to sell 'boot camp' trainers

NO MoT, NO INSURANCE NO LICENCE NO EYES!

Ruki Sayid, Consumer Editor, *Daily Mirror* (16 September 2004)

Jerry Lawton, *Daily Star* (5 September 2006)

headline is therefore eye-catching: it builds towards a climax, taking readers from the ordinary to the extraordinary.

The **structure** of headlines is easily recognisable. Many are **noun phrases**:

m   m   m   h   q
First passenger test flight for new Airbus
num   N   N   N   PrepP

The Independent (5 September 2006, compact)

m   h   q
Conspiracy theory that might even rock Elvis
N   N   RelCl

Jeff Powell, *Daily Mail* (5 September 2006)

Headlines differ from everyday language in their **omission** of many of the grammatical function words, copula verbs and auxiliaries. In the examples considered so far, for instance, determiners are deleted from almost all of the noun phrases. This is one of the characteristic features of headline writing, marking it out as a distinctive variety of English. The structure is often described as TELEGRAPHIC.

Some headlines comprise one **simple sentence**:

S   P   O
(Tourists) (rediscover) (their sea wings)

S   P   O
(Flying boats) (are making) (a comeback)

Richard Owen, *The Times* (15 May 2007, compact)

A   S   P   O
(Why) (we) (can't ban) (Muslim schools)

Chris Woodhead, former Chief Inspector of Schools, *The Sun* (5 September 2006)

Some headlines use the **passive voice** to focus the reader's attention on a particular element:

'Evil' teenager who cried rape is jailed

Simon de Bruxelles, *The Times* (19 September 2006, compact)

This headline uses the full form of the passive verb phrase (*to be* + past participle). By choosing the passive voice, the journalist was able to foreground the object of the active sentence – the fronted complex noun phrase *'Evil' teenager who cried rape*. This emotive term of address has added weight when in the initial position, providing information about the disposition, age and crime of the perpetrator. The use of quotation marks around the pre-modifier reflects the fact that this is a description applied by an external source, not the journalist – in this case, the judge. The omission of the *by + agent* is typical in this kind of headline, in which the focus is on the guilty party and the outcome of the case (*is jailed*), rather than on the legal representatives of the court.

The example below omits the verb *to be*, which is common in passive-voice headlines. It does, however, include the *by + agent* which would have been the subject of an active sentence:

Virgin media called to task by leading investor over poor results
Robert Lindsay and Elizabeth Judge, The Times (15 May 2007, compact)

By using the passive voice, the headline foregrounds the name, drawing attention to the company (*Virgin Media*) rather than to the noun phrase *leading investor*. This is because the journalists wished to highlight the market performance of this particular cable company when it was losing subscribers after dropping five of BSkyB's basic channels.

By omitting the *by + agent*, journalists can leave readers in suspense; and where information is uncertain, they can avoid printing libellous statements or naming suspects:

17-year-old girl stabbed to death in street argument
David Brown and Patrick Foster, The Times (21 June 2007, compact)

'News in Brief' columns often use the passive voice as a shorthand, omitting the verb *to be*, and either the subject of the passive sentence or the *by + agent*:

Saved by footie Star

Trooper 'bullied'
The Sun (16 May 2007)

Ambiguity

Some headlines are **AMBIGUOUS** – they have two meanings. Ambiguity can occur when a word could be interpreted differently depending on its word class; when the different connotations of a word alter the meaning; when word order is altered to make the headline concise; or when punctuation is omitted to prevent a headline from being too long. In some cases the ambiguity is created deliberately, while in others it is accidental:

LOCAL MAN FINDS PICASSO DRAWING IN SHED

10-YEAR-OLD SUSPENDED BY HEAD

IRA BOMB GUTS FACTORY

Each of these examples demonstrates a different kind of ambiguity. In the first, ambiguity occurs in whether the word *DRAWING* is a **verbal noun** pre-modified by *PICASSO* or whether it is a **present participle**. In the second, the ambiguity depends upon the **connotations** of the verb *SUSPENDED*: it is used here as a **subject-specific term** for a kind of punishment used by schools, but could be seen as denoting 'dangling'. The **abbreviation** of 'headmaster' or 'headmistress' adds to the ambiguity – *HEAD* can be interpreted as the part of the body by which the child has been dangled. In the third example, the ambiguity depends on the *–s* inflection that marks plural nouns and third person present tense verbs, and on the meaning of *guts* (*pl. n.* the bowels or entrails, especially of an animal; *v.* destroys the inside of a building, especially by fire). **Changing the function** of the words changes the meaning: if *guts* is the predicator, *bomb* is the head of the subject noun phrase, but if *bomb* is the predicator, *guts* is a noun modifier in the object site.

Typically, tabloids are associated with headlines that are **informal** in tone and that are not always serious. *The Sun* is renowned for outrageous headlines like *'FREDDIE STARR ATE MY HAMSTER'*. Some examples, however, cause concern because they actively seek to persuade readers to react in a particular way. During the Falklands War, for instance, the informal tone of the front-page headline *'GOTCHA'* was censured as mindlessly jingoistic and inappropriate as it seemed to make light of the deaths of four hundred Argentinian sailors. **Alliteration** is common, often adding to the informality of tone. Broadsheets/compacts tend to be more conservative in their lexical choices, although they do sometimes use **puns**.

Reports

The way in which media reports are put together reflects the ideology of the paper as a whole. Reports give a particular view of events, and the information that is **excluded** can be as important as the information that is **included** – in each case journalists and editors are making decisions about what their readers will see. Occasions when a newspaper does not report a certain event while others do, or when it does not report certain features of an event, are examples of SELECTIVE PERCEPTION. This is a form of **bias**. Some newspapers claim to be impartial, but by analysing the lexis and syntax it is possible to identify the ways in which a distinctive point of view is conveyed.

The reports in Figures 11.1–11.3 will be used to show how the lexis and syntax of news reporting can:

- reflect whether a paper is a broadsheet/compact or a tabloid
- influence the reader.

Read through all three reports before considering the points made below. The first two examples are taken from 'News in Brief' columns, while the third is a 'human interest' story.

Lexis

The intended audience dictates the **lexical choices** that journalists make. Vocabulary may be formal or informal: usually broadsheets and compacts will use formal lexis, while tabloids will use informal. In Report 1, *The Sun* uses colloquial nouns such as *CROOK* (l. 2) and *cops* (l. 11), while the lexis from *The Times* in Report 2 is standard, avoiding the informal style of the tabloid. The concrete nouns *pitchfork*, *screwdrivers*, *hacksaw* and *sack* (ll. 23–5) give readers a physical sense of the event, while the abstract noun *scare* (l. 18) suggests its effect. The informal tone of the popular paper's headline helps to create a different kind of relationship with

Figure 11.1 **Report 1**

1

HEIR BRAINED

A CROOK was fined yesterday after armed police caught him "tooled up" for theft on
5 Prince Charles' estate.

Jobless Desmond Kellaway, 55 – a thief for 40 years – said he did not know it was Highgrove, Gloucs, and "any-
10 one could have got in". Two cops held him at gunpoint at 4am on January 30. The dad of five from Bristol got a £100 fine from JPs after admitting going
15 equipped.

The Sun (21 June 2007)

Figure 11.2 **Report 2**

16 ### Royal break-in

Desmond Kellaway, 55, who caused a royal security scare in January after sneaking into the
20 grounds of Highgrove House, pleaded guilty to going equipped for theft. Kellaway, who was carrying a broken pitchfork, two screwdrivers, a hacksaw and a
25 sack, was fined £100 with £40 costs by Cheltenham magistrates.

The Times (21 June 2007, compact)

Figure 11.3 **Report 3**

27 # Kids' junk food run is halted

THE mums selling junk food
30 to schoolkids have stopped after a rollicking from the headmaster.

Shamed Julie Critchlow, 43, and Sam Walker, 41, were
35 hauled into the head's office at Rawmarsh Comprehensive.

Julie said: "We have agreed not to comment and will not be delivering takeaways today."
40 The Sun revealed last week how they sold burgers and chips at a playground fence in protest at healthy school dinners.
45 The mums caused outrage when they blasted TV chef Jamie Oliver for promoting food they claimed kids did not like.
50 Yesterday pupils at the school in Rotherham, South Yorks, were eating jacket spuds, pizza meals and healthy sarnies.
55 Head John Lambert said: "We want to get on with being a school."
The Sun Says – Page Eight

The Sun (19 September 2006)

readers: the broadsheet is factual; the tabloid is tongue-in-cheek. The pun in the headline of *The Sun* juxtaposes the inept attempted break-in with its royal location – Prince Charles' estate at Highgrove. The overlaying of the colloquial idiom 'hare-brained' with the fact that Prince Charles is the 'heir' to the throne creates a headline that underpins the light-hearted tone of the report.

The way in which **participants are named** is another means of distinguishing between the two different kinds of reportage. Both papers use the proper noun *Desmond Kellaway* (ll. 6, 17) and include a parenthetical reference to his age. *The Sun* also refers to the defendant using the emotive noun phrases *A CROOK* (l. 2) and *a thief* (l. 7). These epithets are judgemental and are quite different from the neutral terms of naming in the compact report. The tabloid's use of the pre-modifier *Jobless* (l. 6), the direct quotation of Kellaway's words (ll. 9–10) and the noun phrase *The dad of five from Bristol* (ll. 12–13) provides personal details, giving the report a narrative quality that is absent from the compact which does not include this information.

The naming of the **location** also distinguishes between the two reports. It is assumed that readers of *The Times* will recognise the link between the noun phrase *the grounds of Highgrove House* (ll. 19–20) and Prince Charles. While the repetition of the modifier *royal* implicitly highlights the link, *The Sun* report makes it explicit. The reference to *Highgrove, Gloucs* (l. 9) is preceded by the possessive noun phrase *Prince Charles' estate* (l. 5). This link to an 'élite' person makes the story newsworthy.

The **connotations** of words chosen are often interesting. The colloquial phrasal verb *"tooled up"* (l. 4), for instance, is an implicit reference to the concrete nouns listed in the compact report. The use of quotation marks is a signpost to the reader that the colloquial idiom ('to arm oneself') is functioning as a pun. The language in the compact report is more restrained, but the connotations of the noun *scare* (l. 18) and the non-finite verb *sneaking* (l. 19) are central to our understanding that this incident was not serious. Where the tabloid explicitly adopts a light-hearted and humorous approach, *The Times* hints at the comedy underlying the situation through its choice of lexis. The connotations of *sneaking* are comic in the light of what the defendant was carrying and, where the noun 'threat' would imply a significant breach of safety, a *scare* is a minimal disruption.

Modifiers are used by both broadsheets/compacts and tabloids as they help journalists to provide detail. While the former tend to choose factual words, tabloids often use more emotional and sensational ones. Because 'News in Brief' reports have restricted word counts, modifiers tend to be kept to a minimum. In Reports 1 and 2, therefore, modifiers are usually factual: <u>armed</u> police (l. 3), <u>Two</u> cops (ll. 10–11), <u>a £100</u> fine (l. 13); <u>a royal security</u> scare (l. 18) <u>a broken</u> pitchfork, <u>two</u> screwdrivers (ll. 23–4), <u>£40</u> costs (l. 25). In Report 3, however, we see a more distinctive use of modifiers because the journalist is trying to engage readers in a more narrative account of events. Noun phrases tend to be longer so that they can provide a lot of information in a compact way.

Strings of modifiers can seem excessive unless they actually contribute something to the report. Only where they are used to achieve precision are they effective. In the reports here, the compact uses factual modification and an objective tone – the modifiers are used to establish details of the context.

> h   q
> (Desmond Kellaway), 55, who caused a royal security scare in January after sneaking
> N   RelCl   SCl–ACl
> into the grounds of Highgrove House   (ll. 17–20)

By contrast, Report 3 uses a narrative style with colloquial head words (*mums, rollicking, sarnies*) to set the tone.

> m   m   m   h   m   h
> Kids' junk food run (ll. 27–8)   Shamed (Julie Critchlow) (l. 33)
> N   N   N   N   V   N
>   (past participle)

> m   h
> healthy sarnies (l. 54)
> Adj   N

m   h   q
a rollicking from the headmaster (ll. 31–2)
det   N   PrepP
    (verbal noun)

m   h   q
The mums selling junk food to schoolkids (ll. 29–30)
det   N   NFCl

Many of the noun phrases implicitly suggest a judgement in the connotations of the words chosen by the journalist (*junk food*, *Shamed*, *rollicking*). The effect is more personal and the use of direct speech (ll. 37–9, 56–7) adds to the narrative feel of the piece.

Adverbials are used to add extra detail. They can answer questions like *how?*, *when?*, *where?*, *why?*, *what for?*, *how long?* These kinds of details are often used in broadsheets/compacts to provide accurate information and in tabloids to develop a sense of narrative. Because Report 3 adopts a more narrative-like structure, it uses many adverbials of place: *into the head's office at Rawmarsh Comprehensive* (ll. 35–6); *at a playground fence* (l. 42); *at the school in Rotherham* (ll. 50–1). Adverbs of time (*after a rollicking from the headmaster*, ll. 31–2; *today*, l. 39; *last week*, l. 40) and reason (*in protest at healthy school dinners*, ll. 43–4) are equally important.

Selective perception means that although reports might cover the same event, the information included may not be the same. Both 'News in Brief' reports here include the same basic facts, but *The Sun* develops a more story-like approach by adding personal details. *The Times* avoids the personal, but includes extra factual information about the tools the defendant was carrying (ll. 23–5) and the court case (*£40 costs*; *Cheltenham magistrates*). In Report 3, the paper's editorial view of the incident is clear in the connotations of words such as *Shamed* and in the associated editorial column 'The Sun Says', which (using noun phrases such as *their stupid protest*) makes explicit the judgement that is implicit in the report itself.

Grammar

The **grammar** of newspaper reports varies quite markedly in tabloids and broadsheets/compacts. The former tends to use simple and compound sentences. When subordinate clauses are used, they are kept reasonably short so that readers do not have to retain large amounts of information. Broadsheets and compacts, on the other hand, use a wider variety of sentence structures. Paragraphs in a tabloid paper are rarely more than three sentences long and can be no more than one sentence in length; broadsheets and compacts, however, develop paragraphs more fully. These grammatical differences are not always clear-cut, however, since broadsheets and compacts now use features traditionally associated with tabloids. Linguists therefore need to be able to recognise the distinctive grammatical features of both the popular and the serious press, and also any variations.

While none of the reports here is dominated by simple sentences, the length of the sentences and the number of sentences that make up a paragraph do vary from report to report. Report 1 has two paragraphs, the first of which is a grammatically complete sentence. One sentence is a simple sentence (ll. 10–12), two are complex sentences containing adverbial subordinate clauses of time (ll. 2–5, 12–15), and the other sentence is compound–complex with two coordinated subordinate noun clauses (ll. 6–10):

S P O
(Jobless Desmond Kellaway, 55 – a thief for 40 years –) (said) (ø he did not know
SCl–NCl

O
ø it was Highgrove, Gloucs), (and) (ø "anyone could have got in".)
SCl–NCl   conj   SCl–NCl

The use of dashes to mark the parenthesis divides the long subject, making the sentence seem less dense for the reader. The omission of the subordinating conjunction 'that' in three places also helps to keep the sentence shorter.

In Report 2, the single paragraph is made up of two complex sentences. In the first, there are five clauses: a main clause (*pleaded*); an embedded relative clause (ll. 17–20) which post-modifies the head noun *Desmond Kellaway, 55* and contains an adverbial clause of time (*after sneaking*); and two non-finite clauses (*to going, equipped*):

S
(Desmond Kellaway, 55, who caused a royal security scare in January after sneaking
SCl–RelCl   SCl–ACl
P   C
into the grounds of Highgrove House) (pleaded) (guilty to going equipped for theft).
SCl–NFCl   SCl–NFCl

In the second sentence, an embedded relative clause post-modifies the head word *Kellaway* (ll. 22–5). While the tabloid aims to visually divide the weight of the long second sentence by using dashes and a direct quotation of the defendant's words, the compact requires its readers to link the subjects and the main verbs which are separated by the long relative clauses.

Despite the fact that Report 3 is not taken from the 'News in Brief' section of the paper, its style is closer to Report 1 than Report 2: each paragraph comprises just one sentence, with the most grammatically complicated sentences kept away from the beginning of the report. There is a greater variety of subordinate clauses, however: for example, an embedded non-finite post-modifying clause (*... selling...* ll. 29–30); a noun clause (*how they sold...* ll. 41–4), an adverbial clause of time (*when they blasted...* ll. 46–9), and a non-finite clause with an embedded relative clause (*promoting... ø they claimed...* ll. 47–9). In part, this reflects the different journalistic expectations of a news report as opposed to a 'News in Brief' column.

The formality of the broadsheet/compact style demands much more concentration on the part of the reader. The use of short simple and compound sentences enables the tabloids to develop a chatty approach, where it is appropriate.

In journalists' training manuals, reporters are advised to avoid cramming too many ideas into one sentence: a sentence should communicate no more than one idea or two connected ideas and should not exceed a maximum of thirty words. A successful report, however, will vary the type of sentence structure to retain readers' interest.

Style

There are several ways in which newspapers can reorder the material in their sentences to draw attention to certain elements. **Marked themes** bring clause elements other than the subject to the front of the sentence and give them prominence. Use of the **passive voice** rather than the active also has this effect. In Report 1 from *The Sun*, the passive is used without an agent (l. 2). The name of the court and the magistrate who issued the penalty are not seen to be of interest to readers of the tabloid and are omitted – the object of the active sentence (*A CROOK*) becomes the subject and is therefore given more weight. The report from *The Times*, on the other hand, uses the passive voice with *by* + *agent* (l. 26). The name of the defendant is again given prominence, but the subject of the active sentence (*Cheltenham magistrates*) has semantic emphasis too. The end focus suggests that this is important information for readers of the compact.

Newspapers use both **direct** and **indirect speech** – they may directly quote the exact words spoken by an individual or they may report those words indirectly. By interweaving direct quotations, journalists can vividly recreate the personal experiences of ordinary people, and they can allow eminent people to voice their views accurately and directly without intervention. Tabloids often quote eminent people directly, to encourage a feeling that even the rich and famous are ultimately the same as their readers; and they quote ordinary people to make their readers feel that they have a voice. Broadsheets/compacts tend to use direct quotation to add weight to their arguments, allowing people to prove their points in the words they wish to use. The use of quotations can also vary the pace of an article, making it more interesting to read. Formal speeches can be summarised so that the newsworthy points are highlighted. Interviews with ordinary people unaccustomed to speaking in public contexts can be tidied up, eliminating non-fluency markers.

Direct speech is made up of a **QUOTING CLAUSE** such as *said the Prime Minister* or *the Prime Minister said* and a **QUOTED CLAUSE** which contains the actual words spoken:

> Head John Lambert said: 'We want to get on with being a school.'   (ll. 55–7)
> [quoting clause]   [quoted clause]

Indirect speech can be recognised by the marker *that* which introduces the paraphrase of the actual words spoken. The clause introduced by *that* is called a **REPORTED CLAUSE** and takes the form of a noun clause:

>   S   P   O
> (Jobless Desmond Kellaway …) (said) ([that] he did not know it was Highgrove, Gloucs)
>   [reported clause]
>
>   S   P   O
> (Head John Lambert) (said) ([that] they wanted to get on with being a school).
>   [reported clause]

In most cases, it is possible to delete the marker *that*.

Sources

The **sources** of information are important in newspaper articles and provide another way to distinguish between tabloids and broadsheets/compacts. While a quality paper will often cite official sources – for example, Parliament, the courts, or the police and other emergency services – as the basis for their reports, tabloids quote ordinary people who have no particular authority. Variations in sources can clearly affect the credibility of any statements made.

Summary

All the features discussed above help to indicate the point of view or ideology of a newspaper. By contrasting the approach of two or more reports, a linguist can come to conclusions about the intended audience and the house style of a paper.

It is very easy to stereotype broadsheet/compact and tabloid newspapers by assuming that the characteristic features discussed here can always be found in every report. Linguistic analysis, however, has shown that these are generalisations: journalists adapt their approach to suit each report they write. They consider the target audience, the house style of the newspaper, and the effect they wish to create – linguistic analysis has to take account of this. Although the two distinctive newspaper styles are useful as a starting point, it is important to remember that broadsheets and compacts sometimes use features characteristic of the tabloid style, and vice versa.

11.4 Types of newspaper reports

The introductory paragraph of each report must capture the reader's attention. It should concentrate on exactly what has happened, summing it up in no more than twenty words. The rest of the report (the **NEWS LEAD**) will provide the necessary extra detail.

Action stories

Action stories often package news as entertainment – they create stories from dramatic incidents. Their structure is chronological and they tend to focus on the human results of an event. The introduction establishes what has happened; the news lead develops the narrative chronologically; and the conclusion often provides some kind of assessment or evaluation.

ACTIVITY 11.1

Read through the three versions of the action story in Figures 11.4–11.6 (published on 11 October 2005), and comment on the distinctive linguistic and stylistic features of each report.

COMMENTARY

The event has taken place in Bristol and is directly linked to two well-known animation characters: Wallace and Gromit. It is therefore of interest to British readers because it deals with popular culture and has taken place in a newsworthy location. Not only is a fire a dramatic event, but journalists can also directly connect it with the successful US release of an Aardman Animation feature film, *Wallace and Gromit: The Curse of the Were-Rabbit*, and the sentimentality of the loss of Aardman's entire collection.

All three papers include the same basic facts: details of the fire and the location of the Aardman Animations warehouse; information about what has been

'Wallace and Gromit' creator's clay archive is destroyed by fire

By Cahal Milmo

Morph would have appreciated the cruel irony. The small plasticine man with an ability to melt into a blob of modelling clay was among a host of Britain's best-loved animated characters reduced to ashes by a warehouse fire.

Thirty years of toil, including the creation of the premier couple of "claymation", Wallace and Gromit, were destroyed in the blaze at the archives of Aardman Animations, Britain's largest and most successful animation studio.

News that the archive building had been destroyed came 30 minutes after the company heard that its latest film featuring Wallace and Gromit, *Curse of the Were-Rabbit*, had topped the US box office, taking $16.1m (£9m) during its opening two days.

Executives said the "entire history" of the studio, which started in 1976 with Morph created for the BBC's *Take Hart* programme, had been lost, including sets, figures and props for feature films, shorts and adverts.

Arthur Sheriff, a spokesman for the company, said: "This should have been a day for celebration and instead everything we have done has been destroyed. It really is a bit of a tragedy."

The fire in a Victorian warehouse close to Temple Meads station in Bristol broke out just before 5.30am yesterday, causing all three floors to collapse in the heat.

At the height of the blaze, the flames were 100ft high. Avon Fire Service said that an investigation was under way to establish if arsonists had caused the fire.

Hundreds of figures, including surviving Morph figures and many of the 40-plus Gromits and 30-plus Wallaces needed to make each animation, were in metal cases. A spokesman said nearly all had melted and only a small number of items on loan to an exhibition had survived.

Figure 11.4 **Report 1: *The Independent*, extract (*I*)**

lost; and responses to the loss. The difference between them emerges in the tone of the reports and in the broader references developed by the journalists.

The **headlines** immediately demonstrate the variation in approach of a compact, middle-market paper and a popular tabloid. *The Independent*'s headline uses a passive-voice sentence with an agent. This allows the object of the active sentence (*'Wallace and Gromit' creator's clay archive*) to gain prominence in the initial position. The long pre-modified noun phrase is factual: the proper nouns immediately draw attention because they are familiar characters; the noun *clay* in the context of the fire is dramatic; and the head word *archive* is formal with its connotations of a long-term collection of valuable items. The possessive noun *creator's* does not directly name Nick Park, the creator of Wallace and Gromit, but it does indicate the creative force behind the animations, whereas the other headlines focus exclusively on Wallace and Gromit themselves. The *by + agent* at the end of the sentence adds dramatic impact. The tone is objective and the information provided in brief in the headline is filled out in the report that follows.

The *Daily Star* aims to attract attention by using a capitalised headline and a pun on the name of *Gromit*. The colloquial *GONNIT* relies on the sound association between 'gone', the slang 'goner' (a person or thing beyond help or recovery),

Blaze destroys nation's Plasticine favourites as film hits No 1

Wallace and Gromit: Curse of the inferno

By **Martin Evans**

THE Oscar-winning animators behind Wallace & Gromit were devastated last night after a huge blaze destroyed their "entire history" including virtually all their famous Plasticine models.

Everything, from Seventies favourite Morph to TV's Creature Comforts and the original Wallace and Gromit figures, was feared lost in the inferno which swept through Aardman Animation's Bristol warehouse.

The building housed all the props and sets in the company's 30-year history. Many items can never be replaced.

The collection was likely to have been worth millions – each of the models cost thousands of pounds to build. An investigation was under way last night – and arson has not been ruled out.

Important

The fire occurred on the day Aardman staff should have been celebrating their new film Wallace and Gromit: The Curse of the Were-Rabbit, topping US box-office.

Aardman spokesman Arthur Sheriff said: "Instead, our whole history has been wiped out.

"For us it held everything we had done since day one. It had all the film sets, the props, the models, everything.

"It was very important to us. We used it for tours and exhibitions. It's turned out to be a terrible day."

But Nick Park, creator of Wallace and Gromit, said the fire should be kept in perspective following the tragic earthquake in Pakistan. He said: "Even though it is a precious and nostalgic collection and valuable to the company, in the light of other tragedies today isn't a big deal."

Figure 11.5 **Report 2: *Daily Express*, extract (*DE*)**

and the name of the animated dog. This play on words makes the tone seem less serious than that of *The Independent*, but the overline or strapline uses an alliterative noun phrase (*Hollywood heroes*) to remind us of the celebrity status of the characters. Like *The Independent*, the *Daily Star* uses a passive-voice sentence to bring *Hollywood heroes* (the object of an active sentence) into the initial position. The style is telegraphic because the verb 'to be' is elided. Where the compact uses the neutral *fire* in the *by + agent* at the end of the headline, the tabloid dramatises the incident with the more emotive noun *blaze*.

The *Daily Express* falls between the styles of the compact and the tabloid: it is more dramatic than *The Independent*, but less informal in tone than the *Daily Star*. It parodies the title of the recently-released film *Wallace and Gromit: The Curse of the Were-Rabbit*, immediately forging a link with a US box-office success that is about to be released in Britain. The strapline here uses an active sentence:

S	P	O	A
(Blaze)	(destroys)	(nation's Plasticine favourites)	(as film hits No 1)

SCl–ACl

Hollywood heroes destroyed in blaze

WALLACE & GONNIT

MOVIE heroes Wallace and Gromit were yesterday reduced to a pool of Plasticine goo in a massive fire.

The blaze tore through the warehouse where the pair and their props were stored – just as their first Hollywood film topped the US box office charts.

The Curse of The Were-Rabbit, which hits cinemas here on Friday, raked in £9.1million in its first weekend Stateside.

The inferno wrecked sets, models, and even awards won by Wallace and Gromit, leaving workers at Aardman Animations devastated.

Lost

Cheese-loving inventor Wallace and his faithful canine sidekick Gromit have become a much-loved British institution, helping to earn their creators and animators three Oscars.

Now all the models and sets from past hits A Grand Day Out, The Wrong Trousers and A Close Shave are said to have been wiped out.

Props from other Aardman favourites were also lost, including Chicken Run – featuring the voice of Mel Gibson, 49, as rooster Rocky – Morph, the clay pal of telly artist Tony Hart, 70.

Aardman also makes up to 30 adverts each year, including PG Tips, Nike and Dr Pepper. And it turned Gary Lineker, 44, into Mr Potato Head in an advert for Walkers crisps.

Aardman spokesman Arthur Sheriff said: "Today was supposed to be a celebration, with the new film going in at No1 in the US.

"Instead, our history has been wiped out. The warehouse held everything we had done since Day One.

"It had all the film sets, the props, the models, everything. It really is a bit of a tragedy."

The fire at the warehouse in St Philip's, Bristol, broke out at 5.30am. Arson has not been ruled out.

But Aardman head Nick Park, 46, said the fire was "no big deal" in comparison with the Pakistan quake.

He said: "It was a precious collection, but in the light of other tragedies it isn't a big deal."

Figure 11.6 **Report 3: *Daily Star*, complete report (*DS*)**

The present tense verb (*destroys*) creates a sense of immediacy and, like the *Daily Star*, the *Daily Express* opts for the dramatic noun *Blaze*. The effect is made more emotive by the possessive noun phrase *nation's Plasticine favourites* with its connotations of special preference. The final adverbial clause allows the journalist to make a direct reference to the commercial success of the film.

Ideologically, the three papers have different standpoints, but since this is an action story based on cultural interest the different political viewpoints do not affect the way the story is told. The **intended audience** in each case, however, does affect the approach to reporting. While all three papers convey the drama of the incident, the articles communicate the information in ways that are appropriate to their own readers. *The Independent* provides a factual rather than dramatic account, focusing on what happened and the results. The middle-market *Daily Express* and the popular tabloid *Daily Star* are quite similar in approach, but the *Express* adopts a more formal style than the chatty, personal tone of the red-top. (The term 'red-top' is used to denote the popular tabloid press because of their mastheads: black or white titles printed on a red block.) Both, however, focus on the 'élite' personalities that can be linked to the event and on recent 'popular culture' in a broad sense.

The compact, *The Independent*, uses **modifiers** that give the reader precise information which is factual rather than dramatic. The noun phrases tend to be long and many use post-modification:

> m   h   q
> a host of *Britain's best-loved* characters reduced to ashes by a *warehouse* fire
> det N   PrepP   NFCl
>   (ll. 9–12)

> m   m   m   m   h
> *Britain's largest* and (*most successful*) *animation* studio (ll. 19–21)
>   N   Adj   Adv   Adj   N   N
>   (superlative)   (superlative)

> h   q
> News that the *archive* building had been destroyed (ll. 22–4)
>   N   NCl

The *Daily Express* is more emotive, using some noun phrases that contain dramatic modifiers and others that develop the focus on popular culture:

> m   m   h   m   m   h   q
> a *huge* blaze (l. 8)   the *tragic* earthquake in Pakistan (ll. 60–1)
> det Adj   N   det   Adj   N   PrepP

> m   m   h   m   m   h
> their *new* film (l. 39)   *Seventies favourite* Morph (ll. 13–14)
> det   Adj N   N   Adj   N

> m   m   h   q
> The (*Oscar-winning*) animators behind Wallace and Gromit (ll. 5–7)
> det   N   V   N   PrepP
>   pres. part.

The noun phrases in the *Daily Star* contain modifiers, often multiple, that dramatise the fire and the central characters, Wallace and Gromit. The approach is more narrative than in either of the other papers:

> m   h   m   m   h   m   h   q
> *Movie* heroes (l. 3)   a *massive* fire (l. 6)   a pool of *Plasticine* goo (ll. 5–6)
>   N   N   det   Adj   N   det N PrepP

> m   m   h   m   m   m   m   h
> (*Cheese-loving*) *inventor* Wallace and his *faithful canine sidekick* Gromit (ll. 25–7)
>   N   V   N   N   conj det Adj   Adj   N   N

> m   m   m   h
> a (*much-loved*) *British* institution (ll. 28–9)
> det   Adv   V   Adj   N

In each report, the modifiers contribute to the tone. Where the compact uses post-modifying clauses, the tabloids tend to use pre-modification and prepositional phrase post-modifiers.

The **naming of participants** and **places** tells the reader something about the nature of a newspaper. References to the location of the warehouse are all quite similar in these reports: *Temple Meads station in Bristol* (*I* ll. 49–51); *Aardman Animation's Bristol warehouse* (*DE* ll. 19–21); *St Philip's, Bristol* (*DS* l. 67). Differences in tone emerge, however, in the terms of address. All three papers refer formally to the Aardman spokesman *Arthur Sheriff*, although the middle-market and tabloid papers foreground his role as spokesman for the company, while the compact foregrounds his name. Similarly, the *Daily Express* foregrounds *Nick Park* which is followed with a parenthetical phrase *creator of Wallace and Gromit* (ll. 55–6), while the *Daily Star* pre-modifies the head of the noun phrase *Nick Park* with two noun pre-modifiers *Aardman head* (ll. 70–1). This change of emphasis allows readers who may not recognise the name to identify the significance of Nick Park immediately.

Other employment titles divide the papers more explicitly: the formal *Executives* (l. 32) of *The Independent* has greater status than the collective noun *staff* used in the *Daily Express* (l. 37); both of these references are more formal than the *Daily Star's workers* (l. 21). Probably the most significant difference lies in the number of proper nouns used in the red-top report. The inclusion of contemporary celebrity names (*Mel Gibson*, l. 42; *Gary Lineker*, l. 50), brand names (*PG Tips, Nike, Dr Pepper*, ll. 48–9), familiar Aardman shorts (*A Grand Day Out, The Wrong Trousers, A Close Shave*) and well-known characters (*rooster Rocky*, l. 43; *Mr Potato Head*, ll. 50–1) reflect the red-top tabloid interest in élite persons and popular culture.

All three papers refer to *Morph* (*I* l. 4; *DE* l. 14; *DS* l. 43), a plasticine model linked to a children's art programme in the 1970s. The compact assumes that its readers will recognise the name and therefore does not explain the reference until the second sentence, where the *cruel irony* becomes clear in this long noun phrase:

> m m m h q
> The small plasticine man with an ability to melt into a blob of modelling clay (ll. 5–8)
> det Adj N N PrepP [SCl–NFCl]

The *Daily Express* pre-modifies the head noun with *Seventies favourite* to set a time context and the *Daily Star* uses a parenthetical noun phrase which establishes a wider point of reference:

> m m h q
> the clay pal of telly artist Tony Hart, 70 (ll. 44–5)
> det N N PrepP

The **lexical choice** and **connotations** add to the effects created. All three reports refer to the fire as a *blaze* (*I* l. 18; *DE* ll. 1,8; *DS* ll. 1,7), but the compact keeps this dramatic word away from the beginning of the report. Equally all three refer to the new Aardman film as 'topping' the US box-office (*topped*, *I* l. 29; *topping*, *DE* l. 41; *topped*, *DS* l. 11). This, like *blaze*, is a recognised newspaper shorthand – an example of **journalese**. The papers differ, however in their description of the film's opening: in both tabloid papers it *hits* the screens (*DE* l. 1; *DS* l. 14), while the compact chooses the more formal *opening* (*I* l. 31).

This reflects the dominant tone of the report in *The Independent*. The almost biblical connotations of *toil* (l. 13), the repetition of *archive* (ll. 18, 22) with its connotations of historical reference and museum collections, the literary concept of *irony* (l. 5) and the neologism *"claymation"* (ll. 15–16) are appropriate for the readership of the paper. The *Daily Star*, by contrast, is more informal, with colloquialisms like *goo* (l. 6), *pal* (l. 44), *telly* (l. 44) and *quake* (l. 73). Phrasal verbs are common (*raked in*, l. 15; *wiped out*, ll. 37, 59) and words are often emotive (*massive*, l. 6; *tore*, l. 7; *inferno*, l. 18). As we would expect, the middle-market paper lies between these two extremes. It uses the formal *investigation* (l. 31), but also the emotive *devastated* (l. 7) and *inferno* (l. 3).

The **grammar** of the reports is quite similar, but longer phrases with embedded clauses tend to occur more frequently in *The Independent*. Paragraphs are made up of one or two sentences and those in the red-top tabloid tend to be shortest:

	S		P		A	

(The blaze) (tore) (through the warehouse where the pair and their props were stored)

SCl–ACl (place)

                                               A

– (just as their first Hollywood film topped the US box office charts).   (ll. 7–12, *DS*)

SCl–ACl (time)

   S   P   A

(The fire) (occurred) (on the day that Aardman staff should have been celebrating

SCl–RelCl

their new film *Wallace and Gromit: The Curse of the Were-Rabbit*, topping the US

SCl–NFCl

box-office).   (ll. 36–42, *DE*)

                                S   P   A

(News that the archive building had been destroyed) (came) (30 minutes after the

SCl–NCl   SCl–ACl (time)

company heard that its latest film featuring Wallace and Gromit, *The Curse of the*

SCl–NCl   SCl–NFCl

Were-Rabbit, had topped the US box office, taking $16.1m (£9m) during its opening

SCl–NFCl

two days).   (ll. 22–31, *I*)

Each of the examples here places a different demand upon the reader's concentration. Although tabloids are typically associated with simple grammatical structures, there is evidence of subordination in all three reports. Nevertheless, the sentences in the compact tend to be longer and to have more embedded clauses and a greater variety of clauses.

The sentence organisation is often distinctive. **Marked themes** can be used to dramatise the narrative element of the reports. Although they are not used frequently in these examples, the fronted adverbial *At the height of the blaze* (*I*, l. 55) contributes to the emotive nature of the compact's description, and the foregrounded *Now* (l. 32) in the *Daily Star* draws attention to the harsh realisation of Aardman's losses the day after the fire. As we would expect in tabloids, there are several examples of co-ordinating conjunctions (*And, But*) in the initial position (*DE* l. 56; *DS* ll. 49, 70), allowing the journalist to control the length of sentences.

The **passive voice** is used frequently in all the reports. *The Independent* uses passive verbs in order to bring the object of the active sentence (*clay archive*, l. 2; *a host of Britain's best-loved animated characters*, ll. 9–11; *Thirty years of toil*, l. 13) into prominence at the front of the passive sentence. In most cases, the agent is included to reiterate the drama of the story (*by fire; by a warehouse fire; in the blaze…*). The passive verb phrases *was feared* (ll. 17–18) and *can never be replaced* (ll. 25–6) in the *Daily Express*, however, do not use the agent since the company and the individual animators responsible for crafting the models are less significant in this context than the artistic creations destroyed in the fire.

Direct speech is important in this kind of story because it adds personal feeling to the drama. All three newspapers quote the spokesman for Aardman Animations, although his 'actual' words vary slightly in each version. As a representative for the company, his words add authority to the report of the fire.

The compact cites the least direct speech and Arthur Sheriff's noun phrase *a bit of a tragedy* (l. 47) reduces the relative importance of the event. In the tabloids, reported speech (*DE* ll. 56–61; *DS* ll. 70–3) fulfils the same function since Nick Park juxtaposes the *precious and nostalgic collection* they have lost with the real tragedy of the disaster in Pakistan.

Action stories have a **chronological structure** and this is evident here. Having established the 'victims' and the dramatic event in the first paragraph, each report then recounts the story from beginning to end.

Although compact, middle-market and tabloid newspapers are different in their approaches to reporting, because this is a dramatic story with explicit connections to popular culture and celebrity, differences are not as marked as they would be for a political or economic issue.

Statement and opinion stories

Statement and opinion stories deal with issues rather than just narrative. They attempt to summarise an argument and to provide readers with key information. Although a report may be triggered by a specific event, the event will only be the starting point for a wider consideration of related issues. In other words, such reports give readers more than just a chronological human interest story.

The introductory paragraph usually presents the reader with the most important news points and with supporting direct quotation where appropriate. The rest of the report summarises further points and develops the argument, while the conclusion draws all the points together.

Running stories

Journalists make the most of an ongoing story because they hope that once their readers have become interested they will continue to buy the newspaper to keep up to date with new findings. Tabloids in particular will sensationalise and dramatise stories to keep old readers and attract new ones.

A running story requires the journalist both to report on new information and to recap on what has happened so far. This ensures that readers can keep up to date and understand any new developments in context.

ACTIVITY 11.2

Typically, broadsheet/compact readers are loyal and will probably buy the same paper every day; tabloid readers are more likely to choose the paper that attracts them because of its headline and other front-page information (advertisements for features inside, competitions, photographs, free gifts, and so on). Often tabloids therefore use a dominant headline and photographs, only including part of the report on the front page: readers must turn to inside pages if they wish to finish reading. This means that the headlines, photographs and opening of a report must capture readers' interest, persuading them to continue reading on the inside pages. While the traditional broadsheet newspaper has additional space in which to develop several stories, the new-size compacts are more restricted. Their front page will normally draw attention to one significant story, while a 'News in Brief' column will establish links to other key pages.

The Independent often takes a different approach, selecting one headline to dominate the front page, with a dramatic (often artistic) photograph to highlight what the editorial team see as the most important story. On Friday, 29 September 2006, for instance, the headline *The growth of breast cancer* was accompanied by a much enlarged electron micrograph image of a cell from some breast-cancer tissue. The effect can be very dramatic: in this case, the black background with its white lower-case headline, a 47-word lead-in with pink print to stress key facts, and the striking image which, on first glance, resembled a flower in the fragility of its shape and the intensity of its colour, together caught the eye in a more subtle way than the celebrity photos characteristic of the tabloid papers. Readers were then directed to the pages where full reports could be found.

Each of the three reports in Figures 11.7–11.9 was printed the day after the end of a Labour Party Conference in Manchester (Friday, 29 September 2006). They all contain information about a speech made by John Prescott, then deputy leader of the Labour Party. Each paper makes reference to Prescott's final speech as deputy leader and to the 'running story' of his time in office, which drew media attention on a number of occasions. While including much of the same information, the content is approached from a different angle in each case.

Read through the reports and comment on the distinctive features of each.

COMMENTARY

The three articles here take very different approaches to the same basic information. The middle-market paper (*Daily Mail*) and the popular tabloid (*Daily Star*) are quite similar in approach and the styles of reporting adopted are typical of their individual house styles. *The Guardian* report is different from the accounts in the tabloids because it is written by the paper's political correspondent and treats the story exclusively as political news, whereas the tabloids focus more on the personality behind the politics. The tone is also noticeably different: the tabloids are humorous, whereas *The Guardian* is serious.

The **headline** in *The Guardian* is a factual and non-judgemental introduction to the report that follows. It is a short complex sentence that uses the present tense to communicate a current event:

S	P	O
(Apologetic Prescott)	(prepares)	(to bow out)
	SCl–NFCl	

The modifier (*Apologetic*) and the non-finite clause (*to bow out*) highlight the two elements of the speech that have attracted most press attention: Prescott's apology for his affair and his announcement that he will resign his role as deputy leader of the Labour Party at the same time as Tony Blair leaves office. The presentation of these facts in *The Guardian* is objective – the journalist reports the information without making any moral or political judgements. The cliché *bow out* is reminiscent of the stage and gives Prescott a dignity that is missing in the other reports.

Apologetic Prescott prepares to bow out

Tania Branigan
Political correspondent

John Prescott yesterday apologised for the embarrassment his affair caused Labour activists and announced he would step down as deputy prime minister before next year's party conference.

Mr Prescott began his closing speech to delegates by acknowledging their disappointment over the affair with his diary secretary and by thanking them for their support. But he said he was not leaving politics and went on to issue a stern if coded warning against attacks on Gordon Brown, warning that "disunity destroys" and cautioning against "dangerous and foolish nonsense".

On Wednesday he became the second cabinet minister this week – after Margaret Beckett – to endorse the chancellor as the next prime minister. He told a fringe reception: "There is one man I will be rooting for and that is Gordon Brown."

Yesterday Mr Prescott confirmed the widely held assumption that he will quit when Tony Blair stands down, saying it would be his last conference as deputy leader. "This party has given me everything. And I have tried to give it everything I have got," he said. "I know in the last year I let myself down – I let you down. So conference, I just want to say sorry." He admitted to "robust debates" with Tony Blair, but paid tribute to Labour's most successful prime minister and said he was proud of their joint achievements. The deputy leader warned delegates that the debate over who succeeded Mr Blair had to be conducted in a unified manner.

"I know from my experience over four decades the damage disunity can do. I've seen Labour governments, elected with big majorities, driven out within a few years as the party bitterly divided," he said. Firing a warning shot across the bows of restless Blairites, he added: "I've had it said to me: 'A period in opposition would be good for us.' I've even heard some say they would prefer us to lose a general election rather than see a particular candidate win. That is dangerous and foolish nonsense, usually expressed by individuals who would not feel the full savagery of a Tory government. It would be a betrayal of the millions of people who rely on a Labour government to improve their lives."

Mr Prescott stressed that local, Scottish parliament and Welsh assembly elections were only seven months away and urged colleagues: "Remember who the real enemies are."

In an attempt to smooth troubled waters after Wednesday's angry health debate – when delegates trounced the leadership over the programme to use private contractors in the NHS – he said that party members shared the same values and principles, even if their views differed.

But policy divisions within the party were underlined yesterday when members defeated the leadership for a third time, this time over punishing negligent company directors for deaths at work. A rebel demand for urgent direct investment in council housing was passed on Tuesday. Yesterday delegates overwhelmingly backed a union motion calling for negligent directors to face up to 14 years in jail, despite warnings from the chancellor such a move would be "crazy". A rival motion from the ruling national executive committee went to a card vote.

Unions want the corporate manslaughter and corporate homicide bill – which will be debated in the Commons next month – to be amended.

At present it allows for the prosecution of companies rather than individuals and proposes unlimited fines rather than prison as a penalty. Tony Woodley, T&G general secretary, said the government was "plain wrong" in giving negligent directors "a get out of jail free card". But an aide to Mr Brown warned that introducing jail penalties would wreck the bill, making it impossible to gain cross-party consensus, or the support of business.

Figure 11.7 **Report 1:** *The Guardian* (Berliner; *G*)

Prezza was so sorry for letting them down (the delegates, … not his trousers)

Quentin Letts
on why Two Jags has suddenly become obsolete

NOW we've lost Two Jags. This is turning into an England batting collapse. Another wicket down. John Prescott, voice scraping like a chair leg on concrete, pushed his wobbly bits up the conference hillside one last time and announced he were off. Aye.

'This'll be my last conference as your deputy leader.' Pause. Under his Alan Titchmarsh hairdo he blinked. Another pause.

Come on, you lot, show the Deputy Prime Minister some appreciation! Alas, delegates greeted the news with a sort of toffee-sucking silence. I suppose if they had cheered at this point it might have sounded as though they were relieved the old lump was quitting.

This speech was, in fact, one of Mr Prescott's better efforts. He seemed marginally less furious than normal.

There was a sense of pride as he recalled the way his mum once fought to pay the doctor's bills, and how just a few years later his brother's cleft palate was treated on the NHS.

It helped that the speech had begun – as it needed to – with a clean 'sorry'. He was sorry he had let them down. (By 'them' I mean Labour delegates, not his trousers.)

Pauline Prescott and her perm turned up. We hadn't seen her all week but there she finally was, seated in the front row next to Cherie Blair.

As ever, Mrs Prescott was impeccably tweezered and tonged. What a monument to the British hairdressing profession she is. And those eyebrows. Plucked as carefully as a Sandringham partridge.

Can we really be surprised that Labour quit the seaside for the first time since the 1940s to come to Manchester?

Pauline hates a shore wind. Pauline, I suspect, put down her foot.

Up on stage her very own Ollie Hardy was plopping through the hoops like an overfed Labrador at the village dog show.

He had a bad start when a video of his career highlights refused to play. And his friend Sir Jeremy Beecham said that he'd worked with Two Jags for years and did not know anyone 'with a quicker or keener intelligence'.

Up and down the country television viewers, at this point, may have done the nose trick into their coffee cups.

But back to our hero. He gripped the lectern, stared at the crowd with his Buzz Lightyear jaw, and talked about 'Tory Ypockressy'.

But we had less partisan nonsense than normal. The spite of all those years of anti-Thatcher rhetoric has finally gone.

Labour delegates this week have not quite known what to say about Cameron's crowd and they have normally ended up referring to the Tory leader as 'David' rather than 'Cameron'.

In such a hate-free age John Prescott is not needed. He finished his speech, gave Pauline's thick-powdered cheek a peck, and then left for a retirement of padlocked winceyette pyjamas, meat pies and fond reminiscences of how he wrecked the poncy Home Counties and their once green fields. The day's far more telling event was the performance of John Reid. [...]

Figure 11.8 **Report 2: *Daily Mail* (*DM*)**

The **language** of Report 1 is formal. Although addressing the much-reported liaison with his diary secretary, the journalist uses words with neutral connotations like *affair* (l. 6) and quickly moves towards wider politics issues (the next leader of the Labour Party; local elections; the use of private contractors in the

PREZZA AGREES TO QUIT – AND SAYS SORRY

It's not over 'til Fat Bloke sings

AND HERE HE IS ... IN FULL VOICE

5 TWO Sh*gs John Prescott finally told the Labour conference yesterday: "Fats yer lot, folks."

He agreed to quit after apologising for disgracing the Government over his affair 10 with his diary secretary Tracey Temple, 43.

He also became involved in a row after staying at the Colorado ranch of US tycoon Philip Anschutz, 67, who wants to open a 15 supercasino in the Millennium Dome.

Prezza promised to step down when Tony Blair leaves Downing Street. And he stunned delegates by admitting: "I know in the last year I let myself down. I let you 20 down. So conference, I just want to say sorry."

The 68-year-old has been in high spirits all week – as shown above [*photograph of John Prescott singing*] when he grabbed 25 the microphone and sang to delegates at a party in Manchester.

Cheers

And the biggest cheers yesterday came when footage of his best career blunders 30 was beamed onto a giant screen.

Mr Blair, 53, and Gordon Brown, 55, were left cringing as delegates watched the infamous moment Prezza punched an egg-throwing protestor.

35 More laughter greeted film of him dancing at party bashes.

Then there was the sight of the lardy Leftie playing croquet at his country mansion when he should have been working. 40 He even joined in the jokes by having a pop at TV chef Jamie Oliver, 31, for shaming the Government over school dinners.

Closing the conference, Prezza said: "I'm still a fish and chip man – as some people 45 might even say, I'm fat for a purpose.

"This will be my last conference as your deputy leader. Thank you for electing me and for all the support over the last 12 years."

50 His loyal wife Pauline, 64, appeared on the platform and gave him a kiss.

And that triggered a three-minute standing ovation as Mr Blair and wife Cherie, 52, joined the Prescotts on stage.

The Star Says: Page 6
gary.nicks@dailystar.co.uk

Figure 11.9 **Report 3: *Daily Star (DS)***

NHS; the punishment of negligent company directors). The 'running story' here is not John Prescott and his exploits but the day-to-day political concerns of the Labour Party.

In line with this political emphasis, the **modifiers** are factual. They tend to be linked to politics (*party*, l. 68; *policy*, l. 71; *union*, l. 78) and convey no sense of the paper's attitude. The noun phrases are often long and complex with both pre- and post-modification.

	m		m		h	q	
a	(stern	if	coded)	warning	against	attacks on Gordon Brown	(ll. 15–17)
det	Adj		V		N	PrepP	
			past part.				

m   m   h   q

the (widely held) assumption that he will quit when Tony Blair stands down   (ll. 26–8)

det   Adv   V   N   SCl–NCl   SCl–ACl

           past part.

m   m   h   q

a union motion calling for negligent directors to face up to 14 years in jail (ll. 78–80)

det N   N   SCl–NFCl   SCl–NFCl

The complex structure and factual lexis contribute to the formality of tone throughout the report and this is underpinned by the **naming of participants**. Full names (*John Prescott*, l. 5; *Gordon Brown*, ll. 16–17; *Margaret Beckett*, ll. 21–2) are used for the first reference to a particular politician and subsequent references use the recognised title *Mr* (*Mr Prescott*, l. 10; *Mr Blair*, l. 40; *Mr Brown*, l. 96). A less well-known person is put in context with a parenthetical noun phrase that defines his role: *Tony Woodley, T&G general secretary* (ll. 92–3). Similarly, John Prescott is also referred to in terms of his current role in the Labour party (*The deputy leader*, l. 38). This approach to naming is typical of the more serious papers and clearly sets them apart from the tabloids.

Like the noun phrases, the **sentence structure** tends to be complex, making the paragraphs longer than is customary in the tabloid press. Some paragraphs contain only one sentence, but they are made up of a number of clauses:

S   A   P   O

(John Prescott) (yesterday) (apologised for) (the embarrassment his affair caused

                                             SCl–RelCl

                           P   O

Labour activists) (and) (announced) ([that] he would step down as deputy prime

                    conj   SCl–NCl

minister before next year's party conference).   (ll. 5–9)

Where tabloid papers aim to keep the opening sentences straightforward for their readers, *The Guardian* has used this compound–complex sentence that immediately introduces the two main topics in a succinct manner and establishes the tone of the article that is to follow.

Sentence organisation is designed to guide the reader and there are many instances where **marked themes** are used to create a particular focus. Frequently, they are references to time (*On Wednesday*, l. 20; *Yesterday*, ll. 26, 77; *At present*, l. 89) which set the issues of the report within the timescale of the Labour Party conference. Others set the context in a different way: a long prepositional phrase and parenthetical adverbial clause (ll. 64–8) ensures that readers understand the background to Prescott's juxtaposition of *values and principles* with *views*; and a foregrounded cliché (ll. 46–7) allows the journalist to provide an interpretative comment to accompany Prescott's advice to the delegates.

Most of the report uses simple past tense verbs (*apologised*, l. 5; *confirmed*, l. 26; *stressed* l. 59), but the **passive voice** (*were underlined*, l. 72; *was passed*, l. 77; *will be debated, to be amended*, ll. 86–8) is used where the journalist focuses on events in the conference rather than on John Prescott. In the first and second examples, the reordering of the active sentence enables the object to appear in the subject site of the sentence. This places emphasis on the issue of *policy divisions* (l. 71) and the *rebel demand* (l. 75) for an investigation into council housing. The fourth example places emphasis on the passive verb phrase *to be amended* (ll. 87–8), which occurs in the end position. In an active sentence, it would have been in the middle of an embedded clause in the object site of the sentence:

> S   P   O
> (Unions) (want) (the government to amend the corporate manslaughter and corporate
>   SCl–NFCl
> homicide bill – which will be debated in the Commons next month).
>   SCl–RelCl

By opting for a passive sentence, the journalist can stress the importance of the verb phrase, giving it prominence at the end of the sentence after the parenthetical relative clause. Agents are omitted because the subject of the active sentence is understood and is of less importance than the object.

In this report, there is a lot of **direct speech** since the focus is on John Prescott's last conference speech as deputy prime minister. The tone is formal and authoritative. In most cases, the lexis is subject-specific (*big majorities*, l. 44–5; *opposition*, l. 49; *general election*, l. 51; *candidate*, l. 52), although there is some use of informal collocations (*rooting for*, ll. 24–5; *everything I have got*, ll. 31–2). The quotation of individual words and phrases (ll. 17, 18–19) allows the journalist to underpin reported speech with highlighted key phrases from Prescott's actual words.

Because *The Guardian* moves beyond Prescott's apology for his affair (ll. 32–4), the direct speech includes wider political references: Prescott's support for Gordon Brown as the next Labour leader (ll. 24–5), his warnings about the long-term effects of disunity (ll. 42–55), and his certainty that the electorate should not be let down by Labour politicians (ll. 56–8). The direct speech is often quite extensive, continuing over a number of lines with neutral quoting clauses (*told*, l. 23; *said*, l. 32; *added*, l. 48). The effect is to reinforce the formal content, approach and style of the report with its emphasis on the political rather than the human.

Although there are some informal collocations in the direct quotations from Prescott's speech, a few **clichés** are used in the main body of the report. While the *attempt to smooth troubled waters* (l. 64) is a traditional expression for calming a difficult situation, *Firing a warning shot across the bows* (ll. 46–7) is a naval saying. Its origin lies in the cautionary shot fired to indicate to a ship that it must stop – its relevance here is political since the warning is addressed to the supporters of Tony Blair who may not endorse Gordon Brown as the party's future leader.

Although Prescott's apology is dealt with in this report, it does not form the main body of the content. Instead 'running' political issues such as the next leader of the Labour Party, changes in policy in the NHS and the judicial system, and the need for council housing dominate the journalist's agenda. The *Daily Mail* and the *Daily Star* adopt a very different approach in which the 'running story' is a focus on John Prescott himself. The content is less interested in political issues than in the saga of John Prescott's time as a minister.

The tabloid style of the middle-market and red-top papers is immediately apparent in the **headlines**. Both use the colloquial *Prezza* to set the informal tone that will dominate each report. The *Daily Mail* foregrounds the apology and makes a sexual pun on the colloquial phrasal verb 'to let down' (ll. 1–2). The parenthesis functions as a cataphoric reference for the object pronoun *them*, juxtaposing the nouns *delegates* and *trousers* for comic effect. Where *The Guardian* has been neutral in its approach, the *Mail*, in line with its ideological standpoint, is clearly not impartial.

The headline in the *Daily Star* is also humorous, but the tone is less biting – Prescott is presented as a jovial buffoon who entertains and has good intentions even if he is prone to 'blunders'. The American proverb 'The opera isn't over till the fat lady sings' forms the basis for the main headline with its suggestion that an event has not ended until some essential, significant part of it has taken place. The underlined subheadline develops this with the prepositional phrase *in full voice* (l. 4, *DS*), referring both to Prescott's end-of-conference speech and to his 'vocal' performance at a party earlier in the week. Where the *Mail's* humour is satirical, this is jocular. The strapline (l. 1, *DS*) reinforces this attitude to Prescott by giving prominence to his decision to leave his post as deputy leader, adding information about the apology as an apparent afterthought.

In line with a **'running' story**, both reports fill in relevant details from previous news coverage. In its sardonic naming of Prescott as *Two Jags* (l. 5, *DM*), the *Mail* implicitly reminds readers of media reports criticising his use of two Jaguar cars at a time when as head of the Department for Transport, the Environment and the Regions he encouraged others to use public transport. Satirical references to his wife's hair (ll. 34, 38–41) relate to Prescott's explanation in 1999 that he was driven the 250 metres between the Labour Party conference centre and the hotel because his wife did not like having her hair blown around.

The *Star's* naming of Prescott as *Two Sh*gs* (l. 5, *DS*) is an implicit reference to accusations of sexual harassment and extramarital affairs. The main body of the report, however, makes explicit references to past events in Prescott's career. At the time, media coverage made much of the incidents, with the tabloid press often giving him a **sobriquet** (a humorous epithet attached to a name): in the brawl with a farmer during the general election campaign (May 2001), he was dubbed 'Two Jabs Prescott', and his refusal to leave his 'grace and favour' home in Dorneywood after a cabinet reshuffle (June 2006) earned him 'Two Shacks Prescott'. Other occasions referred to by the *Star* include his involvement in a game of croquet when he should have been working (May 2006), the row over his visit to Philip Anschutz's ranch (July 2006), and the subsequent investigation of this matter by the Parliamentary Commissioner for Standards. Each of these references is used by the journalist to provide a context for discussion of Prescott's speech.

The **lexis** of both reports is informal, but where the *Star* is affable in its mockery, the *Mail* is savage. The satirical parallel between English cricket and Prescott (ll. 5–7, *DM*), the simile comparing his voice to *a chair leg on concrete* (l. 8) and the description of his *wobbly bits* (ll. 9–10), his *Alan Titchmarsh hairdo* (ll. 13–14) and his *Buzz Lightyear jaw* (ll. 61–2) aim to undermine the politician by focusing on his human frailties. He becomes a comic-book character – *our hero* – yet he clearly isn't presented in heroic terms. Instead, he is *the old lump* (l. 20); he is *Ollie Hardy*, bungling, pompous and unaware (l. 48); and he is *an overfed Labrador, plopping through the hoops … at the village dog show* (ll. 49–50). Imitations of his accent (*Aye*, l. 11; *'Tory Ypockressy'*, ll. 62–3) and the undermining of Sir Jeremy Beecham's comment (ll. 53–6) in the supposed response of television viewers clearly reflect the journalist's attitude. This is a very personal piece of journalism in which the first person pronoun is used on a number of occasions in comment clauses (*I suppose*, l. 18; *I mean*, ll. 32–3; *I suspect*, ll. 46–7), which remind the reader that this is a subjective account.

Where the extract from the *Mail* takes the form of a satirical political sketch, that from the *Star* typifies tabloid journalism in which explicit references to past events are used to set the context for current news. The language is informal (*lardy Leftie*, ll. 37–8; *having a pop at*, ll. 40–1, DS); noun phrases tend to be long (*footage of his best career blunders*, l. 29; *the infamous moment Prezza punched an egg-throwing protestor*, ll. 33–4); and the connotations of words tend to dramatise events (*stunned*, l. 18; *grabbed*, l. 24; *blunders*, l. 29). By choosing the noun *embarrassment*, *The Guardian* (l. 6) underplays the effect of Prescott's affair; the *Star*, in contrast, uses the emotive verb *disgracing* (l. 9), with its connotations of shame and dishonour. It implies a moral judgement that is absent from the Berliner report. The *Star* does not, however, belittle Prescott – the modifier describing his wife (*loyal*, l. 50) suggests that he is worthy of support, and the prepositional verb *joined in* (l. 40), the joke he makes at his own expense (ll. 43–5) and the noun phrase *high spirits* (ll. 22–3) all seem to reflect Prescott's willingness to be himself. Indeed, the *Star Says* column on page 6 ends with an emphatic, if typically tabloid, affirmation:

> **He may be a bit of an oaf, but we'll miss him when he's gone!**

The **sentence structure** in these tabloid reports reflects the content and approach of the journalists. The *Mail* is more varied than the *Star* because of the personal engagement of the reporter: imperative (ll. 15, *DM*) and interrogative (ll. 43–5) sentences change the relationship between reader and writer; simple sentences (ll. 5, 22–4, 46, 72–3) and minor sentences (ll. 7, 13, 14, 60) change the rhythm and pace; and marked themes change the balance of information (ll. 5–7, 13–14, 38–9, 72–3). There are also, however, compound–complex sentences that demand more of the reader:

```
      dumS      P        delayed S                                          A
    (There) (was) (a sense of pride) (as he recalled the way his mum once fought to pay the
                          SCl–ACl                    SCl–RelCl                    SCl–NFCl
                                                         A
    doctor's bills), (and) (how just a few years later his brother's cleft palate was treated
                     conj    SCl–NCl
    on the NHS).                                                              (ll. 25–9)
```

There are few simple sentences in the *Star* report, but the journalist uses features such as initial-position conjunctions (ll. 17, 20, 52) or a dash to control the length of sentences:

```
        S            P              C          A                                A
    (The 68-year-old) (has been) (in high spirits) (all week) – (as shown above when he
                                                         SCl–ACl              SCl–ACl
    grabbed the microphone and sang to delegates at a party in Manchester).  (ll. 22–6)
                        conj  SCl–ACl
```

The approach of each report directly reflects the ideology of the paper, the kind of information included, and the angle taken. Where politics is the dominant topic, the issues of Prescott's affair and his apology are dealt with quickly so that the wider political themes can be developed; where interest lies in Prescott himself, the emphasis is on his human failings. The tone and lexis provide readers with signposts, implicitly guiding their response and influencing their attitudes.

11.5 What to look for in newspapers

The following checklist can be used to identify key features in examples of different kinds of newspaper reporting. You will not find all of the features in every report, but the list can be used as a guide. The points made are general, so discussion of specific examples will need to be adapted to take account of the specific context, intended audience and purpose in the given discourse. Remember that you need to evaluate the effect of the features you identify, exploring the ways in which they create meaning.

The following are helpful questions to ask.

Register

1 What is the **mode**?
   • written.
2 What is the **manner**?
   • formal or informal relationship between participants (journalist and reader)?
   • ideology?
   • function (to inform, persuade, entertain, etc.)?
3 What is the **field**?
   • subject matter?
   • journalist's approach?
   • linked to the audience, purpose, and context?

Lexis

Headlines

1 What is noticeable about the **style**?
   • easily readable? simple?
   • appropriate?
   • impact created?
2 What are the **connotations** of words chosen?
3 What kinds of **modifiers** are used?
4 What **point of view** or **ideology** is conveyed?

Reports

1 Are the words chosen **formal** or **informal**?
2 Are the **modifiers** used to express precise detail or to make the report emotive or sensational?
3 How are **participants named**?
   • use of titles? use of first names or surnames?
   • use of abbreviated, familiar names?
4 What are the **connotations** of words?
   • nouns to describe people and things?

- verbs to describe actions and processes?
- associations?

5 What kinds of **adverbials** are used?
- time? place? manner?

Grammar

Headlines

1 What is the **structure**?
- NP?
- simple/compound/complex sentence?

2 Do the **straplines** and **subheadlines** explain or qualify the main headline?

3 Is the **passive voice** used?

4 Is there any **ambiguity**?
- accidental?
- intentional, to create humour or to add interest?

Reports

1 Is the **sentence structure** varied?
- simple/compound/complex? variety?

2 Are there any **initial-position conjunctions**?
- to create a conversational tone?
- to control the length of sentences?

3 Is there any **direct speech**?
- ordinary or authoritative speaker? formal or informal tone?
- to add weight to an argument or to give ordinary people's views?
- to vary the pace?

4 Is there any **indirect speech**?
- to summarise formal speech?
- to paraphrase the speaker's words and make them more fluent?

Style

1 Is the **sentence organisation** designed to influence the reader?
- marked themes to highlight a clause element other than the subject in the initial position?
- foregrounding of adverbials to provide extra information?
- passive voice to alter the position of the object for emphasis?
- are *by* + *agent* included or omitted?

2 Are there any **literary devices**?
- metaphors and similes to establish a narrative atmosphere or to make the report more dramatic or the abstract issues concrete?
- symbolism to force the reader to make connections?
- clever or comic puns?
- unusual or unexpected words or descriptions?

3 Is there any **sound patterning** to underpin meaning, create humour or make a report more memorable?
- alliteration, rhythm or rhyme?

4 Are there any **rhetorical devices**?
  - antithesis juxtaposing words or key concepts for dramatic effect or contrasting particular viewpoints?
  - listing building to a climax or an anti-climax, creating emphasis or developing a serious or comic tone?
  - patterning to emphasise important attributes or contrasts?
  - repetition of words, phrases or clauses to highlight key points and make the report more dramatic or noticeable?

Sources

1 Are there any **official** sources giving authority to evidence?
  - police? emergency services? courts? investigating bodies? the government?
2 Are there any **unofficial** sources that allow ordinary people to have a voice?

Typographical features

1 Does **capitalisation** attract readers?
2 Is there any **variation in print size** to draw readers into the report?
3 Is **colour** used, drawing on wider symbolic associations to enhance meaning?
4 Do **images** dramatise or support the story?

Summary

The **function** of newspaper language is to inform and entertain people, and to present them with a particular ideology and an interpretation of events.

The **impartiality** of the press is often questioned. By considering the language, grammar and sources of headlines and reports it is possible to assess the extent of any media bias.

An editor or a newspaper owner can dictate which stories or facts are to be included or excluded. This **selective perception** may influence the way in which the reader responds to the world and to particular events.

The **relationship between a newspaper and its intended audience** dictates the kind of reporting in its pages. Content, style, typographical features and the use of images are distinctive to each paper, whether tabloid or broadsheet/compact.

Chapter 12

The language of advertising

12.1 The nature of advertising

We are surrounded by **ADVERTISING** in everyday life: **advertisements** directed at general groups of consumers appear on commercial television and radio, at the cinema, on billboard posters and in newspapers and magazines; subject-specific advertisements appear in subject-specific contexts focused on individuals and groups with certain interests; and **direct mail** (often known as **junk mail**) arrives through the letterbox sent straight to named individuals. The aim of all these advertisements is to draw attention to particular products or services through announcements paid for by an individual or a group wishing to inform or influence a particular audience.

In the eighteenth and nineteenth centuries most advertising was straightforward and informative. Its language and style were formal and respectful; its tone was often ceremonious. In the late twentieth century, however, the power of the mass market changed this. Since advertisers aim to **persuade** people to 'buy', 'give' or 'vote for' their own particular product or service, their approach is biased. To succeed in a competitive market, they must be better or more persuasive than their rivals. Their **marketing campaigns** seek to encourage 'customer loyalty' by establishing a clear and distinctive image and identity which will make their products or services stand out from equivalent brands produced by other companies.

Advertisers focus their advertising on particular groups of people. They may divide people by age, gender, race or social class. Traditional **CLASSIFICATIONS** are used. **Age groupings** often fall into these categories:

- 0–15   16–24   25–35   36–55   56+

Social class groupings are equally common:

- A   higher managerial, administrative and professional
- B   intermediate managerial, administrative and professional
- C1   supervisory or clerical and junior managerial, administrative and professional
- C2   skilled manual
- D   semi-skilled and unskilled manual
- E   casual labourers, state pensioners and the unemployed.

Such groupings help advertisers to TARGET the people most likely to buy their products. On commercial television, programming schedules try to 'package' audiences by running certain kinds of programmes at certain times: this encourages advertisers to buy time, because it is easier to focus on a specific audience than on a very general one. For instance, advertisements on television usually promote particular types of household cleaning products, food and drink, services (mortgages, insurance policies, loans) and cars at times when adults may be watching, and toys at times when children may make up the main part of the audience. In newspapers and magazines, the target audience is clearer because publishers and advertisers are more aware of the kind of people who buy each publication. Certain newspapers attract an affluent middle-class audience: because of these readers' spending power, advertisers will be prepared to buy advertising space. This means that although the broadsheets and compacts may not have large circulation figures, they can survive because they can sell advertising space easily. Popular newspapers, on the other hand, have to rely on high circulation figures because advertising revenue is relatively low. People in their target audience do not have the same amounts of disposable income and therefore advertising space is a less saleable commodity.

Advertisements work by raising interest in a product or service. Once a potential customer has the **desire** to 'buy' or 'give', the 'sale' or 'donation' is more likely to happen. The strategies used in each case must be appropriate both to the target audience and to the kind of product or service offered. Some advertisements try to modify the attitudes of the audience: slogans like *Fairy Lasts Longer*, for example, aim to persuade the consumer to buy one particular brand rather than another by convincing them that the product is more successful, more stylish, or better value even if more expensive. Other advertisements have to convince consumers that they want an item that is not essential to everyday living: car and perfume manufacturers therefore use a 'reason why' approach to their advertisements.

Research has shown that people remember particular advertisements if the product is different, if the advertisement itself is unusual, or if the advertisement has some personal relevance. Often the initial impact will be caused by the visual content and the overall design, but it is the **use of language** that will ensure that the product or service identity and the brand name are remembered. Typically, the language of advertising is **positive**, **unreserved** and **colloquial**. Advertisers choose **vivid concrete words** and make their COPY (the words attached to an advert) memorable by using **figurative language** and **non-standard spellings**.

Because advertisements are designed to appeal to 'typical' members of certain groups, they use STEREOTYPES. Women are often portrayed in the house; men are shown driving impressive cars, happy families visit holiday resorts, and good-looking young people enjoy themselves in clubs and bars. More recently, advertisers have begun to reflect changes in society by challenging such stereotypes, and by using a wider range of actors in mainstream advertising campaigns to appeal to an increasingly mixed audience. Advertisements for perfume and clothes, insurance and holidays, healthy eating, exercise and household goods show some recognition of changing gender roles, the growing 60+ age group, and the ethnic mix in Britain today. It could be argued, however, that certain stereotypes persist with 'exotic' and 'size zero' women being presented as sexually desirable, and handsome young men as athletic and fit. The Halifax Building Society advertisements, on the other hand, have created a different kind of role model by using their own employees to front their campaigns.

Alongside this recognition that society is changing and that advertising stereotypes need to reflect this change, companies have also recognised that audiences appreciate seeing 'ordinary' people. Dove, for instance, has promoted its moisturiser with the slogan *Real women. Real curves* in an advertisement containing women who clearly, instead of having the stereotypical physique of models, had self-declared 'love handles', 'muffins' and 'buddha tummies'. Similarly, a Nintendo DS advertising campaign to promote a new games console showed ordinary people of many kinds – black, Asian and white; families and young professionals; and people of all ages, including the 50+ age group.

In Britain there are stringent controls on what is acceptable in advertising. Regulations like the British Code of Advertising Practice and the British Code of Sales Promotion try to ensure that all advertisements are **legal**, **decent**, **honest** and **truthful**. They state that advertisers must show responsibility both to consumers and to society as a whole, and must conform to the principles of fair trading.

Despite detailed codes of conduct, however, people still object to some campaigns. The Advertising Standards Authority acts on complaints made by the general public and can, if necessary, insist that a certain campaign is stopped. Complaints might be based on various features of the campaign.

'Hard sell' tactics or fraudulent claims

Health campaigners have made many complaints about supposedly 'sugar-free' products, for instance, and consumer organisations disputed the allegedly healthy attributes of 'Sunny Delight', a sales marketing phenomenon of the late 1990s. Promoted as a healthy alternative to other soft drinks and sold from the chiller cabinet in supermarkets, its advertising campaign encouraged consumers to associate it with freshly-squeezed fruit juices. It was ruled, however, that its health attributes could not be proven, and when a little girl who had drunk large quantities of 'Sunny Delight' turned orange, its commercial fortunes were reversed. Unfortunately for the company, its situation was compounded by an advertising campaign in which a snowman turned orange – a clever marketing idea that suddenly had an uncomfortable resonance.

The Advertising Standards Agency requires that any claim made in an advertisement must have definitive evidence to support it. When St Ivel suggested that its 'advance milk' could make children cleverer, and Flora claimed that 'Pro-activ' could keep blood vessels healthy as well as lowering cholesterol, the ASA required that the advertisements were not broadcast.

The effect on children

An advertisement for the orange drink 'Tango', in which an orange man gave someone waiting at a bus stop a nasty shock by slapping him round the ears, was taken off the television because its images and its slogan – *You'll know when you've been Tango'd* – were resulting in copycat behaviour.

In 2006, a Wanadoo advertisement was set in a scrapyard full of smashed cars, where young people played around in the wreckage. As research has shown that copycat behaviour is most likely to occur where the behaviour is easy to copy and the scene seems realistic, the ASA banned this advertisement. It was feared that young viewers might emulate the scene portrayed and risk serious injury as a result.

In a more general way, debate has focused on the influence advertising can have on young children as consumers. Concerns about diet and weight have led to discussion of the role of advertising in promoting junk food, which is frequently marketed during children's programmes. In April 2007, junk food advertisements were banned during programmes targeted at seven- to nine-year-olds. By December 2008, channels dedicated to children's programmes will have to phase out all advertisements for foods high in fat, salt and sugar. In addition, there are plans to ban the use of celebrities and licensed characters such as cartoon heroes (Scooby Doo and Yu-Gi-Oh, for instance). Consumer groups believe the new rules are insufficient since they fail to cover advertising during family programmes (*The X Factor, Coronation Street, Ant and Dec's Saturday Night Takeaway*): they are pushing for a complete ban before the 9 p.m. watershed.

The morals apparently promoted

When a famous person is used to promote a certain product, complaints may focus on the way in which the celebrity is portrayed. Gary Lineker's advertisements for Walkers' crisps caused a stir because the football hero was seen taking crisps from a young boy and from a nun. Viewers objected that a positive role model for young children was behaving in a morally unacceptable way, since Gary Lineker might be seen to be endorsing such behaviour.

On related grounds, advertising campaigns for 'Club 18–30 Holidays' have also been widely criticised. Complaints were made about slogans such as *Discover your erogenous zones* which were seen to promote the sexual promiscuity often associated with such holidays.

In June 2005 the ASA received 1671 complaints about a KFC advertisement for 'Zinger Crunch Salad' in which women were shown singing with their mouths full. Complaints focused on the issue of encouraging 'bad manners' and the concern that the advertisement ignored the risk of choking on food. The 'moral' argument in this case was rejected by the ASA, but complaints received in July 2005 about the 'Fanta Z' advertisements were accepted. Some viewers felt that images of young people spitting would encourage antisocial behaviour amongst children, and the ASA agreed, accepting that the advertisement would be appealing to children. The advertisement was not banned completely, but broadcasters were required to schedule it after the 9 pm WATERSHED when fewer children would be watching.

Shock tactics

Benetton, with its slogan *The United Colors of Benetton*, is renowned for its provocative campaigns. It aims to market goods worldwide and its campaigns are meant to reflect this. Its official policy states that its advertisements will raise awareness of key social issues on a global level, thus 'uniting' nations. Many people, however, have complained about Benetton's poster campaigns, believing some to be immoral and distasteful. Billboard posters of a newborn baby still covered with blood, of a man dying of AIDS with his family around him, and of the bloodstained clothes of a dead Croatian soldier, have all been described as 'shock' advertising.

In 2006, a public information advertisement adopted shock tactics in order to influence viewers' behaviour. The campaign to promote awareness of the dangers of drinking and driving was emotive because of the surprising conclusion to its advertisement. Set in the context of a bar, the advertisement shows three young men drinking, chatting about a woman at the bar, and convincing one another that 'one more' won't affect their driving skills. The young woman turns towards them and is suddenly thrown across the room as though hit by a car. The juxtaposition of the ordinary social occasion and the woman slumped and twisted at the foot of the bar is chilling.

Similarly, in advertisements informing viewers about the dangers of passive smoking, the silent movement of smoke through a variety of contexts is disturbing – the advertisement is shot with the dark tones of a horror movie, and we understand its significance only as the advertisement comes to an end. Because advertisements like these are using shock tactics to educate their audience, they are less likely to be banned.

12.2 The function of advertising

The main function of advertising is to **persuade** (**conative** function); its subordinate function is to **provide information** (**referential** function). Different kinds of advertising use different techniques to persuade and inform. Some use the copy to provide information like the size, the brand name, the price, and the address and telephone number of the shop or company, relying on the product itself to promote sales. Other advertisements **highlight a particular background** as more important than the product, so that the **image** of the product is the selling point. Others rely on the **associations between the product and a particular context** – dreamlike fantasies, for instance, may suggest the product's potential for changing an individual's life.

Advertisers appeal to our desire to be a 'successful career man or woman', a 'wonderful lover' or part of a 'happy family'; they exploit our wish to be 'beautiful', 'powerful', 'responsible' and 'knowledgeable'. To persuade viewers or readers to buy a car, an advertisement will try to convince us that we will be stylish, prestigious and exciting if we own that particular model. Advertisements may suggest that buying a certain brand of baby food, supposedly purer or more natural than its rivals, will make you into a 'better' parent; or that wearing certain clothes will make you more desirable or more powerful; or that eating a certain kind of icecream will make you more attractive or more alluring. In each case, the function of the advertisement is to persuade you to buy. Although information may be provided, it will not be neutral because there is an implicit purpose: the advertiser has chosen the content and the language of the advertisement primarily to influence rather than to inform.

Advertisements, however, do more than just sell products – different advertisers have different purposes. Table 12.1 summarises the main kinds of advertiser and their main functions.

Table 12.1 **Advertisers and their functions**

Advertiser	Function
Charities	Collecting funds; attracting support and voluntary helpers.
Commercial companies	Selling goods and services; attracting investment; changing attitudes; creating new desires in a target audience; giving information about a product or service.
Government	Giving information; publicising planning proposals and health and safety issues.
Media	Attracting a target audience; selling advertising space.
Event organisers	Promoting events and demonstrations.
Political parties	Winning votes; attracting members or financial support.
Private individuals	Selling and purchasing goods and services; announcing personal events and occasions.
Schools, colleges, universities	Informing prospective students of courses, facilities, and future career possibilities.

12.3 Features of advertising language

Inevitably, advertisements designed for a visual medium like television or the cinema screen will be dominated by images, and usually these will be more important than any accompanying spoken or written words. However, prosodic features like intonation, pace and rhythm will influence the viewer, and the use of a written slogan can make the product more memorable. In print forms like newspapers and magazines, advertisements rely on a combination of copy and image – it is the balance of the two that is important. Because print is not transient, as an image on the screen is, it can be reconsidered: the written language accompanying the image can therefore be more extensive.

Advertisements for different media use different techniques, but a number of features are common to both spoken and written examples. First, it is always important to establish:

▸ the **advertiser** (logo, slogan, brand name, distinctive colour or image)

▸ the **target audience** (age, gender, social status)

▸ the **function** of the advertisement or its message ('buy this', 'give generously', 'join us', and so on)

▸ the **selling techniques**:
  ◆ a **product-based approach** praises the features of a product or service, hoping to win customers on the strength of the product or service itself
  ◆ an **audience-based approach** tries to convince the target audience that they need a particular product or service: by concentrating on practical needs like

saving time, or psychological needs like the desire to look better or younger, advertisers try to persuade consumers that their lives will be better if they use a certain product or service
- an **impact-based approach** aims to attract attention linguistically or visually.

Having considered these general motivations, it is important to look more closely at the **design** of each advertisement. By focusing on the language and images, it is possible to analyse the way in which the advertisement is intended to influence its target audience.

Design

Often the first thing to influence a viewer or reader will be the overall design of an advertisement. Juxtapositions of **slogan, image, copy** and **logo** contribute to the overall effect. They all work together to create a certain view of a particular product or service.

The **images** will also attract the attention of the intended audience: they are a form of **non-verbal communication**. The people, the settings, the props (objects used in a particular context to create a sense of reality) and the product itself together make up the image. Each element can work in both a literal and a symbolic way. In an advertisement for perfume, for instance, the clothes worn by the actors, the kind of background used, and props like a diamond necklace and a waiting Rolls Royce car, would together symbolise that this perfume is associated with wealth, luxury and status. A reader or viewer would automatically recognise the implicit meaning of the non-verbal signals and would therefore make certain assumptions about the perfume.

Stereotypes

Advertisers use **cultural stereotypes** in their images so that they can be sure that their target audience will associate good things with a product or service. Women are invariably beautiful; children are angelic; men are strong and rugged; and young people are up to date with current trends. Props help to create these stereotypes – glasses symbolise cleverness; books symbolise education; beer has connotations of masculinity; and so on. By breaking down the codes that are used in the images, it is possible to learn something about the advertisers' intentions even before reading the copy.

Language and tone

The **language** of advertising is quite often associated with the language of everyday conversation: the **tone** is often informal and chatty, and colloquial expressions are common. Verbal **contractions** like *we've* and *you'll* are easily recognisable features of informal spoken language that would be inappropriate in a more formal variety. Advertising language is distinct from conversation, however, and other linguistic features make this field a variety in its own right.

A **SLOGAN** is crucial if an advertising campaign is to succeed, because it is the slogan that will stick in people's minds. The structure varies, and may use a noun phrase, a simple sentence or a complex sentence. Advertisers can use puns, disrupt collocations, or work on our emotions, but whatever approach a particular campaign uses, the slogan is always made eye-catching.

Film advertising often uses disrupted collocations and puns to attract our attention. In 2005, *Wallace and Gromit: the Curse of the Were-Rabbit* was marketed using familiar sayings adapted for comic effect. The saying 'there's something funny going on' became:

> dumS   P   delayed S   P
> **(There) ('s) (something bunny) (going on)**

This retains the rhyme of the original adjective while also creating a semantic link with one of the key characters of the film. Another poster declared *It gnaws no fear*, punning on the verb 'knows' pronounced by Wallace as /nɔːs/ and the dynamic verb that characterises the Were-Rabbit. In advertising the second *Garfield* film, the posters punned on a well-known fairytale ('The Prince and the Pauper') in the compound noun phrase:

> m   h   m   h
> **The Prince and the Paw-per**
> det   N   conj det   N

The phonetic make-up of the two words (*pauper/paw-per*) is identical, /pɔːpə/, but the spelling of the advertising slogan explicitly reflects the refocusing of this tale in which cats rather than humans are the main characters.

Heinz ran a campaign with the slogan *THE BEAN AMNESTY IS ON*, parodying amnesties in which the police aim to encourage owners of illegal weapons to hand them in with no fear of repercussions. The juxtaposition of the noun phrase *other beans* with the capitalised *the ORIGINAL AND BEST* drew attention to the focus of this particular amnesty. In the advertisement, a distraught person sat behind a table with a plate in front of her or him and a variation on a simple sentence above. In each case an adverbial of time (*Every hour...*; *Every day...*; *Every year...*) was followed by the dismissive noun phrase *other beans*, a dynamic verb with negative connotations (*spoil*; *wreck*; *tarnish over*), and a noun phrase describing the food on the plate (*countless pieces of toast*; *thousands of jacket potatoes*; *a million fry ups*) – the numerical references emphasised the extent of the problem. The advertiser's direct intentions were communicated in the imperative *Hand in* and the certainty of the modal verb phrase *will swap* alongside the immediately recognisable Heinz bean tin.

The success of campaigns like these is in using sayings or situations that are already well known – when we see the advertisements we are struck simultaneously by the familiarity and the novelty of the campaign. The tone is often tongue-in-cheek, as with the RAC's slogan *Your knight in shining viscose*, which simultaneously elevates the rescue patrols to the status of heroic saviours yet also undermines this image by substituting *viscose* for 'armour'.

Lexical choice

LEXICAL CHOICE is crucial to the effect an advertisement will have since it helps to create a relationship with the audience. The copy of an advertisement can have two functions: modifiers can be used to emphasise the positive attributes of a product in order to **persuade** a consumer to buy it (conative function); or the written text can provide technical facts about the product to **inform** the consumer, of size, power, range of features, price and so on (referential function).

The language of advertising can also **influence the contemporary word stock**. During the period of a campaign, slogans and phrases may become part of everyday usage.

- **Colloquial expressions** can now be heard in everyday conversation, such as *freebies, bangers and mash, c'mon*.
- **Adjective phrases** can become catchphrases, as with the phrase *naughty but nice* (originally used in a campaign promoting real cream), which suggests that something is pleasant even if not really a good thing to do.
- **Sentences** can use distinctive patterns that are memorable. The advertisement for a new product, for instance, may draw on earlier advertisements while introducing a new angle. The marketing of a dark Kit-Kat chocolate bar in October 2006 retained a link to the traditional slogan *Have a Break, Have a Kit-Kat*, but drew on the connotations of additional words to make the new product seem desirable:

(BREAK into) (your DARKER SIDE)

The imperative dynamic prepositional verb is an explicit semantic link to earlier advertising, but the noun phrase introduces the new angle. As well as an explicit reference to the dark chocolate, its connotations of evil (and perhaps the suggestion of Star Wars' *dark side*) suggest that this new version of an old product is dangerously liberating. The comparative form of the adjective prevents it being an outright threat – this is 'danger' and 'evil', but both within a safely controlled environment!

Because advertising language changes so fast, however, coined words and phrases soon become stale and are then replaced with new expressions.

The **structure of noun phrases** is often complex, with strings of pre-modifiers and post-modifiers being used. The use of both kinds of modification provides precise information in a concise way, but the complex noun phrases of advertising can be a substitute for clear and honest description. The information may be technical, but more usually it is emotive and based on opinion rather than fact:

The Citroën C6. A stunning combination of practical innovation, almost indecent comfort and shameless good looks.

Adjective phrases can also be subjective:

	h		h		m		h		m		h		h	q
incredible but true		perfectly shocking and utterly crazy		proud to be different
Adj	conj	Adj		Adv		Adj		conj		Adv		Adj		Adj	NFCl

The **possessive** form of nouns is often used with inanimate objects in advertising language, and this is not common in any other variety:

> the *car's* outstanding performance …   the *food's* aromatic aroma …

Modifiers are a distinctive feature of advertising language because of their power in attracting attention. By using them in strings, advertisers can arouse emotions, stimulate desires, and so on. Because they allow advertisers to evoke the kind of image they want to associate with a particular product or service, modifiers are described as **TRIGGER WORDS**. Some, like *big, long* or *double*, indicate physical qualities that can to some extent be proved; others, like *wonderful, elegant* or *incredible*, are intangible and so cannot be measured. Advertisers often use these quality words precisely because they are vague. The most common adjectives are *good, better, best, free, special, great, real, new* and *big*, all of which create a positive image without really telling the consumer anything about the product or service. Other modifiers relate directly to price: the verb *reduced*, the adjective *cheap* and the noun *bargain* can all modify the noun *prices*. Compound phrases can be used to suggest that products have special features. By combining adjectives, noun, adverb and verb modifiers, advertisers can convey a sense of a product's uniqueness:

> Do you want *radiantly-glowing naturally-coloured full-styled* hair? Then try our new hair-care range.

Because each new campaign must attract attention, advertising language is often **innovative**. Advertisers **coin new words** (**neologisms**) to make a brand more memorable:

The Shoob – fashion's latest craze!	(ankle boot – hybrid of <u>sh</u>oe /ʃuː/ + <u>b</u>oot)
Heelys – the footwear craze of the moment	(shoes that look like trainers with a wheel in the heel)
Incredibubble	(advertising the penguins at Bristol Zoo)
Fry'ghtfully Funny	(advertising a DVD of Stephen Fry and Hugh Laurie)

New words are also coined by using the brand name of an item as the basis for a word. Often **non-standard spelling** will be used to attract attention:

> Diamondz are a Bratz Girl's Best Friend
> Zurich Insurance … Because change happenz

Advertisers use the copy to enhance the associations an image has evoked, with the language working alongside the picture to reinforce the intended message. Each lexical choice must make a particular product or service more memorable because space in print advertisements and time for television advertisements cost money. The lexis must therefore convey the essential points in a concise and dramatic way. This makes the language of advertising almost like a shorthand code – every word included has a specific function.

Grammar

The **grammar** of advertisements is also similar to **informal spoken language**. It can be disjointed and abbreviated. Slogans will often omit verbs to make a catch-phrase more concise and striking:

> Hydra-star (ø) the first moisturising range with a choice of textures.

Imperatives are used frequently because consumers are being urged to 'buy', 'give' or 'join':

> *Plunge* into the warm waters of the Red Sea Riviera. *Chase* rainbow-coloured fish across the tropical coral reefs. *Order* delicious food from the world's favourite cuisines. Or *soak up* the year-round sunshine on pristine, golden beaches.
>
> Red Sea Riviera, Egypt

Through variations in **mood**, the advertisers appeal to their target audience to take notice and to act.

Verb tenses allow the advertisers to implicitly convey differences in the semantics. Simple present tense emphasises features of a product; simple past tense and the perfect aspect allow advertisers to draw comparisons; and future time, often constructed using the modal verb *will*, makes assumptions about what is possible if the consumer uses a particular product or service.

Pronouns help advertisers create a personal relationship with consumers. By using the second person pronoun *you*, advertisements can appeal directly to readers or viewers, aiming to make them feel special. Other **interactive features**, like coupons to save money on a particular product or forms to complete and return, also encourage the consumer's direct participation. Some advertisements use a checklist system of boxes to tick or questionnaires to complete in order to make the customer more active.

Sentence structures are unusual because elements are often left out in order to keep sentences short. **Verbless clauses** are common and sentences are often divided in unexpected ways to keep the copy simple for the reader. This means that sentences can be literally ungrammatical, although they do convey meaning.

Sentences are often **simple** and **co-ordination** is more common than subordination. **Co-ordinating conjunctions** are often used in the initial position, as is typical of informal spoken language:

> S   P   A   A   S   P
> (Free trade) (sounds) (like a great idea). (But) (if it's not between equals) (it) (doesn't
>   conj   SCl–ACl   neg
> work).
>
> The Co-operative Bank

This kind of structure gives a separate emphasis to each clause and is therefore useful since it allows advertisers to highlight a number of key points. **Adverbials** are also placed at the beginning of sentences to emphasise key information:

>   A   S
> (Located at the heart of the Mediterranean basin), (this breathtakingly beautiful island)
> SCl–NFCl
> P   C
> (is) (crammed with things to do and see).
> SCl–NFCl   SCl–NFCls   'Discover Sicily', *The Independent*

Sentence organisation uses grammatical patterning (marked themes, end focus, passive voice) to rearrange the elements of a sentence in order to draw attention to key information. It allows advertisers to control the order in which we receive information.

Advertisements use **literary devices** to attract attention to the product, often 'breaking the rules' of conventional language. They can construct different layers of meaning: **metaphors** link emotive associations to a product, building up an impression that will influence potential consumers; **symbolism** likewise encourages viewers or readers to make certain connections that will colour their view; **personification** or **animation** of inanimate objects can create a mysterious or comic atmosphere; and **puns** can be clever or humorous in their manipulation of language. **Ambiguity** can both create **humour** and provoke interest through the double meanings it promotes. **Sound patterning** (alliteration, rhyme, rhythm) makes slogans and copy stand out.

Rhetorical devices create patterns at the level of words and clauses. **Antithesis** sets key words or ideas in opposition for dramatic effect or to distinguish between different attitudes or brands; **listing** indicates specific features that may attract the buyer; **patterning** balances similar or contrasting features to draw attention to a product or its features; **repetition** highlights key points or a particular brand name.

Typography

The **typographical features** of advertising are also important because they can help consumers to identify certain brands or products. **Print size** and **shape**, **colour** and **layout** are often used consistently throughout a campaign, and these become as significant as the language in persuading readers and viewers to act in the way the advertisers intend.

12.4 Types of advertising

There are many different types of advertising, all using the same techniques but requiring different responses from the intended audience. Advertisements can be **persuasive**, using the 'hard sell' approach, aiming to make consumers go out and buy a product. They can be **informative**, relying on the influence of technical data to help the consumer make an informed choice. Or they can be **competitive**, attempting to gain a new share of the market at the expense of their rivals. Advertisements may be product-, audience- or impact-based; or they may use variations in typeface, juxtapositions of striking images, or emotive appeals to make them eye-catching. Besides distinguishing between advertisements by their approach, however, it is also possible to classify them according to the **content**.

Product advertising

On a very basic level, **CLASSIFIED ADVERTISEMENTS** try to sell products or services to people who already know what they are looking for. They are described as 'unintrusive advertising' because readers seek them. For this reason, they tend to be straightforward. They use the minimum number of words and convey the most relevant information in as concise a way as possible. Because they are so short, **abbreviations** are commonly used. Although they are more likely to be informative than persuasive, some value words may be used:

> Charming 3 bedroom cottage with delightful views. Master bedroom with en-suite WC. GCH and traditional-style dbgl. Extensive gardens and dble garage. Sought after village location. £420,000 NO CHAIN.

> 25YR OLD SINGLE MALE, 6ft, good build, reasonably goodlooking, GSOH seeks female 23–28 for nights in and out. Love? Friendship? Maybe more? Who knows? Are you the lady for me? ALA. Box No. 123456.

> THREE PIECE BEDROOM SUITE consisting of a mirrored teak dressing table and two single wardrobes one of which is mirrored. All VGC. £50 ono. Tel. 01234 1234.

To the reader looking for a partner, a particular piece of furniture or a certain kind of property, the codes are straightforward: *ono – or near offer*; *VGC – very good condition*; *ALA – all letters answered*; *GSOH – good sense of humour*; *GCH – gas central heating*; *dbgl – double glazing*; and *dble – double*. Sometimes there will be 'sales talk', particularly in property small ads, but usually this type of advertisement will be marked by its factual approach. Classified advertisements can be local in community newspapers or national in many daily and Sunday newspapers; the contents of publications like *Exchange and Mart* and *freeADS* are exclusively made up of classified advertisements. The internet has transformed classified advertising, with ordinary people now able to advertise beyond their immediate locality. Ebay is a thriving private sales auction site and many people make a living from buying and selling goods online.

POINT-OF-SALE ADVERTISING is very much the same. Local people write out a card and place it where other local people shop: on a supermarket display board, in a shop window and so on. This kind of advertising is directed specifically at the local community and therefore its target audience is quite limited.

DIRECT MAIL comes straight to people's homes, addressed to individuals whose names have been taken from sources such as the electoral register. The form of advertising is usually a letter which tries to persuade the addressee to buy a particular product. A sample or a 'money off' coupon may be enclosed. The tone is informal and direct address is used to try to create a personal relationship between sender and reader. Famous people may be used to endorse the product.

ACTIVITY 12.1

Read through the letter in Figure 12.1 and comment on the linguistic and stylistic features which make it typical of the field of advertising. Try to establish whether direct mail is different from other kinds of advertising.

Figure 12.1 **Direct mailshot**

www.thesun.co.uk   www.newsoftheworld.co.uk

1   Ref No: 341/7/58356152
    [Name]
    [Address 1]
    [Address 2]
5   [Address 3]
    [Address 4]
    [Address 5]
    [Postcode]   33050

Dear [Name]

10   Get more from your newspaper. Don't miss the front-page exclusives, the juiciest
gossip, amazing real-life stories and the most thrilling sports coverage every day
of the week in our multi-award-winning papers, The Sun and News of the World.
That's a whole lot more than the rest!

We want to give you more, for less money. With the enclosed money-saving
15   vouchers, you can find out what makes us Britain's favourite newspapers.
There are 56 vouchers WORTH £6 for you to use over the next 8 weeks,
starting on Saturday 12th November. Just give your vouchers to your newsagent
when you buy your Sun and News of the World.

HOW TO GET MORE

20   Every week look out for our great money-saving promotions like free CDs and DVDs,
as well as fantastic offers like Holidays from £9.50.

AND THERE'S EVEN MORE – WIN £500

Help us give you more of what you want by telling us a little about yourself in our reader
survey. It'll only take a few minutes. And if you return it to our Freepost address (or complete
25   it online) before Wednesday 25th January, we'll enter you in our free £500 prize draw.

Get more by spending less. Now, that's an offer too good to refuse

Yours sincerely

Rebekah Wade   Andy Coulson
Editor, The Sun   Editor, News of the World

30   PS. Fancy your papers delivered right to your door every morning? If so, see the
back of the voucher booklet for details of how to use your money-off vouchers.

341

1/0611069

1/0611069

£500 Cash Prize Draw – Terms and Conditions
1. All entrants must be resident in the UK and aged 18 or over. 2. Only one entry per person. 3. Entry to the draw is free and entries must be on an official, fully completed entry form. No purchase is necessary. 4. All entries must be returned to £500 Cash Prize Draw, FREEPOST NEA12187 WORKSOP S81 2ZX. 5. The closing date for entries is 25th January. An independent adjudicator will randomly select the winner by 1st February. The winner will be notified by post within 28 days. 6. The prize should be claimed within 28 days of notification. 7. Proof of posting cannot be accepted as proof of delivery, and responsibility cannot be accepted for lost or mislaid entries. 8. No correspondence will be entered into. 9. The single prize is £500 cash. The prize is not transferable. 10. The winner's name and county will be available to those who send a S.A.E. marked £500 Cash Prize Draw Winner, to £500 Cash Prize Draw, PO BOX 87, Worksop S81 1ZG before 5th April. 11. News Group Newspapers Ltd. reserves the right to photograph and use the name of the winner for the purpose of publicity. 12. All applications will become the property of News Group Newspapers Ltd. and will not be returned. 13. Applicants will be deemed to have accepted and agreed to be bound by the Terms and Conditions of which the application instructions form a part. 14. Employees of News Group Newspapers Ltd. and their families, associated companies, agents or anyone professionally associated with the promotion are not eligible for entry. 15. The promoter is News Group Newspapers Ltd. Registered address: 1 Virginia Street, London E98 1XY. 16. Please send entries to **£500 Cash Prize Draw, FREEPOST NEA12187 WORKSOP S81 2ZX.**

The **advertiser** is News Group Newspapers, which publishes *The Sun* and the *News of the World*; the intended AUDIENCE are people who may be persuaded to make a commitment to buying these papers over an eight-week period. The **function** of the letter is to convince readers that as well as great entertainment, these papers can also offer a wide range of additional promotions.

The letter format is used to shape the **overall design** – it is addressed to a particular individual and ends with *Yours sincerely* (l. 27). Because it is apparently sent by two individuals rather than the News Group itself, the advertising seems more personal. The use of the senders' full names, *Rebekah Wade* and *Andy Coulson* (l. 28), reinforces this sense of a personal address, while the use of their respective titles (l. 30) adds authority to the status of the opinions expressed in the letter.

The **mastheads** (title blocks) at the top of the letterhead ensure that the brand is easily recognisable: as red-top papers, each uses a white title printed on a red block of ink. The accompanying illustrations then explicitly demonstrate some of the features highlighted in the text of the letter and reflect the variety of supplements included with *The Sun* and the *News of the World* (sports news; television listings; magazines). They are eye-catching in their use of colour, dramatic headlines, celebrity photographs and emotive language.

The **tone** is personal because the letter is addressed to a specific named individual. It mixes an informal, friendly tone with a more formal offer of good value entertainment and information. The chatty tone is marked by **contractions** (*That's*, l. 13; *It'll*, l. 24); by direct address using **second person pronouns** (*you*) and **determiners** (*your*); and by **colloquial expressions** (*a whole lot more*, l. 13; *what you want*, l. 23; *Fancy...*, l. 31).

The **lexis** mirrors this combination of informal and formal tones, creating a personal relationship between sender and recipient. The **subject-specific lexis** reflects the field of newspapers: *front-page exclusive* (l. 10); *sports coverage* (l. 11); *newsagent* (l. 17). Most of the noun phrases use pre-modification and the **modifiers** are typical of advertising in that they aim to draw attention to the qualities of the product and this particular offer:

	m		h		m	m		h
	Our	(multi-award-winning)	papers		our	great	(money-saving)	promotions
det		Adj	N	V	N	det	Adj	N	V	N
				pres part					pres part	

Most modifiers are subjective rather than factual – they clearly reflect opinions and would be difficult to quantify or prove. Superlatives (*juiciest*, l. 10; *most thrilling*, l. 11), overstatement (*amazing*, l. 11; *fantastic*, l. 21) and commonly occurring adjectives (*great*, l. 20; *free*, l. 25) seek to persuade the reader that this offer is special.

The positive **connotations** of the words in this letter are persuasive, with modifiers such as *multi-award-winning* (l. 12) and *favourite* (l. 15) reminding the reader of the popularity of *The Sun* and the *News of the World*. The lexical field related to money aims to convince us in a different way that this is a genuine offer. The compound modifiers *money-saving* (l. 20) and *money-off* (l. 32), the monetary nouns *money* (l. 14), *vouchers* (ll. 16, 17, 32), *promotions* (l. 20) and *offers* (l. 21), and the verbs *buy* (l. 18) and *spending* (l. 26) all appeal to our love of a bargain. Where the positive lexis is explicit in its persuasive qualities, the repeated pecuniary references appeal to our human nature implicitly.

The **grammar** is more varied than in many advertisements, because of the letter format. The text moves between simple and complex **sentences**, but most are short, making the letter easy to read. The longest sentence (ll. 10–12) may have a sequence of coordinated pre-modified noun phrases in the object site, but it retains a straightforward structure because it comprises only one clause:

> P   O   O   O
> (Don't miss) (the front-page exclusives), (the juiciest gossip), (amazing real-life stories)
>
> neg
>   O   A   A
> and (the most thrilling sports coverage) (every day of the week) (in our multi-award-
> conj
> winning papers, The Sun and News of the World).

The complex sentences tend not to be long, but contain subordinate clauses in the object (ll. 14–15) or adverbial sites (ll. 17–18; 23).

The **mood** juxtaposes present tense statements about the offer (declaratives) with imperatives urging the reader to act in a certain way: *Get* (ll. 10, 26); *Don't miss* (l. 10); *give* (l. 17); *look out for* (l. 20); *Help* (l. 23); *Fancy*; *see* (l. 31). Many direct mailings avoid the explicit commands of other advertising forms, but the frequency of imperatives in this letter creates a tone of urgency. The balance of **personal pronouns**, however, prevents the reader feeling unnecessarily pressured – the direct address (*you, yourself*) and the inclusive first person plural pronouns *we* and *us* establish a co-operative relationship between sender and recipient.

Modal verbs are used to express certainty and possibility. The tentative *can* (l. 15) is persuasive since it offers readers the opportunity to discover for themselves what the editors purport to know already – that *The Sun* and the *News of the World* are *Britain's favourite newspapers*. It underlines the confidence of the noun clause (*what makes us…*) while accepting that some readers may not agree. The verb phrases *'ll… take* (l. 24) and *'ll enter* (l. 25), on the other hand, are certainties: these are facts that can be verified and the company sending the letter can be confident in the assertions they make.

The absence of **literary devices** is to be expected in this kind of letter because the target audience is wide and the purpose is referential rather than poetic. Other **rhetorical devices** are used, however: the **repetition** of *more* (ll. 10, 13, 14) and *less* (l. 14) reflects the dual purpose of the letter in promoting the newspapers and a particular offer; **foregrounded** adverbials draw attention to *the enclosed money-saving vouchers* (ll. 14–15) and the frequency of promotions (*Every week*, l. 20); and **initial-position conjunctions** (l. 24) emphasise additional bonuses.

The **typographical features** are typical of advertising: **bold print**, for instance, is used to highlight the subheadings, which help to divide the text visually; **slogans** (*WE LOVE IT* and *BIG ON SUNDAYS*) establish a brand identity; and colour images attract our attention. Other features are associated specifically with the letter format: the handwritten signatures encourage readers to see this as a personal letter rather than a form of advertising, and the use of a postscript (*PS.*) suggests a familiar afterthought rather than an additional marketing ploy – both are more common in personal rather than official correspondence.

The main differences between direct mail and other forms of explicit advertising are linked to the letter format: the address to a named individual; the use of a named sender; the more varied grammatical structures associated with prose in letters; and the absence of figurative language. In place of implicit imperatives, letters of this kind often enclose a sample or a 'money-off coupon' to encourage the target audience to purchase the product being promoted.

The most far-reaching mainstream source of product advertising can be found in **magazines** and **newspapers**, on **billboards** and on **television**. These kinds of advertisements are an everyday part of our lives and we take them for granted. They use typical rhetorical techniques to influence their intended audience, and juxtapose slogans, copy and images to evoke an appropriate response.

Television product advertisements rely far more heavily on **images**, and because these are often animated by actors the images are far more powerful. The words and actions together aim to reveal new ways of visualising people, places and events. By producing a certain view of the world in this way, advertisers can then suggest that their target audience could be a part of this world too – if only they bought the right product. The **logo** and **slogan** have exactly the same form as they would in a magazine or newspaper advertisement, and this allows advertisers to create a consistent brand identity across a range of media. The copy of a written advertisement might be delivered by a **voice-over** in which an unseen speaker draws attention to certain features of a product. Typical prosodic features of intonation, pace, pitch and so on affect the way the product is received. These can be marked on a commercial script, just as they would be on a transcription, enabling the actor to evoke a certain mood or atmosphere.

Print advertisements cover a wide range of forms and products, so advertisers design different kinds of campaigns depending upon the different audiences they wish to attract. The images, tone and language chosen all reflect the target group, but in each case the variety is distinctive.

ACTIVITY 12.2

The advertisements in Figures 12.2 and 12.3 are examples of product advertising found in broadsheet/compact newspapers. Consider each advertisement in turn:

1 Identify the advertiser and comment on the possible target audience in each case.

2 Identify the function and the main selling technique for each advertisement.

3 Jot down some general points about the design of each advertisement. Consider the juxtaposition of any slogans, images, copy or logos.

4 Comment on the tone and its effect on the relationship between advertiser and reader.

5 Reread each example and identify any distinctive lexical choices. Think about:
   a the slogan
   b the noun phrases and any modifiers used
   c the overall effect of the copy.

6 Reread each example and note any interesting grammatical usage. Think about:
   a minor sentences
   b different moods

c changes in tense

d the use of direct address and any interactive features

e sentence structure

f the techniques used to focus attention on key elements.

7 Identify and evaluate the effects of any literary or rhetorical devices used.

8 Comment on the typographical features. Think about:

a variations in print size or shape

b the overall layout.

COMMENTARY

Although each advertisement is promoting a product, they appeal to their **intended audience** in different ways. In Figure 12.2, the advertiser is Citroën. The manufacturer is promoting a new model and its aim is to convince the target audience that this car not only meets twenty-first century technical and environmental specifications but actually provides the luxury and style of cars that are far more expensive. The approach is product-based, with extensive references to the main selling features. There is also a sense, however, that the advertiser is appealing to a psychological need in the audience – drivers of this model will have class.

The *New Internationalist* (*NI*) advertisement in Figure 12.3 uses an impact-based approach: the image immediately catches our attention because the characters are familiar, and this familiarity is anchored by the slogan. The target audience is not flattered or persuaded that they will be better or more desirable individuals. Instead, the advertisement suggests that this magazine will help people with a particular worldview to keep up-to-date with political, environmental and economic developments in a global context.

The **design** of each advertisement is different and this reflects the overall aim of each advertiser. Citroën choose to let the image of the car and the accompanying slogan dominate the page. There is no attempt to put it in a context – where many car advertisements use the symbolism of a background (a winding mountain road; an elegant European cobbled street; busy urban traffic; an open, wild landscape), Citroën use a bland grey background. Like a model on a catwalk, the Citroën C6 is displayed in a way that focuses on its elegant shape and style: the noun phrases *sleek profile* and *sweeping curves* (ll. 25–6) are reminiscent of a fashion-show voice-over and the **slogan** establishes the 'catwalk' motif. The noun phrase *Haute Voiture* is a pun on 'haute couture' (high fashion), as is explicitly demonstrated in the final italicised noun phrase *couture motoring* (l. 30). It aims to attract attention through its use of the French *Voiture* (car) and its suggestion of high-class exclusivity, which will appeal directly to the readers of the *Daily Telegraph*. Small print at the bottom includes technical details of fuel consumption and emissions in line with government targets to reduce air pollution from vehicles. This is important information if the company is to persuade the target audience that this is a cost-efficient 'luxury' car. A website address allows readers the opportunity to find out more if they are interested.

Figure 12.3 **Product advertisement (in *The Independent*, 31 March 2005)**

The *New Internationalist* advertisement is designed to work in a very different way. The image is an imitation of the famous comic duo Laurel and Hardy. This is immediately recognisable in the body language and stature of the cartoon characters: the bemused Stan Laurel scratches his head, while the pompous Oliver Hardy twiddles with his tie. Since this is an advertisement for a magazine that explores the state of the world in the twenty-first century, however, the image is intended to do more than just entertain us. Its use of caricature is evident in the British and American flags that decorate the traditional 'Laurel and Hardy' hats – Laurel becomes a surprised Tony Blair, then Prime Minister of the UK Labour Government, and Hardy a bombastic George W. Bush, then US President.

The **slogan** also adopts a satirical tone: Hardy's traditional catchphrase ('And that's another fine mess you've got me into') is adapted to reflect the point of view that Blair and Bush have interfered in too many situations that were not their concern, and with devastating results. It is a complex sentence and its exclamatory tone is humorous:

> S   P   C
> (That) ('s) (another fine mess we're in)!
>   SCl–RelCl

As well as making us laugh, however, it is also designed to appeal to readers of *The Independent* who will probably have a similar worldview. The anaphoric reference (*That*) remains general rather than specific and, in conjunction with the determiner *another*, it suggests that this is just one more ill-advised action or decision on the part of the two world leaders. The replacement of the second person pronoun 'you' in the original catchphrase with the first person plural pronoun *we* reflects the relationship between Blair and Bush: they are equally responsible for the *mess*, whereas Ollie invariably blamed Stan.

The **relationship with the target audience** in each case is serious and the **tone** is therefore formal. Citroën combine technical data with an appeal to the emotions – the style is descriptive with long noun phrases and complex sentences. The *NI* advertisement uses a political lexical field to highlight the kind of topics addressed in the magazine; the approach is matter-of-fact rather than descriptive.

The **lexis** of each advertisement reflects the product focus in each case. The repetition of *new* (ll. 6, 19) in the Citroën advertisement and the large print capitalised *FREE* in the *NI* advertisement are typical features of advertising – companies wish to draw attention to the ground-breaking features of their product or to highlight a special offer. Citroën's selection of words with a French origin, however, is distinctive. It is designed to create a mood of sophistication that is mirrored in the abstract nouns *elegance* (l. 27) and *exclusivity* (l. 28). The marketing angle is to sell this model as an everyday car that is good enough to reclaim all the words associated with *automotive luxury*. In the *New Internationalist* advertisement, the language is less stylised and the appeal is more direct.

Subject-specific lexis reflects the product for sale. For the car, subject-specific concrete nouns (*bonnet, windscreen, headlights, diesel V6, gearbox*) are set against abstract nouns (*innovation, comfort, looks, performance, elegance, exclusivity*); technical modifiers (*208hp 2.7 litre, six-speed, 4-mode*) and capitalised trademark modifiers (*Active, Head-up, Lane Departure Warning, Xenon*) are balanced by evaluative modifiers (*stunning, almost indecent, shameless, legendary, luxury, powerful*). The effect is to juxtapose the practical with the psychological – while the former appeal to the head (*the rational reasons*, l. 24), the latter work directly on the emotions (*your heart*, l. 25). In contrast, the political language of the *NI* advertisement is restrained, with no evaluative modifiers and no technical data. Instead, political (*war, terrorism*), environmental (*climate, global warming*), economic (*corporate, WTO* [the World Trade Organisation], *fair trade*) and religious (*Islam*) lexis establishes the range of issues covered. Rather than selling its product with emotive language, the *NI* uses a level-headed, factual approach. The style of the advertisement suggests that the magazine's approach to the discussion of such complex topics will be equally detached and balanced.

The **grammar** also reflects the different approaches of the advertisers: the straightforward style of the *NI* uses shorter phrases and sentences; the long phrases and sentences of Citroën mirror the desire for sophistication. The **noun phrases** linked to the car's technical features tend to be long, with strings of pre-modifiers and post-modification:

> m   m   h   q
> an Active bonnet ... that automatically lessens pedestrian injury in case of an
> det   Adj   N   SCl–RelCl
> accident   (ll. 6–8)

> m   m   m   m   m   m   h
> a dynamic (electronically controlled) springing and damping suspension system
> det   Adj   Adv   V   V   conj   V   N   N
>   past part   pres part   pres part   (ll. 19–20)

In contrast, those in the *NI* advertisement tend to be short – pre-modification does not occur in strings, and post-modification tends to be in the form of prepositional phrases:

> m   h   q   q   m   m   h
> A war in Iraq with no end in sight (l. 3)   a better way (ll. 6–7)
> PrepP   PrepP   det   Adj   N
> m   h
> corporate power (l. 14)
> Adj   N

The longest noun phrase, which has an embedded clause as a post-modifier, is still not complicated to understand because its length is built up from a number of listed short noun phrases following the non-finite verb *including*:

> m   m   h   q
> short snappy sections including country profiles, reviews, news and snippets from
> Adj   Adj   N   SCl–NFCl
> the world's media   (ll. 17–21)

The **sentence structures** in both advertisements tend to be complex. After the sequence of noun phrases, the *NI* magazine promotion opens with an **indirect question** – there is no inversion of the subject and verb. Although short, it is a complex sentence because it has a non-finite clause in the subject site (*invading Iran*). The use of the adverb *Maybe* (l. 5) in the **initial position** is satirical: after international concern about the conflict in Iraq, the possibility of US intervention in Iran caused widespread unease. The first sentence of the copy addresses the issues raised in the noun phrases and the indirect question: the **fronted adverbials** establish a condition that can be resolved by the purchase of the magazine, uniting readers through the comparative noun phrase *a better way*:

>   A   A
> (If you think ø there's got to be a better way) and (ø want to keep on top of the issues
>   SCl–ACl   SCl–NCl   SCl–NFCl   conj SCl–ACl SCl–NFCl
>   S   P   O
> that matter) (you) (need) (the *New Internationalist Magazine*).   (ll. 6–10)
> SCl–RelCl

In the Citroën advertisement, the opening sentence is more straightforward: it has a simple structure with three coordinated complements. Subsequent sentences are more complicated as they include greater amounts of technical information:

>   S   P   Oi   A
> (All the important driving data) (is relayed) (to you) (via a Head-up display on the wind-
>   A   A
> screen) (so that you can give the road ahead your full attention); and (even if fatigue
>   SCl–ACl   conj SCl–ACl
>   S   P
> causes your attention to wander), (the Lane Departure Warning System) (will alert)
>   SCl–NFCl
>   O   P   O   A
> (you) and (restore) (you) (to the straight and narrow).   (ll. 9–14)

The dominant **tense** in each case is the present tense, because the advertisers are promoting products that are currently available. The perfect aspect is used to create a timescale that sets the present within the context of the past: the comfort of Citroën cars that other manufacturers have copied (*have been much imitated*, l. 18); and the elegance of the C6 compared to other equivalent cars (*haven't seen*, l. 27). The *NI* advertisement uses the informal *'s got* ('has got', l. 6), but although present perfect in form, this has the same meaning as a simple present tense. The **mood** is predominantly declarative since the advertisers are making statements about their products. The *NI* advertisement uses an exclamatory tone in the slogan to draw attention to the satirical use of the Laurel and Hardy catchphrase and an indirect question, but these still take the form of declarative sentences (*subject + verb*). Imperatives are used, however, to encourage a direct response to the advertisement from the reader (*subscribe*; *send*). There are both interrogatives (*Have you ever noticed…?*, l. 1; *What does your heart tell you…?*, l. 25) and an imperative (*Welcome to couture motoring*, l. 30) in the Citroën advertisement. These directly engage readers, setting the context for them to agree with the point of view expressed by the advertisement.

Both advertisements aim to draw the reader in through their use of **direct address**. The second person pronoun *you* (*NI* and Citroën) and the possessive determiner *your* (Citroën) engage the reader explicitly – the Citroën advertisement in particular uses direct address repeatedly to give the reader the experience of being a driver in the new C6. The companies promoting their products are also given a familiar face through the first person plural pronoun *we*, which encourages readers to identify with the otherwise impersonal corporate body. Rather than appearing to be detached and faceless corporations, they present themselves as groups of committed individuals who have a personal interest in our experience of 'reading' or 'driving'. Other **interactive features** can be seen in the use of questions (Citroën) and in the direct debit form (*NI*).

Sentence organisation controls the way in which we respond to the advertisements. The **passive voice** is used throughout the car advertisement because it allows the rearrangement of information in the sentence: *is relayed* (l. 9); *is... illuminated* (l. 14); *have been imitated* (l. 18); *is delivered* (l. 21). In most cases, the agent is included after the passive verb phrase and this therefore suggests that the advertisers wished to delay the subject of the active sentence for dramatic effect. In three of the examples here, end focus creates semantic weight on a noun phrase that demonstrates a key feature of the car: *Head-up display* (l. 10); *Xenon dual function directional headlights* (l. 15); *Citroën's proven and powerful 208hp 2.7 litre diesel V6* (ll. 21–2). In the other passive sentence, the rearrangement of information allows the object of the active sentence (*Citroën's legendary levels of ride comfort*, l. 17) a position of prominence at the beginning of the subordinate clause.

Marked themes are used to foreground a particular piece of information: adverbial clauses of condition (*If you think...*, l. 6, *NI*; *even if fatigue...*, l. 11, Citroën); an adverbial clause of contrast (*While Citroën's legendary levels of ride comfort*, l. 17, Citroën); and an adverbial of time (*Now...*, l. 2, Citroën). Each of these allows the advertiser to draw attention to a significant element of its campaign.

Rhetorical devices help to make both examples persuasive. **Listing** suggests the extensive qualities of a product that can be recommended to the reader. In the *NI* advertisement, the asyndetic listing of the noun phrases presents a particular worldview with which readers will identify. The absence of any final co-ordinator and the continuation mark (..., l. 4) suggest that this is merely the beginning of a list that could be far longer. The list is representative of the kind of concerns a potential reader of the *NI* magazine might have. **Tripling** (*practical innovation, almost indecent comfort and shameless good looks*, ll. 4–5) and **parallelism** (*alert you and restore you*, l. 13; *that sleek profile and those sweeping curves*, ll. 25–6) in the Citroën advertisement suggest balance and logic and that these are indicative of the product itself – this is a design that has been carefully considered and tailored to the demands of discerning drivers.

The **typographical features** of each advertisement draw attention to the product. The prominent image, large slogan and italicised subheading of the Citroën advertisement immediately catch the eye, but the advertisers are confident that their target audience will not be put off by the size and extent of the copy. The small print and the use of words with a French origin suggest that their potential customers are sophisticated and will not be daunted by the amount of text. The larger print and prominent cartoon image of the *NI* advertisement are dramatic and aim to persuade readers to look more closely at the advertisement once their attention has been attracted. Both advertisements display the brand logo, but in neither case is it a dominant part of the overall effect – Citroën's company slogan is in very small print:

>   A   P   O
> (JUST) (IMAGINE) (WHAT CITROËN CAN DO FOR YOU)
>   SCl–NCl

Although the ultimate aim of the advertisers is different – Citroën want readers to 'buy' and NI want readers to 'subscribe' – the principles on which they design their advertisements are quite similar. Both rely on words rather than colour; both assume a sophistication in the target audience (a technical knowledge about cars or politics); and both appeal to the human desire to be 'better' (the owner of a more stylish car or a more informed member of society).

Service advertising

SERVICE ADVERTISING is very similar to product advertising except that a service rather than a concrete product is offered. It may be a banking service or a mortgage, a personal service like massage or reflexology, or a range of educational or leisure evening classes at a local school or college. **Classified advertisements**, **point-of-sale advertisements** and **direct mail** can all offer a 'service' to a target audience.

Charity advertising

This kind of advertising is distinctive because it is non-profit making. Although it uses the mass-marketing approach of mainstream product and service advertising, the persuasive techniques are used for a quite different purpose: rather than 'buy', the message is now 'give'. Charities depend upon reminding the public that there is a continuing need for donations, and advertising fulfils this purpose, particularly when the campaigns are emotive or sensational in some way.

In a competitive market, charities have to win their prospective donors and then persuade them to be loyal. They have to find effective ways of encouraging people to give voluntarily. Instead of standing in shopping centres with collecting tins, more and more charities are now opting for a 'brand identity'. By using the same kind of advertising techniques as commercial companies, they are able to create a distinctive image, encouraging donors to identify with a particular 'brand' of charity. Their distinctive advertising campaigns allow them to say something about the people who give, as well as about their own work and aims.

Charities therefore employ advertising agencies just as commercial companies do, and their campaigns are carefully crafted to influence the public. Advertisements such as the Multiple Sclerosis Society's campaign showing images damaged by 'torn edges', and the RSPCA's depiction of a mountain of dead dogs, have a powerful effect on their audiences. This kind of dramatic approach allows the charity to get more public attention because the approach generates more media coverage than the charity could afford to pay for in advertising.

ACTIVITY 12.3

Consider the advertisement in Figure 12.4, and comment on the features that make it successful.

COMMENTARY

The **function** of a charity advertisement can be to encourage donations, to lobby a local MP in order to raise awareness of a particular cause or issue, or to promote joint action of some kind, as in the advertisement in Figure 12.4. The **adver-**

Figure 12.4 **Charity advertisement (in *Change! The Oxfam Campaigner*, Issue 58/autumn 2006)**

tiser** can be identified by the web address given at the bottom. This link explains the context of the Stop Climate Chaos charity organisation: the website lists the 39 charities that make up the coalition, whose aim is to change our behaviour, at domestic, industrial and governmental levels. Well-known members include Oxfam, Greenpeace, CAFOD (Catholic Agency For Overseas Development) and WWF. Because this advertisement appears in the Oxfam campaigning magazine,

Change!, its target audience is specific: people who are interested in global issues and wish to work with Oxfam to create a better working and living environment for people around the world who have no voice of their own. In this advertisement, readers are encouraged to take part in a rally that will persuade the government to take action in the UN climate conference. The **selling technique** is impact-centred and draws attention to the issue by taking a familiar image (a weather forecast) and undermining our expectations.

The **overall design** is eye-catching because it is bold and takes up more than half of the advertisement. Initially the image presents no challenge to our understanding – it is a map of the world with a range of familiar weather symbols and temperatures, and a weather forecaster is pointing out key features. The sub-heading, a post-modifying non-finite clause (*Becoming stranger and stranger*), sets the tone, however – this is not a comfortable world but one in which the pleasure of some is offset by the suffering of others. The comparative adjectives hint at what is to follow.

Although the approach is formal, **contractions** such as *There'll* (l. 3) and *it's* (l. 10) link the copy to spoken language, drawing on the familiar and conversational tone of a television weather forecast. This is reinforced by the use of **direct address** (*you*; *your*) and the inclusive first person plural pronoun (*we*) that unites viewer and forecaster in a common context. The mix of formal and informal is appropriate because although the advertiser seeks to establish a rapport with readers, the subject matter is serious.

The **lexis** is used initially to lure readers into familiar territory and then to shock them out of their complacency. The bold print *Record temperatures* (l. 1) and the adverbial of place *in the north* (l. 2) introduce a positive mood that will not be sustained. We are prepared for the change in mood by the simple sentence *... it's a different story* (l. 10) and the adverbial of place *in the south* (l. 11). In the context of a global map, the reader is forced to recognise that this is more than a geographical division: in a wider political and social context, the north is represented for the main part by the privileged developed countries, while the south is made up of the developing countries where many live in absolute poverty.

The first words we read in the left-hand column are, as we would expect from the opening sentence, mainly positive. The **connotations** of concrete nouns such as *sunglasses, ice cream* (l. 7) and *sun lotion* (l. 8) set a familiar summer scene, while the negative connotations of noun phrases such *hose-pipe bans* and *transport disruptions* (ll. 4–5) are minor irritations rather than anything of consequence. This opposition is symbolised by the juxtaposition of the abstract nouns *discomfort* (l. 3) and *fun* (l. 4) with their proportional prepositional post-modifiers (*for some*; *for most*). The language of the right-hand column, on the other hand, is devastating. Concrete nouns here set a very different mood: *floods*; *drought*; *crop failure*; *livestock deaths*; *food shortages*; *disease* (ll. 12–16). There are no positive references and no qualifying phrases: life here is characterised by the adjective phrase *very uncertain* (l. 12), and everyone is at risk.

Many of the modifiers are factual rather than emotive – they narrow the reference of the noun (*hose-pipe bans*; *transport bans*; *crop failure*; *food shortages*). In the description of the south, however, modifiers are also used for dramatic effect, appealing to our emotions and enhancing the contrast between life in the north and life in the south. The adjective *severe* (l. 13) and the past participle modifier *displaced* (l. 15) are moving because they help to communicate an image that affects us – an image all too easily called to mind of starving children and sprawling refugee camps, in which appalling conditions do little to relieve people's suffering.

The **grammar** in this advertisement is not complicated. **Sentences**, even those containing subordination, tend to be quite short:

> S | A | P | O
>
> (Record temperatures) (in the north) (look) (set to continue).   (ll. 1–2)
> SCl–NFCl

> dumS P   (S)   A
> (it) ('s) (a different story) (in the south where the future looks very uncertain indeed).
> SCl–RelCl   (ll. 10–12)

Where sentences are longer, co-ordinated subjects and listed objects create the length, rather than embedded subordinate clauses (ll. 12–17). This ensures that the advertiser's message is communicated clearly. The most important sentence is set apart from the 'weather forecast', allowing the advertisers to draw attention to their message explicitly:

> S   P   A   A
> (Poor people in developing countries) (will suffer) (as a result of climate change) (long
> SCl–ACl
>
> before we do)   (l. 19)
> SCl–ACl

The **mood** is mostly declarative, but imperatives are used to engage the reader. The commands are made more emphatic by the addition of the auxiliary *do* which stresses the importance of the imperative verbs (*Do take care*... l. 8; *do get ready*... l. 16) and enhances the familiar tone of the weather forecast. Other imperatives are addressed directly to the reader: *GET INVOLVED*... *rally* (ll. 20–1) These are the focus of the advertisement because they urge the reader to take action. In line with the theme of climate change, the **tense** of verb phrases moves between the present, which describes current conditions (*look*, l. 2; *'s*, l. 10; *looks*, l. 11), the progressive, which describes ongoing conditions (*'re seeing*, ll. 5–6; *'re relaxing*, l. 9; *are causing*, l. 13), and future time, which predicts the changes we can expect (*'ll be*, l. 3). The use of the **modal verb** 'will' in the verb phrase *will suffer* (l. 19) indicates a certain truth that the advertisers wish their readers to face. To counter the depressing reality of climate change, the final sentence of the advertisement uses the modal *can* (l. 21) to suggest our ability to do something to help. After the imperative *GET INVOLVED*, this offers readers a way to take direct action to help.

The dominant **rhetorical device** used in this advertisement is **antithesis**: the *north* is set against the *south* in a comparison of weather that initially seems familiar. Lexical sets of positive and negative words, however, and syndetic lists of contrasting noun phrases together set this familiar division of a country against a global background. Perhaps the most moving opposition comes in the almost casual **juxtaposition** of the colloquial *So do get ready* (l. 16) with the apparently neutral verb phrase *to change* and the adverb *dramatically* (l. 17). This is an example of **understatement** (**litotes**) – the horror of what climate change may do is left unsaid.

Because the tone of the copy is conversational, mirroring the spoken language of a weather forecast, **figurative language** would seem out of place. It is important to recognise, however, that the weather forecast has a **symbolic** rather than a literal significance. We are not meant to focus on the numerical and visual detail of the image, but on the underlying social and political issues.

The **typographical features** are effective here because they immediately engage our attention. The image is familiar and therefore unthreatening, and this is reinforced by the sans serif **font** which has a handwritten, personal quality. Our comfort zones are challenged, however, as we read the copy. The larger print at the beginning of each column is the hook to get us reading, and the capitalised *GET INVOLVED* makes the focus of the advertisement explicit. **Borders** around certain parts of the text emphasise important information and mark changes in the approach: the symbolic weather forecast is in one large boxed area, while the non-finite clause *Becoming stranger and stranger*, the capitalised imperative and the call to action are highlighted separately.

Information advertising

Most non-profit-making **INFORMATION ADVERTISING** campaigns are associated with the Government and its various departments. The Government may wish to inform the population in general of some changes in its services. It may wish to educate or warn: passive smoking advertisements, for instance, reflect the dangers of inhaled smoke for those in the company of smokers – especially young children. Shot in dark tones reminiscent of a horror or detective film, the advertisements show smoke curling around a variety of people who are unaware of the danger they are in. Similarly, advertisements on television, on YouTube and on a Government website (www.knowyourlimits.gov.uk) with the caption *Know Your Limits* are to warn teenagers of the risks they face in binge drinking. In one example, a 'superhero' figure climbs up the scaffolding on a building site to rescue a helium balloon for a girl. The advertisement has a dramatic soundtrack and stuntman acrobatics. When the distant figure slips and falls, we see the twisted corpse not of a superhero but of an ordinary young man. The accompanying voice-over says: *Too much alcohol makes you feel invincible when you're most vulnerable*. Every Christmas, the Government and the police promote a campaign to encourage people not to drink and drive. In recent years, the approach has been hard-hitting, emphasising the horrors for the victims and their families and for the driver.

Sometimes a commercial company uses advertising to inform its customers of a change in policy or a problem. Toy manufacturers may discover that a certain product has a fault and place advertisements in national newspapers to alert parents of the potential danger, while also offering a refund or replacement. To advise Tesco customers of a faulty product – a television that might contain a faulty component – the company displayed advertisements and leaflets in the entrance and at the Customer Services desk. Customers were advised about the model numbers affected and were given instructions to follow so that a *free of charge home visit* could be arranged to *check and modify* the set should it be necessary. After a warehouse fire had affected the supply and distribution of Branston Pickle, Crosse &

Blackwell used information advertising to thank their customers for their support and patience. The company took out a full-page advertisement in a range of newspapers (November 2004) to indicate that they were *back up and running, producing great quality, great tasting Branston® pickle.* While offered as a 'thank you', this information advertisement also functioned as a product-based advertisement, encouraging any customers who had used other brands in the intervening period to buy Branston for Christmas.

Non-profit-making bodies like the Government and commercial companies use the same kinds of mass-marketing techniques to disseminate important information. The only difference between this kind of advertising and product, service or charity advertising is in the function: people are no longer asked to 'buy' or 'give' but to 'know'.

12.5 What to look for in the language of advertising

The following checklist can be used to identify key features in examples of advertising. You will not find all of the features in every example, but the list can be used as a guide. The points made are general, so discussion of specific examples will need to be adapted to take account of the specific context, the target audience and the function for a given advertisement. Remember that you need to evaluate the effect of the features you identify, exploring how they create meaning.

The following are helpful questions to ask.

Register

1 What is the **mode**?
   * spoken or written?
   * newspaper, magazine, billboard, radio or television? internet?
2 What is the **manner**?
   * formal or informal relationship between participants (the advertiser and the reader or viewer)?
   * persuasive or informative?
   * personal or impersonal?
3 What is the **field**?
   * advertiser and target audience?
   * subject matter?
   * linked to the audience, purpose and context?

Overall design

1 What kinds of **images** are used?
   * people? settings? props?
   * literal or symbolic? cultural stereotypes?
2 How does the **copy** anchor the **image**?
3 What effect does the juxtaposition of **slogan**, **logo** and **copy** have?

Lexis

1 What is noticeable about the **slogan**?
   * structure? puns? disrupted collocations?

2 Is anything significant about the **lexical choice**?
- positive descriptions of a product? information about an issue?
- formal or colloquial language? subject-specific lexis?
- ambiguity to add interest or amuse the reader or viewer?

3 Are the **noun phrases** simple or complex?
- pre- or post-modification?
- technical or emotive words?

4 Is anything significant about the **modifiers**?
- physical or emotive qualities? trigger words? link to price?
- strings? compound words?

5 Are there any examples of language that has influenced the **contemporary word stock**?
- colloquial expressions? coinages? clichés?

6 Are there any **possessive forms of nouns** used for inanimate objects?

7 Are there any **neologisms**?
- words or phrases which make a brand memorable because the advertising campaign manipulates language?

Grammar

1 Are there any links to **spoken language**?
- contractions or colloquial language?
- abbreviated or disjointed sentences?
- initial-position conjunctions?

2 Does the **mood** change?
- declarative to make statements about a product or service?
- interrogative to involve the reader or viewer in decision-making?
- imperative to reinforce the function of the advertisement?

3 Are there any **tense** changes?
- simple present to establish the key features of a product or the present state of affairs?
- simple past tense and perfect aspect to develop comparisons?
- future time to propose potential changes?
- modal verbs to imply certainty or possibility?

4 Is there anything noticeable about the **sentence structure**?
- verbless clauses to reflect the disjointed and abbreviated grammatical forms of spoken language and to break the copy into easily readable chunks?
- short sentences to avoid alienating readers or viewers?
- longer sentences to reflect the subject matter and the message conveyed?

Style

1 Is the **sentence organisation** designed to influence the reader or viewer?
- marked themes to focus attention on key points?
- foregrounding of adverbials to provide extra information that the advertiser believes is important in making the target audience act in a certain way?
- repositioning of the object in an active sentence to the initial position of a passive sentence to create emphasis?

2 Are there any **literary devices**?
- metaphors and similes to evoke emotive associations in the mind of the reader or viewer?

- symbolism to force the reader or viewer to make connections that will colour the way he or she interprets an advertisement?
- personification or animation to create a mysterious or humorous atmosphere?
- clever or comic puns?

3 Is there any **sound patterning** to create a memorable slogan or phrase or to develop a particular mood?
- alliteration, rhythm or rhyme?

4 Are there any **rhetorical devices**?
- antithesis which sets key words or concepts against each other for dramatic effect or develops a particular point of view?
- listing which suggests the range of a product's features?
- patterning which emphasises important attributes or contrasts products and services?
- repetition of words, phrases or clauses which highlights key points or a particular brand name?

Typographical features

1 Is there anything significant about the **print size**, **shape** and **style**?
- to draw attention to certain elements of the advertisement?
- to encourage the reader to concentrate on longer pieces of text?
- to break the text into easily manageable sections?

2 Is **colour** used effectively?
- to encourage symbolic associations?
- to catch the reader's or viewer's interest?
- to create clear contrasts?

3 Is the **layout** successful?
- size of advertisement?
- balance of copy and images?
- techniques used to attract attention?

Summary

The **function** of advertising language and style is to persuade people to act in a certain way, to make them believe in certain claims, or to inform them of key information.

Advertising uses many features of **informal spoken language** to develop a personal relationship between the advertiser and the 'consumer'. However, the purpose of the advertisement can affect the extent of the informality used – the more serious the issues, the more formal the approach will be.

Advertising **manipulates language**, **images** and **layout** to achieve the best possible results, but most people will be aware to some extent of the ways in which they are being manipulated. In the 1960s, it was commonly believed that the mass media 'injected' their message into passive unsuspecting consumers who were unable to form their own opinions. Now, however, the audience is recognised as being more active – people do not passively accept the mass media messages that they are fed, but make informed decisions based on information taken from a range of sources.

Chapter 13

The language of literature – narrative prose

13.1 The nature of narrative prose

It is difficult to categorise narrative PROSE because prose is so wide-ranging. Above all, it offers opportunities for authors to experiment, to manipulate language in order to create the best possible effects. At the heart of a novelist's work is the desire to create a fictional world which exists alongside the real one. It may be a representation of the past, of the present or of an unknown future; the characters may be realistic or caricatures; the physical and social backgrounds may be familiar or unfamiliar – and ultimately the author must decide whether to draw readers into this created world or to alienate them.

13.2 The function of narrative prose

The words on the page are the novelist's raw material: it is by manipulating language and style that the author can influence the reader. The dominant function of language is therefore **poetic**. Because literature deals with human emotions and states of mind, the **expressive** use of language is also important.

One of the main functions of fiction is to **entertain**, but authors can do much more than this through their creation of an imaginary world. Narrative prose can implicitly raise the reader's awareness about an issue or about the world in general, and can thus educate and inform (**referential** function).

Each short story or novel is different and each author will make decisions about the purpose and style of the prose. Most fiction will not fall neatly into categories, but will have a mixture of functions. It is important to establish what an author is trying to achieve in order to understand the approach adopted and the effects created.

13.3 Features of narrative prose

Novels and short stories can use language in such a wide variety of ways that it is difficult to be specific about linguistic and stylistic features. There are, however, certain features that are worth looking out for.

Manner

The **manner** can be formal or informal, depending upon the relationship the author wants to create with the reader. Often the modern novel will try to re-create the language of everyday, particularly in FIRST PERSON NARRATIVES (stories told from the point of view of one individual, using the first person singular personal pronoun *I*). Older novels tend to be more formal in their address to the reader. It is also important to identify the author's attitude to characters and events: **irony**, for instance, allows the author to write in a contradictory way – what is actually meant is contrary to what the words on the page appear to say. An author may use irony to show the difference between how things are and how they might be, to mock certain characters, to highlight a discrepancy between how characters see a situation and its true nature, or to emphasise that a reader knows more than the characters themselves.

Point of view

The POINT OF VIEW is central to narrative prose because the reader needs to know who is telling the story. In a **first person narrative**, the *I* narrator relates the events she or he experiences. This allows the reader a direct insight into the character's mind. Often the experiences are viewed retrospectively so that there is a difference between the character's mature and immature personalities (for instance, *Jane Eyre*, by Charlotte Brontë; *Great Expectations*, by Charles Dickens; *A Clockwork Orange*, by Anthony Burgess). The choice of a first person narrator produces a personal relationship that tends to encourage the reader to empathise with the main character. Because this approach gives only one person's view of the story, however, it can be biased, showing a limited understanding of the events and other characters.

In a THIRD PERSON NARRATIVE the narrator is often **omniscient** – all-seeing and all-knowing. Such narrators tend to give an overview of the story. Because there is no *I*, the narration is presented to the reader directly without an intermediary. There are two kinds of omniscient narrator: the unintrusive and the intrusive. The **unintrusive narrator** allows the author to tell the story from a distance, without the reader being aware of a persona telling the story or making judgements. The action is presented without many explicit comments or judgements. Graham Greene and E. M. Forster, for example, are known for their invisible narrators. The **intrusive narrator**, on the other hand, explicitly comments on events and characters, often pointing to the significance of what they are presenting and providing a moral interpretation. Authors such as Jane Austen and George Eliot intervene in their novels, explicitly guiding and influencing the reader's judgements.

Normally, third person narrators relate events and make descriptions using the declarative mood. The interrogative or imperative moods can be used to address the reader directly, inviting judgements or opinions on events and characters. Such addresses often involve a change from simple past tense to simple present.

Writers can choose to make their narrators **reliable** or **unreliable**. A reliable narrator is used in realistic novels, in which the writer aims to offer the reader a true picture of life. He or she will provide an accurate picture or interpretation of events. Sometimes characters interpreting the events are limited in their understanding because they are depicted as being aware only of their own beliefs and values. By failing to recognise other viewpoints or possible interpretations, the characters fail to understand what is happening and so the reader is offered an unreliable interpretation. Writers who choose to use an unreliable narrator can draw attention to the complexity of experience by suggesting that there is always a gap between life itself and the way individuals interpret it.

Novelists are interested in more than just events. The thoughts and opinions of characters are central to the creation of a fictional world. In the nineteenth century, many novelists used **INTERIOR MONOLOGUES** to build up the thought patterns of their characters. Although supposedly reflecting a character's thoughts, the author would order and pattern these so that they were fluent and logical. In the twentieth century, writers like James Joyce and Virginia Woolf were some of the first to experiment with **STREAM OF CONSCIOUSNESS** writing, in which thought patterns appear on the page randomly. To show how chaotic and jumbled thoughts often are, writers can manipulate syntax and layout. This approach attempts to convey on the page the complexity of the human mind.

Lexis

The lexis can be simple or complicated, formal or colloquial, descriptive or evaluative. The choices made depend upon the author's intentions. Words may be subject-specific, belonging to a particular field; they may be archaic; they may be idiosyncratic, clearly linked to a particular character; or they may be linked to a real or imaginary dialect appropriate to the setting of the novel. The connotations of the words chosen will build up a particular viewpoint of the fictional world.

Nouns may be abstract or concrete, depending upon whether the prose focuses on events or states of mind. **Proper nouns** may be used to give the fictional world and its inhabitants a concrete basis. The intentional omission of names may create a mysterious atmosphere.

Modifiers may provide physical, psychological, emotive or visual detail. They may focus on colour, sound or noise to create the fictional world. It is through the modifiers that authors can influence the reader – they can describe or evaluate using words with positive or negative connotations which direct the reader to respond in chosen ways. Modifiers are crucial in forming a parallel world; in helping the reader to make decisions about events, characters and places; and in adding depth to any underlying message.

Verbs tell the reader about the kinds of actions and processes occurring. The use of stative verbs suggests that the author's interest lies in description, whether it be of setting or states of mind, whereas dynamic verbs place an emphasis on what is happening, implying that the author is more interested in action than in contemplation.

All consideration of the lexis of fictional prose must take account of the time and place in which the novel is set. Authors' lexical choices will vary depending upon the kinds of worlds and the people they are creating.

Speech

Writers can adopt a variety of approaches to convey the **speech** of their characters on the page. DIRECT SPEECH is an exact copy of the precise words spoken, allowing characters to speak for themselves. This approach gives prominence to the speaker's point of view. If writers vary spelling, vocabulary, word order and so on, it is possible to produce an accurate phonological, lexical and syntactical written version of characters' accents and dialects. INDIRECT SPEECH reports what someone has said, using a subordinate *that* clause. The person who is reporting the conversation intervenes as an interpreter by selecting the reported words. This submerges the original speaker's point of view.

FREE INDIRECT SPEECH is a form of indirect speech in which the main reporting clause (for instance, *he said that…*) is omitted. This merges the approach of both direct and indirect speech. It uses the same third person pronouns and past tense as indirect speech, but reproduces the actual words spoken more accurately. It can be used to create irony because it gives the reader the flavour of characters' words, while keeping the narrator in a position where he or she can intervene. Free indirect speech can also be used to direct readers' sympathy away from certain characters or to indicate changes in the role of a character. Writers can present a character's thoughts in a similar range of ways.

Grammar

The **grammar** of narrative prose will reflect the kind of world created and the kind of viewpoint offered. In many ways, novelists are freer in their potential choices than writers in other varieties – in fiction, non-standard grammar and lexis are acceptable because they are part of a created world and are an integral part of the characters who inhabit that world.

Most fiction is written in the **simple past tense** – extensive use of other tenses or timescales is worth commenting on. The effects created by writing completely in the present tense, for instance, can be quite dramatic. **Mood** will vary depending upon the requirements of the author. Declarative mood is most common, but interrogatives and imperatives are used to vary the pace and change the focus. In fiction, **sentence structures** are often complex. When simple sentences are used, they are often emphatic or striking. Because writers can experiment, there can also be sentences that do not appear to conform to standard grammatical patterns. Writers vary the kind of sentence structure they use, to maintain readers' interest and to make their fictional world seem alive.

Style

Sentence organisation uses grammatical patterning to rearrange the elements of a sentence in order to draw attention to key information. It allows writers to control the order in which we receive information. Marked themes, the passive voice and end focus all throw emphasis onto certain elements of the text, highlighting things that the author considers to be important.

Literary devices are a writer's way of personalising the world created. Metaphors, symbolism and so on tell the reader something about an author's relationship with the fictional world. Such language usage makes the imaginary world real and guides the reader in judging the characters, setting and events.

The **rhetorical devices** a writer chooses persuade readers to involve themselves in or distance themselves from the fictional world. Antithesis, listing, patterning and repetition can be used to influence the reader's perception of characters, settings and events. Whether working at the level of lexis, grammar or phonology, the devices chosen by an author will guide readers' responses.

13.4 Types of authorial intention

To characterise

Writers can allow characters to reveal themselves to the reader by using a first person narrative or they can mediate using a third person narrator who comments and makes explicit judgements. In both methods other linguistic and stylistic techniques inevitably play a part in the effects created overall.

Physical description is the most obvious way in which a character can be given a concrete presence. Such detail may be provided by the author or by other characters. It is important to decide whose view is being given so that the reliability of the description can be assessed.

> 1 Aleph, the 'beauty', was pale in complexion, her skin (of course innocent of make-up) faintly glowing, her face from a large brow tapering into an oval form, her eyes, beneath long, almost straight dark eyebrows, large and dark brown, thoughtful, expressive of sympathy, also of judgment, her hair, a dark shining chestnut colour,
> 5 a lively complex of curls which framed her face and cascaded in orderly disorder to her long slim pale neck.
>
> Iris Murdoch (1919–99), *The Green Knight*

Murdoch provides a lot of detail about the character, distinguishing between the narrator's viewpoint and that of other characters by using inverted commas to highlight the **abstract noun** in parenthesis, *beauty* (l. 1). Certain **modifiers**, like *large*, *long* and *dark* (ll. 2–6), are repeated to emphasise key qualities of Aleph. These physical qualities give a visual image of the girl, but abstract nouns like *sympathy* and *judgment* (l. 4) build up a more complex portrait. Other modifiers like *lively* (l. 5) and the present participle *shining* (l. 4), and the paradox of *orderly disorder* (l. 5), describe the girl's hair but also suggest something about her character. The parenthesis emphasises that this girl is a natural beauty and the adverbial expressing certainty, *of course* (l. 1), suggests that readers should have guessed this for themselves.

In the one long **sentence** here, Murdoch manages to convey precisely many physical and personal details about Aleph. It is made up from a sequence of S P C clauses in which the stative verb *to be* is omitted. No explicit figurative language is used because the portrait relies on literal description, but Murdoch makes sure that readers realise the **symbolic** value of the physical details. The positive **connotations** of the lexis chosen and the asyndetic **listing** of the details about

Aleph's *skin* (l. 1), *eyes* (l. 2), *hair* (l. 4) and *face* (l. 5) persuade the reader to like the character just as the narrator clearly does.

Apart from information provided by the author, what characters **say**, **do** and **think** is also an important means of characterisation. Direct speech and thought (interior monologue and stream of consciousness) reflect the characters as they really are, without apparent intervention by the writer or other characters.

> 1 'It is over! it is over!' she [Anne] repeated to herself again, and again, in nervous
>   gratitude. 'The worst is over!'
>   Mary talked, but she could not attend. She had seen him. They had met. They
>   had been once more in the same room!
> 5   Soon, however, she began to reason with herself, and try to be feeling less. Eight
>   years, almost eight years had passed, since all had been given up. How absurd
>   to be resuming the agitation which such an interval had banished into distance
>   and indistinctness! What might not eight years do? Events of every description,
>   changes, alienations, removals, – all, all must be compromised in it; and oblivion
> 10 of the past – how natural, how certain too! It included nearly a third part of her
>   own life.

Jane Austen (1775–1817), Persuasion

The subject matter here focuses on the main character's response to meeting a former lover. Austen uses an **interior monologue** to convey Anne's emotions: the rhetorical devices and disjointed style reflect her state of mind. The event – the meeting – is insignificant, but Anne's response is an important stage in Austen's characterisation. There are many **abstract nouns** to stress internal rather than external reactions: *agitation* (l. 7) *changes* (l. 9), *alienations* (l. 9) and *gratitude* (l. 2). By contrast, there are no descriptions of actions other than Mary's talking (from which Anne feels distanced) and Anne's summary of the meeting. The sequence of **simple sentences** used to represent the visit emphasises the minor event that has occurred in comparison to the great emotions it has stirred:

> S   P   O   S   P   S   P   A   A
> (She) (had seen) (him). (They) (had met). (They) (had been) (once more) (in the same
> room)!   (ll. 3–4)

Verbs like *banished* (l. 7) and abstract nouns like *oblivion* (l. 9) are dramatic and seem ironic when juxtaposed with such an insignificant occasion.

The **mood** varies frequently to mirror Anne's state of mind. As is usual, declaratives are used to tell the story, but Anne is questioning her own reactions and emotions and therefore interrogatives are common: *What might not...* (l. 8). There are also a number of exclamations to mark Anne's feelings: *How natural, how certain...* (l. 10). By changing from one mood to another, Austen is able to reflect Anne's disturbed emotional state in the style as well as in the lexis.

Direct speech is used at the opening of the extract. The simple sentences are emphatic:

> S P   C   S P   C
> '(It) (is) (over)! (it) (is) (over)!'   (l. 1)

The **repetition** of the S P C structure marks Anne's attempts to regain control. While the rest of the extract emphasises that they have been separated for eight years, the repetition of the third person plural *they* (l. 3) suggests some kind of unity between Anne and the unnamed man. This contradiction underlines the effect the meeting has had on her. As she tries to rationalise what has happened, the sentences tend to be complex because they are conveying Anne's confusion. Austen mirrors the complexity of Anne's thoughts in the style she chooses – this is typical of interior monologue, in which the author orders a character's thoughts on the page:

A	S	P	O		O
(Soon),	(however), (she)	(began)	(to reason with herself),	(and)	(try to be feeling less).
conj		SCl–NFCl			SCl–NFCls

(l. 5)

Some **verb phrases** differ from Late Modern English usage: Austen uses expanded verb phrases like *try to be feeling* (l. 5) and *to be resuming* (l. 7). The use of the **progressive aspects** expresses the depth of Anne's feelings and suggests that there is an ongoing process as she struggles to resume control of her emotions.

The style is very rhetorical. Austen **repeats** the noun phrase *eight years* (ll. 5–6, 6, 8) to draw attention to the length of time since Anne and the man last saw each other. She uses **tripling** to show Anne's thought processes as she tries to sort out her unexpected emotions: *changes, alienations, removals* (l. 9). **Antithesis** juxtaposes Anne's actual responses with the ones she feels to be more appropriate: verb phrases like *to reason* and *try to be feeling less* (l. 5); noun phrases like *agitation* (l. 7) and *oblivion* (l. 9).

The author's main interest is in conveying Anne's inner experience after a brief meeting. She is more concerned with Anne than with the event itself. The **point of view** varies in the extract: Austen allows Anne to present her own thoughts and feelings directly in the form of an interior monologue, but she also provides an authorial overview: *Soon, however, she began...* (l. 5). By using **free indirect thought**, Anne's feelings are given strength: *She had seen him* (l. 3). Her inner feelings are given a 'voice', allowing the narrator to stand back and imply that the character is directly revealing herself to the reader.

Modern authors often use **stream of consciousness** to convey a character's thoughts to the reader in a more realistic way. James Joyce was one of the first to experiment with style in this way.

> 1 Once upon a time and a very good time it was there was a moocow coming down along the road and this moocow that was down along the road met a nicens little boy named baby tuckoo ...
>
>   His father told him that story: his father looked at him through glass: he had a
> 5 hairy face.
>
>   He was baby tuckoo. The moocow came down the road where Betty Byrne lived ...

James Joyce (1882–1941), *Portrait of the Artist as a Young Man*

In this extract, Joyce is trying to re-create a child's-eye view of the world in both the words and the style he chooses. The child's perspective is captured in the focus on senses: the sight of his father's face seen through *glass* (l. 4 – his glasses); the feel of his *hairy* (l. 5) face. Childlike lexis such as *moocow* (l. 1) and *tuckoo* (l. 3) mark the register. Equally, the **syntax** resembles child language: sentences are long and the co-ordinating conjunction *and* is common. The opening sentence uses a traditional adverbial associated with narrative: *Once upon a time* (l. 1). Here the child retells himself the story his father tells. **Repetition** of phrases is also a typical feature of children's stories because it creates a memorable pattern.

The reader's knowledge of the child here seems to come directly from the child himself with no narrator intervention. In the Austen extract, the narrator orders Anne's thoughts so that although the lexis and syntax convey her sense of confusion, the grammatical structures are standard. Joyce, on the other hand, uses lexis and syntax that specifically reflect a child's character – the words and sentence structures have been chosen to suggest the child's actual pattern of thought.

ACTIVITY 13.1

Read this extract from George Eliot's *The Mill on the Floss* and comment on the techniques used to characterise Maggie.

1   You may see her now, as she walks down the favourite turning, and enters the Deeps
    by a narrow path through a group of Scotch firs – her tall figure and old lavender-
    gown visible through an hereditary black-silk shawl of some wide-meshed net-like
    material; and now she is sure of being unseen, she takes off her bonnet and ties it
5   over her arm. One would certainly suppose her to be farther on in life than her seven-
    teenth year – perhaps because of the slow resigned sadness of the glance, from
    which all search and unrest seem to have departed, perhaps because her broad-
    chested figure has the mould of early womanhood. Youth and health have withstood
    well the involuntary and voluntary hardships of her lot, and the nights in which she
10 has lain on the hard floor for a penance have left no obvious trace; the eyes are liquid,
    the brown cheek is firm and rounded, the full lips are red. With her dark colouring and
    jet crown surmounting her tall figure, she seems to have a sort of kinship with the
    grand Scotch firs, at which she is looking up as if she loved them well. Yet one has
    a sense of uneasiness in looking at her – a sense of opposing elements, of which a
15 fierce collision is imminent: surely there is a hushed expression, such as one often
    sees in older faces under borderless caps, out of keeping with the resistant youth,
    which one expects to flash out in a sudden, passionate glance, that will dissipate all
    the quietude, like a damped fire leaping out again when all seemed safe.
    But Maggie herself was not uneasy at this moment. She was calmly enjoying the
20 free air, while she looked up at the old fir-trees, and thought that those broken ends of
    branches were the records of past storms, which had only made the red stems soar
    higher.

George Eliot (Mary Ann Evans, 1819–80), *The Mill on the Floss*

COMMENTARY

The **third person narrator** directly addresses the reader here using the second person pronoun *you*. This kind of narrator is described as **intrusive** because the reader is made explicitly aware of her presence. By revealing her thoughts and speculations on Maggie, the narrator creates a personal relationship with the reader – the tone is almost conspiratorial as they observe Maggie unseen. In the first paragraph, the focus is on Maggie's external features and on what can be deduced from these. The narrator is tentative, using verbs like *suppose* (l.5), *seems* (l.12) and *may* (l.1); adverbs like *perhaps* (l.6); and noun phrases like *a sense of...* (l.14). The second paragraph changes the focus and approach: the narrator is no longer so obvious; Maggie's actions and thoughts are described. Verbs are now stative, describing Maggie as she is, not as she seems to be: *was* (l. 19); they also describe processes: *looked* and *thought* (l. 20).

Initially, **physical description** characterises Maggie. The narrator draws the reader's attention to literal features using complex noun phrases:

m	m	h	m	m	h	m	m	m	h	q
her	tall	figure	... old	lavender-gown	... an	hereditary	black-silk	shawl	of some	wide-
det	Adj	N	Adj	Adj	N	det	Adj	Adj N	N	PrepP

meshed net-like material   (ll. 2–4)

The **modifiers** suggest conformity of dress. Her clothes are not bright or extravagant, but practical and old. **Compound modifiers** allow the writer to provide detailed information in a concise way. Other modifiers describe her face: her eyes are *liquid* (l. 10); her cheeks *brown ... firm ... rounded* (l. 11); her lips *full* and *red* (l. 11).

The author creates a very visual picture of Maggie, but also hints at her mood using noun phrases like *slow resigned sadness* (l. 6) and *hushed expression* (l. 15). A contradiction is built up between the physical details of dress and facial features and Maggie's mood. **Literary language** creates another layer to Maggie's character. The post-modified noun phrase *a sense of opposing elements* (l. 14) summarises the knowledge the reader has gained from the description of Maggie in the first paragraph. The pre-modifier *fierce* and the complement *imminent* (l. 15) used to modify the abstract noun *collision* imply that Maggie's apparent external calm does not reflect her inner state of mind. Such lexical choices prepare the reader for conflict. The **metaphor** of the *damped fire* (l. 18) and the verbs *flash* (l. 17) and *leaping* (l. 18) develop this sense of Maggie's inner strength – she has an inner spark that cannot be quelled by external circumstances like poverty and hardship. By comparing her to the fir trees, Eliot suggests that Maggie has an inner grandeur that will enable her to rise above everyday problems. The modifier *grand* (l. 13), used to describe the trees, can equally be applied to Maggie's ability to cope with a life that does not fulfil her dreams.

The **syntax** reflects the kind of character described. The **present tense** is used in the first paragraph where Maggie is portrayed through her physical characteristics. It unites the reader and writer, while separating them from Maggie. The second paragraph uses the **simple past tense**, which is traditional for narratives. It allows the narrator to return to unintrusive narrative comment. The reader is aware of the narrator's omniscience since although judgements are apparently made on the basis of observations, some of the details describing Maggie's internal state of mind could not be known.

The **sentences** are mostly complex, which is appropriate for the detailed nature of the characterisation. A relationship is created between external details and internal feelings – because the narrator's thoughts are not simple, the sentences are invariably complex:

S	P	A	O
(Youth and health)	(have withstood)	(well)	(the involuntary and voluntary hardships of

		S	P
her lot),	(and)	(the nights in which she has lain on the hard floor for a penance)	(have
	conj	SCl–RelCl	

$$\overset{O}{\text{left}} \text{ (no obvious trace)}; \overset{S}{\text{(the eyes)}} \overset{P}{\text{(are)}} \overset{C}{\text{(liquid)}}, \overset{S}{\text{(the brown cheek)}} \overset{P}{\text{(is)}} \overset{C}{\text{(firm and rounded)}},$$

$$\overset{S}{\text{(the full lips)}} \overset{P}{\text{(are)}} \overset{C}{\text{(red)}}. \hspace{4cm} \text{(ll. 8–11)}$$

The style is **rhetorical** because the author is trying to persuade the reader to react to Maggie in a certain way. The **repetition** of the adverb *now* (ll. 1, 4) suggests that readers are being given a chance to observe Maggie for themselves – allowing them to make their own decisions about the nature of her character. By using **compound phrases**, Eliot gives her style a balance which encourages the reader to accept the conclusions reached: the co-ordinated noun phrase *search and unrest* (l. 7) suggests that Maggie has been forced to accept her life rather than to challenge events; the abstract nouns *Youth and health* (l. 8) are almost personified, implying that despite the hardships of her life, Maggie's physical and psychological nature is strong. **Tripling** is used to list the physical features of Maggie's face so that the writer seems to be scrutinising her. Most importantly, the **antithesis** reminds the reader of the apparent contradictions within Maggie: *hushed … resistant* (ll. 15–16); *involuntary … voluntary* (l. 9); *uneasy … calmly* (l. 19) and so on. These **juxtapositions** imply that although externally Maggie seems to accept her fate, she is repressing her true nature.

Eliot uses several techniques to characterise Maggie. She presents her in a positive light, encouraging readers to empathise with her through the lexis and stylistic features. The contradictions in her character are emphasised – Maggie seems old before her time, yet she has an inner strength and dignity.

To set the scene

Setting the scene is important if the writer wishes readers to immerse themselves in the fictional world created. By providing physical details of time and place, the author can enable the reader to visualise the background. It may just provide a context for characters to interrelate and events to take place, but often it is symbolic. Even literal descriptions can tell the reader something about the characters who are seen in a particular location.

By providing **literal details**, a writer can build up a sense of place. In particular, rooms can tell us something about the characters who inhabit them.

> 1 The room had scarcely altered since their father had furnished it, hastily but not cheaply … The desk was handsome and huge, with an almost military look, its dark green leather glowing, its brass fitments gleaming. Lucas, who scarcely tolerated other people in the house, cleaned the place himself … Bookshelves
> 5 covered the entire wall behind the desk, and also the opposite wall by the door. A large dark brown leather sofa, rarely sat upon, shiny as on the day of its purchase, stretched out beside the door to the garden, above it hung a watercolour of Lake Geneva showing the Château de Chillon. There were several powerful strong upright chairs with leather seats and ladderbacks … There was a huge dark
> 10 Persian carpet now pleasantly worn …
>
> Iris Murdoch, *The Green Knight*

The details here not only **create a background** for the events that are about to occur, but also tell the reader something about Lucas, who has deliberately left the room as it was in his father's time. The **concrete nouns** *desk* (l. 2), *Bookshelves* (l. 4) and *watercolour* (l. 7) all suggest that the owner is an educated person; while the reference to the *leather sofa* (l. 6) and the *Persian carpet* (l. 10) suggest that he is affluent. Although the verb **modifiers** *glowing* and *gleaming* (l. 3) and the adjective modifier *shiny* (l. 6) imply that the owner takes a pride in his environment, the repetition of the modifier *dark* (ll. 3, 6, 9) gives the room a mysterious atmosphere, suggesting that perhaps he has something to hide. Developing this sense of a possibly mysterious side to Lucas, the modifiers *large* (l. 6), *powerful* (l. 8) and *strong* (l. 9) seem to imply that his personality can daunt and dominate the people around him. The military **metaphor** used to describe his desk reinforces the reader's awareness of his power. The description of the furniture thus becomes **symbolic** of the character who inhabits the room.

Some descriptions are more explicitly symbolic: by using figurative language to create a sense of place, an author can develop a theme.

1   It is the long vacation in the regions of Chancery Lane. The good ships Law and
    Equity, those teak-built, copper-bottomed, iron-fastened, brazen-faced, and not
    by any means fast-sailing Clippers, are laid up in ordinary. The Flying Dutchman,
    with a crew of ghostly clients imploring all whom they may encounter to peruse
5   their papers, has drifted, for the time being, Heaven knows where. The Courts are
    all shut up, the public offices lie in a hot sleep, Westminster Hall itself is a shady
    solitude where nightingales might sing, and a tenderer class of suitors than is
    usually found there, walk.
       The Temple, Chancery Lane, Sergeants' Inn and Lincoln's Inn even unto the
10 Fields, are like tidal harbours at low water; where stranded proceedings, offices
    at anchor, idle clerks lounging on lop-sided stools that will not recover their per-
    pendicular until the current of Term sets in, lie high and dry upon the ooze of the
    long vacation. Outer doors of chambers are shut up by the score, messages and
    parcels are to be left at the Porter's Lodge by the bushel. A crop of grass would
15 grow in the chinks of the stone pavement outside Lincoln's Inn Hall, but that the
    ticket-porters, who have nothing to do beyond sitting in the shade there, with
    their white aprons over their heads to keep the flies off, grub it up and eat it
    thoughtfully.

Charles Dickens (1812–70), *Bleak House*

This is a vivid picture of the deserted Inns of Court when the lawyers have left London during the holiday period. The **tone** is formal because the theme is serious: the nature of justice. Even though the lawyers are absent, there is still a sense of the rituals which are linked to the Courts – it is a public world and Dickens's prose reflects this.

He uses a simple sentence in the declarative **mood** to make the time clear:

dumS P   (S)   A
(It) (is) (the long vacation) (in the regions of Chancery Lane).   (l. 1)

To discuss his theme implicitly, he takes a metaphor and develops it, giving a concrete presence to the inactivity he describes in the Inns of Court. His figurative language is used to indirectly criticise what he sees: *Law and Equity* become *good ships* (ll. 1–2) and an **extended metaphor** of the sea is used to make the reader aware of Dickens' view of these institutions. Because it is the vacation, the *good ships ... are laid up* (ll. 1–3), allowing the reader to come close and inspect them. The string of **compound modifiers** suggests something about the nature of the law: *teak-built, copper-bottomed* and *iron-fastened* (l. 2) all imply that the Law is solid and long-lasting, that it has been lovingly created for the safety of those who come into contact with it. The compound modifier *brazen-faced* (l. 2) and the prepositional phrase *not by any means* (ll. 2–3) which pre-modifies the final compound modifier *fast-sailing* (l. 3) create a different kind of response from the reader. Both these examples have negative connotations: the lawyers, the text implies, are shameless – interested only in prolonging legal action rather than in bringing cases to an end. To mirror the inactivity during the vacation, Dickens continues his sea metaphor by referring to *The Flying Dutchman* (l. 3) which has *drifted* (l. 5). The **connotations** of an unmanned ghost ship are appropriate here to describe the aimlessness of Chancery Lane now that the lawyers have gone. The simile *like tidal harbours at low water* (l. 10) suggests that the other law courts are equally unable to do anything constructive. The **lexical set** of the sea continues with verbs like *stranded* (l. 10) and nouns like *anchor* (l. 11), *current* (l. 12) and *ooze* (l. 12).

Having established his metaphor, Dickens can describe the location more literally: the *Outer doors of chambers are shut up* (l. 13), *the ticket-porters … have nothing to do* (ll. 15–16), and so on. The description of small details like the *lop-sided stools* (l. 11) and the *stone pavement* (l. 15) help the reader to build up a visual image running parallel to the metaphorical image of ships moored in a harbour when the tide is out. The present participle *lounging* (l. 11) and the use of the modal verb to describe the grass that *would grow* (ll. 14–15) emphasise the idleness of all who are left behind.

At one level, this extract is no more than a description of a place during the summer: Dickens uses the **present tense** and **stative verbs** to create a strong sense of the Inns of Court. However, the underlying meaning makes this more than just a picture created from words. The theme is the law and its public and private faces: Dickens indirectly suggests that the lawyers are more interested in their fees than in their clients and that the Law is not as efficient as it might be. To convey this message, he uses metaphorical language that forces the reader to make connections and recognise that there is a purpose to the description.

In autobiographical fiction, writers may recall a place of personal significance. Such description will often be distinctive either in its content or in its style because it is based on an individual's memory of a particular place. Authors may pick out small details that seemed important to them at the time, or they may use non-standard lexical and grammatical forms in order to re-create the power of the place.

> 1 August Bank Holiday. A tune on an ice-cream cornet. A slap of sea and a tickle of sand. A fanfare of sunshades opening. A wince and whinny of bathers dancing into deceptive waters. A tuck of dresses. A rolling of trousers. A compromise of paddlers. A sunburn of girls and a lark of boys. A silent hullabaloo of balloons.
>
> Dylan Thomas (1914–53), 'Holiday Memory'

Each **sentence** in this opening paragraph of Thomas's short story is a complex noun phrase:

m   h   q   m   m   h   q

A fanfare of sunshades opening. (l. 2)   A silent hullabaloo of balloons. (l. 4)

det   N   PrepP   det   Adj   N   PrepP

The effect is almost cinematic as the eye sweeps across the sands and sees each group doing something different. Thomas experiments with words as well as sentence structures. He disrupts **collocations**: the 'slap and tickle' of bawdy seaside postcards is linked to the *sea* and the *sand* (ll. 1–2). He creates a powerful sense of the sounds of the beach as well as the sights: the *slap* (l. 1) of the sea; the *wince and whinny* (l. 2) of bathers. However, he also gives sounds to things that are essentially visual: the *ice-cream cornet* (l. 1) becomes a trumpet playing a tune, possibly the jingle of the ice-cream van itself; developing the musical image, the *sunshades* open in a *fanfare* (l. 2) – the association with royal occasions and the arrival of someone significant makes everyone on the beach seem important. Even the jostling of balloons is portrayed in the **oxymoron** *silent hullabaloo* (l. 4).

Thomas's opening description immediately creates an active beach holiday scene in the reader's mind. His individual approach to conveying the sounds and sights is effective: his style may not be familiar, but the scene he offers readers is. The verbless sentences capture life as it is happening – the effect is photographic.

ACTIVITY 13.2

Read the extract below and consider both the techniques used to set the scene and the authorial intention in creating it.

> 1 The house was left; the house was deserted. It was left like a shell on a sandhill to fill with dry salt grains now that life had left it. The long night seemed to have set in; the trifling airs, nibbling, the clammy breaths, fumbling, seemed to have triumphed. The saucepan had rusted and the mat decayed. Toads had nosed their way in. Idly, aim-
> 5 lessly, the swaying shawl swung to and fro. A thistle thrust itself between the tiles in the larder. The swallows nested in the drawing-room; the floor was strewn with straw; the plaster fell in shovelfuls; rafters were laid bare; rats carried off this and that to gnaw behind the wainscots. Tortoise-shell butterflies burst from the chrysalis and pattered their life out on the window-pane. Poppies sowed themselves among the
> 10 dahlias; the lawn waved with long grass; giant artichokes towered among roses; a fringed carnation flowered among the cabbages; while the gentle tapping of a weed at the window had become, on winters' nights, a drumming from sturdy trees and thorned briars which made the whole room green in summer.

Virginia Woolf (1882–1941), *To the Lighthouse*

COMMENTARY

The **lexical repetition** of the first two sentences emphasises a sense of abandonment. The past participles *left* and *deserted* (l. 1) stress the absence of any human life, while the stative verb *was* (l. 1) reinforces the apparent stasis. To make this image more concrete the author uses the **simile** of the shell: just as the snail has left an empty shell, so people have left this house. The comparison links the house to its environment – the sea – and makes it seem fragile. Equally, the abandoned building, like the empty shell, is open for others to take control. The complex noun phrase *The long night* (l. 2) is possibly **symbolic** of death, reminiscent of the phrase 'the dark night of the soul' which describes a time of mental and spiritual suffering before some kind of change takes place. The writer uses the **verb phrases** to mark both the present stasis and the potential for change. Although the perfect aspect in the verb phrase *had left* (l. 2) suggests a finality, the stative verb *seemed* (l. 3) prepares the reader for change.

The scene starts to become more active with the introduction of present participles which imply ongoing movement:

	m	m	h	q		m	m	h	q
	the	trifling	airs,	nibbling (ll. 2–3)		the	clammy	breaths,	fumbling (l. 3)
	det	V	N	V		det	Adj	N	V
		(pres part)		(pres part)					(pres part)

Even though the movement is tentative and apparently linked to the death-like atmosphere of the house, it begins to replace a sense of stasis with a sense of life. The life here, however, is not linked to people – the end of their time in the house is symbolised by the saucepan and mat. The perfect aspect used in the verb phrases *had rusted* and *decayed* (l. 4) indicates that the process is complete – people and their domestic possessions no longer have a place in the house. This mood is reinforced by the adverbs describing the movement of the shawl: *Idly, aimlessly* (ll. 4–5). Even the verb modifier *swaying* (l. 5) suggests only insignificant movement.

The house now becomes a source of new life as the natural world takes over. The verb used to describe the appearance of the toads, *nosed* (l. 4), is tentative, but dynamic verbs like *thrust* (l. 5) and *burst* (l. 8) change the atmosphere dramatically. The use of the **simple past tense** rather than the perfect aspect reinforces the sense of immediacy. The **juxtaposition** of the natural and the domestic highlights the changes occurring. Nouns like *thistle* (l. 5), *swallows* (l. 6) and *rats* (l. 7) are juxtaposed with *the tiles* (l. 5), *the larder* (l. 6), *the drawing-room* (l. 6) and *the wainscots* (l. 8). The house begins to take on a new form – the plaster is crumbling and the floor is covered with straw, but verbs like *nested* (l. 6) have **connotations** of new life rather than destruction.

However, the writer reminds the reader that this will always be a human environment and will never be perfectly adapted for the natural life. The connotations of energy in the verb *burst* (l. 8), for instance, are juxtaposed with the verb *pattered* (l. 9). Ultimately the butterflies are trapped by the windows – although apparently offering a way out, these ultimately destroy them.

The changes in the garden also reflect the end of one kind of order and the beginning of another. The reflexive verb phrase *sowed themselves* (l. 9) reminds the reader that the natural world is now in control. This knowledge is reinforced by the **juxtaposition** of plants in unexpected contexts: *poppies* and *dahlias* (ll. 9, 10); *artichokes* and *roses* (l. 10); *carnation* and *cabbages* (l. 11). The timescale of these changes is highlighted by the description of the *weed* (ll. 11–13). The verbal nouns *tapping* and *drumming* (ll. 11, 12) mark the transition from something weak to something strong, and this change becomes symbolic of the growing power of the natural world and the diminishing power of the human world. The concluding noun phrase emphasises this by using a predicative modifier normally associated with the natural world to describe the room. The use of the adjective *green* (l. 13), with its connotations of new life and growth, contrasts with the earlier descriptions of the house.

The description appeals to the senses. Its attention to detail makes it easy for the reader to visualise. **Noun phrases** are often complex, providing detailed information in a concise way:

m	m	h	
a	fringed	carnation	(ll. 10–11)
det	V	N	

m	h	
Tortoise-shell	butterflies	(l. 8)
N N	N	

m	m	h	q
the	gentle	tapping	of a weed (l. 11)
det	Adj	V/N	PrepP

The focus of the description is the house and yet it is possible to say that the unnamed people who have left the house are also important. The way in which the opening **sentence structure** is grammatically described dictates whether the house itself or the unnamed people should be the focus of the reader's attention. The verb phrase *was left* (l. 1) could be the simple past tense of the verb phrase *to be left*; it could, however, be the passive form of the verb *to leave* with the agent omitted. The first interpretation allows the house itself to gain prominence; but the use of the passive voice suggests that the underlying mystery should be considered. Whichever interpretation is chosen, the extract builds up a clear visual picture of the abandoned house, drawing the reader into the fictional world created.

To evoke a powerful atmosphere

The creation of a range of different atmospheres is essential to the success of fiction. If readers are to believe in the world of the novel or short story, the writer must be able to arouse their emotions. By creating a dramatic, poignant or euphoric atmosphere, writers can persuade their readers to feel as the characters do.

Often a striking atmosphere is created through description mirroring a character's state of mind or a theme.

1 Fog everywhere, fog up the river, where it flows among green aits and meadows; fog down the river, where it rolls defiled among the tiers of shipping, and the waterside pollution of a great (and dirty) city. Fog on the Essex Marshes, fog on the Kentish heights. Fog creeping into the cabooses of collier-brigs; fog lying out
5 on the yards, and hovering in the rigging of great ships; fog drooping on the gunwales of barges and small boats. Fog in the eyes and throats of ancient Greenwich pensioners, wheezing by the firesides of their wards; fog in the stem and bowl of the afternoon pipe of the wrathful skipper, down in his close cabin; fog cruelly pinching the toes and fingers of his shivering little 'prentice boy on deck. Chance
10 people on the bridges peeping over the parapets into a nether sky of fog, with fog all round them, as if they were up in a balloon, and hanging in the misty clouds ....

   The raw afternoon is rawest, and the dense fog is densest, and the muddy streets are muddiest, near that leaden-headed old obstruction, appropriate orna-
15 ment for the threshold of a leaden-headed old corporation: Temple Bar. And hard by Temple Bar, in Lincoln's Inn Hall, at the very heart of the fog, sits the Lord High Chancellor in his High Court of Chancery.

Charles Dickens, *Bleak House*

By opening the extract with a **verbless sentence**, Dickens is able to attract attention to the noun *fog* (ll. 1–3). He further emphasises its importance by **repeating** it throughout the paragraph and by using the basic pattern of subject and adverbial several times. Although **proper nouns** like *Essex Marshes* (l. 3), *Greenwich* (l. 6) and *Temple Bar* (l. 15) give the places described a sense of reality, the fog in fact destroys all individuality and the repetitive grammatical structures seem to mirror the way it makes everywhere look the same.

To emphasise the all-pervading nature of the fog, Dickens uses a range of contrasts: the adverbs *up* (l. 1) and *down* (l. 2); a sequence of sentences starting *Fog on…* and *Fog in…* ; and present participles like *Fog creeping…, fog lying…* (l. 4) and *fog… pinching…* (ll. 8–9). This very patterned approach forces the reader to recognise the power of the fog. **Lexical sets** create a sense of the environment: nouns like *river* (l. 1) and *waterside* (l. 3); nautical nouns like *cabooses* (ships' kitchens, l. 4), *collier-brigs* (l. 4), *rigging* (l. 5) and *barges* (l. 6); legal nouns like *Lincoln's Inn Hall* and *Lord High Chancellor* (ll. 16–17). **Modifiers** like *great* (l. 3) and *small* (l. 6) remind the reader that nothing can escape the fog. Although its effect on the landscape dominates the extract, people are also at its mercy. The noun phrases referring to the people who inhabit these scenes are as wide-ranging as the kinds of landscapes affected: *ancient Greenwich pensioners* (ll. 6–7), *the wrathful skipper* (l. 8), the *shivering little 'prentice boy* (l. 9) and *Chance people* (ll. 9–10). Through the breadth of his references, Dickens creates a microcosm – the fictional world becomes a miniature version of reality.

A verb modifier like *defiled* (l. 2), an adjective modifier like *dirty* and the abstract noun *pollution* (l. 3) all have negative **connotations**. They evoke an atmosphere that is unpleasant, reinforced by verbs like *wheezing* (l. 7), adverbs like *cruelly* (l. 8) and adjectives like *wrathful* (l. 8). Everyone becomes detached, as though suspended in a balloon – all sense of community has gone. The second paragraph then uses **superlatives** like *rawest, densest* (l. 13) and *muddiest* (l. 14) to stress that the worst of all conditions are to be found at Temple Bar (l. 15). By using the prepositional phrase *at the very heart of* (l. 16) Dickens indicates that the fog has more than just a descriptive purpose: it actually becomes **symbolic** of the legal process as a whole.

In evoking this atmosphere, Dickens aims to create a parallel between the landscape and people obscured by literal fog and the legal system. The Law has its own symbolic 'fog' – its impenetrable processes confuse and bewilder the people caught up in its impersonal and uncaring systems.

The extract from Dickens's *Bleak House* uses **repetition** as the main technique for creating an evocative atmosphere. Recurring lexis and syntactical patterns draw attention to the central theme: the deceptive nature of the Law. Writers can also exploit less explicit ways of evoking a mood, such as using modifiers. The choice of words with positive or negative connotations can influence readers, persuading them to immerse themselves in, or distance themselves from, the scene and the events occurring there.

The interaction of characters in a certain context can also create an evocative scene. By focusing on a particular environment, the characters in it, and the way it affects them, it is possible to arouse the reader's emotions.

1 They worked together, coming and going, in a rhythm, which carried their feet and
their bodies in tune. She stooped, she lifted the burden of sheaves, she turned her
face to the dimness where he was, and went with her burden over the stubble.
She hesitated, set down her sheaves, there was a swish and hiss of mingling oats,
5 he was drawing near, and she must turn again. And there was the flaring moon
laying bare her bosom again, making her drift and ebb like a wave.
     He worked steadily, engrossed, threading backwards and forwards like a shuttle
across the strip of cleared stubble, weaving the long line of riding shocks, nearer
and nearer to the shadowy trees, threading his sheaves with hers.
10   And always, she was gone before he came. As he came, she drew away, as he
drew away, she came. Were they never to meet? Gradually a low, deep-sounding
will in him vibrated to her, tried to set her in accord, tried to bring her gradually to
him, to a meeting, till they should be together, till they should meet as the sheaves
that swished together.

D. H. Lawrence (1885–1930), The Rainbow

The atmosphere is created here by the relationship between the characters,
their environment and their task. Harvesting has **connotations** of abundance
and fertility, yet the two characters cannot meet – the very pattern of their task
keeps them separate. Although they are in harmony physically, they are distanced
emotionally. The fact that the characters are unnamed in the extract reinforces
this sense of their detachment – they become secondary to the task they must
complete.

The natural world is given a concrete presence by the **lexical set** that is developed: nouns like *sheaves* (l. 2), *shocks* (l. 8), *stubble* (l. 3) and *oats* (l. 4) all create the
background against which the reader sees the man and the woman. The symbolic
fruitfulness of the harvest mirrors the sexual urges of the man and woman – their
inability to relate to each other is therefore ironic. The noun phrase *the flaring
moon* (l. 5) makes the irony more explicit: traditionally, the moon represents passion, but here, ironically, it makes the woman indistinct. By using the verbs *drift
and ebb* (l. 6), Lawrence is able to contrast the solidity and reality of their task with
the ephemeral nature of their relationship.

The **lexis** is chosen to portray the ritual nature of their work: prepositional
phrases like *in a rhythm* (l. 1) and *in tune* (l. 2) indicate the harmony they achieve.
A sense of balance is also developed through the **antithesis** of verbs like *stooped*
and *lifted* (l. 2) and adverbs like *backwards* and *forwards* (l. 7). References to light
and dark enhance the idea of opposition: nouns like *dimness* (l. 3) and *moon* (l. 5),
and modifiers like *flaring* (l. 5) and *shadowy* (l. 9). The contrast becomes symbolic
of the desire to meet which is not fulfilled.

The **rhetorical patterning** of the sentences helps to create the atmosphere.
The verbs are dynamic: *worked* (l. 1), *threading* (l. 7) and *weaving* (l. 8). The repetition of these and of the sentence structures mimics the repetitive nature of their
task:

```
 S        P       S     P              O              S      P      O       A
(She) (stooped), (she) (lifted) (the burden of sheaves), (she) (turned) (her face) (to the
dimness)                                                                    (ll. 2–3)

      A         S       P         A          S      P
(As he came), (she) (drew away), (as he drew away), (she) (came).           (ll. 10–11)
 SCl–ACl                          SCl–ACl
```

In contrast to their actions, the author uses **free indirect thought** in the man's question: *Were they never to meet?* (l. 11). The move from declarative to interrogative **mood** changes the pace and makes the atmosphere more dramatic because the reader knows that the man is not happy at the distance which remains between himself and the woman. The **repetition** of the tentative verb *tried* (l. 12) marks his attempts to alter the pattern. The use of the subordinating conjunction *till* and the modal *should* (l. 14), however, remind the reader that any disruption to the pattern is hypothetical.

The **figurative language** intensifies the atmosphere because it is poetic. Lawrence uses natural imagery that is appropriate to the context: the woman is compared to a wave; the man thinks of meeting the woman just as the sheaves meet. Juxtaposed with these is the image of the *shuttle* (l. 7). By choosing an industrial comparison, the writer creates a conflict within the literary language which is a parallel to the conflict between the man and woman. They are divided by their work and this is symbolically represented by the shuttle of a loom threading backwards and forwards creating a patterned material.

The power of this writing lies in its intensity. Lawrence uses language poetically and thus creates a scene that is out of the ordinary. The reader is drawn into the pattern of the work, into the inability of the man and the woman to approach each other, by the lexical choices and syntactical patterns.

To experiment with language

By using non-standard language, writers can intensify the effect of the fictional world on the reader. Using variations in language for different characters makes them more authentic and places them more specifically in a time and a place.

Traditionally, non-standard language was confined to dialogue in novels. It was used to reflect the accent and dialect of characters.

> 1 'I'm a goin' to leave you, Samivel my boy, and there's no telling ven I shall see you
> again. Your mother-in-law may ha' been too much for me, or a thousand things
> may have happened by the time you next hears any news o' the celebrated Mr
> Veller o' the Bell Savage. The family name depends wery much upon you, Samivel,
> 5 and I hope you'll do wot's right by it … If ever you gets to up'ards o' fifty, and feels
> disposed to go a marryin' anybody – no matter who – jist you shut yourself up in
> your own room, if you've got one, and pison yourself off hand … '
>
> Charles Dickens, *The Pickwick Papers*

In this example, Dickens is interested in conveying the 'sound' or accent of Samuel Weller's father. There is no unrecognisable lexis, but the spellings are manipulated in order to reflect the pronunciation. The phoneme /w/ is pronounced /v/: *ven* (l. 1); and the phoneme /v/ is pronounced /w/: *wery* (l. 4). Other features mirror the contracted nature of spoken language: *o'* (l. 3) = 'of'; *goin'* (l. 1) = 'going'; *up'ards* (l. 5) = 'upwards'; and *ha'* (l. 2) = 'have'. The spelling of *jist* (l. 6) and *pison* (l. 7) aim to indicate the way in which the RP vowel sounds /ʌ/ and /ɔɪ/ have been altered. The spelling of *wot* (l. 5) tries to mirror the traditional pronunciation in a phonetic-like simplification. Dialect features can be seen in the use of the third person singular verb inflection -*s* with a second person pronoun, *you … hears* (l. 3), *you gets* and *you…feels* (l. 5), and in the use of the archaic present participle *a goin'* (l. 1) and *a marryin'* (l. 6).

Where Dickens deviates from the standard English of his own narrative, the effect is often intentionally comic. The characters who speak using non-standard language are invariably of a lower social class and the features chosen reflect this status. Here the character speaking is a working-class father giving homely advice to his son – the content itself is comic, but when delivered in the non-standard form that Dickens chooses, the comedy is intensified.

Hardy uses non-standard language in more serious contexts: his aim is to create an authentic regional and social background for his characters.

> 'Bring on that water, will ye, you idle young harlican!'
>
> Thomas Hardy (1840–1928), *Jude the Obscure*

The use of the archaic second person pronoun *ye* is representative of the tone here – the address is informal and the speaker is in a position of superiority. The noun *harlican* is a dialect term of abuse, reinforcing the idea that the addressee is being treated as an inferior.

The movement in the twentieth century towards more realistic novels meant that it was important to write in a style appropriate to the characters and settings. Traditionally, minor characters used dialect, but as writers experimented non-standard language became an important means of characterisation. Some writers chose to write whole novels in non-standard English. Although the effects could still be comic, more often writers had serious intentions.

The choice of a particular form of language can make the fictional world more credible, helping the reader to identify and empathise with the characters. In first person narratives, the use of non-standard language appropriate to the *I* character clearly marks the viewpoint. It reminds readers that they are being presented with a subjective interpretation of events.

In *The Color Purple*, Alice Walker's main character is Celie, a young Black American girl living in the South in the 1920s and 1930s. The novel is a first person narrative, using a sequence of Celie's letters as a record of her life. Walker chooses to use non-standard English throughout the novel because it is a form of language more appropriate to Celie than standard English.

> 1 Dear God,
>   Shug Avery is coming to town! She coming with her orkestra. She going to sing in the Lucky Star out on Coalman road. Mr. ——— going to hear her. He dress all up in front the glass, look at himself, then undress and dress all over again. He
> 5 slick back his hair with pomade, then wash it out again. He been spitting on his shoes and hitting it with a quick rag.
>   He tell me, Wash this. Iron that. Look for this. Look for that. Find this. Find that …
>   I move round darning and ironing, find hanskers. Anything happening? I ast.
>   What you mean? he say, like he mad. Just trying to git some of the hick farmer
> 10 off myself. Any other woman be glad.
>   I'm is glad, I say.
>   What you mean? he ast.
>   You looks nice, I say. Any woman be proud.
>   You think so? he say …
>
> Alice Walker (1944–), *The Color Purple*

Alice Walker chooses to write in Black American English since this is a form of English appropriate for Celie. The list below summarises the main non-standard linguistic features.

- Some non-standard spellings reflect pronunciation: *git* (l. 9); *ast* (l. 8). For others, while pronunciation remains the same, traditional orthography is simplified: *orkestra* (l. 2).
- Some words are part of the Black English dialect and are therefore unfamiliar: *hanskers* (l. 8).
- Some words are representative of American English rather than British English: *glass* (l. 4) for 'mirror'.
- The noun phrase *a quick rag* (l. 6) is unusual – in Standard English the adverb 'quickly' would have been used following the pronoun *it*, describing the movement rather than the rag itself.
- Although in narrative the simple past tense is usual, most third person singular verbs here use the base form – since Black English dialects often omit verb suffixes, it is not possible to be certain which tense is intended: *He dress* (l. 3); *He slick* (ll. 4–5); *He tell me* (l. 7).
- Auxiliaries are often used non-standardly or omitted: *She coming* (l. 2); *He been spitting* (l. 5); *I'm is glad* (l. 11). When the auxiliary *to be* is included, it seems to be used to give emphasis.
- Modal auxiliaries are also omitted: *Any other woman be glad* (l. 10).
- Interrogatives are formed without the dummy auxiliary *do*: *What you mean?* (l. 9); *You think so?* (l. 14).
- Some prepositions are used non-standardly: *in front the glass* (l. 4).

A first person narrative always offers a limited point of view and here the reader is immediately aware of this both because of the dialect and because of the choice of a letter format. However, by using this particular form and structure of English, Walker gives Celie an appropriate means of self-expression. The short sentences, the reports of what has been said and the literal nature of the content make the novel immediate and dramatic. Although Celie is uneducated, the way she records her observations and experiences is distinctive. Walker has created a 'real' character and the reader can believe in Celie because she is so obviously a product of the society in which she lives.

Other writers aim to alienate their reader through their choice of language and style. By writing in an unfamiliar form of English, authors can distance readers, forcing them to learn something about both the fictional and the real world.

Anthony Burgess's novel *A Clockwork Orange* uses a partially made-up language to convey the kind of society he visualised for the future.

1 'What's it going to be then, eh?'
  There was me, that is Alex, and my three droogs, that is Pete, Georgie, and Dim, Dim being really dim, and we sat in the Korova Milkbar making our rassoodocks what to do with the evening, a flip dark chill winter bastard though dry …
5 Our pockets were full of deng, so there was no real need from the point of view of crasting any more pretty polly to tolchock some old veck in an alley and viddy him swim in his blood while we counted the takings and divided by four, nor to do the ultra-violent on some shivering starry grey-haired ptitsa in a shop and go

smecking off with the till's guts. But, as they say, money isn't everything.

10   The four of us were dressed in the height of fashion, which in those days was a pair of black very tight tights with the old jelly mould, as we called it, fitting on the crotch underneath the tights, this being to protect and also a sort of design you could viddy clear enough in a certain light … We wore our hair not too long and we had flip horrorshow boots for kicking.

Anthony Burgess (John Burgess Wilson, 1917–), A Clockwork Orange

Much of the text is in Standard English, but certain nouns, adjectives, verbs and adverbs are created specifically for the novel. Many of the non-standard words are of Russian origin. Readers can use their instinctive knowledge of English linguistic structures to guess at the word class of words and to some extent the context can hint at the meaning, but the glossary provided at the back of the novel is an essential part of the decoding process. The list that follows suggests some of the ways in which a reader can begin to decipher Burgess's code:

▸ A noun can be preceded by a determiner and can take an -*s* inflection to mark the plural: *droogs* (l. 2) for 'friends'; *rassoodocks* (l. 3) for 'minds'; *ptitsa* (l. 8) for 'chick'; *deng* (l. 5) for 'money'; *veck* (l. 6) for 'man'.

▸ Verbs can take an -*ing* inflection: *crasting* (l. 6) for 'stealing'; *smecking* (l. 9) for 'laughing'.

▸ A verb infinitive is preceded by the preposition *to*: *to tolchock* (l. 6) for 'to hit' or 'to beat'.

▸ A lexical verb follows a modal auxiliary: *could viddy* (l. 13) for 'could see'.

▸ Adjectives can pre-modify nouns in a noun phrase: *flip* (l. 4) for 'wild'; *starry* (l. 8) for 'ancient'; *horrorshow* (l. 14) for 'good'.

Burgess uses these unusual words in familiar linguistic patterns and therefore the reader can begin to recognise and understand them. Other linguistic games are played too: rhyming slang is used, such as *pretty polly* (l. 6) for 'lolly' or 'money'; and the Standard English associations of a word are inverted – *horrorshow* (l. 14) will probably have negative connotations for the reader, but in this society 'bad' has become 'good'.

The language here is the language of youth. It is a coded form of communication which clearly marks out insiders and outsiders. The novel is about a violent drug-orientated society and Burgess wants to show the reader the way in which language can conceal the truth about what is happening. By using a unique form of English, Burgess forces the reader to remain outside the fictional world he has created – it is very difficult for readers to immerse themselves in the society and its violence because they have to concentrate so hard on the language. Screening of the film version was banned because people were concerned that viewers would do no more than relish the violence. Once the barrier of the created language was removed so that audiences could understand what was going on, the process of alienation itself was removed. Instead of conveying a warning about the potential violence of society, the film actually seemed to promote violence. This shows that the Nadsat language (the teenage vernacular which Burgess' first person narrator uses to tell his story) is absolutely central to the novel – it creates a distinct group within society which lives by its own rules and has its own cultural and social customs.

Debra Chase is a second-rate model, appearing in second-rate beauty contests, but she is unaware of her own limitations. Her purpose in Keith Waterhouse's novel, *Bimbo*, is to correct the untruths told about her in a tabloid paper, the *Sunday Shocker*, but her own version of events appears to be equally sensational.

Read through the extract below and comment on the non-standard language used and the writer's purpose in choosing it.

Chap One

MY EARLY LIVELIHOOD

1

Now it can be told. The biggest majority of the Debra Chase By Herself series in the *Sunday Shocker* which I am sposed to of written was a load of rubbish, a virago of
5 lies from start to finish.

Frinstance it is just not true that I had one-night stands with half the Seathorpe Wanderers team before I was seventeen. If it is of any concedable interest I did not even meet most of the lads until I had been selected Miss South-east Coast and that was when I was eighteen at least as I can prove.

10 Not true that after sex romps with playboy MP Sir Monty Pratt – The Sir as I always called him – I threatenised I would swallow a whole bottle of aspirin to stop him bringing our sizzling romance to an end. I do not even like aspirin, it just so happens it always gives me a headache. All right, so at the death The Sir was pressured into choosing between I and his wife Pussy as all the world now knows – but Debra
15 Chase is still alive and kicking, thank you very much.

And it is defnitely not true that me and rival model Suzie Dawn, reel name Norma Borridge, fought like alley cats over super soap stud Den Dobbs, two-timing minicab driver Terry of the chart-topping series The Brummies, whose reel-life scorching romance with barmaid Sally – raven-haired sexpot Donna Matthews – was the cause
20 of a love-tug punch-up with burly boy friend Bruce Bridges, ex-welterweight boxer who is now a top DJ.

Keith Waterhouse (1929–), *Bimbo*

COMMENTARY

Keith Waterhouse uses a form of English that closely resembles spoken language in order to characterise his first person narrator appropriately. **Colloquial noun phrases** like *a load of rubbish* (l. 4), *one-night stands* (l. 6) and *most of the lads* (l. 8) are typical of informal spoken discourse. Waterhouse also uses **non-standard spellings** to reflect the way in which Debra pronounces words: *sposed* (l. 4), *Frinstance* (l. 6) and *defnitely* (l. 16) show the way in which informal speech elides certain sounds. This elision has an effect on the grammar of Debra's speech when the auxiliary verb 'have', used to construct the perfect aspect in the verb phrase 'have written', becomes *of* (l. 4). In speech, the auxiliary 'have' is pronounced as the phonemes /əv/ and many people mistake it for the preposition *of*.

The language is clearly influenced by the **tabloid newspapers** – Debra dramatises events by using the language of the tabloids. The first chapter opens with a **marked theme**:

A   S   P
(Now) (it) (can be told). (l. 3)

This immediately sets the **tone** and prepares the reader for what is to follow. The stories about the Seathorpe Wanderers, Sir Monty Pratt and the actors in the soap, however, are an anticlimax – the writer wants readers to recognise Debra's limitations even if she cannot see them herself. She sometimes writes in the telegraphic style of headlines: *Not true that...* (l. 10). The **noun phrases** are often complex with sequences of modifiers:

m		h		m	m	h	q
raven-haired	sexpot (l. 19)			a	whole	bottle of aspirin	(l. 11)
Adj	V	N		det	Adj	N	PrepP

m	m	h	q	
reel-life	scorching	romance	with barmaid Sally	(ll. 18–19)
Adj	N	V	N	PrepP

Words typical of tabloids are chosen: modifiers like the present participles *sizzling* (l. 12) and *scorching* (l. 18) describing the head noun *romance* develop the cliché of passion as a fire; the noun phrase *sex romps* (l. 10) uses tabloid 'code' words which are used as a shorthand to signify immediately to the reader a certain kind of affair. The juxtaposition of the nouns *playboy* and *MP* (l. 10) are also typical of tabloidese since they imply something sensational: the authority of a politician is undermined when placed in the sexual context associated with a playboy. Other common tabloid linguistic features are seen in the frequent use of compound words like *love-tug punch-up* (l. 20) and *two-timing mini-cab driver* (ll. 17–18) and in the alliteration of *super soap stud Den Dobbs* (l. 17) and *burly boy friend Bruce Bridges* (l. 20).

The **grammar** is similarly influenced by the tabloids. Sentences are loosely structured – conjunctions are used in the initial position and parenthesis is common:

dumS	P		C	(S)
(And) (it) (is) (defnitely not true) (that me and rival model ... fought like alley cats over				
conj		neg	SCl–NCl	

super soap stud Den Dobbs ... whose reel-life scorching romance ... was the cause
SCl–RelCl

of a love-tug punch-up with burly boy friend Bruce Bridges ... who is now ...)
SCl–RelCl   (ll. 16–21)

Finally, the language is often **idiosyncratic** – it is specifically marked by features that are typical of Debra as an individual. She tries to make herself seem educated by using long words, but often she uses them inappropriately. MALAPROPISMS (similar words used mistakenly in the wrong contexts) like *virago* (l. 4) for 'farrago' and *concedable* (l. 7) for 'conceivable' and PLEONASMS (words used unnecessarily to convey meaning) like *biggest majority* (l. 3) suggest that Debra is not well read. She lengthens words by adding the inflection *-ised* when it is not needed: *threatenised* (l. 11) for 'threatened'. She uses common clichés like *alive and kicking* (l. 15), *fought like alley cats* (l. 17) and *at the death* (l. 13). Grammatically, Debra confuses her subject and object pronouns, using *I and his wife* (l. 14) instead of the object pronoun *me*; and *me and rival model Suzie Dawn* (l. 16) instead of the subject pronoun *I*. All these features suggest that Debra is more familiar with spoken rather than written forms of language, but that she is trying to write in a formal way.

Waterhouse makes Debra seem a somewhat comic character, but the reader is not meant to dislike her. She is sincere in what she writes and is trying to find an appropriate formal style for her memoirs. Although she fails, the reader is aware that society has made her what she is – reading the tabloids and living in a society in which informal spoken language takes precedence over written language, it is inevitable that she writes as she does. Above all, the reader is aware of her liveliness and her basic honesty, and these are more important characteristics than any linguistic inaccuracies.

The form of English Waterhouse has chosen for this first person narrative makes Debra Chase a more realistic character, helping the reader to empathise with her. It makes the fictional world of the novel more credible and allows Waterhouse to suggest something about the nature of Late Modern English itself.

13.5 What to look for in the language of narrative prose

The following checklist can be used to identify key features in examples of prose. You will not find all of the features in every extract, but the list can be used as a guide. The points made are general, so discussion of specific examples will need to be adapted to take account of the specific context and authorial purpose. Remember that you need to evaluate the effect of the features you identify, exploring the ways in which they create meaning.

The following are helpful questions to ask.

Register
1 What is the **mode**?
    - written.
2 What is the **manner**?
    - formal or informal relationship between writer and reader?
    - personal or impersonal relationship?
    - authorial intention (to characterise, describe a place or time, create an atmosphere, convey a message, etc.)?
3 What is the **field**?
    - subject matter?
    - linked to the audience, purpose and context?

Point of view
1 Does the author choose a
    - first person narrative to give a direct insight into a character's mind? (limitations of understanding? signs of bias?)
    - third person narrative to provide an omniscient view of events and characters? (intrusive or unintrusive? informing or evaluating?)
2 Is the narrator **reliable** or **unreliable**?
    - can readers rely on the version of events provided by the narrator or should they mistrust her or him?
3 Are there any examples of **interior monologue** or **stream of consciousness**?
    - are the characters' thoughts ordered or random?

Lexis

1 What kinds of **words** are used?
   * simple or complicated?
   * formal or colloquial?
   * descriptive or evaluative?
   * modern or archaic?
2 Are there any examples of **subject-specific words** or specific **lexical sets**?
3 Has the writer used **non-standard language**?
   * dialect?
   * idiosyncratic linguistic choices?
   * code language identifying insiders and outsiders?
4 Are the **nouns concrete** (to do with the physical environment) or **abstract** (linked to thought or spiritual matters)?
5 Is the **naming of characters** important?
   * first names, surnames, titles?
   * are any names omitted on purpose?
6 Do any words have significant **connotations**?
7 What function do the **modifiers** have?
   * visual and physical to set the scene or to describe a character?
   * psychological to communicate a particular state of mind?
   * emotive to create the mood?
   * evaluative to make judgements?
8 What kinds of actions and processes do the **verbs** describe?

Speech and thought

1 Does the writer use **direct speech** or **thought** to let the characters speak for themselves?
2 Does the writer use **indirect speech** or **thought** to interpret or comment on what characters say?
3 Does the writer use **free indirect speech** or **thought** both to intervene and to give the true sense of a character's words?

Grammar

1 What kind of **grammar** is used?
   * standard or non-standard?
   * formal or informal?
   * modern or archaic?
2 Are there any occasions when the **tense** changes from the simple past?
   * present tense for direct speech or authorial comment, or for dramatic effect?
   * future time to predict events or make contrasts?
3 Do changes of **mood** create any interesting effects?
4 Is the **sentence structure** varied?
   * simple and compound, to create a sense of immediacy or to characterise a child or a childlike individual?
   * complex, to develop a reflective mood, to relate complex events, or to develop a complicated character?
   * minor, to create emphasis or to imitate spoken language?

Style

1 How does the writer persuade the reader to believe in the fictional world created?

2 Does the writer use **sentence organisation** to emphasise certain elements?
   + branching to control the order of information and change the pace?
   + marked themes to focus attention on important information?
   + passive voice to throw emphasis onto the object or to conceal the subject?
   + end focus to delay an important part of the sentence?

3 Does the writer use **images** to give the fictional world physical presence?
   + visual? auditory? tactile?

4 Are there any **literary devices**?
   + metaphors or similes to evoke emotive associations?
   + symbols to encourage the reader to make connections?
   + personification to bring a landscape to life?
   + irony to challenge our relationship with the text?

5 Is **sound patterning** used to underpin the meaning or to enhance the emotional effect of the text?
   + alliteration? assonance? sibilance?
   + plosives? fricatives?

6 Are there any **rhetorical devices**?
   + antithesis to develop contrasts in atmosphere, character, events, settings?
   + listing to build to a climax or an anti-climax?
   + patterning to draw attention to similar or contrasting ideas?
   + repetition to highlight a key feature?

Summary

The **function** of prose is to entertain, but writers can also implicitly or explicitly convey a message about society or life.

The language of fictional prose is very **varied** because writers can manipulate language in order to make their fictional worlds more powerful and credible. Non-standard language can be used to add depth to characterisation, word class boundaries can be broken to create dramatic effects, and poetic techniques can be used to build up the atmosphere.

Authorial intention dictates the kinds of linguistic and stylistic choices made, and the kind of relationship created with the reader.

Chapter 14

The language of literature
– poetry

14.1 The nature of poetry

Like prose, **POETRY** cannot be neatly categorised. Poets can choose a range of structures and techniques; they can manipulate language; and they can, at times, seem almost to invent a special language in which to express their ideas and their individuality. Poetry is a very disciplined genre because of the restrictions that poetic form places on poets. Because thoughts are often compressed into a short space, it can be difficult for readers to understand the message conveyed by a particular poem. Equally, because poets are creating something unique, the language of poetry can deviate from generally observed rules. **POETIC LICENCE** allows poets to experiment: parts of words may be omitted; word order can be altered; archaisms and dialect can be used; the word classes of words can be changed; and lexical and syntactical patterns can be used to reinforce the meaning.

14.2 The function of poetry

The language of poetry is both **poetic** and **expressive**. It has a wide range of functions: it can **entertain, arouse emotions** and **provoke thought**; it can **describe**, **evaluate** or **inform**. The lexis can be poetic and intense, or ordinary and conversational.

By considering the linguistic and stylistic features of a poem it is possible to come to conclusions about the poet's intentions. The content, form and style will give the reader clues to the meaning and often there will be an underlying message or theme which is revealed only on close reading.

14.3 Features of poetry

Each poem is distinctive, so it is important to identify what the poet is trying to convey to the reader and the linguistic and stylistic techniques used to do this. It is not possible to be prescriptive about the kinds of features to comment on, but certain devices and forms are worth looking out for.

The **manner** can be formal or informal, depending upon the relationship that the poet wants to create with the reader. Because poets often convey their message in a concise way, the language of poetry tends to be far more intense than that of everyday conversation. The language of traditional poetry tends to be concentrated and heightened, but there are many examples of poems that aim to mirror the language of speech, creating a very different tone.

Form and structure

The **form** and **structure** tell the reader something about the poet's intentions. STANZA LENGTH and LINE LENGTH, for instance, are chosen to best convey a poem's message. By choosing a particular format, poets can reinforce their messages through the structure. It is therefore useful to be able to identify some of the main poetic structures.

Ballads

BALLADS date back to the **oral tradition** of the late Middle Ages. They are poems in which an impersonal narrator tells a story – the focus is on action and dialogue rather than on interpretative comment. They usually begin abruptly at a point when a tragic event of some kind is about to take place. This single episode is the focus for the whole poem, with only minimal background detail provided. They are usually very dramatic and the poet creates a sense of intensity and immediacy both through the content and the style.

The structure is usually straightforward: the story is told in rhyming QUATRAINS (four-lined stanzas); the language is simple; the poets draw on stock phrases; and ballads are often written in dialect. **Repetition** is used to make the poems memorable – this is typical of poems written in the oral tradition.

Sonnets

SONNETS are fourteen-line poems which have a very structured rhyme scheme and rhythm (usually **iambic pentameter**). Because the form is so disciplined, poets are forced to craft their ideas. Often the subject matter deals with love, with the problems of life or with questions of disorder – poets then use the patterned structure to create an ordered response to complex issues. There are two main kinds of sonnet: the **Petrarchan** (Italian) and the **Shakespearean** (English).

The **PETRARCHAN SONNET** divides the fourteen lines into an **octave** (eight lines) and a **sestet** (six lines), using the rhyme scheme abbaabba cdecde or abbaabba cdcdcd. The octave sets out the problem and the sestet is used to resolve it. The turning point acts as a pivot on which the two sections are balanced – the pause is called the **VOLTA**. The two stanzas allow the poet to explore an issue and reflect or change direction.

The **SHAKESPEAREAN SONNET** divides the lines into three **quatrains** and a **couplet**, using the rhyme scheme abab cdcd efef gg. The quatrains present the ideas or themes to be developed and the final couplet summarises the central theme, rounding off the argument and resolving the tension created.

Odes

ODES are elaborate lyrical poems addressed to a person, a thing or an abstraction able to transcend the problems of life. They may consist of straightforward praise of their subject or they may be more hesitant and philosophical; they may focus on positive celebration or negative feelings. Because they deal with difficult ideas and involved arguments, odes tend to be complex, drawing on many images in a single stanza. The poet often tries to convey an awareness of being trapped in everyday difficulties and of the difference between the ideal and the real. Elevated lexis is used to create a sense of things that transcend the mundane and images are juxtaposed to create a sense of the harsher realities of life.

Blank verse

BLANK VERSE is often used for long narrative poems or lyric poems in which a poet is thinking in a discursive way. It does not have an obvious overall pattern or structure as other poetic forms do, but despite the fact that it does not rhyme, blank verse is a very disciplined form in which each line has ten syllables with five stresses (an **iambic** pattern). Its rhythms are closer to speech than other poetic forms, but it is recognisably more stylised than speech or prose. Although it appears to be less formally contrived than a poem that rhymes, the regularity of the verse implies a search for order. The sentence structure is often complex and the imagery is fully developed.

> We love the things we love for what they are.
>
> Robert Frost (1874–1963), extract from 'Hyla Brook'

Free verse

FREE VERSE is often chosen by modern poets to confront a disorganised world because it acknowledges the untidiness of life and the mind. It is written in irregular lines and has no regular **metre** (the pattern of stressed and unstressed syllables). Rhyme is used infrequently, but repetition of words or phrases is often significant in providing an internal pattern.

Poetic devices

Poets use the same kinds of literary and rhetorical devices common in other varieties of English, but also some distinctive **POETIC DEVICES** particular to poetry.

End stop

An **END STOP** describes a line of verse in which a grammatical break coincides with the end of a line. It is often marked by punctuation.

> Some say the world will end in fire,
> Some say in ice.
>
> Robert Frost, extract from 'Fire and Ice'

Enjambement

ENJAMBEMENT describes a line of verse in which the grammatical structures run on from line to line. This allows the poet to defeat the reader's expectations – the meaning is not complete at the end of the line; punctuation is not used to make the reader pause. This technique can be used to reinforce a poem's meaning.

> My heart leaps up when I behold
>   A rainbow in the sky;
>
> William Wordsworth (1770–1850), extract from 'My Heart Leaps Up'

Metre

Poetic **METRE** is the pattern of stressed and unstressed syllables in a line of poetry. It is one way in which a poet can order language to make it more meaningful. By analysing the metre, a reader can appreciate how the poet is using stress patterns to convey meaning. Variations in the pattern may mark changes in the mood or the poet's attitude.

There are five basic patterns of stress. Stressed syllables are marked ´ while unstressed syllables are marked ˘.

- **IAMBIC**: one unstressed syllable is followed by one stressed syllable (dĕ|líght, ă|bóut):

> Sweet day, sŏ cóol, sŏ cálm, sŏ bríght
>
> George Herbert (1593–1633), extract from 'Virtue'

- **TROCHAIC**: one stressed syllable is followed by one unstressed syllable (gá|thĕr, féel|ĭng).

> Sóft ănd éasў ĭs thў crádlĕ
> Coárse ănd hárd thў Sáviŏur láy.

- **DACTYLIC**: one stressed syllable is followed by two unstressed syllables (há|ppĭ|nĕss, sén|tĭ|mĕnt).

> Síng ĭt ăll mérrĭlў

- **ANAPAESTIC**: two unstressed syllables are followed by one stressed syllable (ĭn|tĕr|rúpt, dĭs|ă|ppéar).

> Wĕ áre théy whŏ rĭde éarlў ŏr láte
>
> J. E. Flecker (1884–1915)

- **SPONDEE**: two stressed syllables (héart|bréak, wíne|gláss).

> Óne twó
> Buckle my shoe
> Threé fóur
> Knock at the door

Having identified the stress pattern, each line of poetry can then be divided into metrical **FEET** (groups of syllables forming metrical units). Each foot consists of a stressed syllable and any unstressed syllables that accompany it. The foot will therefore be iambic, trochaic, and so on.

- 1 foot = **monometer**
- 2 feet = **dimeter**
- 3 feet = **trimeter**
- 4 feet = **tetrameter**
- 5 feet = **pentameter**
- 6 feet = **hexameter**
- 7 feet = **heptameter**
- 8 feet = **octameter**

To SCAN a line of poetry it is necessary first to decide the pattern of the stress, then to count the number of stressed syllables to determine the number of feet, and finally to combine the two.

> She lived | in storm | and strife,
> Her soul | had such | desire
> For what | proud death | may bring
> That it | could not | endure
> The com|mon good | of life
>
> William Butler Yeats (1865–1939), extract from 'That the Night Come'

- stress pattern: ˘ ˘ ´
- number of stresses per line: *three*
- metre: *iambic trimeter.*

> Learn to | speak first, | then to | woo; to | wooing | much per|taineth;
> He that | courts us, | wanting | art, soon | falters | when he | feigneth
>
> Thomas Campion (1567–1620), extract from 'Think'st Thou to Seduce Me Then'

- stress pattern: ´ ˘
- number of stresses per line: *seven*
- metre: *trochaic heptameter.*

This kind of patterning makes poetry very different from speech. If poets want to mimic the rhythms of informal conversation, they choose iambic pentameter because the pattern it creates is closer to the spontaneity of speech.

Pause

The CAESURA (a break or pause in a line of verse) is very important in poetry. It is used to achieve a degree of variety in the metre and rhythm: it can make verse formal and stylised, or it can relax rigid metrical patterns and mimic the rhythms of speech. The position of a caesura is often marked by punctuation, but the natural rhythms of language can also dictate a pause.

> To be or not to be: [caesura] that is the question.
>
> William Shakespeare (1564–1616), *Hamlet*

Rhythm

The RHYTHM of a poem is governed by the language and the way we speak it. It is closely linked to semantics, as meaning dictates the way lines are read. In everyday speech, lexical words bear the **stress** and grammatical or function words are **unstressed**. In poetry, stress patterns are directly linked to metre as well as to the natural stress of words.

Lexical choice

The **lexical choice (DICTION)** depends upon the context and the content. Inevitably, it will determine the relationship created between reader and poet: formal or informal; familiar or polite; personal or impersonal. **Abstract** or **concrete nouns** may be chosen, depending on the subject matter. **Modifiers** can be used to describe places or people in detail, to arouse the reader's emotions, or to evaluate and judge. The kinds of actions or processes the **verbs** describe and the form they take can also tell the reader something about the message the poet wishes to convey.

Dialect words can be used to create a certain social or regional atmosphere. ARCHAISMS can heighten the dignity and solemnity of the language – such lexical choices can remind the reader of the poetic and cultural traditions on which poetry draws. Poets can equally make their lexis very modern by using NEOLOGISMS (invented words) which give their writing a sense of individuality. Sometimes words can seem **incongruous** – poets borrow words from non-poetic registers in order to disrupt readers' expectations. **Collocations** can be disrupted as poets experiment, throwing new light on familiar things and forcing readers to reconsider things previously taken for granted.

Grammar

The **grammar** of poetry is sometimes complicated, particularly when poets manipulate language to conform to the restrictions of traditional poetic forms. Poetic licence equally allows poets to manipulate language structures to achieve distinctive end results. **Sentence structures** are therefore often complex and the omission of clause elements can make a poem difficult to understand.

Changes in **tense** or **mood** also indicate that the poet is highlighting something significant. **Cohesion** is used to establish exact connections because the compression of thought can make the syntax seem disjointed. **Pronoun referencing, ellipsis** and the use of **synonyms**, however, can make the imagery and message stand out more clearly.

Style

Sentence organisation allows a poet to rearrange clause elements in order to draw attention to important information. **Marked themes** are common in poetry because they change the focus and encourage readers to interpret the poem in a particular way. Similarly, **end focus** delays important information, forcing readers to wait. In some cases, however, the rearrangement of a sentence will be directly linked to the prosodic requirements of verse – a poet may need to invert clause elements in order to achieve a particular rhyme or rhythmic pattern.

Literary devices make the language of poetry intense, since poets use them to add layers of meaning beyond what the words on the page literally say. They clarify the poet's message and enhance the emotive impact. **Figurative language** can sometimes be difficult to interpret because poets can invent their own systems of references which readers may not immediately understand. **Images** are used to appeal to the senses, evoking atmosphere in a very tangible way. They can suggest meanings without the poet having to make them explicit. **Metaphors** and **similes** make the abstract concrete or the concrete abstract by referring to one thing either directly or indirectly in terms of another. **Symbols** help poets to widen the range of their references, whether they draw on commonly recognised symbols or create their own.

Sound patterning is fundamental to poetry since the aural quality of words is often as important as their meaning. Poets can evoke different tones through the kinds of sounds they choose: soft sounds can create a sensuous, poignant or reflective mood; harsh sounds can create a bitter, angry or authoritative tone. Alliteration, assonance and rhyme are key poetic devices that can be used to underpin the meaning.

Rhetorical devices also provide extra layers of meaning. **Antithesis** develops contrasts in the language that can be used to establish a theme, change the tone or move a poem in a new direction. **Listing** can be expansive or reductive, allowing the poet to present us with an inspiring range of possibilities or a claustrophobic sense of entrapment. The use of co-ordinators (syndetic listing) or their absence (asyndetic listing) can affect the way we respond to a list. Similarly, the use of a climax or an anti-climax can affect the mood of a poem. **Repetition** and **patterning** are common in poetry because of the tightly structured nature of poetic form. Line length, syllabic patterning of weak/strong syllables, stanza structure and rhyme can restrict the ways in which poets use language – every word therefore has to fulfil a particular semantic or phonological function. Repetition of key words and distinctive linguistic or grammatical patterns will directly underpin the meaning and it is important to explore the effects they have.

Typography and layout

Typographical and **structural features** can also be important in poetry. Variations in **typeface** or **layout** are significant in terms of the poet's intentions.

14.4 Types of poetic intention

To characterise

Poets, like prose writers, can present characters directly to readers or they can allow characters to present themselves; they can intervene and comment on characters or allow readers to make their own judgements from the information provided.

Physical description usually focuses on the external features of a character, but inevitably it also tells the reader something about the inner person too.

> *The Face in the Mirror*
>
> 1 Grey haunted eyes, absent-mindedly glaring
>   From wide, uneven orbits; one brow drooping
>   Somewhat over the eye
>   Because of a missile fragment still inhering,
> 5 Skin deep, as a foolish record of old-world fighting.
>
>   Crookedly broken nose – low tackling caused it;
>   Cheeks, furrowed; coarse grey hair, flying frenetic;
>   Forehead, wrinkled and high;
>   Jowls, prominent; ears, large; jaw, pugilistic;
> 10 Teeth, few; lips, full and ruddy; mouth, ascetic.

> I pause with razor poised, scowling derision
> At the mirrored man whose beard needs my attention,
> And once more ask him why
> He still stands ready, with a boy's presumption,
> 15 To court the queen in her high silk pavilion.

Robert Graves (1895–1985)

In this poem, the poet observes himself in the mirror and the physical features of his face become reminders of past experiences as a World War I soldier and as a sportsman. The **enjambement** (ll. 1–2, 2–3, etc.) seems to parallel the poet's gaze as he moves from eyes to brow to nose, assessing all the features he sees in the mirror. The **lexis** is concrete: *cheeks* (l. 7), *forehead* (l. 8) and *lips* (l. 10). **Modifiers** indicate the way in which the poet sees himself. Some are descriptive – adjectives like *grey* (l. 1), *large* (l. 9) and *high* (l. 8); others are evaluative – the verb modifier *haunted* (l. 1), the adjectives *pugilistic* (l. 9) meaning 'boxer-like' and *ascetic* (l. 10) meaning 'austere'. Together these provide a factual description of the poet and a sense of his character.

The **sentence structure** is disjointed and this reinforces the sense that the poet is immersed in an analysis of his reflection. The first two stanzas are made up of a sequence of head words which are usually both pre- and post-modified:

>   m   h
> (Crookedly broken) nose   (l. 6)
>   Adv   V   N

> m   m   h   q
> Grey haunted eyes, absent-mindedly glaring / From wide, uneven orbits   (ll. 1–2)
> Adj   V   N   SCl–NFCl   PrepP

Verbs are omitted and this draws attention to the things that Graves sees – the language has been reduced to the bare minimum, leaving only the words crucial to our understanding of the poet's external and internal nature:

>   S   C   S   C
> (Cheeks), (furrowed); (coarse grey hair), (flying frenetic);
>   S   C
> (Forehead), (wrinkled and high);   (ll. 7–8)

The omission of the stative verb *to be* intensifies the observations, and the use of predicative modifiers like *furrowed* and *frenetic* (l. 7) instead of attributive modifiers is more dramatic. As complements, they have more emphasis. A grammatically complete sentence is used in the second stanza:

>   S   P   O
> (low tackling) (caused) (it)   (l. 6)

Only in the third stanza does the context of the poem establish itself clearly. The use of the grammatically complete sentence here implies that the reader can now pause with the poet to reconsider the disjointed sequence of observations presented so far:

> S   P   A   A
> (I) (pause) (with razor poised), (scowling derision
>   SCl–NFCl
> At the mirrored man whose beard needs my attention)   (ll. 11–12)
>   SCl–RelCl

The poet does not draw on **figurative language** to describe his face, but the physical features do become symbolic of the life he has led and the effect it has had on him. **Rhetorical devices** are used to enhance the things that the poet sees in his face: **listing** forces the reader to follow the sequence of observations; **repetition** of the S and C clause elements gives a balanced and logical atmosphere to the self-examination. Both these rhetorical techniques suggest that the descriptions are honest and that the poet's self-evaluation can be trusted.

Although the poet basically uses **free verse**, the **rhyme pattern** is very structured: within each five-line stanza the four longer lines rhyme; the shorter third line rhymes from stanza to stanza:

- Stanza 1: the phonemes /ɪŋ/ are used to rhyme *glaring, drooping, inhering* and *fighting*.
- Stanzas 1–3: the phoneme /aɪ/ is used to rhyme *eye, high* and *why*.

The poem appears to be a straightforward physical description of what the poet sees in the mirror, but the reader is aware that it represents more than this. The compression of language and the patterned structure of the poem force the reader to contemplate more than just the appearance of the poet.

Poets can create imaginary characters or use real people as the basis for their poems. Rather than describing and interpreting these characters, poets can allow them to present themselves to the reader. The dramatic monologue gives life to characters because it allows a direct insight into their minds without using physical description. Often the character created will have some significance to the poet and in some ways the poem will be as much about the poet as about the character.

To set the scene

The language of a poem may provide concrete detail of a particular place, but beyond this the setting will often be symbolic, telling the reader something about the poet's mood, about a character's state of mind, or about the place itself. Changes in the description are significant because they indicate a change in mood or attitude.

The natural world can be a backdrop for the poet's experiences and by focusing on key details of place, a poet can recapture important moments. Recollecting a particular place therefore becomes a means of understanding oneself.

```
 1  And in the frosty season, when the sun
    Was set, and visible for many a mile
    The cottage windows blazed through twilight gloom,
    I heeded not their summons: happy time
 5  It was indeed for all of us – for me
    It was a time of rapture! Clear and loud
    The village clock tolled six, – I wheeled about,
    Proud and exulting like an untired horse
    That cares not for his home. All shod with steel,
10  We hissed along the polished ice in games
    Confederate, imitative of the chase
    And woodland pleasures, – the resounding horn,
```

The pack loud chiming, and the hunted hare.
So through the darkness and the cold we flew,
15 And not a voice was idle …

William Wordsworth, extract from 'The Prelude'

The **manner** is formal here, but because the poet is recalling a personal experience which in retrospect he considers to be important, a kind of intimacy is developed between the reader and the poet. The poem captures the exhilaration and excitement of the boy, but the lexical choices reflect the adult's understanding of the event.

The lexis appeals directly to the senses of sight and sound, re-creating the time, place and weather vividly. **Concrete nouns** make the physical environment seem real. References to the *cottage windows* (l. 3) and the *clock* (l. 7) remind the reader that the skating takes place not far from the boys' homes. Some abstract nouns like *season* (l. 1) and *darkness* (l. 14) build up a picture of the time and weather, but others like *summons* (l. 4) and *rapture* (l. 6) reflect the mature poet interpreting the experience. **Modifiers** are used to create the mood: for instance, adjectives like *happy* (l. 4), *Clear and loud* (l. 6) and *Proud* (l. 8); and present participles like *exulting* (l. 8), *resounding* (l. 12) and *chiming* (l. 13). The verb modifiers convey a sense of the children's activity and perpetual movement. The **connotations** of certain verbs develop this: the simple past tense verbs *wheeled* (l. 7) and *flew* (l. 14) suggest the children's freedom. However, juxtaposed with these are the verbs *tolled* (l. 7), with its connotations of a bell ringing to mark someone's death, and *blazed* (l. 3), with its connotations of security and comfort. Both these verbs are linked to the adult world which the children ignore during their games.

The **grammar** is formal, but Wordsworth does manipulate **word order** to draw attention to key words and phrases. In clauses like *I heeded not…* (l. 4) and *That cares not…* (l. 9), Wordsworth forms the negative without using the dummy auxiliary *do*. By choosing what may already have been an archaic structure, Wordsworth places emphasis on the negative *not*, making the children's refusal to respond to their parents' calls seem more purposeful. The **simple past tense** is used to retell the experience. The **pronouns** show that Wordsworth sees himself both as a member of the group and as an individual who experiences things more intensely than others. He juxtaposes the first person plural pronouns *we* (l. 10) and *us* (l. 5) with the first person singular pronouns *I* (l. 4) and *me* (l. 5) to mark his own difference. The **sentences** are mostly complex, although there are some simple structures:

<blockquote>

   A   S   P   A   A

(All shod with steel)/(We) (hissed) (along the polished ice) (in games/… pleasures)

(SIMPLE: ll. 9–12)

        A   A   A

(And) (in the frosty season) (when the sun/Was set) (and) (visible for many a mile/
conj   SCl–ACl   conj   SCl–ACl
                                                      S   P   O

The cottage windows blazed through twilight gloom)/(I) (heeded not) (their summons)

(COMPLEX: ll. 1–4)

</blockquote>

The many **adverbials** provide detail of the environment, and the use of a **conjunction** in the **initial position** makes the extract seem as though the poet is addressing the reader directly.

The **figurative language** helps Wordsworth to reveal the importance of the moment. The **simile** *like an untired horse* (l. 8) becomes a **metaphor** as the young Wordsworth is described as *Proud and exulting* (l. 8). It is developed in the reference to the children being *All shod with steel* (l. 9) and to their games as a hunt in which their voices are like *the resounding horn* (l. 12). They become a pack of hounds *loud chiming* (l. 13), chasing their prey *the hunted hare* (l. 13). The *cottage windows* (l. 3) are **symbolic** of the adult world which calls the children to come in for bed. The use of the **possessive determiner** *their* (l. 4) and the abstract noun *summons* (l. 4) with its legal **connotations** clearly divide the children from their parents.

Rhetorical patterning gives the extract its ordered structure. **Marked themes** reorganise clause elements to draw attention to important words or phrases:

> A   S   P   C
> (for me) / (It) (was) (a time of rapture) (ll. 5–6)

In this example, Wordsworth emphasises that the experience is different for him by placing the adverbial in the initial position. This structure also throws emphasis on the abstract noun *rapture* since it is given end focus. **Repetition** of key words like *time* reinforces the importance of the recaptured moment. **Phonological patterning** contributes to the sounds of the experience: **sibilance** mimics the sound of the skates on ice: *all shod with steel, / We hissed along the polished ice* (ll. 9–10); the **onomatopoeia** of *hissed* reinforces this; **alliteration** of the phoneme /h/ in *hunted hare* (l. 13) adds to the range of sounds.

Semantic patterning builds up the contrasts. **Antithesis** of the verb *blazed* (l. 3) and the noun *gloom* (l. 3) juxtaposes the security of the cottages compared with the growing darkness outside. The two noun phrases

> m   h   m h   q
> happy time (l. 4)   a time of rapture (l. 6)
> Adj   N   det N PrepP

juxtapose Wordsworth's intensified experience of the moment with the ordinary enjoyment of the other children.

The **form** and **structure** of the poem enable Wordsworth to give order to his memory. He chooses **blank verse** in which the **line lengths** are very regular, with ten syllables in each. The **metre** is **iambic pentameter** (one unstressed and one stressed syllable; five stresses or feet per line):

> The có|ttăge wínd|ŏws blázed | thrŏugh twí|light glóom
> Ĭ hée|děd nót | thĕir sú|mmŏns: há|ppy tíme …

ACTIVITY 14.1

Read the poem and comment on the techniques the poet uses to create a sense of time and place, and on the features that make this typical of the language of poetry.

> 1 The winter evening settles down
>   With smell of steaks in passageways.
>   Six o'clock.
>   The burnt-out ends of smoky days.
> 5 And now a gusty shower wraps

The grimy scraps
Of withered leaves about your feet
And newspapers from vacant lots;
The showers beat
10 On broken blinds and chimney-pots,
And at the corner of the street
A lonely cab-horse steams and stamps.

And then the lighting of the lamps.

T. S. Eliot (1888–1965), extract from 'Preludes', I

COMMENTARY

The **manner** is formal in the poem, but the poet wants the reader to feel the same as he does himself about the place he describes. By using the possessive pronoun *your* (l. 7), he therefore places the reader directly into the landscape he creates. The reader is forced to experience the desolation at first hand.

The **lexis** creates a very vivid picture of the place by appealing to the senses of sight, sound and smell. The **concrete nouns** build up the town environment – *passageways* (l. 2), *street* (l. 11), *cab-horse* (l. 12) and *lamps* (l. 13); there is a reference to *a gusty shower* (l. 5); the sounds of the town are developed by the dynamic verb *stamps* (l. 12) which describes the cab-horse and by the minor sentence *Six o'clock* (l. 3) which draws attention to the time, implying that the clock is chiming; while descriptions of the smell of *steaks* (l. 2), the *smoky days* (l. 4) and the cab-horse who *steams* (l. 12) conjure up the smells of the winter evening. The **modifiers** emphasise the mood. Lexical sets of adjective modifiers like *lonely* (l. 12) and *vacant* (l. 8) and verb modifiers like *burnt-out* (l. 4) and *withered* (l. 7) highlight the desolation; others like the adjectives *grimy* (l. 6) and *smoky* (l. 4) draw attention to the darkness and gloominess of the scene. The **connotations** of these words make the reader aware that the poet is describing a decaying and lifeless place.

The **grammar** is straightforward, but some sentences are minor because they are made up of noun phrases standing alone:

    h q   m   m   h   q
Six o'clock. (l. 3)   The burnt-out ends of smoky days. (l. 4)
    num PrepP   det   V   N   PrepP

The other sentences are simple or compound:

         S   P   A   A
(The winter evening) (settles down)/(With smell of steaks) (in passageways). (ll. 1–2)

        S   P   A   A
(The showers) (beat)/(On broken blinds and chimney-pots)/(And) (at the corner of the
                                       conj
              S   P
street)/(A lonely cab-horse) (steams and stamps).   (ll. 9–12)

The **tense** is present throughout and this reinforces the sense that this is all happening now. There are only two **marked themes** and both occur at the end of the poem: the adverbial of place *at the corner of the street* (l. 11) draws attention to the cab-horse, which, other than the reference to the *feet* (l. 7), is the only living thing in the poem; the adverbial of time *then* (l. 13) marks a change in atmosphere as the lamps are lit and everything is illuminated.

The lexis and syntax of the poem are much closer to the language of everyday speech and so the **literary language** is far less complicated than in the Wordsworth extract. This reflects the bleakness of the urban landscape. The evening is **personified** as it *settles down* (l.1) and the noun modifier *winter* (l.1) **symbolises** the lack of life that is typical of the scene Eliot portrays. The title serves as an introduction to the poem as a whole, symbolising the possibility of something developing from the desolation here. A 'prelude' is an event leading up to or preceding another event of greater importance, and here the lighting of the lamps implies that the dispiriting darkness can be diminished by the light. **Structurally**, this suggestion is reinforced by the blank line left between lines 1–12 and line 13. The lighting of the lamps, the first definite human action, seems to lighten the mood of despair.

The main **rhetorical features** used are **phonological**. The **alliteration** of the phoneme /b/ in *beat…broken blinds* (ll.9–10), /g/ in *gusty* (l.5) and *grimy* (l.6), and /l/ in *the lighting of the lamps* (l.13) contribute to the resonance of the poem. **Sibilance** is used to mimic the cooking of the steaks: *…settles /…smell of steaks in passageways./Six…* (ll.1–3).

The **distinctive features** of poetry can be seen:

▸ The longer lines all have eight syllables; the shorter ones have three or four.
▸ The metre is quite regular, with four stresses in each of the longer lines (tetrameter) and two in each of the short lines (dimeter); most lines are iambic (one unstressed and one stressed syllable).
▸ The rhymes are clear, but the pattern does not follow any recognisable form – the phonemes /eɪz/ in *passageways* and *days*; the phonemes /æps/ in *wraps* and *scraps*; the phonemes /iːt/ in *feet* and *beat*; the phonemes /ɒts/ in *pots* and *lots*; and the phonemes /æmps/ in *stamps* and *lamps*.
▸ The language, tone and structure are typical of much modern poetry which aims to move away from romantic considerations of nature, finding the harsh reality of everyday life a more rewarding subject.

To evoke atmosphere

Because of the intensity and compression of the language of poetry, poets can create very powerful atmospheres which will influence the reader. The charged atmospheres they create can then be used to convey a message.

> *Dulce et Decorum Est* (extract)
>
> 1 Bent double, like old beggars under sacks,
>   Knock-kneed, coughing like hags, we cursed through sludge,
>   Till on the haunting flares we turned our backs
>   And towards our distant rest began to trudge.
> 5 Men marched asleep. Many had lost their boots
>   But limped on, blood-shod. All went lame; all blind;
>   Drunk with fatigue; deaf even to the hoots
>   Of gas shells dropping softly behind …
>
> Wilfred Owen (1893–1918)

The **manner** is formal – the poet is revealing the reality of war through a description of soldiers returning from the front line for a rest period. The context is serious; in creating an emotive atmosphere, the poet aims to convey a message to the reader. The Latin title translates as 'it is sweet and glorious to die for one's country'. Owen uses this ironically: his poem proves that war is far from heroic.

The **lexis** is emotive and it is through his choice of words that Owen creates a dramatic atmosphere. **Subject-specific nouns** like *flares* (l. 3) and *gas shells* (l. 8) identify the military context. The poet uses the noun *Men* (l. 5) instead of 'soldiers' and this reinforces the sense that they are ordinary people. The **modifiers** are emotive and build up a disturbing picture of the men: adjectives *lame, blind* (l. 6) and *deaf* (l. 7) suggest that the men are isolated from reality – all their senses have been overwhelmed by the horrific experiences of war; verb modifiers like *Bent double* (l. 1), *Knock-kneed* and *coughing* (l. 2) develop the reader's awareness of the men's physical condition – their state of health does not reflect the stereotypical strength of soldiers. The verb modifier *haunting* (l. 3) becomes symbolic of the whole experience from which the men are now retreating but from which they cannot escape in their minds. The **connotations** of the verbs are also disturbing. Although the dynamic verb *marched* (l. 5) is used to describe the soldiers, it is used in conjunction with the adverbial *asleep*. Other verbs describing their movements are more emotive and less expected: *trudge* (l. 4) and *limped* (l. 6) imply the physical and emotional weariness of the men; *cursed* (l. 2) is used to convey literally the oaths they utter and almost figuratively the way movements are hindered by the mud.

The **grammar** is marked by the compression and omission of grammatical function words that is typical of poetry. It contributes to the intensity of the atmosphere created. The poem uses the **past tense** throughout and is clearly made up of the recollections of one of the soldiers. By using the first person plural **pronoun** *we* (l. 2), the poet reveals that he was one of the men described. While he has shared the experience, however, readers are excluded from the reference. This intensifies the atmosphere in two ways:

- the use of the inclusive pronoun reference links the poet directly to the descriptions, thereby making them more horrific
- because they have been excluded, readers will recognise that they can never fully understand what these men have experienced, and will feel personally committed to ensuring that such appalling conflicts do not happen again.

The **sentence structures** are varied: the poet uses a mixture of simple, compound and complex sentences. This is appropriate because he is both recounting personal experience using a descriptive narrative style and conveying a message about the horrors of war. Simple and compound sentences are emphatic, stating facts in an unemotional way which makes the horror of what is being described all the more brutal:

	S	P	A	
(Men) (marched) (asleep).				(SIMPLE: l. 5)

	S	P	O		P	A	
(Many) (had lost) (their boots) / (But) (limped on), (blood-shod).				conj			(COMPOUND: ll. 5–6)

The complex sentences use many adverbials in order to provide the reader with precise details. The omission of grammatical function words intensifies the effect, leaving the reader with only the emotive lexical words:

$\overset{A}{\text{(Bent double, like old beggars under sacks), }/\overset{A}{\text{(Knock-kneed), }}\overset{A}{\text{(coughing like hags),}}}$

(Bent double, like old beggars under sacks), /(Knock-kneed), (coughing like hags),
SCl–NFCl

S   P   A   A

(we) (cursed) (through sludge) /(Till on the haunting flares we turned our backs) /
SCl–ACl

A

(And) (towards our distant rest began to trudge).   (ll. 1–4)
conj   SCl–ACl   SCl–NFCl

The poem uses **literary devices** to intensify the atmosphere created. **Similes** like the references to *old beggars* (l. 1) and *hags* (l. 2) disturb the reader because they are unexpected comparisons – far from being shown as glorious and heroic, the soldiers are instead shown as physically and emotionally broken. The **neologism** *blood-shod* (l. 6) is equally disturbing: the soldiers have no shoes, but their feet are so covered with blood that they appear to be wearing shoes. The compound noun expresses this graphically in a very concise way.

The **rhetorical patterning** helps to make the poem effective: the juxtaposition between the horror of the content and the order of the poetic structure is dramatic. **Marked themes** like *Bent double...* (l. 1) and **listing** like *All... lame; all blind;/Drunk... deaf* (ll. 6–7) focus attention on the condition of the soldiers. They appear to be oblivious to everything around them, cut off from normal life by the inescapable reality of life at the front. **Antithesis** is used to reinforce this sense of two different worlds: *turned our backs* (l. 3) and *distant* (l. 4) are juxtaposed with the verb modifier *haunting* (l. 3) to emphasise that the men cannot forget what they have seen and experienced just by walking away towards *rest* (l. 4). The **phonological patterning** is what gives the poem its sense of order. The **rhyme scheme** links alternate lines: the phonemes /æks/ in *sacks* and *backs*; /ʌdʒ/ in *sludge* and *trudge*; /uːts/ in *boots* and *hoots*; and /aɪnd/ in *blind* and *behind*.

The poem is written mainly in iambic pentameter. Most lines have ten syllables; the pattern of stressed and unstressed syllables is not always the same but each line has either five or six stresses. The variation in the stress pattern draws attention to the key elements used to build up the atmosphere.

ACTIVITY 14.2

Read the following short poem by D. H. Lawrence and comment on the way content and form help to create the atmosphere.

Discord in Childhood
1 Outside the house an ash-tree hung its terrible whips,
  And at night when the wind rose, the lash of the tree
  Shrieked and slashed the wind, as a ship's
  Weird rigging in a storm shrieks hideously.

5 Within the house two voices arose, a slender lash
  Whistling she-delirious rage, and the dreadful sound
  Of a male thong booming and bruising, until it had drowned
  The other voice in a silence of blood, 'neath the noise of the ash.

D. H. Lawrence

COMMENTARY

The atmosphere created in the poem is one of violence and disruption. It is made more effective because of the juxtaposition of the child's and the adult's perspectives. Although the focus of the poem is on the tree that the child sees and the sounds heard, the adult poet explicitly reveals the connection between the two through his choice of lexis and structure.

The **language** creates a physical background for the conflict between the parents. **Concrete nouns** like *ash-tree* (l. 1) and *house* (l. 1) directly link the two elements of the poet's memory. The poem implies that the child is upstairs in bed, able to see only the tree outside while listening to the parents arguing downstairs. By **naming the participants** using the noun phrase *two voices* (l. 5), the poet dehumanises them, reducing them to what the child hears. The **modifiers** develop the dramatic atmosphere of the poem. The adjective *terrible* (l. 1) describes the tree, but becomes symbolic of the child's feelings about what is happening downstairs. Other modifiers clearly divide the mother and father: *slender* (l. 5) is juxtaposed with *dreadful* (l. 6) to suggest the respective parts played by the parents in the battle the child can only hear. **Noun phrases** are complex, conveying a lot of information and emphasising the effect of the parents' conflict on the child:

> m   m   h   q
> a slender lash / Whistling she-delirious rage   (ll. 5–6)
> det   Adj   N   NFCl

> m   m   h   q   q
> the dreadful sound / Of a male thong booming and bruising   (ll. 6–7)
> det   Adj   N   PrepP   NFCl

Throughout, the **connotations** of words are negative: verbs like *shrieked* and *slashed* (l. 3); nouns like *lash* (l. 2) and *thong* (l. 7); abstract nouns like *discord* (in the title); and modifiers like the adverb *hideously* (l. 4) and the adjective *weird* (l. 4). All these make the atmosphere of the poem disturbing.

The **grammar** intensifies the atmosphere by concentrating the descriptions. Each stanza is made up of a complex sentence:

> A   S   P   O   A   A
> (Outside the house) (an ash-tree) (hung) (its terrible whips) / (And) (at night) (when the
>   conj   SCl–ACl
>   S   P   P   O
> wind rose) (the lash of the tree) / (Shrieked) (and) (slashed) (the wind) (as a ship's/
>   conj   SCl–ACl
> A
> Weird rigging in a storm shrieks hideously).   (ll. 1–4)

The **figurative language** is central to the child's impression of what is happening. The child cannot see the parents, but the tree is visible as it lashes in storms and this becomes symbolic of the sounds coming from below. The concrete nouns *lash* and *whips* describe the tree in the first stanza but become linked to the voices the child can hear in the second stanza. The description of the mother's voice as a *lash* and the father's as a *thong* builds up the connotations of violence and punishment. The conclusion of the argument is made dramatic as noise is replaced by *silence* (l. 8). The effect is intensified by the juxtaposition of this abstract noun with *blood* (l. 8) and the use of the verb *drowned* (l. 7), which suddenly make the violence real rather than figurative. The simile *as a ship's / Weird rigging...* (ll. 3–4) contributes to the child's sense that something unearthly is happening.

The most obvious **rhetorical patterning** is the use of **antithesis**: the roles of the mother and father are contrasted; the tree in a storm is juxtaposed with the parents' discord; and the noise of the argument is contrasted with the silence that follows its violent end. **Marked themes** are used to contrast the content of each stanza: *Outside…* (l.1) and *Within…* (l.5). The **phonological patterning** helps to create the cacophony of sounds: **alliteration** of the phoneme /b/ and **sibilance** mimic the noise of the father and mother respectively. The **rhyme scheme** is different in each stanza and this draws a distinction between the descriptions of the tree and of the parents: in lines 1 and 3, the phonemes /ɪps/ rhyme in the words *whips* and *ships*; in lines 2 and 4, the phoneme /iː/ rhymes in *tree* and *hideously*; in lines 5 and 8, the phonemes /æʃ/ rhyme in *lash* and *ash*; in lines 6 and 7, the phonemes /aʊnd/ rhyme in *sound* and *drowned*.

The poet chooses **free verse** and the number of syllables and stresses per line varies, making this poem closer to the patterns of ordinary speech than older, more structured poetic forms. The end result, however, is more intense than everyday conversation. The atmosphere is heightened in two ways: the violence is made more shocking by the almost matter-of-fact way in which it is revealed; and the literary language is emotive because it is the child's way of understanding what he or she cannot see or be a part of.

To experiment with language and structure

As a variety, poetry is very flexible: by adapting language and form, poets can convey their messages in very personal ways. Traditional ballads often used **dialect**, and this makes them more immediate and dramatic.

> *The Twa Corbies* (extract)
>
> 1 As I was walking all alane,
>   I heard twa corbies making a mane;
> The tane unto the t'other say,
>   'Where sall we gang and dine to-day?'
>
> 5 'In behint yon auld fail dyke,
>   I wot there lies a new-slain knight;
> And naebody kens that he lies there,
>   But his hawk, his hound, and lady fair …
>
> Anonymous

In this extract from a Scottish ballad, it is immediately possible to pick out **dialect words** which mark its origin: *twa* (l.2) for 'two'; *corbies* (l.2) for 'ravens'; *tane* (l.3) for 'one'; *gang* (l.4) for 'go'; *auld* (l.5) for 'old'; *fail* (l.5) for 'turf'; *wot* (l.6) for 'know'; *naebody* (l.7) for 'nobody'; and *kens* (l.7) for 'knows'. Since the poem is basically a record of the conversation between two birds about their next meal, the dialect is appropriate, giving the poem an authentic and unsentimental tone.

The poem opens abruptly, with no time spent building up a background. Only salient details like the *auld fail dyke* (l.5) are included, to emphasise the isolation of the newly dead knight. The **lexis** is simple and direct and the **sound pattern** is distinctive: the quatrains are rhymed in couplets; the feet are predominantly iambic:

Aš í | wăs wál|kĭng áll | ălăne   (l. 1)
ĭ wót | thĕre liés | ă néw|-sláin kníght   (l. 6)

Ballads are a traditional form of oral poetry and it is common for them to be written in dialect. Few of the poets are known, but the dialect forms used tell the reader something about their origins. Modern poets can choose to write in dialect and this makes their approach more distinctive.

Other poets choose to manipulate **structure**, not selecting a traditional form but devising one that suits their particular purpose.

> *Prayer Before Birth* (extract)
>
> 1 I am not yet born; O hear me.
>   Let not the bloodsucking bat or the rat or the stoat or the
>   club-footed ghoul near me.
>
>   I am not yet born; console me.
> 5 I fear that the human race may with tall walls wall me,
>   with strong drugs dope me, with wise lies lure me,
>   on black racks rack me, in blood-baths roll me.
>
>   I am not yet born; provide me
>   With water to dandle me, grass to grow for me, trees to talk
> 10   to me, sky to sing to me, birds and a white light
>   in the back of my mind to guide me ...

Louis MacNeice (1907–63)

These three stanzas are taken from the beginning of a poem whose form draws on liturgical prayer. The **rhetorical repetition** of **grammatical structures** and of **sounds** makes the poem's appeal more powerful. The opening of each stanza reinforces the context. The poem is a plea that people create an appropriate environment in which the child may live and therefore after the declarative mood of the first clause, an imperative is used:

```
  S    P     A    C      P         P           P
 (I) (am not) (yet) (born) ... hear ... console ... provide ...          (ll. 1–8)
      neg
```

The poem also uses the sonorous tones of **prayer** – it is clearly a poem to be read aloud. Although there are no end rhymes, **internal rhyme** is used. The phonemes /ɔːl/ are repeated in *tall walls wall me* (l. 5) and the phonemes /æk/ in *black racks rack me* (l. 7). **Alliteration** is frequent: the phoneme /b/ in *bloodsucking bat* (l. 2) and *blood-baths* (l. 7); /l/ in *lies lure* (l. 6); /g/ in *grass... grow* (l. 9); /s/ in *sky... sing* (l. 10). All of these poetic devices contribute to the rhythmical chant of the poem.

Structurally, the poem is distinctive on the page. The third and any subsequent lines are inset, giving the poem a disjointed and jagged appearance. Stanzas also differ in length – as the appeals of the unborn child become more urgent, so the stanzas become longer.

Both the layout and the structure make the poem distinctive, allowing the poet to draw attention to his plea to make a better world; and because it is the unborn child who actually makes the appeal, the poem is very poignant. The repetitions make the poem seem like a never-ending list which must be addressed if the world is to be made into a more humane place. The liturgical qualities give the appeal a very formal tone.

Whichever structure or style a poet chooses tells the reader something about the kind of relationship the poet wishes to create with the reader and about the kind of message to be conveyed. If a poet chooses a form or layout that is unusual in any way, it makes the message more distinctive and personal.

14.5 What to look for in the language of poetry

The following checklist can be used to identify key features in examples of poetry. You will not find all of the features in every poem, but the list can be used as a guide. The points made are general, so discussion of specific examples will need to be adapted to take account of the specific context and authorial purpose. Remember that you need to evaluate the effect of the features you identify, exploring the ways in which they create meaning.

The following are helpful questions to ask.

Register

1 What is the **mode**?
   * written.
2 What is the **manner**?
   * relationship between poet and subject?
   * relationship between poet and reader?
   * personal or impersonal relationship? formal or informal?
   * poet's intention? (to characterise, to describe a place or time, to create an atmosphere, to convey a message, etc.)
3 What is the **field**?
   * subject matter?
   * linked to audience, purpose and context?

Poetic form and structure

1 Has the poet used a recognisable **poetic form**?
   * sonnet? ballad? ode?
2 Has the poet used **blank verse** (ten syllables and five stresses) or **free verse** (irregular lines with no regular metre)?
3 Are the lines **end stopped** or are there examples of **enjambement**?
4 Is there a noticeable **metre**?
   * pattern of stressed and unstressed syllables?
   * number of stressed syllables per line?
5 Are there any significant **pauses**?
6 Is the **rhythm** striking in any way?
   * very patterned and regular?
   * similar to the irregular patterns of speech?
7 Is anything unusual about the **layout**?
8 Is the poem divided into **stanzas**?
   * regular or irregular?
   * linked to a particular poetic form?
   * to underpin the meaning?
   * to highlight key elements?

Lexis

1 What kinds of **words** are used?
   + simple or complex?
   + formal or colloquial?
   + descriptive or evaluative?
   + modern or archaic?

2 Are there any examples of **subject-specific words** or specific **lexical sets**?

3 Has the poet chosen to use **non-standard language**?
   + idiosyncratic linguistic choices?
   + dialect? archaisms? neologisms?
   + code language identifying insiders and outsiders?

4 Are the **nouns concrete** or **abstract**?

5 Is the **naming of participants** important?
   + first names? surnames? titles?
   + are any names omitted intentionally?

6 Do any words have significant **connotations**?

7 What function do the **modifiers** have?
   + negative or positive?
   + to appeal to the senses?
   + to make judgements?
   + to explore a state of mind?

8 What kinds of actions and processes do the **verbs** describe?

9 Are any **collocations** used?
   + familiar or disrupted?
   + to reassure or to challenge?

Grammar

1 Is the grammar **standard**?
   + formal or informal?
   + modern or archaic?
   + minor sentences?

2 Are there any significant changes of **tense** or **mood**?

3 Is the **sentence structure** varied?
   + simple, compound, complex?
   + minor?

4 Are there any examples of **ellipsis**?
   + telegraphic style?
   + intensifying meaning?

Style

1 How does the poet try to influence the reader?

2 Does the poet use **sentence organisation** to emphasise certain elements?
   + marked themes to draw attention to key words or phrases?
   + passive voice to refocus our attention on the object or to delay the subject?
   + end focus to change the balance of a sentence?

3 Does the poet use **images** to add depth to the description or message of the poem?
  - literal or figurative?
  - visual, aural or tactile?

4 Are there any **literary devices** encouraging the reader to make connections?
  - similes or metaphors?
  - symbols or personification?

5 What kinds of **sound patterning** are used?
  - alliteration, sibilance or onomatopoeia?
  - end rhyme or internal rhyme?
  - to make links between words or to develop a tight structure?
  - to create a certain mood, underpin the meaning, or draw attention to key words or ideas?

6 Are contrasts created through the use of **rhetorical devices** to underpin the meaning?
  - antithesis?
  - patterning: parallelism? tripling? listing? repetition?

Summary

The **function** of poetry is to entertain, but poets can also implicitly or explicitly convey a message about society or life.

The language of poetry is very **varied** because poets can manipulate language in order to make their work striking. Unusual and archaic language can be used to add depth to a characterisation or authenticity to a message; word class boundaries can be broken to create unusual effects; grammatical words can be omitted to intensify the mood of the poem; and rhythm and metre can be used to mark poetry as different from ordinary speech.

The **poet's intention** will dictate the kinds of linguistic, stylistic and structural choices made: poets can use heightened and elevated language or ordinary conversational language; they can use predefined strict forms or freer more personal forms; they can compress language until it no longer seems to conform to standard grammatical patterns or they can use the irregular patterns of speech.

Chapter 15

The language of law

15.1 The nature of legal language

The language of law is very distinctive and its lexical and syntactical patterns owe much to traditional forms of English. Its conservatism is linked directly to the need for unambiguous language that has already been tried and tested in the courts. By retaining traditional lexis and syntax, lawyers can be confident that the language of law is consistent and precise. Campaigners for **PLAIN ENGLISH** – English that is straightforward and easy to understand – argue that legal language could be simplified so that it is both more comprehensible to ordinary people and more practical for lawyers themselves. Many lawyers fear, however, that if changes were made, new simplified language structures could create legal loopholes.

LEGAL LANGUAGE is used in a range of legal contexts in both written and spoken forms. It is marked by complex grammatical structures, technical lexis, archaic expressions and limited punctuation, which together make it quite different from other varieties. Nothing is left implicit and there is perhaps no other variety in which anything not stated explicitly is disregarded. Such linguistic features make it easily recognisable even to people who are not part of the profession.

> I swear by Almighty God to tell the truth, the whole truth and nothing but the truth …
> You may approach the bench …

Legal language is the domain of a specialist occupation and the intended audience comprises people who are experts in the field. Because the same kinds of legal transactions occur regularly, linguistic formulae have been developed. This means that legal language is not spontaneous – it is quite unlike informal speech with its irregular patterns, and quite unlike the language of literature with its personal, often idiosyncratic approach. Instead, it draws on structures that have been predefined and pretested, and uses jargon that is familiar only to the experts and grammatical structures that are difficult to decode.

The **lexis** and **syntax** can make it difficult for an ordinary reader to understand a legal document, as can the **layout**. Traditionally, the contents were often written as a solid block with no paragraphs or spacing to mark out sections of the text. To avoid any ambiguity in the interpretation of written documents, punctuation was used sparingly. Examples of blocked layout and minimal punctuation can still be found, but more recently legal documents have tended to use typographical devices to make the variety less obscure. Capitalisation, underlining, different print styles, numbered lists and paragraphs are now often used to highlight the development of key points.

15.2 The function of legal language

The language of law is used to regulate society by establishing obligations that must be fulfilled and by ensuring that rights are granted. Although legal language can be difficult to understand, we all come into contact with it on a regular basis. Statutes dictate what is and what is not acceptable behaviour in society; contracts are made with insurance companies and mortgage lenders; property conveyancing is completed; and wills are drawn up. The spoken language of the courts is portrayed on television in the numerous courtroom dramas and in live trial coverage.

The main function of legal language is **referential** (to convey information). Its subordinate functions are **conative** (persuasive) and **METALINGUISTIC** (discussing language itself). It is always formal, whether written or spoken, although a meeting between solicitor and client will be less formal than cross-questioning in court.

15.3 Features of written legal language

Modern printing techniques and attempts to simplify legal language have had some effect on the nature of written documents, but for the main part the legal variety has changed little over the centuries. In analysing legal texts, linguists must be aware of both the customary approaches and the ways in which these are being changed in order to make the variety less obscure. For instance, whereas traditional documents used no paragraphing and often used Gothic script for the opening letter, modern documents usually divide the text into distinct units and avoid decorative printing. Such changes are linked to the desire for plain English in all public official language. Despite this, the basic language structures remain unchanged.

Manner

The **manner** is always formal and the language of law has little similarity with the language of conversation. There are, for instance, no contractions for negatives or auxiliary verbs in written documents. Because it is a traditional form of language, it retains archaic features. These, and the many formulaic utterances like *signed in the joint presence of...*, preserve a ceremonial tone. It is a public form of language, but its intended audience is legal experts rather than the general public.

Typography and layout

The **typographical features** are designed to draw attention to key elements of the text. The overall **layout** is often distinctive. Traditional documents are printed in a solid block with no indentation, but more modern examples tend to be indented and subdivided. Although the traditional style gives an overall visual coherence to legal documents, modern layouts are more acceptable to the non-specialist. Variations in **typeface** are used to reveal the structure of the content. Capitalisation, underlining and the use of italic can emphasise important lexical items. References to people, companies or parts of a document may be highlighted by using such techniques.

Punctuation is used sparingly in legal documents because it can cause ambiguity. Commas are often omitted in lists and for clauses in parenthesis; colons and dashes may mark the beginning of a list of subsections, but are also often omitted; brackets are sometimes used to identify parentheses. Sentences in legal documents tend to be very long, and full stops are used only at the ends of key sections or at the very end of the document:

> 1 There is reserved for the benefit of any adjoining property of the Vendors or their predecessors or successors in title the free and uninterrupted passage and running of water and soil and gas and electricity from and to other buildings...

A comma following the past participle *reserved* (l. 1) and following the post-modified noun phrase *successors in title* (l. 2) would make this sentence easier to read. Isolating the adverbial would clarify the relationship between the dummy subject *there* (l. 1) and the delayed subject *the free and uninterrupted passage...* (l. 2).

Lexis

The **lexis** of legal language is very distinctive. There is a mixture of **subject-specific jargon** or **'TERMS OF ART'** like *tort*, *alibi* and *bail*, which all lawyers will interpret in the same way, and other **ordinary words** like *damage*, *malice* and *valid*, which will be interpreted differently depending upon the context. The **specialist terminology** can be divided into two categories: ordinary language used in a specialist way, like *proposal* and *life*, and specialist language used in everyday contexts, like *liable*. The subject-specific lexis contributes to the formal tone of legal language.

ARCHAIC LEXIS like *hereafter* and **collocations** like *it shall be deemed* also make the variety formal. **Synonyms** are common, reflecting the influence of both French and Latin on legal language and the need to be all-inclusive:

> made and signed   make (OE *macian*); sign (Fr *signe*, L *signum*)
> able and willing   able (OFr *ableté*, Fr *habileté*, L *habilitas*); will (OE *willa*)

As would be expected, words marking grammatical relationships are mainly descended from Old English, but there is evidence of many French and Latin **LOAN WORDS** which have since been assimilated into the language:

> proposal: Fr *proposer*   conveyance: OFr *conveier*
> contract: L *contractus*   evidence: L *ēvidēns*

Other borrowings are not used in ordinary discourse but have been retained as specialist terms.

> res gestae   facts relevant to the case and admissible in evidence (L)
> caveat emptor   'let the buyer beware' or 'it's the buyer's lookout' (L)

| estop | to hinder or prevent (OFr *estoper*) |
| estoppel | a conclusive admission that cannot be denied by the person(s) it affects |

Many nouns are **abstract**: *valuation, bonus, evidence* and *policy*. Legal language is not concerned with the creation of mood, nor with description or evaluation, so **pre-modifiers** are used infrequently except where they can provide exact information: *the first premium, the current monthly payment* and *the freehold land*. The determiner site in a noun phrase is nearly always filled: *the Valuer, a Mortgagee, the Lease* and *the Life Insured*. If the determiner is omitted, it is usually because the phrase is part of a formula: *details of proposed occupiers* and *interest accruing*. The use of *said* and *aforesaid* (meaning 'mentioned before') as pre-modifiers allows legal documents to be very precise in any anaphoric references that are made: *the sum of £5000 ... the said sum; the period of 28 days ... the said period*. **Post-modification** is common, however, since it provides factual information like names, addresses and legal conditions. Long sequences of post-modifying subordinate clauses can mean that the head noun of the subject and the predicator are separated, making the text difficult to decipher:

(h)   S

(A *conveyance* of the land in this title dated 23 May 1946 made between 1. Mark
              SCl–NFCl   SCl–NFCl

Stephens and Brian Morris [Vendors] and 2. Julie Mary Ryan and others [Purchasers])

P   O

(contains) (the exceptions and reservations as set out below) ...
                  SCl–ACl

The **verbs** are distinctive in legal language because few other varieties have as many non-finite and modal auxiliary verbs. The auxiliary and lexical verbs are often separated by sequences of phrases and clauses, making the documents difficult to read. The lexical verbs found in written legal documents tend to be limited and the same ones are used regularly: *indemnify, accept, be conveyed, be deemed*. **Adverbials** are used frequently and tend to cluster at the beginning of sentences. They are often linked to the archaic prepositional words like *hereto, hereafter* and *thereof*. The use of adverbials is one of the distinctive features of legal language:

A

(If the loss of or damage to the Insured Vehicle is caused by theft or attempted theft)
SCl–ACl

A

(where the Insured Vehicle has been fitted with an immobilising system or an alarm
SCl–ACl

system recognised by the Company) (and) (where the Insured is in possession of all
    SCl–NFCl   conj   SCl–ACl

A

the keys and/or activating accessories and the Certificate of Installation as provided
                                          SCl–ACl

by the manufacturer of the immobilising system or alarm system) (the excess as

S   P

specified in Section 2 of the Policy) (will not apply).
SCl–ACl   neg

Pronoun referencing is not often used in legal documents, so that any ambiguity can be avoided. Instead, nouns are repeated throughout, as in the previous example where noun phrases like *the Insured Vehicle* and the compound noun phrase *immobilising system or alarm system* are repeated in full. So that references can be all-inclusive, general words focusing on function such as *the Insured Party* or *the Life Insured* are chosen. This avoids words that are marked by gender. Where a pronoun is used, however, it will usually be the third person singular *he* or the third person plural *they*.

Grammar

The **grammar** of legal language is complicated by the length of the sentences. Strings of dependent clauses are used to provide precise information about the legal conditions attached to each transaction, whether it is a life assurance or car insurance policy, a will or a property sale. The embedded clauses make the legal terms of reference clear, but the reader has to retain a lot of information to decode the meaning. The **mood** is almost always declarative, but imperatives are used occasionally. Interrogatives are used in the spoken legal language of the courts, but not in written documents. The **passive voice** is often used:

> If the Insured Vehicle *has been owned* by one owner only since the date of its first registration as new ...

As an active sentence the noun phrase *one owner only* would fill the subject site of the adverbial clause. The passive voice is more appropriate in this example since it brings the noun phrase *the Insured Vehicle* to the front of the sentence. The focus of this insurance policy is the car, so it is logical to bring that lexical item forward. It does, however, make the sentence more difficult to read. Campaigners for plain English believe that the use of the passive voice is one of the linguistic and stylistic features of legal language that unnecessarily complicates meaning.

Sentences in legal documents are long because they have to include all relevant points in a single statement. Although the many co-ordinated phrases and clauses make the variety seem list-like, they insure that it is inclusive. The **sentence structure** is usually complex, compound or compound–complex. Few sentences are simple and none are minor:

> (If the Life Insured shall pay or cause to be paid to the Society or to the duly [A]
> SCl–ACl   conj   SCl–NFCl   conj
> authorised Agent thereof every subsequent premium at the date due thereof) (on the
> [A]
> expiration of the term of years specified in the Schedule hereto or on the previous
> SCl–NFCl   conj
> [S]   [P]
> death of the Life Insured) (the funds of the Society) (shall) (in accordance with the
> [A]   [P]
> terms and conditions of the said Table) (become and be) (liable to pay to him/her or
> conj   conj   SCl–NFCl   conj
> [C]
> to his/her personal representative or next-of-kin the sum due).
> conj

As can be seen in this example, the word order is distinctive: adverbials are often clustered at the beginning; almost all clauses contain adverbials to clarify the meaning; and there are many co-ordinated phrases. Such chain-like constructions make legal language distinctive. **Cohesion** is created through repetition of lexical sets. Because of the interrelated sequences of clauses, sentences in legal language tend to be like self-contained units – they do not need to be linked closely to what has gone before or what follows. This makes anaphoric and cataphoric referencing less important between sentences and avoids any possible ambiguity which might constitute a loophole in the law.

15.4 Types of legal language

Statutes

A **STATUTE** is a formal set of rules or rules of conduct which have to be observed. The Government makes policies that establish general principles for guidance and then legislation makes them into law: *Offences Against the Person Act 1861* and *Theft Act 1968*. The **tone** is formal and each word is important because a statute has to convey its meaning precisely so that it can be upheld in law. **Words used loosely in ordinary conversation** take on special significance. Modal auxiliaries, for instance, each have a specific meaning that dictates the way in which a statute is interpreted and enforced: *may* denotes that you are permitted to do something, while *shall* denotes that you must do something.

Statutes have a distinctive structure. They are named formally:

> *Race Relations Act 1968*
> ELIZABETH II
> 1968 CHAPTER 71
>
> An Act to make fresh provision with respect to discrimination on racial grounds and to make provision with respect to relations between people of different racial origins.
> [25 October 1968]

Complex prepositions like *with respect to* and the number of abstract nouns like *provision, discrimination* and *origins* make the tone public and official. The statute name is made up of the noun phrase *An Act* which is post-modified by two non-finite clauses beginning with *to make…*. The parallelism of the structure and the formality of the lexis are typical of this kind of legal language. The title is then followed by an **ENACTING FORMULA**:

> Be it enacted by the Queen's most Excellent Majesty, by and with the advice and consent of the Lords Spiritual and Temporal, and Commons, in the present Parliament assembled, and by the authority of the same as follows:– …

There is a clear pattern to the structure: an imperative in the passive voice, *Be… enacted*, is followed by a sequence of adverbials: *by the Queen's most Excellent Majesty, by… the Lords Spiritual and Temporal, and Commons, in the present* and *by the authority*. The use of the passive voice allows the sentence to be refocused: the long subject of an active sentence becomes the sequence of *by + agent* adverbials, allowing greater emphasis to be placed on the past participle enacted. The style of the formula introducing the Act adds to the ceremonial tone. It is followed by numbered sections which categorise the different elements of the law:

PART I

DISCRIMINATION

General

1.–(1) For the purpose of this Act a person discriminates against another if on the
5 ground of colour, race or ethnic or national origins he treats that other, in any situation
to which section 2, 3, 4 or 5 below applies, less favourably than he treats or would
treat other persons, and in this Act references to discrimination are references to
discrimination on any of those grounds.

After the official naming of the Act, it opens with a formula. The prepositional
phrase *For the purpose of this Act...* (l. 4) establishes the legal definition of discrimination. Repetition highlights key words and avoids ambiguity: for instance,
the abstract noun *discrimination* (ll. 2, 7–8) and the verb *discriminates* (l. 4), the
abstract noun *references* (l. 7) and the verb *treats* (ll. 5, 6). The example is typical of
legal language in a number of ways: third person pronoun references to *he* (ll. 5, 6)
are seen to be inclusive of 'she'; lists of alternatives like *colour, race, or ethnic or
national origins* (l. 5) ensure that all possibilities are legally covered; there are many
abstract nouns; and the sentence structure is complex with adverbials in each part
of the compound sentence:

$$\overset{A}{\text{(For the purpose of ...)}}\ \overset{S}{\text{(a person)}}\ \overset{P}{\text{(discriminates against)}}\ \overset{O}{\text{(another)}}\ \overset{A}{\text{(if ...)}}\ \overset{A}{\text{(and) (in this}}$$

SCl–ACl conj

$$\overset{S}{\text{Act) (references ...)}}\ \overset{P}{\text{(are)}}\ \overset{C}{\text{(references ...)}}\ \overset{A}{\text{(on any ...)}}$$

ACTIVITY 15.1

Read through this example of a statute taken from the Income and Corporation Taxes
Act 1988 and comment on the distinctive features of legal language.

1

PART I

THE CHARGE TO TAX

Income Tax

4.– (1) Any provision of the Income Tax Acts requiring, permitting or assuming the de-
5 duction of income tax from any amount (otherwise than in pursuance of section 203)
or treating income tax as having been deducted from or paid on any amount, shall,
subject to any provision to the contrary, be construed as referring to deduction or
payment of income tax at the basic rate in force for the relevant year of assessment.

(2) For the purposes of subsection (1) above, the relevant year of assessment
10 shall be taken to be (except where otherwise provided) –

(a) if the amount is an amount payable wholly out of profits or gains brought
into charge to tax, the year in which the amount becomes due;

(b) in any other case, the year in which the amount is paid.

The Taxes Acts, 'Income tax, Corporation tax and Capital gains tax'

COMMENTARY

The **manner** is formal: there are no contractions, and formulaic utterances like
the prepositional phrase *For the purposes of...* (l. 9) are typical in this kind of legal
language. The book from which this extract is taken is clearly written for experts

rather than the general public and this also contributes to the formality of the tone.

The **typographical features** show that this is a modern document since the layout has been divided for easier reading. **Paragraphs** are marked numerically and **subdivisions** make each point clear. **Punctuation** is used more extensively than in more traditional documents. Lists of verbs are divided with commas (*requiring, permitting or assuming*, ll. 3, 4); parenthesis is marked by commas and brackets; and a dash marks the beginning of a list of subsections. These typographical marks help the reader by dividing the text into semantic units that are more easily readable.

The **lexis** is **subject-specific**. **Abstract nouns** like *deduction* (ll. 4–5) and *profits or gains* (l. 11) and **collocations** like *the relevant year of assessment* (l. 9) indicate that the field is financial. Nouns like *assessment* (l. 8) are ordinary words used in a specialist context in tax law. The origins of many words can be traced to Latin and French sources:

> deduction (l. 7): L *deducere*   tax (l. 2): Fr *taxe*, L *taxare*
> assessment (l. 9): L *assidere*   payment (l. 8): Fr *payer*, L *pacare*

The only **pre-modifiers** make the information provided more precise:

> m   h   m   m   h   m   m   h   q
> income tax (l. 5)   the basic rate (l. 8)   the relevant year of assessment (l. 9)
> N   N   det   Adj   N   det   Adj   N   PrepP

Post-modifying prepositional phrases and non-finite clauses are common:

> m   h   q   q
> Any provision of the Income Tax Acts requiring, permitting or assuming ...   (l. 4)
> det   N   PrepP   NFCl

By placing adverbial clauses in listed subsections after the predicator, this example avoids the clusters of adverbials at the beginnings of sentences associated with traditional legal documents. Each semantic unit still begins with an adverbial, however:

> A   S   P
> (For the purposes of ...) (the relevant year ...) (shall be taken to be) ... –
> A   C
> (a) (if the amount is ...) (the year in which the amount becomes due);
>   SCl–ACl   SCl–RelCl
> A   C
> (b) (in any other case), (the year in which the amount is paid).   (ll. 9–13)
>   SCl–RelCl

The **verbs** are typical of legal language: the modal auxiliary *shall* (l. 6) is repeated; there are many non-finite verbs where other varieties would use a finite clause: *requiring, permitting or assuming* (l. 4); and the verbs are part of a limited lexical set that is linked to the field: *deducted* and *paid* (l. 6).

The **grammar** is complicated despite the fact that modern visual features divide the long sentences into discrete units:

> S
> (Any provision of the Income Tax Acts requiring, permitting or assuming the deduction
>   SCl–NFCl   conj
> of income tax from any amount ... or treating income tax as having been deducted
>   conj SCl–NFCl   SCl–ACl

	P	A

from or ø paid on any amount), (shall), (subject to any provision to the contrary), (be
  conj   SCl–ACl   aux   aux

| P | | A |

construed) (as referring to deduction or payment of income tax at the basic rate in
  lex   SCl–ACl   conj

                A
force) (for the relevant year of assessment).   (ll. 4–8)

The **mood** throughout is declarative and all sentences are major. The **passive voice** is used in verb phrases like *having been deducted from* (l. 6), *(having been) paid on* (l. 6) and *be construed* (l. 7). No agent is used, but the implication is that the unnamed agents are members of the legal and accounting professions and the Civil Service who together establish and uphold the rules. In this context, it is not important to include the subject of the active sentence because the document is merely providing the regulations that tax inspectors must follow. **Marked themes** draw attention to information that is important in interpreting the legal conditions: *For the purposes of subsection (1) above ...* (l. 9). **Cohesion** is created through the repetition of key words like *income tax, deduction* and *amount*. Pronoun referencing is avoided so that there can be no doubt about the intended interpretation.

Campaigners for plain English have argued that it is unnecessary to use archaic language, to eliminate punctuation and to conform to traditional block layouts. The example of statute law here is still complicated, but modern approaches to the presentation of legal language have made it more accessible than in traditional documents. The extract is clearly typical of the legal variety with its complex sentence structures, lexical repetition and French and Latin loan words. It is less daunting, however, because it attempts to guide inexperienced readers by dividing the document into smaller semantic units.

Contracts

A legal **CONTRACT** is a written document in which a legal agreement of some kind is undertaken between two or more parties. Contracts determine when a promise or set of promises is legally enforceable. Transactions such as selling houses, leasing property or insuring lives and possessions are covered by legal contracts.

In signing a contract, the participants are agreeing to carry out a series of acts or to fulfil a series of conditions. Because these can be enforced by the law, the language is formal and the syntax complicated:

                A   S
(Where agreed with the Applicant) (the insurance of the property to be mortgaged)
  SCl–ACl   SCl–NFCl

         P   A   A
(will be arranged) (by the Society) (unless the property is leasehold and ø the lease
                                       SCl–ACl   conj   SCl–ACl

contains a covenant to insure through a specified agency).
  SCl–NFCl

A number of linguistic and stylistic features make this extract from a mortgage contract typical of legal language:

- **Subject-specific words** define the nature of the contract: the verb *mortgaged* and the abstract nouns *insurance* and *covenant*.

- The noun *property*, which is used in ordinary discourse in a loose way, is used here in a **specific way** to refer to the building to be insured.
- **Collocations** like *where agreed...* and *will be arranged...* are formulaic.
- **Determiners** are used to pre-modify every noun; in one case additional pre-modification is used to provide precise information:

m   m   h
the specified agency
det   V   N

- **Post-modification** is used on several occasions:

m   h   q   m   h   q
the insurance of the property to be mortgaged   a covenant to insure ...
det   N   PrepP   NFCl   det   N   NFCl

- The **adverbials** provide exact information about the conditions to be met: *insurance arranged <u>by the Society</u>...* ; *Unless....*
- The **passive voice** is used to place the object of the active sentence, *the insurance of the property...*, in the subject site of the passive sentence in order to give it more emphasis.
- To avoid ambiguity, nouns like *property* are **repeated** instead of being substituted by pronouns.

Despite the fact that contracts like this are now divided into subsections to make reading easier, the typical features of legal language are still clear. Contracts are legally enforceable so the language must ensure that there are no loopholes, and this inevitably makes the text complicated.

Wills

A **WILL** is a declaration of a person's intentions concerning the allocation of property after death. It can be altered at any point up to death. It must be a written document and it must be signed *at the foot or end*. Two or more **WITNESSES** must authenticate the signature of the **TESTATOR** (the person making the will).

A will is a formal document and the language is formulaic. Much of the lexis is subject-specific:

devise (N): the arrangements for disposing of freehold land
legacy/bequest (N): the arrangements for disposing of any other possessions
grant of probate (N): an official acceptance that a will is genuine

The structure follows certain patterns, although an official will can be no more than a letter.

ACTIVITY 15.2

Read through the following example of a will and comment on the linguistic and stylistic features that make it typical of the legal variety.

1 I, JONATHAN MOORES, of 123 Wood Lane, Newtown, HEREBY REVOKE all Wills and testamentary documents heretofore made by me AND DECLARE this to be my LAST WILL and TESTAMENT.

1. I DESIRE my body to be donated to medical science.

5 2. I APPOINT my wife *Alice Moores* (hereinafter called 'my wife') to be my sole exec-
utrix of this my will but if the foregoing appointment shall fail for any reason then I
appoint my children *Edward Moores* of 456 Smithfield Road, Newtown and *Louise
Moores* of 789 Church Street, Newtown (hereinafter together called 'my trustees'
which expression where the context admits shall include the trustees or trustee
10 hereof for the time being) to be the executors and trustees of this my will.
3. I BEQUEATH to my wife all my real and personal property whatsoever and where-
soever for her own use and benefit absolutely if she shall survive me by thirty days
but if she does not survive me by the thirty days then
4. I DIVIDE and BEQUEATH all my real and personal property whatsoever and where-
15 soever unto my trustees UPON TRUST that my trustees shall sell call in and convert
into money the same and shall therefore pay my funeral and testamentary expenses
and debts and inheritance tax due and shall stand possessed of the residue of such
moneys (hereinafter called 'my residuary estate') UPON TRUST for my children
Edward Moores and *Louise Moores* in equal shares absolutely PROVIDED ALWAYS
20 that if any shall have predeceased me leaving a child or children who attain the age of
18 years such child or children shall stand in place of such deceased and shall take
by substitution and equally between them if more than one the share of my residuary estate which such a deceased child of mine would have taken if he or she had
survived me.

25 IN WITNESS whereof I the said *Jonathon Moores* the Testator have to this my LAST
WILL set my hand this twenty-first day of May One Thousand Nine Hundred and
Ninety-Five.

SIGNED AND ACKNOWLEDGED by the above-named
Jonathon Moores the Testator as and for his LAST WILL
30 in the presence of us both present at the same time
who at his request in his presence and in the presence
of each other have hereunto subscribed our names as
witnesses:

COMMENTARY

The **manner** is formal and the relationship between writer and addressees is official despite the fact that the participants are well known to each other. There are
no contractions, and formulaic utterances like *IN WITNESS whereof* (l. 25) and
LAST WILL and TESTAMENT (l. 3) add to the formal tone. The document is
legally binding and the language and style are therefore typical of the legal variety.

The **typographical features** are typical of a modern will: each point is clearly
numbered; **capitalisation** is used to highlight key lexical items; **italic print** is used
to draw attention to the names of the trustees; and **block paragraphs** are used
to indicate different sections of the document. **Punctuation** is closer to standard
written usage than in traditional legal documents, but commas are still omitted in
lists like *sell call in and convert* (l. 15) and for much of the parenthesis.

The **lexis** is typical of legal language. **Subject-specific words**, like the verb
REVOKE (l. 1), the plural noun *trustees* (l. 9) and the prepositional phrase *UPON
TRUST* (l. 15), reflect the exact nature of the legal language. Because a will deals with
the theoretical division of property at a time in the future, there are many abstract

nouns like *substitution* (l. 22), *presence* (l. 30) and *shares* (l. 19). **Ordinary words** like the nouns *appointment* (l. 6) and *estate* (l. 23) take on a specific legal meaning in this context. **Archaisms** are typical of the legal variety as a whole: for instance, prepositional words like *hereinafter* (l. 5), *hereof* (l. 10) and *heretofore* (l. 2); and the collocation *set my hand* (l. 26). **Collocations** like *real and personal property* (l. 14) and *SIGNED AND ACKNOWLEDGED* (l. 28), however, are characteristic of wills in particular. Some collocations are made up of **synonyms** – an Old English and a Latin word are used together to ensure that the meaning is all-inclusive:

> will and testament (l. 3): OE *willa*, L *testāmentum*
> divide and bequeath (l. 14): L *dīvidĕre*, OE *becwethan*

Because Latin and French were for a long time the languages of the legal system and the courts, there are many examples of **loan words** that have now been assimilated:

> executor/executrix (ll. 5–6): L *exsequī*   appoint (l. 5): OFr *apointer*
> revoke (l. 1): L *revocāre*   estate (l. 23): OFr *estat*
> residuary (l. 18): L *residuum*   deceased (l. 23): OFr *deces*

Modification provides precise information. Where pre-modification is used it is always factual and never descriptive:

> m   m   h
> the foregoing appointment (l. 6)   medical science (l. 4)
> det   V   N   Adj   N
>
> m   m   m   h
> my real and personal property (l. 11)
> det   Adj   Adj

Post-modification is more common:

> m   h   q
> the residue of such moneys (ll. 17–18)
> det   N   PrepP   N
>
> h   q
> Edward Moores of 456 Smithfield Road (l. 7)
> N   PrepP
>
> m   h   q   q
> the share of my residuary estate which such a deceased child of mine (ll. 22–3)
> det   N   PrepP   RelCl

The **verbs** are distinctive and make up a limited lexical set which is typical of any will: *REVOKE* (l. 1), *APPOINT* (l. 5), *DIVIDE and BEQUEATH* (l. 14) and *DECLARE* (l. 2). **Modal auxiliaries** like *shall* (l. 6) denote actions that have to be undertaken in the future and **adverbials** like the prepositional phrases *UPON TRUST* (l. 15), *by thirty days* and *for her own use* (l. 12) define the exact conditions that must be met.

The **grammar** is less complicated than older legal documents because the text is broken up into smaller units in numbered sections. The **mood** is declarative. The present **tense** is used because the document will be read as a current declaration of intent at the death of the testator. The will does not construct sentences with the **passive voice** because the actor (subject) and affected (object) must be clear if the declared intentions are to be carried out appropriately. Although there are many adverbials, there are few **marked themes**. Most sentences have the subject in the initial position because if the testator's wishes are to be fulfilled after death, the declaration needs to be as clear as possible. Clause elements, therefore, are not often rearranged. Examples like *IN WITNESS whereof...* (l. 25), however, draw attention to the final act of signing the will and therefore officially authorise the declarations it contains.

Sentence structures are often complex:

S   A   P   O

(I, JM of ...) (HEREBY) (REVOKE) (all Wills and testamentary documents ... made ...)

SCl–NFCl

P   O

(and) (declare) (this to be my...)   (ll. 1–3)

conj   SCl–NFCl

S   P   Od   Oi

(I) (divide and bequeath) (all my real and personal property ...) (unto my trustees)

conj   conj

A

(upon trust that my trustees shall sell ... and shall therefore pay ... and shall stand

SCl–NCl   conj   SCl–NCl   conj   SCl–NCl

A

possessed of ...) (provided always that if any shall have predeceased me leaving a

SCl–ACl   SCl–ACl   SCl–NFCl

child or children who attain ... such child or children shall stand ... and shall take ...

conj   SCl–RelCl   conj   conj   SCl–ACl

the share ... which such a deceased child ... would have taken ... if he or she had

SCl–RelCl   SCl–ACl conj

survived me).   (ll. 14–24)

The need to include detailed conditions that must be met after the death of the testator means that the sentence is complicated by numerous adverbials. Many of the clauses are co-ordinated and ellipsis makes it even more difficult to identify the clause structure. The **cohesion** is typical of legal language in using repetition of key lexical items like *trustees* (l. 9) and *property* (l. 11) to avoid pronoun referencing which might cause ambiguity. The use of the first person singular pronoun *I* is appropriate here, however, since the document is a written statement from the testator who is clearly named in the post-modification of *I* in the opening sentence of the will. Object pronouns are used where the reference is clear: *them* (l. 22) is used as an anaphoric reference to the possible future children of one of the testator's own children; and the object pronoun *us* (l. 30) is used as a cataphoric reference to the signatures of the witnesses.

The will has a distinctive format which will only vary slightly from example to example. The language and syntax are typical of the legal variety as a whole, but are also marked by characteristics of this particular kind of legally binding contract.

The language of the courts

The spoken legal language of the courts is governed by complex rules: witnesses are not allowed to say what other people have said (hearsay); they are not allowed to evaluate (opinion); and they are discouraged from showing emotions. Instead all contributors must do no more than respond directly to the questions.

Lawyers are advised to vary the way in which they ask questions in order to draw more from the witnesses and to use different questioning approaches for different kinds of people. For example, a good lawyer will choose different styles for expert witnesses, for the elderly and for the very young. Repetition can be used as a rhetorical device, but overuse can bore the jury. Prosodic features like rhythm, pitch and pace are also important variants if members of the jury are to be persuaded to agree with the particular interpretation of events put forward.

Different kinds of courts deal with different kinds of offences and the manner of a particular hearing is therefore dependent on the legal context. Civil offences are tried in both county courts and the High Court. The county courts are less formal since they deal with local affairs in which small sums of money are involved, social matters like housing and the welfare of children, and undefended matrimonial cases. The High Court deals with problems on a larger scale, like mortgages, bankruptcy and divorce appeals, so hearings are far more formal. Criminal cases are heard in the magistrates' courts and the crown court. In magistrates' courts, there is no jury; people can choose to defend themselves or to be represented by a barrister or solicitor; the justices decide whether the defendant is innocent or guilty and fix a sentence where appropriate. The tone here is less formal than in the crown court, where all serious indictable crimes are dealt with.

The spoken language of the courts is often similar to that of written legal documents, but because it is spoken rather than written it tends to be less complicated. Its formal **manner**, nevertheless, is marked by **formulaic utterances** which are immediately recognisable from the courtroom dramas that appear on television: *You may approach the Bench*; *If your Lordship pleases*; *leading counsel for defence*. The **naming of participants** also contributes to the formality of the setting: the judge is called *My Lord* and *Your Lordship*; lawyers address each other as *my learned friend*; and witnesses are addressed by their full names and title – for example, *Mr Philip White*.

The structure of a court case is patterned and the proceedings of any trial will be opened and closed formally. In a crown court, the clerk of the court will probably begin the hearing by saying:

> Members of the Jury, the Prisoner at the Bar is charged that on _____ s/he _____.
> To this indictment s/he has pleaded not guilty and it is your charge to say, having heard the evidence, whether s/he be guilty or not.

The official tone and the subject-specific lexis immediately mark this as an example of the legal variety. Although not as complicated as a legal contract, the sentence structure is still noticeably complex:

>   S   P   O   A   O   A   S   P
> (Members …) (the Prisoner …) (is charged) (that (on …) s/he …). (To …) (s/he) (has
>   voc   SCl–NCl
>   C   dumS P   C   A
> pleaded) (not guilty) (and) (it) (is) (your charge to say), (having heard the evidence),
>   conj   SCl–NFCl SCl–NFCl
>   (S)
> (whether …)
> SCl–NCl

The number of subordinate clauses makes the sentence structure elaborate and clearly marks spoken legal language as more similar to a written register than to an informal spoken one. The use of the subjunctive *s/he be* is also more common in formal written discourse.

Many lexical items are **subject-specific**, like the nouns *witness-box*, *Common Law* and *jury*, and the verbs *adjourn*, *cross-examine* and *prosecute*. In a spoken as in a written register, legal language uses many **loan words** of French and Latin origin:

> defendant: L *dēfendĕre*   adjourn: OFr *ajorner*
> prosecution: L *prōsequī*   verdict: OFr *verdit*
> evidence: L *ēvidēns*   counsel: Fr *conseil*

Archaisms are less common in court because the language has to be appropriate for the general public as well as the experts. **Questions** often require closed *yes/no* responses, but equally lawyers may force witnesses to develop their answers by framing questions using *wh-* question words.

In a spoken context, there is no time for lengthy reconsiderations of unfamiliar words and complex sentence structures, so although the language is always formal, it is not usually marked by the convoluted style of legal written language.

ACTIVITY 15.3

In October 1960 at the Old Bailey in London, Penguin Books Ltd was charged under the 1959 Obscene Publications Act with publishing an obscene article – D. H. Lawrence's book *Lady Chatterley's Lover*. The court case revolved around the issue of whether the novel would 'deprave' and 'corrupt' its readers. After a trial lasting six days, the jury decided that Penguin Books was not guilty of publishing obscene material.

The following extract taken from the court hearing is part of the fifth day's proceedings, in which Mr Justice Byrne began his summing up for the jury. Read through the court transcript and comment on:

1 linguistic features that are typical of the legal variety
2 ways in which spoken and written legal language are different.

SUMMING UP BY MR JUSTICE BYRNE

1 MR JUSTICE BYRNE: Members of the jury, you have listened with the greatest care and attention to this case, and you have read this book. Now the time is rapidly approaching when you will have to return a verdict …
You will recollect that publication has to be proved: the offence is publishing an
5 obscene article. All that is meant by 'publishing' for the purposes of this case is handing a copy of this book to somebody …
… And you, of course, will not exercise questions of taste or the functions of a censor, but you will decide whether it has been proved beyond reasonable doubt that this book is obscene. That is the first question. How the Statute puts the matter is
10 this: it provides that an article shall be deemed to be obscene if its effect is, if taken as a whole, such as to tend to deprave and corrupt persons who are likely having regard to all relevant circumstances, to read the matter contained in it.
Of course, the first thing you would want to know is, what is meant by the words to 'deprave and corrupt', and you have had those words defined from dictionaries, one was
15 the Oxford Dictionary, and I think it would be quite fair to put it in this way, that to deprave means to make morally bad. To pervert. To debase or corrupt morally.
The words 'to corrupt' mean to render morally unsound or rotten. To destroy the moral purity or chastity of, to pervert or ruin a good quality, to debase, to defile …
Having read the book the question is, does it tend to deprave or corrupt?

20　The next matter you have to consider is this, that you have to decide whether there is in this book a tendency to deprave and corrupt persons who are likely, having regard to all relevant circumstances, to read the matter contained in it.

Now what are the relevant circumstances? Who are the people having regard to the relevant circumstances, who are likely to read the book? ...

25　If you have any reasonable doubt as to whether it has been proved to your satisfaction that the tendency of the book is to deprave and corrupt morals, of course you will acquit, and that would be an end of this case. But, on the other hand, if with your knowledge of the world and with your knowledge now of the book, having read it for yourselves, you are satisfied beyond reasonable doubt that the book has a tendency

30　to deprave and corrupt those who might, in the circumstances, be expected to read it, you, of course, will not hesitate to say so.

And that really is the first limb of this case, and, as I said to you, before 1959, before the passing of the Obscene Publications Act of that year, the defendant company felt, although they wished to do so, that they could not publish that book because, prior

35　to the passing of the Statute under which this charge is made, defendants were not allowed by law to call any evidence with regard to the literary or other merits of the book ...

But in 1959 a change in the law was made, and by virtue of Section 4 of the Statute the defendants are enabled to call evidence.

40　That section ... provides that a person shall not be convicted, that is to say, of publishing an obscene publication, if it is proved that publication of the article in question is justified as being for the public good on the ground that it is in the interests of science, literature, art or learning or other objects of general concern ...

I am going to break off now, members of the jury, because I want to refer you to

45　some of the evidence given by the witnesses who were called on behalf of the defendant company with regard to this second limb about which I have been telling you, that is the question whether the probability is that the merits of the book are so high that they out-balance the obscenity so that its publication is for the public good.

Members of the jury, rather than begin that and then break off again I think we will

50　adjourn now until to-morrow morning. Then I shall not take so very long to complete my observations, and you will then be able to retire to consider your verdict. Will you kindly be in your places again at half-past-ten to-morrow morning, and in the meantime, forgive me once again if I remind you of the warning which I gave you, keep your own counsel.

Before Mr Justice Byrne – Regina v Penguin Books Limited:
Central Criminal Court, Old Bailey, London (Thursday, 20 October 1960)

COMMENTARY

The **manner** is inevitably formal because the trial is taking place in the Central Criminal Court at the Old Bailey. The relationship between the participants is official and the presence of 'experts' makes the context very specific. The language is a mixture of both legal and ordinary words since the spoken register used in court is less convoluted and more familiar than the written legal register. **Formulaic utterances** like the formal opening of the judge's summing up, *Members of the jury* (l. 1) mark the gravity of the occasion.

Since this is a transcript of spoken language, there are no distinctive **typographical features**. Written legal language relies on its layout and typographical features to avoid legal loopholes and to guide the reader through complicated legal conditions. The language of the courtroom, however, is primarily a spoken register which is written down only for official records. Jurors, for instance, do not reach their verdict by reading what has been said in court, but by listening. This means that prosodic features like pitch, pace and rhythm replace changes in typeface, underlining and capitalisation. Transcripts of a trial do not mark the prosodic features because when such records are consulted, **what** is said is more important than **how** it was said.

The **lexis** is still recognisably part of the legal variety, but there are more ordinary words too. **Subject-specific words** like the nouns *jury* (l.1), *offence* (l.4) and *verdict* (l.3) mark the variety, but there are also far more everyday words like the nouns *book* (l.2) and *knowledge* (l.28) and colloquial phrases like *in the meantime* (ll.52–3) and *of course* (l.7). Some **ordinary words**, however, are used in a specialist way: *publication* (l.4) now has a specific legal meaning which is defined by the judge; the meaning of the verbs *deprave and corrupt* (l.14) is also established so that the jury are in a position to interpret the legal test for obscene publications. This is an example of the metalinguistic function of legal language. There are no **archaisms** because these would sound awkward in speech and might unnecessarily complicate the legal judgements being made. **Loan words** from French and Latin are still apparent, but technical legal jargon is used less frequently: *Statute* (l.9) from L *statūtum*; *adjourn* (l.50) from OFr *ajorner*; *doubt* (l.8) from OFr *douter* and L *dubitāre*. While the verb *proved* (l.4) has its origins in OE *prōfian*, OF *prover* and L *probāre*, other words like the verb *deemed* (l.10) and the noun *law* (l.38) have their origins in OE *dēman* and *lagu*.

The legal **collocations** are often familiar because they commonly appear in the media: for instance, jurors have listened with *the greatest care and attention* (ll.1–2); they will have to *return a verdict* (l.3); and they must decide whether they have *any reasonable doubt* (l.25). Other collocations are associated with contexts that are not legal: for instance, *on the other hand* (l.27), *of course* (l.7) and *as I said to you* (l.32). This kind of almost informal language use clearly marks one of the key differences between written and spoken legal language. Another difference can be seen in the absence of any **synonyms**. Where written legal documents use these throughout to ensure that all options have been covered, courtroom language has a different purpose. There are still patterns and formulae that must be adhered to, but rather than being a watertight legal document which must guarantee an individual's or a group's rights, spoken legal language uses the law to make judgements. Even though the language is still used by experts, non-experts are also involved as jurors, witnesses, prosecutors and defendants – the spoken language of the courts must therefore be approachable for the general public too.

Abstract nouns are common because the trial is about concepts of taste and decency: *doubt* (l.8), *quality* (l.18) and *tendency* (l.21), for instance. **Modification** is still restrained, providing factual information rather than emotive or descriptive detail:

m	m	h	
all	relevant	circumstances	(l.22)
det	Adj	N	

Verbs seem to be of a less restrictive lexical set because the discourse is spoken and therefore uses verbs that are appropriate for face-to-face exchanges. **Modal verbs** are used to convey attitude, just as they are in written legal language: for instance, *will* (l. 3) marks a time in the future; *shall* (l. 10) denotes the legal conditions under which an article can be deemed 'obscene'; and *could* (l. 34) marks possibility. While the first two have connotations of certainty, the latter is conditional. The use of the auxiliary *will* to frame questions is both polite and formal: *Will you kindly be in your places...* (ll. 51–2). **Adverbials** defining specific conditions which must be met are not used in the same way and this makes the sentence structures seem less elaborate.

The **grammar** is still formal and standard, but there are features that link it to spoken language. Sentences are still long, but this tends to be because spoken language is less purposefully crafted; direct address makes the manner seem more personal; and adverbs like *Now* (l. 2) and prepositional phrases like *Of course* (l. 13) in the initial position (**marked themes**) give the discourse a less ceremonious tone. The **mood** is a mixture of declaratives, imperatives like *keep your own counsel* (ll. 53–4) and interrogatives like *Who are the people... ?* (l. 23). This variation in mood is typical of the different kinds of exchanges that take place in a trial and is quite different from the declarative mood of most written legal documents. The **passive voice** tends to be used in direct references to the Statute: *shall be deemed* (l. 10); *was made* (l. 38); and *were not allowed by law* (ll. 35–6). This adds to the overall formality and links the language of the court to written rather than spoken language.

The **sentence structure** is quite different from that of written legal language. Simple and compound sentences are more frequent:

                 S   P   A

(Members of the jury) (you) (have listened) (with the greatest care and attention)
    voc

      A   S   P   O   A   C   P

(to this case) (and) (you) (have read) (this book) ... . (Now) (what) (are) (the relevant
             conj

     S

circumstances?)   (ll. 1–2, 23)

Some sentences are grammatically incomplete, which is less likely in written legal language: *To pervert* and *To debase or corrupt morally* (l. 16). Complex and compound–complex sentence structures are common, but they tend to contain fewer dependent subordinate clauses:

                                            A

(If you have any reasonable doubt as to whether it has been proved to your satis-
  SCl–ACl   SCl–ACl

                                                  A

faction that the tendency of the book is to deprave and ø corrupt morals), (of course)
    SCl–NCl   SCl–NFCl   conj   SCl–NFCl

    S   P   S   P   C

(you) (will acquit) (and) (that) (would be) (an end of this case).   (ll. 25–7)
            conj

Repetition is again used as a form of **cohesion**. Key legal lexical items like the noun phrases *reasonable doubt* (l. 8) and *relevant circumstances* (l. 12) are reiterated to ensure that the jury understand the legal implications of the trial. Other repetitions like *first limb* (l. 32) and *second limb* (l. 46) show how the judge is dividing his summing up into discrete sections to clarify the facts that the jurors must consider to reach their verdict.

Spoken and written legal language

The extract from the transcript clearly bears many similarities to written legal language, but also differs in marked ways. The following list summarises the key similarities and differences between spoken and written legal language.

Manner

- The manner is formal in both instances, but in a courtroom context, some informal collocations and speech patterns may be used.

Typographical features

- The typographical features of written legal language are an integral part of the document since they ensure that interpretation is unambiguous. Such features are unimportant in spoken legal language because what is said is more important than how it is said.

Lexis

- In both instances, subject-specific language identifies the legal variety.
- It is common in both written and spoken legal language to find ordinary words used in specialist ways, and also specialist words that have become a part of everyday discourse.
- Archaisms are rarely found in spoken legal language, whereas they are common in written documentation.
- The all-inclusive synonyms of written legal language are less common in courtroom language.
- French and Latin loan words form the basis of both written and spoken technical legal language.
- Abstract nouns are common in both kinds of discourse because both are dealing with abstract issues of justice and law.
- Modification is similar in both contexts since it provides factual information rather than descriptive or evaluative detail.
- Clusters of adverbials tend to be more frequent in written documents, but when judges are summing up they may also list various conditions that must be considered before reaching a verdict.

Grammar

- Modal verbs are common in both legal registers.
- Spoken legal language is less likely to use limited lexical sets of verbs than are written documents, in which the context is far more specific.

- Pronouns are more likely to be used in spoken language because the immediacy of the context will prevent the possibility of ambiguous interpretation.
- The grammatical mood of sentences is more varied in a courtroom because the kinds of exchanges are more diverse.
- The passive voice is less common in the courtroom – rearranging the word order of an active sentence could make interpretation more difficult in a spoken context as it is not immediately possible to reread a complicated sentence.
- In spoken legal language, informal phrases are sometimes used in the initial position. Although inappropriate for written legal language, these marked themes are accepted alongside the formal legal language of the courtroom.
- Repetition is used in both cases to give cohesion to the discourse.
- Simple sentences are more common in spoken legal language.
- Both types of legal language use complex and compound–complex sentences, but the sentences of spoken language tend to be less convoluted.

15.5 What to look for in the language of law

The following checklist can be used to identify key features in examples of legal language. You will not find all of the features in every text or transcription, but the list can be used as a guide. The points made are general, so discussion of specific examples will need to be adapted to take account of the specific context, audience and purpose of the given discourse. Remember that you need to evaluate the effect of the features you identify, exploring the ways in which they create meaning.

The following are helpful questions to ask.

Register
1 What is the **mode**?
   - written or spoken?
2 What is the **manner**?
   - formal? traditional? modernised?
   - relationship between participants?
3 What is the **field**?
   - legal subject matter?
   - linked to the audience, purpose and context?

Typographical features
1 Is the written text in a **block** or divided into **paragraphs** and **subsections**?
2 Are any **typographical features** used to guide readers?
   - capitalisation? underlining? changes in typeface?
3 Is the **punctuation** used standardly?
   - commas omitted?
   - colons or dashes used to mark the beginning of sections?
   - brackets used for parenthesis?

Lexis
1 Is there any **subject-specific vocabulary**?

- general technical terms?
- words typical of a particular branch of the law?

2 Are any **ordinary words** used with a specific legal meaning?

3 Is there any **specialist language** that has become a part of everyday conversation?

4 Are there any **archaisms** that mark out the traditional nature of written legal language?

5 Are there **collocations** or **synonyms** typical of the formulaic patterns of legal language?

6 Are there any examples of French and Latin **loan words** that go back to the establishment of the legal structures in society when English was considered unsuitable for such formal contexts?

7 Are there any examples of **abstract nouns** that link to the abstract nature of law and justice?

8 Are there any examples of **pre-** and **post-modification** used to provide factual information?

9 Do **adverbials** cluster together, defining the legal conditions that must be met or considered?

10 Are there any **limited lexical sets** of **verbs** that indicate the kind of legal context of the example?

11 Are there a lot of **non-finite verbs** and **modal auxiliaries**, a feature that distinguishes the legal variety from other varieties?

Grammar

1 Is the **passive voice** used to refocus the reader on key lexical items by re-arranging the word order?

2 Is the **mood** mainly declarative (written) or does it vary (spoken)?

3 Are **marked themes** used to draw attention to key legal conditions?

4 Are the **sentences** long and complicated?
- sequences of dependent clauses?
- simple or compound sentences?
- structures linked to spoken language?
- structures linked to written language?

5 Is repetition used to create **cohesion**?
- are pronoun references used? anaphorically or cataphorically?
- is any ambiguity created with pronoun referencing?

Summary

The **function** of legal language is to enforce obligations and to confer rights. It must therefore say exactly what is intended. Clear interpretation is crucial, so documents are constructed extremely precisely.

The **audience** for written legal documents is not expected to be ordinary language users – instead such documents are written by one expert for another. The style reflects this and its complexity can alienate the ordinary reader. The spoken legal language of a courtroom context must be accessible, however, since the jury is made up of ordinary people and the witnesses called are not always experts. The differentiation in intended audience is one of the key elements that make spoken and written legal language different.

Tradition plays a large part in making legal language distinctive. The variety is marked by its conservatism. It has preserved forms which, although abandoned in other varieties, have proved successful in legal practice. The ceremonial element of legal language is linked to its use of archaisms.

Legal language is often accused of being **obscure** and **lacking clarity**. Because all its intentions must be externalised to avoid ambiguity, legal language often appears to be unnecessarily convoluted. Paradoxically, while the complexity of the language makes legal documents obscure to the lay person, its precision gives clarity to the expert.

Chapter 16

The language of religion

16.1 The nature of religious language

The language of religion is important in any culture, and in Britain the traditional language of Christianity, with its distinctive lexical and syntactical patterns, has influenced the development of English in many ways. Historically, religious language was at the heart of a community, as literacy was often spread through religious services. In modern society the language of the Church may not be so common in daily conversation, yet it remains a variety that most people can recognise because of its widespread use beyond the specific context of Church services. Over many years Church language has become part of the everyday language for believers and non-believers alike – many writers use biblical quotations in their work, for example, and some common sayings can be traced back to the **BIBLE** in its **Authorised Version** (**AV**, first published in 1611 and also known as the **King James Version**) and the Church of England's **BOOK OF COMMON PRAYER** (**BCP**, dating back to 1544 but best known in its 1662 edition). Other formal varieties of English also draw on some of the archaisms associated with religious language. For instance, we talk of *the blind leading the blind* (Matthew 15:14: 'They be blind leaders of the blind. And if the blind lead the blind, both shall fall into the ditch') and *the powers that be* (Romans 13:1: 'There is no power but of God: the powers that be are ordained by God'); some people use *Jesus wept* (John 11:35, from the story of the raising of Lazarus) as an expletive; and the expressions *Till Death Us Do Part* and *In Sickness and in Health*, familiar from the marriage service, have been used as the titles of BBC television comedies. Despite the varied uses of religious language, it can be recognised by the distinctive features that mark it.

The language of religion generally can be found in many contexts: in religious newspapers and magazines, on Radio 4's 'Thought for the Day', and in local publicity material promoting church events. The specific language of the Church, however, is a very distinctive form of religious language, and to a large extent it has been kept free from the influences of other varieties of English such as the language of newspapers or broadcasting.

Religious language has both written and spoken forms. In all religions, written **SACRED TEXTS** provide the central focus for worship – for Christians, the Bible;

for Buddhists, the **PALI CANON**; for Muslims, the **QUR'AN**; and so on. These texts have a historical significance since they are the basis for the spiritual tradition of each religion. Alterations to a given translation are often considered controversial because they change the revered norms with which people are familiar. Both religious leaders and worshippers expect translations to be historically accurate and faithful to the meaning of the source. Contemporary versions therefore attempt to preserve the linguistic features of traditional translations as far as possible, while also taking account of current social and linguistic trends. Up-to-date translations of traditional texts try to avoid changes that may evoke strong reactions, but seek to bridge the gap between sometimes unintelligible archaisms and the language of everyday speech.

Spoken religious language also is distinctive. It is marked by special pronunciations and by prosodic features such as intonation patterns which play a crucial part in ensuring that the worshippers relate to and understand the spiritual message.

16.2 The function of religious language

The sacred texts of different religions have always been a means of **upholding spiritual belief**. Equally, because their written forms do not substantially change, these traditional documents have protected the sacred knowledge central to each religion. Each type of religious language has a slightly different function, but basically the variety as a whole seeks to **persuade** people to believe and to act in a certain moral way (**conative** function). Religious texts like the Bible also have an **expressive** function since they are partly concerned with an expression of feelings.

Both in public and in private contexts, the function of religious language is to develop a more moral and spiritual outlook. Whether used by a church congregation in a public service or by an individual worshipping in private, religious language **prescribes** a specific attitude to life.

16.3 Features of religious language

Each religion has a body of sacred texts and written **DOCTRINE** which sustain and promote its particular spiritual wisdom. Because Christianity has had such a dramatic influence on the English language, however, the examples discussed here focus on material drawn from traditional Christian sources. The distinctive linguistic features of the writings discussed in this section will often find parallels in texts promoting the spiritual beliefs and values of other religions, and the methods of analysis used can also be applied to other world religions.

In the Christian religion, **PRAYERS** are a special form of polite command or request addressed to God; **LITURGIES** are chants, thanksgivings, hymns and psalms; **SERMONS** are moral statements which aim to promote a certain kind of faith and behaviour through stories or examples; and **THEOLOGICAL TEXTS** are discursive documents with a moral purpose written by biblical scholars, theologians or the clergy – they may contain justifications for certain beliefs and lifestyles, spiritual guidelines, or explanations of religious teachings.

Many of the examples considered here are taken from traditional sources (AV and BCP) because these are marked by the most distinctive linguistic features of the variety as a whole. Although modern versions and improved translations reduce the number of archaisms, provide paraphrases for any subject-specific terms and avoid unnecessarily complicated sentence structures, many of the characteristic features of the traditional versions still remain. In its contemporary forms, therefore, the language of the Church is still formal and distinctive, but less likely to seem alien to its intended modern audience.

The traditional language of the Church, as exemplified by the AV and the BCP, can be summarised as follows.

Manner

The **manner** is usually formal and has little similarity with informal spoken or written language, even though examples of religious language are scattered throughout our everyday usage. In written texts, for instance, there are no contractions for auxiliaries or negatives, and spoken religious language is not marked by the hesitancy and normal non-fluency features associated with informal speech. Because it is a traditional form of language, the language of the Church often retains ARCHAIC linguistic features which add to the formality of the medium. Its main use is in public group contexts, however, so although some features are archaic, religious language must remain accessible to the intended audience. FORMULAIC UTTER-ANCES like *Glory be to God* are common, and these too create a formal tone.

Lexis

The **lexis** is **subject-specific**, with nouns like *disciples* and *parables* and verbs like *pray* and *forgive*. In the narrative of the AV, the vocabulary is often **archaic**: some words no longer have a contemporary equivalent; others have been replaced with modern synonyms; and many are linked directly to a specific person, place or action and take their meaning from the historical situation.

Because of its traditional nature, there are many **formal phrases** and **idioms**: *In the beginning* and *Let there be light* are taken from the written language of the Bible, while *Dearly beloved brethren*, *We are gathered here together* and *Let us pray* are spoken directly to the congregation. The language is often **formulaic**, with openings like *We beseech thee* and closings like *Amen* to mark the beginning and end of a prayer. **Antithesis** is common: *heaven* and *hell*, *sin* and *forgiveness*, and *death* and *resurrection*.

Nominal groups in religious language, particularly in prayers, tend to be quite long. Most nouns have at least one modifier and post-modification and noun phrases in apposition are common. Adjectives are often modified by adverbs:

m	m	h		m	m	h
thine	only	son	Jesus Christ	dearly	beloved	brethren
det	Adj	N	NP in apposition	Adv	V	N

In prayers, post-modification is usually in the form of a relative clause following a vocative or personal pronoun in the subject site. It can also take the form of prepositional phrases or non-finite clauses:

	m	h	q			m	h	q	
Our Father who art in heaven   the kingdom of heaven

m — h — q
Our Father who art in heaven   the kingdom of heaven
det N   RelCl   det N   PrepP

h q
we, worthily lamenting our sins
pron SCl–NFCl

The **naming of the godhead** is important in many religions (though in some other religious contexts, the name of God is seen as being too holy to pronounce and is replaced by a symbolic term). The theological terms which represent God in the Christian religion form a clear focus point, helping to make religious language distinctive from other varieties. Post-modifying phrases or clauses often take a human concept like being a 'father' or a 'king' and use this as an analogy for God: *Almighty God, most merciful Father; O Lord our heavenly Father, high and mighty, king of kings*. A link between the known human world and the unknown theological world is also created through **modifiers** that define divine attributes. Adjectives like *Almighty* denote God's omnipotence, while *merciful* emphasises that God's power is not tyrannical. As belief in God is central to Christianity, many references are made to God and to theological concepts or figures linked to God. This means that more than half of the **determiners** used are possessive. Because of the abstract spiritual nature of religion, many of the nouns are non-count: *heaven, compassion, salvation* and so on.

Grammar

The **grammar** of traditional Church language often resembles older forms of English, particularly in the AV and the BCP. In the AV, for instance, third person singular verbs are inflected with the **suffixes** *-(e)th* and *-(e)st*: *creepeth, mayest* and *doth*; and some verbs still have the older **strong forms**: *sware* for *swore, shewed* for *showed* and *spake* for *spoke*. The use of the **unstressed auxiliary do** to indicate past time is also archaic: *I did eat*. In modernised versions of traditional religious language, many of these features have been replaced with Late Modern English equivalent forms.

The **present tense** is often used in the BCP, while the **simple past** is most common in the AV. The **mood** is rarely interrogative, but frequently declarative: *A false balance is abomination to the Lord; but a just weight is his delight* (AV, Proverbs 11:1). Imperatives are also common: *Give heed unto reading, exhortation, and doctrine. Think upon the things contained in this Book* (BCP, The Consecration of Bishops). The subjunctive is more common in the written language of the Church than in Late Modern English, and this marks the variety as formal since the subjunctive is not commonly used in speech. It can be used to express an intention or a proposal about the future or to convey that something which is supposed to happen is not yet happening. In the subjunctive, verbs that would normally take an *-s* inflection are used in the base form: *For if the first fruit be holy, the lump is also holy* (AV, Romans 11:16); *If any man think himself to be a prophet* (AV, Corinthians 15:37).

Modal verbs are also common, implying contrasts in speaker attitudes. They are often used to convey a certainty in future time or to mark a spiritual command which should be followed: *And the woman said unto the serpent, We <u>may</u> eat of the fruit...* (AV, Genesis 3:2); *So <u>will</u> I send upon you a famine and evil beasts, and they <u>shall</u> bereave thee* (AV, Ezekiel 5:17).

In traditional versions, **pronouns** are distinctive because of their archaic forms: *ye* and *thee* are widely used. In many updated versions, these have been revised and replaced with the contemporary form of direct address, *you*. Pronouns in prayers are often post-modified:

>   h   q
> Thou who takest away the sins of the world
>   pron SCl–RelCl

The first person singular is rarely used in formal prayer, but the first person plural is common. This reflects the public, group nature of worship.

Sentences in the AV are often basically simple, but because of the accumulated strings of co-ordinated finite and non-finite clauses, the structure is ultimately complex:

>   A   S   P   O
> (In the beginning) (God) (created) (the heaven and the earth)   Genesis 1:1

>   S   P   O   Co   S
> (And) (God) (called) (the firmament) (Heaven). (And) (the evening and the morning)
>   P   C
> (were) (the second day).   Genesis 1:8

Such use of **co-ordinators in the initial position** is common in the Authorised Version of the Bible and it is not unusual to see an **inversion of the subject and verb**:

> And Micaiah said, As the Lord liveth, even what my God saith, that *will* I speak
>   The Second Book of Chronicles 18:13

> Then *answered the Lord* unto Job out of the whirlwind ...   Job 40:6

Modernised versions, however, avoid such inversions, making religious language more like that of everyday speech:

> But Micaiah said, 'As the Lord lives, what my God says, that I will speak.'

> Then the Lord answered Job out of the whirlwind ...
>   Revised Standard Version (1971)

Sometimes, the **subject can be separated from the verb** by a sequence of subordinate clauses:

>   S
> (God, who at sundry times and in divers manners spake in time past unto the fathers
>   SCl–RelCl
>   P   A   P   Oi
> by the prophets), (Hath) (in these last days) (spoken) (unto us) ...   Hebrews 1:1–2

Structures like this are also simplified in modern versions:

>   A   S   P   A   Oi   A
> (In many and various ways) (God) (spoke) (of old) (to our fathers) (by the prophets);
>   A   S   P   Oi
> (but) (in these last days) (he) (has spoken) (to us) ...

By contrast, in **litanies**, which are chanted by the congregation after the priest, sentences may be very short:

```
   S        P        Oi        Od                            P        Oi        Od
(We) (beseech) (thee) (to hear us), (good Lord).     (Grant) (to us) (thy peace).
                      SCl–NFCl                voc
```

Prayers too have a distinctive sentence structure:

- they begin with a vocative (a single proper noun which may be preceded by *O* + *adjective* or which may be followed by a post-modifying relative clause)
- they contain an imperative verb which is followed by an object and its dependent clauses
- they conclude with the formulaic *Amen.*

Other optional vocatives and dependent clauses can be used, but this pattern establishes the most common structure.

```
(O God, who hast prepared for them that love thee such good things as pass man's
 voc    SCl–RelCl                          SCl–RelCl                          SCl–ACl
                  P           A                        O
understanding; (Pour) (into our hearts) (such love toward thee), (that we, loving thee
                                                                   SCl–ACl      SCl–NFCl
         A
above all things, may obtain thy promises, which exceed all that we can desire);
                                             SCl–RelCl              SCl–RelCl
through Jesus Christ our Lord. Amen.
```

Imperatives of this length and complexity are rarely found in other varieties of English.

The AV clearly has a different type of sentence structure from that used in prayers and ritual ceremonies in the BCP. The former is more likely to use archaic features such as inversion of the subject and verb or the direct and indirect objects, while prayers are more likely to have long sequences of dependent clauses. Rites are usually more straightforward, often using simple and compound sentences. In each case, the structure is distinctive, helping to classify examples as representative of religious language.

Literary devices

The use of **figurative language** is central to the field of religion. **Metaphor** adds an extra layer of meaning to the stories that provide the spiritual philosophy of a religion. Both the AV and modern versions of the Bible use a range of techniques to give the text depth, underpinning the narrative with a specific moral theology. The figurative description of God's anger as fire, for instance, portrays the power of God to punish those who do not follow the spiritual path:

> and the fire of the Lord burnt among them and consumed them that were in the uttermost parts of the camp.
>
> Numbers 11:1

Symbolism is central to the interpretation of the language of the Church. Although service books like the BCP and its modern equivalents are more literal, rarely using metaphors, all religious language requires believers to look beyond the words to a spiritual framework. Thus in Genesis, *Adam and Eve* represent humanity; *the serpent* represents evil; and *the apple* represents temptation. The symbolism makes the Adam and Eve story more than just a narrative – it becomes a moral lesson exemplifying the spiritual and religious message.

The function of religious texts is perhaps to persuade people to believe and act in a way that is appropriate for a particular religion. **Rhetoric**, the art of persuasion, therefore, is very important. Devices like **antithesis** are central since the nature of religion itself juxtaposes good and evil. Concepts like *heaven* and *earth*, *death* and *life*, and *crucifixion* and *resurrection* form part of the fundamental belief structure. Terms like these are then reiterated throughout the texts in order to emphasise their significance. **Sentence organisation** is also used to draw attention to key elements. In the Bible, many adverbs of time like *now* and *then* are marked themes establishing key moments; other foregrounded adverbials are clauses that convey a condition or reason:

$$A$$

(If any man among you seem to be religious, and brideth not his tongue, but
SCl–ACl   SCl–NFCl   SCl–ACl
                                            S   P   C

deceiveth his own heart), (this man's religion) (is) (vain).   AV, James 1:26
SCl–ACl

                  A   A   S   P

(Therefore seeing we have this ministry), (as we have received mercy), (we) (faint)
SCl–NFCl   SCl–ACl

(not).
neg   AV, The Second Epistle to the Corinthians 4:1

In twentieth-century versions, although the archaic features of the AV are modernised, the fronted adverbials remain:

                                      A

(If any one thinks he is religious and does not bridle his tongue but deceives his own
SCl–ACl   SCl–NCl   SCl–ACl   SCl–ACl
                          S   P   C

heart), (this man's religion) (is) (vain).

             A   A   S   P   O

(Therefore having this ministry) (by the mercy of God), (we) (do not lose) (heart).
SCl–NFCl   neg

Revised Standard Version (1971)

All these techniques help to make the language of the Church persuasive and emotive, but the **PHONOLOGICAL PATTERNING** is just as important. The Bible has a controlled framework of balanced structures and the division of the text into verses makes it easy to read aloud. **Co-ordination** and the frequent use of **pauses** marked by commas give it a sonorous and resonant tone. The Book of Common Prayer and other service books are actually written to be read aloud – part of the text is to be read by clergy who are experienced, while other sections are to be read by the inexperienced congregation speaking in unison. The tone variations are often predictable and the sentences are rhythmically balanced.

Typographical features

Typographical features are often used to help the congregation read the relevant parts of the service successfully. **Paragraphing** and **spacing** split text into units which guide the reader. **Capitalisation** marks proper nouns, personal titles and pronouns referring to the deity. In some texts, **punctuation** has a phonetic value. Full stops are not always used to mark the grammatical end of a sentence, but sometimes imply a major phonological pause; commas can reflect a brief pause; and colons can be equivalent to either.

This variety is quite unlike the language of everyday conversation because even in modernised versions many distinctive features can be traced directly to the traditional religious language of the AV and the BCP. Although both of the traditional texts are marked by archaic language and structures, the 1662 BCP is more innovative in its use of language than the 1611 AV – it was the first systematic attempt to adapt the language of the Church's public liturgy, to

> keep the mean between two extremes, of too much stiffness in refusing, and of too much easiness in admitting, any variation from [the original]
>
> Preface, *The Book of Common Prayer*

Because people are familiar with these traditional forms and are unwilling to see them change dramatically, religious language alters very little. However, much of the language of the Church is to be spoken aloud and it must therefore be appropriate for the worshippers. Although the traditional framework is relatively fixed, there are some variations that aim to approximate everyday English in an attempt to engage contemporary worshippers.

16.4 Types of religious language

Sacred texts

The SACRED TEXTS of each religion provide a focus for believers. They aim to preserve both the essential characteristics of a particular faith and the linguistic features associated with its earliest written forms.

Christianity has the Bible as its core: the Old Testament, which includes the sacred texts of Judaism, was originally written in Hebrew; and the New Testament, which records the life of Christ and the early Christians, was written in Greek. For centuries the English Church used the fourth-century Latin translation of the Bible, the Vulgate. A few handwritten English copies were produced in the 1380s by John Wycliffe and his followers, but reading the Bible in English was still prohibited in the 1430s. The first Bible printed in English was translated by William Tyndale in the 1520s and 1530s, from the original Hebrew and Greek sources. Tyndale tried to use everyday words, aiming for clarity rather than for literal translation. He wrote as ordinary people spoke rather than as the scholars wrote and in many ways his version is therefore distinctively English. Because of his work, Tyndale was tried for heresy in Antwerp and in 1536 was garrotted.

The 1611 Authorised Version borrowed from Tyndale's translation – perhaps 20 per cent shows his direct influence. The AV Bible, however, aimed for a dignified rather than a popular style, often choosing older forms of language and grammar instead of the modern alternatives of the time.

ACTIVITY 16.1 ──────────────────────────────────────

Read the extract from *The Gospel According to Saint John* (AV) and list any features that are distinctive of religious language. Consider tone, lexis, grammar and literary devices.

At the Last Supper, Jesus spoke to his disciples after washing their feet to show that a master is no better than his servant in the eyes of God. In Chapter 15, verses 1–12, having already said that one of the disciples will betray him, he asks that they keep the commandments and love one another.

1 ¹I am the true vine, and my Father is the husbandman.
²Every branch in me that beareth not fruit he taketh away: and every branch that beareth fruit, he purgeth it, that it may bring forth more fruit.
³Now ye are clean through the word which I have spoken unto you.
5 ⁴Abide in me, and I in you. As the branch cannot bear fruit of itself, except it abide in the vine; no more can ye, except ye abide in me.
⁵I am the vine, ye are the branches: He that abideth in me, and I in him, the same bringeth forth much fruit: for without me ye can do nothing.
⁶If a man abide not in me, he is cast forth as a branch, and is withered; and men
10 gather them, and cast them into the fire, and they are burned.
⁷If ye abide in me, and my words abide in you, ye shall ask what ye will, and it shall be done unto you.
⁸Herein is my Father glorified, that ye bear much fruit; so shall ye be my disciples.
⁹As the Father hath loved me, so have I loved you: continue ye in my love.
15 ¹⁰If ye keep my commandments, ye shall abide in my love; even as I have kept my Father's commandments, and abide in his love.
¹¹These things have I spoken unto you, that my joy might remain in you, and that your joy might be full.
¹²This is my commandment, That ye love one another, as I have loved you.

COMMENTARY

The table here summarises the key points that make this text typical of religious language. It lists linguistic features that are commonly found in traditional sacred texts like the AV.

LEXIS

Examples	Comment
beareth not (l. 2), cannot (l. 5)	There are no **contractions** for negative verb forms and the **dummy auxiliary** *do* is not used to make a negative. These make the tone formal.
disciples (l. 13), commandments (l. 15)	**Subject-specific lexis** clearly marks the field as religious.
spoken unto (l. 17), Herein (l. 13)	**Archaisms** give traditional religious language its distinctive tone. Late Modern English simplifies these: the preposition *unto* becomes *to*; the adverb *herein* is replaced by *here*.
Abide in me (l. 5)	The verb *abide* has an archaic ring, but still survives in some phrases (including *abide by the law*). Here it is almost a **collocation**.

	Comment
m h m h the Father (l.14) the vine (l.1) det N det N	The **nominal groups** are mostly simple. Although noun phrases in the *Book of Common Prayer* tend to be complex, here Jesus is speaking and the style to some extent resembles spoken language.
Father (l.1) m m h my Father's commandments (ll.15–16) det N N	The **godhead** is here named in relation to Jesus. The use of 'Father' instead of 'God' emphasises that Jesus is a man like any other. By drawing attention to his humanity, he encourages his disciples to do as he does.

GRAMMAR

Examples	Comment
taketh (l.2), purgeth (l.3), abideth (l.7)	The **archaic form** of the third person singular is used. This gives traditional religious language its distinctive tone.
it *shall* be done (ll.11–12), my joy *might* remain in you (l.17)	**Modal verbs** are used to reflect a range of meanings: *shall* – certainty; *might* – possibility or potential.
ye (l.4), you (l.12)	The **pronouns** almost all reflect Late Modern English usage, but the use of *ye* in the subject site is archaic. In the object site, the standard Late Modern English *you* is used.

Compound:
S P   C   S   P
(I) (am) (the true vine) (and) (my Father) (is)
                   conj
    C
(the husbandman) (l.1)
 	
Complex:
A   S   P   C   A
(Now) (ye) (are) (clean) (through the word which I have spoken unto you) (l.4)
SCl–RelCl
 	
Compound–complex:
      A
(If ye abide in me, and ø my words abide in
SCl–ACl   conj SCl–ACl
   S   P   O   S
you), (ye) (shall ask) (what ye will) (and) (it)
                SCl–NCl   conj
   P   Oi
(shall be done) (unto you). (ll.11–12)
	The **sentence structure** is rarely simple because of the literary tone of the AV, unlike the earlier and more homely style of Tyndale.

P S so (shall) (ye) be my disciples (ll.13–14) Od P S P Oi (These things) (have (I) spoken) (unto you). (l.17)	Often **subjects and verbs are inverted**, making the word order seem quite different from Late Modern English. Objects can also be moved from their standard position after the verb. The **marked theme**

in the second example foregrounds the object of the active sentence. The **anaphoric reference** draws attention to the alternatives offered by Jesus to his hearers.

Examples	Comment
husbandman (l. 1), fruit (l. 2), vine (l. 1)	The extended **metaphor** here is based on a natural image of growth and good husbandry. It is used to represent the idea that someone who follows the Christian teachings of God will lead a productive life. It makes a very abstract spiritual concept concrete.
bringeth forth much fruit (l. 8), withered ... cast ... into the fire ... burned ... (ll. 9–10)	The **juxtaposition of negative and positive** here emphasises the alternatives offered to people. It underlines that they can choose the right way by following the advice Jesus offers, but by ignoring it they risk falling from God's favour. The emphasis throughout is on the positive rewards of faith rather than on punishment for lack of faith.
abideth (l. 7), abide (l. 6); loved (l. 14), love (l. 15)	**Repetition** helps to establish the central message: belief in Jesus and love for one another.
I am the true vine ... (l. 1), I am the vine ... (l. 7); As the Father hath loved me, so have I loved you ... (l. 14)	**Parallelism** is used to link Jesus and God with Jesus and the disciples. Throughout, he asks them to do as he has done. This again reinforces our sense of Jesus as an ordinary man whom we can imitate despite his divine status.

Rituals

Different societies have different cultural practices and religion formalises these in different ways. In most cultures birth, marriage and death, for instance, are treated as especially significant moments in life, and religion marks such occasions by the performance of some kind of **RITUAL** (a ceremony or rite).

The Christian Church has specific ceremonies to mark baptisms and funerals; it can give blessings, exorcise spirits, and so on. Each time a given ceremony is performed, the ritual will be almost identical. Although expressions may be modernised, and versions may vary slightly depending upon the specific church or the minister who leads the ritual, the Church of England takes the basic structure from recognised service books like the BCP.

Liturgical forms are written to be read or sung. They can be invocations, petitions, rosaries, hymns or psalms. They use a distinctive form of religious language, and prayers in particular are recognisable because they are a special form of polite plea addressed to the deity.

ACTIVITY 16.2

Read the communion prayer from the BCP below, and identify the distinctive linguistic and stylistic features.

1 ALMIGHTY God, the fountain of all wisdom, who knowest our necessities before we ask, and our ignorance in asking; We beseech thee to have compassion upon our infirmities; and those things, which for our unworthiness we dare not, and for our blindness we cannot ask, vouchsafe to give us, for the worthiness of thy Son Jesus
5 Christ our Lord. *Amen.*

COMMENTARY

Here the prayer is read by the minister and is addressed to God. The **lexis** is typically religious, focusing on God and Jesus. There are many **abstract nouns** like *wisdom* (l.1), *ignorance* (l.2) and *compassion* (l.2) and these reflect the spiritual nature of the request being made. Most noun phrases are simple, but the vocative consists of a complex noun phrase:

```
      m        h                              q
ALMIGHTY God, (the fountain of all wisdom), who knowest ...
   Adj        N        NP in apposition        SCl RelCl
```

Archaisms like *knowest* (l.1) identify this as a traditional variety and the opening and closing formulae *Almighty God* (l.1) and *Amen* (l.5) are typical of religious utterances. The verb *vouchsafe* (l.4) is now only used in formal contexts and has an archaic ring to it. It means 'to be graciously willing' or, in older contexts, 'to condescend to grant'. Its use here reinforces the sense of the unworthy congregation asking for a wise and merciful God's help.

The sentence structure is typical of a prayer: vocative + S P O. It appears much more complicated than this, however, because of the sequences of dependent clauses:

```
                                                              S        P
(ALMIGHTY God), (the fountain ...) (who knowest ... before we ask ...); (We) (beseech)
      voc            NP in apposition    SCl–RelCl          SCl–ACl

  Oi           Od                                              Od
(thee) (to have compassion ...); (and) (those things, which ..., and ø for our blindness
         SCl–NFCl                  conj         SCl–RelCl        conj    SCl–RelCl
                 P             Oi        A
we cannot ...), (vouchsafe to give) (us), (for the worthiness ...)
```

Ellipsis in several places makes relative clauses difficult to recognise: the direct object *those things* has two post-modifying clauses, only one of which is actually introduced by *which*. The clause beginning with the noun phrase *those things* **inverts the word order**, placing the direct object first and thereby giving it greater emphasis. In common with other examples of religious language, the **pronoun** *thee* (l. 2) is used for the second person in the object site, identifying this variety with archaic forms of the English language.

The **symbol** of *the fountain* (l. 1) is used to portray God as a natural source of wisdom. Traditionally, water is linked with purity and this image implicitly reinforces our sense of God's purity. There are several **co-ordinated phrases and clauses**: co-ordinated noun phrases (*our necessities... and our ignorance*, ll. 1–2); co-ordinated prepositional phrases (*for our unworthiness... for our blindness...*, ll. 3–4); and co-ordinated clauses (*we dare not, and... we cannot ask*, ll. 3–4). These all contribute to the **rhetorical** effects, adding a sense of balance and reason to the plea.

The initial vocative is **capitalised** and **italic print** is used to mark the point at which the congregation join in and say *Amen* after the priest has finished the prayer. The structure throughout is traditional and to a large extent predictable.

Sermons

SERMONS are religious statements based on a particular moral and spiritual view of the world. Ministers may write them as speeches to be delivered to their congregation or they may speak spontaneously on an appropriate topic. Many will craft their sermons carefully, but will then learn them in order to speak in a more immediate and dramatic way. Sermons are varied in their content since they can draw on the whole range of religious writing. They may contain modern or biblical stories, examples, parables, psalms, poetry, and so on. Statements within the discourse will often implicitly be understood as instructions since their purpose is to promote a certain way of life.

In the Roman Catholic Church, individual ministers are required to deliver the same pastoral letter at a particular time. This is a sermon, usually from the Archbishop to every person in his diocese. These pastoral letters are read out exactly from the Archbishop's script and no comments are made on its contents. Personal sermons, or **HOMILIES**, will reflect a priest's individuality, but all sermons in the Roman Catholic tradition are based on specified readings of the day. Current events may be introduced as long as they relate to the day's message. Individual ministers may vary the degree of formality of their approach, some adopting more modern references and forms of speech than others.

ACTIVITY 16.3

The sermon that follows was written for the fourth Sunday of Easter (27 April 2005) by the Reverend Angela Dugdale, a minister in the Church of England. It is clearly an example of religious language and yet it is very different from the traditional language of the Bible and the Book of Common Prayer. In order to involve a modern congregation, the rector chooses language and examples appropriate for the twenty-first century. Read through the text of the sermon and jot down notes on the following key areas:

1 Comment on the register used.
2 Identify lexis which shows this to be an example of religious language.

3 Identify language use that is modern, and comment on its function.
4 Explore the grammar of the sermon, including the use of modal verbs and pronouns, the sentence structure and the mood.
5 Identify any literary or rhetorical devices and comment on their function.
6 Comment on the ways in which the linguistic, grammatical and stylistic features help to transmit the message effectively to the congregation.

1 **WEYBOURNE – MATINS AT 9.15 A.M.   UPPER SHERINGHAM – HOLY COMMUNION AT 11 A.M.**

The fourth Sunday of Easter – say together Psalm 23. B.C.P. p.372
Readings: Acts 2: 42–47 and John 10: 1–10. Hymns and Canticles as set.

May I speak with the help of God the Father, Son and Holy Spirit. Nicholas suggests
5 in 'Link Up' that the readings bring to mind the theme <u>Discernment</u>.

Thinking again of the readings: Acts – written by Luke – 'All who believed were together – shared all things … were in the Temple – broke bread at home with glad and generous hearts – praising God.'

This is a picture of the early Church – the Christian community – 3,000 had just
10 been baptised – and Peter, 'the rock', was looking after them. In St John's gospel and in the 23rd psalm set for today, there is a picture of the Good Shepherd and the abundant life Christ brings.

Both of these pictures are positive and good, but I wonder how difficult the choices were for each of that early Christian group – how did their families and neighbours
15 react …?

Discernment – the word comes from the Latin dis – apart, and cernare – to sepa-rate, therefore discernment means to be able to separate apart – to have the ability to judge well. Surely it's a gift we'd all like to have – life is full of difficult choices.

Shall we acknowledge that we <u>need</u> a shepherd and that living is a serious busi-
20 ness or shall we be silly sheep and follow whatever takes our fancy? Shall we try to live together happily in communities – sharing, loving and praising God or shall we simply live life for ourselves – and get out of it what we can?

In Handel's 'Messiah' there's a chorus 'All we like sheep have gone astray – we have turned everyone to his own way' (Isaiah). The music is fast and cheerful – choirs
25 always sound 'perky' singing it – then each part, each voice, rushes off happily, 'we have turned … everyone to his own way'. Without a shepherd sheep scatter and behave in this frenetic way – but to close the chorus the mood changes utterly – the choir sings strong, slow, firm chords, (no more independent voices) for 'the Lord hath laid on Him the iniquity of us all'. The difference in the actions and mood of the sheep
30 and that of the Lord is made very clear.

In our gospel reading Jesus said that He is our shepherd who comes to give us abundant life – but aren't we still often behaving like Handel's sheep? – we are way-ward and irresponsible and act as if we had no shepherd – think of our divisions and arguments within the church today – think of our lack of sharing with one another in
35 the world – think of our lack of discipline in our lives, homes and schools – then something pulls us up and we remember that it's our Lord and Saviour who bears <u>our</u> sins and we say and mean 'Lamb of God – have mercy on us'.

These last two weeks have given us a lot to think about:–
            the Pope's death – and now the Cardinals' difficult decision
40   the royal wedding
            the general election
The world and the church came together to the Pope's funeral – many apparently drawn by his humanity rather than by his authority.

The blessing of the marriage of Prince Charles and the Duchess of Cornwall was
45 mocked by some in the media – but we <u>all</u> need God's forgiveness – only a megalo-
maniac or a fool could think otherwise – none of us is a clear reflection of God in our
time – we <u>need</u> God's mercy – our choices are so often the selfish ones – we behave
like straying sheep.

If only we could say now – as Luke did of the early church in Acts – 'All who be-
50 lieved were <u>together</u> – and had glad and generous hearts'. Is it true in our parishes?
(of Weybourne?), (of Upper Sheringham?), of the Group?

We each long to be wise – to choose rightly – to discern when to say 'No', when to
say 'Yes' and we each have to take responsibility for our actions. There are so many
areas when it's difficult to discern God's will – but we have to <u>try</u> – we can't just opt
55 out. What can we do to promote an integrated, multi-national multi-faith society?
How best can we help young people? They need a shepherd. What do we think about
abortion, euthanasia, AIDS, same-sex relationships, contraception, women bishops?

We can't pretend it doesn't matter to us that most people think going to church is
a nonsense and pathetic – that drug-misuse and bullying happen so frequently – that
60 religion, we are told, has nothing to do with politics. Of <u>course</u> it has everything to do
– we're thinking about <u>people</u> and Jesus cared deeply for individuals – often the poor
and marginalized.

We pray that, with God's help, we may discern wisely – relying on God's mercy and
having faith in his saving love – we ask that the Holy Spirit will guide the Cardinals, the
65 Royal family and the politicians. We pray for the church – the world and for ourselves
– knowing that not one of us is released from the responsibility to think and act, but
in our anxiety to do what is right we must remember that our first duty is to love and
serve God – and He has given us abundant – full – overflowing life in Him now and for
ever.

COMMENTARY

The **mode** of the sermon bridges both written and spoken language: it is written, carefully crafted on the page, before being delivered orally to a congregation. The text displays many features of formal written language, but by practising 'speaking' the written text, the minister will make the language seem spontaneous. In its spoken form, intonation, pitch, pace and emphasis will help the congregation to focus on key elements of the sermon, even if they are unaccustomed to listening to complex language structures. Underlining signposts words that the minister wishes to stress.

The **manner** is inevitably formal and this reflects the relationship between the minister and her congregation. In essence, a minister is God's representative on earth and in preaching her sermon can be seen in the role of mentor, educator and advisor. With a minister who is known to her congregation, however, there is a personal relationship beyond the formality of the Sunday service.

The **field** is clearly religious even though the traditional archaic language and verb inflections have been replaced by modern English. The sermon becomes almost a literary text with a religious and spiritual message. It adopts traditional prose format, using paragraphs rather than the verse of the Bible, and conveys its message using traditional literary and rhetorical devices.

The sermon opens with an **INVOCATION** (*May I speak with the help of God the Father, Son and Holy Spirit*, l. 4) and a local reference that reflects the personal relationship between minister and congregation (ll. 4–5). The link established between the readings and the theme of the sermon is made explicit in the underlined and capitalised abstract noun <u>*Discernment*</u> (l. 5). The **MORAL MESSAGE** that follows is quite complicated because it is embedded in a philosophical debate about the meaning of the word, its relevance to everyday life and the ways in which it should inform the congregation's religious and spiritual practice. The sermon suggests that society would be a better place if the congregation took responsibility for their own actions and aimed to make informed decisions guided by their faith.

The **subject-specific lexis** immediately identifies this as a religious variety: **proper nouns** such as *Luke* (l. 6), *Peter* (l. 10) and *'Messiah'* (l. 23); **verbs** such as *praising* (l. 21) and *pray* (l. 63); **abstract nouns** such as *blessing* (l. 44), *forgiveness* (l. 45) and *mercy* (l. 47); and **biblical names** such as *Christ* (l. 12); *God* (l. 21) and *the Lord* (l. 30) are all found in the Bible. Using traditional religious **collocations** like *our Lord and Saviour* (l. 36) and *now and for ever* (ll. 68–9) also helps the congregation to make direct links with traditional religious teachings. The **noun phrases** are often complex and these make the variety distinctive even though the sermon is modern:

	m	h	q		
	a picture of	... the	abundant life Christ brings		(ll. 11–12)
	det	N	PrepP	(RelCl)	

	m	h	q	
	our shepherd	who comes to give us abundant life		(ll. 31–2)
	det	N	RelCl	(NFCl)

The repeated modifier *abundant* is linked directly to the central moral lesson of the sermon: that with Jesus's help the congregation can make wise judgements and therefore make full use of the rich life their faith offers them *now and for ever*.

To ensure that members of the congregation are not alienated and to ensure that the sermon relates directly to their lives, **modern references** are introduced. **Proper nouns** such *Prince Charles and the Duchess of Cornwall* (l. 44) and **abstract nouns** such as *the media* (l. 45) indicate that this is a contemporary text. In addition, the minister sets the theme of the sermon, the concept of *difficult choices* (l. 18), in a contemporary context of *the Pope's death – and ... the Cardinals' difficult decision, the royal wedding* and *the general election* (ll. 39–41). These become **symbols** of the need for 'discernment' in all life's decisions – whether public or private. The sermon draws on them in order to make the spiritual message more meaningful in a modern context, in a *multi-national multi-faith society* (l. 55). The idea is broadened in the **asyndetic list** of noun phrases that reflects more general contemporary issues: *abortion, euthanasia, AIDS, same-sex relationships, contraception, women bishops* (l. 57). The omission of a coordinating conjunction implies that this is just the beginning of what could be a significantly longer list. Its significance lies in the fact that these are all issues that require the congregation to 'think' rather than *opt out* (ll. 54–5) – *to choose rightly* (l. 52).

Because a sermon contains a spiritual message reminding the congregation of the way in which life should be lived according to God's will, it uses many **abstract nouns**. Examples such as *discernment/discern* (ll. 5, 16, 17, 52, 54, 63), *discipline*

(l. 35), *decision* (l. 39), *choices* (l. 47) and *responsibility* (ll. 53, 66) all build up the central theme of the sermon. Juxtapositions then develop the concept of choice through contrasting **modifiers** such as *serious/silly* (ll. 19–20), *wayward and irresponsible/wise* (ll. 32–3, 52) and *selfish/glad and generous* (ll. 47, 50); and contrasting **adverbials** *together/for ourselves* (ll. 21–2). These form the basis for a sermon which aims to encourage the congregation to *discern wisely* so that they follow the example of Jesus rather than the sheep.

The **grammar** is no longer archaic – verbs do not use *-eth* inflections; word order is standard. The sentences move between simple, complex and compound–complex depending upon the effect the minister wishes to create. Where the content is reflective, the structure will be complex. The final paragraph, which brings the central theme to a climax, is a compound–complex sentence made up of a sequence of subordinate and coordinate clauses. Its dense style is appropriate for the formality and gravity of the statement it makes.

> S   P   O   O   A
> (We) (pray for) (the church) – (the world and for ourselves) – (knowing that not one of
>   phrasal verb   conj   SCl–NFCl
>   A
> us is released from the responsibility to think and act) (but) (in our anxiety to do
>   SCl–NFCls   conj   SCl–NFCl
>   S   P   O
> what is right) (we) (must remember) (that our first duty is to love and serve God) – (and)
> SCl–NCl   SCl–NCl   SCl–NFCls   conj
> S   P   Oi   Od   A   A
> (He) (has given) (us) (abundant – full – overflowing life) (in Him) (now and for ever).
>   (ll. 65–9)

When the content consists of a certainty rather than reflection, however, simple sentences are emphatic and direct:

> S   P   C   S   P   O
> (life) (is) (full of difficult choices) (l. 18)   (we) (need) (God's mercy) (l. 47)
>
> S   P   A
> (we) (behave) (like straying sheep) (ll. 47–8)

Dashes are used to control the length of sentences, allowing the sermon to be delivered in a way that resembles spontaneous speech – it is broken up by the use of pauses into smaller units that are more manageable for the congregation.

The **mood** moves between declarative statements (ll. 9–12, 23–30), interrogatives that force the congregation to engage with the minister's contemplation of modern life (ll. 14–15, 19–22, 55–6), and imperatives that allow the minister to direct her congregation (ll. 33–5) and solicit God's help (l. 4). The variation in mood allows the minister to engage her congregation – they are required to take an active part, albeit mentally rather than physically. The questions are rhetorical since they require no direct answer, but they are designed to provoke thought in line with the sermon's focus on discernment.

Modal verbs occur frequently. The tentative *May* (l. 4) of the opening sets the tone by invoking the spiritual guidance of the Holy Trinity, while in the final paragraph (l. 63) it suggests a possibility that can be fulfilled with God's help. The repetition of *shall* (ll. 19–21) introduces clauses of doubt that offer the congregation the alternatives between which they must choose. Other modals include the use of *can* (ll. 55–6) to indicate possibility, *will* (l. 64) to express a desire in the form of a polite request, and *must* (l. 67) to communicate an obligation on the part of the congregation.

Pronouns help to create a personal relationship between minister and congregation. By using the first person pronoun *I*, the minister first establishes her own role as leader of the congregation (l. 4), and then introduces the concept of 'difficult choices' with a personal comment clause *I wonder* (l. 13). In the rest of the sermon, however, first person plural references unite minister and congregation. The pronouns *we* (subject) and *us* (object) and the possessive determiner *our* recur throughout the text, suggesting that both minister and congregation are subject to the difficult choices of life.

The **literary devices** are crucial to the emotive appeal to the congregation to lead thoughtful lives. The **metaphor** of the *shepherd* is a traditional religious **symbol** of guardianship. It is developed here with explicit references to ordinary people as the *silly sheep* who fail to understand the importance of *sharing, loving and praising God* (ll. 20–1). It forms a cohesive link through the sermon, recurring in different forms to remind us of the importance of having someone to guide us.

The reference to Handel's *Messiah* also fulfils a **symbolic role** in developing the metaphor. The direct quotation from Isaiah (ll. 23–4) neatly illuminates the minister's theme of communal responsibility. The negative connotations of *astray* ensure that the prepositional phrase *to his own way* is interpreted as an example of selfishness rather than commendable independence. Similarly, although the description of the music uses positive modifiers (*fast, cheerful, perky*, ll. 24–5), the summative modifier *frenetic* (l. 27) suggests chaos and anarchy. The music thus becomes symbolic of the 'sheep' with no shepherd to guide them. To remind her congregation of the theme, however, the minister describes the change in mood at the end of the chorus. The modifiers *strong, slow, firm* (l. 28) have a solemnity that allows her to establish the concept of Jesus as a saviour who will redeem those who follow him. The language draws a direct contrast between the good judgement of Jesus and the *wayward and irresponsible* nature of his followers.

Sentence organisation allows the minister to draw attention to elements of her sermon that she considers important. The **marked themes** reorganise the information in a sentence: foregrounded prepositional phrases remind the congregation of the day's readings (ll. 10–11, 31–2), introduce an example to illuminate the theme (l. 23) and foreground the central idea of life lived with no guide (ll. 26–7); and a foregrounded conditional clause (ll. 49–50) expresses a regret about the current lack of 'togetherness' in society.

The sermon uses **rhetorical devices** because it is trying to persuade people to act in a certain way. Other forms of **patterning** are used throughout the sermon for dramatic effect. **Repetition** of key words is cohesive and helps to develop the central theme (*shepherd/sheep; responsibility; choices*). **Listing** focuses attention on important concepts, often using tripling for rhythmic balance (*sharing, loving and praising; lives, homes and schools; for the church – the world and for ourselves*). Recurring clause structures such as the imperatives *think of our divisions... think of our lack of sharing... think of our lack of discipline* (ll. 33–5) have an accumulative effect, forcing the congregation to address the issues that the sermon raises. Similarly, the parallel interrogatives *Shall we acknowledge... or shall we be silly* *sheep?… Shall we try… or shall we simply live…* (ll. 19–22) present the congregation with some of the 'difficult choices' that the minister wishes them to contemplate. The overall effect of such features is persuasive since they encourage participation – this is a sermon that requires active reflection.

The sermon is effective because it is related to matters familiar to the congregation. Musical references, contemporary events, the behaviour of the media, and recognition of the big 'issues' we face in the twenty-first century all serve to illustrate the religious theme. The linguistic patterning makes the lesson more memorable, leaving the congregation to reconsider the choices offered to them.

ACTIVITY 16.4

The following text was written by Dr Mona Siddiqui for *Thought for the Day* on BBC Radio 4 (10 October 2006). This is a daily slot on the morning magazine programme *Today* in which a range of speakers with differing religious viewpoints take a contemporary event as the basis for a moral reflection. It aims to make us think about our lives and experiences from a common ground – not as Christians, Muslims or Jews, but as human beings. The text is a copy of the speech Dr Siddiqui broadcast, which was slightly different from the written version found on the *Thought for the Day* website.

Dr Mona Siddiqui is a Professor of Islamic Studies and Public Understanding in the Department of Theology and Religious Studies, Glasgow University. She has been a regular contributor to *Thought for the Day* since 1997 and is a primary contact for the media on religious and ethical matters.

Read through the text and make notes on:

1 any distinctive linguistic features that make this an example of a religious variety
2 any features identifying this as an example of a contemporary moral reflection
3 the ways in which this differs from a sermon written by an individual minister for a local congregation.

1 Last week, a small American community, known for its distinctly frugal way of life, mourned the deaths of 5 small girls in a school shooting. When children die, it's tragic, but when they are killed in such a terrible way, it's heartbreaking. And yet as I watched the slow, dignified funeral procession on Sunday, the parents' solemn acceptance of
5 their fate, I felt terribly moved. Moved because here there seemed to be no tears, no calls for retribution, no cries to God 'why my child?' just a sober reflection, the quiet face of forgiveness and forbearance.

But these events were almost eclipsed by that other story of faith and difference – Muslim veiling. Both stories are in some ways about the differences we can accept
10 and those we find disturbing. Veiling has become such an iconic image, an image of everything the west has struggled against that its mere visibility is seen as a threat. And seen through the blurred prism of terror, the threat becomes even more magnified. And yet, the Amish too are very different, easily stereotyped and a minority in the way they practise their Christian faith. We can all accept them because they are
15 peaceful, non-threatening and their humble values don't encroach on anyone else's life even if their own lives may seem insular and extreme. The choices they make in their enclosed environment affect no-one else but themselves.

But what the wider community has recognised is a depth of faith so powerful that it has given this small community an extraordinary ability to forgive. Sadly, most of our
20 own current debates about faith are less about God and more about communities

and representation. Everyone wants to be heard yet no-one is prepared to debate the real issues. With too much rhetoric and too little humility, we are at risk of hurtling towards a destruction of what really binds us as people.

Acceptance of difference may hold us together as society but it is not what ties us
25 to one another as human beings. And perhaps this is where we are going wrong, over-emphasis on community identity and social cohesion and not enough understanding of individual worth. The Prophet's saying, 'none of you truly believes until he loves for his brother what he loves for himself' emphasises not an abstract love for fellow man, but a real sympathy. I know what makes me feel British, I know what makes me feel
30 Muslim, but it has taken me some time to understand what really ties me to a common humanity. Compassion, compassion even for those suffering in distant lands, to whom I feel drawn, and where I see neither colour nor creed – only people who with all their differences are, just like me.

COMMENTARY

The **mode** mixes written and spoken registers, but *Thought for the Day* is primarily a written text although it is delivered orally. The **manner** is formal because the speaker is an academic addressing a wide audience who are not known personally. The **field** is perhaps reflective rather than religious: Dr Mona Siddiqui focuses on two apparently separate media stories – the shooting of five girls in an Amish school in America and their funeral, and the issue of Muslim veiling. In her consideration of the events, she finds common ground that reveals something of the human condition. The quotation from the Qur'an, the Muslim sacred text, indicates the spiritual framework that underlies the ideas that Siddiqui is exploring. It comes in the final paragraph of the piece and allows her to draw her arguments together, both as a Muslim and as a human being.

Subject-specific lexis reinforces the field here: proper nouns such as *American* (l. 1), *Muslim* (ll. 9, 30), *Amish* (l. 13), *Christian* (l. 14); abstract nouns such as *acceptance* (ll. 4, 24), *retribution* (l. 6), *forgiveness, forbearance* (l. 7), *faith* (ll. 8, 14, 18, 20), *difference* (ll. 8, 9, 24, 33), *representation* (l. 21), *identity* (l. 26), *sympathy* (l. 29) and *compassion* (l. 31); modifiers such as *different* (l. 13), *peaceful, non-threatening and... humble* (l. 15); and religious names such as *God* (ll. 6, 20) and *The Prophet* (l. 27). All the lexis is explicitly linked to the theme of 'compassion', a compassion that exists beyond religious, cultural or racial boundaries.

The **pronouns** lead us from a personal response to a particular tragedy (*I*, ll. 3, 5) to a point of unity (*we*, ll. 9, 10, 14, 22, 25; *us*, l. 24) from which we can together recognise the difference of the Amish who are set apart with third person plural pronouns (*they/them*, ll. 14–16) and determiners (*their*, ll. 14–16). Siddiqui points out that it is easy to 'accept' this distant religious group whose differences do not affect us – but far harder to see beyond the media headlines to the individuals behind the veil in our own community. In the final lines of the text, she returns to first person singular pronouns (ll. 29–33) since her reflection has led her towards an understanding of what it really means to feel for another human being.

As this text is dominated by written features, the **noun phrases** tend to be long and complex. They contain a lot of information and allow the speaker to explore her theme:

> m   m   m   h   q
> a small American community, known for its distinctly frugal way of life   (l. 1)
> det Adj   Adj   N   NFCl

> h   q
> compassion even for those suffering in distant lands to whom I feel drawn and
>   N   PrepP   NFCl   RelCl
> q
> where I see neither colour nor creed – only people who … are just like me
> RelCl   RelCl
> (ll. 31–3)

Because this is a very personal text, an individual response to a topical event, Siddiqui tends not to use traditional religious collocations. Adverb phrases such as *Last week* (l. 1) and *on Sunday* (l. 4) and the modifier *current* (l. 20) locate the monologue firmly in a contemporary context, while the repetition of words (*acceptance/accept*, ll. 4, 14, 24; *difference*, ll. 8, 9, 24; *compassion*, l. 31) highlights her central concerns. These form the structural framework for her argument just as biblical collocations in a sermon remind the congregation of the wider context in which the sermon can be understood.

The **grammar**, although formal, shows evidence of spoken language in its use of initial-position conjunctions (*And yet*, ll. 3, 13; *But*, ll. 8, 18; *And*, ll. 12, 25) and minor sentences (ll. 5–7, 31–3). The number of subordinate clauses and the use of the passive voice (*were… eclipsed*, l. 8; *is seen*, l. 11), however, remind us that this is, ultimately, a formal field. Most sentences are complex or compound–complex, reflecting the theoretical and spiritual nature of the text:

> S   P   S   P   O   A
> (We) (can) (all) (accept) (them) (because they are peaceful, non-threatening) (and) (ø
>   modal aux   lex   SCl–ACl   conj
>   A
> their humble values don't encroach on anyone else's life even if their own lives may
> SCl–ACl   SCl–ACl
> seem insular and extreme).   (ll. 14–16)

Because most of the clause structures are long, where they are short, the effect is dramatic. The delayed main clause reflecting the speaker's response to the Amish funeral, for instance, suggests the sincerity of her response:

> S   P   C
> (I) (felt) (terribly moved).   (l. 5)

The isolated noun phrase *Muslim veiling* (l. 9) is a cataphoric reference to the long noun phrase *that other story of faith and difference* (l. 8). Its brevity is emotive in drawing the listener's attention to the second theme of Siddiqui's reflection. Use of the passive voice, which places the subject of the active sentence in the end position after *by*, brings the appositional phrase *Muslim veiling* to a place of prominence. In both examples, the simplicity of the structure changes the pace of the delivery: the first example highlights a personal response to a distant tragedy; the second draws attention to an individual religious choice that has for some people become symbolic of cultural separation and the threat of terrorism.

The **mood** is dominated by the declarative since the speaker is formally presenting a personal viewpoint on a topical subject. The only change from this is in the embedded interrogative *'why my child?'* (l. 6), which is presented as the typical response to such a tragic event. There are no imperatives since the speaker is reflecting on a state of affairs rather than urging her audience to adopt a certain kind of behaviour. A sermon promotes a certain kind of lifestyle and requires its congregation to adhere to certain principles, but *Thought for the Day* has a less didactic purpose. Rather than directly commanding or beseeching, its aim is to promote active contemplation which may indirectly affect the way we live our lives.

Rhetorical devices are used to guide the audience through the logical development of the speaker's commentary and to persuade listeners to identify with the point of view being offered. **Juxtapositions** remind the audience of the opposing choices: *retribution* or *a sober reflection… forgiveness and forbearance* (ll. 6–7); *threat/non-threatening* (ll. 11, 15); *an abstract love/a real sympathy* (ll. 28–9). If we are to understand the central argument, we must recognise the opposition of the two stories (Amish and Muslim) and the discrepancy in the way we respond to them. **Patterning** creates a sense of balance and is often emotive. The compound–complex sentence in lines 2–3, for instance, with its fronted adverbial clauses, creates a parallelism between the two simple clauses *it's tragic* and *it's heartbreaking*. The use of predicative modifiers places a lexical stress on the adjectives *tragic* and *heartbreaking* – the latter, with its emphatic end position in the sentence, is particularly poignant because of its intensely personal connotations. Tripling (*no tears, no calls… no cries*, ll. 5–6; *what makes me feel British… what makes me feel Muslim… what really ties me to a common humanity*, ll. 29–31), compound phrases (*community identity and social cohesion*, l. 26) and other parallel structures (*less about… more about*, l. 20; *Everyone… no-one*, l. 21) all add to the tight development of the speaker's case.

There are few examples of **figurative language** since this is more like a formal speech than the poetic prose of many religious texts. The only example here is in the metaphor of *the blurred prism of terror* (l. 12) which allows Siddiqui to give a very physical presence to the prejudice that faces many Muslim women wearing the veil. The concrete noun *prism* becomes the symbol of our distorted view of a culture that is 'different' and the pre-modification further emphasises the slanted version of reality that the fear of terrorism has created. It is developed in the comparative adjective phrase *even more magnified* (l. 12) – the *visibility* (l. 11) of the veil makes it an easy target.

The **marked themes** allow Siddiqui to control the order in which we receive the information. The opening fronted adverbial *Last week* (l. 1) draws attention to the timescale, and the fronted non-finite clause *seen through the blurred prism of terror* (l. 12) to the context in which Muslim veiling becomes a 'threat'. Other foregrounding reflects the speaker's personal viewpoint (*Sadly*, l. 19) and her own assessment of the situation (*With too much rhetoric and too little humility* l. 22).

The speech here focuses on the nature of society in the twenty-first century with its emphasis, as the speaker sees it, on *community identity and social cohesion* (l. 26) at the expense of an *understanding of individual worth* (ll. 26–7). She is exploring the concepts of 'difference' and 'acceptance' just as the personal sermon considered earlier (Activity 16.3) addresses the importance of personal choice, of making informed decisions and leading a responsible life. Despite the fact that both texts are designed to make the audience reflect on what has been said and on their own lives, there are marked differences in approach between the two:

▸ The **tone** is quite formal in each text, but the different relationships with the intended audience in each case affect the speakers' lexical and structural choices: the minister is speaking to her congregation face to face; the *Thought for the Day* speaker has no direct contact with her listeners and must adhere to the tight time restrictions of broadcasting.

▸ The **style** is less poetic in the *Thought for the Day* text: the minister is engaging with a congregation who are known and can be seen, and she has a longer period of time to deliver her sermon, which can therefore range more widely; the *Thought for the Day* slot is broadcast to an unknown audience who are likely to be doing other things as they listen to the radio, and it must be complete in less than three minutes.

▸ The **function** is different in each case: the minister's sermon is written to mark a particular date in the religious calendar (the fourth Sunday of Easter); *Thought for the Day* marks a personal response to a public event which the speaker uses as a springboard for a reflective meditation. Both, however, aim to give people the opportunity to think about the kind of life they are leading – one within an explicitly Christian framework, and the other implicitly underpinned by the Muslim faith though 'humanitarian' in its general appeal.

16.5 What to look for in the language of religion

The following checklist can be used to identify key features in examples of religious language. You will not find all of the features in every text or transcription, but the list can be used as a guide. The points made are general, so discussion of specific examples will need to be adapted to take account of the specific context, audience and purpose of the given discourse. Remember that you need to evaluate the effect of the features you identify, exploring the ways in which they create meaning.

The following are helpful questions to ask.

Register

1 What is the **mode**?
   ◆ written?
   ◆ spoken by the congregation or the minister?

2 What is the **manner**?
   ◆ formal or traditional?
   ◆ relationship between participants?

3 What is the **field**?
   ◆ religious subject matter?
   ◆ linked to audience, purpose and context?

Lexis

1 Is there any **subject-specific vocabulary**?
   * general?
   * typical of a certain ceremony or a particular religion?
2 Is lexis **archaic** or has it been modernised?
   * words with no contemporary equivalent? words with modern synonyms?
   * words linked to specific people, places or events?
3 Are there any **abstract nouns** that convey spiritual and theological concepts?
4 Are there any **formulaic phrases and collocations** that contribute to the traditional and formal tone of religious texts?
5 Are there any **sequences of post-modified relative clauses** in prayers which make the nominal groups particularly long?
6 How is the **godhead named**?
   * with variations?
   * using human qualities to describe the divine?

Grammar

1 Is the grammar **archaic** or has it been modernised?
2 Are there any examples of the archaic **third person singular inflection** *-eth/-est*?
3 Are there non-standard **past participle strong forms**?
4 Is the **dummy auxiliary** *do* used to indicate past time?
5 Which **moods** are used?
   * declaratives for stories from a sacred text?
   * imperatives for prayers?
   * interrogatives to make a congregation reflect?
6 Is the **subjunctive** used to express possible or potential processes?
7 Are **modal verbs** used to express certainty, possibility, etc.?
8 Are any of the **pronouns archaic**?
   * second person forms *thou* and *thee*?
9 Are the **sentence structures** varied?
   * basically simple, but with sequences of dependent clauses to make the structure more elaborate?
   * simple sentences to make points emphatically?
   * compound sentences to create a balanced argument?
   * complex sentences to deal with spiritual concepts?
   * minor sentences to emphasise a key concept or to mirror the patterns of speech?
10 Are there any **initial-position co-ordinators**?
   * to create emphasis?
   * to divide long sentences into smaller units?
11 Are **vocatives** used in prayers to address the godhead?
12 Is the **word order** archaic?
   * inversion of subject and predicator?
   * use of the object as a marked theme?

Style

1 Is the **sentence organisation** used to draw attention to important lexical items?
  - marked themes to order the information and manipulate audience response?
  - end focus to create emphatic weight at the end of a sentence?
  - passive voice to alter the semantic significance of the subject or object?

2 Are any **literary devices** used?
  - similes and metaphors to help represent abstract, spiritual matters in a concrete way?
  - symbolism to draw on wider associations?
  - personification to animate abstractions or difficult concepts?

3 Is there any noticeable **sound patterning**?
  - alliteration, sibilance, assonance?

4 Are **rhetorical devices** used to engage the audience?
  - antithesis to create contrasts between good and evil, or between believers and non-believers?
  - listing to suggest a range of possibilities or to build to a moral or spiritual climax?
  - patterning to develop a sense of balance or to add weight to the message?
  - repetition to highlight a central moral point or theme?

Typographical features

1 Are any words **capitalised**?
  - proper nouns? other key words? vocatives?

2 Is the text **divided into verses** to make reading and understanding easier for the congregation?

Summary

The **function** of religious language is to preserve and promote a particular spiritual belief system, and to persuade the congregation or individual worshippers to live their lives in a certain way.

To a large extent, **traditional texts** such as the AV and the BCP play an important role in defining the nature of religious language – archaic features provide links with the past, and well-known phrases and clauses from the Bible embedded in everyday conversation mean that religious language is recognised even by non-believers.

Semantically, the language of the Church must be accessible, so although it changes very little, it must adapt in some ways to the expectations of a modern congregation. Religious utterances can be statements of belief, prayers of supplication, narratives with spiritual or moral messages, celebrations of important days or occasions, or philosophical reflections on current events and attitudes.

Chapter 17

The language of politics

17.1 The nature of political language

In 1946, George Orwell wrote 'Politics and the English language', an essay in which he discussed the nature of **POLITICAL LANGUAGE**. He criticised politicians for failing to use *a fresh, vivid home-made turn of speech* and instead choosing *ready-made phrases*. Through a metaphor of mechanisation, he suggested that speakers had turned themselves into machines and were no longer aware of the importance of what they were saying. He believed that political language had become mechanical instead of reflecting individual speakers, and that meaning was often concealed by the *lifeless, imitative, style* which, in his view, was common. At the beginning of the twenty-first century, it may seem that little has changed.

Political language is often accused of trying to conceal the truth and euphemism is one common way of making a harsh reality more palatable. **EUPHEMISMS** are words or phrases that substitute mild or vague language to soften the harsh reality of an event – for example, *pushing up the daisies* or *passing away* for *dying*; *letting someone go* for *sacking*. The euphemistic expression *ethnic cleansing* conceals the bitter reality of one ethnic group killing another because of their origin – the verb has positive connotations that at a linguistic level appear to give an unacceptable act an air of respectability. *Conflict* replaces *war*, and when bombing raids hit civilian rather than military targets, the result is described as *collateral damage*. No longer are the *dead* brought home, but the *body bags* are returned. All these examples conceal the horror of war: they make the whole issue less unpalatable. Government reports replace phrases like *health and inequality of the elderly* with *differential ageing among social sub-groups*. In an example like this, the focus changes – instead of being drawn to the key word *inequality*, readers are faced with far more objective terms like *differential* and *social sub-groups*. These kinds of changes make the political reality of the noun phrases less human and therefore make financial restrictions easier to impose.

Many people believe that language influences thought: if language is manipulated, therefore, so are the very processes of thought. In other words, politicians can influence the way we think about the events happening around us, and the words they choose are a crucial part of that process.

Each politician has a particular **IDEOLOGY** or way of seeing the world. The concept of 'ideology' refers to a body of ideas or a belief system which is organised from a specific **POINT OF VIEW**. For instance, Conservative and Labour politicians think about society in different ways, and because they have different ideologies, they approach political issues from different angles and often propose contrasting solutions to the same political problems. Through their use of language they encourage voters to identify with their own particular ideology or world view.

17.2 The function of political language

Linguists are interested in the words and structures politicians use to create a certain view of the world. This world view will be directly linked to their purpose and audience and will affect the language they choose in order to achieve a set goal. Lexical and syntactical choices can affect the voters, persuading them to vote for certain policies or personalities. By analysing these, it is possible to identify occasions when politicians try to subvert or obscure issues, evade questions or arouse audience emotions.

As well as the actual words and structures used, however, linguists are also interested in the pragmatics of political language. **PRAGMATICS** considers the meaning beyond what has actually been said and concentrates on the way meaning is constructed in different contexts. The focus here is therefore wider than just the lexis and syntax itself, since the factors influencing a speaker or writer's choices are analysed.

Political language can be recognised in a variety of forms, but in each case lexical and syntactical choices are directly linked to the audience, purpose and context of the discourse. Speeches are scripted as part of an election campaign or a fundraising event; unscripted responses are made in reply to questions in the House of Commons or in a media interview; manifestos are circulated as part of information campaigns; motions are drafted for debate; a written record (Hansard) is made of everything that occurs in Parliament; and so on.

Political language can be informative (**referential** function) or persuasive (**conative** function) and is often rhetorical. It is always useful to consider the **speaker** or **writer**, the **audience**, the **purpose** and the **context** of any example since each of these factors can change the nature of the language used.

17.3 Features of political language

There are many examples of political language in everyday life and it is possible to categorise some linguistic features that are common to most of these.

Manner

The **manner** is usually formal, and there tend to be **FORMULAIC UTTERANCES** which add to the formality. In the House of Commons, for instance, phrases like *I beg to move…* and *the honourable Lady* are common.

Sometimes **informal language** is used and the change in tone is obvious. From looking at the daily records of what takes place in the House of Commons, it is possible to explore parliamentary attitudes to language. The Speaker's role is to adjudicate in any instances where inappropriate language or behaviour is used, and the intervention or non-intervention of the Speaker draws attention to contemporary linguistic standards in the House.

In 1994, the Speaker, Betty Boothroyd, objected to the phrase *ripped off* when it was used in relation to one particular MP (Business of the House, Hansard, 3 March) – it was described as *a grossly disorderly expression* and the MP who had used it was ordered to withdraw immediately and was banned from all other parliamentary debates for the day. An extract from Hansard in 2006 would suggest that parliamentary attitudes to language may have changed, reflecting changes in society as a whole. John Prescott, for instance, who was then the Deputy Prime Minister of the Labour Party, responded after several interruptions from the floor to William Hague (Conservative MP for Richmond, Yorkshire) in an unexpectedly informal way:

> I notice from the papers and on television today that the Tories have now brought in a new person to get people to vote Tory, and I could not help noticing that the person is named, as I saw on the website, "Mr Tosser". I do not know which person on the Front Bench this man is modelled on, but let me tell the right hon. Gentleman that I always thought that his party was full of them, and that is why they have lost three elections.
>
> Prime Minister's Questions, Hansard, Column 1082 (29 November 2006)

While Prescott does not explicitly use the colloquial and abusive term of address, his meaning is clear. The Speaker, Michael J. Martin, however, did not intervene except to require order from the House as a whole. On another occasion, in a debate on the introduction of authorised casinos into Britain, John Prescott described James Duddridge (Conservative MP for Rochford and Southend, East) as *a busted flush* (Prime Minister's Questions, Column 307, Hansard, 19 July 2006). MPs responded to this with calls for him to withdraw and the Speaker intervened:

> Order. It is difficult for me to be fair if I cannot hear what is going on. I shall take advice on what has just been said and make a ruling ...

The term *busted flush* is both subject-specific (a poker term for a player's hand that contains an incomplete flush – usually four cards of the same suit) and a general idiom (someone or something that had great potential but ended up as a useless failure). In the context of the debate, it was seen by many as inappropriate.

There are other instances, however, when the Speaker's response is more certain. In a debate on antisocial behaviour, the Conservative MP Nick Herbert (Arundel and South Downs) was reprimanded by Sylvia Heal (Madam Deputy Speaker) for his use of a phrase that he was quoting from a report in *The Times*:

> **Nick Herbert:** Summary justice can also lead to injustice. The Minister (Mr Lindsay Hoyle, Labour MP for Chorley) knows, because I have raised the matter with him before, that a stallholder at the Royal Norfolk Show in July 2006 was fined £80 and given a penalty notice for disorder by the police. His offence was that he displayed a T-shirt that the report in *The Times* said bore the slogan "Bollocks to Blair".

> **Madam Deputy Speaker (Sylvia Heal):** Order. I remind the hon. Gentleman about the use of parliamentary language. He has not been in the House very long, but I think that he knows that that is unacceptable.
>
> Hansard, Antisocial Behaviour Debate, Column 959 (18 January 2007)

After an apology for *reading out* what he describes as *the prohibited phrase*, Nick Herbert paraphrased the slogan as *"Testicles to the Prime Minister"* and was allowed to proceed with his speech.

In some cases, although the Speaker does not intervene, an MP might ask for clarification of the acceptability of what has been said. In a debate about the accuracy and use of statistics (Orders of the Day, Hansard, Columns 61–2, 8 January 2007), Fiona Mactaggert (Labour MP for Slough) used informal language which led to a sequence of interventions:

> Not every local authority can drum up the resources that Westminster council had at its disposal to produce evidence that the statistics on its population were flawed. Slough's evidence is compelling. The council has even counted the amount of shit that goes through our local sewers, which is considerably greater than it was 10 years ago. [*Interruption.*] I am sure that was not a parliamentary word. I am sorry.

Paul Flynn (Labour MP for Newport West) asked the Deputy Speaker (Sir Michael Lord) whether, since he had made no ruling on the word, it was *appropriate to use that word as a noun, but not as an adjective*. The Deputy Speaker's response made it clear that his lack of intervention indicated that *it was appropriate to use the word in this way*. Before the debate could continue, Peter Bottomley (Conservative MP for Worthing, West) took the opportunity of making a humorous political point:

> Was the hon. Lady saying that there was more waste under Labour?

In 1995, Betty Boothroyd made a statement drawing attention to the expected tenor of parliamentary language:

> Good temper and moderation are the characteristics of parliamentary language. I do hope that in future interventions, all members will bear that in mind and we shall make use of the richness of the English language to select elegant phrases that express their meaning without causing offence to others. I have to tell this House that I know only too well from my postbag that some of the exchanges across the floor of this House do not enhance it in the eyes of our electorate.
>
> Hansard (8 February 1995)

Members of the public expect politicians to choose language that reflects the formal parliamentary context and most do. When the manner is changed, inevitably some people complain because informal language is seen as inappropriate in the formal and public field of politics.

Lexis

The **lexis** is usually **subject-specific** and **abstract nouns** are quite common since discussions are often theoretical, even though they may be directly linked to a proposed plan of action. Politicians aim to represent society as it really is, but as has already been seen they can use language to adapt reality to suit their purposes. It is therefore useful to identify any use of **implication** or secondary meaning. This allows politicians to state the truth while using words that can be interpreted in more than one way. For example, if someone were to say that a room was 'too warm', the intention could in fact be to imply that the heating should be turned off. In a social context, it might be considered more polite not to make the request more directly; in a political context, the implication might represent an attempt by a politician to evade a direct answer.

The **naming of politicians** is often significant: sometimes their **role title** is used rather than their **name**. This can be appropriate when their individual identity is irrelevant because the actions associated with the role would be the same whichever individual was involved. However, the use of the role title instead of an individual name can also be used to direct the focus away from the person. In redirecting the audience's attention, a politician can sometimes deflect personal responsibilities:

> David Cameron, the new leader of the Conservatives, will take the party in a new direction.

> The new leader of the Conservatives, David Cameron, opposed the Government's standpoint.

In the first example, the focus is on the **name** of the new party leader, because David Cameron will affect the way in which the Conservative Party represents itself to the electorate; in the second, the focus is on the **role** of the party leader, since any new Opposition leader would adopt the same stance.

In 2006, there was a campaign against the Labour Party policy of shutting special schools and providing places in the state school system for children with a range of disabilities. Many parents and practitioners felt that for a number of children this was not an appropriate educational, social or emotional environment. The Education Secretary at that time was Ruth Kelly, so when in January 2007 she decided to send her own child to a private school, the newspapers exploited what they saw as a double standard. Her position was made particularly awkward by the fact that at that point her successor as Education Secretary, Alan Johnson, was about to announce a programme of one-to-one tuition for children in the state sector who were struggling with Maths and English. Newspaper coverage suggested that as an individual Kelly was failing to set an example to other parents and was undermining the status of her local school, and that as a government minister (she was by then the Communities Secretary) she was advocating one policy in public while pursuing a different policy in private. In this case, the former role and the action of the individual politician were apparently at odds: the newspapers emphasised this, juxtaposing Kelly's former title, Education Secretary, with her choice of school.

Grammar

The **grammar** of political discourse varies, depending upon whether the utterances are spoken or written – inevitably, written statements tend to be more complex than speeches that have been written to be spoken or oral replies to questions.

However, the use of **pronouns** is significant in that pronominal choices often reflect the ideology of individual politicians by conveying their personal negative and positive attitudes. The connotations of the pronouns selected are not always predictable, but politicians with the same world view will probably choose the same kinds of pronouns.

> This is the very reason *we* want to increase training – but *he* has pledged to cut that investment.
>
> Tony Blair, in response to a question from David Cameron in
> Prime Minister's Questions, Hansard, Column 300 (6 December 2006)

Here Tony Blair, the Prime Minister, clearly distances the Labour Party from David Cameron, the leader of the Conservative Party, by using the third person singular pronoun *he*. The fact that the pronoun is singular also suggests that David Cameron is acting alone, without the support of his party. In contrast, the use of the possessive pronoun *we* unites the Labour Party politicians. This choice reinforces the underlying message: Blair implies that while the Labour Party works for the good of all, the Conservative Party is interested only in the good of the few.

The choice of pronouns in the next example illustrates a more subtle divide than that of Conservatives versus Labour.

> *We* have been entirely vindicated and it would be nice to get a message from the government that *they* were wrong and *we* were right.
>
> Ian Davidson (Labour MP for Glasgow South West)
> 'Labour MPs on Iraq', *The Guardian Online* (26 September 2005)

Although the first person plural *we* unites the speaker with other Labour Party members who identify with his own viewpoint on the war in Iraq, Ian Davidson and like-minded MPs remain distanced from the leadership of the party. By using the third person plural *they*, he suggests that the leadership and those continuing to support the party's policy on Iraq have failed to face the truth of what has happened.

Linguists need to think about the formality or informality of the pronouns used; the personal involvement of the speaker or writer; and whether their status, class or sex makes any difference. Pronouns enable politicians to accept, deny or distance themselves from their responsibilities, to encourage their supporters, to distance the opposition, and to give a personal touch to their discourse.

The **framing of questions** is also important. In a democracy, the very nature of alternative parties, and therefore alternative ways of tackling issues, is central to the whole process of government. The right to ask questions, whether it be in Parliament or in the domain of the media, is a fundamental principle of a democracy. Questions are rarely straightforward and they use techniques that allow the speaker to clearly establish the context and to manipulate the addressee: sentences in declarative mood precede the question and convey the speaker's own attitudes; the adverb *so* is commonly used to suggest that the proposition following is a logical consequence and should be automatically accepted; and negative forms that are sometimes contracted like *don't* allow the questioner to lead by suggesting that the truth of the proposition is already taken for granted.

> Does the Prime Minister share the widespread concern around the world at the unilateral action of the United States in bombing Somalia a couple of days ago and again yesterday? *Does not he think* that the bombardment will merely intensify the already desperate situation for the people of Somalia, when what is required is not foreign intervention but a peace process in Somalia?
>
> Jeremy Corbyn (Labour MP for Islington, North)
> Prime Minister's Questions, Hansard, Column 281 (10 January 2007)

Interrogative *wh-* words are often used to frame questions:

> *What* recent progress has been made in reducing relative child poverty; and *what* additional steps he plans to take to reduce child poverty further?
>
> David Kidney (Labour MP for Stafford)
> Oral Answers to Questions, Hansard, Column 3 (8 January 2007)

Questions demanding a *yes/no* reply are more common. These are less open and presuppose a particular answer to the question as more acceptable than any other possible ones. The use of *yes/no* questions is an attempt to force politicians to accept or deny the allegations made:

> Is the hon. Lady honestly saying that Health Ministers do not try to spin figures to suggest that things are better in the health service? Is she saying that the Home Office is not trying to spin criminal statistics to suggest that things are better than they are?
>
> Brooks Newmark (Conservative MP for Braintree)
> Orders of the Day, Hansard, Column 59 (8 January 2007)

When questions start with the modal *will*, they imply that because of the added politeness associated with the verb, any rejection of the request made will seem unnecessarily rude. By using it, politicians try to get the addressees to commit themselves to action:

> The Prime Minister is making a statement today about national security in Northern Ireland. *Will* he assure the House that the measures that he is announcing will not in any way compromise national security or undermine the capacity of our security services to combat terrorism, whether domestic or international?
>
> Jeffrey M. Donaldson (DUP MP for Lagan Valley)
> Prime Minister's Questions, Hansard, Column 281 (10 January 2007)

Literary devices

Literary devices are a significant part of the rhetoric used by politicians to persuade their audience, and the more original the image created, the more effectively the idea will be conveyed. **Metaphors** help explain complex arguments since one element is used to develop understanding of another element. Politicians use metaphor to prove a point, to provide light relief, and so on. The repetition or development of a single metaphor can be a powerful means of reinforcing a message.

> Does not the Prime Minister's complete lack of judgement in trusting the Deputy Prime Minister show that it is high time *he and his deputy saddled up and rode off into the sunset*?
>
> David Cameron, leader of the Conservative Party
> Prime Minister's Questions, Hansard, Column 313 (19 July 2006)

There are a number of political *minefields* that I could *step on* in answering that question.

Tony Blair, Prime Minister
Prime Minister's Questions, Hansard, Column 863 (12 December 2006)

The vain hope that Ministers will want their statistics to be awarded a quality kite-mark is wishful thinking; I suspect that *pigs will fly* before Ministers scramble to *fly their kite-marks*.

Brooks Newmark (Conservative MP for Braintree)
Orders of the Day, Hansard, Column 74 (8 January 2007)

Individual politicians have their own ways of speaking and writing, and analysis should focus on the choices made in each case. Discussion of linguistic features should be linked closely to pragmatics because it is these wider factors that often dictate the lexical and syntactical choices made. By considering the distinctive linguistic and pragmatic features it is then possible to come to conclusions not only about the individual in question but about political language in general.

17.4 Types of political language

Manifestos and campaign statements

Voting is central to our political system and politicians are therefore accustomed to producing statements that enable the electorate to make informed decisions at the ballot box. Candidates for general elections produce material presenting the views of their party, but also convey their own personal stance in order to give their campaign a distinctive identity. Such documentation will be read by people who oppose the viewpoint put forward, by those who support it, and by those who may be persuaded to agree with it. The main function is therefore **conative**. The **referential** function is subordinate, but it is often the information included in the statement which may persuade 'floating' voters to support the party in question.

Most of the documentation will be written for campaign leaflets which will be delivered to the local constituents in their homes. As technology has become more accessible, however, many MPs also use email and blogs in order to communicate directly with their potential supporters.

ACTIVITY 17.1

Read the following email sent by Simon Hughes, Liberal Democrat MP for North Southwark and Bermondsey, during the leadership campaign which followed the resignation of Charles Kennedy in January 2006. It was sent to members of the Liberal Democrat Party in order to generate support for his campaign.

As you read, think about the following features of the text and make notes on the effects they create:

- the intended audience, the purpose and the context (pragmatics)
- the lexis
- the grammar
- the rhetorical devices.

From: Lib Dems Hughes News [mailto: ld-hughesnews-l@LISTS.LIBDEMS.ORG.UK]
On behalf of Simon Hughes MP
Sent: 18 February 2006 17:07
To: ld-hughesnews-l@LISTS.LIBDEMS.ORG.UK
Subject: [SIMON HUGHES] A personal message from Simon Hughes MP

Dear friend,

With only a little over a week left until the result of our party's leadership contest is known I want to say thank you to my supporters, and indeed everyone I have met on the campaign trail, for all the support you have shown me.

You have turned up in your hundreds to the hustings meetings up and down the country. From Plymouth to Newcastle, from Swansea to Cambridge it has been a pleasure to meet with many of you and listen to your views on the future direction of our party. Today I am in the Midlands before further hustings and visits in Edinburgh, Wales, Devon and Cornwall, Manchester and London next week. I look forward to seeing many of you at these events too.

Who could have imagined when this campaign started that we would have enjoyed such a successful result in Dunfermline? I was there on the day the by-election was called and then through other visits, right up until my final return on polling day itself. I saw how Willie Rennie and hundreds of Liberal Democrats working together made the real difference. Just think where the Party can go when we have settled this three way leadership contest.

People sometimes say political debate is dead in this country. I can testify that it is not! One of the real joys of this campaign has been discussing the ideas and themes that I have advanced as a way forward for the party. If you haven't seen them do go to my website www.simonhughesforleader.com and have a look – and feel free to let me know what you think.

I want to lead a Party not afraid to trumpet its principles, a party that is true to its values and a party that is built on freedom, fairness and sustainability. We have achieved a lot in the last 50 years but we can't wait, and more importantly Britain can't wait another 50 years for the party to make progress. We need to be out there every day, in every region, in every city, in every town and every parish making our case and encouraging people to join us. I pledge that when elected leader I will not seal myself away in Westminster, but will be there with you on the streets, in the TV and radio studios both in London and the regions and out campaigning with you so that we make that real breakthrough.

I need your support to do that. I realise that some of you may have already voted – and if you have done so I hope it was for me – but **please do contact your party friends and colleagues this weekend**, check that they have voted and encourage them to join with you and I in building a party for the 21st century led by a leader in it for the long haul, with campaigning experience both in the Westminster village and the wider world outside. I want to do that – I hope you will give me your support to do that.

When Charles stood down at the beginning of this year I had not decided whether to throw my hat in to the ring. It was the encouragement of many people, including some of you who are listed on my site – the largest number of names of any candidate – that made me decide to run for leader. The past three weeks have shown that it was the right decision.

I was grateful when eighteen months ago you overwhelmingly elected me as your Party President. Now I want to lead our Party to even greater success. For over 28 years I have been working with people like you all around the country and together we have got more Liberal Democrats elected, and got our message out on to the streets more than ever. Now I want to do that as Leader.

With best wishes,

Simon Hughes MP

55 Printed and published by Chris Davies on behalf of Simon Hughes, Leadership Campaign Office, 103 Gaunt Street SE1 6DP

This email was sent to you by the Simon Hughes campaign for party leader. If you do not wish to receive emails from our campaign in future, please email liza.coffin@gmail.com. Please note that our records are separate from the party's own records, which are kept confidential and have not been provided to any cam-
60 paign.

COMMENTARY

Since this was sent directly to the email addresses of Liberal Democrat support-ers, the **intended audience** is clearly party members who will be taking part in the leadership election. The **purpose** of the email is therefore to persuade the voters to choose Simon Hughes rather than the other candidates who are stand-ing in the leadership campaign. The **context** is formal, although there are some features that suggest a familiarity between sender and recipient, which is typical of email communications. The lexical and syntactical choices reflect this blurring of boundaries.

The **lexis** is **subject-specific** – often linked to the political context. Nouns such as *contest* (l. 7), *campaign trail* (l. 9), *hustings* (ll. 10, 13), *by-election* (l. 17), *polling day* (l. 18) and *candidate* (ll. 45–6) establish the political focus of the email, while **proper nouns** such as *Plymouth, Newcastle, Swansea, Cambridge, Midlands, Edinburgh* and *Westminster* (ll. 11–14) establish the geographical boundaries of the context. Because the content is balanced between physical events (visits and meet-ings) and principles (the policies of the Liberal Democrats and Simon Hughes' personal viewpoint), the language of the email moves between the concrete and the abstract. **Abstract nouns** such as *support* (ll. 9, 36) and *encouragement* (l. 44) reflect the main purpose of the email; *views* (l. 12), *debate* (l. 22) and *decision* (l. 47) suggest the process by which the political democratic process is carried out; *pleas-ure* (l. 11) and *joys* (l. 23) create a personal touch that humanises the politician; and *freedom, fairness* and *sustainability* (l. 28) represent the underlying principles of the Liberal Democrat Party. The tone of the email is logical and the style balanced so that readers are thereby encouraged to participate in the leadership campaign.

Most of the **modifiers** used in the noun phrases are directly linked to the political theme: *leadership* contest (l. 7), *hustings* meetings (l. 10), *political* debate (l. 22). There are a few, however, that indicate Simon Hughes' response to events. The positive connotations of the adjective *successful* (l. 17), the superlative *larg-est* (l. 45) and the comparative *even greater* (l. 49) help Hughes to communicate his sense of purpose, encouraging the reader to be positive about his leadership campaign.

Similarly, the **pronouns** both promote his individual case and encourage a sense of unity. The repetition of the first person singular pronouns *I* (subject) and *me* (object) and the possessive determiner *my* throughout the email draws attention to Hughes' personal commitment to the campaign, emphasising what he can offer to the Liberal Democrat Party. This is balanced by the use of direct address (*you*, ll. 9, 10–15, 36–41) which engages readers and makes them an integral part of the political process. By uniting himself and the party members in the inclusive first person plural pronoun (*we*, ll. 28–30), Hughes reinforces the importance of ordinary voters in the leadership campaign and in the wider context of the Liberal Democratic Party's political success in recent elections. The compound phrase *you and I* (l. 39) aims to highlight the bond between the email recipient and the sender. However, it is an example of **hypercorrection**, as the subject pronoun *I* is used instead of the grammatically standard object pronoun *me*. This is a common variation from the standard since it is often considered impolite to use 'me'. The absence of third person singular ('he') and plural ('they') pronouns reflects the very positive approach of the campaign – Hughes focuses on his own potential as a candidate rather than on the limitations of the other participants.

As a written text, the **sentence structures** tend to be long and complicated, with more compound and complex sentences than simple. There are lots of adverbials and in places the sentences are lengthened by the use of dashes that are indicative of the familiar tone of the email. The grammatical complexity reflects the writer's serious approach to his subject.

> S P A A A
> (You) (have turned up) (in your hundreds) (to the hustings meetings) (up and down the
> country). (SIMPLE: ll. 10–11)

> A S P A A
> (For over 28 years), (I) (have been working) (with people like you) (all around the
> A S P O P P
> country) (and) (together) (we) (have got) (more Liberal Democrats) (elected), (and) (got)
> conj conj
> O A A
> (our message) (out on to the streets) (more than ever). (COMPOUND: ll. 49–52)

> S P O S P O
> (I) (want) (to do that) – (I) (hope) (you will give me your support to do that).
> SCl–NFCl SCl–NCl SCl–NFCl
> (COMPLEX: ll. 41–2)

> A
> (With only a little over a week left until the result of our party's leadership contest is
> SCl–NFCl SCl–ACl
> S P Od Oi A Oi
> known) (I) (want) (to say thank you) (to my supporters), (and) (indeed) (everyone ø I
> SCl–NFCl
> A A
> have met) (on the campaign trail), (for all the support ø you have shown me).
> SCl–RelCl SCl–RelCl
> (COMPOUND–COMPLEX: ll. 7–9)

Because of the serious style and tone of the email, the verb phrases reflect a wide range of **timescales**. Simple past is used to describe events that are complete (*was*, l. 17); simple present to indicate a current event (*am*, l. 13); the present perfect progressive (*have been working*, l. 50) to suggest an ongoing event that has both past and present relevance; the perfective (*have advanced*, l. 24) referring to something that happened leading up to the current campaign; and future time (*will not seal*, ll. 32–3) to look beyond the leadership election. In two sentences, the verb phrase is **passive** (*is known*, ll. 7–8; *was called*, ll. 17–18) with no agent. This allows the writer to move the object of the sentence in each case (*the result of our party's leadership contest; the by-election*) to a more prominent position in the sentence, drawing attention to the events rather than to the people responsible for them. While the **grammatical mood** of the email is dominated by the declarative, there are examples of the interrogative (ll. 16–17) and the imperative (ll. 20, 24–6, 37–8). The first is a rhetorical question that is designed to engage the reader; the imperatives aim to encourage direct action.

There are no examples of **figurative language**, but there are 'dead' metaphors – figurative use of language that has become so widely used that we no longer think of such phrases as metaphors: *political debate is dead* (l. 22); *a Party not afraid to trumpet its principles* (l. 27); *throw my hat in to the ring* (l. 44). Many **rhetorical devices**, however, can be identified here, all of which add to the persuasive nature of the text. **Listing** allows the writer to suggest a range of possibilities: adverbials of place (ll. 11, 13–14, 31) show his commitment to the country as a whole; adverbials of time (ll. 17–18) show his commitment to the party. The neat balance of **parallelism** underpins the rational tone of the email: *up and down the country* (ll. 10–11); *to meet... and listen...* (l. 12); *a Party... a party* (l. 27); *can't wait... can't wait...* (ll. 29–30); *have got... and got...* (l. 51). **Tripling** is emphatic: *freedom, fairness and sustainability* (l. 28); *contact... check... and encourage...* (ll. 37–8). All these features help to create a tightly structured appeal to readers that aims to persuade them to take a particular course of action.

Sentence organisation is distinctive, with many **marked themes** where the writer rearranges clause elements in order to bring the lexically most important item to the front of the sentence. Many are fronted adverbials of time (l. 7) or place (l. 11). The sentence beginning *I pledge* (ll. 32–5), however, consciously keeps the adverbial of time (*when elected leader*) away from the beginning of the sentence in order to allow the emotive subject and verb prominence in the initial position. This is the writer's personal commitment to those who vote for him and is therefore of great semantic importance.

The reference to the campaign **internet address** (l. 25), which can be immediately accessed from the email, represents one of the ways in which campaigning has changed with developments in modern technology. It means that Simon Hughes does not have to include policy statements in the email as they can be explored in more detail at the click of a button. In an age of 'spam' and circular emails that are often deleted without being read, the use of **bold print** (ll. 37–8) ensures that the main paragraph is eye-catching – even if nothing else is read, it is likely that readers will glance at this paragraph which emphasises the importance of participation and encouraging others to support the Hughes campaign.

The lexical, grammatical and rhetorical features of this written political statement make it a typical example of political language. The overall structure is clearly defined, with each paragraph focusing on a different theme. Simon Hughes' explicit thanks to those who have visited the hustings, his description of public interest in the campaign and his reasonable and balanced approach are aimed to persuade readers that he is 'the best man for the job'. Email is an excellent means of communication for politicians in the twenty-first century since it is fast, efficient, cost-effective and clearly targeted.

ACTIVITY 17.2

Read the following extracts taken from direct mailings representing two of the candidates in the 2005 General Election. Use the questions that follow to identify any differences or similarities in the approaches of Kim Howells (Labour) and Quentin Gwynne Edwards (Welsh Conservatives).

1 Jot down the audience, purpose and context for these written campaign statements.
2 Comment on the tone.
3 Identify any subject-specific lexis. Is there anything which could be considered typical of the party each candidate represents?
4 Identify any abstract nouns and comment on their significance.
5 Comment on the use of proper nouns and on the ways in which people or parties are named.
6 Discuss the use of first person singular and plural pronouns and the possessive determiners *my* and *our* in each statement.
7 Find examples of a range of sentence types and comment on your findings.
8 Find examples of the following rhetorical devices and comment on their effects:
   a listing
   b repetition
   c marked theme.
9 Jot down any other interesting features in each written statement and try to decide which you consider to be more effective overall.

KIM HOWELLS (KH) ....

1   # Caring for all of our People

Dr Kim Howells is one of the best-known and most experienced government ministers. For sixteen years he has been a hard-working Member of Parliament for the Pontypridd Constituency, dedicated to improving our communities for
5 **young and old alike.**
        He has been a key member of a government that has brought us the lowest mortgage interest rates for more than 30 years, the highest number of people in employment for half a century, record amounts of money going into Health and Education and into tackling anti-social behaviour and crime.
10   This is a government that has forced employers to give millions of hard-working men and women the dignity of a decent minimum wage. It has ensured higher Winter Fuel Allowances, free bus passes and eye-tests for our pensioners and free television licenses for those most in need. Kim Howells has been at the heart of all this and much more.

15   **KIM WORKING FOR YOU**
                        [* * *]
        It has been a privilege to have served as your Member of Parliament. Over the years, we have seen great changes, a general increase in prosperity and in people's expec-

tations. The constituency now has a state-of-the-art, brand-new hospital, the Royal
20 Glamorgan, staffed with the best professionals. We have a terrific network of doctors, paramedics, health professionals and carers in our communities. We should be proud of them.

There are more law officers on our streets than ever before and they are turning the tide in the fight against those who prey on the decent and vulnerable. We are cleaning
25 up our environment, protecting our woodland and transforming our rivers and streams from the filthy, polluted water courses that they were just a few years ago. Fish and otters have returned and, once more, red kites are gracing our skies in numbers.

Great tasks remain: we must renew and revitalise the commercial hearts of towns like Pontypridd and Tonyrefail. We must control the commercial sprawl that threatens
30 to engulf our remaining green areas and choke-up our roads.

We must protect the beauty of our parks and countryside. These are causes I believe in. If I am fortunate enough to win your vote, I will continue to fight for them.

QUENTIN GWYNNE EDWARDS (QGE) ....

Your Choice – Your Government

1

On May 5th you have a choice: more tax and waste with Labour or less tax and accountable investment in our Health and Education with the Conservatives. More lies, spin and deceit with Labour, or clear, honest and accountable commitments
5 with the Conservatives. More of your freedoms lost in legislation and meddling or smaller government, reduced bureaucracy and more independence with the Conservatives.

Labour is all talk. They have promised so much but not delivered, even though they have spent a huge amount of our money and raised our taxes 66 times.

10 ## "I would fight for efficient, honest and accountable government."

This is a real choice for you because the Conservatives and Mr Blair believe in different things. Mr Blair wants to control our lives and meddle; Conservatives do not. Labour think they as a Government can spend our money better than we can; we do
15 not. They believe in big government, federal Europe, state control and centralising power; we do not.

The choice before voters on May 5 is very clear: they can either reward Mr Blair for eight years of broken promises and vote for another five years of talk; or they can vote Conservative, to support a party that's taken a stand and is committed to action
20 on the issues that matter to hard working Britons.

- One in ten schools in England and Wales have disciplinary problems according to OFSTed.
- One third of primary age children in Wales leave their school unable to write properly.
25 - One fifth of children expelled from schools by Headteachers are put back in those schools by appeal to cause more trouble.
- Five thousand people died last year from infections they caught IN hospital.
- The Police are so busy filling forms they don't have time to fight crime.

Labour cannot blame every one else after 8 years in power. This is their record.

In response to the questions raised above, you may have picked up on some of the following points.

PURPOSE

The **purpose** here is very specific: to encourage readers to take the opportunity to vote for a local MP and thus to influence the make-up of Parliament. Since Kim Howells has been the MP for this constituency for sixteen years, the two campaign statements adopt very different approaches: where Kim Howells can emphasise the nature of his achievements to date, Quentin Gwynne Edwards has to stress the supposed disadvantages of having a Labour MP. The campaign statements are addressed to local residents in the constituency, delivered as direct mail and designed to appeal to ordinary members of the public.

TONE

The **tone** of the Howells campaign is positive and aims to draw attention to the improvements that have taken place under Labour; the Edwards campaign, on the other hand, tends to be negative. Both statements have been written to be read and they are inevitably formal – the content is serious and the style rhetorical. Both candidates use direct address, however, to engage the audience and to establish a personal relationship between sender and recipient.

SUBJECT-SPECIFIC NOUNS

In both statements there are many **subject-specific nouns** which are commonly associated with politics: *government* (l. 2, KH; l. 1, QGE); *Health and Education* (l. 8, KH; l. 3, QGE); *Member of Parliament* (l. 3, KH); *Conservatives* (l. 3, QGE); *Labour* (l. 2, QGE). In Kim Howells' statement, there are also many nouns that can be specifically associated with Labour Party policy (*minimum wage, Winter Fuel Allowances*, ll. 11–12, KH). They tend to occur in long noun phrases which use modifiers to emphasise Labour's achievements:

m m m m h q the *lowest* mortgage interest rate for more than 30 years det Adj N N N PrepP	(ll. 6–7)
m m h q the *highest* number of people in employment for half a century det Adj N PrepP PrepP PrepP	(ll. 7–8)
m h q q q *record* amounts of money going into Health and Education and ø into tackling anti- N N PrepP NFCl NFCl NFCl social behaviour and crime	(ll. 8–9)
m m h h q *free* bus passes and eye-tests for our pensioners Adj N N conj N PrepP	(l. 12)

These form the basis for the Labour campaign since they highlight the positive achievements at a national level. Unlike the earlier examples, they are not directly linked to the political field, but in the context of a campaign statement, they have clear political significance.

There are numerous examples of **abstract nouns** in both statements because the purpose of the texts is to promote philosophical debate as well as to deal with everyday life: *privilege* (l. 17, KH); *prosperity* (l. 18, KH); *commitments* (l. 4, QGE); *freedoms* (l. 5, QGE). The Conservative Party text, however, uses more abstract nouns: it cannot report on the Party's day-to-day achievements, so instead it explores the political differences between the two parties. The Labour Party is associated with negative abstract nouns – the connotations of *waste* (l. 2), *lies, spin and deceit* (l. 4) are used to persuade voters that they will have an effective government only if they vote Conservative. Abstract nouns linked to the Conservative Party use modifiers with positive connotations to help to establish the field of reference:

| m | m | m | h |
| *clear*, | *honest* and | *accountable* | commitments | (l. 4)
| Adj | Adj | Adj | N |

| m | h | m | h |
| *reduced* | bureaucracy | *more* | independence | (l. 6)
| V | N | det | N |
| past participle | | | |

| m | m | m | h |
| *efficient*, | *honest* and | *accountable* | government | (ll. 10–11)
| Adj | Adj | Adj | N |

The modifiers (in italics) allow the Conservative campaign to promote what this Party sees as its potential strengths – having no concrete evidence of the result of its policies in this particular constituency, it aims to win voters through the positive connotations of the lexis.

The **proper nouns** used in each campaign statement reflect the approach of each candidate. Kim Howells is named immediately in the opening paragraph: he is well known in his constituency and will attract votes on a personal as well as a political level. This personal tone is reinforced by the references to local places, which remind readers that Kim Howells is a local man with local experience: *Royal Glamorgan* (ll. 19–20); *Pontypridd, Tonyrefail* (l. 29).

The Conservative candidate is not explicitly named in his statement at all: there is just a small captioned photograph on the leaflet. This is probably because, although known within the Welsh Conservative Party, he may be unfamiliar to local residents. This is why the statement tends to focus on the differences between the parties rather than on a personal appeal to voters. Other proper nouns include the repetition of *Labour* and *Conservatives* which underpin the structural divide.

Both statements use a range of pronoun forms, but in slightly different ways. The Kim Howells text uses the third person (*Kim Howells; he*) in the opening paragraphs (ll. 2–14) to present an apparently objective account of his time as Member of Parliament for Pontypridd. This is replaced (ll. 17–32) by a first person account, which unites reader and politician through first person plural pronouns (*we*) and possessive determiners (*our*):

> *We* are cleaning up *our* environment, protecting *our* woodland and transforming *our* rivers ...   (ll. 24–5)

The change in pronoun references reinforces the personal tone of the text since it establishes a common desire: to value, protect and improve the constituency. It can also be seen in the use of the adjective *proud* (l. 21) in the stressed predicative position, together with the modal verb *should* with its connotations of something that is right and desirable. The emphasis is on the unity between reader and sender: a team which can continue to improve the constituency if voters elect Kim Howells again. The final lines use singular first person pronouns (l. 32) to remind the reader that Kim Howells is the candidate who can fulfil his promises.

Where the Kim Howells campaign is personal in its approach, the Quentin Gwynne Edwards campaign is impersonal. Singular first person pronouns are used only once (l. 10) to develop a sense of the candidate as an individual, while first person plural pronouns are repeated to establish a sense of the Conservative Party as a whole. The juxtaposition of the third person plural *they* (the Labour Party) with the first person plural *we* forms the basis for the extended comparison of the two main political parties (ll. 14–16). Direct address aims to engage the reader in debate, but the second person pronoun *you* (ll. 2, 12) and the possessive determiner *your* (ll. 1, 5) are replaced in later paragraphs with the third person plural *they* (the voters). This adds to the impersonal tone of the text as a whole, in spite of the occasional use of the inclusive possessive determiner *our* (ll. 9, 13, 14).

SENTENCE STRUCTURE

Because these are written statements of intent, the **sentence structure** is mostly complicated. Each text opens with a simple sentence, however, in order to engage the reader:

S   P   C
(Dr Kim Howells) (is) (one of our best-known and most experienced government ministers).   (ll. 2–3, KH)

A   S   P   O
(On May 5th) (you) (have) (a choice) ...   (l. 2, QGE)

Other simple sentences tend to be emphatic, stressing a key point about the candidate (ll. 13–14, KH; ll. 10–11, QGE), underlining political divisions (l. 8, QGE) or expressing an attitude (ll. 21–2, KH).

Both candidates use a range of compound, complex and compound–complex sentences to communicate their viewpoint. These kinds of structures are effective because they enable candidates to link significant issues in the mind of the reader:

dumS   P   (S)   A   (S)   S
(There) (are) (more law officers) (on our streets) (than ever before) (and) (they) (are
                                                       conj

P   O   A
turning) (the tide) (in the fight against those who prey on the decent and vulnerable).
                                        SCl–RelCl
                                              (ll. 23–4, KH)

S   P   O   P   A
(They) (have promised) (so much) (but) (not delivered) (even though they have spent a
                              conj   neg   SCl–ACl

huge amount of our money) (and) (ø raised our taxes 66 times).   (ll. 8–9, QGE)
                              conj   SCl–ACl

The intention of politics is to persuade people to support a certain view of the world and to act in accordance with it: a formal tone, serious content and long sentences are therefore typical.

SENTENCE ORGANISATION

Marked themes are used to draw attention to an element of the sentence which is not the subject. In Kim Howells' statement, two of the marked themes foreground adverbials of time, allowing the campaign to draw attention to his experience: *For sixteen years…* (l. 3); *Over the years…* (l. 17). The other marked theme (l. 32, KH) foregrounds an adverbial clause of condition – the event described in the main clause is dependent on the condition described in the adverbial clause. Here, it allows the campaign statement to end on a note of humility, recognising that any MP is dependent upon the support of his constituents.

The only marked theme in the Conservative statement is used to emphasise the importance of the election date: *On May 5th* (l. 2).

RHETORICAL DEVICES

The texts use a range of **rhetorical devices** to underpin their message. Both Edwards and Howells use **listing** to emphasise things that they think are important. The syndetic listing of the noun phrases *higher Winter Fuel Allowances, free bus passes and eye-tests… and free television licenses [sic]…* (ll. 11–13, KH) and the clauses *are cleaning up…, protecting… and transforming…* (ll. 24–5, KH) provide the reader with evidence supporting the argument being put forward. The Conservative text uses listing of modifiers to emphasise the difference between the two parties: the tripling of *lies, spin and deceit* (l. 4, QGE) is set against *efficient, honest and accountable* (ll. 10–11, QGE).

Repetition is also used by both candidates. Howells repeats the modal verb *must* (ll. 28–9, 31) to emphasise the joint obligation to build on the work already done in the last 16 years; Edwards repeats *can* (ll. 17–18) to develop a sense of the possibilities that will exist if the voters elect a Conservative rather than a Labour MP. The repetition of the abstract noun *choice* (ll. 1, 2, 12, 17) in the Conservative statement underpins this – the emphasis throughout the text is on the need to make a decision based on the evidence provided. Where Kim Howells can refer directly to his achievements, the Welsh Conservatives have to rely on communicating political principles – hence the repetition of the stative verb *believe* (ll. 12, 15).

Because Edwards' statement relies on dividing the political principles of the two main parties, **parallelism** and **antithesis** are the dominant rhetorical devices used. The balanced parallel phrases of the headline *Your Choice – Your Government* (l. 1) immediately establish the importance of the individual in electing a government. This is developed in the parallel *they can either… or they can…* (ll. 17–18), which seems to offer voters an objective choice. The connotations of the words, however, reflect the Conservative bias: the antithesis of *broken promises* and *taken a stand* and of *talk* and *action* underline the political leanings of the statement. This juxtaposition can also be seen in the way that Labour Party 'beliefs' are set against the emphatic negative simple sentences: *Conservatives do not* (l. 13); *we do not* (l. 16).

Both written statements are interesting for different reasons and they will have appealed to different voters for different reasons. While Kim Howells seems to speak directly to the reader in a personal way, Quentin Gwynne Edwards aims to highlight political and ethical differences between the parties. His use of pronouns is less personal and there is less sense of him as an individual than as a party representative. Although highlighted by a typographical change (ll. 10–11), the fact that he only once uses the first person pronoun *I* distances him from the local election process.

Kim Howells, on the other hand, emerges from the statement as a man who has practical knowledge of his community: the hospitals, the police, the landscape and the wildlife. References to *woodland, rivers and streams, Fish and otters* and *red kites* (ll. 25–7) are concrete – quite unlike the abstracts of the Conservative statement. In addition, the use of figurative language contributes to the personal tone of the text: phrases such as *the commercial sprawl* (l. 29) and the collocation *turning the tide* (ll. 23–4) may be dead metaphors, but the present participle *gracing* (l. 27) is poetic in style. The verbs are also emotive, setting the positive connotations of *renew and revitalise* (l. 28) against the negative *engulf… and choke-up* (l. 30). Stylistic features like these add another layer to the text, moving it beyond the impersonality of the Conservative statement.

The basic difference in approach is reinforced in the final paragraph of each text. For Edwards, the emphasis is on the failure of Labour. The two simple sentences (l. 29) function as a summary to the listed bullet points that catalogue what the Conservative Party sees as evidence of Labour's inefficiency:

> S   P   C
> (This) (is) (their record).

The anaphoric reference (*This*) directs readers back to the bullet points and it is this information that is intended to influence voters – rather than underlining Conservative potential, the statement ends with statistics that are supposed to undermine local support for Kim Howells. It is a statement designed to appeal to voters who have become disillusioned with the Labour Party.

The Labour Party statement ends with a more direct and personal appeal to the reader (ll. 31–2): the inclusive *we*, the integrity implied by the abstract noun *causes* and stative verb *believe*, the heartfelt repetition of the first person pronoun *I* and the emphatic use of the modal *will* are persuasive. The final three sentences function structurally and semantically as a link to the headlined non-finite clauses: *Caring for all our people* (l. 1) and *working for you* (l. 15). Readers are left with the sense of an impassioned appeal to their judgement – a vote for Kim Howells will result in continued change for the constituency because he has a genuine interest in the area.

Both Quentin Gwynne Edwards and Kim Howells employ typical features of political language here. Although there are many differences in their approaches, the end result is effective in each case. The most important thing to recognise is that the individual focus in each will attract different voters.

Any speech which has been prepared ahead of delivery has been consciously planned – the politician is involved in the selection of lexical, syntactical and rhetorical features and in the overall organisation. Like a campaign statement, choices are made in advance to achieve the maximum possible effect on the audience. It is likely, however, that a politician will attempt to use some techniques that reflect formal spoken language. The first person pronoun is often used more frequently and **SPONTANEITY MARKERS** like *I know* or *you know* may be chosen to make the manner seem less formal than it actually is. The overall effect will inevitably depend upon the audience and context, but in analysis of a scripted speech it is important to first identify the features of 'speeches written to be read' and then to consider any features that seem to resemble spoken language.

ACTIVITY 17.3

The following speeches were both written to be read aloud in a formal context. The first was delivered by the Prime Minister, Tony Blair, at the Labour Party Conference in Brighton on 26 September 2006; the second was a speech by Cheryl Gillan, Conservative MP for Chesham and Amersham and the Shadow Secretary of State for Wales, at the Centre for Policy Studies on 16 January 2007. In both cases, the speeches contain many examples of formal written language, but there are also features which can be linked to informal spoken language. Only the conclusions of these speeches are printed, and these do not include examples of all the features that can be adopted by politicians to make their speeches seem more spontaneous than written statements.

Read through the two examples and list:

1 lexical, syntactical and rhetorical features
2 techniques used to make the speech seem like spoken language.

TONY BLAIR (TB: EXTRACT) --

1 The first rule of politics: there are no rules. You make your own luck. There's no rule that says the Tories have got to come back. David Cameron's Tories? My advice: get after them.

His foreign policy. Pander to anti-Americanism by stepping back from America.
5 Pander to the Eurosceptics through isolation in Europe. Sacrificing British influence for Party expediency is not a policy worthy of a Prime Minister.

His immigration policy. Says he'll sort out illegal immigration, but opposes Identity Cards, the one thing essential to do it.

His energy policy. Nuclear power, but "only as a last resort". It's not a multiple choice
10 quiz question, Mr Cameron. We need to decide now otherwise in 10 years time we will be importing expensive fossil fuels and Britain's economy will suffer.

He wants tax cuts and more spending, with the same money.

He wants a Bill of Rights for Britain drafted by a Committee of Lawyers. Have you ever tried drafting anything with a Committee of Lawyers?

15 And of course the policy for the old lady terrorised by the young thug is that she should put her arm round him and give him a nice, big hug.

Built to last? They haven't even laid the foundation stone. If we can't take this lot apart in the next few years we shouldn't be in the business of politics at all.

The Tories haven't thought it through. They think it's all about image. Now it's true

20 we've changed our image. We created a professional organisation. But I tell you
something else that's true. If I'd stood in 1997 on the policies of 1987 I would have
lost. And it's the same now. If you don't mind, enough talk of hung Parliaments.

The next election won't be about image unless we let it be. It'll be about who has
the strength, the judgement, the weight and the ideas for Britain's future in an uncer-
25 tain world. And if we show belief in ourselves, the British people will feel that belief
and they'll sense it and they'll be given confidence.

Something else I've learnt. Politics is also about a Party's character. The characters
of the people in it and I'll give you two examples. Dennis Skinner. He's watching
from his sick bed. Get well soon. Never agreed with a policy I've done. Never once
30 stopped him knowing the difference between a Labour Government and a Tory one.

And people like Janet Anderson and George Howarth and Mike Hall. Good
Ministers, but I asked them to make way. And they did. Without a word of bitterness.
They never forgot their principles when in office; and they never discovered them
when they left it.
35 This is the Party I am proud to lead. From the day I was elected and until the day
I leave, they'll always try to separate us of course. "He's not Labour." "He's a closet
Tory." In the 1980s some things done were necessary it's true. Saying it doesn't make
you a Tory. I'm a progressive and the true believer, the true progressive believes in
social justice, in solidarity, in help for those not able to help themselves. They know
40 the race can't just be to the swift and survival for the strong. But they also know that
these values, gentle and compassionate as they are, have to be applied in a harsh,
uncompromising world and that what makes the difference is not belief alone, but the
raw courage to make it happen.

You know they say I hate the Party, and its traditions. Well I don't. I love this Party.
45 There's only one tradition I ever hated: losing. I hated the 1980s not just for our irrelevance, but for our revelling in our irrelevance. And I don't want to win for winning's
sake but for the sake of the millions here that depend on us to win, and throughout
the world.

Every day this Government has been in power, every day in Africa, children have
50 lived who otherwise would have died because this country led the way in cancelling
debt and global poverty. That's why winning matters. So keep on winning. Do it with
optimism. With hope in your hearts. Politics is not a chore. It's the great adventure of
progress.

I don't want to be the Labour Leader who won 3 successive elections. I want to
55 be the first Labour Leader to win 3 successive elections.

So: it's up to you. Take my advice. Don't take it. It's your choice. Whatever you do,
I'm always with you. Head and heart. You've given me all I have ever achieved, and all
that we've achieved, together, for the country.

Next year I won't be making this speech. But, in the years to come, wherever I am,
60 whatever I do. I'm with you. Wishing you well. And wanting you to win.

You're the future now. So make the most of it.

CHERYL GILLAN (CG: EXTRACT) ··

1 I have outlined the problem: a selfishness that permeates our society. I have outlined
the contribution made by Labour's materialist philosophy. So what can we do about
it?

What are the Conservatives thinking, and how are we approaching our policy-
5 making process?

We think the wrong answer would be trying to tell people what to do, nannying and regulating. But I believe that David Cameron is helping to find the right answer. It is social responsibility – the big idea at the heart of modern Conservatism, which we explored in a fascinating conference yesterday.

10   The idea behind social responsibility is that the state alone is not able to sort out all of society's problems – only society can do that. And by 'society' I mean each one of us. Social responsibility can be led by politicians, but it can only be delivered by people themselves. ...

At our conference yesterday, David quoted Archbishop Oscar Romero of El Sal-
15   vador: "aspire not to have more, but to be more." And I think that is part of our philosophy of social responsibility.

This is part of an embryonic trend in our country, and we need to build on it. For example, I particularly like the phenomenon known as Guerrilla Gardening – informal bands of residents who furtively, under cover of darkness, go out and improve areas
20   of public space neglected by the council. But there's also a huge resurgence of more traditional social action – from supplementary schools helping the children of immigrants, to charities helping the elderly and unemployed.

I believe that politicians need to be part of this trend. I am not going to instruct people how to spend their money or their time. But I do believe that politicians can
25   help to change the culture – indirectly, by putting in place the right frameworks and incentives. ...

... I want to explore how we engage more people in their local communities. I believe that government can help stimulate a greater culture of volunteering, especially in the fight against poverty.

30   As the interim report from Iain Duncan Smith's Social Justice Policy Group demonstrated last month, one of the trickiest challenges for us is to find ways of increasing state funding of charities and other independent organisations, without at the same time increasing the power of the state and diminishing the independence of the organisations we are funding. A possible way of doing this is to ensure that some of
35   the money the state spends on the voluntary sector is allocated by citizens themselves, rather than by government officials with all sorts of strings attached.

Therefore, on behalf of David Cameron and the Shadow Cabinet, I am today submitting a policy proposal to Iain Duncan Smith and the Social Justice Policy Group. We would like Iain and his colleagues to investigate the idea of Volunteering Vouchers –
40   taxpayers money which you can "earn" for the charity of your choice by volunteering for it. This would not represent an increase in spending, but a reallocation of existing funding. Rather than the state controlling this money, we believe that individuals and communities could be in charge of it.

There's a song in the charts at the moment by the singer Just Jack. It's called *Starz*
45   *in their Eyes* – and it's a savage attack on the cult of celebrity, and the cynicism of a media which makes money out of the gullible dreams of the young.

I believe that this song is part of a new culture in our country. People are beginning to see through the hollowness of our selfish society. They want more than the glitter and the false magic of the adman. And they want more than the greed and material-
50   ism which has developed under Labour.

As politicians we need to capture this new mood. Our role is to provide the framework for society and communities to flourish. We need to practise the politics of inclusion rather than allowing the culture of selfishness and greed to prosper. More than ever under David Cameron, this imperative is forming part of mainstream conserva-
55   tive thinking.

An intrinsic part of Conservatism has always been a sense of duty and service and social responsibility. Now we are translating those principles into a modern prospectus to encourage a society and a country we are all happy to live in and contribute to.

COMMENTARY

There are numerous features here that are typical of political language. Some of the main examples are included in the table below.

LEXIS

Examples	Comment
politics (l. 1, TB), politicians (l. 12, CG), election (l. 23, TB), government (l. 28, CG)	This **subject-specific language** is typical of all kinds of political discourse. It marks no specific political ideology, but is used by all politicians.
Dennis Skinner (l. 28, TB), Janet Anderson (l. 31, TB), David Cameron (l. 7, CG), Iain Duncan Smith (l. 30, CG)	The use of these **proper nouns** identifies each party through direct reference to its MPs.
Tories (l. 2, TB), Conservatives (l. 4, CG)	The use of the abbreviated **name** of the Conservative Party by Tony Blair reflects his lack of sympathy with the party, while Cheryl Gillan's use of the full name is a mark of respect.
expediency (l. 6, TB), belief (l. 25, TB), social responsibility (l. 8, CG), poverty (l. 29, CG)	**Abstract nouns** are common in both speeches because the speakers are discussing philosophical issues and party viewpoints to them.
Guerrilla Gardening (l. 18, CG), Just Jack (l. 44, CG), Starz in their Eyes (ll. 44–5, CG)	Gillan uses these **proper nouns** as contemporary references that will give her speech a topical relevance.

GRAMMAR

Pronouns

Examples	Comment
This is the Party *I* am proud to lead (l. 35, TB)	Blair foregrounds the Labour Party, referring to himself in a **post-modifying relative clause** i.e. 'the Party that I am proud to lead'.
I tell you … (l. 20, TB), You've given *me* … (l. 57, TB)	The use of **first person singular pronouns** gives the speech a personal tone. Since this is to be Blair's last conference speech as Party leader, he emphasises his individual experiences rather than his political role.
we shouldn't be in the business of politics … (l. 18 TB), *we*'ve changed *our* image (l. 20, TB)	The use of the **first person plural** *we* and the possessive determiner *our* reminds us that Blair is part of a team as well as having an individual role as Prime Minister.
hope in *your* hearts … (l. 52, TB), it's up to *you* … (l. 56, TB)	The **direct address** links Blair and his audience – party delegates who have come to hear his last conference speech as Party leader – more personally.

His immigration policy... (l.7, TB), He wants... (l.12, TB), They haven't even laid the foundation stone... (l.17, TB)	Third person singular and plural pronouns and possessive determiners allow Blair to distance himself and his party from the opposition.
I have outlined... (l.1, CG), what can we do... (l.2, CG), They want... (l.48, CG)	By balancing first person singular and plural pronouns, Gillan can move between an expression of a personal opinion and party policy; third person plural pronouns distinguish between the Party and the general public.
our conference... (l.14, CG), our philosophy... (ll.15–16, CG)	Possessive determiners reinforce the unity between Gillan and her Party.

Verbs

Examples	Comment
get after them (ll.2–3, TB), take this lot apart (ll.17–18, TB)	Blair uses colloquial verbs – prepositional (get after); phrasal (take apart) – to underpin the personal, familiar tone. He is speaking to a supportive audience with whom he has a personal relationship (albeit in a very broad sense).
I was elected (l.35, TB)	The passive verb phrase allows Blair to foreground the first person singular I which would have occurred as 'me' after the verb in an active sentence.
know (l.40, TB), hate... love (l.44, TB), think (l.6, CG), believe (l.7, CG)	Stative verbs are common because the content is reflective rather than physical.
Social responsibility can be led by politicians... be delivered by people... (ll.12–13, CG)	By using the passive voice, Gillan can foreground the key concept of her policy speech: *social responsibility*. In the initial position, it has more significance than if it occurred after an active verb phrase as the object. The agent is included because the contrast created between *politicians/people* is fundamental to the point being made.

General

Examples	Comment
Have you ever tried...? (ll.13–14, TB), So what can we do...? (ll.2–3, CG)	Interrogatives enable the speakers to engage directly with their audiences. These are rhetorical questions, however, since the speakers provide their own answers.
Take my advice. Don't take it (l.56, TB), make the most of it (l.61, TB)	Blair's use of the imperative mood is designed to persuade his audience to respond, to carry on the work he has begun.
will feel... 'll sense... 'll be (ll.25–6, TB), can be led... can... be delivered... (l.12, CG), We would like... (ll.38–9, CG)	Modal verbs allow the speakers to communicate shades of meaning: certainty (will), possibility (can), intention (would), and so on.

Sentence structure is very varied in each speech, as would be expected since such variety guarantees that the audience will be kept interested. However, Tony Blair's speech contains far more **simple sentences** than Cheryl Gillan's and this adds to the rhetorical effect:

```
 dumS    P    (S)      A              A                      A
(There) ('s) (a song) (in the charts) (at the moment) (by the singer Just Jack). (l. 44, CG)
```

```
  S     P       A    P        O
(They) (haven't) (even) (laid) (the foundation stone).                    (l. 17, TB)
```

Tony Blair's use of simple and minor sentences makes his speech seem emphatic: it adds a sense of certainty and enhances the informality of his relationship with the audience. The tone is almost conversational:

```
  S    P      C        A       P         O
(You) ('re) (the future) (now). (So) (make) (the most of it).            (ll. 61, TB)
                                  conj
```

Both speakers also use **compound** and **compound–complex** sentences in which elements from the first main clause are omitted in the second, allowing speakers to link ideas together for their audience. In this kind of public context where a pre-scripted speech is delivered orally, compound–complex sentences are common. To control the length and make it easier for the audience to understand, the grammatical unit may be divided into two with an initial-position conjunction. Compound–complex sentences reflect both the formality of the occasion and the reflective nature of the content:

```
                     A                    S           P        O
(And) (if we show belief in ourselves) (the British people) (will feel) (that belief) (and)
conj   SCl–ACl                                                                          conj
  S     P    O     S     P        O
(they) ('ll sense) (it) (and) (they) ('ll be given) (confidence).          (ll. 25–6, TB)
                          conj
```

```
 S    P      P                          O                                O
(I) (am) (not) (going) (to instruct people how to spend their money) (or) (ø their time).
          neg          SCl–NFCl                SCl–NFCl                conj SCl–NFCl
  S     P                                        O                                    A
(But) (I) (do believe) (that politicians can help to change the culture) – (indirectly),
conj        SCl–NCl                    SCl–NFCl
                    A
(by putting in place the right frameworks and incentives).                (ll. 23–6, CG)
SCl–NFCl
```

Complex sentences place a greater demand upon listeners because they need to remember the key elements – they are unable to look back, as readers can.

```
                     A                        A         A          S      P
(Every day this Government has been in power) (every day) (in Africa) (children) (have
    SCl–RelCl
                              S                                          A
lived) (who otherwise would have died) (because this country led the way in cancel-
       SCl–RelCl                       SCl–ACl                             SCl–NFCl
ling debt and global poverty).                                          (ll. 49–51, TB)
```

```
                                                  A
(As the interim report from IDS's Social Justice Policy Group demonstrated last month),
SCl–ACl
                  S                          P                              C
(one of the trickiest challenges for us) (is) (to find ways of increasing state funding of
                                              SCl–NFCl        SCl–NFCl
```

charities and other independent organisations, without) (at the same time) (increasing

SCl–NFCl

C

the power of the state) (and) (ø diminishing the independence of the organisations

conj   SCl–NFCl

we are funding).   (ll. 30–4, CG)

SCl–RelCl

Complex sentences such as these are appropriate because the context is formal. Although each one provides a lot of information, listeners will already have had both knowledge of and an interest in the issues raised. This helps them to process the content. Each speaker's aim is to prove the relative merits of a particular ideological standpoint – each must convince the audience that it is beneficial to continue supporting the party that he or she represents.

SENTENCE ORGANISATION

Examples	Comment
From the day ... (l. 35), Next year (l. 59, TB) At our conference yesterday (l. 14), As the interim report ... last month (l. 30–1), Now ... (l. 57, CG)	Marked themes are used to indicate a specific time, drawing a distinction between past and present. This shows how far each party has come in terms of its achievements or successes.
Therefore, on behalf of ... (ll. 37–8, CG) If we ..., If I'd ..., If you ..., if we ... (ll. 17, 21, 22, 25, TB)	Other marked themes highlight key points to be considered alongside the one being made at the time. Gillan sets her submission of a policy proposal in the context of the Shadow Cabinet she represents; Blair establishes 'conditions' which affect our understanding of the delayed main clause.

RHETORIC

Examples	Comment
His foreign policy ... His immigration policy ... His energy policy ... (ll. 4–9, TB)	The patterning of the noun phrase minor sentences provides an overall framework for the point that Blair is making – that Conservative Party policy is ill-conceived and ineffective.
... the strength, the judgement, the weight and the ideas ... (l. 24, TB)	The listing of abstract nouns allows Blair to set philosophical principles against the superficial concept of *image* (l. 23). The syndetic list is emphatic and the suggestion is that these positive concepts are more closely allied to Labour than to the Conservatives.
I have outlined the problem ... I have outlined the contribution made by Labour's materialist philosophy ... (ll. 1–2, CG)	The repetition of this S P O clause structure provides a springboard for Gillan to explore Conservative attitudes to social issues. The three interrogatives that follow (ll. 2–5) are rhetorical; they allow the speaker to address party policy explicitly.

social responsibility (ll. 8, 10, 12, 16, 57, CG) election (ll. 23, 54–5), elected (l. 35), win/won (ll. 46–7, 54–5, 60), winning (l. 51, TB)	Each speaker has a central theme or themes, and **repetition** of a word or phrase reminds listeners of the focus of the speech.
the politics of inclusion ... the culture of selfishness and greed ... (ll. 52–3, CG)	The **antithesis** of these two noun phrases brings the speech to a climax: they represent current social attitudes and what the Conservatives see as the way to counteract them.

SPOKEN LANGUAGE

When a speech is delivered before an audience, listeners have the benefit of intonation patterns, stress patterns and other such prosodic features to help them understand what is being said. Unless actually transcribed for linguistic analysis, however, the written record of a speech does not mark these variations. Nevertheless, even in the written language it is possible to identify certain features that are included in order to make the speech seem more like the spoken than the written word.

Examples	Comment
I want to be the first... (ll. 54–5, TB) *I* believe that... (ll. 23, CG)	Use of the **first person singular pronoun** is more frequent in spoken language and gives a speech a more personal feel.
it's up to *you* (l. 56, TB)	The direct address of the **second person pronoun** is personal because it makes those in the audience feel that they are being individually involved by the speaker.
can't (l. 17), it's (ll. 19, 22), won't, It'll (l. 23, TB) there's (l. 20), It's (l. 44, CG)	**Contractions** are commonly associated with the spoken word and are seen as being quite informal.
If you don't mind (l. 22), You know (l. 44, TB)	Some words or phrases may seem quite **conversational** compared with the formality of the context.
And of course... (l. 15), But, in the years to come... (l. 59, TB) But I believe... (l. 7), And by 'society'... (l. 11, CG)	**Conjunctions** used in the **initial position** are associated with informal spoken language. Their use in a formal context creates a more relaxed manner.
..., gentle and compassionate as they are, ... (l. 41, TB) ..., under cover of darkness, ... (l. 19, CG)	**Parenthesis** is used to add extra information. It gives the sentence in which it is included a looser structure, which is again reminiscent of conversation.
Dennis Skinner (l. 28), Without a word of bitterness (ll. 32–3), Wishing you well (l. 60, TB) ... – only society can do that (l. 11), – indirectly, by putting in place... (l. 25, CG)	**Minor sentences** and the use of **dashes** as a loose form of coordination contribute to the conversational tone of the speeches.

Both of the texts reproduced here are extracts from written copies of speeches composed to be spoken. In fact, their style remains very similar to that of the manifestos and campaign statements in the previous section. The main differences lie in features which can be linked to informal spoken language. Because of the formal context and informed audience in each case, however, these informal features are less dominant than those associated with the more formal register of the written word.

The Houses of Parliament

Although pre-scripted speeches and debates are a central part of Parliament, many of the exchanges are not scripted. Everything that is spoken is recorded in **HANSARD**, and this provides language students with interesting examples of political language in use.

Much of the language is formulaic and traditional patterns are used time and time again. This can be seen in the **framing of a motion for debate**. For example, Hansard records the motion on 5 December 2006 from Andrew Lansley, Conservative MP for South Cambridgeshire, which was to introduce a debate on public health:

> 1 I beg to move,
>   That this House notes the Government's failure to improve public health out-
>   comes and to reduce health inequalities; believes that the gap between the pub-
>   lic health of the UK and that of comparable health economies is unacceptable;
> 5   identifies obesity, smoking, sexually transmitted disease, infectious disease
>   control, teenage pregnancy, alcohol and substance abuse, the promotion of
>   healthy lifestyles and screening for treatable disease as areas of particular con-
>   cern; supports frontline staff striving in adverse circumstances to improve the
>   health of the nation; is concerned about the shortage of public health staff due
> 10 to the Government's financial mismanagement; joins with the Chief Medical
>   Officer in condemning the use of public health funds to tackle NHS deficits;
>   and calls on the Government to ensure that funds for public health are spent on
>   addressing remediable health issues.

The formulaic *I beg to move* (l.1) is the traditional opening to a debate. The verb phrase *beg to move* allows the speaker to provide a number of objects in the form of a noun clause introduced by *that* which is often omitted after the first clause:

> S   P   O   O   O
> (I) (beg to move) (That this House notes…); (ø believes…); (ø identifies…);
>   SCl–NCl   SCl–NCl   SCl–NCl
>   O   O   O   O
> (ø supports…); (ø is concerned…); (ø joins…); (and) (ø calls…).   (ll.1–12, AL)
>   SCl–NCl   SCl–NCl   SCl–NCl   conj   SCl–NCl

The **repetition** of the nouns *health* and *disease* establishes the focus of the motion, while references to *financial mismanagement* (l.10), *funds* and *deficits* (l.11) reflect the fact that this is a Conservative motion which aims to challenge the Government's position on health. The use of several words with **negative connotations** underlines the political purpose: *failure* (l.2); *inequalities* (l.3); *adverse* (l.8); *shortage* (l.9).

A later intervention by the Minister of State for the Department of Health, Caroline Flint MP, after thirty-seven minutes of debate, replaces Andrew Lansley's motion with the following version:

> 1 I beg to move, To leave out from "House" to the end of the Question, and to add
>   instead thereof:
>   "welcomes the Government's trebling of investment in the NHS by 2008 which
>   is crucial to improving public health and tackling health inequalities; notes that
> 5 this extra investment has enabled a huge expansion in preventative services
>   including extending breast cancer screening to women aged 65–70 which has
>   helped increase the number of breast cancers detected by 40 per cent. since
>   2001 and the first ever national bowel cancer screening programme which will
>   detect around 3,000 bowel cancers a year when fully rolled out; acknowledges
> 10 that this Government has done more than any previous government to help
>   people give up smoking, including banning smoking in all workplaces and pub-
>   lic places from 1st July 2007; further welcomes the help and support being
>   given to people to live healthier lives including two million 4 to 6 year olds now
>   receiving a free piece of fruit or portion of vegetables, new healthier standards
> 15 for school meals, clearer food labelling, new health trainers and NHS life checks;
>   and recognises the unprecedented action this Government has taken to tackle
>   the root causes of ill health and health inequalities including helping more peo-
>   ple to find work, lifting a significant number of children out of relative poverty
>   and taking action to tackle poor housing."

This motion provides a complete contradiction in terms of ideology, but the basic structure remains exactly the same. While subject-specific **noun phrases** such as *public health* and *health inequalities* occur in both motions, the tone and content are quite different. The negative connotations of words in the Conservative motion are replaced here by **positive verbs** (*trebling*, l. 3; *improving*, l. 4; *extending*, l. 6; *increase*, l. 7), **nouns** (*investment*, ll. 3, 5; *expansion*, l. 5) and **adjectives** (*extra*; *huge*, l. 5; *healthier*, l. 14; *unprecedented*, l. 16). **Comparative adjectives** such as *healthier* and *clearer* (ll. 14–15) implicitly contrast the present Government's achievements with those of previous governments. With their connotations of 'amplification', these all contribute to Caroline Flint's praise for the Government's action. Because the noun phrases are long, she is able to list the range of actions the Government has taken to improve the health of the nation in **post-modifying clauses** (*including*, ll. 6, 11, 13, 17; *which*, ll. 3, 6, 8):

m		m		h	q		
the unprecedented	action	this	Government has taken to tackle	the root causes of
det	V		N	RelCl		NFCl	
	(past part)						

	q		
ill health and health inequalities	including	helping more people to find work	
NFCl	NFCl	NFCl	(ll. 16–18, CF)

This is in direct contrast to the connotations of verbs such as *is concerned about* (l. 9) and *condemning* (l. 11) and nouns like *failure* (l. 2) in the first motion.

These examples of political language are pre-scripted and they follow a very precise pattern. They bear little resemblance to spoken language because of their formulaic structure. The speech turns are not equal because the speaker introducing the motion dominates, allowing interventions when she or he considers this appropriate. The verb phrase *to give way* is used to mark the points in the debate at which the speaker allows another politician to make a statement or to ask a question. The speech following the introductory motion is scripted, but interventions from the floor are unlikely to have been prepared. Although they are still formal because of the context in which they take place, interventions may sometimes be introduced by phrases that seem rather informal. Phrases like *just one second* or clauses like *you know* are described as **spontaneity markers** because they reflect the unscripted nature of the language.

One of the most important features of parliamentary language is the **framing of questions**. The first question asked in the House of Commons was in 1721, and since then questioning has become a central part of parliamentary procedure. Each week there are timetabled sessions in which questions are addressed to the Prime Minister. Because of the nature of these sessions, questions are structured in a particular way. They do more than just request information: often they are used to make statements, and may criticise or praise the speakers to whom they are addressed. Usually speakers each have only one chance to ask a question, so questions are carefully constructed for maximum effect.

Questions are rarely straightforward: they must include appropriate facts, establish the nature of the question, address a minister's knowledge of the issue, and provide a conclusion linked to the speaker's own viewpoint. Such complexity forces the politician being questioned to provide a more detailed answer. If ministers give a straightforward answer to a complicated question, they may find that they have committed themselves to a sequence of propositions with which they do not actually agree.

All the exchanges take place orally, but they are recorded exactly in Hansard. Because questions are often pre-scripted, however, their structure is closer to written rather than to spoken language. Responses are not pre-scripted, but because of the complexity of the questions addressed and the necessity for a detailed reply, the answers also resemble written language. Although parliamentary questions are marked by the structure and style of formal written speeches, some features can reflect spoken discourse.

ACTIVITY 17.4

Questions and answers will usually convey a certain ideology and will follow party lines. MPs of the party in government will ask questions that enable ministers to respond in a positive way, showing their knowledge of a subject, the strength of Government policy, and so on. Opposition MPs, however, will try to test ministers, revealing any weakness in their approaches or gaps in their knowledge, and so forth.

Read the two exchanges below, which took place in January 2007 when the Labour Party was in government and the Conservative Party in opposition. In the first extract, the Labour MP Keith Vaz (Leicester, East) addresses the Prime Minister, Tony Blair; in the second extract, David Cameron, Leader of the Conservative Party, questions the Prime Minister. Comment on:

1 the attitude towards the Prime Minister in each case
2 the structure of the questions
3 any features that are typical of political language.

1 **Keith Vaz:** Will the Prime Minister join me in condemning racism and xenophobia in any form, including on the so-called reality television show "Big Brother", which has prompted 13,000 individual complaints? Does not he agree that it is important that broadcasters take great care before broadcasting any such prejudices to millions of
5 people throughout the country?

The Prime Minister: First, let me tell my right hon. Friend that I have not seen the programme in question and I cannot therefore comment on it. Of course, I agree entirely with the principle that he outlines: we should oppose racism in all its forms.

Prime Minister's Questions, Hansard (17 January 2007)

1 **Mr Cameron:** Violent crime has doubled, and we have been telling the Prime Minister to build prisons for the last 10 years. Now, is it the Government's policy to split the Home Office into two entirely separate Departments?

The Prime Minister: The issue about the future structure in the Home Office arises,
5 the right hon. Gentleman knows, from the review announced by the Home Secretary last October, which is to do with terrorism and security, not prison places. Let me just remind him that since 1997, 20,000 extra prison places have been created, which has required an investment running into billions of pounds. It is in part as a result of tougher sentencing that there are more people in prison, and I repeat: every single
10 measure of tougher sentencing and investment he has opposed.

Mr Cameron: The Lord Chancellor said that splitting the Home Office in two was a "very, very serious proposal", and indicated that he thought that it was time to do it. Can the Prime Minister tell us whether the Chancellor of the Exchequer agrees with splitting the Home Office in two?

15 **The Prime Minister:** I have already explained that as a result – [*Interruption.*] As a result of the review that was announced by the Home Secretary – [*Interruption.*]

Mr Speaker: Order. Let the Prime Minister answer.

The Prime Minister: The review announced last October is about the structures of the Home Office to do with security and terrorism. There are proposals that the Home
20 Secretary has made, and we will make an announcement on those in the next few weeks. However, whatever the different structures in the Home Office, there is only one way in which we shall be able to deal with the problems in our prisons – to build more prison places and make sure that we have violent, serious and persistent offenders behind bars. Let me repeat once again: all of that investment – all of it – has
25 been opposed by the right hon. Gentleman. Incidentally, since we are talking about this Government's record on crime, according to the British crime survey of all recorded crime, crime has fallen; it doubled under the Tories.

Mr Cameron: I think that the Prime Minster will find that the Chancellor does not want to break up the Home Office – he just wants to break up the Home Secretary. There
30 is no point considering this proposal unless the Chancellor has agreed it. The Prime Minister is not going to be here for very long, so let me ask him again – he can ask the Chancellor now – does the Chancellor back splitting the Home Office, yes or no?

The Prime Minister: As I have just explained to the right hon. Gentleman, proposals were put forward by the Home Secretary. The Government will come to a view on
35 those within the next few weeks, and we will make an announcement to the House in the normal way. However, when the right hon. Gentleman is talking about the relation-

ship between the Home Office, prisons and policing, let me make it clear that there is absolutely no way that we can deal with the current issues in respect of places unless we are going to build more. We are building 8,000 more prison places, but the invest-
40 ment necessary to do that is investment that he voted against, as he did tougher sentences. So it is no use his coming to the Dispatch Box and saying, "Make sure that no serious or violent offenders are let out of prison." They are in prison precisely because of this Government, and he opposed the measures.

Hon. Members: Answer the question!

45 **Mr Cameron:** It is a pretty simple question: does the Chancellor want to break up the Home Office – yes or no? [*Interruption.*] We have got prisoners on the run, weak borders – [*Interruption.*]

Mr Speaker: Order. Let the Leader of the Opposition speak.

Mr Cameron: We have got overcrowded prisons, and all that the Government can do
50 is float half-baked schemes for breaking up the Home Office that they cannot even agree about. Have not this Government now become like the ship stranded off the Devon coast? They are washed up and broken up, and they are just scrabbling over the wreckage.

Prime Minister's Questions, Hansard (24 January 2007)

COMMENTARY

Controversial television footage in which the Bollywood actress Shilpa Shetty was subjected to bullying became an issue of international debate. Keith Vaz's question aims to show that the Labour Party and its individual members have a unified approach to dealing with racism. The post-modifying clause *including...* allows him to move from 'racism' in general to a specific and topical instance that provoked approximately 42,000 complaints to the television regulator, Ofcom. (This was the greatest number that the regulator had ever received on one matter.)

As well as publicly addressing the nature of the incident (ll. 1–3), Vaz also raises an ethical question about whether broadcasters should be allowed to air such footage for entertainment (ll. 3–5). Blair answers the first question emphatically with a simple sentence:

S	P	O	A	
(we)	(should oppose)	(racism)	(in all its forms).	(l. 8)

Although he declines to comment on the ethical issue since he has not seen the programme, he does directly answer the question.

By using the **modal verb** *Will* (l. 1), Vaz suggests that he expects his request to be fulfilled. This immediately marks the question as one that will be acceptable to the Prime Minister. A similar effect is achieved in the use of the archaic *Does not he agree...?* (l. 3). The questions allow the *Big Brother* incident to be addressed formally in Parliament; and the Prime Minister's use of the first person singular and plural pronouns (*I*, l. 7; *we*, l. 8) ensures that, both personally and as the leader of the British Government, he can dismiss any allegations that British society is inherently racist.

David Cameron's questions, on the other hand, are clearly more demanding. Far from offering an opportunity to show the party in a positive light, they constitute an attack on Labour policy. The questions are not as simple as they would appear – although they apparently demand only a *yes/no* answer, to give a simple reply would compromise the Prime Minister. If his response to Cameron's first question (ll. 2–3) were 'yes', Blair would be making an announcement on behalf of his Government that had not yet been discussed in Cabinet. If he were to answer 'no', he would be dismissing the findings of the review announced by the Home Secretary, John Reid, before fully assessing them.

In each case, Blair evades a direct answer by avoiding the key words in the question. The first asks him directly whether the Home Office will be split into *two entirely separate Departments* (l. 3). Blair sidesteps the question by using a long noun phrase that refocuses the issue:

> m   h   q   q
> the review announced by the Home Secretary last October, which is to do with
> det   N   NFCl   RelCl   NFCl
> terrorism and security, not prison places. (ll. 5–6)

This attempts to bring the debate back to a discussion of prison places and over-crowding, allowing Blair to avoid addressing the issue of the Home Office. The second question (ll. 13–14) is even more challenging since it requires Blair to address his political relationship with Gordon Brown, the Chancellor, as well as the issue of splitting the Home Office. He deflects it in the same way: by referring to *the review* (ll. 16, 18–19) and to *the problems in our prisons* (l. 22). Because he does not answer with the requisite *yes/no* answer, David Cameron repeats the question (ll. 31–2; 45–6) and there are calls from the floor of the House for the Prime Minister to answer (l. 44). Tony Blair, however, attempts to turn the situation to his advantage by attacking the Conservative Party for their opposition to policies that are designed to help the prison situation (ll. 39–43).

Cameron moves from the polite modal *Can the Prime Minister tell us whether*... (l. 13) to the more emphatic *does the Chancellor back*... (l. 32) and *does the Chancellor want to break up*... (l. 45): as the Prime Minister continues to avoid answering, the questions become more insistent. Cameron's repetition of *yes or no?* (ll. 32, 46) is designed to force Blair to recognise the straightforward nature of the answer that is required.

The formality of the context is reflected in the **TRADITIONAL TITLES** used to address people. A politician who is also a Privy Counsellor is referred to using the phrase *the right hon. Gentleman* (l. 5), while one who is a barrister will be called *the learned Gentleman*. In this extract we also see references to *the Home Secretary* (l. 5), *The Lord Chancellor* (l. 11) and to *the Chancellor of the Exchequer* (l. 13). The use of titles is significant since in this debate the role is more important than the individual. However, Cameron's reference to the Chancellor is part of his attempt to undermine the Prime Minister, whose sometimes stormy relationship with Gordon Brown often made news headlines. This implicit attack on Blair is reinforced by the satirical reference to the fact that he will soon be standing down from the role of Prime Minister and will, therefore, no longer be in charge of Labour Party policy.

Subject-specific lexis such as *the Home Office* (l. 4), *the Home Secretary* and *the Dispatch Box* (l. 41) indicate that this is a political field, but the **connotations**

of certain words suggest something about the political persuasion of the speaker. Tony Blair's repetition of *opposed* (ll. 10, 25, 43) implies that the Conservative Party is against Labour in terms of its response to the problems of violent crime and overcrowding in prisons: the suggestion is that whereas the Labour Party is trying to do something to mitigate the problems, the Conservatives are voting against positive action. As Leader of the Opposition, David Cameron has to challenge the Government's position. He does this through emotive noun phrases: *Violent crime* (l. 1), *prisoners on the run, weak borders* (ll. 46–7), and *overcrowded prisons* (l. 49). As well as challenging the proposal to split the Home Office, he aims to make a party-political point.

The register here is primarily influenced by the written word, but there are examples of **colloquial language** which would probably not have appeared in pre-scripted speeches. Clichés such as *just wants to break up the Home Secretary* (l. 29) and *half-baked schemes* (l. 50) are more commonly associated with spoken language. Their presence here reminds us that this is a written record of an oral exchange. Cameron's **simile** of the Government *like the ship stranded off the Devon coast* (ll. 51–3) is a topical analogy – the *Napoli*, a 62,000 tonne container ship, had recently been deliberately run aground off the Cornish coastline after suffering structural damage in storms (January 2007). The negative phrasal verbs *washed up* and *broken up* are used figuratively to describe the Conservative view of a Labour Party that is no longer governing efficiently. The satirical comparison is continued in the verb *scrabbling* and the prepositional phrase *over the wreckage*.

Grammatically, because of its complexity the structure of the speech utterances here resembles written language more closely than spoken language. **Sentence structures** are rarely simple and usually complex:

> S   P   O
> (The Lord Chancellor) (said) (that splitting the Home Office in two was a "very, very
>   SCl–NCl SCl–NFCl
>
>   P   O
> serious proposal"), (and) (indicated) (that he thought it was time to do it).
>   conj   SCl–NCl   SCl–NCl SCl–NFCl
>
>   (ll. 11–12, DC)

>   A   A   dumS P   (S)
> (However), (whatever the different structures in the HO), (there) (is) (only one way in
>
>   C
> which we shall be able to deal with the problems in our prisons) – (to build more
> SCl–RelCl   SCl–NFCl   SCl–NFCl
>
>   C
> prison places) (and) (ø make sure that we have violent, serious and persistent offen-
>   conj SCl–NFCl SCl–NCl
>
> ders behind bars).   (ll. 21–4, TB)

Such complexity is not usually associated with spoken language. The sentence structure here is complex because each speaker wishes to provide a lot of qualifying information and this makes both the questions and the answers complicated.

The **pronoun referencing** is typical of political language. Tony Blair's use of the first person singular pronoun is emphatic: *Let me just remind…* (ll. 6–7); *I repeat…* (l. 9); *Let me repeat…* (l. 24); *I have already explained…* (l. 15); *As I have just explained…* (l. 33); *let me make it clear…* (l. 37). It allows him to reinforce his status as leader of the Government in Prime Minister's Questions. Where he uses the first person plural (ll. 20, 22, 23, 35, 38, 39), the emphasis is on the role of the Government as a democratic body in which discussion precedes decisions about policy – it promotes a view of the Government as a 'team'.

17.5 What to look for in the language of politics

The following checklist can be used to identify key features in examples of political language. You will not find all of the features in every text or transcription, but the list can be used as a guide. The points made are general, so discussion of specific examples will need to be adapted to take account of the specific context, audience and purpose in the given discourse. Remember that you need to evaluate the effect of the features you identify, exploring the ways in which they create meaning.

The following are helpful questions to ask.

Register

1 What is the **mode**?
   * spoken – a spontaneous response or read aloud from a script?
   * written – to be read or spoken?
2 What is the **manner**?
   * formal or informal relationship between participants?
   * the same or different ideologies?
   * supporting or opposing a particular point of view?
3 What is the **field**?
   * political subject matter?
   * linked to the audience, purpose and context?

Lexis

1 Are there any examples of **subject-specific language**?
   * general?
   * typical of a certain ideological stance?
2 Are there any **abstract nouns** that reflect beliefs or political policy?
3 How are the participants **named**?
   * using titles, first names or surnames?
   * to focus on the role or the person?
   * to reveal the relationship between the speaker, the topic and the audience?
4 Is there anything significant about the **connotations** of words?
   * positive or negative?

Grammar

1 Are there any **pronouns that create a sense of distance**?
   * using *those* to divide the speaker and audience?
   * using *it/they* to dehumanise the reference and make it seem faceless and threatening?
   * using *they* to convey a sense of opposition?
   * using *one* as a first person or second person personal reference to create a very formal tone (often associated with high social status)?
   * using *one* to distance the speaker from an action or convey a sense of authority?

2 Are there any **pronouns that bring the speaker and audience together**?
- repeating or 'blocking' *I*, particularly with mental-process verbs (*think, feel, believe*), to create an individual tone and suggest sincerity?
- using *I* to establish rapport with the audience?
- using *his, hers, theirs* to link issues and policies to a particular person and to place emphasis on people rather than policies?
- using *we* to focus on the institution as well as the individual, to include the speaker or to suggest personal support for actions or policies?
- using direct address (*you*) to draw in the audience?

3 Are there any **pronouns that convey degrees of responsibility**?
- using *I* to mark the speaker as the instigator of an action or process?
- using *I* to show an acceptance of responsibility?
- using *we* to make the degree of responsibility less clear?
- using *they* to place responsibility at a distance or to explicitly exclude the speaker?

4 How are **questions** framed?
- negatives which allow questioners to lead an addressee to a particular answer by suggesting that the question's proposition is undeniable?
- modal verbs (*will*) which suggest that any rejection will seem unacceptably rude, and which encourage the addressee to commit himself or herself to action?
- adverbs (*so*) which suggest that the proposition is logical and should therefore be accepted?
- closed *yes/no* questions which attempt to force the addressee to accept or deny a proposition directly?
- *wh-* words which require a more focused answer?
- embedded statements within a question which enable the speaker to establish a context or point of view?

5 Is the **sentence structure** varied?
- simple sentences which make direct and emphatic statements?
- compound sentences which balance arguments?
- complex sentences which explore abstract concepts?
- minor sentences which create a conversational tone or highlight key issues?

Style

1 Is **sentence organisation** used to draw attention to important lexical items?
- branching to control the order of information?
- marked themes to highlight key information?
- end focus to delay information and create weight at the end of a sentence?
- passive voice to refocus the audience's attention on certain sentence elements or to conceal a person's responsibility for an action?

2 Are there any examples of **literary devices**?
- similes and metaphors which establish a direct link between abstract theories and concrete examples?
- extended metaphors which emphasise a particular message or underpin a particular viewpoint?

3 Are **rhetorical devices** used?
- antithesis to create contrasts between political parties or candidates in an election?
- listing to emphasise important issues or principles?

- tripling to add weight to a particular point of view?
- parallelism to create a sense of balance and reason?
- repetition of key words, phrases or clauses to highlight a topic, party viewpoint or political principle?

Summary

The **function** of political language is to make people believe in a certain world view and to persuade them to a certain course of action.

To a large extent, **tradition** plays an important role in defining the nature of political language: in the Houses of Parliament, certain formulaic utterances add to the formality of the field; in speeches, traditional rhetorical techniques are used to manipulate audience response.

Semantically, written and spoken words often have **underlying meaning or meanings**. Answers to direct questions are often non-committal, even evasive; by using implications, politicians can avoid direct answers and statements of belief and make implicit points that are quite different from what is apparently being said.

Chapter 18

The language of broadcasting

18.1 The nature of broadcasting language

BROADCASTING can be defined as the sending of messages via **television** or **radio** with no technical control over who receives them. These messages are sent to a **MASS AUDIENCE**, the unknown individuals and groups who watch and listen to the transmissions. Broadcasters use codes to organise and convey meaning, and the audience interpret these in order to understand the programmes.

Between 2007 and 2012, the traditional analogue system of broadcasting will be replaced in the UK by digital technology. The change from analogue to digital signals allows many more television and radio channels to be broadcast. In order to interpret these digital signals, however, viewers need a digital receiver, which can be built into the television set or purchased separately as a set-top box.

While some believe that the digital system provides higher-quality pictures and sound, a greater variety of channels, and the opportunity to interact with programmes, others see the change from analogue as an unnecessary expense. The Government argues that it is costly to run two parallel services and that analogue broadcasting should be shut down so that frequencies can be reallocated. Frequencies no longer needed for existing analogue channels can then be sold off for other uses, such as new digital channels, mobile phones and mobile television.

Broadcasting uses three main **CODES**: **image**, **language**, and **symbol**. Different kinds of broadcasting use these three codes in different proportions – for television, visual codes are often more important than linguistic ones, as the images provide messages that are not transmitted by the words; radio, on the other hand, can use no visual codes and relies exclusively on linguistic ones. Both television and radio use symbolic codes, allowing broadcasters to convey extra layers of meaning – on television, body language, the use of colour and props can be symbolic; on the radio, sound effects and prosodic features fulfil the same function.

The **form of communication** between participants is distinctive: communication is direct from the media source to the target audience, but there is no visual contact. The broadcasting process is therefore primarily one-way: the viewer or listener has no direct means of questioning or redirecting the messages that are conveyed. Modern technology does, however, offer viewers and listeners some opportunity for intervention: telephone numbers, email and website addresses, online message boards or the use of buttons on the remote control enable the audience to comment on programmes, ask questions, get or provide follow-up information or vote. Digital copying to a hard drive, podcasts, 'listen again' and 'view again' facilities and services such as Sky+ also give the audience some control of the broadcasting process because they can enjoy their favourite programmes when and where they choose. Despite such innovations, this kind of delayed participation is quite unlike the informal interaction that takes place in ordinary conversation. Even where the relationship between participants seems informal in broadcasting, the public context means that in reality the **tone** tends to be formal.

Public broadcasting began in the 1920s and since then has developed significantly, becoming a national institution with which most people are familiar. The overall variety of 'broadcasting' can be subdivided into a number of distinctive categories, each with its own characteristic features. Newsreaders, sports commentators, continuity announcers, weather readers and DJs all have distinctive styles which viewers and listeners can recognise. Typical codes and conventions in each category allow broadcasters to organise and transmit messages that viewers and listeners can interpret.

In the early period of broadcasting it was possible to describe **BBC ENGLISH** as the medium of communication. The BBC originally adopted **RECEIVED PRONUNCIATION** for its announcers because this was thought to be the form of English most likely to be understood universally and least likely to be criticised. From the 1990s, however, both television and radio used a wider range of **REGIONAL** and **SOCIAL ACCENTS**. As broadcast programmes are received by a vast audience, people have become increasingly familiar with accents and dialects that would not be heard locally. The language of broadcasting is now as diverse as its programme schedule, and it is impossible to define just one recognisable kind of language use – in each case, the purpose and style of the communication dictate the nature of the language used. While some welcome these developments, the frequency with which regional accents and informal or colloquial language are now heard in broadcasts has inevitably attracted complaints from people who believe this to be further evidence that the standards of spoken English are slipping.

Because most viewers and listeners hear the linguistic codes only once as a programme is transmitted and cannot ask for clarification, the language of broadcasting needs to be **easily understandable**. Utterances must be carefully organised and are often made up of short, uncomplicated units. The language of broadcasting is **seldom completely spontaneous**, although it may be presented as if it were. People who work regularly in the medium of television or radio learn to speak in a way that emulates the spontaneous spoken word, even if they are in fact reading aloud. When ordinary people appear in programmes, editing will often have eliminated many of the false starts, hesitations and repetitions that are characteristic of truly spontaneous informal conversation. In drama, the writers and actors will actually 'write' such non-fluency markers into the script in order to emulate the structures of normal interaction.

The language of broadcasting is an unusual mix of **spoken** and **written language** – like written language it can be polished and edited, yet it is usually delivered as though it were spontaneous speech. Because it is written to be 'read' aloud to a very diverse audience, the language must be **easy to articulate**, **fluent** and **approachable**. Although each kind of programme has its own distinctive lexical, grammatical and prosodic features, certain characteristics can be identified as typical of broadcasting as a whole.

18.2 The function of broadcasting

Just as broadcasting covers a wide range of programme types, adopting different kinds of language to meet the requirements of each type, so it has a number of **functions**. Documentaries and discussion programmes can **inform** the audience; schools' services, the BBC *Learning Zone* and programmes linked to the Open University can **educate**; situation comedies and soaps can **entertain**; and advertising can **persuade**.

Language choice, grammatical structures and prosodic features depend upon the kind of programme, its purpose, the intended audience, and the time of transmission. An informative feature for children shown at teatime on a programme like *Blue Peter*, for instance, will be quite different from a documentary for adults such as *Horizon* or *Dispatches*, shown after the nine o'clock watershed; the content and language of a drama shown during 'family' viewing hours will be very different from those of a mini-series broadcast late at night; and although the six o'clock news may report the same material as the ten o'clock news, it will always include a warning before any disturbing images are shown.

In order to analyse the language of broadcasting effectively, it is important to establish some background information first. Linguists need to start by asking themselves the following questions:

- Is the **medium** television or radio?
- What **type** of programme is it?
- What is its **purpose**?
- Who is the **intended audience**, and what kind of **relationship** is established with them?
- What **time** is the programme broadcast?
- On which **channel** is the programme broadcast?
- Is the **tone** serious, comic or somewhere in between?

Answers to these questions will provide the basis for a closer focus – having identified the broadcasting framework, linguists can then consider how these affect the lexical, grammatical and prosodic choices made by writers, actors and programmers.

18.3 Features of broadcasting language

The language of broadcasting covers such a wide range of linguistic forms that it is difficult to draw up a definitive list of language features. Nevertheless, it is possible to identify a number of distinctive features that mark it out as different from other varieties.

Mode

The **mode** will often be both written and spoken. There will, however, be examples of truly spontaneous speech (unprepared answers in a debate; live interviews and commentaries) and of language that is written with no attempt to mimic spontaneous speech (short stories read on the radio; written statements read out when the people concerned are unable or unwilling to attend in person). The language and structure of each programme will display features associated with speech or writing or both, depending upon the balance the broadcasters aim to create between the two modes.

Manner

The **manner** will also vary depending upon the kind of programme transmitted. Although there is rarely any direct interaction between broadcasters and their audience, they do create a relationship with their unknown viewers and listeners. Just as in face-to-face communication, this may be formal or informal depending upon the content, purpose and time-slot of the programme. News programmes, documentaries and serious drama establish a largely formal relationship with their audience, while situation comedies, game shows and soaps establish an informal relationship.

Status

The relative STATUS of a programme and its audience is directly linked to the relationship created between them. The broadcasters may use 'experts' who are in the role of advisers or educators (*Moneybox*; *Grow Your Own Veg*; *It's Not Easy Being Green*). They may imply that the people on television or radio are no different from the viewers and listeners, using ordinary people as an integral part of the programme (*Cash in the Attic*; *Ready Steady Cook*; *Location, Location, Location*). In other forms of programming, the audience become 'flies on the wall', overhearing and overlooking everyday life as it goes on (soaps; video diaries; reality television). The relative status assigned to the audience will inevitably affect the linguistic and prosodic choices made.

Topics

A programme may have one or more TOPICS. A documentary will focus on a particular issue, for instance, while a soap will cover a different story for each set of characters. The kind of topic and the depth of coverage it is given will depend upon the goal of the programme. An informative documentary on the financial, emotional and physical difficulties of being a single parent would provide a wide range of information and sources; the news, addressing the same topic, might focus on a newly released report or on new government legislation; and a drama, tackling the topic in a more individual way, might describe the problems encountered by one particular fictional character and depict the views of other characters affected by her or his situation.

Where more than one issue is addressed, TOPIC SHIFTS will be clearly marked. On programmes like the news or the consumer rights programme *Watchdog*, linguistic and prosodic clues will indicate that one topic is coming to an end and that another is about to start. Speakers on these programmes will use the same approaches as speakers in formal situations would use to mark the end of a topic. Because the links are pre-written, most topic shifts will be smooth. They will rarely be challenged, as they might in informal conversation, because the structure is predefined.

The end of a topic is equally carefully organised. Timing is crucial because of pre-published programming schedules, which are available in television and radio listings magazines like *The Radio Times*, in national daily newspapers and in free local papers. If time is running out, presenters may have to break off a discussion by explicitly reminding participants that the programme is about to end; they may use stock phrases like *and I'm afraid I'll have to stop you there…* or *and we'll have to leave it there…*, or technicians can literally 'fade out' the sound as they carry on talking. Pre-recorded programmes do not have the same problems because scriptwriters and editors have already established the cut-off point. They will nevertheless ensure that each episode or section concludes at an appropriate moment – the audience may be left with a cliffhanger encouraging them to watch or listen to the next programme, or a neat summary which finalises the issues covered.

Structure

The STRUCTURE of a programme depends on its type – if it is part of an ongoing series, characters, storylines and locations will run from episode to episode; if it is a one-off programme, its structure must be self-contained. In either case, the overall structure is very carefully planned so that maximum use can be made of the time-slot allocated in the programming schedule.

Some programmes are marked by distinctive structural features. The **opening** and **closing** of the news or a documentary, for instance, will always follow a predefined pattern. For instance, the news will start with a formal greeting, an indication of the specific programme being broadcast and the newsreader's name; it will end with a summary of the main news and a formal closing (*and that's all we have time for… (.) from _____, goodnight*). A documentary is less likely to address its audience directly. Instead, it will start with a general introduction to the topic on which the programme will focus and conclude with a summary of the key issues. Intonation patterns will indicate to the audience that the programme is coming to an end.

Other programmes are structured around very organised forms of TURN-TAKING. Programmes like quizzes (*Mastermind*; *University Challenge*) and game shows based on asking the contestants questions (*Deal or No Deal*; *The Weakest Link*; *Never Mind the Buzzcocks*) require participants to behave according to certain 'rules' which enable communication to take place effectively. Although there may be interruptions, overlaps or digressions, **adjacency pairs** establish the basic structure of such programmes.

Prosodic features

Because broadcasting relies on the spoken word to communicate effectively with its audience, **PROSODIC FEATURES** play an important part in conveying meaning. Although most of the programmes will exist first in a written form, actors, presenters and other kinds of speakers use their voices to bring the words to life. **Intonation patterns** reinforce the meaning of the words spoken. Changes in intonation can indicate different attitudes and moods, mark grammatical structures like questions or commands, and help to establish a rhythm by drawing attention to grammatical boundaries in utterances. **Pitch variations** underpin intonation changes, allowing speakers to reinforce their attitudes and responses. **Loudness** and **pace** also contribute to the meaning system, allowing speakers to reflect the relative importance of what they are saying in a dramatic way. Information programmes are more likely to adopt an average sound level and pace, but any programme that attempts to re-create real speech or that involves ordinary people in an informal context will use variations in the prosodic features to enhance meaning. **Vocal effects** play a similar role: they are more likely to be found in less formal contexts, but even in pre-scripted, pre-recorded programmes there may be some evidence of throat-clearing or coughing which has not been edited out.

Stress patterns and **pauses** allow speakers to draw attention to certain lexical items. Viewers and listeners sometimes complain about the way in which stress is used by the people involved in television and radio broadcasting. Newsreaders in particular are sometimes accused of stressing inappropriate syllables and words and of pausing after grammatical function words. Many people think that television and radio are very influential, and they see such 'inaccuracies' as eroding the standards of English. They argue that because prestigious people are heard eliding final consonants, pronouncing words with the emphasis on the 'wrong' syllable and stressing words that are insignificant in terms of the meaning, the individuals who make up the audience may do the same. In the eyes of the prescriptivists, the 'error' is perpetuated, slowly changing the 'correct' form.

Lexis

The **lexis** is directly linked to the content of the programme. Some will be subject-specific and the language will reflect this; other parts will be based on ordinary informal interaction and the language will therefore be far more wide-ranging. In order to assess the nature of the language used, it is important to come to some conclusions about:

- the **kind** of programme
- the **intended audience** (age, gender, educational or cultural background)
- the **subject** matter
- the **approach** (formal or informal? serious or comic? detailed or general? one-off or a series?).

From this starting point, analysis can focus specifically on the kind of words used and the effects created.

Grammar

The **grammar** is also linked to the kind of broadcast, the target audience, the topic and the approach. The more serious the context, the more likely that the grammar will be both formal and complex. Equally, where a broadcast is imitating the structures of informal conversation, the utterances are more likely to be incomplete and the grammatical structures more likely to be straightforward.

Accents and dialects

Accents and **dialects** will vary according to the kind of programme, the participants and the regional and social background. Newsreaders are more likely to speak SE with an RP accent, although it is now common to hear reporters and correspondents with regional accents. Programmes that are geographically located will use an appropriate regional accent for many of the characters: most characters in *Coronation Street* have Northern accents; in *Byker Grove*, they have Tyneside accents; in *EastEnders* London accents; and in *Neighbours* Australian accents. Because individuals all speak in different ways, however, the variation from character to character is quite significant. The accents and dialects of characters vary according to their age, gender, social class, and occupational and educational background.

Normal non-fluency features

Normal non-fluency features are apparent in certain kinds of programmes only, because in many cases editing will have eliminated evidence of hesitancy, repetition and lack of fluency. Live broadcasts are more likely to contain such features, but even in these many speakers will be polished and articulate. While politicians are accustomed to speaking spontaneously about a range of subjects in a formal context, ordinary people have usually had less experience. Where inexperienced speakers take part in a broadcast, therefore, their speech will often be marked by non-fluency features. Programmes that aim to mirror reality (drama, situation comedies and soaps) can use non-fluency features to make characters seem more real or to create comedy.

As in informal conversation, **repairs** in television and radio broadcasts can take a number of forms. Editing will sort out many of the problems in pre-recorded programmes, but in live contexts participants must assess the cause of any breakdown in communication and then act accordingly. In live contexts there is considerable pressure on participants to communicate effectively within a limited amount of time, and this can lead to problems that require immediate repairs (misunderstood questions in an interview; participants talking simultaneously in a debate; unexpected silences in a discussion). On the whole, however, because the structure of spoken interaction in any broadcast is quite tightly defined and because most participants follow the expected patterns of behaviour, few examples of interaction will show any evidence of substantial breakdown.

* * *

In order to analyse the 'language of broadcasting', linguists use the key features of spoken language covered in Chapter 10. By identifying and commenting on the way in which language use is both similar and dissimilar to that of spoken language, it is possible to assess the way in which broadcasting language draws on both spoken and written registers.

18.4 Types of broadcasting language

The news

The news will vary in form and structure depending upon the time of its transmission, its intended audience and whether it is broadcast on radio or television. Each individual news programme, however, will be recognisable by its format and length, its presenter and its distinctive approach to presenting news stories.

The dominant **function** is to **inform**, although there will often be some stories that **entertain**. The **tone** will be directly linked to the function – the light-hearted topics may be marked by more varied prosodic features, while the serious ones will usually be delivered in a level or neutral tone and pitch, with few volume or pace changes.

The **structure** is distinctive. After an opening social greeting addressed directly to the audience, a summary of the programme's main features will draw the viewer or listener's attention to the subject matter that will be covered. On television news, these news 'headlines' will be accompanied by film footage which will encourage continued viewing. The main body of the news programme will be made up of more detailed coverage of the headline events. Each topic will be introduced by the news reporter and then interviews, on-the-spot reports or comment by 'expert' correspondents will develop the coverage. On television, voice-overs may accompany images to provide the audience with important information.

Stories will be **selected** depending upon the range of possible stories for a particular broadcast, the relative impact of available film images (for television), and the need to balance serious and light items. Stories selected will have cultural, social and geographical relevance to the intended audience; they will usually focus on celebrities or current issues; and their content will usually be negative. The order of broadcasting will affect the way the audience interprets events: by juxtaposing certain stories, it is possible to create implicit links that influence the way the audience responds.

Many people would say that the news is objective, presenting information in a neutral and unbiased form. Because news stories are selected and presented in a certain way, however, there will always be evidence of subjectivity. There are many ways in which it is possible to recognise **bias** in news broadcasts: certain stories are included at the expense of others; priority is given to some stories by placing them first in the running order; words are chosen to convey the intended message in a way that suits the particular media institution; and the images which accompany television news can be chosen to influence the audience emotively rather than intellectually.

It is important to realise that the news does not present us with reality but with a view of events that has been **ordered** and **constructed**. Words, prosodic features and the images accompanying television news are used to influence the target audience. While the content may disturb the viewer or listener, the continuity of the programme structure, the fluency of the programme as a whole and the stability and order of the studio are all designed to reassure.

ACTIVITY 18.1

The following extracts are taken from three different kinds of news programme: *Newsbeat* (BBC Radio 1, 5.45 pm), the *ITV News* (ITV, 10.30 pm) and *Newsround* (BBC 1, 5.25 pm). The programmes are transmitted at different times and are aimed at different audiences. *Newsbeat* will appeal mainly to the 16–24 age group (11 per cent of the population and the most ethnically-diverse demographic group) to whom the station is directed – it adopts a dynamic form of presentation to attract their attention. It is transmitted at 5.45 pm, sandwiched between popular music programmes. The news coverage is fitted into just 15 minutes, which means that the treatment of each story is brief. As a national programme broadcast at 10.30 pm, the *ITV News* will appeal to a wide range of people. It is transmitted after the nine o'clock watershed, which means that its images and reporting may be more disturbing than earlier news programmes. *Newsround* is broadcast at the end of the CBBC children's television slot that runs from 3.25 pm. It is specifically designed to engage children with topical news stories of the day – the focus is often on the way in which a story affects children. Its 10-minute format means that the treatment of each story is brief. A linked website encourages children to read more about particular stories and to make their own comments.

The transcripts below record the opening and closing sequences for each of these three news programmes broadcast on 5 April 2007. Read through the texts and comment on the following:

1 any structures used to mark the opening and closing of the programme
2 the relationship created with the intended audience
3 the topics summarised in the headlines
4 the prosodic features used to attract audience attention.

Only the most prominent prosodic features are marked on the transcripts. A key to the symbols can be found on page 93.

TRANSCRIPT 1: *NEWSROUND* ....

Newsround, CBBC (*NR*), read by Lizo Mzimba (LM).

1   LM hello I'm <u>Lízo</u> and (.) wélcome (.) to Néwsround (.) <u>here's</u> (.) what's coming your wáy (.) <u>this</u> ↑afternoon↑ (1) théy're <u>bàck</u> (.) the British sailors held <u>cáptive</u> in <u>Irán</u> are home (2) <u>plus</u> móuntain on <u>fìre</u> (.) a vólcano that ↑<u>keeps on erûpting</u>↑

5   * * *

            LM well that's it we're back here on <u>Tûes</u>day but our wébsite (.) and the búlletins on the CBBC chánnel will (.) keep you up to date all <u>óver</u> the hóliday ↑<u>wèekend</u>↑ and (1) don't forget <u>Spórts</u>round on Saturday on

'accel'   CB́BC2 (.) Jake will be 'coming <u>live</u> from the Cricket World Cup in the

10   Càribbean' have a <u>great</u> <u>Easter</u>

Newsbeat, BBC Radio 1 (*NB*), read by Georgina Bowman (GB); with DJ Scott Mills (SM), Leading Seaman Faye Turney (FT), *Newsbeat* reporter Jonathan Blake (JB), Barnsley teenager Katie (K), sports reporter David Garrido (GD), and a Royal Navy representative of the 15 Britons held captive in Iran (RNR).

1	SM	it's 5.4<u>5</u> on Radio 1 (2) let's get Newsbeat with Georgina Bowman =
	JINGLE	= digital (.) FM Online (.) this <u>is</u> Radio 1 =
	GB	= <u>back</u> (.) on (.) <u>British</u> soil (1) the 15 Navy crew held captive in Irán are <u>back</u> with their <u>families</u> at làst =
5	FT	= it was just so wonderful (1) I shall just put my arms around him and cover him in kisses (1) just tell him how much I <u>love</u> hìm =
	JB	= this is Newsbeat's Jonathan Blake in Plymouth where the <u>cele</u>-<u>brations</u> look set to go on áll nìght =
'rall'	GB	= the excitement's been <u>over</u>shadowed by the deaths of 'four <u>British</u>
10		<u>soldiers'</u> in <u>Iraq</u> we've got a <u>special</u> <u>report</u> from <u>Basra</u> =
	JINGLE	= Newsbeat =
	GB	= also before six we're in ↑<u>Barnsley</u>↑ home to the newest ↑<u>drugs</u>↑ craze (1) <u>wheelie</u> <u>bins</u> =
	K	= well a couple of people have said they get high off it better than
15		drúgs for some (.) strange reason God knows whý (.) it's kind of smoking coming out of the bìn (.) crázy =
	GB	= David's got the spórt =
	DG	= it could be bad news if you like watching <u>Heineken</u> <u>Cup</u> <u>Rugby</u> plus we're in Spain for Tottenham's UEFA Cup tie against ↑Sevilla↑ =
20	GB	= and Michael Jackson's <u>stuff</u> goes up for auction in the ↑States↑ trouble ìs (1) he doesn't want to ↑sell↑ it =
	JINGLE	= Radio 1 Newsbeat
		* * *
	GB	= tónight's top stòry (.) the British Navy crew released by <u>Iran</u> have
25		been réunited with their fàmilies (.) they arrived báck in the <u>UK</u> after
'rall'		being 'captive for <u>thirteen</u> dáys' (.) in the last few minutes ↑we've↑ had a státement from them =
'leg'	RNR	= 'touching down at Heathrow this morning was (.) for all of us a dream come trùe' (.) and the welcome home that we've enjoyed
30		today (.) is one <u>none</u> of us will ever forget and we wish to thank every-one (.) for their <u>thoughts</u> (.) kind <u>words</u> (.) and <u>prayers</u> (.) it meant so múch to us àll =
	GB	= Tony Blair <u>insists</u> no deal was done to secure their rélease but <u>Irán</u> says Britain's <u>apologised</u> for what hàppened (1) ↑<u>lots</u> of sun↑ for the
35		Easter weekend should be mainly drý and wàrm <u>too</u> (.) <u>cold</u> at night thóugh =
	JINGLE	= Radio 1 Newsbeat national Radio 1

ITV News at 10.30, ITV (*ITVN*), read by Alastair Stewart; with tsunami witness Toby Diggens (TD) and ITV Wales presenter Juliet Piper (JP), speaking during a regional news insert into the national news broadcast.

1		AS the homecoming (1) the fifteen British <u>sailors</u> and <u>marines</u> are <u>re-united</u> with their <u>families</u> (1) <u>relief</u> and ↑tears↑ after two weeks in Iran it was ↑in their words↑ (1) a <u>dream</u> come true (1) <u>and</u> for Faye Turney (.) a reunion with the ↑daughter↑ <u>she</u> had left behind (.) but ↑tonight↑
5	'rall'	concerns about their ↑treatment↑ (.) and claims that despite the pictures (1) they were '<u>held</u> (1) in solitude'

[THEME MUSIC] (6)

AS a bittersweet return to Britain for the servicemen seized at <u>gunpoint</u> (.) and paraded as <u>apologetic</u> <u>pawns</u> by Iran (.) as concerns deepen
10 over ↑how well↑ they were <u>really</u> treated by their captors and <u>more</u> <u>grim</u> news from the region as also tonight (1) two women one a medic are among the four British soldiers killed in a bomb attack in Iraq (1) <u>more</u> football violence in <u>Europe</u> (.) now ↑<u>Spurs</u>↑ fans are involved in <u>clashes</u> on the continent (2) and the moment a <u>tsunami</u> struck the
15 Pacific (1) and the British <u>backpackers</u> who ↑witnessed↑ it =

'stacc' TD = sure enough on the horizon (.) you know (.) something over on 'the reef (.) just (.) big (.) white (.) explosion'=

JP = in Wales fifteen captured Royal ↑Navy↑ personnel including three from Wales have returned home safe and well there were emotional
20 scenes as they were reunited with ↑their↑ families

[MUSIC] (3)

AS good evening

* * *

AS <u>now</u> for a look at tomorrow's <u>front</u> pages the Independent says the
25 return of the captives from Iran was overshadowed by events in Iraq (.) it says (.) the deaths of <u>four</u> British soldiers ↑<u>shattered</u>↑ whatever hopes had emerged (1) of better relations (.) with (.) <u>Iran</u> the Guardian shows the aftermath of that attack it says (.) as the marines and sailors celebrate <u>their</u> release (.) it shows (.) the <u>bloody</u> <u>reality</u> of the
30 conflict in which (.) <u>they</u> were embroiled (.) the Telegraph says Iraqis were pictured ↑<u>gloating</u>↑ over the wreck of the Warrior armoured vehicle (.) it points out that (.) never before have <u>two</u> women died (.) in the <u>same</u> incident (.) on the <u>front</u> line and the Mirror shows former captive Faye Turney <u>reunited</u> with her <u>baby</u> (1) after the <u>killings</u> in
35 'rall' Basra it says (.) it was a day of '<u>unfettered</u> <u>joy</u> and (1) of <u>untold</u>
'accel' <u>griefs</u>' 'and that is' (.) the news (.) this <u>Thursday</u> <u>night</u> (1) <u>so</u> from me (.) and the whole team here (2) a very good<u>night</u> to <u>you</u>

C O M M E N T A R Y

Both *Newsround* and *Newsbeat* **open** with direct references to their respective titles: *Newsround* and *Newsbeat*. Radio 1 also has a reference to the time, an introduction from the DJ and an instantly recognisable jingle. The late-night television news has no spoken reference to the title; instead it relies on familiar thematic images of a clock face displaying the time at 10.30 and our recognition of the ITV newsreader. The *Newsround* (10 minutes) and Radio 1 *Newsbeat* (15 minutes) news slots are both shorter than the 30-minute ITV programme, and this difference in time allocation is reflected in the overall approach of each broadcast.

While the opening of *Newsround* relies entirely on the presenter to engage the target audience, *Newsbeat* and *ITV News* provide variety by including other contributors alongside the main newsreader. Both programmes intersperse their headlines with the words of key participants: Faye Turney (ll. 5–6, *NB*), Katie (ll. 14–16, *NB*) and Toby Diggens (ll. 16–17, *ITVN*). In addition, *Newsbeat* draws on specialist reporters: Jonathan Blake for an outside broadcast from Plymouth (ll. 7–8) and David Garrido for the sports news (ll. 18–19).

All three programmes use linguistic signals to mark the **end** of the broadcast: *well that's it* (l. 6, *NR*); *tonight's top story* (l. 24, *NB*); *and that is the news this Thursday night* (l. 36, *ITVN*). A summary of the main features follows, drawing attention to stories that have been given the most prominence. *ITV News* does this through its discussion of some of the next day's front pages, which are accompanied by a printed quotation on the screen. *Newsround* also tells viewers about other ways in which they can keep up to date with news (*our website and the bulletins on the CBBC channel*, ll. 6–7) and about the related programme *Sportsround* (l. 8). Radio 1's *Newsbeat* includes a brief summary of the weather (ll. 34–6). The different approaches indicate something about the audience for each programme: children are less likely to use broadcast listings than adults and reminding them about the website and CBBC programming may encourage them to use some of the additional facilities offered by the BBC children's service; the late-night audience will be specifically interested in current news and in the way different newspapers have presented it for the morning issues; and listeners to *Newsbeat*, many of whom will be on the way home from work, may find the weather summary for the holiday period useful in making plans for the long Easter weekend.

SOCIAL TOKENS often precede the title music. While *Newsround* adopts the informal *have a great Easter* (l. 10), the *ITV News* chooses the more formal *a very goodnight to you* (l. 37). It is a reflection of the familiar relationship between the viewers and the presenter in *Newsround* that social tokens are also used in the opening: *hello I'm Lizo and welcome to Newsround …* (l. 1). This encourages children to engage with a named individual who can make the topical and factual programme, which is quite different from much of the programming broadcast in the children's slot (3.20 pm–5.35 pm), more approachable. *Newsbeat* offers no social greetings but the newsreader is named before she begins to speak, and the closing jingle names the programme. *ITV News* can rely on viewers' recognition of the presenter, who will have been named by the continuity announcer.

The **relationship** created between the target audience and the newsreader in each broadcast is quite different. The use of first person plural pronouns in *Newsbeat* and *Newsround* makes the news teams seem less impersonal (*we*, ll. 10, 12, *NB*; l. 6, *NR*). This is reinforced by the use of first names for reporters: *Jake* (l. 9, *NR*) for CBBC presenter Jake Humphrey, and *David* (l. 17, *NB*) for sports reporter David Garrido. *Newsround*'s use of possessive determiners (*our*, l. 6), direct address (*your*, l. 2; *you*, l. 7) and imperatives (*don't forget*, l. 8), and *Newsbeat*'s use of informal contractions (*excitement's*, l. 9) and colloquial language (*stuff*, l. 20; *trouble is*, l. 21) underpin the familiar and personal tone of these news programmes. *ITV News*, however, remains impersonal: it avoids familiar references until the final words: *from me and the whole team* (ll. 36–7).

All three programmes cover the **topic** of the return of fifteen British sailors after a two-week detention in Iran and it is placed first in the running order in each case. In the ITV broadcast, it also takes precedence in the Welsh regional news, which focuses in particular on the three crew members from Wales. *Newsbeat* and *ITV News* then contrast this 'good news' story with news of the death of four British soldiers in the conflict in Iraq. For emotional and dramatic effect, both stations draw attention to the women involved in what is often perceived as a traditionally male-dominated environment. *Newsbeat* does so implicitly in Faye Turney's statement (ll. 5–6), while the *ITV News* is explicit (ll. 3–4, 11–12, 32–3, 34). *Newsround* avoids this topic, which is probably a reflection of the very different target audience, focusing instead on one of the world's most active volcanoes (Piton de la Fournaise or 'Mountain of the Furnace', on Reunion Island in the Indian Ocean).

Beyond these main topics, the headlines summarise quite different news. The children's broadcast only deals with two stories, but Radio 1 also includes a regional story (*Barnsley – the newest drugs craze*, ll. 12–13, *NB*), sports news (ll. 18–19) and a 'celebrity' story (*Michael Jackson*, ll. 20–1). Because of the newly released statement by a representative of the British sailors, its summary covers only the main news item. The time reference *in the last few minutes* (l. 26) suggests that Radio 1 listeners are the first to hear the statement. The *ITV News* headlines are dominated by topics that have a relevance internationally (*football violence* in international games, ll. 13–14; the *tsunami* that *struck the Pacific*, ll. 14–15). These topics are reinforced by the summary of newspaper articles that also focus on the two main stories. The topics are all serious and the tone is formal.

The **prosodic features** are distinctive. The beginning and end of many utterances are marked by rising and falling intonation patterns. This ensures that the meaning is clear for viewers and listeners. Stress is far more frequent than it would be in informal conversation and it allows newsreaders to draw attention to key words. In the *Newsbeat* and *Newsround* bulletins there are examples of consecutive stresses that make the delivery emphatic and rhythmical and directly engage the audience (ll. 4, 10 *NR*; ll. 9–10, 18 *NB*). While there are no examples of lowered pitch, raised pitch is used to highlight significant information. The mood is serious in all three broadcasts; on other occasions news programmes may end with a trivial or light-hearted story when time permits and more serious issues do not dominate.

Because of the consistency of the mood, changes in pace and volume are not common. In the examples here, changes in pace are directly related to the tight scheduling demands which require that a programme finish at precisely the same time each day (*'accel'*: l. 9, *NR*; l. 36, *ITVN*), or to the need for an emphatic delivery of serious information (*'rall'*: l. 9, *NB*; l. 26, *NB*; l. 6, *ITVN*; l. 35, *ITVN*). In addition, headlines are usually pre-written, so although newsreaders may alter word order or adapt the script so that it sounds more spontaneous, ultimately they are delivering material that is quite inflexible. This also contributes to the even quality of the utterances. It is noticeable that in the speech of contributors the pauses may be longer (ll. 5–6, *NB*); there may be pauses in the middle of grammatical units (l. 15, *NB*); and delivery may be uneven (ll. 16–17, *ITVN*).

Documentaries try to present real life in as **objective** a way as possible without fictionalising an issue or using professional actors (except for dramatic reconstructions). They focus on **facts** and attempt to provide useful information on a chosen subject. The **field** may be political, social, educational or cultural, and the documentary makers will try to draw on as many sources of information as they can. **Contributors** may be ordinary members of the public or experts who can discuss an issue from an academic or practical point of view.

It is important to remember, however, that although a documentary may seem to be an objective presentation of the facts, the material has been **selected** and **presented** in order to promote a certain view of the subject. By omitting certain details or examples, by juxtaposing certain scenes or by inviting particular people to contribute, programmes may provide a **subjective** rather than an objective interpretation. Equally, **editing** of contributors' utterances or the framing of an image in a certain way can alter audience response. Voice-overs can add authority to the words spoken, encouraging viewers or listeners to agree; music can be used to engage the audience's emotions rather than their intellects; 'leading' questions can be asked, forcing interviewees to say things they did not really mean or did not wish to deal with; and speakers with non-standard accents and dialects may be presented as having a less valid viewpoint.

In order to identify any bias or underlying viewpoint, it is important to look closely at the lexis, the grammatical choices and the overall structure of a documentary. This kind of linguistic analysis will reveal the angle adopted by the programme, providing evidence to show whether the presentation of a particular topic is positive or negative. While the news aims to cover regional, national and international events in an objective way, documentaries aim to provide an interpretation of events and this is inevitably subjective.

ACTIVITY 18.2

Read the following extract from a BBC1 documentary in the *Panorama* series. The programme focused on the problem of antisocial behaviour in our communities and our own role as individuals in managing such behaviour. Jeremy Vine, the *Panorama* presenter, discussed the problem with Barry and Kym Ledgar, whose post office had been targeted by robbers four times in fifteen years. Entitled 'Should I fight back?', the programme, which was broadcast on 5 February 2007, was produced by Judith Ahern and edited by Sandy Smith.

The transcript below shows how an apparently seamless programme is in fact put together from lots of smaller units of language and image. Annotations mark new speakers, the kind of images selected and the way in which the spoken word is used. It uses the normal conventions of written language, rather than those associated with linguistic analysis. The key below explains the technical terms marked on the extract.

As you read, jot down notes on the following:

1 the register
2 the kind of people who contribute to the discussion
3 the grammatical structures used by different speakers

4 the overall structure of the extract

5 the viewpoint(s) presented

6 any distinctive features of formal or informal speech.

KEY

SYNC	the synchronisation of image and spoken word	CAPTION	a printed title appearing at the bottom of the screen
V/O	the superimposition of a voice over an image when the actual speaker is not seen	MS	medium-range shot
		CU	close-up
		MCU	medium close-up

Extract from *Panorama* transcript:

1	CU Jeremy Vine	**SYNC JEREMY VINE:** Good evening. I'm Jeremy Vine and this is Panorama.
5	CCTV footage	**V/O JEREMY VINE** Two robbers with knives attack an elderly newsagent. He instinctively fights back. Is he a hero or just plain foolish?
	CCTV footage	**V/O JEREMY VINE** Put yourself in this man's shoes: he went to the aid of two teenagers being attacked by a gang. Do you join in or walk on by?
10	CU Tony McNulty MP, Minister for Police and Security	**V/O JEREMY VINE** You see a young man looking aggressive, shouting at an old woman. What do you do? Do you retreat and ring the police? *[Theme music]* (8)
15	MCU Jeremy Vine	**SYNC JEREMY VINE** It's a split-second decision that any of us could face at any time: whether to intervene or turn away. It's happened to me, maybe it's happened to you. Tonight we're asking if we don't take action when we see crime and antisocial behaviour happening right in front of our eyes, who will?
20	CAPTION: Should I fight back? MS urban streets	**V/O JEREMY VINE** I've been meeting people who have fought back against criminals with vastly different consequences. But as individuals, just what is the right thing to do when we are confonted by violence or antisocial behaviour?
25	CAPTION: Stoke on Trent CCTV footage	**V/O JEREMY VINE** Here an armed robber runs into a busy street.
		SYNC ROBBER Oi, put the money in the bag. Put the money in the bag or you get it through the head. Now. Quick.
30		**V/O JEREMY VINE** Kym Ledgar, the sub-postmistress, was terrified.
	CAPTION: Kym Ledgar	**SYNC KYM LEDGAR** I saw this figure all in black and couldn't even see like the whites of his eyes.
35	CCTV footage	**V/O KYM LEDGAR** And he'd got a shotgun, he'd pointed it at me and then he moved it to the customer and he said, in a very threatening strong voice.
		SYNC ROBBER Put the money in the bag. Put the money in the **** bag. Quick.
40	MCU Kym Ledgar at home	**SYNC KYM LEDGAR** So I just got up and did exactly as he said.

| CCTV footage | V/O JEREMY VINE |
| | Her husband, Barry, a former soldier, walked straight into the middle of the robbery. |

45 MCU Barry Ledgar in the PO — **SYNC BARRY LEDGAR**
CAPTION: Barry Ledgar — Uh, it was an instant decision. Well, we came into contact right by the counter here, he started to turn, I grabbed hold of the barrel of the shotgun and as he turned, I got with me other hand I grabbed his collar.

CCTV footage — **V/O JEREMY VINE**
Barry, in beige, grabbed the robber, who's wearing a hood.

50 **V/O KYM LEDGAR**
I remember giving out a blood-curdling scream because I thought I could well lose him.

V/O BARRY LEDGAR
He was pulling away, I was pushing. It was a struggle for the gun.
55 Control of the gun.

V/O KYM LEDGAR
I knew Barry wouldn't let go. I just knew how determined he would be.

CU Kym Ledgar at home — **SYNC KYM LEDGAR**
I was just in fear of his life.

60 CCTV footage — **V/O BARRY LEDGAR**
And we bounced off one or two of the walls.

MCU Barry Ledgar in Post Office — **SYNC BARRY LEDGAR**
And then he threatened to kill me, all part and parcel of it.

CCTV footage — **V/O BARRY LEDGAR**
65 Then he let go of the gun and leapt up and he was out through the door.

V/O JEREMY VINE
Barry, who has a serious heart condition, cracked a rib in the vicious struggle.

70 **V/O KYM LEDGAR**
I thought I might have lost him actually.

MCU Kym Ledgar at home — **SYNC KYM LEDGAR**
He'd gone an ashen colour and his lips had gone purple, and I was very, very concerned that he was going to have a heart attack.

CU Photofit
75 picture of robber — **V/O JEREMY VINE**
The robber was Sasha Markovic, a heroin addict and persistent offender. Barry was given a bravery medal by the police but confusingly they tell others not to follow his example.

CU Paul Clews in office — **SYNC CHIEF INSPECTOR PAUL CLEWS**
80 CAPTION: Chief Inspector Paul Clews — We generally advise in such a serious incident like that people shouldn't get involved, but I'd certainly not be critical of Barry for his bravery.

MS family images — **V/O JEREMY VINE**
For Barry, it's not really about bravery. He feels he simply can't look
85 on while the family post office is targeted by robbers. Four times it's happened in fifteen years. So next time?

MCU Kym and Barry Ledgar — **SYNC BARRY LEDGAR**
If I was confronted by a criminal in similar circumstances I would hope I would do the same. It depends on the situation. It's not something you
90 can give a general advice to. If you can avoid it, then by all means if you think it's dangerous, don't do it. Phone the police and let the police handle it, they're trained for it.

The **register** of this extract is typical of many documentaries. The **field**, of course, will be directly linked to the subject of each individual broadcast – in this extract the focus is on antisocial behaviour. A lexical set of related words is developed to provide lexical cohesion: *fights back* (l.5), *attacked* (l.8), *antisocial behaviour* (ll.17,22), *shotgun* (ll.35,47), *struggle* (ll.54,68), *robber* (ll.24,49,75).

The **mode** is clearly spoken and although contributors may have planned what they were going to say beforehand, their utterances are marked by the normal non-fluency features typical of informal conversation. This is more likely to be evident in the turns of non-professional participants. The format of the documentary predefines the structure of turn-taking: each turn latches smoothly onto the next, and there are no adjacency pairs because the programme is not made up of the question-and-answer patterns of an interview. Where interrogatives are used (ll.5,8,11,16–18,21–2), their effect is rhetorical – we do not expect a direct answer, but we know that the programme will go on to explore the issues raised.

The **manner** is formal because the tone is serious and the programme is targeted at a public audience who will be unknown to the participants. The range of contributors will provide an appropriate breadth of information on the topic – their relationship with the subject matter may be personal, academic or professional. By ensuring that a documentary is made up of speakers who develop the discussion in quite different ways, producers can target their programme at a mass audience. If an issue such as 'antisocial behaviour' were approached exclusively from an academic standpoint, for instance, the programme would appeal to a more limited audience. To engage their target audience, therefore, broadcasters encourage viewers to see the utterances as spontaneous and 'real' rather than theoretical and pre-planned.

The **broadcast slot** for *Panorama* plays a fundamental role in developing a wide-ranging audience: the 30-minute presenter-led format aims to engage viewers with serious and thought-provoking issues that have a direct effect on their lives. Broadcast on Mondays at 8.30 pm, immediately after the popular BBC soap *EastEnders*, the programme aims to put investigative journalism at the heart of prime-time television. First launched in November 1953, *Panorama* is the longest running public affairs television programme in the world: by broadcasting at this new time and in a shorter format than previously, the BBC hopes to establish a new audience base. While new viewers may initially drift into watching because they had tuned to the previous programme on BBC1, it is hoped that they will be engaged by what they see and go on to become regular viewers with an active interest in current affairs.

The **speakers** are identified by name and, where appropriate, professional role, on a caption which is printed at the bottom of the screen. Kym Ledgar is first seen on CCTV footage in the post office where she is the sub-postmistress: we are told who she is by the voice-over of the presenter (l.30) and a caption (ll.31–2). The juxtaposition of the dramatic CCTV footage and the shots of Kym Ledgar at home enhances the horrifying nature of what took place. Her contribution to the discussion is based on personal experience, and the images, together with her own account of events, directly engage the audience.

This personal perspective is developed in the contributions of Barry Ledgar, who is also introduced by the presenter (l. 42) and a caption (ll. 46–7). The introduction of Chief Inspector Paul Clews, however, provides a different perspective: he is in a professional role, offering people advice about the best way to behave in situations where antisocial behaviour may threaten their safety. The caption, therefore, includes not only his full name but his title as well (ll. 80–2). The other professional contributor (ll. 9–12) does not speak in this extract and is not introduced until later in the programme, when he is able to address the issues Vine raises. While he too is a professional, his role as a government minister means that his relationship with the issue is more theoretical than practical.

The dominant speaker is the presenter, Jeremy Vine, whose contributions provide the framework for the programme. There is no caption to establish his identity because of his direct reference to his name in the opening (l. 2) and his familiarity to viewers as the regular presenter of the programme. While we see him when he introduces himself (l. 2) and when he directly introduces the topic (ll. 13–18), the majority of his utterances are delivered as voice-overs. These comment on the CCTV footage, which provides the concrete evidence for the programme.

The speakers in this extract are not engaged in a dialogue with each other, but their contributions are all linked thematically. Although there is no linguistic interaction between them, their comments have been edited so that they follow on logically. The contributors' different experiences and their different relationships with the issue of 'antisocial behaviour' provide the audience with a range of responses from which to establish their own standpoint.

The **structure** of the extract engages the audience on many layers. The juxtaposition of images and the spoken word, the organisation of speech turns and the distinctive grammatical patterns of each speaker all contribute to the overall effect of the documentary. Images are used to reinforce and develop the words that accompany them: CCTV footage of violent scenes is made more dramatic by the accompanying first person narration of a participant. The editing process ensures that each new speaker latches smoothly onto the end of the previous turn. For instance, Kym Ledgar concludes her account of her husband's struggle with the robber (ll. 72–3), whom Jeremy Vine then identifies (l. 75). His turn ends with a summary of the police response (ll. 76–7), which is immediately followed by the Chief Inspector's advice (ll. 79–80) and his recognition of Barry Ledgar's bravery (l. 80). Jeremy Vine then questions whether it is 'bravery' that has motivated Barry Ledgar's actions (ll. 84–6).

The **grammatical structures** of the speakers are typical of spoken language. Despite the fact that the manner is formal, their speech is marked by the features of informal conversation. Clauses are often long and complex with several embedded subordinate clauses – spoken language tends to be loosely structured, unlike the tighter structures associated with the written word which can be redrafted and polished.

S	P	A	A	A	S	P	O	S
(Well)	(we) (came)	(into contact)	(right by the counter)	(here),	(he)	(started)	(to turn),	(I)
linking Adv								SCl–NFCl

	P		O				A	S	P	A

(grabbed hold of) (the barrel of the shotgun) (and) (as he turned), (I) (got) (with me

conj   SCl–ACl

	S		P		O

other hand) (I) (grabbed) (his collar).   (ll. 45–7)

An utterance like this has features that resemble spoken language: it begins with the colloquial linking adverb *Well*; it has an incomplete grammatical unit (*I got ø with me other hand*); and the structure is loose as the speaker tries to communicate to his audience the speed of the encounter. Where there are simple sentences, they tend to be used rhetorically for dramatic effect:

	S		P		O	S	A	P

(Two robbers with knives) (attack) (an elderly newsagent). (He) (instinctively) (fights

P   S   C

back). (Is) (he) (a hero or just plain foolish)?   (ll. 4–5)

Some utterances are incomplete, but this does not affect our understanding – we are accustomed to hearing disjointed structures in spontaneous speech:

O   A

(Control of the gun).   (l. 55)   (So) (next time?)   (l. 86)

conj

Each of these utterances is directly connected to the previous one: Barry Ledger qualifies his post-modified noun phrase *a struggle for the gun* (l. 54); Jeremy Vine raises a question about the future of the Ledgar family in the light of past events (ll. 84–6). His rhetorical question makes a direct link to the moral choice that underpins the programme as a whole: *Do you join in or walk on by?* (l. 8).

The **viewpoints** presented in this extract encourage viewers to engage with the issue of antisocial behaviour and to consider their social and moral responsibilities. Most documentary presenters will have no personal connection with the content of the programme – their role will be those of detached professionals who have researched a topical issue and recorded their findings in a formal context. Jeremy Vine's personal reference (*it's happened to me*, l. 15), however, suggests that this issue is one that affects us all. The use of direct address (*you*, ll. 8, 10–11, 16) and first person plural pronouns (*we*, l. 16–17, 22; *us*, l. 14) emphasises the importance of engaging directly, of recognising that we cannot afford to ignore antisocial behaviour. This viewpoint is reinforced by the fact that all the examples given at the start of the programme (ll. 4–11), like Barry and Kym Ledgar's account of the violent incident in their post office, are based on the personal experiences of ordinary people. Contributors such as Paul Clews and Tony McNulty, however, are speaking from a professional point of view – the captions draw attention to their official titles. As a Member of Parliament and a Minister in the Cabinet, Tony McNulty must present the view of his political party, supporting Labour policy on antisocial behaviour; as a Chief Inspector, Paul Clews must advise people against getting involved in incidents in which the outcome may be fatal.

The speakers do not address the issue in the same way, nor do they explicitly develop each other's argument. Nevertheless, they all have one thing in common – each argument places antisocial behaviour and its consequences at the centre of the debate. This enables broadcasters to convey a convincing argument by presenting viewers with a persuasive case: real-life evidence; an emotive commentary that re-creates the experience of two ordinary people; a presenter who has a personal relationship with the topic; and experts who speak from theoretical (Tony McNulty) and practical (Paul Clews) standpoints.

Documentaries combine the features of **formal** and **informal spoken language** in a distinctive way. The context is formal because of the public nature of the transmission, and many documentaries resemble a form of lecture – they provide experts in a particular field with a public platform where they are able to discuss a specific subject. In this extract, abstract nouns such as *decision* (ll. 14, 45), *consequences* (l. 21), *violence* (l. 22) *incident* (l. 79) and *bravery* (ll. 80, 84) are typical of a theoretical consideration of the topic. Similarly, the formal approach of the documentary is reinforced by the use of parenthesis (ll. 30, 42–3, 67–8) and rhetorical features such as parallelism (*join in or walk on by*, l. 8; *intervene or turn away*, l. 15; *It's happened to me, maybe it's happened to you*, ll. 15–16) and juxtaposition (*Two robbers/an elderly newsagent*, l. 4; *hero/just plain foolish*, l. 5; *two teenagers … a gang*, ll. 7–8; and *a young man looking aggressive … an old woman*, l. 10). The emphasis is on the opposition created between aggressor and victim. The moral choice seems quite clear cut until the issue is complicated by the real-life example, which demonstrates the potential consequences of intervention.

Panorama, however, is consciously aiming to broaden its appeal, and alongside these characteristics of formal speech there are many features that are more commonly associated with informal spoken language: the colloquial filler *like* (l. 32); initial-position conjunctions (ll. 21, 35, 61, 63); the adverb *Well* (l. 45) used at the start of a sentence to provide thinking time; the repetition of the adverb *just* (ll. 57, 59) for emphasis; colloquial collocations such as *part and parcel* (l. 63); the tautological repetition of *such … like that* (l. 79); and the repetition of the adverb *then* (ll. 35, 63, 65) as a time marker in an oral narrative.

There are examples of informality in the utterances of all the participants, but they are most common in the turns of the Ledgars as they narrate the sequence of events that took place in their post office. Interestingly, however, there is only one example of a voiced hesitation (l. 45), although these occur frequently in spontaneous speech. Because a documentary is created from edited statements and images, the producers can polish the end product even when the contributors are unaccustomed to speaking in public. Although the speech may be spontaneous rather than scripted, it is nevertheless very different from everyday interactions in which the spoken word cannot be recalled and reconsidered.

The **function** of a documentary is to educate, inform or enlighten. Because the information is conveyed through a medium that is commonly associated with entertainment, however, documentaries are quite unlike academic lectures. Rather than targeting an expert audience, they aim to appeal to a wide range of people. The mix of expert and ordinary viewpoints means that they do not alienate viewers. By balancing facts and theories with the experiences of ordinary people, programme makers engage their audiences and make abstract issues more approachable.

Drama

While documentaries aim to discuss the 'truth' of real issues, radio and television dramas **dramatise** life, considering the possible consequences of real events in a fictional context. Some dramas aim to be realistic, portraying life as it really is; others create an obviously fictional version of reality in which characters, places and events are sanitised.

The use of **sets** and **locations** gives a concrete background to the fictional world created, helping to establish both the characters and the audience as part of a reality which runs parallel to real life. In television drama, characters rarely address the camera or the audience directly and this reinforces our sense that the fiction is real rather than something created. Dramas, just like documentaries, are presented to their audiences as a seamless whole in which there is no evidence of the way the end result has been achieved. The world created, however, is **manipulated** – in both television and radio drama, volume levels are adjusted so that audiences never really hear sounds or speech in the distance; shots and scenes are edited smoothly so that the audience is unaware of the movement from one to another; cameras and microphones move so that the audience becomes omniscient, seeing and hearing things that would be impossible to see or hear in a real context.

A general knowledge of the ways in which television and radio dramas manipulate their audiences is useful in assessing the 'reality' of an extract. As well as commenting on the **spoken language**, it is important to consider the kinds of **shots** or **sound effects** that accompany the spoken word, and the ways in which the end product is created from a wide range of **visual** and **aural source material**.

The kind of **speech** used will depend directly upon the geographical location, the historical period, the cultural and social background of individual characters and the function of the communication. Like speakers in real life, fictional characters will have a range of repertoires and they will vary their speech according to their audience, purpose and context. Where characters do not, the results will often be comic. **Prosodic features** tend to be exaggerated so that audiences recognise the mood and attitude of speakers.

There are three main types of television and radio drama: single plays, series, and serials.

Single plays

Single plays often have transmission times of 45 minutes or longer and are self-contained. While plays have been traditionally associated with serious art (such as presentations on BBC Radio 3 of traditional and modern classics), in the twenty-first century one-off dramas have become a popular form of entertainment – there are 45-minute radio plays daily on Radio 4, afternoon television dramas on BBC1, and prime-time dramas with well-known actors on both BBC and ITV television channels. Digital broadcasting has also expanded the possibilities with dramas on the spoken-word channel BBC7.

Series

Series have recurring sets of characters and are usually set in the same locations over a number of episodes: *Casualty* (BBC); *Life on Mars* (BBC); *Lewis* (ITV); *Doctor Who* (BBC); *House* (Five). Each programme is based on a different story, but there may also be some running strands that enhance our understanding of the main characters. Each narrative is usually completed within the weekly broad-casting slot, but may be shown in two parts on consecutive nights.

Serials

Serials have continuity of action, character and location, with stories that run from episode to episode. Often each programme ends with a cliffhanger to encourage viewers to watch the next transmission. Dramatisations of classic novels (*Bleak House*, BBC; *Northanger Abbey*, ITV), soap operas (*EastEnders*, BBC; *Coronation Street*, ITV) and large-scale dramas (*Ugly Betty*, C4; *Heroes*, BBC 2) fall into this category.

ACTIVITY 18.3

A transmission script records details such as sound effects and tones of voice (radio and television), camera shots and facial expressions (television), and the actual words spoken. The extract that follows is taken from the transmission script for a 45-minute radio drama *Once a Friend*, broadcast on BBC Radio 4 (24 August 2007). The play takes a real event, the murder of three police officers next to the common land of Wormwood Scrubs, West London, in 1966, and imagines its effect on the lives of two fictional characters: Leo and John, 11-year-old boys at the time of the murders.

The focus is on these childhood friends as they meet 37 years after the murder case. The play explores their attempt to re-establish a friendship and understand the way in which their lives have been shaped by past events. As the drama unfolds, we learn that John was assaulted in the park on the day of the murders. He has believed ever since that Leo went for help and that the police did not come to his assistance because of their involvement in the murder of their colleagues. What their meeting reveals, however, is that Leo did not reach the police: after stumbling upon the murdered officers, he fled from the horror of the scene. References to *Secrets* (l. 41) and *Past indiscretion* (l. 53) in the opening scene therefore have a wider semantic significance within the context of the play as a whole.

Read through the text and jot down notes in response to the following questions:

1 What technical information does the transmission script provide?
2 Will an audience be aware of the technical processes in the polished end product?
3 How will the written descriptions of character and setting be conveyed to the audience in the broadcast version?
4 How does the structure engage the audience?
5 How realistic is the dialogue?
6 What will the dialogue gain by being spoken aloud rather than read?

KEY

GRAMS	music sound track	FX	sound effects
ARCH	news bulletin taken from the BBC archive	/ /	interrupted turn
		(BEAT)	timed pause
* * *	11 minutes omitted from script		

Extract from the first 17 minutes of *Once a Friend*, written by Stephen Phelps and directed by Toby Swift.

	1		The action takes place in July 2003.
			CAST
	LEO		Teacher, 48, clever, slightly untidy. A little highly-strung.
	JOHN		48, Leo's childhood best friend. Street smart.
5	WAITRESS (ELLIE)		19, harassed, overworked.

SCENE 1.

GRAMS: **KEEP ON RUNNING (Spencer Davis Group)**

ARCHIVE OF 2003 NEWS BULLETIN ANNOUNCING THAT HARRY ROBERTS WILL SEEK A JUDICIAL REVIEW OF HIS

10   **LIFE SENTENCE IN THE HIGH COURT**

TODAY (ARCH: A, P1/16)

            (MUSIC HELD UNDER)

            (MUSIC MIXES INTO ...)

F/X: **ACOUSTIC: A BUSY CITY CENTRE BAR**

15	LEO	John! (BEAT) Over here ...
	JOHN	Is that ... ?
	LEO	Yes, it's me, Leo. Good Lord, you haven't changed a bit.
	JOHN	Come onnn!
	LEO	No. Good-looking as ever – just that sort of *Unforgiven* look now.
20	JOHN	Unforgiven?
	LEO	Clint Eastwood in *The Unforgiven*.
	JOHN	You mean thirty years older than *Fistful of Dollars*?
	LEO	Well ... (BEAT) Thirty years? Doesn't seem possible.
	JOHN	More. Trust you to find a place with 60s music.
25	LEO	Great isn't it? Never found anything I liked better, myself. There's a juke-box full of it. (BEAT) What can I get you? I'm on lager. It's Polish – good though ...
	JOHN	That's fine. Wouldn't be ordinary beer, English beer, would it? Not for Leo. First kid in the class to go "abroad" for his holidays. Motoring down
30		to Spain in the Jag.
	LEO	France, actually. Côte d'Azur.
	JOHN	That was it! That was the one thing I hated about you. Bloody languages. You found it all so ridiculously easy. Even when we were "first years".
	LEO	Well since we've gone straight into things we *didn't* like, how do you
35		think the rest of us felt when you showed up with a girlfriend? And we were barely out of short trousers ...
	JOHN	Well yes, I always did seem to find *that* easy.

F/X: **LAUGHTER (OFF)**

	JOHN	It's good to see you. You're looking well.
40		* * *
	JOHN	Never let you go, do they? Secrets ...
	LEO	Do you remember when we cheated in the exams?
	JOHN	At primary?
	LEO	That's it. And Kenny Baldock got caught up in it ... and it cost him a
45		place at Grammar School.
	JOHN	Kenny Baldock! The ginger kid? With one sticky out ear?
	LEO	But it wasn't him, it was me ...
	JOHN	I'd forgotten all about that.

	LEO	I didn't. I carried it around with me for years. And then finally, not long
50		ago, only about three years, I had to go and find him and own up. He was
		fine about it. Didn't care. Not a bit. He's making a fortune, doing very nicely
		thank you. Estate Agent, or a chain of them actually. Living in Surrey.
	JOHN	(PAUSE) Is this what it's like getting on for fifty? Past indiscretion coming
		up to bite you?

<table>
<tr><td>55</td><td>F/X:</td><td>SHARP, QUICK, BREATHING. FEET RUNNING THROUGH
UNDERGROWTH</td></tr>
<tr><td></td><td>JOHN (1966)</td><td>Leeoo! Help me! …</td></tr>
<tr><td></td><td>WAITRESS</td><td>You guys ok there?</td></tr>
<tr><td></td><td>LEO</td><td>We're fine thanks. For now.</td></tr>
<tr><td>60</td><td></td><td>ARCHIVE OF 1966 NEWS BULLETIN ANNOUNCING THE
ARREST OF TWO MEN AND THE MASSIVE POLICE HUNT
FOR A THIRD (HARRY ROBERTS – UNNAMED) (ARCH: C,
P53/55)</td></tr>
<tr><td></td><td></td><td>SCENE 2.</td></tr>
<tr><td>65</td><td></td><td>JOHN IS RETURNING FROM THE LAVATORY</td></tr>
<tr><td></td><td>JOHN</td><td>(SITTING DOWN) That's better. Goes right through you, this lager. P'raps
that's why they call it Pils.</td></tr>
<tr><td></td><td>LEO</td><td>(DISTRACTED) Huh?</td></tr>
<tr><td></td><td>JOHN</td><td>Spelling mistake. Wrong consonant. Something like that …</td></tr>
<tr><td>70</td><td>F/X:</td><td>SLOW, HEAVY BREATHING. RUSTLING UNDERGROWTH:</td></tr>
<tr><td></td><td>LEO (1966)</td><td>(SHOUTING) John! Johhhnnn!</td></tr>
<tr><td></td><td>F/X:</td><td>FOOTSTEPS RUNNING, PUSHING THROUGH UNDER-
GROWTH. CLOSE BREATHING, FAST AND HEAVY.</td></tr>
<tr><td></td><td>LEO (1966)</td><td>(LOW) Run, come on, run …</td></tr>
<tr><td>75</td><td>F/X:</td><td>FOOTSTEPS RUNNING</td></tr>
<tr><td></td><td>LEO</td><td>I don't understand …</td></tr>
<tr><td></td><td>JOHN</td><td>Just a joke. A bad joke. Pils, piss, missing consonant, you know.</td></tr>
<tr><td></td><td>LEO</td><td>Oh. Yeah, sorry (BEAT) I was just thinking about that day. That extraordi-
nary day – on the common.</td></tr>
<tr><td>80</td><td>JOHN</td><td>Nothing was ever quite the same after, it's true.</td></tr>
<tr><td></td><td>F/X:</td><td>LAUGHTER OFF</td></tr>
<tr><td></td><td>LEO</td><td>That's why your parents moved away – wasn't it? So soon afterwards.</td></tr>
<tr><td></td><td>JOHN</td><td>The police were bloody useless.</td></tr>
<tr><td></td><td>LEO</td><td>I know. That's awful. But then, they had so much/</td></tr>
<tr><td>85</td><td>JOHN</td><td>/Thank god you were there. I mean we were kids. They should've come,
shouldn't they? For kids. Shouldn't have turned you away like that. Not
when there's kids. Not without helping.</td></tr>
<tr><td></td><td>LEO</td><td>It had to be that day, didn't it? Any other day, and things would have
been different …</td></tr>
<tr><td>90</td><td>JOHN</td><td>Nobody really talked about it in our house, and I certainly didn't want to
… except with you.</td></tr>
<tr><td></td><td>LEO</td><td>I kept dreaming about it. That day. Just me. On my own. And the bodies
– the dead policemen. Like I had something to do with it. Like it was my
fault somehow.</td></tr>
<tr><td>95</td><td>JOHN</td><td>It was never mentioned in our house, not once.</td></tr>
</table>

COMMENTARY

The script clearly marks **technical information** by capitalising the scene number, the location and the sound effects. It uses subject-specific terms such as *GRAMS* (l.7), *HELD UNDER* (l.12), *MIXES INTO* (l.13), *F/X* (l.14) as an indication of the points at which sound will be used to create a sense of time and place. Because the radio broadcast is pre-recorded, listeners hear no evidence of the units in which the play has been produced. Editing ensures that individual scenes fade into each other in a polished and seamless whole. The audience is presented with a context in which the participants John and Leo interact and a sequence of revelations unfolds. During the broadcast, listeners immerse themselves in the fictional world, believing in the credibility of the discourse.

In a television transmission script, **written descriptions** of character and place are often detailed, but they are ultimately communicated through images. Camera angles and the physical appearance of each actor bring the verbal descriptions to life. Facial expressions and other details of body language are picked up by close-up shots; scenes cut from location to location to provide the appropriate backdrop. These all become part of the way in which meaning is conveyed.

In a radio broadcast such as this, on the other hand, the audience is reliant on sound: the prosodics and the background sound effects. The cast list (ll. 3–5) uses noun and adjective phrases to provide information about each of the characters:

h		h	m	h		m	m	m	h
Teacher		clever,	slightly	untidy		Leo's	childhood	best	friend
N		Adj	Adv	Adj		N	N	Adj	N
NP		AdjP	AdjP					NP	

The descriptions highlight the characteristics, the relationships or state of mind of the participants. They are details that will be revealed through the prosodics – the intonation patterns, pace, volume and pitch of the speakers. Similarly, a pre-modified noun phrase establishes the context:

m	m	m	m	h
A	busy	city	centre	bar
det	Adj	N	N	N

This indicates the kind of sound effects that will be used to build up a sense of place: bottles or glasses being put down on the table; background laughter and conversation.

The **structure** of this extract is complex: the play interweaves archive news bulletins (ll. 8–11, 60–3), the boys' experiences from 1966 when they are 11, and their meeting in 2003. The juxtaposition of real-life news with fictional characters gives a hard edge to the play, blurring the boundary between fiction and reality. The movement between the different layers enhances the drama by intriguing the audience, who do not immediately have all the information they need to make connections. The sound effects used to create a sense of the boys' experience in 1966 are atmospheric, building tension and changing the mood.

The formality of the news bulletins, the informality of the two men's conversation in the bar, and the fear communicated by the sound effects (ll. 55–6, 70, 72–3, 75) work together to give the drama layers of meaning which will ultimately converge. The structure, therefore, draws listeners on by moving them from a position of confusion to one of understanding – we continue to listen because we want to understand the relationship between the different layers.

The **dialogue** aims to imitate real conversation by adopting features of spoken language. Verbal contractions are common: *it's, haven't* (l.17), *That's* (l.66), *should've* (l.85). Minor sentences such as *No.* (l.19), *Unforgiven?* (l.20), *More.* (l.24), *Motoring down to Spain in the Jag.* (ll.29–30), *Just a joke.* (l.77) reflect the looser structure of spoken language; informal modifiers (*bloody*, ll.32,83), John's joke (ll.66–9,77) and initial-position conjunctions (ll.35,44,84,92) reflect the informal manner.

The opening greetings are also typical of informal speech. Vocatives personalise the discourse (*John!* l.15) and complete adjacency pairs (*Is that …? / Yes, it's me* ll.16–17) and an other-related comment (*you haven't changed a bit*, l.17) create a co-operative mood. References to the Clint Eastwood films (ll.19–22), to music (ll.24–6) and to past experiences (ll.29–37) establish the men's shared history.

As in most informal contexts in which the participants are friends, the topics emerge co-operatively with references to the past (school; the murder of the policemen) and the present (physical appearance; *Kenny Baldock, Estate Agent … Living in Surrey*, ll.44,52). The only point at which there is a breakdown in the communication is when Leo fails to understand John's joke. The stage directions referring to Leo's state of mind (*DISTRACTED*, l.68), his admission that he has not understood (l.76) and his apology (l.78), however, are practical approaches that repair the breakdown. The change in mood then moves the conversation away from comfortable topics (music, holidays, beer, old schoolfriends) to the difficult issues surrounding *That extraordinary day* (ll.78–9) and its ongoing impact on their lives. It is the point at which we begin to recognise the dramatic connection between events in the past, the atmospheric sound effects (ll.55–6,70,72–3,75) and the three lines of dialogue linked to Leo and John as boys (ll.57,71,74). The fact that these utterances are all exclamatives or imperatives increases the tension.

A change in the style mirrors the change in mood. The staccato effect of the minor sentences (ll.85–7, 92–4) reflects the men's strong emotional response even after 37 years:

> S   P   A   P   O
> (They) (should've come) (shouldn't they). ø (For kids). ø (Shouldn't have turned) (you)
>   tag question
>   A   A   A
> (away like that). ø (Not when there's kids). ø (Not without helping).   (ll.85–7)
>   SCl–ACl   SCl–NFCl

The mood is intensified by the use of ellipses (…, ll.89,91); by tag questions (ll.82, 86,88), which suggest Leo and John's uncertainty and their need to understand; and by repetition of the informal noun *kids* (ll.85–7), which emphasises their vulnerability.

The dialogue clearly conforms to our linguistic expectations. Scripted dialogue differs from everyday conversation in that it lacks the normal non-fluency features: here there is no evidence of false starts or voiced hesitations, and only one example of an overlap. This reflects the very ordered nature of a drama – the playwright has a fixed time-slot in which to introduce characters, create a sense of context, and develop and resolve a plot. The effect is therefore stylised.

In a real city-centre bar, **interaction** would probably be far less orderly, with more evidence of other customers in the background, more frequent overlaps, and noticeable interruptions in the conversation. In order to make communication clear for listeners and viewers, however, radio and television dramas structure speech acts so that latching is smooth and the meaning of utterances is not lost. Although there may be background noise, such as music (ll. 12–13) or laughter (ll. 38, 81), meaningful utterances that further the development of the narrative are always clear. This does not accurately mimic the linguistic features of spontaneous informal conversation, and underlines the fact that drama is basically an orderly written form of spoken language.

The transmission script has been written to be **read aloud**. Actors animate the words, drawing attention to the meaning of the written text with their use of prosodic features. Changes in volume, pitch, pace and intonation bring characters and events to life. In places, the written script attempts to mirror pronunciation by using non-standard spelling such as lengthened words (*onnn*, l. 18; *Leeoo*, l. 57; *Johhhnnn*, l. 71) and the contraction of *P'raps* (l. 66) which inserts a linking /r/ at the boundary of the two syllables:

/pə'hæps/ → /præps/

Most of the variations are introduced as individual actors develop their particular roles according to the geographical, social or historical context. Accents reflect local pronunciations and idiosyncratic features make characters distinctive in a way that the words on the page cannot. This is particularly important in radio drama because we have no visual clues to rely on – as we see in this extract from *Once a Friend*, sound effects and the voices of the actors must build our sense of character, time and place, developing a narrative and engaging the audience in the fictional world of the play.

ACTIVITY 18.4

The following transcript is an extract from the ITV soap *Coronation Street*, from the episode broadcast on 2 April 2007. It records a sequence of scenes that begins with the sentencing of Tracy Barlow for the murder of her partner, Charlie Stubbs.

Read the transcript and jot down notes on the following:

1 the relationship between the speakers
2 the way in which the speakers interact
3 the prosodic features
4 the difference between a transmission script and a transcription.

A key to the symbols can be found on page 93. The participants are listed below:

- Judge Alderman (JA)
- Tracy Barlow (TB), a young mother who has killed her partner
- Deirdre (DB) and Ken Barlow (KB), Tracy's mother and stepfather
- Claire (CP) and Ashley Peacock (AP), Tracy's neighbours
- David Platt (DP), a troubled teenager
- Emily Bishop (EB), an old friend of the Barlow family
- Blanche Hunt (BH), Tracy's grandmother
- Adam (AB) and Peter Barlow (PB), Ken Barlow's grandson and son

- Liz McDonald (LM), a friend of the Barlow family
- Steve McDonald (SM), the father of Tracy's child Amy
- Wiki Dankowska (WD), a Polish worker
- Sean Tully (ST), Hayley Cropper (HC), Janice Battersby (JB) and Joanne Jackson (JJ), workers at the local factory
- Betty Williams (BW), a long-serving barmaid at the *Rovers Return* pub
- Jerry Morton (JeM) and his daughter Jodi Morton (JoM), who run the local take-away
- Kevin Webster (KW), a local car mechanic.

Transcript from an episode of *Coronation Street*, written by Joe Turner and directed by Neil Alderton.

1			INTERNAL: COURT ROOM
	'leg'	JA	Tracy Barlow (2) 'you have been found guilty of murder for which there is a mandatory sentence of life imprisonment' =
		DB	= ↓óh↓ Tràcy =
5	'leg'	JA	= 'I've heard submissions from defence and prosecution and I am recommending that you serve a minimum term of fifteen years in prison before you will be eligible for parole' =
		TB	= ↑no↑ =
		JA	= take her down please =
10	'accel'	TB	= ↑no no I have a child 'I was protecting my child' what's the matter
	'cresc'		with you 'why can't you see that' =
	'cresc'	CP	= ↑it's not fair↑ =
		TB	= ↑he's the one that was the monster not me he '<u>terrorised</u> me he <u>attacked</u> me'↑ =
15		DP	= you're all <u>mad</u> =
		JA	= order =
'accel'/'cresc'		TB	= ↑'I was defending myself' I was 'defending my child' please help↑ (4)
		DB	[*crying*] =
		TB	= ↑no no I have a <u>child</u>↑ (2)
20			INTERNAL: ROVERS RETURN
		WD	but what did I do <u>wróng</u> =
		ST	= oh nothing <u>listen</u> Janice Battersby could cause an argument in an <u>empty</u> hòuse =
		HC	= I think that's right Betty =
25		BW	= oh thánks love =
		HC	= you come and <u>join</u> us =
		JB	= ↓<u>no</u> tà↓ =
		HC	= Jó =
		JJ	= I'm alright <u>hère</u> =
30		HC	= she's (.) really nice (.) and funny once you get to know 'er you know =
		JB	= she'll have us ↑áll↑ out of a <u>jòb</u> in tíme Hàyley yóu mark my wòrds (3) look at her (1) nosey cow [*pulls face*] =
		JJ	= [*laughs*] (2)
35			EXTERNAL: OUTSIDE COURT
	'dimin'	EB	'I don't suppose you could give me (.) a líft <u>home</u>' =

		AP	= we'll get a <u>cab</u> you can come with us =
		EB	= thank you (1)
40	'forte'	BH	what's wrong with them are they <u>stupid</u> I bet most of them <u>never</u> <u>made</u> it <u>through</u> <u>school</u> 'what kind of a <u>system</u> <u>trusts</u> <u>justice</u> to that <u>shower</u> of rèprobates' =
		AB	= gran cóme òn =
		PB	= look can you take er Blánche I'd better go er with dàd and Deirdre =
		AB	= alright (2)
45	'accel'	CP	it's not right (.) there must have been a <u>mistake</u> 'we can appéal we'll start a cámpaign' (2) Déirdre =
		KB	= I think we should get hòme =
	'dimin'	AP	= 'cóme àway' =
		CP	= ↑whát↑ =
50		AP	= just give 'em a bit of space hey =
		CP	= I just <u>can't</u> believe it I <u>really</u> <u>cán't</u> (2)
	'rall'	BH	can't we <u>go</u> and <u>see</u> her can't we 'at least <u>say</u> gôodbye' =
		AB	= it's going to be fìne c'mon (4)
		LM	ohh [*sigh*] what can you say (1) I feel for hèr (.) I really <u>do</u> (2) right
55			where've you put the cár =
		SM	= round the bàck =
		LM	= rìght (2)
		DB	it's all my <u>fault</u> [*crying*] =
		KB	= <u>you</u> didn't kill Charlie Stubbs =
60		DB	= I've just <u>sent</u> my <u>daughter</u> to <u>prison</u> [*crying*] =
	'dimin'	KB	= 'let's go home hey' (5)

INTERNAL: TAKE-AWAY

		JoM	that's one twenty please mate =
		KW	= cheers =
65		JeM	= no not <u>todày</u> (.) on the hóuse (.) <u>Kevin</u> isn't ìt (.) from the gàrage =
		KW	= uh yeah what's going ón =
		JeM	= well you missed our grand ópening so you missed out on a <u>compli-</u><u>mentary</u> kebáb and I <u>hate</u> to think of anybody missing <u>out</u> =
		KW	= alright cheers =
70		JeM	= so you know about cárs =
		KW	= oh I hope so =
		JeM	= yeah I've got some mates in the <u>trade</u> =
		KW	= oh yéah =
		JeM	= but I like to stay <u>local</u> you know make new <u>contacts</u> you see my
75	'accel'		mates 'always make sure I get a good <u>deal</u>' =
		KW	= what you after =
		JeM	= I'm looking for a car =
		KW	= oh yéah =
	'accel'	JeM	= yeah you know relìable, econòmical, sáfe 'the sort of car you might
80	'dimin'		want to buy for an eighteenth birthday prèsent' (.) 'sort of car you want to buy for one of your own kids' =
		KW	= how much we looking at =
		JeM	= eh (.) let's go and have a chát Kev

The transcript records a sequence of scenes in which characters interact in different **contexts**. The formal court scene is defined by the official and ritualistic nature of legal language and the gravity of the sentencing process. The lexical set of legal terms (*guilty*, l. 2; *mandatory sentence, life imprisonment*, l. 3; *defence and pros-ecution*, l. 5; *minimum term*, l. 6; *parole*, l. 7; *take her down*, l. 9) and the detached, unemotional tone of the judge dominate the opening scene of this extract. This ensures that the **relationship** between participants is formal: where informal inter-ruptions (ll. 12, 15) and Tracy Barlow's emotional outbursts (ll. 10–11, 13–14, 17–19) disrupt the formality of the court, the judge calls for order (l. 16). The naming of participants reinforces the formality of the relationship between the judge and defendant: Tracy's mother uses her first name (l. 4), but Judge Alderman uses her full name (l. 2).

The formality of the courtroom scene is juxtaposed with the informality of the local pub and the take-away. In these contexts, the language and tone are conversa-tional, reflecting the familiar **relationships** of people who are known to each other. Social tokens (*thanks*, l. 25; *ta*, l. 27; *cheers*, ll. 64, 69), informal contractions (*that's*, ll. 24, 63; *'er*, l. 30; *what's*, l. 66), high-frequency clauses (*you know*, l. 74) and col-loquial pronunciations (*yeah*, ll. 66, 72, 73, 78) are common. The use of first names (*Betty*, l. 24; *Jo*, l. 28; *Hayley*, l. 32; *Kevin*, l. 65), abbreviated names (*Kev*, l. 83) and familiar direct terms of address (*love*, l. 25; *mate*, l. 63) reinforces the informality of the exchanges. The use of Janice Battersby's full name (l. 22), on the other hand, is dismissive: it reflects the tone of criticism implied by the collocation *could cause an argument in an empty house* (ll. 22–3).

The scene that takes place outside the court falls between these two extremes: the relationship between the participants is informal, but the context is still for-mal and the tone is sombre. The language moves between formal abstract nouns (*system, justice*, l. 40; *mistake, appeal*, l. 45; *campaign*, l. 46) and informal conver-sational features such as contractions (*'em*, l. 50; *c'mon*, l. 53; *where've*, l. 55), minor sentences (ll. 44, 56) and informal sentence connectors (*look*, l. 43). Where a full name is used (l. 59), the tone is disparaging – the reference to the murder victim *Charlie Stubbs* emphasises his exclusion from the community. Although the jury has not accepted Tracy Barlow's claim of self-defence in a context of domestic violence, none of the characters have any sympathy for the dead man, who had a reputation as a violent bully and a relentless liar.

The **topics** of conversation in the formal and informal contexts are quite dif-ferent. The verdict and sentence inevitably dominate the court-based scenes, but in the local pub and take-away the conversation focuses on topics that are directly relevant to the participants. In the pub, the focus is on the social conflict created by the arrival of Polish workers in the fictional community of Weatherfield; in the take-away, the conversation revolves around an introduction and buying a car. The formality of the judge's professional role in the courtroom is in direct contrast to the informality of the practical expertise offered by Kevin Webster.

The **turn-taking** in this extract is very ordered: turns are rarely long and speakers latch on smoothly. This is typical of a scripted conversation which elimi-nates the untidy nature of spontaneous conversation. Most turns are similar in length because of the equal status of the participants, but the longer turns fulfil a specific purpose within the development of the narrative: the judge delivers the formal ritualistic sentence (ll. 2–3, 5–7); Tracy's grandmother questions the nature of justice (ll. 39–41); and Jerry Morton defines the kind of car he wishes to buy (ll. 79–81). The structure of the judge's utterances reflects the formality of her role:

> S   P   O   S   P
> (I) ('ve heard) (submissions from defence and prosection) (and) (I) (am recommending)
>   conj
>   O   A
> (that you serve a minimum term of 15 years in prison) (before you will be eligible for
>   SCl–NCl   SCl–ACl
> parole)   (ll. 5–7)

The grammatically standard structure of this compound-complex sentence is quite unlike the loose structure and grammatically incomplete utterances of Jerry Morton:

>   C   O
> (yeah) (you know) ø (reliable economical safe) ø (the sort of car you might want to buy
>   comment clause   SCl–RelCl   SCl–NFCl
>   O
> for an eighteenth birthday present) ø (sort of car you want to buy for one of your own
>   SCl–RelCl   SCl–NFCl
> kids)   (ll. 79–81)

The different style in each case reflects the character of the speaker and her or his audience, purpose and context.

Because the interactions are co-operative, adjacency pairs are usually complete (ll. 21/22, 43/44, 55/56, 66/67, 70/71) unless the questions are rhetorical (ll. 39–40, 54). The one incomplete adjacency pair (l. 52) reflects the difficulty of the situation for the family of Tracy Barlow: Adam Barlow cannot answer Blanche Hunt's question without increasing the emotional strain of the moment. His response, although it fails to complete the adjacency pair, aims to ease the tension by providing reassurance.

Unlike real informal conversation, there are no examples of speaker turns overlapping. The turns latch smoothly onto the end of the previous speaker's words. At the end of some turns, however, there is a pause. These pauses indicate either a change of location (ll. 19, 34, 61) or a change in the camera shot from one group of characters to another (ll. 38, 44, 51, 53, 57). Where a radio script will often develop longer turns which allow listeners time to identify voices, a television script can move quickly from group to group because we have visual as well as aural clues. In the 3½ minutes' transmission time for these four scenes, the viewers see twenty-two different characters in four different contexts.

The **prosodic features** quite closely resemble those found in informal spoken language. Changes in intonation mark questions (ll. 21, 43, 70); the grammatical end of utterances (ll. 23, 47, 54); and add emphasis to key words (ll. 36, 45, 79). Stress is used to draw attention to lexical items that are important semantically: *terrorised, attacked* (ll. 13–14); *what kind of a system trusts justice to that shower of reprobates* (ll. 40–1); *local* (l. 74).

The raised pitch in the courtroom scene reflects Tracy Barlow's emotional state, as do the increased pace (ll. 10, 17) and volume (ll. 10, 13, 17) of her utterances. These changes intensify the dramatic atmosphere of the scene and are in direct contrast to the polished, smooth, objective delivery of Judge Alderman's extended turns. Similar variations mark the utterances delivered outside the court as the characters are all responding emotionally to the sentence that has just been passed. The informal scenes, on the other hand, are marked by few distinctive prosodic changes – the conversations aim to imitate the insignificance of everyday spoken acts.

Normal non-fluency features appear in all kinds of spoken language: few speakers can sustain a turn without hesitation of some kind. In this transcription, however, there are very few examples. Although there are some voiced hesitations (ll. 43, 66, 83), there is no evidence of repetitions, incomplete words or pauses in unexpected places. This fluency and polish reminds us that this is not real conversation but something that has been first scripted and then spoken aloud.

While a **transmission script** records the written text and the scene cuts, a **transcription** aims to record the way in which the words are delivered. It adds extra information to show how a written script is made into a meaningful spoken interaction. The prosodic features demonstrate the different ways in which individual actors interpret their roles and communicate with their audience. Their personal interpretation of the written word makes the interaction seem more real.

Children's television

Children's television was first broadcast in the 1940s. Initially just one 25-minute programme went out on a Sunday, but within two years an hour a week of broadcasting time was dedicated to children. By 1954, this had grown to an hour a day, consisting of stories and songs for young children (*Watch With Mother*), magazine programmes (*Studio E; Blue Peter*), live dramatisations of classic novels (*The Railway Children; The Secret Garden*) and serialisations (*The Adventures of Robin Hood*). By the late 1960s, children's television had been recognised as a significant part of the broadcasting timetable, even though it was catering for a small percentage of the total audience. As a result of this, the range of programmes designed for children was extended: the addition of news, quizzes, travel programmes, cartoons and Saturday morning entertainment meant that by the 1970s the schedule for children had become a small-scale version of the adult service.

With the addition of satellite and cable channels from the late 1980s and Freeview digital broadcasts by ITV and BBC in the early twenty-first century, broadcasting for children has become very widely available. There are now hours of programmes each day on the BBC and all-day services on a dozen satellite channels.

While the BBC has developed two parallel services for children, on its principal channels (BBC1 and BBC2) and on its additional digital channels (CBeebies and CBBC), ITV has dropped its terrestrial programming except at the weekend (Saturday 6.00–11.30 a.m. and Sunday 7.25–11.00 a.m.), focusing instead on broadcasting on CITV Freeview. Five has also announced cuts in spending on broadcasting for children. These decisions have raised concerns about reduced investment in public service children's television. It is thought that recently imposed restrictions on food advertising when young children are watching television may have affected the income of commercial channels, and that in consequence there may be less money available for the production of children's programmes.

Despite this, television and radio broadcasting schedules in the twenty-first century contain a variety of programmes for children. Children's digital channels are broadcast for much of the day: 6.00 a.m.–7.00 p.m. (CBeebies, CBBC); 6.00 a.m.–6.00 p.m. (CITV); 6.00 am–12.00 midnight (Disney, Disney Cinemagic); and 6.00 a.m.–11.00 p.m. (Nickelodeon). Television programmes for children on other channels tend not to appear at peak transmission times but at certain points during the day, such as in the late afternoon (3.30–5.30 p.m.) and early in the morning at the weekend. Radio broadcasts specifically aimed at children are less wide-ranging, with *Go For It* (BBC Radio 4) on Sunday evening at 7.15 p.m. for 30 minutes, *Big Toe Books* (BBC 7) daily at 7.00 a.m. for an hour, and CBeebies (BBC 7) at 2.00 p.m. daily for three hours.

There are five main types of programme which are specifically aimed at a target audience dominated by children.

Programmes for pre-school children

CBeebies broadcasts programmes for a pre-school audience, including *Teletubbies* for babies, *Fimbles* for toddlers, *Tweenies* and *Tikkabilla* for reception-age children. It aims to combine games, stories, songs and activities that will entertain them and provide the foundation for later formal schooling. The programmes and their acompanying websites are designed to correspond to national targets set by the Government (Sure Start for 0–3-year-olds; Early Learning goals for 3–5-year-olds). As well as basic numeracy and literacy skills, the programmes encourage the development of personal, social and emotional skills.

The language used is appropriate for the target audience and the content is directly linked to the children's own experience of the world. The emphasis is on joining in, through songs, movement, creative activities and imaginative role-play.

Schools television

Schools programmes are designed for clearly defined target audiences: infants (5–7-year-olds), juniors (7–11-year-olds) and secondary (11–16-year-olds). This allows the content of the programme and the method of delivery to be appropriate for each specific age group. Titles are explicit, indicating the nature of the subject matter: *Pathways of Belief* (religious and spiritual education); *BBC Primary History*; *BBC Primary Geography*; *English Express*; *Look and Read*. While the main broadcasting takes place between 10.30 a.m. and 12.00 noon during school hours, the BBC's *GCSE Bitesize* programmes are broadcast in the early hours of the morning (2.00–6.00 a.m.) for recording. These programmes are designed to support students studying for specific examination syllabuses, and the BBC's 'Schools' website (www.bbc.co.uk/schools) provides additional help with advice on revision, subject-based information and interactive activities.

The language and content reflect the target audience: for primary-school children, the tone is often personal and familiar; for older students it is more detached. Programmes for the younger audience aim to engage them by creating a direct relationship. This may be achieved by using a lively and personable presenter, by dramatising the information, or by using comedy. GCSE programmes, on the other hand, aim to present information in a formal manner: the language is subject-specific and the tone formal – there is a presenter, but his or her role is to make the material accessible rather than to create a personal relationship. Subject-based information, methodology and examples help the target audience to understand. Captions, written examples and working may be shown on screen.

Information or magazine programmes

Programmes such as *Blue Peter* (first shown in 1958) and *Newsround* (first shown in 1972) provide information in a format that is appropriate for children. By changing the presenters and adapting the programme to take account of social trends and technological developments, the programmes have been able to capture the interest of children on a long-term basis.

In the twenty-first century, programmes aim to appeal to a wide-ranging audience by choosing presenters with a variety of regional accents. Although the language is formal, the tone is familiar. Close-up camera shots develop this personal approach because the presenters seem to be speaking directly to their audience.

While *Newsround* deals with topical stories, its focus tends to be on issues that have direct relevance for children. Its treatment of sensitive news always takes into account its target audience. On-screen captions highlight key points for reinforcement, and the linked website (www.bbc.co.uk/cbbcnews) encourages children to follow developments, to get involved by contributing to the blog or reviewing films and books, and to explore key topics (the world, sport, animals, science and technology, and music).

Blue Peter covers a broad range of subjects. Experts are invited to the studio to talk about their specialism, and presenters participate in cultural, sporting and career-based activities. Competitions encourage active engagement from the target audience; the linked website (www.bbc.co.uk/cbbc/bluepeter) provides additional information, live webchats with the presenters and guests, access to the book club, a 'Things to do' section and interactive games.

Serialisations

Dramatisations of novels and 'soaps' form the basis for storytelling on children's television, along with the return of *Jackanory*, which originally appeared between 1965 and 1996. The language and tone of such programmes is varied – they aim to engage the viewers through a direct appeal to their imagination and emotions.

While classic serials (*The Secret Garden*; *The Borrowers*) used to form the main body of children's drama, more recent productions have been based on modern stories that deal with topical issues (*Tracy Beaker*; *Featherboy*) or that mix realism and fantasy (*The Queen's Nose*; *Johnny and the Bomb*; *Maddigan's Quest*). Such dramatisations encourage reading, as children often search out the novels on which the programmes were based.

Soaps like *Byker Grove* and *Grange Hill* have brought a harder realism to children's television, dealing with topics such as teenage pregnancy, bullying, rape, heroin addiction, and attempted suicide. The recognisable characters and hard-hitting storylines engage viewers, who identify with the fictional world that is being portrayed.

Animations

Animations form a large proportion of the output for children's television, many having been imported from America. Some use stop-motion techniques that require the animator to physically readjust the scene between shots (*Shaun the Sheep*; *Roary the Racing Car*); some use traditional two-dimensional graphics that are hand-drawn and then scanned into a computer (*Pokemon*; *Horrid Henry*; *The Simpsons*); and others use computer graphics (*Bratz*).

The language used is often subordinate to the images shown, particularly in programmes targeted at a younger audience. Actors provide voice-overs for the characters, and it is their interpretation of a script that helps to create a sense of individuality. Catchphrases (such as Homer Simpson's *Doh*) and recurring character traits (Wallace's fascination with inventing machines in *Wallace and Gromit*) ensure that viewers quickly build up a familiarity with each individual. These animated characters are often directly linked to merchandise (*Thomas the Tank Engine*; *Teenage Mutant Ninja Turtles*). Each storyline is completed within a single episode.

ACTIVITY 18.5

The following extracts have been taken from the magazine programme *Blue Peter* (28 February 2007) and the pre-school *Teletubbies* (6 May 2007). Read through the two extracts and consider the ways in which language and image are used together to entertain and educate the target audience.

You may like to think about:

1 the register
2 the content and its organisation
3 the language
4 the grammatical structure
5 the link between the visual and the aural.

KEY

V/O	images with voice overlaid	CU	close-up
SYNC	spoken direct to camera	DR	dramatic reconstruction
LS	long-range shot	(.)	micro-pause
MS	medium-range shot	(1)	timed pause

EXTRACT 1: *BLUE PETER*

1 LS outside Edinburgh
   Medical School (EMS)

   MS GJ outside EMS   V/O GETHIN JONES (GJ)
                                Edinburgh's famous medical school is in the heart of the city.
5   It's a solid, respectable place. (1) But, if only walls could talk.

	CU inside EMS	
	MS GJ inside EMS	SYNC GETHIN JONES Back in 1828 a scandal took place here which brought terror to the city and rocked the medical world. (3)
10	MS GJ in the lecture theatre	This is one of the lecture theatres where the students are taught. Part of their training involves cutting open dead bodies – the best way for them to learn about the human body. (6)
15	CU painting of dissection; model of chest cavity	[atmospheric music]
	MS GJ in EMS Anatomical Museum	SYNC GETHIN JONES Today, the bodies used by students are donated by people after they die, but back in the 1820s, when there was a desperate need to discover more about how the body works,
20		the only corpses available came from executed criminals. (2)
	CU skeleton; preserved brain; skull	V/O GETHIN JONES As that meant a limited supply, a horrendous new trade began here in Edinburgh. Body-snatching. (2)
25	MS graveyard (night) Dramatic reconstruction (DR)	Under the cover of darkness men would break into graveyards across the town and dig up dead bodies. As there was no law against stealing them it happened more and more often. It became such a problem that patrols were set up and
	MS watch tower next to graveyard	some graveyards even had watch towers built next to them. (1)
30	MS/CU GJ in streets (night)	SYNC GETHIN JONES So body-snatching became riskier and fewer people attempted it, but this only pushed up the price of bodies even further so now there was serious money to be made. (2)
35	CU two men; DR	V/O GETHIN JONES Two men called Burke and Hare fell into the grisly trade almost by accident. (1)
	CU GJ in streets (night)	SYNC GETHIN JONES Hare owned a lodging house. One of his tenants died owing him £4 which was a lot of money back then. (1)
40	MS graveyard; DR CU picture of Knox	V/O GETHIN JONES Hare decided to get his money back by selling the tenant's body to Doctor Knox who was in charge of the Medical School. (1)
45	CU hands exchanging money; DR	Knox paid £10. (2) Together with his friend Burke, Hare had found a willing buyer. Now they decided to supply more dead bodies and murder was easier than grave robbing. The pair selected their victims from the poorest people in Edinburgh – often homeless and with no-one to care if they disappeared. They would befriend
50		them, get them drunk and then murder them in the dead of night. (2) [Screams]
	MS GJ in graveyard (night)	SYNC GETHIN JONES For a nightmare year, Burke and Hare kept to their hideous
55		trade and throughout Edinburgh fear and suspicion grew to whispers. Whispers grew to rhymes.
	LS graveyard; DR	V/O REPEATED WHISPERED Burke's the butcher,
60		Hare's the thief, Knox is the boy who buys the beef.

```
 1  LS Teletubby land
    MS Tinky Winky (TW)          TINKY WINKY
                                 Eh-oh.

                                 V/O NARRATOR
 5                               One day in Teletubby Land Tinky Winky stood on one leg.
    CU TW's feet; MS TW          TINKY WINKY
                                 Stand on one leg. (10)
    CU flowers                   FLOWERS
                                 Do be careful! Mind you don't fall. Be careful. (3)
10  MS TW                        TINKY WINKY
                                 [laughs]
    CU flowers                   FLOWERS
                                 Nearly. Nearly did it. Nearly. Nearly did it.
    MS TW; CU feet; MS TW        TINKY WINKY
15                               Again. Again. (8)
    CU flowers                   FLOWERS
                                 Oh look! Oh! Very clever!
    MS TW                        V/O NARRATOR
                                 Very graceful. (3)
20  CU flowers                   FLOWERS
                                 Very well done! Very graceful! Very graceful!
    MS TW; CU TW                 TINKY WINKY
                                 Very graceful. (2) Very graceful. (6) [falls over] Oh dear!
                                 [laughs]

25                               *  *  *

    LS Teletubby Land
    MS Po (P); CU P              PO
                                 Eh-oh.
    MS P on scooter              V/O NARRATOR
30                               One day in Teletubby Land Po stood on one leg.
    CU P's feet; MS P; CU feet   PO
                                 Oh! Stood on one leg. [laughs] (3) Ooh. Uh-oh. [laughs] (11)
    CU flowers                   FLOWERS
                                 Oh look! Oh look at that! Yes, how clever. (6)
35  MS P                         V/O NARRATOR
                                 Very graceful!
    CU flowers                   FLOWERS
                                 Well done! Oh it's very graceful. Very graceful. Excellent.
    MS P; CU P                   PO
40                               Very graceful! Oh. Oh. Uh-oh! Oh. [laughs] Oh dear (8).
                                 SUN (6)

    LS Teletubby Land
    MS all Teletubbies           TINKY WINKY/DIPSY/LA-LA/PO
                                 Eh-oh.
45                               V/O NARRATOR
                                 One day in Teletubby Land all the Teletubbies stood on one
                                 leg together.
    MS all Teletubbies; CU of feet  TINKY WINKY/DIPSY/LA-LA/PO
                                 All together. One leg. Stand together. [laughter] (10) Uh-oh.
50                               (13)
```

CU flowers	**FLOWERS** Oh look! Look. They've done it. Well done. Oh they did it all together.
MS P on scooter	Oh (4) [*Po rolls down hill on scooter*]
55 CU flowers	**FLOWERS** Oh my goodness! Oh! I can hardly look!
MS P on scooter	**PO** Hurry! Hurry! Hurry! Hurry!
MS P on scooter; Teletubby 60 house	**V/O NARRATOR** What a very graceful way to ride a scooter! (6)
MS/CU other Teletubbies	**TINKY WINKY/DIPSY/LA-LA** Oh very graceful! Oh! Very graceful! Yes. [*laughter*] (4) Very graceful. [*laughter*]
MS Teletubby house 65	**V/O TELETUBBIES** Hug! Hug! Big hug!

COMMENTARY

The **register** of each extract is directly related to the target audience: 6–12-year-olds for *Blue Peter*; pre-school children, many of whom are only just acquiring language, for the *Teletubbies*. Both programmes are shown at times when children will be watching (5.00–5.25 p.m. Tuesday to Thursday for *Blue Peter*; 6.00–6.30 a.m. and 12.00–12.30 midday on Saturday and Sunday for the *Teletubbies*). They combine entertainment and education in a way that is appropriate for the targeted age group.

The dominant **mode** in each case is written since the words are delivered from a script, but both use features of informal spoken language to engage the audience – non-standard sentence structures, for instance, are common. The **manner** mixes the formality of public broadcasting with the familiarity of speaking to a 'known' audience. The personable nature of the presenter in the *Blue Peter* extract suggests that he is chatting with friends rather than delivering a formal lesson on the body-snatching trade in Edinburgh in the 1820s. The juxtaposition of image and spoken word and the use of exophoric references (*here*, ll. 8, 23; *This*, l. 10) that draw us into the scene enhance this. Similarly, the social greetings in the *Teletubbies* extract (ll. 3, 28, 44) help to create a bond between programme and viewer – particularly since the broadcast is dominated by long pauses in which children have time to respond or imitate the words and actions.

The **content** is dictated by the nature of the target audience. Where *Blue Peter* deals with a topic of historical interest, the *Teletubbies* focus on a physical action – balancing on one foot. Each programme aims to educate its target audience, but the methods are very different. The 6–12-year-old viewers are able to listen to large amounts of speech, processing the information as they watch the accompanying images. Subject-specific language (*medical school*, l. 4; *students*, ll. 10, 17 *bodies*, ll. 12, 17, 25, 46; *graveyards*, ll. 25, 28; *trade*, ll. 35, 55) clearly establishes the field and the repeated rhyme (ll. 58–60) brings the first half of the feature to a climax. The *Teletubbies* programme, on the other hand, relies on the repetition of a single action so that young viewers begin to recognise and anticipate the pattern.

Both extracts use narrative as a means of making information more approachable: *Blue Peter* recounts the 'story' of Hare and Burke's activities along with the atmospheric footage of a dramatic reconstruction; *Teletubbies* creates a narrative framework in which the traditional elements of time (*One day*), place (*in Teletubby Land*) and character (*Tinky Winky ... Po ... all the Teletubbies*) engage the viewers in a magical world where the Teletubbies do things that the target audience will recognise (*stood on one leg*, l. 5).

The **organisation** of the content also reflects the age of the viewers. *Blue Peter* establishes the context of its feature on body-snatching by filming its presenter in the Edinburgh School of Medicine, the centre of the story it is about to tell. The juxtaposition of the current references to medical students and the *scandal* (l. 8) of the past engage the audience immediately: the adverbials *Today* (l. 17) and *back in the 1820s* (l. 18) highlight the contrast. The use of atmospheric images and the dramatic reconstruction of events described by the presenter brings history to life. The extract ends with the repetition of a children's rhyme: a piece of local history recalling the effect of Burke and Hare's activities on the inhabitants of Edinburgh.

Where the *Blue Peter* extract adds additional new information throughout its 3-minute broadcast, the *Teletubbies* programme reworks the same basic structure three times. The opening Tinky Winky narrative takes 1 minute and 10 seconds. The structure is then repeated for Po and all the Teletubbies together (the total running time of the extract is just over 3½ minutes). The broadcast aims to educate through reinforcement – in each segment, the narrator introduces the character or characters: they try to stand on one leg; the flowers provide a commentary, which is reinforced by a comment from the narrator. In the full 6-minute feature, the framework is also repeated for the other Teletubbies, Dipsy and La-La. Reiteration of the content in this way encourages children to join in as they begin to recognise the pattern. It also allows the introduction and reinforcement of a word (*graceful*) which may be unfamiliar to the young viewers.

As would be expected, the **language** in each extract reflects the target audience: the linguistic range and variety of the *Blue Peter* feature are in direct contrast to the repetition and limited language of the *Teletubbies*. While their purposes are similar – to educate and entertain – the age of the audience affects the kind of information presented and the language used to convey it.

The *Blue Peter* script balances objective neutral language (*lecture theatres*, l. 10; *training*, l. 11; *discover*, l. 19; *corpses*, l. 20) with emotive words that enhance the drama of the tale. The juxtaposition of the positive modifiers *famous*, *solid* and *respectable* (ll. 4–5) with the sensational abstract nouns *scandal* and *terror* (l. 8) and the colloquial verb *rocked* (l. 9) prepares us for a story that will challenge our expectations. Emotive modifiers such as *horrendous* (l. 22), *grisly* (l. 35) *nightmare* and *hideous* (l. 54) and the connotations of nouns such as *Body-snatching* (ll. 23, 31), *graveyards* (ll. 25, 28), *murder* (l. 46) and *grave robbing* (l. 47) engage the viewers directly in the horror of this historical sequence of events. It is an approach that will be familiar to readers of the *Horrible Histories* series, where traditional versions of history are accompanied by the 'nasty bits' that are usually left out. A lexical set of words and phrases related to finance emphasises the business-like nature of the enterprise: *money* (ll. 33, 39, 41), *trade* (ll. 35, 55), *selling* (l. 41), *paid* (l. 44), *buyer* (l. 45). In the context, these apparently neutral terms become representative of the detached way in which Burke and Hare went about their business.

The pre-school programme deals with a very different scenario in language that will be familiar to the viewers. Repetition is a dominant feature and many words are monosyllabic. The programme has been criticised for failing to extend the language use of the target audience – some people believe that the 'baby-talk' used by the Teletubbies (reflected here in the social greeting *Eh-oh* and the exclamative *Uh-oh*) fails to develop the language skills of viewers. Linguistically, however, the familiarity of the Teletubbies' immature speech can be seen as a point of engagement for young children, who respond to the colourful bodies, stylised faces and distinctive speech patterns of each character. In addition, formal language structures are provided by the narrator and the animated flowers. The relationship between the two levels of language mirrors what happens in the home: young children may not use formal patterns and pronunciations themselves, but they hear them used by the adults with whom they interact. For instance, the replacement of the irregular past tense *stood* with the simple present *stand* (l.7) and the omission of the first person subject pronouns 'I' and 'we' (ll. 7, 32, 49) is a common feature of child language.

Proper nouns linked to place (*Teletubby Land*, ll. 5, 30, 46) and character (*Tinky Winky*, l. 5; *Po*, l. 30) and catchphrases (*Eh-oh, Again. Again, Oh dear, Uh-oh, Big hug*) will be familiar to viewers as they appear in all episodes of the programme. Other language is directly related to the activity: the concrete noun *leg*, the verb *stood/stand* and the cardinal number *one* are repeated as each character tries to perform the task; adjectives such as *careful, clever, graceful* and *Excellent* are used to comment on their actions. The relationship between participants is positive – the narrator and the animated flowers provide the kind of encouragement and reassuring feedback that enhances learning.

The **grammar** of each extract is also very different. The *Teletubbies* script is dominated by short phrases, whereas the *Blue Peter* narrative tends to use longer phrases with pre- and post-modification.

m h	m h	m h	
One day (l. 5)	Very graceful. (l. 21)	Big hug. (l. 65)	*Teletubbies*
num N	Adv Adj	Adj N	

The only exception is the complex exclamative phrase used by the narrator:

m   m   h   q
What a (very graceful) way to ride a scooter! (l. 60)
pron det Adv   Adj   N   NFCl

Blue Peter, on the other hand, uses a wider range of phrases:

m m m h	m h q
Edinburgh's famous medical school (l. 4)	the bodies used by students (l. 17)
N Adj Adj N	det N RelCl

h q	
Doctor Knox who was in charge of the Medical School (ll. 42–3)	*Blue Peter*
N RelCl	

In line with this, the programme for younger viewers uses minor and simple sentences, while the grammatical structures of the programme for the older audience are more complex, consisting of complete formal grammatical units:

A   A   S   P   A   (S)   P   A

(One day) (in TL) (TW) (stood) (on one leg). (l. 5)   ø (Stand) (on one leg). (l. 7)

(S)   A   P   O   S   P   O   S P O   A

ø (Nearly) (did) (it). (l. 13)   (They) ('ve done) (it) … (they) (did) (it) (all together) (ll. 52–3)

There is no subordination in the *Teletubbies* extract, but the grammatical mood is often imperative (*Do be careful!* l. 9; *Oh look!* l. 17) or exclamative (*Very well done!* l. 21; *Oh my goodness!* l. 56), which is in keeping with the interactive nature of the programme.

The extract from *Blue Peter* uses a far wider range of sentence structures – the content is more detailed and the delivery more varied. The speech must communicate information in a clear and concise way; it must engage the viewers by creating a dramatic version of events. Simple sentences are used for emphatic statements, but the majority of sentences are complex or compound–complex:

S   P   A

(Edinburgh's famous medical school) (is) (in the heart of the city).   (SIMPLE: l. 4)

A   S   P   A   A

(Today) (the bodies used by students) (are donated) (by people) (after they die) (but)

             SCl–RelCl   SCl–ACl   conj

A

(back in the 1820s) (when there was a desperate need to discover more about how

             SCl–ACl   SCl–NFCl   SCl–NCl

             S   P   A

the body works) (the only corpses available) (came) (from executed criminals).

(COMPOUND–COMPLEX: ll. 17–20)

The five subordinate clauses carry additional information, and use of the passive voice (*are donated*) adds to the density of the sentence. Subordination is used often to communicate a lot of information in a restricted time-slot. Foregrounding is common because it allows the speaker to place emphasis on a particular piece of information (ll. 22, 25, 45) or the time (ll. 8, 17, 46), or to dramatise events (ll. 24, 54). The minor sentence *Body-snatching* (l. 23) and the initial-position conjunctions *But* (l. 5) and *[and] So* (l. 31) are used for dramatic effect.

In line with the target audience and the complexity of the subject matter, the extract from *Blue Peter* uses a wide range of grammatical structures. The mood is declarative: the presenter communicates information to his viewers and there is no interaction with the audience. The extract builds to a climax in the repetition of the haunting rhyme which is typical of playground songs. The rhythm is mainly trochaic (a strong–weak beat), throwing emphasis onto the names, and the lexis is dominated by monosyllabic words. The emotive language (*butcher*), the full rhyme (*thief/beef*) and the figurative use of *beef* for the murdered bodies together make a dramatic end to this section of the feature.

The link between the **visual and linguistic content** of each programme is directly related to the target audience and the subject matter. In the *Teletubbies*, the long shots of Teletubby Land place the event in a physical context; the medium and close-up shots of Tinky Winky, Po and the animated flowers help to develop a relationship between the viewers and the characters, enhancing the narrative elements of the programme; close-ups of the Teletubbies' feet as they try to balance on one leg focus attention on the activity and encourage children to try themselves. These shots underpin the educational elements of the programme. The visual therefore directly underpins the spoken – it develops an active rather than a passive relationship between the viewers and the programme.

Although the content and approach are more complex, the same principles govern the link between speech and image in *Blue Peter*. Long- and medium-range shots of the Edinburgh Medical School, one of its lecture theatres and its Anatomical Museum create a concrete physical background against which the history of Burke and Hare can be played out. They give an immediacy to the facts about body-snatching: viewers can see that this all took place in a setting where students still need corpses to learn about the human body. A lot of information is delivered in this 2 minute 50 second extract, and medium and close-up shots of Gethin Jones, a familiar presenter, help the target audience to engage with the facts. By alternating voice-overs and direct-to-camera pieces, the programme aims to maintain viewers' interest. Atmospheric night shots, emotive graveyard backdrops and a grainy quality in the filmed re-enactments create a sense that history is being brought to life. The drama of the images reinforces the drama of the story being told: viewers are engaged by the linguistic and visual elements, which together present history in a form that is both academic and approachable.

18.5 What to look for in the language of broadcasting

The following checklist can be used to identify key features in examples taken from different kinds of broadcasts. You will not find all of the features in every extract or transcript, but the list can be used as a guide. The points made are general, so discussion of specific examples will need to be adapted to take account of the specific programme, its context, purpose and target audience. Remember that you need to evaluate the effect of the features you identify, exploring the ways in which they create meaning.

The following are helpful questions to ask.

Programme type
1 Is the transmission on **television** or **radio**?
2 What kind of **programme** is it?
3 What is the **purpose** of the broadcast?
4 Who are the **intended audience**?
5 What **time** is the programme transmitted?
6 Is the **tone** serious, comic, or somewhere in between?

Register
1 What is the **mode**?
   + spoken?
   + written to be read aloud?
2 What is the **manner**?
   + the relationship between participants, and their relative status?
   + direct or indirect address?
   + formal or informal?
   + personal or impersonal?

3 What is the **field**?
  * subject matter?
  * linked to audience, purpose, context?

Structure

1 Is the programme part of an **ongoing series** with a running story, or a self-contained **one-off broadcast**?
2 How is the **opening** marked?
  * a formal greeting? a summary of the topic(s) to be considered? a general introduction?
  * distinctive intonation patterns?
3 How is the **closing** marked?
  * a summary? a formal closing phrase? a cliffhanger?
  * distinctive intonation patterns?
4 Is there anything distinctive about the **turn-taking**?
  * adjacency pairs? interruptions? overlaps? latchings? digressions?

Topic management

1 What is the **goal** of the programme?
  * to convey information?
  * to question?
  * to entertain?
2 Is the **topic range** broad or narrow?
3 Are there any **topic shifts**?
  * prosodic or lexical clues to mark the changes?
  * smooth changes?
4 How is the **end of a topic** marked?
  * stock phrases? fade-out? a cliffhanger? a summary?

Prosodic features

1 Do **intonation patterns** vary?
  * to reinforce the meaning of the words spoken?
  * to indicate different attitudes?
  * to mark grammatical structures?
  * to draw attention to grammatical boundaries?
2 Does the **pitch** change to reinforce speakers' attitudes and responses?
  * for emphasis?
  * for comic effect?
  * to express emotion?
3 Is **stress** used to draw attention to certain lexical items?
  * distinctive or unusual patterns?
4 Does the **volume** change significantly to enhance the meaning of utterances?
5 Does the **pace** change to draw attention to key parts of utterances?
6 How are **pauses** used?
  * emphasis? drama? hesitation? breathing? grammatical breaks?
7 Is the transcript or transmission script marked with any **vocal effects** or **para-linguistics**?
  * relationship to the words actually spoken?

* reflection of the speaker's mood?

Lexis

1 Is the language **formal** or **informal**?
  * subject-specific or general?
  * serious or comic?
2 Are there any examples of **high-frequency conversational clauses, colloquial idioms** or **collocations**?

Grammar

1 What is the **grammatical structure** of utterances?
  * simple? compound? complex? a mixture?
2 Are **loosely co-ordinated or subordinate clauses** more common?
3 Are there any **minor sentences**?
4 Are **phrases** complex or simple?
  * relationship to the topic and manner of the programme?
5 Are **different grammatical modes** used to add variety?
  * direct speech? reported speech?
  * changes in grammatical mood and voice?
6 Are there any **grammatically non-standard or incomplete utterances**?
  * ignored or commented on by participants?
7 Are there any **marked themes**?

Normal non-fluency features

1 Are there any **overlaps** in the speech turns?
  * frequency? length? cause?
  * intentional challenges? supportive minimal vocalisations? mishearing of linguistic clues?
  * participants' responses?
2 Are there any **voiced hesitations**?
  * to prevent interruptions? to prolong a turn? to allow thinking time?
3 Are there any **false starts** or **repetitions**?

Repairs

1 Has the **editing** produced a seamless, polished programme?
2 Are there any **repairs**?
  * self-correction? other corrections?
3 Are there any **topic loops**?
4 Are speakers aware of **listener responses**?
  * self-monitoring? direct address? questions? rephrasing or restating points?
5 Are there any **silences**?
  * lack of responses? failure to introduce a new topic? utterances misheard?

Summary

The language of broadcasting, whether live or pre-recorded, ultimately has more in common with spoken than written language because it is marked by prosodic features. Although it is primarily spoken rather than written, however, it is important to recognise the difference between spontaneous and scripted language. Scripted language is often written in such a way that it mimics many of the characteristics of speech; spontaneous commentaries, on the other hand, are automatically less formally organised and more random.

Accents and **dialects** vary according to the kind of programme, the participants and their regional and social backgrounds. Other variants will also affect the kind of language used: age, gender, occupational background and status; time of broadcast, target audience, and so on.

Having recognised the features that the language of broadcasting has in common with spoken language, it is important to identify characteristics dictated by the **genre**. Documentaries, dramas, comedies and news programmes, for instance, all have distinctive features that mark the overall structure, the topic management, and the lexical and grammatical choices.

Chapter 19

The language of humour

19.1 The nature of the language of humour

HUMOUR is the broad term used to describe situations, characters, speech, writing or images that amuse us. At a physical level, it is no more than an involuntary respiratory response to a stimulus – **laughter**. Although we can imitate this in social contexts where we feel an obligation to be polite, genuine laughter comes upon us spontaneously; it is beyond our control. It may be a motor response, but we seek out experiences that will result in laughter, and if we don't get the physical reaction, we don't feel that we have been amused.

Laughter is a central characteristic of human behaviour which allows us to signal that we are part of a group. Anthropologists believe that the first human laughter may have begun as a gesture of shared relief at the passing of danger – the moment at which the fight-or-flight response is replaced by relaxation. Laughter is, therefore, a SOCIAL SIGNAL. Psychologists see it as a physical response to our need to 'belong' to a group. It may help us in social interaction as it can mark a conscious connection with other people and an acceptance of a particular shared viewpoint.

Researchers now believe that the ability to laugh can also contribute to our physical and emotional well-being, reducing the levels of stress hormones, boosting our immune systems, lowering blood pressure, and providing a physical workout. Increasingly, mental health professionals are suggesting that because laughter is **cathartic**, 'laughter therapy' can help people to cope with difficult situations: it can allow us to release negative emotions (anger, sadness, fear) in a harmless way.

In this sense, we can understand the origin of the word 'humour'. It is directly linked to the Latin *humor* (moisture) and the Hippocratic tradition of the 'humours' or bodily fluids (blood, phlegm, yellow bile and black bile), the specific combination of which was thought to determine each person's nature. The writers of the Middle Ages and the Renaissance created characters whose personalities were dictated by a particular mix of humours which controlled their disposition, their mind, morality and temperament. Familiar sayings such as 'ill-humoured', 'good-humoured', 'green with envy' or 'in a black mood' all stem from this view of human physiology.

A sense of humour is very personal – because people laugh at different things, the language of humour can be quite diverse. Nevertheless, there are certain common elements. Humour is based on **everyday observations** – if we find something funny, it is because we recognise some kind of truth in the heightened and often exaggerated version of the human condition with which we are presented. The comedian Catherine Tate has described comedy as 'eight parts recognition, one part shock and one part exaggeration'. The **element of surprise**, of the unexpected, is often crucial to our appreciation of comedy, yet we can also find satisfaction in the fulfilment of our anticipation. In the 'Andy and Lou' sketches in *Little Britain*, for instance, we laugh at the ways in which the 'expected' is delivered to us. We know that Andy will change his mind about the video or holiday he has chosen; we know that he will get out of his wheelchair – the humour is in waiting for our expectations to be realised.

There must be **honesty** and **frankness** in the comedy: we must feel that writers or comedians are describing things as they see them, and we must feel some kind of empathy in their representation of the world. We may also laugh, however, when we are presented with a view of the world that is contrary to all decent values – our laughter is directed at the characters whose viewpoints are made to seem ridiculous. Borat Sagdiyev, 'Kazakhstan's sixth most famous man', creation of comedian Sacha Baron Cohen, is infamous for his inappropriate statements; *Little Britain's* Maggie, the Women's Institute member, vomits profusely in what can only be described as a homophobic and racist response to ordinary events; and Catherine Tate's bigoted provincial couple express their horror at examples of 'world cuisine' that have reached as far as Dudley. All these comic creations challenge **political correctness** by behaving in an inappropriate manner – because they are so blatantly distasteful, our laughter is tempered by an awareness that we would not like to display such behaviour ourselves. This is humour that shocks, forcing the audience to recognise the limitations of the characters that they are observing.

Universal values underpin all societies: we know how we should behave towards others and we know how we should respond in certain situations. In comedy, we laugh at foolish behaviour and at inappropriate responses because the context is not threatening: we laugh at Oliver Hardy slipping on a bar of soap because we know that he has not really been hurt; we laugh at the pomposity of Mr Elton in Jane Austen's novel *Emma* because we know that he is a fool; we laugh at the self-importance of the put-upon son Sanjeev in the comic interviews of *The Kumars at No. 42* because he is naïve and often out of his depth. In each case, humour is created because we recognise the characters and their personality traits – while the contexts may change in time, place or culture, our basic human values remain the same.

19.2 The function of humour

The basic **function** of humour is ENTERTAINMENT – to make its intended audience laugh. There is often a secondary function, however, in that the comic discourse will aim to **improve its audience** in some way, making them less pompous, for instance, or more politically aware. Comedy can expose the vices, follies and weaknesses of individuals and the society in which they live and, in laughing at these, we can aim to avoid the same pitfalls in our own lives.

Humour often pushes at the boundaries of what is acceptable, challenging us to look at familiar things in new ways. It can aim to **shock** us into thinking about things we take for granted: politics and politicians; social stereotypes; religion; music, film and literature. It can **embarrass** us and make us **feel uncomfortable**, and it can generate a **moment of recognition** when we are presented with something that we had already experienced or felt ourselves. Ultimately, however, if it does not make us laugh, it will have failed – we are more likely to see things differently if we find the humour funny.

Humour can be a **unifying** or an **isolating SOCIAL EXPERIENCE**. When individuals share a sense of humour, they feel a sense of camaraderie: it creates social bonds between them. Yet it can also be used as a means of control within a group: as an exercise of power, a dominant individual may use laughter to humiliate a subordinate group member, to undermine an individual who may threaten her or his social dominance, or to dictate the emotional mood of a group.

Laughter can function as a **conciliatory gesture**, reducing the tension in a confrontation or remedying an embarrassing situation. If you arrive late at a meeting, for instance, a self-uglifying grimace or exaggerated tiptoeing may serve as a remedial action. Such behaviour will often provoke laughter, pre-empting an accusation of lateness and functioning as a non-verbal apology. The comic performance is based on the recognition that you are making yourself into the fool that you have become by arriving late. Much comedy is based on the need to make up for a **faulty social performance** such as tripping over or hailing a taxi that drives straight past. The exaggerated behaviours that accompany such events (looking intently at the pavement; smoothing your hair as though you never had hailed the taxi anyway) become comic acts – remedial performances that aim to mask social awkwardness.

Because 'humour' can occur in so many different spoken and written forms, it is important to establish some background information before discussing it. To analyse the language of humour effectively, linguists need to start by asking themselves the following questions:

- Is the **medium** print, television, film, radio, pre-recorded CD or DVD, or live performance?
- What **type** of text, programme or performance is it?
- What is its primary **purpose**? Is there an underlying or secondary purpose?
- Who are the **intended audience**, and what kind of **relationship** is established with them?
- What **time** is the programme broadcast or the performance staged? In what kind of **publication** does the printed text appear?
- Is the **tone** formal or informal, familiar or impersonal, tolerant or caustic, or somewhere in between these extremes?

Answers to these questions will provide the basis for a closer focus – having identified a framework, linguists can then consider how the answers affect the lexical, grammatical and prosodic choices made by writers, comedians and programmers.

19.3 Features of the language of humour

The language of humour covers such a wide range of forms that it is difficult to draw up a definitive list of linguistic features. Nevertheless, it is possible to identify a number of distinctive qualities that mark it out as different from other varieties.

Mode

The **mode** is often both written and spoken. There are, however, examples of truly spontaneous speech (ad-libbing; responding to hecklers; improvising) and of language that is written with no attempt to mimic spontaneous speech (comic passages in novels; parodies; poems). The language and structure of a comic discourse therefore displays features associated with speech or writing, depending upon the balance the writers and comedians wish to create between the two modes.

Manner

The **manner** will also vary depending upon the kind of context in which the comedy takes place. In written and broadcast comedy, there is usually no direct interaction between the writers or comedians and their audience. When television or radio recordings are pre-recorded with an audience, however, interaction is very often 'guided' by production managers who explain exactly what is required of the audience in terms of participation. The addition of a 'canned' laughter track to the final edited version of a programme aims to provoke laughter in the audience at home since laughter is infectious. In public performances, a relationship is established that may include direct interaction (audience participation; the humiliation or taunting of individuals; heckling). Just as in face-to-face communications, this relationship may be formal or informal depending upon the content, purpose and time of the performance.

The relative **status** of a programme or performance and its audience is directly linked to the relationship created between them. In a comic context, the performer will often imply that there is no distance between comedian and audience – the emphasis is on observations of everyday life from an ordinary perspective (the stand-up routines of comedians like Jo Brand or Peter Kay; sitcoms such as *My Family* or *The Royle Family*). The comedy works because of the common ground created between the audience and performers. In other types of comedy, however, the audience can become part of the comic process: humiliated in mock interview shows (Rob Brydon's 'Keith Barret'; Caroline Aherne's 'Mrs Merton') or the butt of jokes in stand-up (Ross Noble; Jack Dee). In examples such as these, the comedian adopts a comic sense of superiority that allows him or her to exploit apparent vulnerabilities in particular members of the audience. The relative status assigned to the audience inevitably affects the linguistic and prosodic choices made.

Context

The **context** in which the language of humour takes place is critical to our understanding of the comedy. The period, the geographical region, the social and cultural background and our own personality and personal experiences affect the way in which we respond.

While some humour can exist outside its own **period**, other examples are no longer funny to an audience that is not contemporary. We can still laugh at the comedic scenes in Shakespeare's comedies, even though some of the wordplay and the wider comic associations have lost their relevance and we fail to pick up on the subtleties of the comic references. The larger-than-life character Bottom in *A Midsummer Night's Dream*, for instance, has the enthusiasm and concentration span of a child, dropping one thing as soon as another seems more interesting. His determination to be the centre of attention remains comic because it expresses a human quality that we can still recognise:

> If I do it [*play the part of the lover Pyramus*], let the audience look to their eyes; I will move storms, I will condole in some measure. To the rest. Yet my chief humour is for a tyrant; I could play Ercles rarely, or a part to tear a cat in, to make all split … .
>
> An I may hide my face, let me play Thisby [*the lady whom Pyramus loves*] too. I'll speak in a monstrous little voice … Let me play the lion too. I will roar, that I will do any man's heart good to hear me. I will roar, that I will make the duke say, 'Let him roar again, let him roar again.'
>
> (Act 1, scene 2, ll. 19–23, 43–4, 59–61)

In addition to this comedy of character which is still relevant to a twenty-first century audience, there is a level of humour that is lost on us. There is evidence to suggest that Shakespeare was drawing on the well-known characteristics of Kempe, the clown who probably first played Bottom. Some critics believe that Bottom's desire to play all the parts and his insistence on being the leader may have been a satirical comment on Kempe's tendency to add his own material to the scripted part and his reputation for being difficult to work with. Similarly, descriptions of Bottom roaring *as gently as any sucking dove* or *any nightingale* (Act 1, scene 2, ll. 69–70) and having *a very paramour for a sweet voice* (Act 4, scene 2, ll. 11–12) satirise Kempe's supposedly loud mouth.

While we can still appreciate the comedy of recognisable human traits, we need knowledge of the period to make us laugh at the contemporary satirical references that Shakespeare's audience and cast would have understood in *A Midsummer Night's Dream*. If you are presented with a comic discourse that was written or performed in the past, therefore, you may need to do some research in order to understand the comedy. Whether it is a ten-year-old or a hundred-year-old text, as modern readers we may be missing some of the references that would have immediately appealed to a contemporary audience's sense of humour.

Humour with a **geographical** or **regional identity** has the same limitations: those who live outside the region will often fail to appreciate the nuances. Dialect words, distinctive grammatical structures and local pronunciation can be used to create comedy that works on two levels: 'insiders' can laugh at their ability to confuse others; 'outsiders' can laugh at the bewildering and unfamiliar sounds of a language that is quite alien.

This provides a rich field of humour and numerous regional dialect books have been written to 'translate' a particular English dialect for outsiders. They create humour in the non-standard spelling that reflects pronunciation and in the formal

Standard English paraphrases that interpret the informal idiom of the dialect. One such example is *Teach Thissen Tyke* (1989) by the Labour MP for Grimsby, Austin Mitchell. The emphasis is on the ignorance of the Southerner who needs help in understanding *the Tyke tongue*. The comic effect is intensified because the format follows that of a 'teach yourself' book:

> *First test your tonsils to see if there are any structural weaknesses. Say this Test Piece:*
>> Ah were bahn dahn us ginnel as pictures wor loosin'
>> It wer black as t'coil oil and mucky as t'tip,
>> I saw t'rag and bone man all brussen wi'boozin'
>> Tweltin' t'osses ower t'eads wi' t'whip.
>
> *Translation:*
> I was making my way down a narrow passage as the crowds were exiting from the cinema. It was extremely dark and there was mud underfoot. I saw a scrap metal merchant somewhat the worse for drink and he was belabouring his trusty steeds on their heads with his whip.
> *Obviously you need language classes. So read on and TEACH THISSEN TYKE.*

The humour here lies in the juxtaposition of formal and informal registers. The imperatives (*test, Say, read on*) and the subject-specific vocabulary (*Test Piece, Translation, language classes*) are typical of the genre, but other words are used for comic effect (*tonsils, structural weaknesses*). Similarly, the formality of the Standard English (*somewhat the worse for drink, belabouring*) is juxtaposed with the colloquial expression (*wor loosin'*), unfamiliar dialect words (*ginnel, brussen, Tweltin'*), the non-standard spelling (*bahn, dahn, t'osses*) and the pronunciation (*t'coil, ower, t'eads*).

Accents and **dialects** can be an essential part of the language of humour. A stand-up comedian from a particular region can unite a local audience by finding humour in local traditions, events or places. This kind of humour creates insiders and outsiders since those not part of the community do not appreciate the nuances of the comedy – they are alienated by the regional references as well as the lexicon.

Accents can also be used to distinguish between characters in a comic novel or a drama, a sitcom or a sketch show. In Shakespeare's plays, for instance, the comic characters are often rural, speaking prose in a style that is lexically and grammatically different from the verse of the main characters; in a Charles Dickens novel, the comic characters are marked out by a regional, social or idiosyncratic form of English. Similarly, in sitcoms such as *The Vicar of Dibley* (rural) or *Kath and Kim* (Australian) we are presented with comedy that exploits different regional varieties of English.

Stereotypical accents can also be used for comic effect: a mock German accent will imitate the phonology (*Ve hav vays off making zem tok*); a mock Scandinavian accent will imitate the consecutive rising and falling tones; a mock Oriental accent will elide /r/ and replace it with /l/ (*velly hot*). Such features are exaggerated and taken out of context – they become caricatures of a type of speech, imitating individual broad features and failing to capture the subtleties of a language.

In a Catherine Tate sketch in which the central character offers to be a translator in a business meeting, comedy is created because she is clearly incapable of speaking any language except English – in spite of her catchphrase *I can do that*. She addresses each of the international representatives in a form of language that captures the phonological patterns and pitch of the native language while meaning nothing. The sketch is humorous because of the character's total inadequacy – we laugh at her vain attempts to cover up her ignorance. What adds to the humour is that Tate has managed to capture the sound patterns of each language so that we can recognise each one.

It is important to understand, however, that where imitation of an accent becomes the focus of the comedy it is inappropriate. Comedy created from imitating English spoken with an international accent must be perceived as antisocial. As was seen in a controversial series of *Celebrity Big Brother* (January 2007), the imitation by two of the housemates of Shilpa Shetty, the Bollywood actress, was considered to be malicious rather than humorous. There was no comic intent since the apparent function was to mock rather than to entertain. It appeared to be an act of imitation that sought to emphasise Shetty's position as an outsider while reinforcing the participants' sense of 'belonging'.

The **social and cultural background** of a writer or performer can work in a similar fashion to create comedy. By drawing on culturally specific topics that are directly related to a particular audience's experience of life, the humour can be exclusive – it emphasises the unity of those who understand and excludes those who do not. In such cases, the semantic and linguistic features of the humour only amuse the audience if they 'belong' to the group. Jewish jokes, for instance, usually depend upon a knowledge and understanding of the cultural and religious life of the Jewish community. Without this background, a non-Jewish audience would not recognise the impulse behind the joke.

Jewish jokes often focus on the community's traditional celebrations and their use of Hebrew, the official language of Israel. Without an understanding of these, the jokes do not 'work' – we need a gloss to help us appreciate the humour. This is the case in the following example which depends on both a knowledge of the Jewish Passover celebration and an understanding of Hebrew.

> You know that Abe Shapiro? You know, he takes deportment lessons and lays out a fortune on morning dress and tails? You know, he's been awarded high honours? Well, today he alights from his Rolls Royce at Buckingham Palace for his Investiture. You know what? He waves at us all, then he goes inside and kneels before the Queen. She touches his shoulder with the sword and says, 'Sir Abraham Shapiro, arise.'
>
> Suddenly, in the midst of all this ceremony, all the elocution and deportment lessons disappear and Abe is stuck there, paralysed. There is a silence. A terrible silence. He has forgotten the Latin and can only think of the words that every good Jewish boy knows: 'Ma Nishtana ha-lahylah ha-zeh mi-kol ha-layloht.'
>
> Puzzled, the Queen looks at her equerry and says to Abe's astonishment, 'Why is this knight different from all other knights?'

To the non-initiated this joke fails to deliver because the **PUNCH LINE** has no resonance – it is a Jewish joke that relies on knowledge of the traditional celebrations at Passover, in which the youngest child at the Passover Seder table asks four questions of the elders. In order to appreciate the humour, we need to know about the cultural traditions associated with the celebration.

The 'Four Questions' are actually one question with four clauses which represent a complete overview of the Passover story as told in the Passover Haggadah (a book containing the order of service of the traditional Passover meal). The four clauses and their answers demonstrate the uniqueness of the Passover holiday compared to other times of the year. The aim is to encourage future generations of Jews to inquire about their history.

Why is it that on all other nights:
- we eat either bread or matzoh, but on this night we eat only matzoh?
- we eat all kinds of herbs, but on this night we eat only bitter herbs?
- we do not dip our herbs even once, but on this night we dip them twice?
- we eat either sitting or reclining, but on this night we eat in a reclining position?

The answer for each question describes specific events in the Passover story and their symbolic meaning in relation to the Passover holiday. The first two questions and their answers remind the Jewish community of the burdens of slavery, and the second two symbolise the glory of freedom.

The main question recited before each of the four clauses can be translated as *Ma Nishtana* [*What is different*] *ha-lahylah ha-zeh* [*this night*] *mi-kol ha-layloht* [*from all other nights*], and the joke relies on the *night/knight* pun. As homophones, the two words have different semantic functions in the two juxtaposed contexts: for the Queen, the investiture makes Abe Shapiro a 'knight'; for the Jewish audience, he has slipped into the Hebrew of his childhood and is asking what is different about this particular 'night'. The humour lies in the Queen's apparent understanding of Hebrew and in the ambiguity – he is different from other knights because he has failed to stand up after his dubbing.

While this kind of cultural joke strengthens community bonds, there are other instances in which cultural stereotypes can be used divisively to isolate religious, social or cultural groups. In such cases, humour becomes antisocial and the jokes are often racist or homophobic: they poke fun at ethnic or social groups who are less likely to have a dominant role in the power structure of society. Their function is no longer to entertain, but to mock and humiliate. This kind of antisocial humour becomes a means of expressing the inexpressible, and most people will be shocked rather than amused.

Content

The **content** of the language of humour is incredibly diverse. It may focus on one particular **topic** or it may range more widely. A comic novel or play, for instance, will be driven by a particular set of characters within a particular context, and the topic will be directly linked to these and the kind of events taking place. Similarly, in sitcoms, the domestic (family life in *Malcolm in the Middle*, BBC2; flatmates in *Men Behaving Badly*, BBC1), the workplace (a Slough-based paper company in *The Office*, BBC2; a hospital in *Green Wing*, C4; a government department in *The Thick of It*, BBC2) or a group of people (the Ladies' Guild in *Jam and Jerusalem*; the parish council in *The Vicar of Dibley*, BBC1) provide the basis for topics that evolve from the context and the character interaction. Often, each episode develops one particular topic that provides cohesion and focuses the comedy.

Topic shifts tend to be marked by a change of character and context. A sketch show such as *The Catherine Tate Show*, for instance, will range from topic to topic with no explicit underlying connection. Each character will become familiar over the course of a series and, while each topic will be relevant to the character, there will be no real sense of cohesion. In addition to the familiar behaviour of characters, the *Little Britain* sketch show uses a narrative voice-over to link disparate sketches – the emphasis is on the 'people of Britain' and the lives of 'ordinary British folk'. This adds to the humour, of course, as the characters with whom we are presented are invariably larger-than-life caricatures and the scripted voice-over delivered by Tom Baker is absurd.

In many turn-based comedy shows there is an overarching **theme** or **subject** which provides a general framework to underpin topic shifts: a topical slant on the week's news (*Mock the Week*, BBC 2; *Have I Got News For You*, BBC 2; *The Now Show*, BBC Radio 4); or questions or 'tasks' on panel games (*QI*, BBC 2; *Just a Minute*, Radio 4; *I'm Sorry I Haven't a Clue*, Radio 4). For a stand-up comedian, on the other hand, topic shifts are often marked by lexical association – a particular word will form a link between one context and another.

The **end of a topic** is clearly signposted because the language of humour often occurs in spoken contexts (broadcasts and performances) and is therefore subject to tight time schedules. Because it is mostly pre-written or improvised on a pre-pared structure there will usually be an explicit cut-off point. Where programmes are part of a series, each episode will conclude with an appropriate 'hook' to encourage the audience to watch or listen to the next part. In prose and poetry, the language of humour uses the traditional conventions of the written word to mark the end of a topic, while jokes have a distinctive structure indicating the climax with a punch line or a recognised sequence of question and response.

Structure

The **structure** of a humorous discourse depends upon its type. If it is a SITCOM, a group of characters in a particular context will run from episode to episode; if it is a one-off PERFORMANCE, the structure will be self-contained; if it is a JOKE, the format will be dictated by a predefined pattern; if it is a PARODY, it will follow the structure of the original on which it is based. In each case, the overall structure is tightly organised so that the maximum use can be made of the allocated time-slot or written genre.

Some programmes are marked by distinctive structural features. The **opening** and **closing** of a sitcom, for instance, always follow a predefined pattern in that the main characters probably appear in a familiar context. A joke may begin with a recognisable opening statement that is followed by an answer or a logical conclusion – for this to work, the punch line must be easily recognisable so that the intended audience know when to laugh. A stand-up comedian may directly address his or her audience with a specific regional reference to mark the location of a gig; the closing of a performance will probably include a reference to the quality of the audience and some form of polite 'thank you'.

Other programmes are structured around a very organised form of **turn-taking**. Comic programmes such as *Never Mind the Buzzcocks* and *Have I Got News For You* (*HIGNFY*) are based on the formality of **adjacency pairs**: the quiz master asks questions and the panellists provide answers. Because the context is humorous, however, the initial response is often at odds with the question or exploits some comic **ambiguity**. Interruptions, overlaps and digressions are common – the primary purpose of the interaction is to amuse the audience rather than to achieve the greatest score. *QI* represents the comic quiz show in its most extreme form: tangential discussions, non sequiturs, frivolous conversations and humorous anecdotes lie at the heart of the comedy.

Prosodic features

Because much of the language of humour is spoken, **prosodic features** play an important part in communicating meaning. Although a great deal of the material first exists in written form, performers will use their voices to bring the words to life. **Intonation patterns** reinforce the meaning: rising intonation can mark out a question or suggest an uncertainty; falling intonation can change the mood or mark the end of a grammatical unit; moving repeatedly between rising and falling intonations can parody an accent or create a caricature. **Pitch variations** underpin intonation changes, allowing speakers to reinforce their attitudes or responses. While a raised pitch can indicate excitement or amazement, a lowered pitch can suggest a depressed or automatic response. **Loudness** and **pace** also contribute to the communication of meaning, allowing speakers to reflect the relative importance or insignificance of what they are saying. Because the language of humour is often dependent upon extremes of reaction, variations in the prosodic features are common. **Vocal effects** fulfil a similar role in underpinning the comedy: laughter, humming and non-verbal utterances such as groans and ironic throat-clearing are used to enhance the comic effect.

Stress patterns and **pauses** allow performers to draw attention to certain lexical items. Stressed words may be pronounced in a consciously comic way or may be used inappropriately for comic effect; repeated stresses or unexpected patterns of stresses can create humour by distorting the meaning and throwing semantic weight onto insignificant lexical items. In formal spoken language, pauses are kept to a miminum; in comedy, they can be used to exploit a moment of discomfort, to elaborate on a point with gesture or facial expression, to create suspense before a comic climax, or to allow time for audience laughter to run its course. Such features intensify the effect of the comedy by exaggerating the lexical and structural patterns with which we are familiar.

Lexis

Comedy at its most basic is **physical**: the slapstick of the pantomime dame slipping on a banana and the custard pie in the face both work at a universal level. As well as fixing comedy more firmly in a particular geographical context, the use of **language** also adds additional layers of entertainment.

The **lexis** will be directly linked to the content, the context, the characters or performers, and the intended audience. Frequently, comedy is created by the **juxtaposition** of lexical opposites: formal and informal, the expected and the unexpected, the logical and the ridiculous. It may be distinctive because of a particular register, period or regional influence; it may exploit a semantic ambiguity, sexual innuendo, or a conflict of interest. The language of humour is all about finding undiscovered connections and seeing hidden patterns.

Often the language of humour relies on audience recognition of familiar **lexical patterns**: collocations, idioms, connotations, and so on. In Figure 19.1, most readers will follow the lexical clues and recognise their comic implications.

Figure 19.1 **Part of a cartoon strip (*The Independent*)**

Adapted from: Neil Kerber, *The Independent* (29 July 2006)

In Figure 19.1 the images of a mother and father shouting at their child and the use of the disparaging vocative *Young man* establish the context for us. This is reinforced by the language: the connotations of the noun phrase *these disgusting magazines*, the adverbial *under your bed*, the exclamative adjective phrases *Filth! Absolute filth!* and the abstract noun *Shame* lead us to assume that we have guessed the boy's crime. The father's simple sentence only reinforces our certainty that we have understood the situation:

	S	P	C	A
	(I)	(was)	(the same)	(at his age).

If we look at the complete second frame, however, we find that our expectations have not been fulfilled (Figure 19.2).

Figure 19.2 **The complete cartoon strip**

Neil Kerber, *The Independent* (29 July 2006)

The humour lies in the false leads that the cartoonist has created in his lexical choice: the boy's crime is not reading 'dirty' magazines but reading advertising material from the bank that promotes poor-value loans. The subject-specific lexis juxtaposes the positive connotations of *a huge loan* with the negative *long-term repayments* and *a high rate of interest.* Once we know the title of the cartoon strip (*The Cost of Living*) and the context (it was published in the business pages of *The Independent,* 29 July 2006), we can understand the significance of the financial register. The cartoon is making a serious point: at a time when many people are in debt, promotional material offering additional money with conditions that appear to benefit the bank rather than the borrower can only cause further hardship.

WORDPLAY is common because we can find humour in the gap between the real and the potential meaning. Tabloid newspaper headlines exploit such semantic possibilities on a daily basis, but sitcoms, comic novels and stand-up comedians do much the same. In the following extract taken from a circular email, complete with voice-over and stills, the supposed conversation between President Bush (PB) and his National Security Advisor, Condoleeza Rice (CR), is marked by comic misunderstanding:

CR G'morning, Mr President.
PB Oh, Condoleeza, nice to see ya. What's happening?
CR Well, Mr President. I have the report here about the new leader in China.
PB Great, Condi. Lay it on me.
CR Mr President, Hu is the new leader of China.
PB Well, that's what I want to know.
CR But that's what I'm telling you, Mr President.
PB Well, that's what I'm asking you, Condi. Who is the new leader of China?
CR Yes.
PB I mean the fella's name.
CR Hu.
PB The guy in China.
CR Hu.
PB The new leader of China.
CR Hu.
PB The Chinaman!
CR Hu is leading China, Mr President.
PB Whaddya asking me for?
CR I'm telling you Hu is leading China.
PB Well, I'm asking you, Condi. Who is leading China?
CR That's the man's name?
PB That's who's name?
CR Yes.
PB Will you or will you not tell me the name of the new leader of China?
CR Yes, sir.
PB Yasser? Yasser Arafat is in China? I thought he was in the Middle East.
CR That's correct?
PB Then who is in China?
CR Yes, sir.
PB Yasser is in China?
CR No, sir.
PB Then who is?
CR Yes, sir.
PB Yasser?
CR No, sir.

The comedy lies in the phonological matches between the relative pronoun *who* and the Chinese leader's name (Hu), and between the American pronunciation of the polite affirmative *yes, sir* and the then leader of the Palestinians, Yasser Arafat. The fact that Bush has a reputation for linguistic faux pas and gaffes (often described as 'Bushisms') adds to the humour – although all the adjacency pairs are complete, each participant fails to understand the other. The discourse requires repair, but neither speaker provides the necessary clarification and so the topic loop continues.

Because humour is often a direct challenge to our understanding of the society in which we live and its attitudes, the lexis is non-conformist. Topics such as sex, sexuality, politics, race and relationships provide a rich lexical field. As well as making us laugh, the language of humour aims, in many cases, to open our eyes to a particular discrepancy or to make us think about some piece of received wisdom that is commonly taken for granted. The lexical choice reflects this by representing things in a way that will jolt us from our apathy. We can expect to be shocked by language that seems inappropriate and, at times, offensive.

In order to assess the nature of the language of humour, it is important to come to some conclusions about:

> - the **kind of discourse** (spoken or written)
> - the intended **audience** (age, gender, educational or cultural background)
> - the **subject matter**
> - the **approach** (formal/informal? personal/detached? narrative/sequential? one-off/series? shocking? ironic? enlightening? observational?)

From this starting point, analysis can focus specifically on the kind of words used and the effects created.

Varieties of English

Comedy can be created by juxtaposing different **varieties of English** in unexpected ways. It can work at a very simplistic level: using an exaggerated regional accent in a context where we would expect the formality of RP (a documentary voice-over using a broad accent and dialect); seeing a well-known character who then speaks using an unexpected variety (the Queen, for instance, using an urban street dialect). A comic effect can also be created by using a word or phrase that has distinct meanings in particular contexts – often one of these meanings relies on sexual **INNUENDO**, as in the following example by Spike Milligan:

> Are you going to come quietly or do I have to use earplugs?

The humour lies in the fact that our expectations are not fulfilled. We understand the first part of the quotation within a formal register as part of a collocation used by the police at the point of an arrest – we expect the final word to be 'handcuffs'. The substitution of *earplugs* is humorous because it is unexpected, but also because it forces us to reassess the register of the beginning of the sentence. The infinitive *to come* must now be seen as part of an informal register because the joke is dependent upon sexual innuendo: the denotation or dictionary definition of the verb when used as slang.

The Monty Python team frequently set a formal register against an informal one. In *Monty Python and the Holy Grail,* one scene uses a biblical register to describe throwing a grenade at a man-eating rabbit. The context is SURREAL and the effect of the language ABSURD:

KNIGHT	we have the Holy Hand Grenade =
KING ARTHUR	= of course (1) the Holy Hand Grenade of Antioch (1) 'tis one of the sacred relics Brother Maynard carries with him =
KNIGHT	= bring out the Holy Hand Grenade
	[*PLAINSONG* (20)]
KING ARTHUR	how does it um (4) how does it work =
KNIGHT	= I know not my liege =
KNIGHT	= ↑Consult↑ the Book of Armaments =
MONK 1	= Armaments Chapter 2, verses 9 to 21 (3)
MONK 2	↑and Saint Ati-la raised the Hand Grenade up on high saying, Oh Lord, bless this thy Hand Grenade that with it thou mayst blow thy enemies to tiny↑ ↓bits↓ in thy mercy (1) ↑and the Lord did <u>grin</u> and the people did feast upon the <u>lambs</u> and <u>sloths</u> and <u>carp</u> and <u>anchovies</u> and <u>orang-utangs</u> and <u>breakfast cereals</u> and <u>fruit bats</u> and ‖<u>large</u>↑
MONK 1	‖skip a bit Brother (5)
MONK 2	↑and the Lord spake saying (2) 'First shalt thou take out the holy↑ ↓pin↓ (2) ↑then shalt thou count to↑ ↓three↓ (1) no <u>more</u> (1) no <u>less</u> (1) ↑three shalt be the number thou shalt count (2) and the number of the counting shalt be↑ ↓three↓ ↑four↑shalt thou ↓not↓ count <u>neither</u> ↑count thou <u>two</u> excepting that thou then proceed (1) to↑ (1) ↓three↓ ↑five is right out↑ (3) ↑once the number three (1) being the third number be reached (2) then lobbest thou thy Holy Hand Grenade of Antioch (1) towards↑ ↓thy foe↓ (2) ↑who being <u>naughty</u> in my sight↑ ↓shall snuff↓ it =
ALL	= amen

The overlaying of varieties here creates comedy because the effect is absurd: the familiarity of the religious register and the basic chronological instructions for preparing the hand grenade are set against lexis that is out of context, circumlocutary explanations and informal expressions. The archaic grammatical features create a biblical resonance: archaic inflections (*mayst, shalt, lobbeth*); irregular past-tense forms (*spake*); the use of the primary verb *do* for the past tense (*did grin ... did feast*); and the absence of *do* for negatives (*know not*). Religious lexis (*the Lord, bless, holy, Amen*), archaic pronouns (*thou*) and determiners (*thy*), religious formulaic expressions (*Chapter 2, verses 9 to 21*; *in thy mercy*) and fronted co-ordinating conjunctions (*And*) all enhance our sense of this as a religious variety.

Because the religious features of the discourse are out of context, however, we know that the intention is comic rather than serious. The biblical features are set against informal verbs (*lob*, throw; *snuff it*, to die), childlike adjectives (*naughty*) and the language of conflict (*blow ... to bits, enemies, foe*). The syndetic list of animals is also humorous: it begins with animals that make sense in the context and have a biblical resonance (*the lambs*), while the following concrete nouns are quite unconnected; the repeated use of the conjunction creates a comic emphasis; and the consecutive stresses on the nouns draw attention to their incongruity.

Similar effects can be seen in the use of subtitling that paraphrases a character's actual speech in an informal and comic version. In the 2007 *Epic Movie*, the albino assassin (a comic parody of the monk in the film version of Dan Brown's novel *The Da Vinci Code*) speaks Latin – a language appropriate to his religious status. The subtitles on the screen, however, adopt a colloquial urban style, translating his austere and incomprehensible words into a recognisable street dialect.

Other parodies adopt a similar juxtaposition of styles. The BBC spoof of 1970s and early 1980s educational and schools programmes, *Look Around You* (Series 1, 2002; Series 2, 2005), sets a formal scientific register against content that is often nonsensical. Each episode, or *module*, focuses on a different scientific subject, and its success lies in the use of realistic approaches to fictional items. Lexical jokes ('germs' come from Germany), the labelling of all items (hairdriers, magnets), the dated colour and look of the film and the creation of an apparently authentic 'educational' website (www.bbc.co.uk/comedy/lookaroundyou) all contribute to the humour. The website advertises the *Look Around You* book that is supposedly *an invaluable tool for the scientific student* – references to its author, the leading biochemist E. W. Whitmarsh, his work on *bemins* and *cemins*, and his discovery of *memims* are clearly nonsensical.

Quizzes on the website offer internet users the opportunity to test their own knowledge. These too follow the pattern of traditional topic-based questions, but are nonsensical. The example below is taken from the Maths Quiz:

QUESTION 1
If 1 Greek Drachma (Gk Dr) is worth 1½ Greek Drachmas, how many lamps can be bought from the market, if each lamp is 4 times the cost of each other lamp, the cost being the same as it was the year before last?

ANSWER
The market does not sell lamps. It sells fruit, vegetables, traditional carvings, dishcloths, badges, pottery, lamps, silverware, butterflies and butter.

While the style is reminiscent of a traditional maths problem, the information provided does not make sense and the answer is tangential – it merely negates the question rather than attempting to untangle it. The humour of *Look Around You* lies in the fact that on first viewing it is (almost) possible to believe that you are watching a schools programme.

Grammar

The **grammar** is linked to the kind of humour, the context, the intended audience, the topic and the approach. In written varieties, the grammatical structures will tend to be more formal and complex; in informal spoken varieties, they are more likely to be characterised by incomplete utterances and non-standard grammar, using prosodics and body language to underpin the meaning.

In order to analyse the grammatical features of the language of humour it is first necessary to decide whether the discourse is written, spoken, or written to be spoken. This focuses the analysis since we are then able to explore features that are distinctive to written or spoken language and to consider the ways in which they are an integral part of the language of humour in a particular context.

Normal non-fluency features are only apparent in certain kinds of comic discourse. Many broadcast programmes are pre-recorded and editing will have eliminated evidence of hesitancy, repetition and lack of fluency. Sitcoms, however, often demonstrate features that have been written into the script in order to mimic the less polished feel of spontaneous conversation. Certain characters may even be characterised by their use of normal non-fluency features: in *The Vicar of Dibley*, for instance, Jim Trott's stammering repetition of *no-no-no-no-no-no* is a preface to every sentence. Such features are often exaggerated for comic effect – we never know whether Jim is against something or not, as the repetition of the negatives is often followed by *yes*. In stand-up routines, comedians prepare a basic script but may ad lib, improvising with a topical theme or a local reference, or going off at a tangent. There may, therefore, be evidence of non-fluency features, but since the speakers are polished performers these will often be limited unless used self-consciously to enhance the comedy.

As in informal conversation, **repairs** can take a number of forms in live and pre-recorded broadcasts. A breakdown in communication can provide a rich source of comedy, however, and often repairs are delayed in order to exploit the comic possibilities of the misunderstanding. Ambiguity, incomplete adjacency pairs, lack of co-operation in turn-taking, failure to take account of a topic, extended topic loops and non sequiturs can all create comedy in a humorous context. In most comic discourse, there will eventually be a repair of some kind so that the situation can develop, but exaggeration of the problem is a primary source of comedy.

19.4 Types of humour

Jokes

JOKES represent humour at its most basic. Frequently, they are not original, but are part of a shared tradition, passed on in playgrounds, pubs, informal gatherings, and even within the formality of occasions such as after-dinner speeches and wedding celebrations.

The dominant **function** is to entertain, although there will be some instances in which a joke is intended to mock or humiliate. The **tone** is directly linked to the function – the light-hearted joke will be delivered in a humorous tone, while those that are antisocial or unethical will be marked by a more dismissive and aggressive tone. The context in which such jokes are told and the impulse behind them dictate whether the effect is humorous or immoral:

> What do you call three estate agents at the bottom of a river? – *A good start*.

In this occupation-based joke, for instance, we know that nobody is seriously suggesting that the target group should be harmed in reality.

There are no political dimensions here – although estate agents may be seen by some as not earning the money they get for selling a house, there is no suggestion that drowning is a real proposal for eliminating them. If the joke were reworked with a racist or homophobic reference, however, its impulse would be very different: in laughing at the concept of racist or homophobic violence, the teller and audience would be united in turning the reality of aggressive acts against these kind of minority groups into a matter of amusement. Because of the moral and political dimensions, such a joke could not be seen as humorous.

The **structure** of a joke is dependent upon the kind of joke being told. Many have a distinctive formula: *Knock, knock. Who's there?*; *Have you heard the one about the…?*; *There was an Englishman and an Irishman…*; *Why did the…?* The structure often depends upon adjacency pairs: a question will be followed by a negative statement, or a repeated question and an answer:

> PARTICIPANT 1   What do short-sighted ghosts wear?
> PARTICIPANT 2   I don't know. What *do* short-sighted ghosts wear?
> PARTICIPANT 1   Spooktacles.

When we hear the opening lines, we know that a joke is about to be told and we anticipate what is to follow. While some jokes are short, others take on the form of a **'SHAGGY-DOG' STORY** (a long rambling joke, often ending in a deliberate anticlimax). All jokes have a recognisable conclusion – the punch line functions as a signpost to the audience that a joke is complete and that the speaker's turn has ended. Since joke-telling is a social activity, interaction from the audience is customary. This is often informal (affirmations; non-verbal feedback such as groans and laughs) but may also be formal – some jokes require participation (answers; reiterated questions).

The **content** of jokes is wide-ranging. As well as 'playground' jokes (*Why did the chicken cross the road?*; *Did you hear about…?*; *Doctor, doctor…?*), political, religious, ethnic and professional jokes represent a substantial body of the genre. Such jokes rely on undermining the status of a particular individual or group based on stereotypes or on creating a hierarchy (for example, physicists may joke about chemists, who may joke about biologists, who may joke about astrophysicists).

The appropriateness of such jokes depends upon who is telling them, upon the impulse behind them, and upon whether the target group has social status or not. A joke about the stereotypical dumbness of blondes, for instance, is considered less politically incorrect than one about a religious or ethnic group who actually are victims of prejudice and social inequality. When one social group is currently at the bottom of the comic hierarchy, therefore, numerous jokes will make fun of what is perceived as the stereotypical behaviour and language of that group.

Humour is often a challenge to the status quo, and **'DIRTY' JOKES** are based on **taboo** subjects, using material and vocabulary that society deems inappropriate. **META-JOKES** turn humour on itself, creating a joke that is self-referential:

> A priest, a rabbi and a leprechaun walk into a bar. The leprechaun looks around and says: 'Saints preserve us! I'm in the wrong joke!'

> Knock knock. *Who's there?* Boo. *Boo who?* Don't cry – it's only a knock-knock joke.

IN-JOKES between a group of friends, viewers of a particular television series or cult film, professionals in a certain field and so on, depend upon a prior knowledge of some kind which unites them and enables them to find humour in material that may not seem funny to others. Jokes are often dependent upon the audience making wider associations – they need to recognise a contextual link to another word, idea or object.

Linguistically, the **humour of jokes** can be created in a variety of ways. Many exploit semantic or grammatical ambiguity, playing on the ways in which the meaning of a word or the structure of a sentence can create two distinct responses. Others explore the phonology of words: **homophones**, **substituted phonemes**, **segmental phonology** (elision and liaison) and **accent** can all form the basis for jokes.

> Knock knock.
> *Who's there?*
> Oliver.
> *Oliver who?*
> Oliver double helping of cabbage, please!

In this joke, the humour is dependent upon the audience making an association with the name *Oliver* and with the scene in Charles Dickens's novel *Oliver Twist* in which the young orphan boy asks for more. There is then a phonological wordplay in which the phonemes of the name /ɒlɪvə/ represent an elided form of the clause 'I'll have a': /aɪl/ /hæv/ /ə/.

ACTIVITY 19.1

The following jokes and their answers depend upon different kinds of lexical, phonological and grammatical patterns. Each demonstrates one main linguistic technique for creating humour.

Read through each joke and explore the technique used in each case. You may like to think about the use of:

- phonemes, segmental phonology and accent
- homophones
- semantic and grammatical ambiguity.

JOKE 1

What happens when you throw eggs at a Dalek?

It's eggs-terminated.

JOKE 2

Why are glow-worms good to carry in your bag?

They lighten your load.

JOKE 3

What do snowmen sing at parties?

'Freeze a jolly good fellow.'

JOKE 4

What happened when the chicken ate a big pile of sage, onion and breadcrumbs?

It was stuffed.

JOKE 5

What do you call a vampire who likes to relax in a bloodbath with a good book?

Well red.

JOKE 6

What's the best thing about deadly snakes?

They've got poisonality.

COMMENTARY

Each of the jokes here relies on an adjacency pair to complete the structure, but the linguistic device used to create humour is different in each case.

PHONOLOGY is the study of the function of sounds and the ways in which sounds create meaning. What we see in Joke 1 is the way in which **a change of phoneme** can create humour. The audience is expected to engage with the contextual associations created by the reference to *a Dalek* (from the BBC's *Doctor Who*) – an alien life-form intent on destruction, whose defining cry is 'Exterminate!' The joke works because of the phonological associations between the verb *exterminate* and the neologism *eggs-terminate*. Phonemically, the two words are very similar – their difference lies in the first phoneme: /eks/ and /egz/. The substitution of the voiced velar /g/ for the voiceless velar /k/ and the voiced alveolar /z/ for the voiceless alveolar /s/ change the semantics of the word, creating a direct link to the question's 'egg' reference.

The semantics of a word can change according to its context or word class. In Joke 2, the verb *lighten* provides the source of humour: a **lexical tension** is created between its different denotations and the context provided by the reference to *glow-worms*. A dictionary will define the meaning of *lighten* in a number of ways:

> **lighten**[1] *vb*
> *1.* to become or make light *2.* to shine; glow *3.* to flash
>
> **lighten**[2] *vb*
> *1.* to make or become less heavy *2.* to make or become less burdensome or oppressive; mitigate *3.* to make or become more cheerful or lively

Within the semantic framework of the joke, we can see that the two contrasting meanings have a resonance: literally, the *glow-worms* create light, but, in addition, a pun on the other meaning of *lighten* suggests that they will make your bag less heavy and burdensome.

SEGMENTAL PHONOLOGY is a study of the ways in which a particular language uses and adapts phonemes in continuous speech. The humour in Joke 3 is created by **liaison** and **elision**, two of the distinctive features of segmental phonology, and by our recognition of the title of a well-known celebratory song, 'For He's a Jolly Good Fellow'. The lexical fields of winter (*snowman, freeze*) and social celebrations (*parties, sing*) are brought together in the song reference. In continuous speech, the distinct phonemes /fɔː/ (*for*) and /hiːz/ (*he's*) are changed at the boundary point where a linking /r/ is inserted between the words. This process is called liaison and the inserted /r/ is a vocalised link between the phonemes: /fɔːriːz/. The phonological similarity between this and the verb *freeze* forms the basis of the humour: with the elision of /ɔː/ in informal speech, both phonemes can be represented as /friːz/.

GRAMMATICAL AMBIGUITY can also create humour: interpreting the function of elements in a clause in different ways can change the meaning. The tabloid headline *DO YOU WANT A WOMAN VICAR*, for instance, can be described as grammatically ambiguous:

> P   S   P   O   P   S   P   O
> (Do) (you) (want) (a woman vicar)?   (Do) (you) (want) (a woman) (vicar)?
> aux   lex   aux   lex   voc

In the first version, the pre-modified noun phrase *a woman vicar* represents a central issue in a serious debate about the ministry of women in the Church. The second follows in a long tradition of jokes that depend for their effect on innuendo. In this version, the simple noun phrase *a woman* is followed by a vocative and the interrogative becomes a direct request. Joke 4 works in a similar way: a grammatical ambiguity results in two different meanings.

| S | P | C | S | P |
| (It) | (was) | (stuffed). | (It) (was stuffed). |

In the first version, the colloquial past participle *stuffed* functions as a modifier – it is a complement telling us that the chicken was full after eating *a big pile of sage, onion and breadcrumbs*. In the second version, the verb *stuffed* has a specific meaning: 'to fill (food such as poultry or tomatoes) with a filling'. It is linked semantically to the list of nouns which, we realise, are the ingredients of 'sage and onion stuffing'. The passive voice (*to be* + past participle) with no agent indicates that the chicken has been prepared by an unnamed person. The humour lies in the fact that in one version the chicken itself has eaten and in the other it is about to be eaten.

Wordplay based on sound is the root of many jokes and, in Joke 5, the use of **HOMOPHONES** creates humour. Again there is tension between two lexical sets: horror (*vampire, bloodbath*) and reading (*relax in a… bath, a good book*). The word *red* functions as a colour adjective in the first lexical set and as a phonemic transcription of the verb past participle 'read' in the second. As the meaning of *red* changes, so too does the function of the adverb *well*: in the context of the horror genre, it is a colloquial intensifier pre-modifying the adjective; in the context of reading, it is part of a collocation 'well read' (having read widely and intelligently; erudite). The joke works because the two lexical sets are overlaid – we understand both meanings simultaneously.

Joke 6 depends upon **ACCENT**. We understand the semantic link between the noun phrase *deadly snakes* and the lexical root of the neologism *poisonality*. The joke only truly makes sense, however, when we recognise that the answer has to be delivered in an exaggerated Bronx accent. If we adopt the appropriate pronunciation, the noun becomes more than just a link to 'poison':

/pɔɪsənælɪtɪ/ 'poisonality' → personality /pɜːsənælɪtɪ/

The change of the phoneme /ɜː/ to /ɔɪ/ creates a phonological link between 'poisonality' and 'personality': the humour lies in the overlaying of the neologism and the pronunciation of the word in a non-standard accent. In addition, the pronunciation is comic because it is a **CARICATURE** rather than a realistic imitation of a New Yorker: the replacement of the /ɜː/ vowel with /ɔɪ/ is now perceived as old-fashioned and extreme.

Jokes form the basis for social interaction – they are designed to be told rather than read. In analysing them, we destroy their spontaneity, but gain an understanding of the way in which they work linguistically. The activity here diffuses the humour of the jokes, yet it is interesting to explore the different ways in which they aim to amuse.

Farce

Traditionally, **FARCE** is a type of comedy in which unlikely and often extravagant situations, larger-than-life characters and slapstick elements are used for humorous effect. It is also known as 'laughing comedy' and its function is to provide entertainment at a basic level of physical comedy, with characterisation and dialogue less important than plot. It is often described as 'low' comedy and focuses on what lies beneath the apparently decent surface of society.

PLOTS tend to be intricate and fast-moving, with disguise and mistaken identity central to the comedy. Events are usually improbable and surprises in the form of unexpected appearances and comic revelations are common. Adultery, sexual intrigue, contemporary manners and social climbing dominate the content. Frequently, there is only one **SETTING** – often a drawing room with many doors that permit the numerous entrances and exits.

The **characters** of farce tend to be vain, irrational and highly sexual individuals whose transgressive behaviour is amusing rather than threatening. The main protagonists are always presented sympathetically so that the audience hope for their success – although often rogues, they are lively, witty, spontaneous and creative. There is generally a happy ending in which all problems have been resolved in some way. The main protagonist, however, often gets away with his 'crimes' – fleeing the scene with the potential to begin again in another place.

The **language** is commonplace, but draws on puns and sexual innuendo for comic effect. Dialogue is fast-paced and the dominant means of characterisation: the way characters speak tells the audience a lot about the kind of people they are.

Farce has a long **history** and is often used in serious plays as **COMIC RELIEF** (as a humorous interlude to release tension). In the seventeenth century, Ben Jonson's plays often used farcical episodes and *Bartholomew Fair* (1614) is an excellent example of farcical comedy. The wit and bawdy sexuality of **RESTORATION COMEDY** later in the century (1660–1699) broadened the form further, exposing the gap between public and private behaviour.

By the eighteenth century, the supposed amoralism of Restoration farce was seen as distasteful and drama moved in a new direction – **SENTIMENTAL COMEDY** emerged as a reaction against the bawdy exposure of human vices. It aimed to exhibit the virtues of private life, emphasising the difficulties people face, rather than their weaknesses. While the function of farce is to entertain, sentimental comedy is didactic, focusing on improving its audience through the intentional **PATHOS** (the quality of arousing feelings of pity and sorrow) of the emotional content. In the second half of the eighteenth century, comedy moved away from the emotional and didactic leanings of sentimental comedy. Instead, it combined features of farce, satirical comedy and the **COMEDY OF MANNERS** (comedy focusing on the behaviour and attitudes of people living under a specific social code).

In the twentieth century, however, successful farces, often called '**BEDROOM FARCES**', with their emphasis on sexual infidelity and amorous escapades, have again drawn huge audiences. John Cleese's performance in *Fawlty Towers* brought the exaggerated characters, absurd situations and misunderstandings of farce to television, and many sitcoms continue to draw on the same traditions.

ACTIVITY 19.2

Read the following extract from *The Rivals* (1775), by Richard Sheridan. The play is set in Bath, where Captain Absolute, son of Sir Anthony and heir to £3000 a year, has assumed the character of the penniless Ensign Beverley in order to court Lydia, a sentimental heroine. Lydia's aunt and Sir Anthony desire a match between Lydia and the Captain, but Lydia thinks it more romantic to love a poor lieutenant than a rich man. No one knows of Absolute's deception, so comic misunderstandings, mistaken identities, surprises and discoveries underpin the plot.

Explore the way in which comedy is created here. You may like to think about:

- the register and the context
- the structure
- the characterisation
- the language and grammar.

1   *Enter Lucy in a hurry.*
    Lucy   O Ma'am, here is Sir Anthony Absolute just come home with your aunt.
    Lydia They'll not come here. – Lucy, do you watch.   [*Exit Lucy.*
    Julia Yet I must go. – Sir Anthony does not know I am here, and if we meet,
5   he'll detain me, to shew me the town. I'll take another opportunity of pay-
             ing respects to Mrs. Malaprop, when she shall treat me, as long as she
             chooses, with her select words so ingeniously *misapplied*, without being
             mispronounced.
                                        Re-enter Lucy.
10 *Lucy*   O Lud! Ma'am, they are both coming up stairs.
    Lydia Well, I'll not detain you Coz. – Adieu, my dear Julia, I'm sure you are in
             haste to send to Faulkland. – There – through my room you'll find another
             stair-case.
    Julia Adieu. – [*Embrace*]   [*Exit Julia.*
15 *Lydia* Here, my dear Lucy, hide these books. – Quick, quick. – Fling *Peregrine
             Pickle* under the toilet – throw *Roderick Random* into the closet – put *The
             Innocent Adultery* into *The Whole Duty of Man* – thrust *Lord Aimworth*
             under the sopha – cram *Ovid* behind the bolster – there – put *The Man
             of Feeling* into your pocket – so, so, now lay *Mrs. Chapone* in sight, and
20   leave *Fordyce's Sermons* open on the table.
    Lucy   O burn it, Ma'am, the hair-dresser has torn away as far as *Proper Pride.*
    Lydia Never mind – open at *Sobriety*. – Fling me *Lord Chesterfield's Letters.*
             Now for 'em.   [*Exit Lucy.*
                        Enter Mrs. Malaprop and Sir Anthony Absolute.
25 *Mrs. Mal.* There, Sir Anthony, there sits the deliberate Simpleton, who wants to dis-
             grace her family, and lavish herself on a fellow not worth a shilling!
    Lydia Madam, I thought you once –
    Mrs. Mal. You thought, Miss! – I don't know any business you have to think at all –
             thought does not become a young woman; the point we would request
30   of you is, that you will promise to forget this fellow – to illiterate him, I say,
             quite from your memory.
                                            [...]
    Lydia What crime, Madam, have I committed to be treated thus?
    Mrs. Mal. Now don't attempt to extirpate yourself from the matter; you know I have
35   proof controvertible of it. – But tell me, will you promise to do as you're
             bid? Will you take a husband of your friend's choosing?

                                                    (Act 1, scene 2, ll. 154–94)

The **register** is formal since this is a play that has been written to be spoken (**mode**) – it is a one-way communication in that the participants and the audience have no direct interaction (**manner**). The relationships between the characters on the stage, however, reflect the age, social status, personality and role of the individuals, providing a rich source of comedy.

For the twenty-first century audience, there may, on first reading, be little that appears funny: a young woman and her maid servant rushing around hiding books; an aunt and her charge arguing about appropriate suitors; out-dated comments about girls who should do as they are told and avoid thought at all costs. To appreciate the humour, therefore, we need to know something about the **context** in which the play was written. An understanding of eighteenth century comedy, contemporary social attitudes and cultural expectations will enable us, as a modern audience, to appreciate the comedy of the extract.

The play is an example of 'laughing' comedy, a form that puts its emphasis on entertainment rather than improvement. It draws on the tradition of farce and has numerous entrances and exits, intrigue, fast-paced dialogue, and misunderstandings. In the extract here, there are six entrances and exits within 30 lines and this creates an atmosphere of comic chaos as a backdrop to the dialogue. As a modern audience, we feel uncomfortable with Mrs Malaprop's comments on young women, but it is likely that a contemporary audience would have found them funny. We know that they are not intended by Sheridan as a serious social comment since they have been delivered by the ridiculous Mrs Malaprop – the role of a character within a play inevitably affects the way in which we are intended to respond to what they say. The play was written at a time when the novel was emerging as a major literary form and when circulating libraries were making novels easily accessible. It was contemporary practice to attack these libraries and the supposedly immoral behaviour they encouraged by promoting the reading of novels. Such attitudes are demonstrated here in the desperate attempt to hide Lydia's books.

The **structure** of the extract is based on the interaction of characters and the changes in topic. The first section focuses on Lydia and Julia, who talk about Sir Anthony Absolute and Mrs Malaprop; the second on Lydia and Lucy, who talk about books; and the third on Lydia and Mrs Malaprop, who discuss Lydia's love for Ensign Beverley (a disguised Captain Absolute). Lucy's entrance and her warning of the arrival of Mrs Malaprop and Sir Anthony Absolute (l. 2) create a disruption and set the scene for physical comedy (hiding the books); Mrs Malaprop's entrance and her criticisms of Lydia create verbal comedy. The turn-taking is co-operative in the first and second sections, reflecting the relationships between Lydia and her cousin Julia and between Lydia and her maid Lucy. In the third section, Mrs Malaprop's position of authority is seen in her extended turns, in her interruption of Lydia's turn (l. 28), and in her failure to answer Lydia's question (l. 33) – the incomplete adjacency pair is indicative of her dominant position.

The **characterisation** is developed in the interactions between characters and in the linguistic and grammatical features of the dialogue. The relationship between Lydia and her aunt falls into a traditional thematic pattern: a young girl is prevented from fulfilling her dreams by an authoritative older figure. The interaction here is comic rather than tragic because both are limited by their own self-deception. Mrs Malaprop thinks herself *queen of the dictionary*, but is made ridiculous by her word blunders; Lydia is deluded by her novel-reading and the false ideals these novels encourage, which colour her view of the world and love. The interactions between Lydia and Julia and between Lydia and Lucy, on the other hand, are marked by the similarity in their ages and outlooks. The comedy relies on the topic (Mrs Malaprop; books) and the action (hiding the books).

The **language** of the extract creates comedy on a number of levels. The humour in Mrs Malaprop's misuse of words is explicit. Mrs Malaprop has become the most well-known character from Sheridan's play and her name has become a byword for the unintentional misuse of a word that has been confused with one of a similar sound, particularly when the effect is ridiculous (**MALAPROPISMS**). The name originates in the seventeenth-century French 'mal à propos', meaning 'not to the purpose'. In this extract, she uses *illiterate* (l. 30) for 'obliterate', *extirpate* (l. 34) for 'extricate' and *controvertible* (l. 35) for 'incontrovertible'. The humour is explained by Julia before we see Mrs Malaprop – her words are *so ingeniously misapplied*, but not *mispronounced*.

The titles of the novels that Lydia and Lucy so studiously conceal from Mrs Malaprop and Sir Anthony are also designed to amuse the audience. *Roderick Random* (1748) and *Peregrine Pickle* (1751) are by Tobias Smollett, whose declared purpose in writing was to arouse *generous indignation* in his readers. His novels were often controversial because of the libellous passages, the episodes set in scenes of squalor and violence, and his tendency to write about passion in a way that did not conform to eighteenth-century affectations. Just as Smollett's works were controversial for their content, so too were the sentimental novel *The Man of Feeling* (1771) by Henry Mackenzie and *The Innocent Adultery* (1771), contemporary works dramatising the romantic view of life that produced the sentimental Lydia who yearns for the romance of an elopement and a penniless husband. Such novels were seen by some to encourage the false ideals that restrict Lydia's understanding of the world.

Sheridan enhances the comedy by juxtaposing these romantic novels with the religious and educative texts that would have been approved reading matter for young women: *The Whole Duty of Man* (1659), an extensive religious handbook which continued to be published throughout the eighteenth century; *Fordyce's Sermons to Young Women* (1765), which reflect his disapproval of novels; and *Lord Chesterfield's Letters* (1774), which was described by its author as *a famous, highly improving work*. The comedy of concealment is enhanced by the juxtaposition of the popular and respectable reading material of the time. The incidental comment by Lucy that the hairdresser has used the pages of Fordyce as far as *Proper Pride* (l. 21) is an example of period humour – as a twenty-first century audience, we may need to have a gloss to understand that they have been used for curling papers and that the *toilet* is a dressing-table.

The **grammatical features** are not an explicit part of the comedy, but they do have a role to play in defining the characters: Lydia and Mrs Malaprop speak in very different ways and it is Sheridan's use of grammar that underpins this. The dynamic verbs of the imperatives (*fling, throw, thrust, cram*), for instance, reflect

Lydia's vitality, while Mrs Malaprop's exclamatives (ll. 24, 26) and interrogatives (ll. 32–3) reflect her authoritative role as guardian. The contrast establishes the thematic divide of the play between the young and the old, and the audience recognises the relationship as a comic one. In this extract, Lydia's physical energy is set against Mrs Malaprop's ridiculous use of language and her blustering attempts to be authoritarian. Similarly, Lydia's sentences tend to be simple or compound – the use of dashes to divide them into grammatical units is another means of communicating her energy on the page:

    A   P   O   A   P   O
(Here), (my dear Lucy), (hide) (these books). – (Quick, quick.) – (Fling) (*Peregrine Pickle*)
           voc

     A   P   O   A
(under the toilet) – (throw) (*Roderick Random*) (into the closet)

The long-winded complex and compound–complex sentences of Mrs Malaprop are in direct contrast. Where the style adopted for Lydia suggests a breathless excitement, the style of Mrs Malaprop is verbose and staid. Her sentences are marked by numerous clauses, parentheses and a general verbosity:

S   P   O   S   P
(I) (don't know) (any business ø you have to think at all) – (thought) (does not become)
  neg   SCl–RelCl   SCl–NFCl   neg

        O   S   P   C
(a young woman); (the point we would request of you) (is), (that you will promise
                       SCl–RelCl   SCl–NCl

                 C   A
to forget this fellow) – (to illiterate him), (I say), (quite from your memory).
SCl–NFCl   SCl–NFCl   commentCl

To understand the way in which comedy is created in this extract, we need to recognise three key areas: the staging of the scene; the characterisation and the ways in which lexical and grammatical features develop our sense of character; and the importance of contextual knowledge. The interaction between the physical activity and the changes in dramatic pace, the comic contrasts created between characters, and an appreciation of contemporary attitudes and expectations together ensure that an audience will find Sheridan's play amusing.

Parody

A **PARODY** is an imitation of the words, style, attitude, tone and ideas of a discourse, which often aims to make the original seem ridiculous by exaggerating its defining features. There has to be a subtle balance between the original speech or writing and the distorted version – for the parody to be successful, the intended audience must immediately see the semantic and stylistic links. The most informal parodies are often described as **SPOOFS**.

Although **grammatical structures** will be recognisably similar to those of the original, the parody may include contemporary features that link it to the context in which it was written. The **language** is often informal, and puns, slang, sexual innuendo and expletives are common. The **tone** is light-hearted rather than serious. **Direct address** to the reader and the author's incidental use of the **first person** enhance the comic effect as they self-consciously challenge the reality of the fictional world.

Parody has a long **history**. One of the first English parodies can be found in Chaucer's *Canterbury Tales* (1387), where the 'Tale of Sir Thopas' is a comic imitation of the characteristics of medieval romances. Poets like Dryden (1631–1700) and Pope (1688–1744) used parody as a form in which they could mock particular individuals or contemporary attitudes. They adopted a grand and serious style, often parodying the great classics, and set it in opposition to the content, which dealt with an insignificant or frivolous subject. It is a style often referred to as the **MOCK-HEROIC**. The parody of serious novels can be seen in the lively reworking of Samuel Richardson's gloomy epistolary novel *Pamela* (1740). The parody *Shamela Andrews* (1741), written by Henry Fielding but first published under a pseudonym, aimed to challenge what Fielding saw as the pompous moralising and hypocrisy of the original.

Written parodies of contemporary popular novels are common: *The Asti Spumante Code: A Parody* (2005), by Toby Clements, parodies Dan Brown's bestseller *The Da Vinci Code* (2003); *The Chronicles of Blarnia* (2005), *Barry Trotter and the Shameless Parody* (2003), *Barry Trotter and the Unnecessary Sequel* (2004) and *Barry Trotter and the Dead Horse* (2004), by Michael Gerber, parody C. S. Lewis's 1950s classic *The Chronicles of Narnia* and J. K. Rowling's bestselling *Harry Potter* series. In such books the irreverent tone, footnotes and asides addressed to the reader, puns on the names of characters, and contemporary references are all designed to entertain – their originality as well as their humorous take on familiar texts makes us laugh. Although often reworking books read by children, the parodies are for a very different audience. With their use of sexual innuendo, expletives and potentially offensive content, the intended audience for these novels is clearly adult.

SPOKEN PARODIES appear in sketch shows and as full-length features. The *Epic Movie* team have addressed the genres of romantic comedy (*Date Movie*), horror (*Scary Movie*) and fantasy (*Epic Movie*) on the big screen, while Dawn French and Jennifer Saunders have parodied *Titanic, Braveheart, The Lord of the Rings* and *Brokeback Mountain*. Radio shows such as *Radio Active* and *The Sunday Format* parody local commercial radio and 'lifestyle journalism' respectively; on television, *The Office* parodies small businesses and their self-important managers.

The **purpose** of parodies is to entertain their intended audience by drawing on key features of the original and exaggerating them; any serious point made is of secondary importance. **POLITICAL SATIRE** often draws on parody in order to highlight apparent discrepancies in policy, failure to answer direct questions or a tendency for linguistic faux pas; but whereas a parody points to such discrepancies for entertainment value, a satire aims to promote change. In the poem 'Reading Scheme' (*Making Cocoa for Kingsley Amis*, 1986), Wendy Cope parodies the repetitive style and structure of traditional school reading-scheme books. The result may implicitly suggest that such books lack the narrative excitement we need to make us real readers, but this educational issue is not central to the poet's purpose or our enjoyment. Cope exploits the format because she knows that her readers will immediately recognise it and will be amused by the way in which she pokes fun at it.

Cope's poem draws on the named characters (*Peter, Jane, Mummy, Daddy*), the concrete lexis (*doll, ball dog*) and the short simple sentence structures (*Here is Peter... . They like fun./Jane has a big doll.*) of the original. The humour of her poem lies in the juxtaposition of the original content with her reworked version in which the mother entertains the milkman until they are interrupted by the arrival of the father with a gun. Although the content has been made adult with the implicit references to sexual intrigue, the style throughout imitates the tone of the reading-scheme books. Cope's version, however, has to draw on a wider range of vocabulary and sentence structure, and uses interrogatives, the exclamative and some minor sentences. These additions to the original are necessary because her poem develops a more complicated narrative.

In Figure 19.3, the writers of the *Simpsons* comic (January 2005) use parody as a celebration of an original and inventive poem, 'The Jabberwocky' by Lewis Carroll. As suggested by the lead-in (*"Nothing beats the nonsensical narrative of Lewis Carroll!"*), their cartoon-strip version is not intended as a mockery of the original, but as an appreciation of its creative spirit. The first page of the comic version parodies the first six lines of the poem:

Jabberwocky (*extract*)

'Twas brillig and the slithy toves
    Did gyre and gimble in the wabe;
All mimsy were the borogoves,
    And the mome raths outgrabe.

'Beware the Jabberwock, my son!
    The jaws that bite, the claws that catch! ...

The **title** of the comic story is immediately recognisable as a parody of the original: the /æ/ and /ɒ/ vowels have been exchanged and the initial phoneme /dʒ/ has been replaced by /sl/ to change the meaning of the word. Where the original is nonsensical, the semantic link created between a monster and the noun 'slobber' (to dribble; to speak or write in a maudlin or sentimental way) is comical.

The main text accompanying each image closely follows the style and structure of the poem. It keeps the archaisms (the contraction *'Twas* and the past tense verb form *Did cheat*) and the line structure and rhythm, but substitutes a **lexical set of words** directly linked to the Simpsons to replace the language of epic fantasy. Proper nouns (*Wiggum, Moe, Nelson*) relating to characters and adjectives (*slimy, tipsy*) and verbs (*cheat, stole*) establishing their characteristics will be familiar to the intended audience.

The **content** has been adapted so that it focuses on an event (*Springfield Annual Picnic*) that is appropriate and the images develop the detail of the occasion. Speech bubbles and capitalised onomatopoeic words (*BLAM! BLAM!*; *GLUG! GLUG! GLUG!*) add to the humour. The parody of the vicious Jabberwocky of Carroll's poem in the form of a monster with the face of Barney, a regular at Moe's Tavern, creates comedy. Barney is renowned for his love of alcohol and his distinctive loud belch – the noun phrases that describe him replace the threatening lexis of the original (*bite, claws, catch*) with words that have humorous connotations in the context (*drool, paunch, sags*). As the monster of the cartoon strip, Barney is not intimidating, but ridiculous. The juxtaposition of the newspaper headline (*STOLEN DUFF TRUCK STILL MISSING*) and Moe's speech bubble (*I WONDER*

Figure 19.3 **Extract from *Simpsons Comics* (January 2005)**

WHERE BARNEY IS?) create an important contextual link that reinforces Barney's status: he is not busy rampaging, but is hidden in the forest with the stolen Duff truck, enjoying its contents.

ACTIVITY 19.3

Read through the two extracts below. The first is taken from a modern parody, *The Chronicles of Blarnia* by Michael Gerber (2005), and the second from the opening of C. S. Lewis's *The Lion, the Witch and the Wardrobe* (1950).

How does the parody adapt the original text to create humour? You may like to think about the following:

- ▶ the register and the context
- ▶ the content
- ▶ the lexis
- ▶ the grammatical features.

EXTRACT 1: *THE CHRONICLES OF BLARNIA* (B)

1 Once there were four children named Pete, Sue, Ed and Loo, and this story is about something that happened to them when their parents sold them for medical experiments. Well, *rented* them, actually – we must be fair.

Early one morning, quite against their will, Pete, Sue, Ed and Loo were carefully
5 packaged up in brown paper and delivered to the house of an old Professor. The Professor, who had purchased his credentials over the Internet, lived in the absolute a***-end of the country, ten long miles from the nearest police station – and there was a very good reason for this. Some of the things that went on in the house were somewhat shady, but scientific progress can be like that. The Professor had no wife,
10 which was a bit of a giveaway, and lived in a large, heavily guarded mansion with a housekeeper named Mrs Macbeth and several servants, each of whom were much too low-class to figure in the story, or even have proper names. Don't worry, I won't mention them again.

The Professor had white hair and large frightening muttonchop whiskers that the
15 children had only seen once before, in terrifying pictures of Isaac Asimov. He wore a white lab coat and carried a stethoscope which he used constantly, even on things like tables and chairs. When the Professor came to the front door to unwrap and frisk them, the four Perversie children felt an urge to flee, like their insides were filled with wriggling bubbles. But it seemed impolite to run, especially since the charwomen had
20 Uzis under their aprons.

The Chronicles of Blarnia

EXTRACT 2: *THE LION, THE WITCH AND THE WARDROBE* (LWW)

1 Once there were four children whose names were Peter, Susan, Edmund and Lucy. This story is about something that happened to them when they were sent away from London during the war because of the air-raids. They were sent to the house of an old Professor who lived in the heart of the country, ten miles from the nearest railway
5 station and two miles from the nearest post office. He had no wife and he lived in a very large house with a housekeeper called Mrs Macready and three servants. (Their names were Ivy, Margaret and Betty, but they do not come into the story much.) He himself was a very old man with shaggy white hair which grew over most of his face as well as on his head, and they liked him almost at once; but on the first evening
10 when he came out to meet them at the front door he was so odd-looking that Lucy

(who was the youngest) was a little afraid of him, and Edmund (who was the next youngest) wanted to laugh and had to keep on pretending he was blowing his nose to hide it.

The Lion, the Witch and the Wardrobe (Chapter 1)

COMMENTARY

Although both extracts have a written **mode**, the **manner** in each case is quite different. Extract 2 has a formal style that reflects the period in which it was written. The third person narration maintains the credibility of the fictional world in which the reader is expected to believe and there are no references to the narrator/ writer or to the audience. Extract 1, on the other hand, moves between the formal and informal, creating humour by juxtaposing unexpected registers. There are no examples of direct address, but the writer's use of pronouns implies a familiarity between himself and his audience. First person singular (*I*, l. 12) and plural (*we*, l. 3) subject pronouns suggest a collusion between author and reader that challenges the conventions of traditional narrative.

The **title** for each novel also reflects the manner, as the tone of each underlines the relationship between reader and writer. The formality of the original work is marked by the seriousness of its title, which draws attention to three crucial, although apparently unconnected, elements of the story. It functions as a **hook** since the reader wants to understand the link between such disparate concrete nouns. The title of the parody adopts a very different tone, preparing us for the informality of the style. The juxtaposition of the formal noun *Chronicles* with the nonsensical neologism *Blarnia* prepares us for this. Punning on the fictional world 'Narnia' in which C. S. Lewis's narrative takes place, Gerber substitutes the phoneme /bl/ for /n/ – changing the sound and the meaning ('blarney' is 'flattering talk' or 'nonsense'). Linked to the Blarney Stone in south-west Ireland, which supposedly endows whoever kisses it with the skills of flattery, the connotations set the tone of the parody that is to follow.

The **context** of each extract is directly linked to the period in which it was written. The original looks back to the time of the Second World War when children were being evacuated from London. The direct reference to this (ll. 2–3) explicitly sets the context and provides the reason for the children's change of location. Extract 1 sets the narrative in a very different context. There are no explicit references to the period, but a lexical set of contemporary words creates the background for the narrative that is to follow: *Internet* (l. 6), a global computer network which evolved from the US Defense Department's linked computer system (1986); *Isaac Asimov* (l. 15), a Russian-born American writer and professor of biochemistry (1920–92), who was a prolific and highly-esteemed writer of science fiction and popular science books; and *Uzis* (l. 20), automatic guns that are seen as status symbols in the world of drug-dealing (1980s). These set the scene at some point in the late twentieth and early twenty-first century and the author uses this change of context to create humour.

The **content** is directly linked to the two distinct contexts, the characters and the plot. The contrast between the two creates humour because the author of the parody relies on his readers' familiarity with the original. The sequence of events in each case is very similar: we are told why the children are sent away; where they go; and something about the Professor and his household. It is the context of Extract 1 that enables the writer to create humour: in both cases, the children arrive in a bizarre household where nothing is quite what it seems, but in Extract 1 the unexpectedness of the references creates comedy. There may be no world war threatening the security of the characters in the parody, but it creates an absurd fictional world in which medical experiments on children are authorised by their parents. Since the tone is not serious, however, we are intended to find this funny rather than terrifying.

The **naming** of the characters is immediately comic: the informality of the abbreviations reflects the tone of Extract 1 and the rhyming of *Sue* and *Loo* is humorous – particularly because of the connotations of 'loo' as an informal word for toilet. In addition, their family name, *Perversie* (l. 18), with its connotations of deliberately deviating from what is regarded as normal, characterises the children as very different from their period counterparts (whom Gerber describes as *four plucky English schoolkids*).

The **lexis** of the parody is dominated by **informal expressions** that mark it as a product of the twenty-first century: the colloquial linking adverb *Well* (l. 3); the expletive *a**** (l. 7); and colloquialisms such as *somewhat shady* (l. 9), *a giveaway* (l. 10) and *frisk* (l. 17). The **lexical set** of scientific words such as *medical experiments* (ll. 2–3), *scientific progress* (l. 9), *white lab coat* and *stethoscope* (l. 16) could suggest a serious topic, but the juxtaposition of these noun phrases with the words around them establishes the tone as humorous. The semantic link between the subject (*their parents*), the predicators (*sold … rented*) and the adverbial *for medical experiments*, for instance, undermines any potential for a serious scientific content by presenting us with an apparently ludicrous situation. We can laugh because we know that the impulse behind the humour is not based on circumstances which actually exist. Similarly, humour is created by the link between the adjective phrase *somewhat shady* and the concept of *scientific progress*, and in the reference to the stethoscope which is used on inanimate objects.

The author plays games with the **denotations of words**, taking a verb such as *sent* (l. 3, *LWW*) from the original and narrowing its meaning to create humour. Rather than interpreting it in the general sense of 'to cause or order a person or thing to be taken, directed or transmitted to another place', Gerber focuses specifically on the associations linked to 'sending by post'. In this context, the language is humorous because the children are literally treated as parcels – subject-specific lexis (*carefully packaged up in brown paper*, ll. 4–5; *delivered*, l. 5; *unwrap*, l. 17) is funny because it is used in an unexpected and surreal context.

Contemporary concepts amuse the reader because they are so distant from the world of the 1950s original. The satirical reference to *credentials* that have been *purchased … over the Internet* (l. 6) will be recognised by modern readers as an increasing problem in the twenty-first century, when computer-based scams are so easy to initiate. The juxtaposition of *Uzis* and *charwomen* (ll. 19–20) makes us laugh because it is an absurd overlaying of unexpected nouns.

The **grammatical features** of the original story reflect the formality of the genre. Although the story was written for children, the sentences are long and there are no simple or minor sentences:

    S   P   C

(He himself) (was) (a very old man with shaggy white hair which grew over most of his
SCl–RelCl

face as well as on his head), (and) (they) (liked) (him) (almost at once); (but) (on the first
conj   S   P   O   A   conj   A

evening) (when he came out to meet them at the front door) (he) (was) (so odd-looking
A   SCl–ACl   SCl–NFCl   S   P   C

that Lucy who was the youngest was a little afraid of him), (and) (ø Edmund who was
SCl–NCl   SCl–RelCl   conj   SCl–NCl   SCl–RelCl C

the next youngest wanted to laugh and had to keep on pretending he was blowing his
SCl–NFCl   SCl–NFCl   SCl–NFCl   SCl–NCl

nose to hide it).   (ll.7–13)
SCl–NFCl

The style is typical of the period – the punctuation and parenthesis guide the reader through the sequences of co-ordinating and subordinate clauses. Where the original provides the reader with all the information in one paragraph of fewer than 200 words, the parody uses three paragraphs and approximately 270 words. The length reflects the addition of extra narrative detail rather than greater complexity of style. Although there are still long compound–complex sentences, the text is made more manageable by the use of a minor sentence (l.3), a dash (l.7), a simple sentence (ll.12–13) and an initial-position conjunction (l.19), all of which contribute to the informality of the tone. In addition, the final sentence of the C. S. Lewis story is divided into four separate sentences in the parody, thus spreading the information and making it easier for the reader to process. Sentence 1:

>   S   P   O
> (The Professor) (had) (white hair and large frightening muttonchop whiskers that the
>   SCl–RelCl
> children had only seen once before, in terrifying pictures of Isaac Asimov).

Sentence 2:

>   S   P   O   P   O
> (He) (wore) (a white lab coat) (and) (carried) (a stethoscope which he used con-
>   conj   SCl–RelCl
> stantly), ...

Sentence 3:

>   A   S
> (When the Professor came to the front door to unwrap and frisk them), (the four
> SCl–ACl   SCl–NFCls
>   P   O   A
> Perversie children) (felt) (an urge to flee), (like their insides were filled with wriggling
>   SCl–NFCl   SCl–ACl
> bubbles).

Sentence 4:

>   S   P   C   A
> (But) (it) (seemed) (impolite to run), (especially since the charwomen had Uzis under
> conj   SCl–NFCl   SCl–ACl
> their aprons).

The change in style contributes to the humour because Gerber can make sure that any comic or unexpected references occur in places of grammatical importance – near the beginning or the end of a sentence.

A change of **grammatical mood** can also create humour. In the original story the passive verb phrase *were sent away* (l. 2, *LWW*) reflects the fact that it does not matter to the reader who was responsible for the decision – the change of setting is just a necessary function of the plot. Gerber, however, uses the active verb phrase *sold* (l. 2, *B*) since he wishes to emphasise the underlying comedy: the humour depends upon the reader's understanding that it is the children's parents who have placed them in danger.

The informality of tone is enhanced by the writer's use of **asides** and **parenthesis**. The prepositional phrase *quite against their will* (l. 4), the relative clauses *which was a bit of a giveaway* (l. 10) and *each of whom were much too low-class to figure in the story...* (ll. 11–12), and the comment clause *Don't worry* (l. 12) are humorous because they develop our sense of the authorial voice – a tongue-in-cheek commentary that signposts the changes to the original.

We know that the impulse behind this kind of humour is entertainment and that the parodied text has a literary status that makes it a worthwhile target. The parody is not meant to be taken seriously, so we can enjoy the implicit mockery. What makes us laugh is the way in which the original has been taken out of one context and put into another. By highlighting the changes in content, language and grammar, writers can ensure that we make the most of the comedy.

Satire

SATIRE is a style of writing in which the follies of society are mocked in an indirect way: criticisms are hidden beneath a veil of **IRONY** in which the writer's words appear to say the opposite of what is actually meant. It is a form of comic writing, but the difference between comedy and satire lies in the **purpose**: where comedy believes that people are ultimately absurd and therefore funny, satire implicitly expresses a desire to 'correct' through ridicule. The **content** is wide-ranging, but will usually be topical, focusing on a very specific target: a particular individual (politician, celebrity, journalist, writer), an event or a particular kind of behaviour. In order to satirise the subject, the writer must represent views that are shared by a substantial proportion of the intended audience, who must also believe that the target has transgressed the accepted codes of behaviour.

The **form** of satire is varied since writers can choose to adopt the conventions of speech (sketches, songs) or writing (poetry, prose, drama, cartoon strips), and parody is common. The **tone** is often ironic, accompanied by an undercurrent of mock-approval that makes the satire seem less threatening. Exaggeration and distortion are used to draw attention to the particular characteristic or behaviour that is the satirist's target. The **grammatical structures** are formal or informal depending upon the register, and the **lexis** often mixes subject-specific language, expletives, colloquialisms and topical references for comic effect.

While shock may be the immediate **audience response** to the use of informal language or the apparent poor taste of the content, there will also be amusement if a balance between humour and satirical comment is achieved. In a film like Sacha

Baron Cohen's *Borat*, for instance, the **'MOCKUMENTARY'** style satirises fictional characters from all walks of life. Cohen has been criticised for the film's politically incorrect central character, Borat, but most audiences have recognised that the satire is also directed at him.

The **history** of satire begins with the early Greek poets – Hipponax criticised his targets so viciously that some committed suicide. The two distinct approaches to satire, however, can be seen in the work of the Roman poets Horace and Juvenal. While the former adopted a tone of amused tolerance, mocking himself as satirist as well as his victims, Juvenal was bitter and indignant, raging against what he saw as the vices of his age. Both were to influence the development of English satire.

In the Middle Ages, Geoffrey Chaucer (*c.*1343–1400) used satire as a means of criticising what he saw as the corruption of the Church – a wealthy and very powerful institution. His portraits of religious figures in *The Canterbury Tales* depict individuals who have lost sight of their true spiritual purpose. The Pardoner, for instance, becomes a representation of the deceitful nature of those who sell worthless relics to gullible people who fear for the future of their souls:

But with thise relikes, whan that he fond	*With these relics, whenever he found*
A povre person dwellynge upon lond,	*A poor parson living in the country,*
Upon a day he gat hym moore moneye	*In a day he got more money*
Than that the person gat in monthes tweye;	*Than the parson would get in two months;*
And thus, with feyned flaterye and japes,	*And so, with his false flattery and jests,*
He made the person and the peple his apes.	*He made fools of the parson and the people.*

The emphasis on money is satirical since, in Chaucer's opinion, a man of God should be less concerned about personal wealth and more about his spiritual state of mind. Chaucer's portrait of the Pardoner is clever because his attack is subtle: while seeming to praise him for his beautiful Church readings and his singing of the offertories, he is critical of his intentions:

For wel he wiste, whan that song was songe,	*For he well knew, that when that song was sung,*
He moste preche and wel affile his tonge	*He'd have to preach and make his speech smooth*
To wynne silver, as he ful wel koude	*To win silver – as he knew he could*

Chaucer was probably the first English satirist, but the great age of satire began with the poet and playwright John Dryden (1631–1700) and continued into the eighteenth century with the work of Alexander Pope (1688–1744) and Jonathan Swift (1667–1745). They often adopted the elegance and irony of Horace, using satire as a weapon against both institutions and individuals.

More recently, television and radio have continued to use satire as a form of **political** and **social commentary** – satirists can usually avoid censorship because their attack is not explicit. In the twenty-first century, celebrities and other people in the public eye recognise that they are legitimate targets and most accept the satire with good grace. There are situations, however, where libel cases may be based on suppositions underpinning the satire.

On television, we find satire in political sketch shows, but it can also be used to create humour in other contexts. A single line in a drama can satirise a particular **social trend**. In ITV's *Primeval*, a Saturday-night family drama in which extinct animals are appearing in contemporary London because of time anomalies, two students, Tom and Duncan, come across a dodo. It becomes the source of some satirical comments: they decide to keep the bird for its money-making prospects, enthusiastically pronouncing *'Student loans will be a thing of the past!'*; when the bird is sick, one says: *'Don't contaminate it! We can sell dodo sick on eBay.'* The comments satirise social trends in the twenty-first century: students worrying about paying off their university debts and people who use the internet to try and make money from their own unwanted possessions.

Satire attacking **individuals**, **groups** and **institutions** can be found in satirical magazines such as *Private Eye*. Newspaper parodies often satirise politicians: for example, Ruth Kelly MP became the subject of an article headlined *WOMAN WITH SPECIAL NEEDS GIVEN PLACE IN CABINET* by the Education Correspondent *Conrad Blackboard* (January 2007), following publicity surrounding Kelly's decision to send her child to a private school for children with disabilities. The satire is directed against the apparent conflict of interest and the hypocrisy of the Government – having received *one-to-one tuition by her teacher Mr Blair*, Kelly will soon know *exactly what to say and think on all matters*. The satire is brought to its climax with an explicit statement of the *special needs* of Cabinet members: *such as a huge salary, a large car and the chance of appearing on the Today programme*.

Sketch shows like *The Now Show* on Radio 4 use satire to comment on **topical issues**. Mitch Benn's satirical song, for instance, tackles political issues such as the war in Iraq or social issues like 'size zero' supermodels. The satire is gentle rather than biting and we laugh at the neat rhymes and clever phrasing of the song, but the content is always thought-provoking.

> Well she's up on the catwalk twice nightly,
> Wouldn't say she's as skinny as hell,
> But it's true that she makes Keira Knightley
> Look a bit like the late Orson Welles.
>
> All the press wonder if she's bulimic
> Or if she's ever eaten or supped.
> Well you know what they say in this business –
> Whatever goes down must come up.
>
> She's a size zero
> With a midriff as thick as a wrist.
> She's a size zero
> If she gets any thinner she'll technically cease to exist.
>
> They say she's a dreadful role model
> In the papers, but also we find
> They complain that the kids are all too fat these days
> How I wish they would make up their minds.
>
> Fashion writers feign fear and anxiety
> And call her condition obscene,
> But they won't be caught dead with a fat bird
> On the cover of their magazines.
>
> So she's still a size zero
> 'Cos this year it's in to look dead.
> She's a size zero
> Or she could be a normal-sized girl with a really big head.

> She's a size zero
> She's almost translucent it's true.
> She's a size zero
> And if beauty's skin deep, she's beautiful all the way through.

The Now Show, BBC Radio 4 (2 March 2007)

The song raises contemporary concerns about: bulimia in the fashion world; the controversy over 'size zero' models; the emphasis in magazines on women who do not represent a normal body image; the effect unrealistically thin models may have on a child's self-image; and overweight children. While the issues are serious, the tone is not – informal language (*kids, bird*), colloquial expressions (*as skinny as hell, caught dead, it's in*) and contractions (*she's, she'll, 'Cos*) reflect the song's conversational tone. Satirical mockery focuses on the suspect practices of the fashion industry (*you know what they say in this business/Whatever goes down must come up*) and its hypocrisy (*Fashion writers feign fear and anxiety*); and on the headline-chasing newspapers that use supermodels as front-page news while berating them as *dreadful role models* and deploring the obesity of today's children.

Straight humour can be found in the light rhymes (*supped/come up; obscene/magazines*), the comparisons (*Keira Knightley/Orson Welles; a normal girl with a really big head*), the unexpected use of words (*supped, midriff*), and the reinterpretation of a familiar saying (*beauty's skin deep*). The audience laugh spontaneously at these features because they are immediately funny, but they also laugh because they recognise the underlying truth that the song reveals about our society. Although the satire is not bitter and the tone is light-hearted rather than indignant, the implicit criticisms are pointed.

ACTIVITY 19.4

Read the following extract from the television programme *Dead Ringers* (12 June 2006), in which two of the team's comedians take on the roles of the Prime Minister Tony Blair (TB, Jon Culshaw) and the BBC's Political Editor Nick Robinson (NR, Kevin Connelly). A key to the symbols can be found on page 93.

Explore the ways in which comedy is created in this sketch. You may like to consider:

- the register and the context
- the content
- the lexical and grammatical features
- the spoken features.

```
 1  NR  problems this week (.) contínue to mount for ↓Tony Blair↓ (.) from record NHS
        déficits (.) to the botched terror raid in Forest Gàte (1) ↑Prime Minister↑ (1) ↑you↑
        must be extremely cóncêrned =
     TB  = yeah (.) yeah (.) ↓whatever↓ =
 5  NR  = starting with the (.) crisis in the (.) ‖ NHS
     TB                                           ‖ twénty (1) nìneteen (1) ‖ éighteen
     NR                                                                    ‖ uh Prime  Minister
         ‖ uh
     TB  ‖ don't mind me (2) just go ahead (.) and ask (.) whatever you were going to ask
10      (1) seven (1) six (1) five =
```

```
NR  = ↑does the ‖ NHS↑
TB                ‖ ↓two↓ (1) ↑one↑ (1) made it [music; English flag lowered behind Prime
      Minister] the World Cup has started (1) now nobody will give a toss (.) about
      anything other (.) than (.) Wayne Rooney's foot (1) Peter Crouch's dance (1) and
15    Sven Goran Eriksson's (.) diamond formation (.) in (.) midfield =
NR  = I don't think that's quite right Prime ‖ Minister
TB                                           ‖ talk to the ↑flag↑ Nick cos the nation ain't
      ↑listening↑
```

COMMENTARY

This sketch uses the **form** of a televised political interview and as such we would
expect certain linguistic features: a formal relationship between participants who
both have professional status; a formal tone; and appropriate subject-specific
lexis. In terms of the structure, we would expect an opening that clearly signposts
the topic, and turn-taking based on complete adjacency pairs and smooth latching with few interruptions. Since it is a satire, however, our expectations are not
fulfilled. The **register** mixes a formal and an informal manner and this is what
immediately creates comedy in the extract – the language and the content of this
scripted 'spontaneous' interview are designed to challenge the audience.

In a wider **context**, we need to understand the relevance of the references that
are made if we are to appreciate the satirical points that underpin the mock interview. The *Dead Ringers* show is topical, with certain sketches written or re-drafted
on the day of broadcast. This particular sketch focuses on criticism of the Labour
Party in June 2006 when the NHS was failing to balance its finances and the
Government was under attack for another apparently unnecessary anti-terror raid
on the home of an Iraqi family in London, after which no charges were ultimately
brought. This political context forms the basis for the satirical attack: Tony Blair is
presented as being more interested in avoiding than in addressing the issues.

The opening is typical in clearly establishing the **content**. As we would expect,
the interviewer introduces the topic (problems for the Labour Party, ll. 1–2), but
the 'Prime Minister' does not co-operate. Instead of addressing the issues raised,
he ignores the opportunity to defend his Party's record, ultimately introducing a
topic of his own choosing later in the extract (the Football World Cup, ll. 13–15).

The **language** used by 'Nick Robinson' conforms to our expectations of the
reporter's role: familiar noun phrases such as *NHS deficits, terror raid* (ll. 1–2) and
crisis in the NHS (l. 5) function as a journalistic code, succinctly summarising running stories that have continued to interest political commentators and the general
public. The modifiers linked to these noun phrases (*record; botched*) suggest that a
judgement is being made – the negative connotations should instigate a defence of
the Labour Party by its leader.

The formal vocative, *Prime Minister* (l. 2), is in keeping with the tone set by the
interviewer, but when 'Tony Blair' does respond, the repetition of the colloquial
yeah, the dismissive *whatever* and his persistent counting mark a breakdown in the
discourse. His choice of lexis creates humour: it seems inappropriate for the formal context and for the age of the participants. The audience laughs at this repre-

sentation of 'Blair' adopting the language of the younger generation in an attempt to distance himself from the political realities with which he is being presented. This humour reaches its climax in his use of the colloquialism *give a toss* (l. 13) and the parody of teenage signage: 'speak to the hand 'cos the face ain't listening' becomes *talk to the flag . . cos the nation ain't listening* (ll. 17–18). As this is a code that defines insiders and outsiders, 'Blair' chooses this form of communication to distance himself from the interview.

With the introduction of the second topic (l. 13), the comedy is intensified – 'Blair' now dominates the conversation and political language is replaced by a lexical set for football. The possessive noun phrases *Wayne Rooney's foot, Peter Crouch's dance* and *Sven Goran Eriksson's diamond formation in midfield* (ll. 14–15) are contemporary references intended to demonstrate the Prime Minister's understanding of popular culture. We recognise the satirical point underpinning the sketch when we sense the relief expressed in the colloquial *made it* (l. 12) – this is avoidance behaviour in which 'Blair' is characterised as more interested in avoiding political debate than in football. His use of a familiar term of address (*Nick*, l. 17) and the non-standard *ain't* characterises the informality of his tone.

The **grammatical structures** are dominated by incomplete and minor sentences. The formal opening, as we would expect, uses a complex sentence to establish the topic followed by an emphatic simple sentence that signposts the end of the interviewer's turn:

> S   A   P   O   (S)   A
> (problems) (this week) (continue) (to mount) (for Tony Blair) (from record NHS deficits
> SCl–NFCl
>
>   S   P   C
> to the botched terror raid in Forest Gate) (Prime Minister) (you) (must be) (extremely
>   voc
> concerned)

The Prime Minister's failure to adopt the tone established by the interviewer and the fact that his minimal responses (ll. 4, 6) are minor sentences highlight for the audience that this is comedy. The change of grammatical mood from declarative to imperative (*don't mind … go ahead … ask*, l. 9) reinforces this since the status of the participants has been reversed and the interviewer is no longer in the dominant position. With the introduction of the second topic, the simple sentences are emphatic, reflecting the Prime Minister's jubilant tone:

> S   P   A   S   P   O
> (the World Cup) (has started) (now) (nobody) (will give) (a toss about anything other
> than WR's foot PC's dance and SGE's diamond formation in midfield)

The **spoken features** of this scripted interview contribute to the comedy because they frequently challenge our expectations. In a formal interview, we would expect the turn-taking to be co-operative, but in this satirical sketch, the 'Prime Minister' interrupts the interviewer on four occasions (ll. 6, 9, 12, 17) and his uncooperative approach means that the interviewer also interrupts (l. 7) as he tentatively attempts to re-establish the formality of the occasion by reiterating the formal vocative *Prime Minister*. The number of interrupted turns adds to the comedy – we know that they are not spontaneous, but scripted to characterise 'Tony Blair' in a comic manner. Similarly, the hesitancy of 'Nick Robinson' is emphasised by the incomplete interrogatives (ll. 5, 11), the normal non-fluency features (*uh*, ll. 7, 8) and the tentative comment clause *I don't think that's...* (l. 16).

The sketch is clearly satirical because it is making a political comment rather than just using the official status of a Prime Minister to create comedy. We laugh at the ludicrous caricature of the Prime Minister and at the linguistic and structural challenges to our expectations, but we recognise the underlying point that is being made about the Government.

Sketch shows

Sketch shows are made up of a sequence of usually unconnected scenes which focus on the development of a particular character or group of characters. In some shows there is a thematic framework that provides cohesion, linking the sketches through a particular location (*The League of Gentlemen*'s serialised sketches of individual characters whose stories do not overlap), an over-arching narrative voice (*Little Britain*), or a political or topical focus (*Dead Ringers*).

The **purpose** of most sketch shows is to entertain – they create comedy at a basic level that aims to make us laugh. Life is represented in a magnified cartoon-style and there is no underlying serious point to the humour. Where the sketches are linked by a common thematic focus, however, there is often a secondary purpose – they aim to make us think about a particular political or social issue. This kind of sketch show will often be satirical.

The creation of **character** dominates most sketch shows, with writers developing distinctive mannerisms, language and spoken features for each individual role. The characters are often stereotypes, larger-than-life people with exaggerated characteristics that are memorable. Most recur from episode to episode and this encourages the audience to become familiar with them. The sketches are funny because we anticipate the way in which a scene will unfold, based on our knowledge of a particular character, and we laugh when those expectations are fulfilled. Equally, however, comedy can be created when our expectations are not fulfilled: we usually associate certain characters with certain contexts, for instance, and if they are placed in a new situation, humour can be created either because they do not adapt to the new context or because they behave out of character in a self-conscious attempt to fit in. Where the comedy is at its most successful, the audience will recognise the caricatures as people from everyday life – they may be distorted and exaggerated, but there is an essential truth in the characterisation that strikes a chord.

The **context** of a sketch show is very varied because characters often inhabit very different physical spaces. The formality or informality of the background, our assumptions about the way in which we ourselves would expect to behave in such a place, and the way in which the character actually does behave all contribute to the comedy. Inevitably, the wider context – the broadcasting or performance time of a sketch show and its intended audience – has a significant effect on the kind of comedy created. Before the nine o'clock watershed, the **content** must be suitable for children, avoiding topics that may offend and focusing on physical slapstick and basic linguistic misunderstandings rather than on sexual innuendo and more sophisticated juxtapositions of register. The emphasis on a comic imitation of real life means that the content can address anything that may affect us on a day-to-day basis.

The **language** of sketch shows is directly linked to the range of characters represented. Most speak in a style that reflects their characterisation: the language may be informal or formal, standard or non-standard, subject-specific or general. Accents and distinctive pronunciations help to individualise the characters, placing them in a specific regional, social or cultural context.

Comedy can be created by using an unexpected linguistic style for a particular character or by juxtaposing the language type and context for comic effect. What is most noticeable, perhaps, is that the majority of characters in a sketch show have their own CATCHPHRASES. Contemporary shows such as *Little Britain* and *The Catherine Tate Show* have created numerous catchphrases that have become part of the modern lexicon, often used by young people as a conversation-stopping device. Tate's *How very dare you* and *Am I bovvered?*, and David Walliams and Matt Lucas's *Nobutyeahbutno, I'm a lady, The computer says 'No'* and *I'm the only gay in this village* have embedded themselves in the modern psyche. These phrases have been so successful because they neatly encapsulate the characters who utter them and communicate a particular mood or attitude.

In many sketch shows the content is SUBVERSIVE in that it challenges the customs and conventions, even the fundamental values, of society. They explore the comedy of sexuality, sex, politically incorrect attitudes and other 'unseen' elements of our culture, and the language is often colloquial, therefore, with expletives and sexual innuendo making many shows unsuitable for pre-watershed broadcast.

The overlaying of different **registers** is sometimes used for comic effect. In one *Dead Ringers* sketch, for instance, the Queen speaks using a teenage urban street dialect. Similarly, a representation of the fictional Gandalf from *Lord of the Rings* in which he offers customers in a department store advice on which saucepans are the best buy is humorous because he is out of context and using a form of language (persuasive sales talk) that is out of character. In each case, our immediate visual recognition of the 'character' leads us to expect a certain kind of language – when our expectations are not fulfilled, we laugh.

The **grammatical features** also tend to be informal since sketch shows use a spoken mode even though they are usually based on a written script. The structures vary, however, depending upon the kind of character who is speaking: the more formal the character, the more likely she or he is to use standard grammatical patterns. Differences in grammatical structure can be used to underpin characterisation, to develop contrasts or to reflect changes in context (region, period, situation). Often sentences are short with simple and minor structures because of the spoken nature of the form. However, rambling, loosely structured sentences can also be used to characterise particular individuals. The main focus of grammatical analysis should be on understanding the kind of character developed and the ways in which the grammar underpins the comedy, whether fulfilling or challenging our expectations.

Spoken features are often exaggerated for comic effect. Sudden or frequent changes in pitch or intonation, an overstated use of stress or pause, and unexpected variations in volume and pace are, like the characters, often more dramatic than in everyday conversation and therefore make us laugh. Turn-taking is important since most sketches use the framework of spoken interaction to dramatise a situation. The relationship between the participants and the ways in which turn-taking is organised will often contribute to the humour.

ACTIVITY 19.5

Read the following extracts. One was transcribed from an episode of *Ronni Ancona & Co.* (BBC 1, 29 May 2007) in which two teenagers talk about their friends; the other from an episode of *That Mitchell and Webb Look* (BBC 2, 12 October 2006) in which a group of marketing executives discuss a new product. A key to the symbols can be found on page 93.

Explore the way in which comedy is created in each scene. You may like to think about:

- the register and the context
- the use of stereotypes
- the lexical and grammatical features
- the spoken features.

EXTRACT 1: RONNI ANCONA & CO.

```
 1                        ZOE    ↑Calara↑ ‖ ↑ahh↑
              CALARA                     ‖ ↑ahh↑
                                 [girls jump up and down and hug] (3)
                          ZOE    my god I have so missed you what have you been doing (.)
 5                               since lunch =
              CALARA    = didn't you get my text =
                          ZOE    = no no =
              CALARA    = I texted you =
   'accel'       ZOE    = [looks at phone] I seriously didn't get it 'send it again
10                               you've got to send it again'=
              CALARA    = no [looks at phone] I've deleted it [sound of mobile bleep-
                                 ing] ohh =
                          ZOE    = [reads text] oh my god that is just (.) so unbelievable =
              CALARA    = what =
15                        ZOE    = totally done my head in (1) look [shows text] (3)
              CALARA    [reads text] ↑oh my god↑ I don't believe it Jessica's already
                                 there (.) ↑she's already ‖there↑
                    ZOE                              ‖↑ah I know↑ =
              CALARA    = ↑how did that happen↑ =
20                        ZOE    = I don't know it's like mad isn't it she must have like (2)
   'rall'                        left 'early' or' something =
   'accel'   CALARA    = 'text her back text her back' =
                          ZOE    = shall I text her back =
   'accel'   CALARA    = text her back and er ask her (1) 'let's think about this' (1)
25                               ask (.) her (.) how long she's been there for and is [indis-
                                 tinct] there too (2)
                                 [phone bleeps – both look at their phones]
              CALARA    ahh ahh ohh (.) what's wrong (2)
```

<pre>
          ZOE   [reads text] oh my god oh my god =
30   CALARA   = ↑what's wrong↑ =
          ZOE   = it's Piper (.) oh my god oh my god ↑oh my god ‖ oh my
       CALARA   ‖ what's
                  wrong [mouthed]
          ZOE   god oh my god oh my god↑ it's Piper she's <u>split</u> <u>up</u> with
35   Árcher =
'rall' CALARA   = 'that is so <u>depréssing</u>' they were <u>made</u> for each óther =
          ZOE   = I knów they've been like going out for (.) áges like what
                  was ít like (2) 3 wéeks (1)

                  [phone bleeps]

40   CALARA   [looks at phone] ah ohh =
          ZOE   = [reads text] oh my gód it's Piper again =
       CALARA   = ↑oh my gód has she self-harmed cos of the split↑ =
          ZOE   = she's going out with N<u>oah</u> ↑ahh that is so cool↑ =

                  [girls jump up and down and hug]

45   CALARA   = so cool they're so brilliant [phone bleeps] ah is that yours
                  ag<u>áin</u> =
          ZOE   = [reads text] oh my god it's Píper (1) she's <u>dumped</u>
                  Nóah =
'rall' CALARA   = oh nó that is so 'áwful (.) poor Nóah' I can't <u>béar</u> ìt [phone
50   bleeps] ehh [looks at phone] (2)
          ZOE   [reads text] it's Nóah (.) ohh god he wants to go <u>out</u> with
                  m<u>é</u>

                  [soundless laughter] (5)

'rall' CALARA   that is 'so (.) brilli<u>ant</u> (.) for y<u>ou</u>' (2)
55   ZOE   bye

                  [ZOE runs off leaving CALARA looking at phone and pre-
                  tending to take call]
</pre>

EXTRACT 2: *THAT MITCHELL AND WEBB LOOK* ·······························

<pre>
         GROUP   <u>1994</u> (.) the year of putting a bit of a k<u>i</u>nk in the <u>handle</u> (.)
         LEADER   s<u>á</u>les up by <u>8%</u> (.) 1991↑ (.) the year of putting s<u>ó</u>me of
60   'leg'   the bristles in di<u>á</u>gonally (.) sales up by 1<u>2½%</u> (.) '2002
                   your <u>finest</u> hour Ch<u>á</u>z' (.) the year of putting in some b<u>lúe</u>
                   bristles to tell them when they need to buy a <u>new</u> òne (.)
                   for the <u>first</u> <u>time</u> people are actually <u>taking</u> órders (.) from
                   their t<u>òothbrush</u> (.) sales up by <u>26%</u> (2) gúys (1) it's 2006 (.)
65   I have one <u>question</u> for yòu (2) <u>what's</u> <u>next</u> (2)
          CHAZ   éhhm =
     G. LEADER   = Ch<u>á</u>z =
          CHAZ   = nò =
     G. LEADER   = <u>come</u> ↑on↑ guys th. this is ↑serious↑ (.) people are out
70   there <u>right</u> <u>now</u> buying <u>toothbrushes</u> that <u>we</u> didn't <u>make</u> =
       FEMALE   = I think (1) we have to realise (.) we may have run out of
    EXECUTIVE   things we can tell them they need on their tòothbrush (3)
'rall'   GUS   I think (1) we could get them (1) to '<u>brush</u> their <u>tongues</u>' (4)
     G. LEADER   no (.) no (.) I admire your reach Gus but (1) no they're not
</pre>

going to <u>brush</u> their <u>tongues</u> =

GUS = I <u>think</u> they <u>will</u> (1) I think that if we <u>tell</u> them (.) to brush their tongues (2) they'll <u>brush</u> their <u>tongues</u> =

CHAZ = is there any <u>health</u> benefit to brushing your tóngue =

'accel'/'rall'   GUS = I have no ìdea (.) but (.) 'show me your tóngue' (1) '↓errh↓
80 (.) yeah' you sée (.) <u>dìrty</u> (.) he's got a <u>dirty</u> tongue =

FEM. EXEC. = has hè =

'accel'   GUS = 'no (.) ↑course he hàsn't↑' but you thought he <u>might</u> have
'accel' (.) and when it's not me saying it but (.) a 'Scottish <u>brunette</u>
in <u>rectangular</u> glasses and a <u>làb</u> coat' (2)

85   G. LEADER I <u>think</u> you <u>míght</u> <u>have</u> something (.) they <u>might</u> <u>actually</u>
'rall' 'brush their tóngues' =

'Scottish   GUS = of course they <u>will</u> (2) '↑did you knów that up to 68% of
accent/piano' us suffer from <u>dirty</u> <u>tongue</u> (.) over time microscopic anti-
tonguenoids build up a gritty (.) [*indistinct*] surface which
90 might very well mean (.) that people laugh at you behind
your back (.) and secretly find you <u>repùlsive</u>↑' =

G. LEADER = got to market it at <u>mén</u> <u>tóo</u> Gus =

'Scottish   GUS = '↑which might very well mean that that's why you're not
accent/piano' getting enough <u>sèx</u>↑' (1)

95 'accel' FEM. EXEC. so (.) whât we'd 'put something on the back of the tôoth-
brush' =

'accel'   GUS = <u>could</u> do (.) doesn't <u>matter</u> 'I mean people aren't actually
going to brush their tongues' trying to brush your tongue
makes you retch everybody knows that but when they're
100 buying the toothbrush they'll forget it they'll forget everything except the <u>Scottish</u> <u>brunette</u> telling them that's why
they're not getting enough <u>sex</u> =

'dimin'/'accel'/   G. LEADER = 'they <u>will</u>' (.) '↑they <u>will</u>↑' they'll <u>brush</u> their '<u>goddam</u>
'forte' <u>tongues</u>' and if we can get them to <u>brush</u> their <u>tóngues</u> (2)
105 'rall/dimin' we can get them to do (1) '<u>ànything</u>'

COMMENTARY

The **register** of each extract is marked by the features of spoken discourse: although the sketches have been scripted, they are performed as spontaneous speech encounters. While the manner of Extract 1 is informal, Extract 2 is formal. This is mirrored in the relationship between participants – the familiar friendship of the girls is informal; the working relationship of the marketing executives is formal. The audience will recognise these characters – the humour lies in the use of **stereotypes** that represent larger-than-life versions of recognisable individuals. Although the speech patterns and behaviour are exaggerated, the portraits of the teenage girls (age and gender stereotypes) and of the market research team (occupational stereotypes) represent a version of reality that has been distorted for comic effect.

The **context** provides an appropriate backdrop for the characters. The sub-urban setting of Extract 1 places the teenage girls and their obsessive texting in a comfortable middle-class environment where insignificant events assume a comic importance. The humour of the sketch lies in the juxtaposition of the apparently inconsequential content of their conversation (texting and relationships) and the marked intensity of their responses. In Extract 2, the formality of the conference room is set against the comic nature of the marketing proposal and the ease with which consumers can be manipulated for financial gain.

The **language** of each sketch is directly linked to the context and the participants: where one mirrors the language of a specific age group, the other re-creates an occupational variety. In Extract 1, the language is consciously informal: it uses a variety that is social rather than regional, a teenage 'lingua franca' that functions as a 'code' to establish insiders and outsiders. While it may confuse parents and teachers, it reinforces social bonds between its users. The lexis moves between widely recognised informalities (*split up*, l. 34; *made for each other*, l. 36; *dumped*, l. 47) and repeated exclamatives (*oh my god*), and lexis that is specific to 'teen speak' with its adverb intensifiers (*seriously*, l. 9; *totally*, l. 15; *so*, ll. 4, 13, 36, 43, 45, 49, 54), colloquial fillers (*like*, ll. 20, 37, 38) and trendy modifiers (*cool*, ll. 43, 45; *brilliant*, ll. 45, 54). The humour works on two levels: some of the audience will laugh because they recognise the language use (insiders); some will laugh because it is so alien (outsiders).

The language in Extract 2 is more formal, with serious subject-specific terms linked to the product (*handle*, l. 58; *bristles*, l. 60, 62; *toothbrush*, ll. 64, 70, 72, 95–6, 100; *brush/brushing*, ll. 73, 76, 78, 86, 98, 103, 104) and to the field of marketing (*sales*, ll. 59, 60, 64; *8%*, l. 59; *buy/buying*, ll. 62, 70; *make*, l. 70; *health benefit*, l. 78; *market*, l. 92). Humour is created by pushing the central marketing idea to extremes and by exploiting a familiar approach to advertising – the psychological appeal to our need to look better (ll. 90–1) and to be more attractive to potential partners (ll. 93–4). Similarly, the proposed use of *a Scottish brunette in rectangular glasses and a lab coat* (ll. 83–4) is humorous because it is a familiar marketing stereotype: surveys have associated the Scottish accent with reliability and dependability; the glasses and lab coat are associated with intelligence and authority. We laugh because we recognise the way in which the team aim to manipulate their target audience – there is an underlying 'truth' which enhances the comedy of the sketch. References to *taking orders* (ll. 83–4), the repetition of *tell/telling* (ll. 62, 72, 76, 101) and the emphatic modal verb *will* (ll. 77–8, 87, 100, 103), and the climax of the sketch (*we can get them to do anything*, l. 105) create humour in a more direct way by focusing on the gullibility of the consumer.

The **grammatical structures** are typical of the speech encounter that is taking place – in Extract 1, the loosely structured simple sentences of girls' informal spontaneous conversation; in Extract 2, the longer, more tightly structured sentences associated with the formality of an occupational variety:

S	P	S	P	C	S	P	P	C
(I)	(don't know)	(it)	('s)	(like)	(mad)	(isn't it)	(she)	(must have)	(like)	(left)	(early)	(or)
	neg			filler		tag question				filler		conj

C
(something)   (ll. 20–1)

S	P					O
(I)	(think)	(ø we have to realise ø we may have run out of things we can tell them they
		SCl–NCl	SCl–NFCl	SCl–NCl		SCl–RelCl	SCl–RelCl

need on their toothbrush)   (ll. 71–2)

In each sketch, the grammar is standard – the humour lies in the stereotypical way in which the participants' language use is exaggerated for comic effect. The girls' informal speech, for instance, is marked by the use of colloquial fillers and tag questions. Simple sentences are used in strings, and there are only two examples of co-ordination (ll. 24–6) and none of subordination. The grammatical simplicity of the style underpins the comic insignificance of the content.

Extract 2, in contrast, uses a very different grammatical style: the number of subordinate clauses reflects the participants' target audience (fellow professionals), their purpose (marketing a new product) and their context (a meeting room):

S	P	O		A

(they) ('ll brush) (their goddam tongues) (and) (if we can get them to brush their
                                          conj   SCl–ACl   SCl–NFCl

tongues) (we) (can get) (them) (to do anything)   (ll. 103–5)
 S   P   Oi   Od
                              SCl–NFCl

Although often associated with informal conversation, minor sentences are used in this sketch as part of the stylised opening:

(1994) (the year of putting a bit of a kink in the handle) (sales) (up by 8%)   (ll. 58–9)
 NP   NP   NP   AdvP

The leader's formal presentation sets the context and establishes the field using an intentionally telegraphic style to focus attention on the key elements: marketing choices that we recognise (*a bit of a kink in the handle*, l. 58; *some of the bristles in diagonally*, ll. 59–60; *some blue bristles*, ll. 61–2); financial information critical to the ongoing success of the company. It is the introduction of an unexpected marketing feature that creates the humour.

The **spoken features** of Extract 1 are central to the comedy of the extract. Associated with New Zealand and Australian English since the 1960s, the repeated use of rising intonation at the end of all utterances has become increasingly prevalent in British English, particularly amongst teenagers. We usually mark the end of a grammatical statement with a falling tone, but in this sketch the frequent rising intonations contribute to the humour: the adult target audience laugh because these teenagers use a stereotypical variety of English that is markedly different from their own. In addition, raised pitch reflecting excitement (ll. 1–2) and disbelief (ll. 16–19), consecutive stresses (ll. 13, 16–17, 19) and elongated syllables (ll. 4, 11, 35–7, 43, 54) contribute to the linguistic stereotype at the heart of the comedy.

The formal speech encounter of Extract 2 uses stress and intonation patterns that are closer to everyday usage – they do not form the basis for the comedy, but add a sense of realism to the discourse. For the comedy to work, the audience has to be convinced that this meeting could take place. Stress patterns highlight key words (ll. 59, 60, 73, 83–4, 85–6, 103–5); most rising intonations mark questions (ll. 67, 78, 81) and most falling intonations indicate the grammatical end of an utterance (ll. 72, 94, 96, 105). Changes in pace focus our attention: the introduction of Gus's idea is marked by a decrease in pace and emphatic stress (l. 73); his enthusiasm and determination to convince his colleagues are marked by an increase in pace (ll. 82–3, 97). Where spoken features occur together, the effect is often humorous. The use of a Scottish accent (ll. 87–91, 93–4), a quieter volume and a higher pitch, for instance, underpin the stereotype of the trusted female scientist.

Similarly, at the end of the extract, the changes in volume and pace (ll. 103–5), the raised pitch, pauses and frequent stresses create a comic climax.

The **turn-taking** is co-operative in both sketches. As we would expect, the formality of the meeting is dominated by smooth latching with few timed pauses. Initially the group leader is the dominant speaker, but Gus's turns become longer as he explores his idea. The climax of the comedy is established in the group leader's emphatic affirmation (ll. 103–5): the timed pauses move us beyond the product and its new feature to a comic recognition of the control marketing has over the consumer.

Whereas the participants in Extract 2 move towards agreement, the discourse in Extract 1 moves towards a breakdown in communication. In the opening, the girls appear to be equally matched – their turns are of similar lengths and most turns latch smoothly to the next. Zoe, however, is the dominant speaker: it is she who dictates the topic as the texts arriving on her phone establish the direction of the conversation. Overlaps are minimal (ll. 1–2, 17–18, 31–2) and adjacency pairs are complete (ll. 4–7, 14–15, 19–21, 23–4, 28–9, 30–1, 42–3), but viewers begin to feel a distance between the two girls. The vocal effects of Calara as each text arrives (ll. 12, 28, 40, 45, 50) reflect her disappointment, building to an ironic climax in her pretended enthusiasm (l. 54) for Zoe's news about Noah. The juxtaposition of the girls' enthusiastic greetings (ll. 1–3) and their over-the-top responses with the final lines of the sketch adds to the humour of the linguistic stereotyping: we laugh at their linguistic mannerisms, the emptiness of their conversation, their heightened emotions, and their capricious and volatile relationships.

In each case, the linguistic and discourse features are appropriate for the participants and the context. Our familiarity with the stereotypes allows us to enjoy the comic exaggeration: the humour depends on us recognising the characters and their distinctive linguistic styles, and the ways in which the writers and performers distort these.

Situation comedies

SITUATION COMEDIES, or **SITCOMS**, are television comedies that entertain us by holding up a mirror to real life and revealing something that we can all recognise. They aim to explore the human condition and to shed light on specific kinds of experience through humour. While most are predominantly light in tone, some sitcoms aim to make us think. The four series of *Blackadder*, for instance, were researched by the writers so that key period details and references were embedded in the fictional world. In the final series, *Blackadder Goes Forth*, the focus on World War I works on two levels. It treats life in the trenches and the absurdity of many of the commands humorously, but it also reveals something about the nature of war itself. The poignancy of the silence at the end of the last episode, as Blackadder and his men go over the top to almost certain death, is a haunting conclusion to a sitcom that has been both hilarious and painful.

The **characters** must have their roots in reality, but they are inevitably larger-than-life individuals with exaggerated gestures, speech mannerisms or attitudes. Most are likeable despite their flaws and many are stereotypical: the grumpy old man (Victor Meldrew, *One Foot in the Grave*, BBC); the womanising doctor (the anaesthetist Dr Guy Secretan, *Green Wing*, C4); the trouble-prone son-in-law (Howard Steel, *Worst Week of My Life*, BBC1); bungling burglars (Bex and Ollie, *Thieves Like Us*, BBC3); a drunken foul-mouthed priest (Father Jack Hackett, *Father Ted*, C4); a ruthless government spin doctor and enforcer (Malcolm Tucker, *The Thick of It*, BBC4); British holidaymakers in Spain (*Benidorm*, ITV). Comedy is often created by an interaction between antithetical characters.

The **context** will focus on one or two main settings which form the backdrop to the stock situations that evolve. We do not usually gain any insight into the settings since they are merely a means of drawing together a group of related characters. Sometimes the context will be geographical, with rural (*Jam and Jerusalem*; *The Vicar of Dibley*), urban (*Only Fools and Horses*) or overseas (*Benidorm*) settings. In other instances, it establishes a work-based background such as a hospital (*Green Wing*), an office (*The Office*; *The Thick of It*), backstage at a film recording (*Extras*) or in a hotel (*Fawlty Towers*), or a domestic environment (*My Family*; *The Royle Family*). Writers often exploit the comic discrepancy created where the behaviour of characters seems to be at odds with the environment in which they find themselves.

The **content** is directly linked to the context and the kind of characters that are brought together. It usually addresses everyday events rather than social or political issues since the function of a sitcom is to entertain. Events may be heightened for comic effect and the plot will often revolve around a sequence of misunderstandings, deceptions or chance happenings that lead towards the climax. In most cases, each episode is self-contained and a resolution to the problem is achieved within the 30-minute structure. There are exceptions, however, in which running themes or plot motifs recur. In its one-hour format *Green Wing* maintained an overarching narrative and an ongoing love triangle, providing cohesion to the absurd and surreal style that won a cult following.

The **language** and **grammatical structures** of a sitcom are linked directly to the kind of characters and their setting. **Spoken features** dominate and the **tone** is usually informal. An understanding of character helps us to appreciate the way in which speech patterns and structures underpin audience response. As well as physical comedy, the use of unexpected language, expletives or other informal lexis, long pauses, uncooperative turn-taking and exaggerated prosodics can also make us laugh.

Stand-up

STAND-UP COMEDIANS perform alone, delivering a comic **monologue** that is designed to provoke laughter. This is a pressurised form of entertainment because audiences are notoriously unforgiving and, if the comedian fails to provoke laughter, hecklers will exploit any apparent vulnerability. Many popular comedians have begun their careers doing stand-up in small venues where they have had to earn respect as they perfect their comic skills.

The **context** plays a significant role in establishing the nature of a performance. In small club venues and bars, audiences are often rowdy and the comedian has to work hard to engage their attention. Performing in theatres tends to be a very different experience since the audience are more respectful and performers have already attained a popular reputation. People buy tickets because they already like the comedian and know what they are going to see. Similarly, the recording of a television comedy is very organised: an audience is invited and audience responses normally guided by specific instructions from a floor manager, so that unexpected noise does not interfere with the recording.

Because of the potential for audience interaction, the **register** is informal. Despite the size of some venues and the awkwardness of some audiences, often a familiar relationship is developed between the stand-up comedian and his or her audience as the comedian speaks directly to them, whether using them as a source of comic material or confronting hecklers and creating comedy from their interruptions.

The **content** frequently relies on a sequence of narrated anecdotes and jokes with stories based on close observations of situations that are familiar to many people. Sometimes performers go off at a tangent, developing an association with a word or an idea. The comedy lies in the fact that everybody can identify with the observations made – comedians put into words what we feel but have not articulated. The everyday nature of the subject matter underpins the informal tone. Domestic (over-flowing dustbins; no-one cleaning the toilet or replacing the toilet roll) and social (relationships; gender) themes, however, are often accompanied by political comment. Although the tone is usually light-hearted, the comment can be satirical.

Some stand-up comedians tell traditional jokes using stock comic themes such as 'mothers-in-law' or 'her indoors'. The content is often mildly risqué and the comedian is more interested in entertainment than in social observation. The content is less challenging than that associated with the more satirical **'ALTERNATIVE' COMEDY**, but may offend because of its tendency towards a stereotypical view of gender roles.

The **language** is usually informal. Colloquialisms and examples of contemporary language are common (often forming the basis for humour about language change) and some performances are marked by the frequent use of expletives. Stand-up comedians use linking expressions to move from one topic to another (*so... yeah*; *have you ever noticed that...*). These allow them to create cohesion in what can be a diverse monologue.

Because stand-up comedy is performed in front of a live audience, the **grammatical structures** are dominated by features we associate with spoken language. Long loosely-constructed sentences coexist with short and minor sentences as the performer controls the pace and mood of the delivery. The grammatical mood varies according to the nature of the discourse: comic monologues are dominated by the declarative, but interrogatives may be used to engage the audience and imperatives to harangue them for comic effect. When direct participation is encouraged by the performer, adjacency pairs may sometimes be completed by the audience as a whole.

Spoken features are often exaggerated because, although the relationship created with the audience is informal and familiar, the public nature and scale of a performance may require a larger-than-life delivery. The **pace** is often fast, with overstated changes of **volume**, **intonation** and **pitch**. **Pauses** can create comedy where they are extended uncomfortably or where they are used frequently to make the delivery staccato. **Vocal effects** such as silly sounds, rude noises, exaggerated normal non-fluency features or self-conscious laughter can create explicit comedy, while **paralinguistics** can develop visual humour.

Most stand-up comedians have perfected their routines prior to performance and there are few examples of **normal non-fluency features**, unless they are consciously used to develop a comic character or to create a comic hesitancy. In some situations, however, amateur comedians are given the opportunity to perform in 'open mike' events: since these performers are still developing their skills, normal non-fluency features are common.

Frequent **topic changes** reflect the nature of the variety – a performer needs to be able to maintain a consistent delivery for a specified length of time and topic changes provide a new source of material. **Topic loops** may be used structurally to provide cohesion or to regain momentum – if the audience have enjoyed a particular topic, a comedian may decide to return to it in order to recapture the mood.

Listener response is critical in stand-up because there is no other interaction taking place on the stage. Where a comic play or sketch show can create comedy through characters or events, the stand-up comedian must engage the audience with his or her view of the world. If there is no laughter, the comedian has failed – it is a challenging and demanding form that requires the ability to judge the mood of an audience and then to improvise and adapt material accordingly.

If the audience is not responding, if hecklers interrupt or if there is a technical hitch of some kind, **repairs** may be required. In the most polished performances, such problems will be embedded in the routine as a source of spontaneous comedy. The comedian will improvise material, aiming to make the audience laugh and thereby avoiding a breakdown of communication.

ACTIVITY 19.6

Read the following extract (3 minutes 20 seconds) by the comedian Eddie Izzard from the Comic Aid *Benefit for the Asian Tsunami Appeal*. The *Benefit* was performed at the Hammersmith Apollo in London and broadcast on BBC 1 and then BBC 2 over a two-hour period on Saturday, 26 February 2005, starting at 9.15 pm. The extract below is a broad transcript that takes account of only the most prominent features. Audience laughter is recorded only when it occurred during a pause. A key to the symbols can be found on page 93.

Analyse the way in which Izzard uses the stand-up format to entertain his audience. You may like to think about:

▸ the context
▸ the register
▸ the content
▸ the language and grammatical structures
▸ the spoken features.

1   'accel' and spiders are dangerous and we <u>know</u> 'that they want to suck our brains' out we know that and when women say <u>get</u> in the bathroom

'rall' there's a spider in there u̇nderstand that 'men are scáred as you'
they're completely and I'm on the boys' side of this being action
transvestite (laugh 3) if we were not scared we would go in and go
[mimes pulling legs off spider] ↑oh↑ there's a huge spider it's fine
come on the legs off (muttered speech) but in fact we tend to go in
there's a **** [stamping action] spider and the óne thing worse than
seeing a spider is not seeing a spider [looking on floor] (laugh 3) see
'accel' a spider spider spider not see a 'where's the spider whére's the
spider' [mimes spider going into ear and sucking out brain] (laugh 4)
we know that the African jumping spider came to this country at one
point it came in on a boat on a banana you know they come in they
they live on bananas they came in on a banana boat they don't live
'rall/dim' on bananas [mimes eating banana] they don't li. 'on bananas'
'cresc'/'rall' (laugh 5) '↑horses↑' when I w. when you 'were a kid you and I' probably you might have done horse riding and in fact we ↑didn't↑ what
we experienced was actually horses doing child wèaring (laugh 8)
'adopts a I've seen a ↑dócumentary↑ where horses say 'yes I've joined
character the stáble it's fantastic they give you a child and you strap it on your
voice' back (laugh 2) and you go out on the hills you eat the grass you
drink the water (2) and they they tickle you in the ribs and things
with their little feet and they pull on your neck sort of exercise [leans
backwards and forwards] I thínk it is (2) come back down and you
take the children awáy and they shoot them out of a cànnon (laugh 3)
'accel' I believe' (1) 'being an action transvestite' I was you know a bíg fan
'accel' of Steve McQueen and who was action 'not transvestite' and he did
'American all those fílms with you know those things 'ay you'd better ride out
accent' of here otherwise you know I'm gonna be an. annoyed n stùff' (laugh
2) and then he would he would go off on a horse looking very
cóol looking doing mainly thát sort of gallopy thing I mainly learnt
to uh this this thing [mimes rising trot] trotting (2) if you ever Steve
'American McQueen never did that he never said 'you'd better ride out of here
accent' ever come back n stuff' [mimes rising trot] (laugh 7) and the now the
trai. interesting on the training cos the training used to be whips and
things ↑woah woah↑ there boy [sound of whips cracking] and they
would train like that and now the horse whisperers these these guys
these amazing guys just uh whisper no-one knows what they say
it's all [repeatedly mimes stroking horse while speaking] woah there
'dimin' (laugh 3) woah there óoh 'no-one knóws what they say' (laugh 2) ↑I↑
don't know what they say èither it's obv. it's obviously something
amazing oah there (4) I don. yeah (2) hello (laugh 3) uh it's it's uh it's
'direct to very tricky but uh th. uhhh um well (laugh 4) 'I'm looking for some-
audience' thing funny to put there and [laughs] I still haven't worked it out it's a
great build-up there isn't it I get to there and I can do that for hours'
woah there woah there and the expectation is huge woah I just
'forte' don't know what to **** say because what ↑what↑ do they say 'stop
'piano' running about' 'all right don't shout' what what can they sáy just
'accel' ↓'don't run or I'll shoot you with this gun'↓ something like that I didn't
see The Horse Whisperer

The **context** here is very specific: popular comedians appeared for no fee in a charity show that was broadcast on BBC1 and later sold on DVD to raise money for the victims of the Indian Ocean earthquake (December 2004). In this context, therefore, the comedy has a serious purpose – to raise money through donations and merchandise.

In spite of the size of the venue, the **register** is informal. As is typical of stand-up, Eddie Izzard speaks directly to the audience, engaging them through his pronoun references: inclusive first person plural references (*we*, ll. 1, 2, 17) and direct address (*you*, ll. 3, 16). Although he does not individualise members of the audience, they are included in the observations that he makes – the emphasis is on a commonality of experience. In addition, he personalises the observations by exploring his own attitudes. The repeated use of the first person singular *I* establishes a direct connection between Izzard and the topics he addresses: *I'm on the boys' side* (l. 4); *I was… a big fan* (l. 26); *I mainly learnt…* (l. 31). In the final section, Izzard comes out of role and speaks to the audience as himself, exploiting the humour of his own failure to complete the line (ll. 43–5). His candour contributes to the comedy; his laugh (l. 44) mirrors the informality and collective good mood of the occasion.

The **content** is made up of a narrative containing two distinct topics: spiders and horses. In the first part of the monologue, Izzard explores our fear of spiders, something that many people will recognise. His focus is on the domestic (*bathroom*), but, as is typical of Izzard's comedy, he quickly moves from the expected to the unexpected. Here the juxtaposition of the ordinary and the surreal (*spiders are dangerous… they want to suck our brains out*, ll. 1–2, 11) underpins the comedy. The initial statement *spiders are dangerous* (l. 1) forms an implicit link between 'brain-sucking spiders' and the change in direction that introduces the new subtopic of the *African jumping spider* (l. 12). The humour of this topic emerges not as a result of the content, however, but in the linguistic confusion that results in the comic pause (l. 16) and the abrupt introduction of a completely new topic.

Izzard creates comedy from his second topic by presenting us with a new way of viewing horse riding. He adopts an unexpected angle – the horse's perspective – and reinterprets things we take for granted: the emphasis is on the insignificance of the child on the back of the horse who proceeds to do exactly as it wishes. This topic sub-divides into a discussion of riding in Westerns and horse training. In each case, the humour lies in the comic juxtaposition that Izzard develops: trotting (awkward and childlike) versus galloping (sophisticated and stylish); training with whips (rough and physical) versus horse whisperers (mysterious and psychological).

The different personas that emerge in the monologue also contribute to the comic effect of the piece as a whole. Izzard is first the 'scared man' who must confront the spider with great bravado; he is then the horse who casually, in the style of a Nick Park animation, describes his experiences at the stable (ll. 19–26); his use of an American accent (ll. 28–9, 33–4) characterises him as the cool Steve McQueen cowboy; and finally the horse whisperer with his low tones and calming repetitive lexis (l. 39). Each change of voice presents the audience with a comic juxtaposition – the brave man who pulls the legs off spiders versus the fearful coward; our perspective of riding versus the horse's.

The **language** of the extract is for the most part ordinary. Repetitions of concrete nouns such as *spider, banana* and *horse* are directly linked to the main topics and Izzard develops lexical sets of words associated with these. Comment clauses (*you know*, ll. 13, 26, 28) and informal expressions such as *done horse riding* (l. 17), *that sort of gallopy thing* (l. 31), *stuff* (ll. 29, 34), or *these guys* (l. 37) underpin the conversational tone of the performance. Since it is broadcast after the nine o'clock watershed, the language includes expletives (ll. 8, 47).

Comedy is created, however, when ordinary language is used unexpectedly. The reference to a *documentary* (l. 19) in which a horse tells viewers about his experience is explicitly comic. The neologism *child wearing* (l. 18), along with the verb *joined* (l. 19) with its connotations of active choice, and the surreal reference to children being shot out of a cannon (l. 25) underpin the humorous change of perspective. Similarly, the long build-up to the common greeting *hello* (ll. 36–42) is comic – its normality after the suggestion of the mysterious powers of the horse whisperers results in a humorous anti-climax. Unexpected expressions can also make us laugh because they challenge the way we see the world. Izzard is well known for his belief in the rights of men to wear whatever clothes they wish to and the noun phrase *action transvestite* (ll. 4–5, 26) amuses us because it neatly overlays the concept of the 'action hero' with his own preferences for wearing dresses as well as traditionally male clothes. We laugh at the comic context (facing a spider) and the linguistic associations.

The **grammatical structures**, as we would expect, include long, loose sentences alongside incomplete or minor sentences. The monologue represents non-stop speech and as such there is little sense of the discrete structures we find in organised written language. The repetition of the co-ordinating conjunction *and* contributes to the length of utterances:

>   S   P   C   S   P   O
> (and) (spiders) (are) (dangerous) (and) (we) (know) (that they want to suck our brains
> conj   conj   SCl–NCl   SCl–NFCl
>   S   P   O   A   (P   A   dum S P   (S)   A)
> out) (we) (know) (that) (and) (when women say get in the bathroom there's a spider in
>   SCl–ACl
>   P   O
> there) (understand) (that men are scared as you)
>   SCl–NCl

Stand-up comedy encourages this kind of loosely structured discourse because the single participant has to sustain an extended turn for sometimes 30–45 minutes. Equally incomplete structures (*they're completely*, l. 4; *if you ever*, l. 32) and minor sentences (*spider spider*, l. 10; *on a banana*, l. 13; *horses*, l. 16) characterise the conversational tone.

The grammatical mood is dominated by the declarative, but Izzard uses interrogative and imperative sentences as he develops each different scenario. We laugh at the movement between the confident imperative (*see a spider*, ll. 9–10) and the repeated hesitant interrogatives (*where's the spider*, ll. 10–11) because this challenges the 'brave hunter' male stereotype. Similarly, the horse whisperer's imperatives (*stop running, don't run*, ll. 47–8, 49) are amusing because they counter the image of the calm, controlled secretive interaction that takes place between horse and whisperer.

Spoken features dominate this extract. The pace is fast throughout, with Izzard delivering approximately 650 words in 3½ minutes. There are almost no pauses – even the micro-pause that usually marks the end of a grammatical utterance is absent here. Despite this, the pace is increased for comic effect in a number of places: to highlight the surreal (l. 1), to characterise (l. 10) and to juxtapose comic concepts (*action transvestite/not transvestite*, ll. 26–7). Where it does slow down, the effect is either for comic emphasis (ll. 3, 16) or to draw attention to the comedy of a linguistic confusion (l. 15).

The relentless delivery, the changes in volume and the vocal effects (ll. 6, 36, 44) all enhance the linguistic comedy. It is, in addition, a very visual performance with physical actions to accompany the words (ll. 6, 8, 9, 11, 15, 23–4, 32, 34, 39). The exaggerated nature of the actions provokes laughter at a basic level – Izzard is a performer who exploits the potential for comedy in gesture as well as language.

Because stand-up is a spontaneous form of live comedy in which performers improvise on a basic structure, there are often examples of **normal non-fluency features**. In this extract, incomplete words (*li.*, 15; *w.*, l. 16; *an.*, l. 29), fillers (*uh*, ll. 38, 42; *uhhh, um*, l. 43), false starts (*when I w.*, l. 16; *and the now the trai.*, ll. 34–5) and repetitions (*they they*, ll. 13–14; *he would he would*, l. 30) reflect the spontaneous and informal nature of the discourse. They are typical of stand-up and do not affect our response to the comedy – we are almost unaware of them in the speed and confidence of the delivery as a whole.

The **topic changes** in this extract contribute to the comedy since they are apparently quite unconnected. As Izzard draws to a halt on the sub-topic of dangerous spiders and their arrival from Africa on banana boats, he uses the dramatic change of direction for comic effect. The pause (l. 16) followed by a change of pitch and volume on the minor sentence ↑*horses*↑ emphasises the abrupt and apparently illogical transition – Izzard makes comedy out of the fact that he has tied himself in linguistic knots and uses a new topic to extract himself. Similarly, he later draws attention to the comedy of his failure to complete the climax of the horse whisperer narrative (ll. 43–7). His direct address to the audience, the lack of fulfilment of audience expectations and the comedian's potential to draw that expectation out indefinitely are essential to the comedy.

This extract creates comedy in a range of ways. Izzard observes the comedy of everyday events, he exploits the humour of physical performance, he plays games with words and perspectives, he exaggerates prosodics for comic effect, and he uses the performance itself as a source of humour. The most important element of stand-up, however, is the relationship between the audience and the performer – Izzard engages his audience directly, and they respond by laughing at the view of the world with which he presents them.

19.5 What to look for in the language of humour

The following checklist can be used to identify key features in examples taken from different kinds of humour. You will not find all of the features in every extract or transcript, but the list can be used as a guide. The points made are general, so discussion of specific examples will need to be adapted to take account of the specific form of comedy, its purpose and target audience. Remember that you need to evaluate the effect of the features you identify, exploring the ways in which they create comedy.

The following are helpful questions to ask.

Type of comedy

1 What kind of **discourse** is it?
   * a traditional joke, a farce, a parody, a satire, a sketch, a sitcom, stand-up?
   * a mixture of several forms?
2 What is the **purpose** of the comedy?
3 Who is the **intended audience**?
4 What **time** is the broadcast or performance?
   * pre- or post-watershed?
5 What is the **date** of the text?
6 What is the **tone**?
   * light-hearted and exuberant? mocking and bitter? somewhere in between?

Register

1 What is the **mode**?
   * spoken? spontaneous or planned?
   * written? written to be read or to be spoken aloud?
2 What is the **manner**?
   * relationship with the intended audience? relative status?
   * formal or informal?
3 What is the **field**?
   * subject matter?
   * linked to the audience, purpose, and context?

Context

1 In which **period** was the discourse written or performed?
   * past or contemporary? historical background?
2 In which **geographical region** does it have its roots?
   * accent? dialect?
3 Which **social** or **cultural background** informs the discourse?
   * expectations? inclusive or exclusive?

Content

1 What **relevance** does the content have?
   * personally linked to the speaker or writer? linked to the intended audience?
   * contemporary issue? political or social comment? focus on a celebrity or a particular event? observations on everyday life? fictional?
2 Is the **topic range** broad or narrow?
   * single subject? linked subjects? unconnected subjects? wide-ranging?
   * who chooses the topics?

Structure

1 Is there a noticeable **framework** to provide an underlying structure?
   - openings and closings? adjacency pairs or incomplete adjacency pairs? topic shifts? topic loops? repairs?
   - listener responses?

2 How is the **turn-taking** organised?
   - dominant speaker? even turns? extended turns? smooth latching? interrupted turns?

Prosodic features

1 Do the **intonation patterns** reinforce the comedy?
   - rising or falling tones? pitch? volume? exaggerated variations?

2 Is the **rhythm** consciously used for comic effect?
   - changes in pace? emphatic stress? exaggerated or frequent pauses?
   - normal non-fluency features?

3 Are **vocal effects** used to underpin the comedy?
   - laughing? sighs? silly sounds? rude noises? groans?

4 Do **paralinguistics** add a physical layer to the humour?
   - hand gestures? facial expressions? movement?

5 Is there any evidence of **normal non-fluency features**?
   - unconscious or intentional?

Lexical features

1 Is the **tone** informal?
   - colloquialisms? expletives? contemporary expressions?

2 Is the **language** distinctive in any way?
   - the denotation(s) and connotations? ambiguity?
   - subject-specific?
   - monosyllabic or polysyllabic? formal or colloquial? dialect?
   - collocations? neologisms?
   - names?
   - unusual, unexpected or inappropriate words? catchphrases? puns or wordplay?
   - codes identifying insiders and outsiders?
   - etymology?

3 Are any recognisable **varieties** used?
   - subject-specific?
   - overlaying of different varieties?

4 Is the **sound** of words important?
   - pronunciation? regional or social accent? idiosyncratic speech mannerisms?
   - contractions? elision? homophones? rhyme? alliteration? onomatopoeia?

Grammar

1 What is noticeable about the **grammar**?
   - standard or non-standard? modern or archaic? formal or informal? ambiguous?
   - closer to speech or to writing?

2 What kind of **phrase structure** is used?
   - type? long or short? pre- or post-modification? tense? modality?

3 What **types of sentences** are used?
  * simple? compound? complex? compound–complex? minor? a mixture?
4 Are there any changes in **mood**?
  * declarative? interrogative? imperative?
  * linked to meaning?

Style

1 Is **sentence organisation** designed to influence the way in which the audience receives meaning?
  * foregrounding? initial-position conjunctions? passive voice?
2 Are there any examples of **literary devices**?
  * metaphors? similes? symbols?
3 Are there any examples of **rhetorical devices**?
  * antithesis? listing? repetition? patterning?

Summary

The primary **function** of the language of humour is to entertain, but humour can also challenge our view of the world and force us to readdress things we take for granted. Because it evokes a very personal response, not everyone finds the same things funny. Our sense of humour may be shaped by our cultural or social background, our peer group, or our own individual personalities.

The **intended audience** and the **context** affect the content and style of the language of humour. Because comedy often pushes at boundaries, it has the potential to shock or offend. The television watershed, film certification and bad-language warnings are therefore designed to ensure that younger or more sensitive viewers and readers are not exposed to expletives and potentially offensive content.

The **style** and **tone** are often informal, with the patterns of spontaneous speech more prominent than written conventions. Linguistic and prosodic features are exaggerated for comic effect and the juxtaposition of unexpected varieties is common.

The language of humour is a very broad variety. It can be spontaneous or scripted, formulaic or original, conventional or ground-breaking. To work as humour, it must evoke an immediate response in its audience – to explore its linguistic, grammatical, semantic and prosodic features, however, is to open up a whole new way of experiencing it.

Chapter 20

Other varieties

20.1 How to classify other varieties

There are so many distinct varieties of English that it would be impossible to cover every kind. It is, however, possible to establish a framework so that unfamiliar varieties can be analysed in the same way that newspapers, legal language or advertising have been tackled in earlier sections.

Different linguists classify texts in different ways. For instance, texts can be **chronological** or **non-chronological**. The structure of a chronological text is based on a sequence of events that occur in a logical order; the verbs often describe actions and events; and time adverbs like *then*, *next* and *after* are common. A non-chronological text is not structured by time, but by a logical relationship between its parts – comparison, contrast, or logical development of an argument. Another method of classifying texts describes **EXPRESSIVE WRITING** (personal jottings that really represent no more than 'thinking aloud' on paper), **TRANSACTIONAL** or **FUNCTIONAL WRITING** (texts that get things done, aiming to inform, persuade, instruct or advise), and **POETIC WRITING** (creative texts that entertain).

Although such categories provide a useful starting point, they are difficult to apply because they show few distinctive linguistic or stylistic features. The examples covered in this section are therefore divided into categories based on **content**, since this allows a range of similar text types to be studied together. The notes that accompany each section aim to provide at least a general idea of the linguistic and stylistic features for which it is worth looking.

20.2 Instruction texts

INSTRUCTION TEXTS have the following characteristics.

- They have a **practical purpose**. They tell the reader how to do something – how to change a spark plug, make a cake, hang wallpaper, fill in an application form, and so on.
- The **mode** is **written**, but the texts are **interactive** because they require the reader to perform a sequence of activities. The **manner** (the relationship created between reader and writer) is formal. The writer is distant and assumes

the dominant role as an expert in the discourse. Despite the interactive response to the instructions, the communication is one-way since the reader obeys and cannot directly question the writer. The **field** dictates the kind of language used – the lexis relates directly to the activity being carried out.

▸ The **tone** is impersonal: there is seldom any mention of the reader or the writer. Instruction texts do not often provide encouragement or develop a relationship between writer and reader – there is no need to employ persuasive techniques because the reader has already decided to carry out a particular activity independently.

▸ Instruction texts are **chronological** – the sequence of the instructions is dictated by the order of the process and this cannot usually be altered. Each part of the process must be clear and unambiguous if it is to be completed successfully.

▸ The **lexis** and **grammar** are often repetitive because the focus of an instruction text is always narrow: the completion of a particular task or activity. The mood is usually imperative, so there is no need for a grammatical subject. The second person pronoun references *you* are omitted because the process is seen to be more important than the creation of a relationship between writer and reader.

▸ Usually reading will be interspersed with action, so the **layout** is often distinctive, with numbered paragraphs dividing the text clearly into a sequence of actions. This makes it easy for readers to re-find their place in the text quickly. The instructions are brief and illustrations may be provided to clarify instructions.

▸ The process is designed to produce the same **end result** each time the instructions are followed.

▸ An **expert writer** is writing for an audience who may not be experts but who share some subject-specific knowledge (an appropriate vocabulary; relevant equipment; some understanding of the processes involved).

Some examples of instruction texts

Recipes

The **layout** is distinctive: the title often uses bold print to draw attention to the particular dish to be made. A list of ingredients and relevant quantities (often in parenthesis) precedes the instructions. Abbreviations are used as a shorthand recognisable to the reader: *tsp* for *teaspoon*; *tbsp* for *tablespoon*. Paragraphs are often numbered. Drawings or photographs may show the end product. Diagrams may explain any complex processes.

The **lexis** is subject-specific: *heat, boil, mix.* Often words are used with a narrower reference than is usual in everyday speech: *rub in* specifically refers to the process of mixing butter and flour, for instance. Many nouns are concrete, based on the ingredients and the equipment: *flour, butter, spoon, bowl, whisk.* Nominal groups tend to be long so that references are very precise:

m	m	m	h	m	m	m	h
100 g	sieved	wholemeal	flour	20 cm	round	cake	tin
num	V	Adj	N	num	Adj	N	N

Modifiers are used to give the reader clear guidance, ensuring that earlier processes have been carried out:

> P   O   m   m   m   h
> (grease) (the baking tray) → the greased baking tray
>   det   V   V   N

> P   O   A   m   m   h
> (place) (half the sugar) (in the bowl) → the remaining sugar
>   det   V   N

Usually modifiers are attributive: *the beaten yolks*. Predicative modifiers, however, are also used:

> P   O   A
> (cream) (the butter and sugar) (until the mixture is smooth)
>   SCl–ACl

Determiners are used distinctively: the indefinite article is used to refer to equipment, since any bowl or implement will be appropriate (*a bowl*; *a skewer*); definite articles are used to refer specifically to the ingredients listed at the beginning of the recipe (*the cornflour*; *the grated rind and juice of the lemon*). However, determiners are often omitted.

The **grammar** is also distinctive. Verbs tend to be dynamic and the mood is almost always imperative. There are lots of non-finite verbs functioning as modifiers and adverbial non-finite clauses (*when cooked…*; *by folding*). Clause structures are often repetitive (P O, P O A, A P O):

> P   O   P   O   A
> (Grease) (the tin) (and) (line) (it) (with greaseproof paper)
>   conj

> P   A   A
> (Bake) (until the cake is firm to the touch) (and) (ø a skewer inserted into its centre
>   SCl–ACl   conj   SCl–ACl   SCl–NFCl
> comes out clean).

Verbs are usually transitive because the process involves an action that is done to something; phrases or clauses are often compound because a recipe involves combining ingredients. Cohesion is created by repetition of nouns and anaphoric references to the list of ingredients and processes already completed. Adverbials make the instructions precise by focusing on details of time, place and manner:

> P   O   A=place   P   A=time   A=time
> (place) (the dough) (on a floured surface)   (leave) (for one hour) (or) (until risen)
>   conj   SCl–ACl

> P   O   A = manner   P   O   A=manner
> (fold in) (the flour) (gently)   (shape) (the pasties) (by pinching the edges)
>   SCl–NFCl

The adverbials give details of length of time, speed, place.

Word-processor user's manual

The **layout** is made distinctive by the combination of text and diagrams. Bold print may highlight the particular process being explained (***Printing blocks***) and definitions succinctly describe its nature (*This function allows you to print a marked block of text*). Numbered paragraphs enable readers to carry out prescribed sequences of actions without losing their place as they move between reading and carrying out instructions. Cross-references ensure that readers can easily pinpoint instructions in other parts of the manual, which may be a necessary part of the process they are currently carrying out (*Define a block, as described on page 70*). Graphics underpin and clarify textual explanations; for example, marginal symbols may show the reader exactly which key or combination of keys needs to be pressed:

> RETURN CODE * UNDO

Capitalisation and bold print also draw attention to the keys to be selected.

The **lexis** is subject-specific (*cut sheet feeder; printer; keyboard*), and some nouns are used with a narrow field of reference that makes them semantically quite different from everyday usage (*menu; window*). Modifiers make references very precise, and post- as well as pre-modification is used:

m	m	h	q		m	m	h		m	h
a	marked	block	of text		letter-quality	print		draft	setting
det	V	N	PrepP		N	N	N		N	N

The verbs tend to be part of a limited set: *press; select; cancel; return*.

The **grammar** is less disjointed than that found in a recipe or knitting pattern. Because the reader might not be an expert, each grammatical utterance must be complete with no abbreviations and no ellipsis since these could cause confusion. Equally, a user's manual is long and contains information which will be used over a period of time. Rather than a sequence of actions that will produce one complete product, it has to cover a wide range of possible processes. The verbs are usually dynamic and the mood is imperative (*insert; check; print*). Because there are explanations as well as commands, however, the declarative is also used frequently. A more personal relationship is created between reader and writer in this kind of text with the use of second person pronoun references (*you can shade text to make it stand out*). This makes the whole process seem less daunting to a beginner. The use of contractions like the negative *won't* and the imperative *let's* contribute to the friendly approach. Adverbials are common:

as described on page 275   A = cross-reference to another
SCl–ACl   instruction

press any key *to enter the program*   A = reason
                      SCl–NFCl

If you want to print a page, press ____   A = condition
SCl–ACl

Sentences in the imperative mood tend to have a P O A clause structure:

P	O	A		P	O	A
(Insert)	(a sheet of paper)	(into the printer).		(Follow)	(this procedure)	(to shade text).
						SCl–NFCl

Explanations in the declarative mood also tend to have at least one adverbial:

S	P	A
(The cursor)	(will be displayed)	(at the word).

S	P	A	A
(All shading directions)	(are displayed)	(on the screen)	(as the same pattern).

Modal verbs like *will* conveying certainty and *can* conveying ability occur in many declarative sentences. Marked themes are common, particularly in the form of adverbial clauses:

(If you don't move the cursor to the beginning of the text), (scanning) (will start) (from
the current cursor position).

Sentence structures are far more varied in this kind of guide than in recipes and knitting patterns. Cohesion is created by the numbered step-by-step processes described; by the typographical features like diagrams, symbols and bold print; and by the use of the definite article, which makes reference specific.

20.3 Information texts

Information texts have the following characteristics.

- They may have a **physical purpose** – such as encouraging you to visit a historic site or persuading you to see a particular film at the cinema – but often the result is more closely associated with **education**. An information text can help you to gain knowledge or to change your attitudes.
- The **mode** may be written or spoken, depending upon the context. Communication is usually one-way, with the information conveyed from an **expert** writer or speaker to a specific audience. However, developments in computer technology, the internet and the availability of CD-ROMs and DVDs can now make even reading an encyclopaedia an interactive process.
- The **manner** is usually formal: a distant writer is linked to readers only by the text; a speaker in a large lecture hall cannot form a close relationship with individuals. Nevertheless, a writer can choose to use techniques that make the text seem less impersonal (using second person pronoun references and contractions), and a speaker in a smaller room may establish direct links with individuals by inviting questions. The manner of some leaflets is also informal, and although they would describe themselves as 'informative', some are in fact covert advertisements – they are more concerned with persuasion than with education and use many of the features of advertising language (such as direct address, grammatically incomplete utterances, and informal language).
- The **tone** is usually impersonal and formal in a textbook or a large-scale lecture, but may be more personal and informal in promotional material or seminars and tutorials.
- Where the discourse is primarily interested in **conveying information objectively** for academic and intellectual purposes, there is less need to use persuasive techniques. In examples like Tourist Board leaflets or entertainment news sheets, however, the information is used in order to persuade readers to visit certain places or do certain things.
- Some information texts are **chronological** (explaining chemical processes, recording historical events, or lecturing on the structure of a play); others are **non-chronological** (describing places of interest in a certain area).
- Information texts must be **clear** and **unambiguous** if the facts are to be conveyed effectively.
- The **lexis** and **grammar** are usually subject-specific, linked directly to the **field**. Modifiers in formal information texts are technical, numerical and

factual. In less formal examples that are really covert advertisements, modifiers are descriptive and evaluative, aiming to convince readers of the value of a particular place or event. Sentence structures in texts with an academic purpose are more likely to be complex; in a leaflet, they are likely to be short and often grammatically incomplete.

- The **mood** is usually declarative, although in advertisements framed as information texts, imperatives may be used to urge the reader to *visit* ____ or *see* ____.
- **Layouts** vary. Textbooks have chapters, subheadings, numbered sections and subsections, and a 'contents' list to guide the reader. They may have photographs, diagrams or tables to reinforce the information provided in the text. Leaflets are more likely to use visual effects such as colour and montage (pictures made by superimposing images) and to keep the written text brief.
- Usually the writer or speaker is an **expert**, but the way in which information is conveyed will depend upon the target audience. The approach needed to present a scientific theory to other experts, for example, will be different from the simplified approach needed to present the same theory to a first-year A-level group; the lexis and sentence structure used by a university lecturer on a law degree course talking about legal precedents will be different from that of a policeman talking about bicycles and road safety to junior-school children. In analysing an information text, it is therefore important to establish the function and the intended audience.

Some examples of information texts

Science textbooks

In a science textbook, the **mode** is written and the **manner** is usually formal. The writer is dominant and often has more expertise in the field than the intended audience. The communication is one-way and the **field** depends upon the specific area of physics, chemistry, biology and so on.

The **layout** uses a mixture of written, symbolic and diagrammatic codes. Paragraphs are likely to be long and may be numbered in subsections for clarity: *1.1, 1.2.* Symbols like H_2O and equations like

$$CuO \quad + \quad H_2 \quad = \quad Cu \quad + \quad H_2O$$
(copper   (hydrogen)   (copper)   (water)
oxide)

are used as a technical shorthand understood by an audience with shared knowledge. Diagrams may clarify processes or the arrangement of equipment. Bold print may highlight key words. Italic print may be used for special purposes: *Erithacus rubecula*, the robin; the radius *r*.

The **lexis** is subject-specific and technical: *electrolysis*; *concentrated sodium chloride solution*. Some general words are used in a subject-specific way: *interference*; *light*; *waves*; *reflection*. Modifiers are technical rather than evaluative or descriptive, and both pre- and post-modification are common:

m	h		m	h	
bimetallic strip			potassium permanganate		
Adj	N		N		N

bimetallic strip — m: Adj, h: N
potassium permanganate — m: N, h: N

m	h	q	m	h	q	m	h	q
the	rate	of diffusion	the	molecules	of liquid	the	gas	dispersed in the flask
det	N	PrepP	det	N	PrepP	det	N	SCl–NFCl

The **grammar** is standard, in line with the formality of the tone. There are many stative verbs (*found; involves; notice*) and dynamic verbs describe processes (*heat; melt; test*). Modal verbs like *will* describe certainties (*sound will travel through liquid*) and *may* describes possibilities (*a catalyst may be used to increase the rate of the reaction*). The passive voice is common and is typical of the impersonal nature of scientific texts. By refocusing the elements of a sentence, the object of an active sentence can be foregrounded – this is appropriate in scientific writing, because the person carrying out the procedure is less important than the objects being tested:

Passive: Substrate concentration can *be increased* if necessary.
Active: *The chemist* can increase the substrate concentration if necessary.

Some modern textbooks, however, choose a less formal approach, using the active voice and direct address.

Many passive constructions are formulaic:

It is found …   It has been suggested …
It can be seen that …   It would be expected that …

Many adverbials are conditional (*If iron and steam are heated…*). Others, however, supply information about time (*when heating; within a few minutes*) or place (*in a Petri dish; in secondary cells*). The mood is usually declarative since scientists are dealing with explanations and records of processes carried out. Sentence structures are usually complex or compound–complex:

dumS   P   (S)
(It) (is found) (that the potential difference across the terminals of a cell decreases)
                SCl–NCl
                                A
(as larger values of current are taken from it).
SCl–ACl

                        A   S   P
(If only one coil is used and the motor is not self-starting), (the coil) (may come)
SCl–ACl   SCl–ACl
                        A
(to rest with the brushes across the break of the split ring) (and) (the armature)
SCl–NFCl   S
        P   A
(will have to be moved) (to start it).
        SCl–NFCl

Many sentences have long sequences of dependent clauses. **Cohesion** is created by the repetition of subject-specific lexis, by the chronological order of events described, and by the sequence of conditions that must be fulfilled.

Science writing for children is distinctive in quite different ways. The tone is usually personal and direct address is used. Writers are also likely to include themselves in references by using the first person plural: *Let's start…*. Imperatives are common because writers tend to try and make the text interactive. Sentences are often shorter and have fewer dependent clauses:

     S   P   C
(Every plant) (is) (a chemical factory).   (SIMPLE)

                S   P   C   A
(The unexposed parts of the leaf) (turn) (brown) (when sunlight does not reach them).
                                                      SCl–ACl   (COMPLEX)

Publicity leaflets

In publicity leaflets, the **mode** is written and the **manner** is often quite informal. Although the writer is in a position of authority, recommending and advising the reader, the text does try to establish a relationship between the participants. Because leaflets are often covert advertisements, the **tone** often has more similarities with the field of advertising than with other more formal information texts. The **field** may be subject-specific, relating to new cinema releases, classical concerts or particular geographic areas, but the lexis will probably not be technical.

The **layout** is often striking. Colour adds interest and variations in print size attract readers' attention. Leaflets are often produced on A4 paper, but folded in half or in thirds to divide information into units that can be easily manipulated. Images are often dominant and logos and symbols are used as a shorthand to make the message or promoter clear. Usually more details can be obtained by contacting the promoter or the venue, so telephone numbers and addresses are a crucial part of the information provided. Dates, times, admission prices and other factual information are commonly included as part of the promotion.

The **lexis** is marked by the use of lexical sets linked to the subject matter: *exhibition, gallery, artist-in-residence*; *cinema, screening, film*. Long nominal groups are a distinctive feature of this kind of information text because the language must persuade the reader to do certain things. The modifiers therefore tend to be evaluative and descriptive:

    m   m   m   h   m   m   m   h
    the top tourist attraction   a superb adventure playground
    det   Adj   N   N   det   Adj   N   N

    m   m   h   m   m   m   h
    The controversial novelist _____   a powerful and (bitingly humorous) film
    det   Adj   N   del   Adj   Adv   Adj   N

Both pre- and post-modification are common:

    m   h   q   q
    a night of music and performance with outstanding performance poets and writers
    det   N   PrepP   PrepP

The **grammar** is also similar to the field of advertising: most sentences are in the active rather than the passive voice; the declarative mood is common, although some imperatives are used (*Visit _____ and enjoy _____*); sentences are often not grammatically complete; non-finite clauses are common (*Controversial playwright and novelist _____ reading a selection of her most outrageous offerings*). The modal auxiliary *will* is used to persuade the reader by communicating a sense of certainty (*You will experience the ride of a lifetime*). Determiners are often omitted (*Workshops by local artist*) and verbal nouns are common (*opening; screening;*

reading). Adverbials give details of time (*tonight*; *on January 4*) and place (*in the park*; *at your local cinema*), and are often used in strings. Sentence structures are varied, though publicity leaflets tend not to have the strings of dependent clauses that are typical of scientific textbooks:

>   S   P   C
> (The local church) (is) (a building of great interest).   (SIMPLE)

>   A   S   P
> (Originally built by the Normans in the 12th century), (the motte and bailey castle) (was
>   SCl–NFCl
>   A   A
> rebuilt) (in stone) (in 1275).   (COMPLEX)

Marked themes are used to draw attention to information considered important:

>   A   S   P   O
> (Over the centuries) (this old town) (has seen) (a number of famous faces including
>   SCl–NFCl
> ____ who have all left their mark).
>   SCl–RelCl

Lectures

In a lecture, the **mode** is spoken and the **manner** depends upon the size of the event. In a large lecture hall, the relationship between speaker and audience is impersonal. The lecturer is dominant as an **expert** in a particular field and the communication is usually one-way. On a smaller scale, however, in a seminar or tutorial, a more personal relationship can be created between the lecturer and individuals: communication can become a two-way process and the lecturer can invite questions and comments from the audience. The **field** is directly linked to the subject matter: physics, literature, history and so on.

Presentation is marked by prosodic features: intonation, pitch, pace and rhythm add variety to the lecture, attracting and holding audience attention. Written handouts may be used to reinforce the content of the lecture. Slides and computer-based presentations (for example, with PowerPoint®) can use images, tables, diagrams, animations or video clips to clarify points made. Some lecturers deliver pre-written essays orally, while others speak more spontaneously from notes. The first approach results in a form that more closely resembles a formal speech; the second has similarities to spoken language – there may be false starts, normal non-fluency features, repetitions or repairs.

The **lexis** is subject-specific (*Shakespeare*; *revenge tragedy*; *ghost*). If the context is more personal, the language is more likely to be similar to everyday formal spoken usage, and will include examples of ordinary language as well as subject-specific jargon. Modifiers are related to the topic:

>   m   m   h   m   m   h   q
> Austen's distinctive style   a descriptive approach to language
>   N   Adj   N   det   Adj   N   PrepP

The **grammar** is formal, whether the tone is impersonal in a large lecture hall or more personal in a smaller-scale seminar. The most common mood is the declarative, although imperatives may be used to direct the audience's attention to handouts and the like. Most sentences are active and the sentence structures are often long. In a lecture that is read from a written essay, the sentences are more likely to be complex and to have many embedded clauses: in one delivered from notes, they will tend to be looser in construction:

$$\underset{\text{P}}{\text{(Look)}}\ \underset{\text{A}}{\text{(at Chapter 1).}}\ \underset{\text{S}}{\text{(Austen)}}\ \underset{\text{P}}{\text{(uses)}}\ \underset{\text{O}}{\text{(irony)}}\ \underset{\text{SCl–NFCl}}{\text{(to characterise Sir Walter)}}\ \underset{\text{conj}}{\text{(and)}}\ \text{(her}$$

P　　　　A　　　　　　　　　S　　P　　O　　　　　　　　　　　　　A
(Look) (at Chapter 1). (Austen) (uses) (irony) (to characterise Sir Walter) (and) (her
　　　　　　　　　　　　　　　　　　　　　　　　　　　SCl–NFCl　　　　　　　　　conj

S　　　　　　P　　　O
approach) (portrays) (him) (as an unpleasant person who thinks only of himself and
　　　　　　　　　　　　　　　　　　　　　　　Co
　　　　　　　　　　　　　　　　　　SCl–RelCl

his position). 　　　　　　　　　　　　　　　　　　　　　　　(SPONTANEOUS)

　　　　　　　　　A　　　　　　　　　　　　　S　　　　P　　　　　　　　　O
(By using metaphorical language), (an author) (can ensure) (that readers appreciate
SCl–NFCl　　　　　　　　　　　　　　　　　　　　　　SCl–NCl
　　　　　　　　　　　　　　　　　　　　　　　　　　　　　　　　　　　　O
the sub-textual meaning of a novel), (that they understand both the literal and
　　　　　　　　　　　　　　　　　　　SCl–NCl
　　　　　　　　　　　　　　　　　　　　　　　　　　　　　　O
symbolic implications of plot and character) (and) (ø make appropriate structural
　　　　　　　　　　　　　　　　　　　　　　conj　　　SCl–NCl
connections). 　　　　　　　　　　　　　　　　　　　　　　　(SCRIPTED)

Both examples here are compound–complex sentences, but the rhetorical patterning of the second clearly marks it as closer to written than to spoken language.

20.4 Personal texts

Personal texts have the following characteristics.

▸ This kind of writing is concerned with the expression of personal ideas, aims, attitudes, and so forth. The **purpose** depends on the writer and on his or her relationship with the text. Some personal texts, such as letters, are written for a wider audience; others, such as diaries and journals, are intended only for the eyes of the author.

▸ The **mode** is usually written, although 'video diaries' are now a popular source of personal material on the television. At the time they are written, diaries are usually a form of one-way communication: the content is not intended for a wide audience and there is little interaction once each entry is complete. It is important to remember, however, that the diaries of famous people are often published subsequently, revealing the private side of public figures. Samuel Pepys' diary has become well known as a historical document because it recounts key events such as the Fire of London from one individual's point of view. In more recent years, politicians have published their diaries. Tony Benn's reflections, for example, are interesting because they are spoken diaries, taped recordings of his years in politics: as well as having been broadcast on BBC Radio 4, they have been made publicly available by the BBC in their 'Radio Collection'.

　　A letter is another form of one-way communication, although the recipient may respond later. The writer is not always dominant – informal letters, for instance, are usually written to equals.

▸ The **manner** may be formal or informal, depending upon the relationship between participants and the purpose of the communication. An official diary of appointments or a job application will be formal and impersonal; in correspondence between friends or in a personal record of events, the writer's feelings will often be informal and personal.

- Personal writing can be **informative**: factual details on a curriculum vitae will be formal, whereas details about a holiday and the places visited will be informal. It can also be **descriptive** or **evaluative**: a letter to a friend comparing two different social occasions will be informal, while an artist's account of a place that later formed the basis of a painting may be more formal.
- Personal writing may be **chronological** (focusing on dates and times) or it may treat events **non-chronologically** (focusing on arguments and comparisons).
- Texts that are written for a formal context like a job application must be **unambiguous**. Personal letters and diaries, however, may adopt the same spontaneous approach as everyday conversation and may therefore be **ambiguous** at times. Such texts may contain non-fluency markers like repetition, grammatical inaccuracies and spelling mistakes which parallel the kinds of non-fluency associated with informal spoken language.
- The **lexis** depends on the purpose and the intended audience. The language used in a job application will be formal and subject-specific. It will be marked by distinctive uses of language: collocations like *I enclose a CV as requested…* and *In response to the advertisement in* ____; terms of address like *Dear Sir/Madam, Yours faithfully, Yours sincerely*; and subject-specific lexis like *bookkeeping, accounts, cashing-up*. A letter to a friend, on the other hand, will be marked by informalities: colloquialisms like *well, you'll never guess what…* and terms of address like *Dear Sue, Hi!, Love Miguel*.
- The **grammar** of personal writing is directly linked to the purpose and intended audience – the more formal the context, the more complicated the grammar is likely to be. The mood of sentences varies: in informal personal writing, declaratives, interrogatives and imperatives are common; in formal personal writing, declaratives are the usual choice. Sentence structures tend to have a looser construction in informal examples: co-ordination is more common and sentences resemble the more rambling structure of spoken utterances. In formal writing, subordination is more common.
- The **layout** for personal writing is dictated by convention. In formal writing, traditions are followed carefully in order to make a good impression; in informal texts, however, each individual writer can make decisions about the way the text will appear on the page.
- The **context**, **audience** and **purpose** dictate the writer's role in each case.

Some examples of personal writing

Letters

In a letter, the **mode** is written. The **manner** can be at any point on a sliding scale between formal and informal. Choices are made depending upon the intended **audience** and the **purpose** of the communication: a job application or a letter to an MP will be formal; a holiday postcard or a letter to a friend will be informal. The **field** may be subject-specific in formal examples, but is often everyday or conversational in informal examples.

The **layout** is more likely to be individualistic in an informal letter because writers are free to alter traditional structures to suit themselves. The patterns of spoken language can be mirrored because recipients are more likely to accept inaccuracies (in spelling, punctuation or grammar) without making judgements about the sender. A formal letter needs to make a positive impression, however, so the conventions of written language are often adhered to far more strictly. Recipients expect paragraph structures to be logically developed, sentences to be controlled, and spelling to be accurate. The use of headed notepaper or logos help the reader to identify the sender immediately and add to the formality.

Formal letters should have a traditional layout, with the sender's address and telephone number and the date in the top right-hand corner, the recipient's name and address below on the left, a formal greeting (*Dear Sir/Madam*) and a formal closing (*Yours faithfully*). Traditionally, if a formal letter is addressed to a named person (*Dear Mr Brown*), it has a different closing (*Yours sincerely*). Informal letters do not have to include the recipient's address and they start less impersonally (*Dear Elena*; *Dear all*); they also conclude with more personal phrases (*Love from Jo*; *See you soon, Suresh*).

The **lexis** is dependent upon the purpose. Some types of letter are subject-specific, but many are not.

The **grammar** reflects the manner. If the letter is formal and impersonal, the grammar is more likely to be complicated and the sentences complex. The following extract is from the letter of resignation sent by Labour MP Clare Short to the Labour Party Whip, Jacqui Smith, dated 6 October 2006:

> S   P   C   A
> (I) (am) (sorry ø it has come to this), (but) (after a lifetime of service to the Labour Party)
>   SCl–NCl   conj
>
>   A   S   P   O
> (and) (ø 23 years in the House of Commons) (I) (think) (ø I am entitled to discuss
> conj   SCl–NCl   SCl–NFCl
>
> what has gone wrong with the government and our political system in my remaining
> SCl–NCl   conj
>
> years as an MP).

An informal letter is more likely to use simple and compound sentences. Where subordination is used, strings of embedded clauses are less common:

> A   P   S   S   S   P
> (Here) (is) (a belated birthday present) (and) (something for Joseph's room). (I) (hope)
>   conj
>
> O
> (you like it).
> SCl–NCl

Letters can mix a formal and an informal manner. An artist writing to a friend, for example, may discuss his work, creating a theoretical discourse on the nature of art and the artist in a personal context. Although the relationship between the participants can be described as informal, the content is subject-specific and formal. The following extract is taken from a letter that Vincent van Gogh sent to his brother Theo in the 1880s, in which he discusses his painting *Potato Eaters*:

> S   P   O
> (I) (have tried) (to emphasise that these people eating their potatoes in the lamplight,
>   SCl–NFCl   SCl–NCl   SCl–NFCl

have dug the earth with those very hands they put into the dish) (and so) (it) (speaks
SCl–RelCl   conj

O   O

of) (manual labour) (and) (how they have honestly earned their food).
conj   SCl–NCl

The complexity of the clause structure here is typical of a formal rather than an informal letter. Although Van Gogh is writing to his brother, he treats his correspondence as an integral part of his art, so the content and style are formal.

Figurative language can be used to personalise both formal and informal letters. In examples where the style closely resembles spoken language, however, figurative language is less common. When used in formal correspondence, it can make a letter distinctive and personal without it becoming informal. The following extract is taken from the letter of resignation sent by the Conservative MP Quentin Davies to the Leader of the Conservative Party, David Cameron, dated 26 June 2007:

> ... under your leadership the Conservative Party appears to me to have ceased collectively to believe in anything, or to stand for anything.
> It has no bedrock. It exists on shifting sands. A sense of mission has been replaced by a PR agenda.

The letter has a formal purpose: the announcement of Quentin Davies' resignation from the Conservative Party and his defection to the Labour Party. The language is therefore formal, using abstract nouns (*leadership, mission, agenda*) and stative verbs (*appears, to believe, exists*). The figurative language adds a concrete visual element to Davies' argument. The juxtaposition of *bedrock* and *shifting sands* in two antithetical simple sentences implies that Conservative policy is no longer based on permanence and stability but on the ephemeral, dictated not by principle but by concerns for public relations. The images underpin Davies' suggestion that under Cameron's leadership the Conservative Party has lost its sense of direction.

Diaries and journals

In diaries and journals the **mode** is usually written and the **manner** may be formal (work appointments), informal (a personal record of ideas), or anywhere on the scale between the two extremes. The **field** depends upon the writer and his or her purpose – a diary may contain a record of homework due or interview times, or may be a description of day-to-day activities, thoughts and feelings. Usually they are private and not for publication, but historians can use diaries of both ordinary and famous people to get an impression of what life was like at a particular time. Novelists can use diaries as a means of characterising people: the *Adrian Mole* novels by Sue Townsend use a diary format to allow the reader to see directly into Adrian's private thoughts – the reader seems almost to be invading his privacy.

The **layout** varies. At one extreme, a diary will be made up of no more than lists of times, dates and events; at the other end of the scale, it may be written in detailed prose. Divisions into days, weeks and months are common. Private, secret diaries may be written in a shorthand or code that is understandable only to the writer. The length of entries may vary considerably.

The **lexis** may be subject-specific or very personal. It is often distinctive.

The **grammar** reflects the nature of the writer and the content. Since diarists often use a personal shorthand, ellipsis of determiners and verbless clauses are common. Grammatical words are omitted, leaving the focus on lexical items:

> (Day of rest)! (In garden) (later). (Evening) (tranquil). (Remarkably clear view of coast).
> NP   PrepP   AdvP   NP   AdjP   NP

Verbs are usually in the past tense since a diary records events, feelings and attitudes after they have occurred. First person pronouns are dominant because the text is specifically related to the writer. The mood varies depending upon the writer's intentions: declaratives are most common, but imperatives and interrogatives may also be used.

Diaries or journals can be kept for practical reasons (listing birthdays) or for more artistic purposes. Factual diaries vary very little from person to person in terms of their content and structure, but a personal diary is often idiosyncratic, revealing much about the person who is keeping it. Dorothy Wordsworth, sister of the Romantic poet William Wordsworth, kept a diary in which she recorded details about the weather, domestic tasks, natural observations and the people who surrounded her. Sometimes the entries are written in a shorthand and many sentences are made up of noun phrases or verbless clauses. Where sentences are composed of grammatically complete clauses, they are all simple sentences. Even at these times, however, the style is clearly poetic:

> *Friday, [31st] October 1800*
>   S   P   A   S   C   S   P   O   A
> (W. and S.) (did not rise) (till 1 o'clock). (W.) (very sick and very ill). (S.) (drank) (tea) (at
>   neg
>   P   A   A   C
> Lloyds) (and) (came) (home) (immediately after). (ø) (ø) (A very fine moonlight night).
>   S   P   A
> (The moon) (shone) (like herrings in the water).

At other times, the sentence structure is complex to match the content. Where Dorothy Wordsworth's style becomes more expressive and literary, the grammatical utterances are more often complete and the prose is therefore more fluent:

> *Friday 23rd April, 1802*
>   S   P   O
> (William) (observed) (that the umbrella Yew tree that breasts the wind had lost its
>   SCl–NCl   SCl–RelCl
>   O
> character as a tree) (and) (ø had become something like to solid wood). ... (We) (left)
>   conj   SCl–NCl   S   P
>   O   A   A   S   P   A
> (William) (sitting on the stones) (feasting with silence) – (and) (C. and I) (sate) (down)
>   SCl–NFCl   SCl–NFCl
>   A   C   S   P   A
> (upon a rocky seat) – (a Couch) (it) (might be) (under the Bower of William's Eglantine,
> Andrew's Broom).

The style here is quite different – subordination is common, strings of adverbials give details of the environment, and a marked theme throws emphasis on the complement of the sentence.

20.5 Narrative texts

Narrative texts have the following characteristics.

- In narrative texts, **expression** is usually personal. Although the content will reflect the writer's interests, experiences and attitudes, there is a greater sense of audience than in other personal writing. Unlike diaries and journals, which are written for the writer's eyes only, and letters, which are written for a clearly defined audience, narrative texts have a wider and more diverse audience. The style is often poetic, although authors can also choose to mirror the language of everyday conversation.

- The **mode** is usually written, although stories can also be recorded and we all tell narratives in our everyday speech encounters. The **manner** depends upon the intended audience and on the author's purpose – a narrative written for an examiner may adopt a more formal approach than a controversial script written for the Edinburgh Fringe Festival. Usually the audience is not directly engaged in an active way, although implicitly the authors draw the reader into the fictional worlds they create. The **field** is linked to the subject matter: science fiction; a particular historical period or country; people of different social classes.

- The **function** of a narrative text is to entertain, but it can also educate and inform. Plays can focus on topical issues such as AIDS, the environment, or war; a comic strip format can be used for educational purposes. In the ____ *For Beginners* series (*Feminism for Beginners*; *Freud for Beginners*), for instance, a comic format is used to introduce complex issues and key historical figures.

- Narratives are **chronological**, but authors do not have to relate events in order. They can use flashbacks, retrospective reflection, parallel timescales, and so on. Children's first narratives tend to be chronological, moving from the beginning to the end in a straightforward linear development.

- **Ambiguity** can be used intentionally to create suspense: some novels, like B. S. Johnson's *House Mother Normal*, have to be read to the end before everything makes sense.

- The **lexis** links to the kinds of character speaking, the locations and the different relationships established. Choices are dictated by authorial intention.

- The **grammar** of narrative texts is varied since authors can use a wide range of techniques to influence readers. However, most prose narratives are in the past tense, while comics and playscripts use the present tense.

- While the **layout** is distinctive for comic strips and playscripts, most prose narratives use the traditional conventions of written language. Since authors are creating something personal, however, they can alter conventions to make their end product more distinctive.

- The writers of narratives are **creative**: they therefore manipulate lexis and language structures in order to influence their readers.

Some examples of narrative texts

Playscripts

Although the **mode** is written, a playscript is essentially made up of language to be spoken. The **manner** is formal, but some playwrights or particular kinds of performance may aim to create a more informal relationship with the audience. Pantomimes, for instance, make the audience less passive by encouraging participation: *He's behind you!* Because there is no omniscient narrator, as there is in a novel, the audience must also actively make connections, interpret the subplot, and deduce things about the characters. The **field** is linked directly to the topic of the play: it may be issue-related or profession-related, or mirror everyday usage.

The **layout** is distinctive. Often the names of speakers are in capital letters, the text running on but with second and subsequent lines indented:

> HELEN   Well! This is the place.
> JO   And I don't like it.
>
> Shelagh Delaney (1939–), A Taste of Honey: Act 1, Scene 1

Italic print may be used to mark stage directions:

> Scene one. *A hotel lounge. Crumbling grandeur. Cane chairs. A great expanse of black-and-white checked floor stretching back into the distance. Porticos. Windows at the back and, to one side, oak doors. But the scene must only be sketched in, not realistically complete.*
>
> David Hare (1947–), A Map of the World: Act 1, Scene 1

Parenthesis is used to show any specific instructions about the way characters should deliver their lines or move:

> THIRD WORKER (*coming on*). I shouted to him to run.
> FOREMAN (*coming downstage*). Go back, go back! Work!
>   FOURTH WORKER *goes off again*.
> THIRD WORKER. You heard me shout!
> FIRST WORKER. He says he's dead.
> FOREMAN. Work!
> SOLDIER (*to* FIRST WORKER). You! – make yerself responsible for 'andin' in 'is pick t' stores. (*Suddenly he sees something off stage and runs down to the others.*) Cover 'im! Quick!
> FOREMAN (*points to tarpaulin*). Take that!
>
> Edward Bond (1934–), Lear: Act 1, Scene 1

The **lexis** chosen by the playwright is dependent on the play's content, characters and context. **Characterisation** is developed through a combination of language, prosodics and movement; **tone** (comic or tragic; elevated or colloquial) is directly linked to the context and the lexical choices; the **context** (geographical, social, historical) is established in the stage directions (concrete and abstract nouns; modifiers). Because scripts do not usually have an omniscient narrator to make implicit points explicit, the audience must interpret language and gesture themselves in order to understand characters and their relationships. Subjective thoughts and feelings may be revealed in a monologue, but more often paralinguistics and prosodics guide audience response. Figurative language and rhetorical techniques can also tell the audience something about a character.

The **dialogue** is initially written rather than spoken, but in most modern plays dramatists want it to sound like spontaneous speech rather than formal prose. Despite this, most scripts are more formally structured than everyday conversation.

The **prosodic features** are an important means of making the written text seem spontaneous. Characters express their feelings in a more exaggerated way on stage – each response is heightened so that the audience can appreciate subtle changes. Variations in pace may be linked to emotions and actions; silence and pauses can be used to create dramatic effects; and intonation patterns are different for each character and context. Through the prosodic techniques, actors bring the words on the page to life.

The **grammar** may be formal or informal, depending upon the character who is speaking. If the script mimics the looser patterns of speech, grammatical structures may be incomplete; if the script is in verse, word orders may be manipulated in order to conform to a particular rhythmic pattern. Lines imitating everyday speech may use minor sentences and utterances may overlap; a verse play will have a heightened style, adopting poetic rather than spoken conventions. If the character speaking is idiosyncratic, the grammar will be distinctive; if the character comes from a particular historical period or geographical context, the grammar may be marked by archaisms or dialect features.

When considering an extract from a script, you will also need to think about: **changes in scene**; the **centre of interest**; the **location** in **time** and **place**; the **relationship** created between the **characters** and **audience**; any **dramatic use of language** to create **atmosphere**; any references to **costume, sound effects** and **music**.

Comic strips

In a comic strip, the **mode** is written. The **manner** is often informal. A personal relationship is created between the reader, the writer and the artist – the tone may be colloquial, satirical or informative. The **field** is subject-specific – traditional girls' comics focus on make-up, boyfriends, and dieting; traditional boys' comics focus on futuristic societies, superheroes, sport and practical activities. Where the comic strip is used as an educative medium, the **lexis** will reflect the topic: drugs, politics, sexism.

The **layout** combines text and image. Each page is divided into strips or unequal sections, making the reading process less demanding than it would be for a page of dense prose. The words are usually clearly marked out: narrative comment or description which sets the scene is placed in a box; direct speech is placed in a bubble; onomatopoeic words such as *BANG* or *HISS* are capitalised and have a larger print size. Stories in a particular comic may use a distinctive print style that is immediately recognisable to regular readers. Comics are often dominated by bright colours, and photo stories are common. Although words are an important part of the storyline, the main means of communication is visual.

The **lexis** is directly related to the content. Photo stories in girls' comics aim to re-create the language of their intended audience, so 'cult' words and colloquialisms are common. Science-fiction comics like *Judge Dredd* create a new language which is appropriate for the fictional world of a particular story (see Figure 20.1). The language in these publications is idiosyncratic – writers do not aim to mirror reality and their lexical choices are therefore distinctive. The world created in futuristic stories is often male-dominated, and the language tends to be linked directly to violence and male superheroes. Text is used to build up atmosphere, provide comment, set the scene or develop characters. Direct speech attempts to reflect the spontaneity of informal conversation. These kinds of comics are often accused of having ugly, crude and vulgar language.

On the other hand, comics can be subject-specific and linked directly to a particular topic (see Figure 20.2). Although comic strip is traditionally associated with non-serious material, the format can also be used to communicate sophisticated ideas to a wide audience. In educative comic strip the tone is still usually informal, but images are accompanied by text that uses technical or factual language as an integral part of the communication.

The **grammar** varies depending upon the kind of publication. Direct speech is often made up of grammatically incomplete utterances, particularly in comics that create fictional worlds. Informative comic strip is more likely to use grammatical utterances, but verbless clauses and noun phrases are still common. The sentence structures are more likely to be complex in educative comic strip texts:

> | A | S | P | O |
> (Based on his writings and ideas), (one third of humanity) (practises) (Communism)
> SCl–NFCl
>
> | A |
> (while the other two thirds keep arguing about them) …   (Figure 20.2)
> SCl–ACl   SCl–NFCl

In comic strip that is basically narrative, sentences tend to be simple, often marked by typical non-standard usage:

> | S | P | A | P | O |
> (The M.I.A.S.) (are) (in the open)! (Go) (chain guns)!   (Figure 20.1)

Comics aim to create a personal relationship with their readers. They are often described as 'alternative' because they do not conform to expectations of traditional narrative.

20.6 What to look for in an unfamiliar variety of English

The following checklist can be used to identify key features in an unfamiliar variety. You will not find all of the features in every text, but the list can be used as a guide. Remember to evaluate the effect of the features you identify, exploring the ways in which they create meaning.

The following are helpful questions to ask.

Register

1 What is the **mode**?
   - spoken or written?
2 What is the **manner**?
   - personal or impersonal relationship between the participants?
   - formal or informal?

Figure 20.1 **Extract from *Judge Dredd***

Figure 20.2 **Extract from *Marx for Beginners***

- one-way or two-way communication?
- the purpose of the communication?
- the relative status of the participants?

3 What is the **field**?
- subject matter?
- linked to the audience, purpose, and context?

Lexis

1 Is the language **distinctive**?
- formal or informal?
- subject-specific or colloquial?

2 Are the **nouns** concrete or abstract?

3 Are the **verbs** dynamic or stative?

4 What kind of **modifiers** are used?
- descriptive/evaluative?
- factual/technical?
- pre- or post-modification?

5 Are the **nominal groups** long or short?

6 Are there any recognisable **collocations**?

7 What kinds of **adverbials** are used?
- time? place? manner?

8 Are any **abbreviations** or **codes** used?

9 Does the language reflect a specific **person**, **place** or **historical period**?

Prosodics

1 Are there variations in **tone, pitch** or **pace**?
- to indicate a speaker's attitude, thoughts or feelings?

2 Are there rising, falling, rising–falling or falling–rising **intonation patterns**?
- to mark a speaker's intentions?
- to make utterances distinctive?

3 Is **stress** used for effect?
- to draw attention to key lexical items?

4 How are **pauses** used?
- to mark the end of a grammatically complete utterance?
- to enhance meaning?

Grammar

1 Are **grammatical utterances** complete or incomplete?

2 Are there any links with **spoken language**?
- contractions? colloquialisms? abbreviated or disjointed sentences?

3 Does the **mood** change?
- declarative to make statements?
- interrogatives to question?
- imperatives to instruct?

4 Is anything noticeable about the **tense of verbs**?
- simple present for playscripts, comics or information texts?
- simple past for narratives, letters or diaries?

5 Is the **sentence structure** varied?
  - simple, compound, complex, or compound–complex?
  - verbless clauses?
  - minor sentences?

6 What kinds of **subordinate clauses** are used?
  - NCl? ACl? NFCl? RelCl?

7 Are any **modal verbs** used?
  - linked to meaning?

8 What kinds of **cohesion** are used?
  - repetition of lexis?
  - pronominal references?
  - chronological sequences?

Style

1 Are there any examples of **literary devices**?
  - metaphors? similes? symbols?
  - personification or animation?
  - puns? ambiguity?

2 Is there any **phonological patterning**?
  - alliteration? rhythm? rhyme?

3 Are there any examples of **rhetorical devices**?
  - listing? repetition? juxtaposition? patterning?

4 Is **sentence organisation** designed to influence the way in which the audience receives meaning?
  - foregrounding? initial position conjunctions? passive voice?

Graphological/typographical features

1 Is the text **handwritten** or **typed**?

2 Is there anything distinctive about the **graphology**?
  - style of the handwriting?
  - child's or adult's?
  - abbreviations? capitalisation?

3 Is there anything significant about the **typography**?
  - print size? shape? style?

4 Is **colour** used?

5 Is the **layout** distinctive?

Summary

Comment on the **function** of the discourse. Then consider the **effect** of the linguistic and stylistic features, and the ways in which these aim to influence the target audience. Concentrate on what makes the discourse **distinctive** – that is, different from other varieties.

Be open-minded and avoid approaching texts with rigid expectations. The material in this section establishes general expectations, but writers can draw upon a range of techniques, mixing formats and styles to communicate effectively with their intended audience.

Chapter 21

Preparing for a language examination

The information covered in Parts II and III can be used in a variety of ways and you need to be versatile in your approach. Initially, you should make sure you feel confident about the reference material in Part I, so that you can respond to questions using the appropriate terminology. When you can recognise and discuss lexical, grammatical, phonological and stylistic features, you are ready to focus on the specific demands of coursework and examination questions. If you intend to sit a language examination, check the requirements of the syllabus and look at past papers so that you know exactly what kind of tasks you will be expected to tackle.

You should be able to analyse spoken, written and multi-modal texts using relevant linguistic approaches; to explore a range of original writing tasks for specific audiences and purposes; to undertake a practical investigative study; and to evaluate your own work. When completing coursework tasks, you should note the word limit set by the examination board. Teachers and moderators will discontinue marking once the prescribed word limit has been reached, so exceeding the stated limit will affect your mark. Remember that the quality of your written expression is assessed in all elements of your course.

21.1 Coursework

Coursework offers you the opportunity to explore elements of the syllabus in more detail and to practise using the linguistic approaches and frameworks. You can begin to identify areas of personal interest and to develop your knowledge and understanding. Most AS and A2 courses contain a coursework unit. Take time to check the requirements of your syllabus so that you know exactly what is expected of you – the word limit is of particular importance.

Original writing

As well as being able to analyse other writers' texts, language courses require students to develop their own writing skills. To produce effective texts, you need:

‣ to know how audience, purpose and context affect speech and writing
‣ to understand how lexical and grammatical patterns shape meaning

- to be sensitive to the effects that literary and rhetorical devices can create
- to be able to recognise and use a range of genres.

Selecting appropriate linguistic structures will enable you to create effective texts in a range of genres for different audiences and purposes.

Some AS and A2 coursework requires you to use language creatively to entertain your intended audience – to write a poem, a script, the opening or closing chapter of a novel, or a short story. You may also be required to write in other literary forms (such as autobiography or the dramatic monologue) or to produce writing inspired by a text you have studied (such as the biography of a fictional character, or additional chapters adopting the style and tone of the original).

Other tasks may require you to adopt a functional approach to persuade, inform, advise or instruct your intended audience. You may have to produce an information or an instruction text, a letter or a speech, a newspaper report or a magazine article, a scripted interview or a guide, advertising material or a review. In each case, you must select an appropriate layout; the lexis and grammar must demonstrate an understanding of your target audience and purpose; and the register and style must reflect the variety.

In original writing tasks, you will be assessed on your ability:

- to demonstrate your expertise and creativity
- to select and use a range of linguistic methods and approaches
- to show your knowledge using appropriate terminology
- to write coherently and accurately.

Evaluating your writing

Often you will be asked to provide an evaluation of the writing task you have completed, explaining the techniques you have used. You may find the framework below a useful starting point, but you should adapt it to suit your particular task and the requirements of the syllabus you are following. Your discussion could focus on these features of your writing:

1 **INTRODUCTION**
   Your knowledge of similar **text types** and the **distinctive features** of the form you have chosen.

2 **CONTENT**
   The **selection of appropriate material**; your **approach** to making it suitable for your chosen format and audience; any **omissions or additions**.

3 **LINGUISTIC, GRAMMATICAL AND STYLISTIC CHOICES**
   The reasons behind **lexical and grammatical choices**; any points at which the **tone changes**; the **effects** created by any **rhetorical or literary devices**.

4 **DIFFICULTIES AND SUCCESSES**
   Areas of the writing that caused **problems**; areas that seem to have been particularly **successful**; links to **audience expectations** and **responses**.

5 **CONCLUSION**
   Your overall **aims**; an **assessment** of how far you have met them.

In your original writing and commentary, you will be expected:

- to study a range of text types to inform your writing
- to demonstrate your understanding of genre and register
- to engage your audience
- to show a clear sense of purpose
- to manipulate language, grammar and style to create appropriate effects
- to use redrafting strategies to develop your material effectively.

Language investigation

This part of your course offers you the chance to undertake a practical and investigative study of an area of personal interest. You need to demonstrate a good understanding of the area you have chosen, and your investigation should show your ability to apply linguistic knowledge to the spoken data or written material you have collected.

Your primary language data may focus on a wide range of language use. Topics could include: the differences between reading schemes and stories for young readers; the linguistic features of children's writing; the formulaic structure of jokes; language acquisition; sports commentaries; political language; attitudes to language; language stereotyping; accent and dialect; stand-up comedy.

In the investigative writing, you will be assessed on your ability:

- to select and use a range of linguistic methods and approaches
- to show your knowledge using relevant terminology
- to write coherently and accurately
- to understand and explore the ways in which meaning is constructed
- to analyse and evaluate the influence of contextual factors
- to show knowledge of the key constituents of language.

Choosing your topic

The first stage of your investigation is to establish an appropriate **TOPIC** or **AREA OF STUDY**. It is then important to carry out some general research so that you have a good basic knowledge of the topic or variety you intend to study. This will involve **PRIMARY SOURCES**, for example watching television interviews (spoken), reading a range of newspapers (written), or observing the interaction between word, image and sound in a film (multi-modal); and **SECONDARY SOURCES**, for example reading a textbook that explores the linguistic features of television interviews, listening to a radio discussion of the ways in which different newspapers have approached a particular story, or watching a film review programme.

Defining your field of reference

Having decided on your topic, you need to define a **FIELD OF REFERENCE**. You may like to ask yourself:

1 What do I want to find out?
2 What data will I need in order to find it out?
3 How should I collect this data?
4 How should I analyse it?

Try to decide whether you wish to focus your study around a hypothesis or around a research question. A **HYPOTHESIS** is a tentative statement that proposes a possible explanation of a particular feature – it can be tested for its accuracy and will often include a prediction. For instance:

> If children read only reading scheme books, then their creative writing will be less original and will demonstrate a narrower range of grammatical and stylistic features than stories written by children who read a wide range of fiction.

A **RESEARCH QUESTION** observes a distinctive way in which language functions, and then explores examples to see whether this is true in a range of cases:

> How do politicians communicate their opinions and what techniques do they use to influence their audience?

Provided that the question you pose is meaningful, you will be able to find a method to prove whether or not it is true.

Collecting material

The next step is to begin collecting the kind of material your examination board requires. If you are going to carry out a study of spoken or multi-modal language, it is important to spend time getting the transcript as accurate as possible before working on your analysis of the data. If you use symbols to mark significant prosodic features, remember to provide a key.

Writing up your investigative study

Your coursework needs to provide an objective assessment of the material you have collected. Some examination boards list the key sections that should be used to structure your work; if yours does not, you may find the framework below a useful starting point. Adapt it to suit your particular task or the requirements of the syllabus you are following. Remember to label and index all sections.

1 **INTRODUCTION**
   Outline your **topic** and your reason for choosing it. Develop a **hypothesis** or **research question**. Establish your **aims**.

2 **METHODOLOGY**
   Give an account of your approach to **data selection**. If you have encountered any **problems**, discuss these.

3 **ANALYSIS**
   Interpret your material or materials using appropriate **linguistic concepts** – lexical, grammatical, and stylistic. Explore the **effects** of the **contextual influences** and discuss any relevant **linguistic issues**.

4 **CONCLUSION**
   Summarise your **findings** and **assess** whether or not you have answered your research question or proved your hypothesis. Explain what you have learnt from your investigation.

5 **EVALUATION**
   Briefly **evaluate** the success of your investigation and the validity of your find-

ings. Explore the possibility of **further research** to support or expand your conclusions.

6 **BIBLIOGRAPHY**

Record all **primary** and **secondary sources** that you have used in your investigation.

7 **APPENDICES**

Include copies of the written or spoken **data** you have collected and any practical analysis that has formed the basis for your findings.

In your investigative work, you will be expected:

- to establish a context for your analysis
- to present your findings in an accessible way, using diagrams, tables and graphs where appropriate
- to focus your discussion clearly
- to use appropriate terminology and language frameworks
- to balance linguistic analysis with appropriate theoretical knowledge of the topic you are studying.

Analytical studies

Some AS units require you to analyse the key features of one or two texts. You may be given a free choice or you may need to focus on a specific mode. It is sensible to choose texts that interest you: written (for example, travel writing, magazine articles, leaflets, letters, diaries), spoken (for example, transcripts of political speeches, stand-up comedians, voice-overs, chat shows, film dialogue), or multimodal (for example, music videos, cartoons, web-based texts, illustrated books, television broadcasts).

In your analytical writing, you will be assessed on your ability:

- to select and use a range of linguistic methods and approaches
- to show your knowledge, using appropriate terminology
- to write coherently and accurately
- to demonstrate and explore the ways in which meaning is constructed
- to analyse and evaluate the influence of contextual factors.

This kind of writing task tests your ability to read closely and to plan and structure an essay. You need to identify the variety and know the distinctive features usually associated with it. Then think about the content and the way in which it has been presented. It is important to make notes or text-mark written material so that you can gather evidence to support the points you make. If you are focusing on spoken texts, transcribe your material and provide a key to show the meaning of any symbols you have used.

In your analytical writing, you will be expected:

- to show an understanding of audience, purpose and register
- to explore any social, cultural, geographical or historical contextual influences
- to discuss the way in which meaning is constructed
- to analyse and evaluate the phonological, lexical, grammatical and stylistic features using appropriate terminology.

Adaptive writing

In some AS units you may be required to present a text in another form, for a new audience or with a different purpose. For example, you might be asked to adapt an interview so that there is little intrusion from the interviewer or so that the interviewee is presented in a particular way; to re-present a tabloid report in the form of a compact or broadsheet report; to adapt a television documentary originally shown after the nine o'clock watershed to a form appropriate for a younger audience; to convert an extract from a novel into a radio script; or to rewrite an information leaflet as a television advertisement.

To prepare for this task, you need to be confident about the distinctive features of a range of text types. Use your knowledge to help you choose an appropriate form and style. Remember to think about the register, the purpose and the context of your writing.

Having completed your adaptation, you will probably need to write a commentary that explores the changes you have made. You could use a plan similar to the one on page 580 ('Evaluating your writing') to organise your ideas.

In your adaptive writing tasks, you will be assessed on your ability:

▸ to demonstrate your expertise and creativity in a range of different contexts
▸ to select and use a range of linguistic methods and approaches
▸ to show your knowledge using appropriate terminology
▸ to write coherently and accurately
▸ to understand and explore the ways in which meaning is constructed.

21.2 The examination

All AS and A2 courses contain external examinations. Look at past papers so that you are familiar with the layout, the number of questions you should answer, the sections from which these should be taken, and the way in which your time should be divided.

Tackling data-based examination questions

Many of the tasks in your examination papers will be based on the analysis of data. You may be presented with a single text or with a range of texts linked by genre, theme, audience or purpose. The texts may be spoken, written, electronic or multimodal; they may be from the present day or from the past – probably no earlier than the transitional period between Middle English and Early Modern English. The accompanying questions will help you to decide how to approach the passage or passages.

To tackle these analytical tasks successfully, you need to develop close reading skills and an ability to understand and apply appropriate linguistic methods. You will be required to analyse the passage or passages in detail, so be prepared to identify, explain and evaluate language constituents, using appropriate linguistic terminology, methods and approaches. As well as the intended **audience**, the **purpose** and the **variety**, you should also consider:

- **register** – the mode, manner and field
- **phonology** – sounds and the way they are combined
- **morphology** – the structure of words
- **lexis** – the choice of words and their denotations and connotations
- **grammar** – the relationship between words in phrases, clauses and sentences
- **prosodics** – intonation, pitch, pace and volume
- **discourse** – whole texts in context.

Remember to provide **examples** to support the points you make and to discuss the **effects** of the language choices you have identified. Thinking about the following questions may help you:

1 How are the language and structure used to create meaning?
2 How does the writer or speaker convey ideas, attitudes, thoughts, opinions, points of view or values?
3 How do the contextual factors (social, cultural, historical, geographical) influence the language and form?

Your knowledge of the key language constituents, linguistic approaches to analysis and the characteristics of different varieties will help you to understand the way in which language is being used in the texts you are given. Use appropriate terminology, and plan your answers before you begin to write.

Read the question carefully so that you know exactly what you need to include in your essay. **Comparative** questions require you to compare (discuss similarities between) and contrast (discuss differences between) texts from different periods, genres and types. The **focus** of your analysis will usually be given in the question and you will need to organise your answer appropriately. Other questions may require you to **evaluate** the influence of contextual factors, the writers' and speakers' techniques, the ways in which different audiences and readers might respond, or the linguistic frameworks you have used.

Tackling topic-based examination questions

Some questions may require you to move beyond analysis of specific texts to a wider consideration of a **particular language issue**. For instance, you may study the way in which language is affected by some of the following: power and identity; culture; occupation; gender, social and economic class, and age; historical, geographical and social variation. Other topic areas, such as child language acquisition (spoken and written), English as a world language, and attitudes to language change, are also common. You will cover a number of topics in your study of language and it is therefore sensible to check the requirements of the examination syllabus you are following.

Topic-based questions require you to **demonstrate your knowledge** of a particular topic area and to provide appropriate examples. Your response therefore needs to show that you can engage with the issues and sustain an **informed critical judgement**.

Time can be a problem in an examination, but drawing up a brief plan ensures that your response is clearly focused. Before you start, always **underline the key words in the title** so that you know exactly what the question requires you to do.

Check how long you should spend on the task and remember that the quality of your written expression will be assessed.

Your plan should be made up of the following sections:

1 INTRODUCTION

Establish a starting point by jotting down some key points that provide you with a **general framework** for your essay.

2 BODY

- Define **three key areas** to make up the main body of your essay. Give each area a title so that you can make sure you focus on only one idea or concept at a time. Use these headings for your notes only.
- Under each heading, jot down the **key points** you wish to make. Try to group similar ideas together, and find links between the different areas.
- Choose appropriate **examples** to substantiate the points you make – **evidence** is crucial to the development of your case.

3 CONCLUSION

Round off your discussion with a **strong statement**. Jot down some new related points that bring your discussion to an **emphatic end**. Avoid repeating or summarising the argument that has made up the main body of your essay.

Be prepared to use relevant information and examples, and include your own opinions as well as the special and non-specialist viewpoints you have explored in the course of your study. Successful essays will show your ability to cross-reference, to evaluate ideas and attitudes, and to explore relevant linguistic frameworks.

In topic-based examination questions, you will be assessed on your ability:

- to select and use a range of linguistic methods and approaches
- to show your knowledge using appropriate terminology
- to write coherently and accurately
- to demonstrate and explore the ways in which meaning is constructed
- to analyse and evaluate the influence of contextual factors.

Tackling 'original writing' in examination questions

In most cases your original writing will be completed as part of your coursework. Some syllabuses, however, include a writing task within the examination. The task tests your ability to produce a **literary or non-literary text in a particular form**. It may be linked to source material printed on the examination paper that explores a topical language issue.

A **WRITING BRIEF** will indicate the specific genre, audience and subject matter for your writing. This information will dictate the way in which you should re-present the subject matter and communicate the ideas so that they are appropriate for your intended audience, purpose and context.

In the original writing questions, you will be assessed on your ability:

- to demonstrate your expertise and creativity
- to select and use a range of linguistic methods and approaches
- to show your knowledge using appropriate terminology
- to write coherently and accurately.

You may need to write a **commentary** on the text you produce. A commentary allows you to explore the distinctive features of the variety. Choose examples from your writing to demonstrate the way in which you have used your linguistic knowledge to meet the demands of the task. In some cases, you may be required to compare your text with some of the source material provided on the paper. The aim of your commentary is to show how genre, audience and purpose affect the lexical choices, the presentation of the subject matter, the grammatical structure, the style and the layout. You must be prepared to describe, explain and evaluate the linguistic features of your writing.

In the commentary, you will be assessed on your ability:

- to select and use a range of linguistic methods and approaches
- to show your knowledge, using appropriate terminology
- to write coherently and accurately
- to demonstrate and explore the ways in which meaning is constructed
- to analyse and evaluate the influence of contextual factors
- to show knowledge of the key constituents of language.

Revising for the examination

REVISION is a crucial part of any examination preparation. You need time to look back at work covered in order to establish what you feel confident about and what causes you problems. If you do this in plenty of time you can immediately begin to fill any gaps in your understanding, avoiding last-minute panics. Plan ahead and organise your time effectively, remembering that few people can sit for hours on end learning topic after topic.

In the course of your study you will have covered all kinds of linguistic terminology. You need to be able to use this as a shorthand to describe the linguistic patterns and processes you identify. Use the Glossary (pages 612–24) to establish what you know, then work through the unfamiliar terms logically. Your starting point should be Part I, since this defines and explains the grammatical, phonetic, phonological and stylistic terms that have been used in the rest of the book.

The next stage in your preparation should be to focus on the key areas of linguistic debate. Re-read Part II and draw up lists of key points and appropriate evidence for each topic covered. Add examples and any other relevant information from your own study of language. These checklists should form the framework for your revision – wider reading will help to broaden your basic knowledge.

Alongside your knowledge of language topics, you need to develop your personal understanding of the different varieties of English. Make lists of key points that will help you to identify the characteristic features of specific text types (spoken, written and multi-modal). These key points will form the basis for your analysis of a range of source material in the examination, but be prepared to have a general approach that can be applied to unfamiliar varieties.

Thorough revision will help you to succeed in your examination, but it is crucial that you are also able to apply your knowledge in new contexts. You must be versatile in your approach so that you can:

- discuss language topics knowledgeably
- make cross-references and develop links between different areas of language study
- analyse examples of spoken, written and multi-modal texts
- cope with unfamiliar topics and examples, applying knowledge and analytical frameworks in new contexts
- explore the ways in which meaning is constructed
- evaluate the influence of contextual factors
- write accurately and coherently.

In the examination

When you are actually sitting with the examination paper in front of you, read the **rubric** before you start. Make sure you know **how many questions** you have to answer, **which sections** they should come from, and **how long** you should allocate to each. Then work out the times at which you should start and finish each question.

Choose questions carefully, making sure before you start writing that you know exactly what they require you to do. To focus your mind, always underline the key information. Spend time planning: good organisation will always be rewarded. It is better to focus closely on three key areas than to cover everything in such a general way that your answer is rambling and vague. If you do feel you have tackled the wrong question, think very carefully before abandoning a half-finished answer – it is usually easier to refocus what you have started than to begin again from scratch.

21.3 Examination-style questions

Examination questions can be divided into **topic-based questions, 'attitudes and opinions' questions, theme-based questions** and **variety-based questions**. This section gives you some material on which to practise your analytical and writing skills. Each examination board sets slightly different kinds of questions, so you may not see examples of all the types here in the course that you are following. To tackle the questions effectively, follow the procedures outlined above.

1 Topic-based questions

Texts 1A and 1B below address the nature of language use in two specific contexts. Read through the source material and complete the following tasks.

TASK 1.1 ━━━━━━━━━━━━━━━━━━━━━━━━━━━━━━━━━━━━━━━

To what extent do the writers raise important issues about language use in modern society?

By close references to both passages, make a detailed critical analysis of the linguistic approaches used by the writers. You should also analyse and evaluate the influence of contextual factors.

Write about the different ways in which language can be used to communicate.

In your answer, pay close attention to the passages below and also draw on your own knowledge and research.

TEXTS

TEXT 1A

Text 1A is taken from a book called *Watching the English: The Hidden Rules of English Behaviour* by the social anthropologist Kate Fox. She explores what it means to be 'English', through her observations of our linguistic, cultural and social behaviour.

1 The mobile phone has, I believe, become the modern equivalent of the garden fence or village green. The space-age technology of mobile phones has allowed us to return to the more natural and humane communication patterns of pre-industrial society, when we lived in small, stable communities, and enjoyed frequent 'grooming talk'
5 with a tightly integrated social network of family and friends. In the fast-paced modern world, we had become severely restricted in both the quantity and quality of communication with our social network. Most of us no longer enjoy the cosiness of a gossip over the garden fence. We may not even know our neighbours' names, and communication is often limited to a brief, slightly embarrassed nod, if that. Families
10 and friends are scattered ... We are constantly on the move ... These factors are particularly problematic for the English, as we tend to be more reserved and socially inhibited than other cultures; we do not talk to strangers, or make friends quickly and easily.
    Landline telephones allowed us to communicate, but not in the sort of frequent,
15 easy, spontaneous, casual style that would have characterised the small communities for which we are adapted by evolution ... Mobile phones – particularly the ability to send short, frequent, cheap text messages – restore our sense of connection and community, and provide an antidote to the pressures and alienation of modern urban life. They are a kind of 'social lifeline' in a fragmented and isolating world.
20   Think about a typical, brief 'village-green' conservation: 'Hi, how're you doing?'
'Fine, just off to the shops – oh, how's your Mum?' 'Much better, thanks' 'Oh, good, give her my love – see you later'. If you take most of the vowels out of the village-green conversation, and scramble the rest of the letters into 'text-message dialect' (HOW R U? C U L8ER), to me it sounds uncannily like a typical SMS or text exchange: not
25 much is said – a friendly greeting, maybe a scrap of news – but a personal connection is made, people are reminded that they are not alone. Until the advent of mobile text messaging, many of us were having to live without this kind of small but psychologically and socially very important form of communication.

Kate Fox, *Watching the English: The Hidden Rules of English Behaviour*
(Hodder & Stoughton, 2004), pages 86–7

TEXT 1B

Text 1B is taken from a self-help book called *The Essential Mars and Venus* by John Gray, an expert in the field of communication and relationships. The book explores the different ways in which men and women relate to each other, and offers advice on the best ways to develop a successful relationship.

4. Be direct.

Women often think they are asking for support when they are not. A woman may present the problem but not directly ask for his support. She expects him to offer his support.

Not Recommended	*Recommended*
"The kids need to be picked up and I can't do it."	"Would you pick up the kids?"
"The mail hasn't been brought in."	"Would you bring in the mail?"
"We haven't gone out in weeks."	"Let's do something fun. Would you plan a date?"

Men always respond best to direct requests
as opposed to implied requests.

5. Use correct wording.

By using correct wording, a man will be more motivated to provide what a woman wants.

One of the most common mistakes in asking for support is the use of "could" and "can" in place of "would" and "will." "Could you empty the trash?" is merely a question gathering information. "Would you empty the trash?" is a request.

Use the "w" words. The "c" words sound too
untrusting, indirect, weak and manipulative.

John Gray, *The Essential Mars and Venus* (HarperCollins, 2003), pages 104–5

---

2 'Attitudes and opinions' questions

The writers in the three texts below (Texts 2A–2C) each express distinctive attitudes and opinions. Read through the source material and complete the following tasks.

TASK 2.1

Analyse the language use in the three texts.

You should apply relevant frameworks that you have studied, including lexis, grammar, style and the construction of meaning.

Your answer should include some consideration of the following:

▶ comparisons and/or contrasts between the texts
▶ the intended audience and purpose in each case, and the effect these have on the style and structure
▶ the different styles
▶ the ways in which attitudes, opinions and points of view are expressed.

TASK 2.2

Imagine that these opinions have provoked correspondence in the letter pages of a quality national newspaper.

Write a letter to the editor for publication in the newspaper, expressing your opinions on <u>one</u> of the points of view expressed in the extracts (at least 300 words).

You should:

- present your viewpoint clearly and persuasively
- think about the audience, purpose and context of your letter
- plan your content carefully and provide examples to support the points you make.

When you have completed your letter, write about the language you have used (approximately 400 words).

Drawing on your knowledge of language frameworks and linguistic features, you should explain and comment on the language choices you have made. Comment particularly on the ways in which you have made the language and syntax appropriate for a persuasive letter to the editor of a quality national newspaper.

TEXTS

TEXT 2A

Text 2A is from the controversial best-selling book by Richard Dawkins. It addresses the nature of belief and non-belief from Dawkins's position as an evolutionary biologist and an atheist.

1   ... The presence or absence of a creative super-intelligence is unequivocally a scientific question, even if it is not in practice – or not yet – a decided one. So also is the truth or falsehood of every one of the miracle stories that religions rely upon to impress multitudes of the faithful.

5   Did Jesus have a human father, or was his mother a virgin at the time of his birth? Whether or not there is enough surviving evidence to decide it, this is still a strictly scientific question with a definite answer in principle: yes or no. Did Jesus raise Lazarus from the dead? Did he himself come alive again, three days after being crucified? There is an answer to every such question, whether or not we can discover it in

10   practice, and it is a strictly scientific answer. The methods we should use to settle the matter, in the unlikely event that relevant evidence ever became available, would be purely and entirely scientific methods. To dramatize the point, imagine by some remarkable set of circumstances, that forensic archaeologists unearthed DNA evidence to show that Jesus really did lack a biological father. Can you imagine religious

15   apologists shrugging their shoulders and saying anything remotely like the following? 'Who cares? Scientific evidence is completely irrelevant to theological questions ... . We're concerned only with ultimate questions and with moral values. Neither DNA nor any other scientific evidence could ever have any bearing on the matter, one way or the other.'

20   The very idea is a joke. You can bet your boots that the scientific evidence, if any were to turn up, would be seized upon and trumpeted to the skies.

Richard Dawkins, *The God Delusion* (Bantam, 2006), pages 82–3

Text 2B is from the editorial column of *The Sun*. It expresses the newspaper's attitude to a police chief, Richard Brunstrom, who had suggested a controversial method for dealing with drug addicts and the crimes related to drugs.

1 # Potty cop

WELSH police chief Richard Brunstrom seems more interested in making headlines than nabbing crooks.

5   He persecutes motorists, but leaves 94 per cent of burglaries unsolved.

    He wastes police time pursuing Tony Blair for anti-Welsh "racism", but makes Wales a laughing stock by parading as a 10 druid.

    Now Brunstrom has strayed way out of line by urging legalisation of ALL drugs – and heroin be provided on the NHS.

    That might drive the drug peddlers out of 15 business – but it would cause a massive rise in young drug addicts.

    This is a sensitive and highly-charged debate.

It isn't helped by attention seekers like
20 **Brunstrom strutting around TV studios in uniform contradicting official government policy.**

The Sun (16 October 2007)

Text 2C is from a nineteenth-century book of essays by John Ruskin (1819–1900), an art and literary critic. He was also a passionate social reformer who challenged what he saw as the dominating principles of greed and self-interest in Victorian life.

1 17. I have already alluded to the difference hitherto existing between regiments of men associated for purposes of violence, and for purposes of manufacture; in that the former appear capable of self-sacrifice – the latter, not; which singular fact is the real reason of the general lowness of estimate in which the profession of commerce 5 is held, as compared with that of arms. Philosophically, it does not, at first sight, appear reasonable (many writers have endeavoured to prove it unreasonable) that a peaceable and rational person, whose trade is buying and selling, should be held in less honour than an unpeaceable and often irrational person, whose trade is slaying. Nevertheless, the consent of mankind has always, in spite of the philosophers, given 10 precedence to the soldier.

    And this is right.

For the soldier's trade, verily and essentially, is not slaying, but being slain. This, without well knowing its own meaning, the world honours it for. A bravo's trade is slaying; but the world has never respected bravos more than merchants: the reason it

15 honours the soldier is, because he holds his life at the service of the State. Reckless he may be – fond of pleasure or of adventure – all kinds of bye-motives and mean impulses may have determined the choice of his profession, and may affect (to all appearance exclusively) his daily conduct in it; but our estimate of him is based on this ultimate fact – of which we are well assured – that put him in a fortress breach,

20 with all the pleasures of the world behind him, and only death and his duty in front of him, he will keep his face to the front; and he knows that his choice may be put to him at any moment – and has beforehand taken his part – virtually takes such part continually – does, in reality, die daily.

John Ruskin, *Unto This Last* (Collins, 1860), pages 38–9

3 Theme-based questions

Texts 3 A–D all create a strong sense of character. Read through the source material and complete the following tasks.

TASK 3.1

By close reference to the passages, make a detailed critical analysis of the different linguistic approaches used to create a sense of character.

Your answer should include some discussion of the following:

- the key features of the different varieties
- the register
- the distinctive linguistic and grammatical features
- comparisons and contrasts between texts
- any other points that you find interesting.

TASK 3.2

Comment on the relationship between language and personal identity in Text 3 A.

You should show an awareness of the contextual factors that have influenced the text and refer to your wider study of language. Provide appropriate examples to support your discussion.

TEXTS

TEXT 3 A ....

Text 3 A is from a contemporary urban novel by Tony White. It is set in the Bangladeshi East End and is told in a distinctive patois that creates a strong sense of the story's narrator and its urban context.

1 They got proper names them two init but everyone still call them by there tags what are everywhere on all them like stairwell and flats and playground round here – least where they aint been wash off yet or paint over. And they are Ruji-Babes and Foxy-T. Both of them girl work up the E-Z Call phone shop and internet up Cannon Street

5 Road. That is they switch on all the computer them and log on or whatever then switch on the network and get them phone meter running so like at whatever time you can see who is in like booth number two calling Russia or back home wherever and how much it cost.

* * *

10 Ruji-Babes is real skinny and small and she look much younger than she is. That girl use to wear glasses I think when she was at school. Man can tell because her eyes always look a bit too small and a bit watery and a bit dark and dry around her eyelid them like if you got flu. Only now she have like contacts what she always lose or stick on the end of her finger and wave around when she talking and thats probaly
15 because she think it look cool to do that like on Friends or whatever. And because the E-Z Call is own by her uncle she is like the manager really until he come back at some point. Which mean that she probaly does all the stuff like pay bills and that. And thats just as well because Foxy-T some time act a bit scatty and a bit of a feather brain what is just useless at that kind of business side of thing. And Ruji-Babes uncle is
20 like a business man init deal with property all over and like import export and him let her take over the shop while him away because him look out for him own family but also because him a bit worry about her long term prospect or whatever because she always been a bit sickly.

Tony White, Foxy-T (Faber & Faber, 2003), pages 3–4

TEXT 3B ....

Text 3B is from a nineteenth-century book of sketches and tales by the American writer Washington Irving (1783–1859). Written after a visit to England, the book was published under the pseudonym 'Geoffrey Crayon, Gent'. In this extract, Irving discusses *John Bull*, the personification of a typical Englishman, a common representation of the English at the time.

<h3 style="text-align:center">John Bull</h3>

1 THERE is no species of humour in which the English more excel than that which consists in caricaturing and giving ludicrous appellations, or nicknames. In this way they have whimsically designated, not merely individuals, but nations; and, in their fond-
5 ness for pushing a joke, they have not spared even themselves. One would think that, in personifying itself, a nation would be apt to picture something grand, heroic, and imposing; but it is characteristic of the peculiar humour of the English, and of their love for what is blunt, comic and familiar, that they have embodied their national oddities in the figure of a sturdy, corpulent old fellow, with a three-cornered hat, red waistcoat,
10 leather breeches, and stout oaken cudgel. Thus they have taken a singular delight in exhibiting their most private foibles in a laughable point of view; and have been so successful in their delineations, that there is scarcely a being in actual existence more absolutely present to the public mind than that eccentric personage, John Bull.

Perhaps the continual contemplation of the character thus drawn of them has con-
15 tributed to fix it upon the nation; and thus to give reality to what at first may have been painted in a great measure from the imagination. Men are apt to acquire peculiarities that are continually ascribed to them. The common orders of the English seem wonderfully captivated with the *beau ideal* which they have formed of John Bull, and endeavour to act up to the broad caricature that is perpetually before their eyes [...]
20 [...] often as he has been described, I cannot resist the temptation to give a slight sketch of him, such as he has met my eye.

John Bull, to all appearances, is a plain, downright, matter-of-fact fellow, with much less of poetry about him than rich prose. There is little of romance in his nature, but a

vast deal of strong natural feeling. He excels in humour more than in wit; is jolly rather
25 than gay; melancholy rather than morose; can easily be moved to a sudden tear, or surprised into a broad laugh; but he loathes sentiment, and has no turn for light pleasantry. He is a boon companion if you allow him to have his humour, and to talk about himself; and he will stand by a friend in a quarrel, with life and purse, however soundly he may be cudgelled.

Washington Irving, *The Sketch Book of Geoffrey Crayon, Gent*
(Cassell's Red Library, 1820), pages 308–10

TEXT 3 C

Text 3 C is an extract from Peter Riddell's political analysis of Sir Menzies Campbell's leadership of the Liberal Democrats after Campbell's sudden resignation on the previous night. It was published in *The Times* (16 October 2007).

₁ First casualty of the non-election

Peter Riddell

Analysis

Sir Menzies Campbell is
5 the first victim of Gordon
Brown's decision to delay
an election. Whatever the
suddenness of last night's
dramas, his long-term
10 position became
unsustainable once an
election was put off until
next year or later, when Sir
Menzies would have been
15 68 or 69. Speculation was
fuelled by the fall in the
party's poll ratings.
By going now, he offers
his party the chance of
20 relaunching under a
younger leader, to fight off
the squeeze from Gordon
Brown and David
Cameron. Such a
25 resignation was just what
the Tories were dreading
because their recent rise in

the polls has come mainly
at the expense of the Lib
30 Dems.
Time was never on the
Lib Dem leader's side. It
was not that he did
anything wrong as leader:
35 he stabilised and rallied
the party in the turmoil
after Charles Kennedy's
resignation in January last
year. A charming and
40 cultivated figure, he
promoted a number of
younger MPs and
encouraged a rethinking of
policy that had been largely
45 absent in the Kennedy era.
Under his leadership, the
Lib Dems have produced
wide ranging plans on
shaking up the tax system
50 to increase taxes on
pollution and cut those on
income. Indeed, some of
their proposals, on aircraft
duty and inheritance tax,

55 were taken up by Alistair
Darling last Tuesday.
Throughout his 18
months in charge, however,
Sir Menzies battled against
60 a public image of being too
old and out of touch, unfair
though this appeared to
many colleagues. His rating
in the polls was always
65 much lower than the other
party leaders and Mr
Kennedy. He could never
change that perception.
While most of his MPs
70 would have accepted him
staying on to fight an
election this autumn or next
May, the situation looked
very different once the date
75 had been put off until 2009
at the earliest. He would
then have been near his
70th birthday. The high
drama yesterday will stir
80 recriminations like those of
early last year. [...]

TEXT 3 D

Text 3 D is a transcript of two brothers (Harry, aged 15, and Zac, aged 10) discussing characters from an anime, *Full Metal Alchemist*, that they have watched online. Edward and Alphonse have attempted to restore their dead mother to life through alchemy, and they have had to sacrifice parts of their body in the process: Ed now has a left leg and right arm made of metal; Al, having lost his whole body, has had his soul fixed to a suit of armour. The conversation takes place in Zac's bedroom while he is playing the Nintendo DS game version of the anime (animated manga cartoons).

KEY

(.)	micropause	=	smooth latching
(2)	timed pause	‖	overlapping turn
bod.	incomplete word	'rall'	getting slower
tall	stressed word	'accel'	getting faster
cúte	rising intonation	↑whot↑	raised pitch
Grèed	falling intonation		

1		ZAC he's really cúte because (1) compared to his <u>big spiked</u> armour
	'accel'	n he's like really <u>tall</u> n (2) 'compared to his brother Ed he's actually
		the eldest' but really short [*indistinct*] =
	HARRY	= but it is partly <u>because</u> (1) Al is (.) in a gigantic robotic ‖ suit
5	ZAC	‖ yeah but
		that's not the point it's like the <u>contrast</u> (.) but he's so cute =
	HARRY	= yes but in an unexpêcted ‖ manner you wouldn't think it but he's
	ZAC	‖ yeah
	HARRY	the gentlest character in the ‖ whole programme
10	ZAC	‖ here's one of my favourite lines from
		the game when they go into the gráveyard he's just sháking and
		he ‖ always is like (.) and he's buying cakes at one point he's just
	HARRY	‖ yeah
	'rall' ZAC	like 'mmm' which one and also ‖ whén a baby is born because
15	HARRY	‖ he's so cute
	'assumes ZAC	he's lost his body and his soul's been put in his armour '↑whén
	character	I was born was I all soft and warm like that↑' cute (.) but sad yeah
	voice'	um but ↑also↑ <u>Hárry</u> you know the homunculi who would you say
		is your <u>fâvourite</u> =
20	HARRY	= I don't know but then who's <u>yóur</u> favourite =
	'rall' ZAC	= probably '<u>Wrath</u>' =
	HARRY	= yes I can certainly say you'll relate ‖ to h<u>i</u>m (.) a lót =
	ZAC	‖ [*laugh*]
	ZAC	= and who do <u>you</u> relate tó =
25	'accel' HARRY	= I don't really think I relate to ány (.) but (.) <u>I</u> (.) 'do like Grèed' =
	ZAC	= yeah um now ↑whot↑ in it goes good (.) Greed (.) Lust and
		‖ Wrath (.) yéah =
	HARRY	‖ Wrath
	HARRY	= yèah =
30	ZAC	= so (2) ‖ um
	HARRY	‖ but then Zác =
	ZAC	= what would you say ‖ about
	HARRY	‖ you say you're like Wrath do you (.) so can
		you absorb things and turn your muscles into thém =
35	ZAC	= what are the powers they have again Príde can see ‖ <u>every</u>thing
	HARRY	‖ Lust
	'rall' ZAC	that's going on everywhere in the wòrld (.) Lúst can 'do spéar
		àrms' =
	HARRY	= cos her arms are claws =
40	ZAC	= okay (.) claws =

```
'accel'  HARRY  = Greed turns his bod. skin into cárbon so he 'can't be húrt' and
                ‖Sloth is lit. aqueous so she uses the water in the human bódy
         ZAC   ‖Envy
         HARRY  to (3) wátery èffect =
45  'accel'  ZAC   = and Envy 'can shape-shift' =
         HARRY  = yeah then do you know w. who I think the unsung hero ís =
         ZAC   = whó =
         HARRY  = Black Hàyate ‖ [indistinct] whatever he's ‖ called
         ZAC              ‖ yeah            ‖ yeah I mean he's so
50            cúte ‖ puppy he may be
         HARRY      ‖ but then he's a puppy =
         ZAC   = an army puppy =
         HARRY  = yéah he definitely ìs =
         ZAC   = I love the way Hawkseye disciplines him
```

4 Variety-based questions

Texts 4A–F illustrate different varieties of language use. Read through the source material and complete the following tasks.

TASK 4.1 ————————————

Discuss various ways in which these texts can be grouped, giving reasons for your choices.

Your answer should include exploration and analysis of some or all of the following:

▶ text type
▶ register
▶ lexical and grammatical structures
▶ how the writers use language to convey thoughts and feelings, opinions, attitudes and viewpoints
▶ similarities and differences between texts
▶ any other points that you find interesting.

TASK 4.2 ————————————

Imagine that you work for the New Zealand Tourist Board.

Write the copy for a television advertisement, encouraging people to visit New Zealand (approximately 100 words).

Write the opening of a novel that is set in New Zealand, using the information given in Text 4B (approximately 250 words).

Analyse and comment on the main features of language and style in the texts you have written (approximately 500 words).

You should use appropriate terminology and draw on your knowledge of linguistic features and frameworks to explain and comment on your language choices and style.

Text 4A is taken from a screenplay of *The History Boys*, by Alan Bennett. It is the story of a group of sixth-form boys and their teachers as the boys try to gain a place to study history at Oxford or Cambridge.

1 EXT. SCHOOL. DAY.

Titles and credits.

As the autumn term begins. Boys of all ages arrive; teachers get out of their cars; the History Boys, now in uniform, greet each other. Hector [a maverick English teacher]
5 *roars through the school gates on his motorbike.*

INT. MRS LINTOTT'S CLASSROOM. DAY.

The first lesson of the new term. Mrs Lintott [the history teacher] and the eight Boys.

MRS LINTOTT

You are entitled, though only for five minutes, Dakin, to feel pleased with your-
10 selves. No one has done as well – not in English, not in Science, not even dare I say it, in Media Studies. And you alone are up for Oxford and Cambridge. So. To work. First essay this term will be the Church on the eve of the Reformation.

TIMMS

15 Not again, miss.

MRS LINTOTT

This is Oxford and Cambridge. You don't just need to know it. You need to know it backwards. Facts, facts, facts.

With a groan, pulling textbooks from their bags, they set to work.

20 INT. HEADMASTER'S STUDY. DAY.

The Headmaster is talking to Mrs Lintott.

HEADMASTER

They're clever but they're crass, and were it Bristol or York I would have no worries. But Oxford and Cambridge. We need a strategy, Dorothy, a game
25 plan.

MRS LINTOTT

They know their stuff.

HEADMASTER

But they lack flair. Culture they can get from Hector, and history from you …
30 but (I'm thinking aloud now) is there something else …

MRS LINTOTT

Properly organised facts are …

HEADMASTER

This is Oxford and Cambridge, Dorothy. Facts are just the beginning.

35 *Fiona [the Headmaster's Secretary] has come in.*

Think charm. Think polish. Think Renaissance Man. Leave it with me, Dorothy. Leave it with me.

He goes back to his desk and takes out Irwin's application with his photograph from beneath his blotter.

40 *A knock at the door.*

Come.

Wilkes is in gym shoes, tracksuit bottoms: plainly the PE master.

Wilkes, ah yes. An innovation to the timetable. PE.

WILKES

45 Yes, Headmaster.

HEADMASTER

For the Oxbridge set. Surely not, you say. But why not? This is the biggest hurdle of their lives and I want them galvanised.

WILKES

50 Galvanised, yes, Headmaster.

Headmaster leads Wilkes out of the office.

TEXT 4 B

Text 4 B is from a travel guide, *The Rough Guide to New Zealand in Spring*. It gives readers advice about places to visit, places to stay and eat, and things to do.

1 **The glaciers**
   Roughly midway along the West Coast (which is defined and isolated by the Southern Alps running down the backbone of the South Island) two blinding white rivers of ice force their way down towards the thick rainforest of the coastal plain – ample justifi-
5 cation for inclusion of this region in Te Wahipounamu, the South West New Zealand World Heritage Area. The glaciers are stunning viewed from a distance, but are even more impressive close up, generating a palpable connectedness between the coast and the highest peaks of the Southern Alps, a sensation heightened by one being able to walk on the glaciers on guided trips. Within a handful of kilometres the terrain
10 drops from over 3000 m to near sea level, bringing with it **Franz Josef Glacier** and, just a few kilometres away, **Fox Glacier**, the two largest and most impressive of the sixty-odd glaciers that creak off the South Island's icy backbone, together forming the centrepiece of the rugged **Westland National Park**.

Rough Guides, The Rough Guide to New Zealand in Spring (2003), pages 72–3

TEXT 4 C

Text 4 C is from *Teach Yourself Speaking on Special Occasions*. It gives advice to readers who may have to speak in public on a formal or informal occasion. The extract here focuses on giving a speech to a club or organisation.

1 The following is a very abbreviated summary of some of the main points to remember.
   • **Timing** This is very important. Ask the organizers in advance how long they want you to speak for, and then make your own judgement. Do not speak for too long.
5 Prepare slightly more than you expect to need, and have one or two self-contained sections that can be left out.
   • **Humour** This will nearly always improve the impact of the speech. As well as entertaining the audience it should make the serious points more memorable. This was covered in some detail in Chapter 4.
10 • **Anecdotes** One or two well-chosen anecdotes that are relevant and memorable, can be the high points of a speech. They can certainly make it memorable and may well be worth including. This, too, was covered in detail in Chapter 4.

- **Technical terms, statistics and jargon** These are the ruin of many otherwise good
speeches. Technical terms and statistics should be used sparingly. Jargon should
15   not be used at all. Do not overestimate the audience's ability to absorb technical
terms and statistics. It is a very common mistake. If the detail is very important,
make the speech simple and give all the details in a written handout.
- **Topical references** Do not be afraid to depart from your script and say something
topical. Perhaps something in the day's news is relevant to your speech. The audi-
20   ence will probably respect you for referring to it.
- **Speak with authority** This is partly a matter of confidence. You will sound confident if you are confident. You will be much more confident if you know that you
have prepared thoroughly and checked your facts. Do not let the audience catch
you out over a mistake with the facts, especially if you are speaking as an expert.
25   Authority also depends on the way that you speak and this was covered in detail in
Chapter 6 ... .

Roger Mason, *Teach Yourself Speaking on Special Occasions* (Hodder Arnold, 2003), pages 128–9

TEXT 4D ──

Text 4 D is from a story told to a group of primary school children by a visiting storyteller.

KEY

(2)	timed pause	'forte'	loud
(.)	micropause	'rall'	getting slower
<u>lake</u>	stressed word	'dimin'	getting quieter
twó	rising intonation	'cresc'	getting louder
sàme	falling intonation	'accel'	getting faster
↑lake↑	raised pitch	'leg'	drawled pronunciation
'piano'	quiet	'stacc'	clipped pronunciation
ST	storyteller	C	children

```
 1                              [MUSIC] (26)
 'dimin'/'cresc'  ST  'ónce' (2) there was a ↑láke↑ (1) and 'in this lake' there lived (1)
                       ↑péople↑ and amongst them there were twó (2)
        'piano'   C   'sisters' =
 5                ST  = and these sisters wére (1)
        'cresc'   C   'twins' =
                  ST  = and they looked <u>exactly</u> ↑the↑ (1)
        'forte'   C   'sàme'
                               [MUSIC] (6)
10      'accel'   ST  both were 'very very' beautiful (2) and the <u>king</u> fell in <u>love</u> with one
                       of them and (.) he (.)
                  C   married (2)
                  ST  now these two twins had <u>always</u> shared éverything <u>before</u> (.) so
        'accel'        they saw no reason why they 'shouldn't share the king' as well
15      'rall'         which is <u>exactly</u> what they <u>dìd</u> (2) 'the king's suspicions were
                       <u>aroused</u> when' one day (.) his beautiful wife who also had the
                       most béautiful (1)
                  C   vòice =
        'accel'   ST  = one day had a 'dreadfully sore throat' there was nothing unusual
```

20		in <u>that</u> except that the following day (.) she was able to ↑sing↑ to
	'stacc'/'accel'	him 'as béautifully as ever' before and the king 'thought it strange'
		that on the <u>first</u> day (1) her voice was fine (.) on the <u>second</u> day
	'dimin'	she had a dreadful sore throat and on 'the <u>third</u> day' (.) her voice
	'accel'	'was fine again' and able to sing to him (1) so he asked her (1)
25	'stacc'	wow '↑yóur↑ sore throat' certainly got better <u>soon</u> (.) and she said
	'accel'	↑whát↑ sore throat ↑my throat's fine↑ 'thank you very much' ↑I
		haven't had↑ a sore <u>throat</u> (1) and that's (.) when she <u>realised</u> (1)
	'rall/dimin'	that she'd put 'herself (.) in (.) a hole' (.) she couldn't get out of
	'leg'	because the '<u>king</u> knew that she was <u>lying</u>' (.) he kept an éye on
30	'rall'	them <u>both</u> and <u>one</u> dáy (.) he saw them 'swáp the ring' that he
		had given (.) the sister that he'd married and as time went by he
		noticed (.) that the <u>ríng</u> was <u>tíght</u> on the finger of one of them (.)
	'rall'	and the <u>ring</u> was <u>lóose</u> on the finger of the other 'and that was
	'accel'	<u>próof</u>' for him so 'he called the two sisters to him and he said'
35	'dimin'	you count yourselves very lucky I'm not having you <u>killed</u> (1) 'yet'
		(2) go (2) leave my land and <u>never</u> (.) <u>ever</u> come back (.) if you
	'stylised/accel'	ever return 'I'll have your head chópped' (1)
	C	off

[MUSIC] (12)

TEXT 4E ···

Text 4E is the voice-over for a 30-second television advertisement shown after nine o'clock during a one-off comedy drama on ITV.

KEY

V/O   images with voice overlaid   **SYNC**   spoken direct to camera

1 V/O PENELOPE CRUZ
To stay feeling young, we take care of ourselves.

SYNC PENELOPE CRUZ
So I invest in my skin.

5 V/O PENELOPE CRUZ
I'm always searching for my perfect moisturiser. I've discovered Derma Genesis. Only l'Oréal Paris Derma Genesis has Pro-Xylane and Hyaluronic Acid. Everybody's talking about it. It intensely moisturises for younger looking skin and nurtures cells in the top skin layers. Skin feels plumped up, tautened with a dewy glow.

10 V/O MALE ACTOR
New l'Oréal Derma Genesis. For your free sample, visit lorealdermagenesis.co.uk.

SYNC PENELOPE CRUZ
Because we're worth it.

TEXT 4F ···

Text 4F is from the web page of a publisher specialising in academic books.

Copyright © 2007 Macmillan Publishers Limited
Houndmills, Basingstoke, Hampshire, RG21 6XS, England
USA & Canada site | Australia site | Legal Notice | Privacy Policy | Contact us

Palgrave Macmillan (2007): www.Palgrave.com/resources

21.4 Conclusion

It is impossible to cover every area of interest in one book, but the information and suggested approaches here should help you to embark on your study of English with confidence. As you become familiar with the frameworks, you will find that you see interesting examples all around you – in the television that you watch, the newspapers that you read, the billboards that you pass. It is a fascinating study that reveals the complexity and versatility of language, and helps us all to be more effective participants in written and spoken discourse.

Appendices

Part IV

Appendices

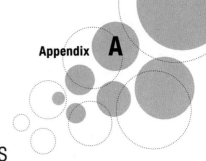

Answers to activities

Activity 1.1 (page 6)

1 Nouns: *December, Monday, Christmas Eve, kid, fact, trauma, parents, existence, Santa Claus, age, bit, God, things, earthquakes, famines, motorway crashes, bed, blankets, word, Tog rating, quilts, heart, palms, anticipation, Beano album.*

2 Proper nouns: *Christmas, Santa Claus, Beano.*
   Common nouns: *parents, existence, quilt, heart, trauma, bed, anticipation.*
   Concrete nouns: *parents, quilt, heart, bed.*
   Abstract nouns: *existence, trauma, anticipation.*

Activity 1.2 (page 8)

1 Modifiers: *gloomy, glorious, ancient, crimson, far, lower, redder, calm, calmest, long, tiny, seaweed-edged, glowing, flying, careless, young, old, harsh, rotting, solemn, lonely, sad, despairing, customary, large, golden, little.*

2 a Descriptive adjectives: *gloomy, glorious, calm, careless, harsh, solemn, lonely, sad, customary.*
   b Size or distance adjectives: *far, long, tiny, large, little.*
   c Age adjectives: *ancient, young, old.*
   d Colour adjectives: *crimson, redder, golden.*
   e Comparative and superlative adjectives: *lower, redder, calmest.*
   f Noun or verb modifiers: *seaweed-edged, glowing, flying, rotting, despairing.*

Activity 1.3 (page 12)

1 a *had* (aux) *gone* (lex)
   b *had* (lex)
   c *can* (aux) *do* (lex)
   d *did* (aux) *like* (lex)

2 a *flapped*: finite; past tense; third person; plural.
   b *laughs*: finite; present tense; third person; singular.
   c *have*: finite; present tense; second person; singular.
      gone: non-finite; past participle.
   d *carried*: finite; past tense; first person; singular.
   e *was*: finite; past tense; third person; singular.

croaking: non-finite; present participle.

  f *chased*: finite; past tense; first person; plural.

  g *have*: finite; present tense; second person; singular.
    been: non-finite; past participle.

  h *has*: finite; present tense; third person; singular.
    been: non-finite; past participle.
    happening: non-finite; present participle.

  i *does*: finite; present tense; third person; singular.
    know: non-finite; base form.

3 a The boat *was lifted* above the dangerous sandbank *by the strong waves*.

    b The bells *were rung by the monks* to warn the surrounding villagers of the impending danger.

    c After the disturbance, the pub *was shut by the police*.

4 a The prisoners *were beaten*.

    b The child *was left* face down in the playground.

    c The way to split the atom *was discovered* and the first atom bomb *was created*.

In each case the person or persons responsible for the action of the verb is or are omitted. In the passive sentences, therefore, the reader no longer knows who is accountable.

Activity 1.4 (page 13)

1 Verbs: *was woken, refusing to start, know, should have gone, helped to push, seemed to be doing, must be, flinging, were … pretending to be, went … to sleep, licked, took, was(n't), must … be staying, passed, was kicking, seemed, stopped to talk, asked, (I)'d had.*

2 a Two lexical verbs: *asked, licked.*

    b Two stative verbs: *be, seemed.*

    c Two dynamic verbs: *kicking, passed.*

    d Two primary auxiliary verbs: <u>*was*</u> woken, *'d* [*had*] *had.*

    e Two modal auxiliary verbs: *should, must.*

3 Passive voice: *I was woken at dawn by the sound of Grandad Sugden's rusty Ford Escort refusing to start.*
    Active version: *The sound of Grandad Sugden's rusty Ford Escort refusing to start woke me at dawn.*

4 Progressive aspect: *were … pretending.*
    Perfective aspect: *I'd had.*

5 Present tense: *I know.*
    Past tense: *I stopped.*

6 Two finite verbs: *I was, He seemed.* Two non-finite verbs: *refusing, woken.*

Activity 1.5 (page 16)

1 Circumstance adverbs: *brightly, well, again, here, anxiously, generally, recently, often, around, warily, sometimes, desperately, properly.*

2 Degree adverbs: *completely, really, very.*

3 Sentence adverbs: *nevertheless, however, perhaps, actually.*

Activity 1.6 (page 18)

1 Personal pronouns: *we, it, I, me, he, she, her*.
2 Possessive pronouns: *ours, mine, hers*.
3 Reflexive pronoun: *myself*.
4 Demonstrative pronouns: *this, that*.
5 Interrogative pronouns: *who* (or *to whom*), *what*.
6 Relative pronoun: *which*.
7 Indefinite pronouns: *everyone, some, everything, something*.

Activity 1.7 (page 19)

1 Articles: definite – *the*; indefinite – *a, an*.
2 Possessive determiner: *her*.
3 Demonstrative determiners: *this, that*.
4 Indefinite determiners: *any, either, many, both, every, some, more*.
5 Numbers: *one, two, second*.

Activity 1.8 (page 20)

1 *out*: particle.
2 *into*: preposition.
3 *out of*: prepositions.
4 *on*: particle.
5 *in*: particle.
6 *towards*: preposition.
7 *down*: particle.
8 *above*: preposition.
9 *up*: particle.
10 *down*: preposition.
11 *out*: particle.

Activity 1.9 (page 21)

1 *While*: subordinating conjunction (time).
2 *and*: co-ordinating conjunction (addition).
3 *but*: co-ordinating conjunction (contrast).
4 *Because*: subordinating conjunction (reason).
5 *Unless*: subordinating conjunction (condition).
6 *and*: co-ordinating conjunction (addition).
7 *if*: subordinating conjunction (condition).
8 *Wherever*: subordinating conjunction (place).
9 *Because*: subordinating conjunction (reason).
10 *since*: subordinating conjunction (reason).
11 *than*: subordinating conjunction (comparison).

Activity 1.10 (page 22)

1 *un-* (bound) + *justify* (free) + *-able* (bound).
2 *summa(ry)* (free) + *-ative* (bound).
3 *mid-* (bound) + *night* (free).
4 *day* (free) + *-ly* (bound).
5 *negative* (free) + *-ity* (bound).
6 *un-* (bound) + *like* (free) + *-ly* (bound).
7 *pity* (free) + *-ful* (bound).

Activity 1.11 (page 23)

The answers here are single possibilities only – many other words could be cited as valid examples.

1 *re- + present*.
2 *hospital + -ise*.
3 *calm + -ly*.
4 *child + -less*.
5 *glorifi + -cation*; *audit + -or*; *act + -or*.

Activity 1.12 (page 25)

1 *-s*: plural noun inflection.
2 *-ed*: past tense inflection.
3 *-s'*: plural noun inflection and possessive inflection; *-s*: plural noun inflection.
4 *-ing*: present participle inflection.
5 *-'s*: possessive inflection.
6 *-s*: present tense third person singular inflection.

Activity 1.13 (page 25)

1 *greatness* (N): free = *great* (Adj); bound = *-ness* (derivational).
2 *multigym* (N): free = *gym* (N); bound = *multi-* (derivational).
3 *declaration* (N): free = *declare* (V); bound = *-ation* (derivational).
4 *delimited* (V): free = *limit* (V); bound = *de-* (derivational); bound = *-ed* (inflectional).
5 *inter-rivalry* (N): free = *rival* (N); bound = *inter-* (derivational); bound = *-ry* (derivational).
6 *illogical* (Adj): free = *logic* (N); bound = *il-* (derivational); bound = *-al* (derivational).
7 *predetermination* (N): free = *determine* (V); bound = *pre-* (derivational); bound = *-ation* (derivational).
8 *horrifying* (V): free = *horrify* (V); bound = *-ing* (inflectional).
9 *institutionalise* (V): free = *institute* (V); bound = *-ion* (derivational); bound = *-al* (derivational); bound = *-ise* (derivational).
10 *reassesses* (V): free = *assess* (V); bound = *re-* (derivational); *-es* (inflectional).

Activity 1.14 (page 28)

pre-mod (The first summer's) *day*   pre-mod (my) *curtains*   pre-mod (the new dawn's) *sunlight*

pre-mod (the) *paths* post-mod (of dust) (which lay on the ancient sea chest) pre-mod (the) *scratches*

post-mod *tribute* (to a life of hardship)   *I*

pre-mod (the interesting) *stories* post-mod (which were linked to the marks)

pre-mod (the drowned) *men* post-mod (who had owned this chest)   pre-mod (their own) *versions* post-mod (of events)

them   pre-mod (the) *wall*   pre-mod (another withered) *mark* post-mod (of the past)   pre-mod (this) *time*

pre-mod (the faded rose) *wallpaper*   pre-mod (The) *memory* (of another place)   pre-mod (my hazy) *mind*

me   *connections*   pre-mod (that first disturbing) *visit* post-mod (to the ruined cottage)

pre-mod (it's ongoing) *effects*   pre-mod (This second historical) *link* post-mod (waiting for me)

Activity 1.15 (page 28)

1 the interesting stories which were linked to the marks
   m   m   h   q
   det   V   N   RelCl

2 their own versions of events
   m   m   h   q
   det Adj   N   PrepP

3 the wall
   m   h
   det N

4 the faded rose wallpaper
   m   m   m   h
   det V   N   N

5 This second historical link waiting for me.
   m   m   m   h   q
   det   num   Adj   N NFCl

Activity 1.16 (page 29)

h   h   m   h   m   h   q
deep and white   rather sad   quite sure of his need for company
Adj   Adj   Adv   Adj   Adv   Adj PrepP

m   h   q   h   m   h
very sincere about the purpose of his journey   isolated and very bleak
Adv   Adj   PrepP   V   Adv Adj

     m   h   m   h   q
Surprisingly fierce   quite certain that he had made the right decision
    Adv   Adj   Adv   Adj   NCl

m   m   h   q
so unbelievably withdrawn that I could not agree with his interpretation of events
Adv   Adv   Adj   NCl

h   m   h   h   q
unsure and rather quiet   certain he wished he had not come.
Adj   Adv   Adj   Adj   ø NCl

Activity 1.17 (page 36)

  S   P   C   S   P   Od
(He) (was) (a very strong and good-looking man), (but) (he) (had) (a red face and rather
                                         conj

          S   P   C   P   C   A
reddish hair). (He) (was) (not) (a good man) (and) (was) (cruel to his people). (Like his
                            neg   conj

       S   P   Od   A   S   A   P
father), (he) (enjoyed) (hunting animals). (One day) (the Red King's arrow) (just) (missed)
  Od   S   P   C   P   O
(a big deer). (William) (was) (very excited) (and) (called out to) (his friend, Walter).
                                  conj

   S   P   Od   A   S   P   A   S
(Walter) (fired) (an arrow), (but) (by accident) (it) (stuck) (in the King's eye) (and) (he)
                  conj   conjs

  P   C   S   P   C   S   P   A   S
(fell) (dead). (Walter) (was) (very frightened) (and) (he) (rode) (away). (The King's body)
                               conj

  P   A   A   A   S   P   A   A
(lay) (in the forest) (all day). (In the evening) (it) (was carried) (away) (in a workman's
            P   A   A
cart) (and) (buried) (in the big church) (at a town called Winchester).
    conj

Activity 1.18 (page 41)

when we arrived   *because* things were not quite *what* they seemed   *Looking* back
ACl   ACl   NCl   NFCl

the key *which* did not fit   *leaving* us stranded   nothing for us *to do*
            RelCl   NFCl   NFCl

The fact *that* we were helpless   *since* we were stuck outside
         NCl   ACl

Although we could do nothing for the moment   *obliged to act*
ACl   NFCl   NFCl

rushing around like a headless chicken *while* the rain fell steadily
NFCl   ACl

so that we could go into the house and (ø) wait for the removal van in the dry
ACl   ACl

that it was on its way at last   *as* we settled into a bare and disorganised house
NCl   ACl

what was *to come* next
NCl   NFCl

Activity 2.2 (page 56)

1 a [f]: labiodental.
  b [n]: alveolar.
  c [m]: bilabial.
    d *th* [θ]: dental.
    e *sh* [ʃ]: palato-alveolar.
    f [k]: velar.

2 a [p]: voiceless.
  b *ch* [tʃ]: voiceless.
  c [d]: voiced.
    d *ng* [ŋ]: voiced.
    e [l]: voiced.
    f *dge* [dʒ]: voiced.

3 a [g]: voiced velar plosive.
  b [ʃ]: voiceless palato-alveolar fricative.
  c [v]: voiced labiodental fricative.
    d [p]: voiceless bilabial plosive.
    e [m]: voiced bilabial nasal.
    f [h]: voiceless glottal fricative.

Activity 2.3 (page 59)

1 [i]: close front spread.
2 [ɔ]: half-open back moderate rounding.
3 [a]: open front neutral.
4 [o]: half-close back slightly rounded.
5 [u]: close back rounded.

Activity 2.4 (page 59)

1 [ʌ]: The centre of the tongue is just below half-open position with the lips in a neutral position.
2 [iː]: The front of the tongue is in a close position with the lips spread.
3 [uː]: The back of the tongue is in a close position with the lips closely rounded.
4 [æ]: The front of the tongue is just above open position with the lips in a neutral position.

Activity 2.5 (page 60)

1 [eɪ]: The front of the tongue moves from between half-open and half-close to just above half-close position with the lips moving from neutral to loosely spread; it is a closing diphthong.

2 [əʊ]: The centre and then the back of the tongue move from between half-open and half-close to just above half-close position with the lips moving from neutral to rounded; it is a closing diphthong.

3 [ʊə]: The back and then the centre of the tongue move from just above half-close to between half-open and half-close position with the lips moving from rounded to neutral; it is a centring diphthong.

4 [aʊ]: The back of the tongue moves from open to just above half-close position with the lips moving from neutral to rounded; it is a closing diphthong.

Activity 2.6 (page 63)

1 _cot_ /kɒt/, _got_ /gɒt/; _hackle_ /hækəl/, _haggle_ /hægəl/; _back_ /bæk/, _bag_ /bæg/.

2 _more_ /mɔː/, _nor_ /nɔː/; _limit_ /lɪmɪt/, _linnet_ /lɪnɪt/; _comb_ /kəʊm/, _cone_ /kəʊn/.

3 _sot_ /sɒt/, _shot_ /ʃɒt/; _massing_ /mæsɪŋ/, _mashing_ /mæʃɪŋ/; _puss_ /pʊs/, _push_ /pʊʃ/.

4 _bat_ /bæt/, _vat_ /væt/; _rebel_ /rebəl/, _revel_ /revəl/; _Job_ /dʒəʊb/, _Jove_ /dʒəʊv/.

Activity 2.7 (page 64)

1 _is the train coming?_ [ɪs ðə treɪŋ kʌmɪŋ]: alveolar nasal /n/ in _train_ becomes velar nasal /ŋ/ before velar plosive /k/ in _coming_.

2 _he sails ships_ [hiː seɪlʃ ʃɪps]: alveolar fricative /s/ in _sails_ becomes palato-alveolar fricative /ʃ/ before palato-alveolar fricative /ʃ/ in _ships_.

3 _what do you want?_ [wɒt dʒuː wɒnt]: alveolar plosive /d/ in _do_ becomes palato-alveolar affricate /dʒ/ before palatal-approximant /j/ in _you_.

Activity 2.8 (page 66)

1 _she should have gone home_: /hæv/ → /əv/.
Elision: Word-initial /h/ frequently undergoes elision in informal conversation.
Reduction: Vowels in unstressed syllables are often reduced to /ə/.

2 _she'll be here in an hour or two_: /æn/ → /ən/ [aʊərɔː tuː].
Reduction: Vowels in unstressed syllables are often reduced to /ə/.
Liaison: Word-final unstressed vowel /ə/ followed by initial vowel /ɔː/ is often linked by insertion of /r/ in speech.

3 _the train came in late_: [treɪŋ keɪm].
Assimilation: Word-final alveolar nasal /n/ becomes velar /ŋ/ before velar plosive /k/.

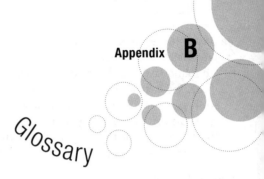

Glossary

This glossary contains brief definitions of the key words used in this book. **Key words** are printed in bold type and *examples* in italics.

abstract A term used in grammar to denote nouns that have no physical qualities (*courage*; *idea*).

accelerando ('accel') A term used to describe speech that is getting faster.

accent A set of distinctive pronunciations that mark regional or social identity.

acceptable A term that denotes any usage that native speakers feel is allowed.

accusative case In an inflected language, an inflection that marks the object of a verb.

active voice A grammatical structure in which the subject is the actor of a sentence.

adjective A word that defines attributes of a noun (*The blue flower*) and that can usually express contrasts of degree (*The smallest boy was the fastest*).

adjunct An adverb that relates directly to the meaning of the verb, giving details of time, manner and place.

adverb A word that describes the action of the verb (*The girl laughed loudly*); that can act as an intensifier (*very fierce*); and that can function as a sentence connector (*Somehow, I did not believe him*).

adverbial A term to denote words, phrases or clauses that function as adverbs.

affix A bound morpheme that can be attached to other words to create new words (*un- + pleasant + -like*), or to mark a grammatical relationship (*go + -ing*). See also **prefix**; **suffix**.

affricate A term used to denote consonants in which a complete closure of the vocal tract is followed by a slow release characteristic of a fricative (*church*).

agent A linguistic form describing who or what is responsible for the action of a verb (*The little dog laughed... and the dish ran away with the spoon*).

agreement A term used to describe the grammatical relationship between words in which the choice of one element determines the form of another (*The girl runs; he talked to himself regularly*). Also called **concord**.

allegro ('alleg') A term used to describe speech that is articulated quickly.

alliteration The repetition of the same consonant sound in the initial position, or in a stressed syllable, in a sequence of words.

alveolar A term used to denote consonants produced by raising the tongue to the alveolar ridge ([t]).

ambiguous The term used to describe a word, phrase, clause or sentence with multiple meanings.

anapest A unit of poetic metre made up of two unstressed syllables followed by a stressed syllable (*ǔn·ǎ·líke*).

anaphoric A form of referencing in which a pronoun or noun phrase points backwards to something mentioned earlier in a discourse (*The film was breathtaking and the audience watched it in silence*).

antonyms Words that are opposite in meaning (*hot/cold; fast/slow*).

apposition A sequence of nouns or noun phrases, often separated by parenthetical commas, that describes the same thing or person (*my neighbour, the builder, came to see me yesterday*).

appropriate A term used to describe any language use that is seen as suitable for the context in which it occurs.

approximant A term used to denote consonants in which the organs of speech approach each other but do not get sufficiently close to produce a plosive, nasal or fricative ([l]; [j]). Also called a **frictionless continuant**.

archaism A word or phrase no longer in current use.

article A word that indicates whether a noun is definite (*the*) or indefinite (*a/an*).

articulation The movements of the speech organs modifying the air flow in order to produce speech sounds.

aspect The timescale of the action expressed by a verb, which may be complete (**perfect**) or in progress (**progressive**).

aspiration The term used to denote audible breath accompanying a sound (*pʰeople*).

assimilation 1. In phonology, the way in which the sounds of one word can change the sounds in neighbouring words. 2. The process by which native inflections are added to loan words as they become part of the general word stock.

assonance A repetition of the same or similar vowel sounds.

asyndetic The linking of linguistic units without a conjunction (*The girl sang quickly, hesitantly, fearfully*).

attributive A term used to denote adjectives or other modifiers that precede the noun in a noun phrase (*the red apple*).

auxiliary verb A verb that precedes the lexical verb in a verb phrase (*I can go; I have gone*).

baby talk A simplified form of speech used by adults to children, or the immature language forms used by children.

base The minimal form of a word to which affixes can be added (*sad, write, man*).

bilabial A term used to denote consonants formed with both lips ([b], [m]).

blank verse Unrhymed poetry with a very disciplined verse form (iambic pentameter) in which each line usually has ten syllables and five stresses.

blend A word composed of the parts of more than one word (*guess + estimate → guesstimate*).

borrow To introduce a loan word from one language into another.

bound morpheme A morpheme that can occur only attached to other morphemes, not by itself (*un-; -ing*).

broad A term used to denote a phonetic or phonemic transcription of spoken language that shows only the functionally important features.

caesura The natural pause in a line of verse, which often follows the strongest stress.

cardinal number The basic form of a number (*one; two; three*).

cardinal vowels A set of reference vowels that are used as a means of describing, classifying and comparing vowel sounds.

caretaker speech The distinctive speech of adults when they talk to children; also called **motherese**.

cataphoric A form of referencing in which a pronoun or noun phrase points forwards to something mentioned later in a discourse (*It was lovely, a day to remember*).

centring diphthong A diphthong in which the second element moves towards the unstressed (schwa) vowel [ə].

clause A group of words, usually with a finite verb that is structurally larger than a phrase. Clauses may be described as **main** (independent) or **subordinate** (dependent).

clear l A lateral consonant which resembles the vowel [i] with the front of the tongue raised (*leg*); a dark *l*, however, resembles the vowel [u] with the back of the tongue raised (*deal*).

cliché An image that has become meaningless because of overuse (*we'll leave no stone unturned*).

close A term used to denote a vowel sound made with the tongue in the highest position ([i], [u]). Vowels may also be described as **half-close**.

closed-class words Words with a grammatical function such as prepositions, determiners and conjunctions: new words are seldom added to the existing stock.

closing diphthong A diphthong in which the second element moves towards a closer vowel like [ɪ] or [ʊ].

cohesion Links and connections which unite the elements of a discourse or text.

coinage The construction and addition of new words to the word stock.

collective noun A noun that refers to a group of people, animals or things (*family, government*). They may agree with a singular or a plural verb, depending on whether the noun is seen as a single collective entity or as a collection of individual entities.

collocation Two or more words that frequently occur together as part of a set phrase.

command An utterance intended to get other people to do something.

comment clause A commonly occurring clause which adds a remark to another clause in parenthesis (*I can come, you know, but I'm not sure I want to*).

common noun A noun that refers to a general group of objects or concepts (*table, happiness*).

comparative See **degree**.

complement A clause element that adds extra information about the subject or object of the clause after a copula verb (*The girl was beautiful*).

complex sentence A sentence made up of one main and one or more subordinate or dependent clauses.

compound A word or phrase made up of at least two free morphemes (*skateboard, washing machine, come in, in accordance with*).

compound–complex sentence A sentence that contains both co-ordination and subordination.

compound sentence A sentence made up of at least two main clauses joined together by a co-ordinating conjunction.

concrete noun A noun that refers to physical things like people, objects, places, or substances.

conjunct A sentence adverb that has a linking function (*however, otherwise*).

connotations The associations attached to a word that go beyond its dictionary definition.

consonance A repetition of consonant sounds in the same position in a sequence of words.

consonant A speech sound produced when the vocal tract is either completely blocked or sufficiently blocked to cause noticeable friction ([p], [d]).

consonant cluster A series of consonants occurring at the beginning or end of a syllable.

contact language A marginal language created by people with no common language who need to communicate.

context The circumstances (social, cultural, geographical, historical, physical) in which speech and writing take place.

continuant A sound that can be made without interruption until the air in the lungs is exhausted ([l], [s], [θ]).

continuant, frictionless See **approximant**.

contraction A shortened word (*can't, you're*).

contrastive stress An emphatic stress placed on a particular linguistic item to draw attention to its significance (*The boy has gone; the boy has gone*).

convergence A process in which accents and dialects move closer to each other, reducing the difference between them.

conversation analysis A study of the key features of informal spoken interaction.

co-ordinating conjunction A word that joins elements of equal rank (*and, or, but*).

co-ordination The linking of lexical items that have the same grammatical status (*The girls and the boys; ran and jumped; slowly and proudly*).

copula A linking verb used to connect other clause elements (*The sky became overcast*).

corpus A collection of spoken and written material gathered for linguistic analysis.

count noun A noun that refers to things that can be counted and occurs with forms such as *a, many, two* (*cats, lorries*).

creole A pidgin language that has become the native tongue of a speech community and is learned by children as their first language.

crescendo ('cresc') A term used to describe speech that is getting louder.

critical age The period between early childhood and puberty during which children can acquire language without instruction.

dactyl A unit of poetic metre made up of one stressed syllable followed by two unstressed syllables (*rá·pǐd·lў*).

dark *l* See **clear *l***.

dative case In an inflected language, an inflection that marks the indirect object of a verb.

declarative A grammatical mood used to express a statement (*I live in a flat*).

decreolisation The process of modification by which creole languages are made more like the standard language of an area.

degree A comparison of adjectives or adverbs: **comparative** (*louder, more intelligent*) and **superlative** (*loudest, most intelligent*).

deictic, deixis Terms used to denote words or expressions that rely on the context to convey meaning (*now, over there, you*).

demonstrative A term used to describe determiners or pronouns that distinguish one item from other similar ones (*this/that, these/those*).

denotation The dictionary definition of a word.

dental A term used to describe consonants made when the tongue touches the inside of the teeth ([ð] or [θ]).

dependent clause See **clause; subordinate clause**.

derivation A morphological process of word formation in which affixes are added to create new words.

descriptive A term used to denote an approach to language based on observation of language in use, focusing on appropriateness and acceptability rather than on concepts of 'right' and 'wrong'. Compare **prescriptive**.

determiner A lexical item that specifies the number and definiteness of a noun (*the, a, some*).

diachronic A term used to describe the study of language change over time.

diacritics Marks added to phonetic symbols to specify various sound qualities, such as length, tone, stress, and nasalisation.

dialect A language variety, marked by distinctive grammar and vocabulary, that is used by a group of speakers with common regional or social backgrounds.

dialect levelling A decrease in dialect differences caused by language contact and possibly by the mass media use of one dialect.

dialogue Language interaction with two or more participants.

diminuendo ('dimin') A term used to describe speech that is getting quieter.

diphthong A vowel sound in which there is a change of quality during its articulation.

direct object A clause element that is directly affected by the action of the verb (*The dog ate a bone*).

direct speech The actual words spoken by a person, which are recorded in a written form enclosed in quotation marks ('*You know I love books*,' *he said*).

discourse Any spoken or written language that is longer than a sentence.

disjunct A sentence adverb giving the speaker or writer a chance to comment on the content or style of a sentence as a whole (*Regrettably, he died last night*).

disyllabic Having two syllables.

divergence A process in which accents and dialects move further apart, increasing the difference between them.

double negative A structure in which more than one negative is used in one verb phrase (*I haven't done nothing*).

dummy word A word that has no specific meaning but that has a grammatical function (*Do you like reading?; It was the train on Platform 1 that I was meant to catch*).

dynamic A verb that expresses an action rather than a state and that can be used in the progressive (*run/running; fly/flying*).

elision The omission of sounds in connected speech.

ellipsis The omission of a part of a sentence that can be understood from the context.

embedded clause A subordinate clause which functions as a subject, object, complement or adverbial within a sentence (*The man who lives next door is very friendly*).

end-stopped A term used to describe a line of verse in which there is a natural pause in the meaning or phrasing at the end of a line.

enjambement The overlapping of meaning from one line of verse to the next.

etymology A study of the origins and history of words.

euphemism A word that replaces a term seen by society as taboo, socially unacceptable or unpleasant.

existential *there* A sentence in which *there* is a dummy subject rather than an adverb of place. It is followed by a delayed subject after the verb *to be* (*There were people everywhere*).

exophoric A form of referencing in which a lexical item points directly to the wider linguistic context (*That man there*).

field An area of meaning (for example, *medicine*) which is characterised by common lexical items (*GP, surgeon, nurse, injection, clinic*).

figurative language The term used to describe any language use that is non-literal, using devices such as metaphor, simile and oxymoron to create poetic and descriptive effects.

filled pause A voiced hesitation.

finite A term used to denote verbs marked for tense, person and number (*the boy sings, they sing, he sang*).

first language The language acquired by children as a native tongue and used as a main language in writing and speech.

focus The arrangement of clause elements so that attention is focused on a particular linguistic item (*it was the red car that broke down; the house was sold*).

foot A poetic unit of measure containing one or two stressed syllables and a variable number of unstressed syllables.

foregrounding A change in the sequence of clause elements in order to draw attention to a particular linguistic item, which is brought to the front of a sentence.

form The word class and structure of a word (*living*: a present participle verb).

formulaic A term used to denote language that is patterned and that always occurs in the same form (*Yours sincerely; Wish you were here!*).

forte A term used to describe speech that is articulated loudly.

free morpheme The smallest meaningful unit of written language that can occur on its own.

free variants Different phonetic realisations of a phoneme in which the substitution of one sound for another has no consequent change in meaning (*neither* → /naɪðə/ or /niːðə/). The choice of one variant as opposed to another may be linked to geographical, social, historical or cultural factors.

fricative A term used to describe consonants where air escapes through a small passage, making a hissing noise ([v] or [f]).

frictionless continuant See **approximant**.

fronting The movement of a clause element other than the subject to the beginning of a sentence.

full stop A punctuation mark that signals the end of a sentence in written language.

function The role of words or phrases within a clause (*subject, object, complement*).

function word A closed class word (a conjunction, a preposition or a determiner) that expresses a grammatical relationship.

future time A verb phrase that refers to actions and states that have not yet occurred. In English, we do not inflect the base form of the verb, but use a range of verb phrases: a modal auxiliary + a lexical verb (*we will go to town tomorrow*); the compound verb phrase *to be* + *going to*; or the simple present in subordinate clauses (*if it rains, the picnic will be called off*). Because there are no inflections, many linguists do not refer to a 'future tense' in English.

genitive case In an inflected language, an inflection that marks possession.

glottal stop A sound produced when air stopped completely at the glottis by tightly closed vocal cords is released.

glottis The opening between the vocal cords.

gradable An adjective or adverb that can be compared (*happier, happiest*) or intensified (*so happy*).

graphology A study of the writing system.

half-close/half-open Terms used to describe vowel sounds that are articulated with the tongue between close and open positions.

head word The main element in a phrase.

hexameter A line of verse containing six feet.

historic present The use of the present tense to narrate events which took place in the past.

holophrastic The stage of child language acquisition at which children produce grammatically unstructured single-word utterances.

homonyms Words with the same form but different meanings.

homophones Words that are pronounced the same but that have different meanings.

hyperbole Exaggeration used to heighten feeling and intensity.

hypercorrection A process of overcompensation whereby speakers who are trying to modify their accent or dialect produce a linguistic form that does not occur in the standard variety.

hypercreolisation The use of pure creole forms as a challenge to standard language.

hyponymy The relationship between words in which the meaning of one form is included in the meaning of another (*tree* ↔ *oak, ash, beech; drink* ↔ *wine, coffee, water*). The inclusive term (*tree, drink*) is called the **superordinate**.

iambic A unit of poetic metre containing an unstressed syllable followed by a stressed syllable (*ă·gó*).

idiolect An individual's own distinctive way of speaking.

idiom An expression in which the meaning of the whole conveys more than the meaning of the parts (*put your foot in it*).

imagery A descriptive or figurative use of language which creates a vivid picture.

imitation The adoption of linguistic features copied from the language of other users.

imperative A grammatical mood expressing a directive (*commanding, warning, requesting, inviting, pleading,* etc.). Usually there is no subject and the verb is in the base form.

inclusive A term used to describe a first person plural reference that includes the speaker as well as the addressee(s).

independent clause See **clause; main clause**.

indirect object An animate being that receives the action of a verb (*he gave her a present; the woman told the story to her neighbour*).

indirect speech The words of a speaker reported in the form of a subordinate clause introduced by *that* (*He replied that everyone was well*), instead of being quoted directly (*He replied, 'Everyone is well.'*)

infinitive A non-finite verb that is in the base form, often preceded by the preposition *to* (*to live; to sleep*).

inflection The marking of a grammatical relationship with an affix (*-ing; -ed; 's*).

initial position A term used to refer to the first linguistic unit in a word (the phoneme /d/ in *dog*), in a phrase (the determiner *the* in *the dog*), or in a sentence (the adverb *Suddenly* in *Suddenly, the dog barked*).

intensifier A word or phrase that adds emphasis (*so; very; incredibly*).

internal rhyme The repetition of rhymes within a line of a verse.

International Phonetic Alphabet See **phonetic alphabet**.

interrogative A grammatical mood expressing a question in which the subject and verb are inverted.

interrogative word A question word used at the beginning of a clause to mark a question. Also known as a **wh- word**.

intonation The quality or tone of the voice in speech.

intransitive A term used to denote a verb that does not have a direct object (*The children laughed*). Many verbs can be used both transitively (*We left the school*) and intransitively (*We left*).

intuition Instinctive knowledge about the acceptability or appropriateness of language use.

inversion Reversing the order of clause elements (*he laughed*; *did he laugh?*).

irony A way of writing or speaking in which what is meant is the opposite of what the words appear to say.

irregular A term used to denote language forms that do not conform to the standard pattern.

isogloss The boundary line defining a regional accent and dialect area and separating it from another.

labial A term used to describe consonants articulated with the lips ([m], [p]).

labiodental A term used to describe consonants produced by touching the bottom lip to the upper teeth ([v] or [f]).

language acquisition The process of learning a first language as a child, or of learning a second or foreign language.

language change The process of change in a language over a period of time.

lateral A term used to describe consonants made by the flow of air around one or both sides of a closure made in the mouth (*clear l*; *dark l*).

legato ('leg') A term used to describe speech that is marked by drawled or elongated pronunciation.

lento A term used to describe speech that is articulated slowly.

lexical diffusion The gradual spread of linguistic change.

lexical verb A verb conveying an action, an event or a state. Also called a **main verb**.

lexical set A group of words that share a specific form or are related in meaning.

lexis The term used to describe the vocabulary of a language. Also called **lexicon**.

liaison A process that changes the pronunciation of words at boundary points.

lingua franca The main language used in an area in which speakers of more than one language live.

linking The introduction of a sound between two syllables to make pronunciation easier (**linking r** in *here and now*: /hɪə/ /ænd/ /naʊ/ → /hɪrənaʊ/).

litotes A deliberate understatement.

loan word A word borrowed from another language.

main clause A clause that is not dependent and that makes sense on its own. Also known as an **independent clause**.

malapropism A misuse of words that sound similar (*description* for *prescription*).

manner The relationship between participants in a language interaction.

metalanguage Language used in talking about language.

metaphor A descriptive use of language in which one thing is directly seen in terms of another (*a sea of troubles*).

metonymy The use of an attribute for the thing meant (*the Crown* for *royalty*).

metre The pattern of stressed and unstressed syllables in a line of verse.

micro-pause A very brief pause in spoken language. Pauses of one second or more are described as **timed pauses**.

minimal pair/set A pair or set of words that are identical except for one phoneme occurring in the same place that alters the meaning (*s̲it, b̲it, k̲it, l̲it, f̲it*).

minor sentence A sentence or utterance that lacks one or more of the clause elements and that occurs often as an unchanging formulaic structure (*Thanks*; *Great party!*).

modal Auxiliary verb that marks a contrast in attitude such as obligation, possibility and prediction (*must, can, will*).

mode A term used to denote the medium of a language interaction (spoken or written) and its format (such as newspaper, playscript, commentary).

modification The use of one linguistic item to specify the nature of another (*the b̲l̲u̲e̲ sea*; *the lion roared l̲o̲u̲d̲l̲y̲*).

monologue Speech or writing produced by a single person.

monometer A line of verse containing only one foot.

monophthong A simple or pure vowel sound.

monosyllabic Having one syllable.

mood Main clauses can have one of three moods: the **declarative mood** is used to make statements; the **imperative mood** is used to give orders and make requests; and the **interrogative mood** is used to ask questions.

morpheme The smallest unit of meaning.

morphology The study of the structure of words in terms of free and bound morphemes.

motherese See **caretaker speech**.

narrow A term used to denote a transcription that records the phonetic properties of spoken language in great detail.

nasal A term used to describe consonants produced with an open nasal passage, which allows air to escape through the nose as well as the mouth ([m] or [n]).

native speaker A speaker who uses a first language or mother tongue.

negation The use of negative forms to convey disagreement or to contradict (*not, never, nothing*).

neologism The creation of a word from existing lexical items (*bodified; zeroised*). Also called **coinage**.

nominative case In an inflected language, an inflection that marks the subject of a sentence.

non-count noun A term which refers to things that cannot be counted and that usually have no plural form (*heaven, happiness, summer*).

non-finite Verbs which are not marked for tense, person or number, such as present and past participles and infinitives.

non-rhotic See **rhotic**.

non-segmental phonology The analysis of prosodic and paralinguistic features in connected utterances of speech.

non-standard Any variety that does not conform to the standard prestige form used as a norm by society.

noun A word class with a naming function which can be used as a subject or an object in a clause.

noun phrase A phrase, which usually has a noun as the head word, that can function as subject, object, complement or adverbial in a clause.

nucleus The main syllable in a tone unit, which is stressed and carries a tone. Also called the **tonic syllable**.

number A grammatical classification marking singular and plural (*I/we, book/books*).

octameter A line of verse containing eight feet.

onomatopoeia The term used to denote words that imitate sounds.

open A term used to describe a vowel sound made with the tongue in the lowest position ([æ], [ɒ]); vowels may also be described as **half-open**.

open-class words Lexical words (adjectives, nouns, verbs and adverbs), new examples of which can be added to the existing stock.

ordinal number Numbers that indicate the order of a sequence (*first; second; third*).

orthography A study of spelling and the ways in which letters are used in a language.

over-generalisation The process used by children and learners to extend the meaning of a word (*dada* as a reference to all men). Also called **over-extension**.

oxymoron The use of apparently contradictory words in a phrase (*delicious poison*).

palatal A term used to denote consonants made by raising the front part of the tongue to the palate ([j]).

palato-alveolar A term used to denote consonants made by placing the tongue at the front of the hard palate near the alveolar ridge ([ʒ] or [ʃ]).

paradox A statement which although apparently ridiculous or self-contradictory contains a truth.

paragraph A unit of written discourse made up of sentences and marked either by indentation or by a blank line before and after it.

paralinguistics The study of non-verbal communication, including vocal effects (giggling, sighing), gestures, posture and facial expressions.

parallelism The patterning of pairs of sounds, words or structures to create a sense of balance and logic in spoken and written discourse.

paraphrase The expression of the same thing in other words.

parenthesis In written language, the use of brackets, dashes or commas to mark out an optional element of a sentence.

participle The non-finite form of verbs which can occur after an auxiliary verb (*was running* – present participle; *had run* – past participle), or before a head noun in a noun phrase (*the running boy*; *the completed essay*). Present participles end in *-ing* and past participles usually end in *-ed* or *-en*.

particle A grammatical function word which never changes its form, like an adverb in a phrasal verb (*cleared up*, *kicked down*) or a preposition in a prepositional verb (*look after*, *believe in*).

passive voice A grammatical structure in which the subject and object can change places in order to alter the focus of a sentence. In the passive voice, the object of an active sentence occurs in the subject site followed by *to be + past participle* (*the bone was eaten*). The subject of the active sentence can be included following *by* (*the bone was eaten by the dog*).

pentameter A line of verse containing five feet in which a caesura can occur between the two halves.

perfect/perfective The perfect aspect is made up of *to have + past participle* and has two forms: **present perfect**, describing a past action with present relevance (*the girl has finished her dinner*); and **past perfect**, describing an action completed before a specific time (*the girl had finished her dinner*).

person A grammatical term used to describe the number and kind of participants involved in a situation: **first person** references relate directly to the speaker or writer or to a group of people including the speaker or writer (*I*, *we*); **second person** references relate to the person or people addressed by the speaker or writer (*you*); and **third person** references relate to other people, animals or objects (*he*, *she*, *it*, *they*).

personal pronouns Subject pronouns (*I*, *you*, *he*, *she*, *it*, *we*, *they*) replace a noun phrase in the subject site of a sentence, and object pronouns (*me*, *you*, *him*, *her*, *it*, *us*, *them*) replace a noun phrase in the object site.

personification A device in which something non-human is given personality and human qualities.

phatic A term used to denote language that establishes an atmosphere or develops a social contact (greetings, comments on the weather, enquiries about health).

phonemes The smallest distinctive sound segments in a language.

phonemics The analysis of phonemes.

phonemic transcription A broad transcription recording phonemes, concentrating on meaning in language rather than on details of articulation.

phonetic alphabet Symbols and diacritics designed to represent exactly the sounds of spoken language. Also known as the **International Phonetic Alphabet** or **IPA**.

phonetics The study of spoken sounds and the way in which they are produced, transmitted and received.

phonetic transcription A detailed transcription using IPA symbols, concentrating on the physical details of pronunciation.

phonology The study of sounds in a particular language and the way in which they are combined to create meaning.

phrasal verb A verb made up of a lexical verb and a particle (an adverb).

phrase A group of words that has no finite verb (except for a verb phrase) – a **noun phrase** (*the green tree*), an **adjective phrase** (*very blue*); a **verb phrase** (*has gone*), or an **adverb phrase** (*quite slowly*).

piano A term used to describe speech that is articulated quietly.

pidgin A simple but rule-governed language which emerges as the basis for communication between speakers with no common language.

pitch The level of a sound: **low**, **medium**, **high**.

place of articulation The point at which the airstream is stopped in the mouth to produce consonantal sounds (bilabial, labiodental, dental, alveolar, palato-alveolar, palatal, velar, glottal).

pleonasm The use of unnecessary words or ineffective repetition in an expression (*safe haven*; *cheap bargain*; *hear with your ears*). Also called **tautology**.

plosive A term used to denote consonants made by a complete closure of the air passage followed by a sudden release of air ([p] or [t]).

plural A grammatical expression of more than one in number (*cars*, *they*).

polysyllabic Having more than one syllable.

possessive A word or inflection signalling possession (*Julie's*; *hers*).

post-alveolar A term used to denote the consonant [r], made by moving the tongue towards the alveolar ridge without touching it.

post-creole continuum The range of creole forms existing when creole speakers adapt their native language to conform to the standard.

post-modification Lexical items that follow the head in a phrase (*the path down the mountain*).

pragmatics The study of how context influences a speaker's or writer's lexical choices.

predicative The term used to denote adjectives or other modifiers that follow a copula verb in a noun phrase (*the girl appeared sad*; *the children seem happy*; *the plants grew tall*).

predicator The verb phrase that fills the verb site in a clause.

prefix A bound morpheme that occurs before a free morpheme (*un-*; *re-*; *dis-*).

pre-modification Lexical items that precede the head in a phrase (*the serious incident*; *very fast*).

preposition A closed-class word like *in*, *on* or *by* which precedes a noun phrase, pronoun or other lexical item to express a relationship between it and the rest of a clause.

prepositional phrase A grammatical structure made up of a preposition and a noun phrase (*in the car*).

prescriptive A term used to denote an approach to language that dictates rules of usage, focusing on concepts of 'right' and 'wrong' rather than 'appropriateness' and 'acceptability'. Compare **descriptive**.

primary verb A verb that can function as a lexical or an auxiliary verb (*be*; *have*; *do*).

progressive An aspect used to describe an event which is in progress. It is made up of *to be* + *present participle* (*the girl is eating*; *the girl was eating*).

pronoun A closed-class word that can replace a noun phrase.

pronunciation The way in which sounds, syllables or words are articulated.

proper noun A name of a distinctive person, place or other unique reference. In written language it is marked by a capital letter.

prosodic features The use of pitch, volume, pace and rhythm to draw attention to key elements of spoken language.

pun Wordplay that uses the different meanings of a word, or two words with similar forms and different meanings, for comic effect.

punctuation The use of graphic marks in written language to signal different sections of a sentence.

pure vowel A vowel made up of only one sound.

qualifier A word or phrase that post-modifies a head word (*the tree in the orchard*; *the baby crawling in the garden*).

question A sentence or an utterance that requests information or some kind of response.

quotation marks Punctuation marks in written language which indicate direct speech or an extract cited from another text.

raising The pronunciation of a vowel in which the tongue is raised higher than in RP.

rallentando ('rall') A term used to describe speech that is getting slower.

rank The hierarchical arrangement of words, phrases, clauses and sentences whereby phrases are made up of words, clauses are made up of phrases, and sentences are made up of clauses.

Received Pronunciation An English accent which has a high social status and is not connected to a specific region. Also known as **RP**.

reduction The process in which front and back vowels are replaced by weak central vowels in monosyllabic function words or unstressed syllables of polysyllabic words.

reduplication A structural repetition within a word (*baba*; *dada*; *pell-mell*).

reflexive pronoun A grammatical function word ending in *-self* or *-selves* in which the subject and object are directly related (*I cut myself*).

register A variety of language defined according to use. It can be described in terms of **mode** (speech or writing; format); **manner** (participants; levels of formality); and **field** (content).

regular A term used to denote linguistic forms that conform to the rules of a language.

relative pronoun A grammatical function word which marks the beginning of a relative clause post-modifying a noun phrase (*the weather which was unpredictable*; *the man who was red with anger*).

repair The correction of a mistake or misunderstanding in conversation.

repertoire A speaker's range of spoken and written language forms.

repetition A device that emphasises an idea through reiteration.

rhetoric The use of dramatic or persuasive words and structures in spoken and written language to manipulate the intended audience.

rhetorical question A question that does not require an answer.

rhotic Accents that pronounce /r/ after vowels. If /r/ is not articulated, the accents are described as **non-rhotic**.

rhyme The arrangement of word endings that agree in vowel and consonant sounds.

rhythm The pattern of stressed and unstressed syllables in language.

rounded The shape of the lips where the corners come together and the lips are pushed forward to make vowel sounds like [u].

rule A principle of language structure that prescriptivists use to dictate 'correct' and 'incorrect' usage.

schwa The unstressed centre vowel [ə] which occurs at the end of words (*actor* [æktə]) or as the vowel in unstressed syllables (*can* [kən]).

segmental phonology The analysis of speech into distinctive units or phonemes.

semantics The study of meaning.

semi-vowel A consonant such as [w] and [j] which, although it sounds like a vowel, has many of the characteristics of a consonant. Semi-vowels are also known as **approximants** or **frictionless continuants**.

sentence A grammatical structure made up of one or more clauses. In written language the beginning is signalled by a capital letter and the end by a full stop; in conversation analysis, linguists usually refer to **utterances** rather than sentences.

sibilant Consonantal sounds like affricates and alveolar and palatal fricatives which are articulated with a hissing sound.

simile A device which makes a direct comparison between two things using *like* or *as* (*the boy was fierce like a lion*).

slang Distinctive words and phrases associated with informal speech. Slang tends to be used within clearly defined social or age groups and is often short-lived.

social tokens Language use that has a phatic function, such as greetings, politeness markers and leave-takings (*hi*; *cheers*; *have a great birthday*).

sonnet A traditional fourteen-line verse form in which rhyme and stanza divisions are usually observed strictly according to two distinct patterns: the **Italian** or **Petrarchan sonnet** or the **English** or **Shakespearean sonnet**. It was originally a medium for the expression of love, but its scope has widened considerably.

source language The language from which loan words have been borrowed.

speech community A regionally or socially defined group of people who have a language or variety in common.

split infinitive The separation of the preposition *to* from the base form of a verb (*to loudly ring*).

spondee A unit of poetic metre containing two stressed syllables (*child·like*).

spontaneity markers Language use, including comment clauses, informal expressions or fillers, that marks spoken discourse as unscripted and spontaneous, and that can be used to make a speech seem less formal (*You know*; *wait a second*; *um*).

spread The shape of the lips where the corners move away from each other to make vowel sounds like [iː].

staccato ('stacc') A term used to describe speech which is marked by an irregular delivery.

standard The form of a language considered to be the norm and used as the medium of education, government and the law. Varieties which differ from this are said to be **non-standard.**

standardisation The process of making non-standard usage conform to the standard, prestige form of a language.

stative verbs Verbs that express states of being or processes in which there is no obvious action (*know; believe*).

stops Sounds like [p] and [m] in which the air flow is briefly stopped in the mouth.

stress The comparative force, length, loudness and pitch with which a syllable is pronounced. Syllables may be **stressed** or **unstressed.**

strong verb A verb that does not follow the regular pattern, but instead changes a vowel to mark the past tense (*hang → hung; swim → swam*).

stylistics The study of lexical and structural variations in language according to use, user and purpose.

subject A noun phrase or pronoun which is usually the actor of the verb in a clause.

subjunctive A grammatical mood used to express something hypothetical or tentative. It is no longer used widely, but occurs in formulaic expressions like *Heaven forbid* and following *if* in structures like *If I were to come.*

subordinate clause A clause that cannot stand as a sentence on its own, but needs another clause to complete its meaning. Also known as a **dependent clause.**

subordinating conjunction A conjunction used to introduce a subordinate clause (*because; while; until*).

substitution The replacement of one lexical item, such as a noun phrase, with another, such as a pronoun (*the unhappy girl → she*).

suffix A bound morpheme that occurs after a free morpheme (*-ly; -ness*).

superlative See **degree.**

superordinate See **hyponymy.**

syllabic A term used to denote a consonant that can stand alone as a syllable.

syllable A word or part of a word that can be uttered by a single effort of the voice. Patterns of stressed and unstressed syllables constitute the rhythm of a language.

symbol A device in which a word or phrase represents something else (*dove* for *peace*).

synchronic The study of language at a particular point in time.

synecdoche A device in which a part is used to represent the whole (*There were several new faces at the meeting tonight* for *There were several new people at the meeting tonight*).

synonyms Different words with the same or nearly the same meaning (*valiant* and *brave*).

syntax The study of the grammatical relationships between words in sentences.

tag question An interrogative structure (made up of an auxiliary verb and a pronoun) attached to the end of a sentence that expects a reply. If the main clause is positive the tag will be negative, and vice versa (*It's nice today, isn't it?*; *I don't want to go, do you?*).

tautology See **pleonasm.**

telegraphic speech Spoken or written language that omits function words (*Boy go school*).

tense A change in the structure of a verb to signal changes in the timescale. There are two tenses in English: **present** and **past.** The present tense uses the base form of the verb, except for the third person singular which is inflected with an *-s*; it refers to actions in the present time and describes habitual actions. The past tense is formed by adding an *-ed* inflection to regular verbs; it refers to actions or states that have taken place in the past. See also **future time.**

tetrameter A line of verse containing four feet.

timed pause A pause of one second or more. A very brief pause is called a **micro-pause.**

tone The distinctive pitch level of a syllable. Tones can be **rising**, **falling**, **rising–falling** or **falling–rising**.

tone units A segment of spoken language consisting of one or more syllables with a series of rises or falls in tone and with one particularly marked syllable.

tonic syllable See **nucleus**.

topic The thing or person about which something is said in a sentence; the focus of a written or spoken text.

transcription A written record of spoken language, which can use symbols and markings to illustrate the distinctive nature of speech.

transitive A term used to describe verbs that have to be followed by an object.

trimeter A unit of poetic metre containing three feet.

trochee A unit of poetic metre containing a stressed syllable followed by an unstressed syllable (*tém·pĕr*).

turn-taking The organisation of speakers' contributions in a conversation. Turns may be equal, or one of the participants may dominate.

typography The study of features of the printed page.

under-extension The use of a word in a limited way which does not recognise its full meaning – young children may use *dog* to refer only to the family pet.

utterance A stretch of spoken language which is often preceded by silence and followed by silence or a change of speaker. It is often used as an alternative to 'sentence' in conversation analysis since it is difficult to apply the traditional characteristics of a written sentence to spoken language.

variety Language use which has distinctive features because of its context, intended audience and purpose (*religious language*; *legal language*).

velar A term used to denote consonants produced by raising the back of the tongue to the soft palate or velum ([g] or [k]).

verbal noun A noun derived from a verb (*The driving is hard work*).

verbless clause A clause that contains no verb (*wherever possible*; *what about a drink?*).

verb phrase A group of verbs consisting of a lexical verb and up to four auxiliaries.

verbs Open-class words that express states, actions or processes. They can be marked for tense, aspect, voice and mood.

vernacular The native language of a speech community.

vocabulary The words of a language or text.

vocal organs The organs of speech used to articulate sound.

vocative The words used to name or refer to people when talking to them (*Do you want a drink, Alex?*; *Hey you, come over here!*).

voiced sounds Sounds made when the vocal cords are drawn together and the air from the lungs has to push them apart, creating a vibration.

voiceless sounds Sounds made when the vocal cords are spread apart so that the air can pass between them without obstruction.

volume Contrasting levels of loudness in speech, which may be described as **loud**, **quiet**, **getting louder** or **getting quieter**.

vowel A sound produced by the free flow of air through the mouth. In written language, a letter that can be used alone or in combination to represent a vowel sound (*a, e, i, o, u*).

wh- questions Questions introduced by *wh*-words, which can be used alone or in a sentence. They expect new information in the reply (*Where did you go?*).

word The smallest grammatical unit that can stand alone. Words can be divided into two groups: **lexical** and **function** words.

word class Groups of words with characteristic features (nouns, adjectives, verbs, determiners).

word formation The process of creating words from bound and free morphemes (*dis- + order + -ly*).

word order The arrangement of words in a sentence.

yes/no questions Questions marked by the inversion of the subject and the first verb in a verb phrase. They expect *yes* or *no* for an answer.

Wider reading

Grammar

- K. Ballard (2007), *The Frameworks of English: Introducing Language Structures*, 2nd edn (Palgrave Macmillan).
- D. Crystal (1996), *Discover Grammar* (Longman).
- D. Crystal (2004), *Making Sense of Grammar*, 2nd edn (Longman).
- D. Crystal (2004), *Rediscover Grammar*, 2nd edn (Longman).
- D. Graddol (1994), *Describing Language*, 2nd edn (Open University Press).
- G. Leech, S. Conrad, B. Cruickshank and R. Ivanic (2001), *An A–Z of English Grammar and Usage*, 2nd edn (Longman).
- G. Leech, M. Deuchar and R. Hoogenraad (2005), *English Grammar for Today: A New Introduction*, 2nd edn (Palgrave Macmillan).

Phonetics and phonology

- P. Carr (1999), *English Phonetics and Phonology: An Introduction* (Blackwell).
- J. Clark, C. Yallop and J. Fletcher (2006), *An Introduction to Phonetics and Phonology*, 2nd edn (Blackwell).
- M. Davenport and S. J. Hannahs (2005), *Introducing Phonetics and Phonology*, 2nd edn (Hodder Arnold).
- P. Roach (2000), *English Phonetics and Phonology: A Practical Course*, 3rd edn (Cambridge University Press).

Style

- P. Simpson (2004), *Stylistics: A Resource Book for Students* (Routledge).
- P. Verdonk (2002), *Stylistics* (Oxford University Press).
- K. Wales (2001), *A Dictionary of Stylistics*, 2nd edn (Longman).
- L. Wright and J. Hope (1995), *Stylistics: A Practical Coursebook* (Routledge).

General

- J. Aitchinson (2004), *Linguistics*, 6th edn (Teach Yourself).

- N. F. Blake and J. Moorhead (1993), *Introduction to English Language* (Palgrave Macmillan).
- B. Bryson (1991), *Mother Tongue: The English Language*, revd edn (Penguin).
- D. Crystal (2002), *The English Language: A Guided Tour*, 2nd edn (Penguin).
- D. Crystal (2002), *A Dictionary of Linguistics and Phonetics*, 5th edn (Blackwell).
- D. Crystal (2003), *The Cambridge Encyclopedia of Language*, 2nd edn (Cambridge University Press).
- D. Crystal (2007), *Words Words Words* (Oxford University Press).
- V. Fromkin, R. Rodman and N. Hyams (2006), *An Introduction to Language*, 8th edn (Heinle & Heinle).
- J. Humphries (2005), *Lost for Words: The Mangling and Manipulating of the English Language*, revd edn (Hodder & Stoughton).
- L. Truss (2003), *Eats Shoots and Leaves: The Zero Tolerance Approach to Punctuation* (Profile).
- L. Truss (2005), *Talk to the Hand* (Profile).
- G. Yule (2005), *The Study of Language*, 3rd edn (Cambridge University Press).

Aspects of English

Language and society

- J. Aitchinson (2000), *Language Change: Progress or Decay?*, 3rd edn (Cambridge University Press).
- A. Coultas (2003), *Language and Social Contexts: Routledge A Level English Guides* (Routledge).
- D. Crystal (2000), *Who Cares About English Usage?*, 2nd edn (Penguin).
- A Goddard and L. MeDan Patterson (2000), *Language and Gender* (Routledge).
- A. Hughes, P. Trudgill and D. Watt (2005), *English Accent and Dialects: An Introduction to Social and Regional Varieties of English in the British Isles*, 4th edn (Hodder Arnold).
- M. Montgomery (1995), *An Introduction to Language and Society*, 2nd edn (Routledge).
- L. Thomas, S. Wareing, I. Singh, J. Stilwell Peccei, J. Thornborrow, J. Jones (2003), *Language, Society and Power: An Introduction*, revd edn (Routledge).
- P. Trudgill and J. Hannah (2002), *International English: A Guide to the Varieties of Standard English*, 4th edn (Hodder Arnold).
- R. Wardhaugh (2005), *An Introduction to Sociolinguistics*, 5th edn (Blackwell).

The history of English

- A. C. Baugh and T. Cable (2002), *A History of the English Language*, 5th edn (Routledge).
- D. Freeborn (2006), *From Old English to Standard English: A Course Book in Language Varieties Across Time*, 3rd edn (Palgrave Macmillan).
- R. McCrum, R. MacNeill and W. Cran (2002), *The Story of English,* revd edn (Faber & Faber).

Child language acquisition

- D. Crystal (1989), *Listen to Your Child: A Parent's Guide to Children's Language* (Penguin).
- J. Stilwell Peccei (2005), *Child Language: A Resource Book for Students* (Routledge).

Varieties of English

- K. Ballard and A. Beard (2005), *Interpreting Texts: Routledge A Level English Guides*, revd edn (Routledge).
- A. Beard (2003), *How Texts Work: Routledge A Level English Guides* (Routledge).
- N. F. Blake (1990), *Introduction to the Language of Literature* (Palgrave Macmillan).
- R. Carter and S. Cornbleet (2001), *The Language of Speech and Writing* (Routledge).
- R. Carter, A. Goddard, D. Reah, K. Sanger and M. Bowring (2001), *Working with Texts: A Core Book for Language Analysis*, 2nd edn (Routledge).
- D. Freeborn, P. French and D. Langford (1993), *Varieties of English: An Introduction to the Study of Languages*, 2nd edn (Palgrave Macmillan),
- A. Goddard (2002), *The Language of Advertising: Written Texts*, 2nd edn (Routledge).
- G. Leech and M. Short (2007), *Style in Fiction: A Linguistic Introduction to English Fictional Prose*, 2nd edn (Longman).
- F. Pridham (2001), *The Language of Conversation* (Routledge).
- D. Reah (2002), *The Language of Newspapers*, 2nd edn (Routledge).

Original writing

- A. Goddard (2003), *Writing for Assessment: Routledge A Level English Guides* (Routledge).
- S. Morkane (2004), *Original Writing: Routledge A Level English Guides*, revd edn (Routledge).
- S. O'Toole (2003), *Transforming Texts: Routledge A Level English Guides* (Routledge).

Index

abstract nouns 5

accents 110, 154, 171, 177–8, 462, 482, 506, 520
  broad 152, 155, 156, 170–1
  modified 98, 156
  personal 155–6
  regional 110, 152, 154, 157–71, 457
  social 152, 154, 156, 457

acceptability 99–101

active voice 11, 75

adjacency pairs 216, 235, 460, 472, 481, 486, 510, 513, 517

adjectives 7–8, 173
  phrases 28–30, 301–2

adverbials 32, 35, 73, 75

adverbs 14–16, 173
  adjunct 14
  conjunct 14
  degree 14
  disjunct 14
  phrases 32

advertising 293–324
  charity 317–21
  classified 305
  complaints 295, 296–7
  design 299, 307, 310, 319
  direct mail 293, 305–9
  effect on children 295–6
  grammar 303, 308, 314–15, 320
  'hard sell' tactics 295
  information 321–2
  lexis 301–2, 307–8, 313–14, 319–20
  literary devices 304, 308

  products 305–17
  rhetorical devices 304, 308, 316, 320
  services 317
  slogans 300, 308, 309, 313
  typography 304, 308, 316, 321

affixes 22

affricates 54

alliteration 82

allophones 55

alveolars 52

ambiguity 267–8, 393, 508, 510, 511, 519–20

American English 122, 124

anaphoric references 45

Anglo-Saxon Chronicle, The 131, 132–4

anti-climax 84

anti-language 119

antithesis 83

appropriateness 99–101

approximants 55

articles 18

articulation 48–56
  manner 53–6
  organs of speech 48–50
  place 52–3

aspect 11

aspiration 167

assimilation 64, 68, 155

assonance 82

asyndetic lists 84–5

attributive adjectives 7

audience 99, 294, 298–9, 372, 428, 456–7, 461, 467, 504, 507–8, 523, 548–9

Australian English 124, 545

Authorised Version of the Bible (AV) 394, 397–8, 399, 401–4, 418

auxiliary verbs 9

babbling 186

'baby words' 183

base forms 9, 10, 42

BBC English 97, 457

'Beowulf' 131

bias 268, 463, 469

Bible 394, 399, 401–4

bilabials 52

Birmingham accent 162–3

Black English 117–23, 343–4

Black English Vernacular (BEV) 117

blank verse 353, 361

blogs 126–7

book hand 139

Book of Common Prayer (BCP) 394, 397, 401, 404–6, 418

borrowing 134, 137, 138–9, 142

branching 83–4

British National Corpus 213

broadcasting language 456–500
  accents and dialects 457, 462, 500
  children's television 487–97
  documentaries 469–75
  drama 475–87
  formal *vs* informal 475
  grammar 462, 473–4, 495–6
  lexis 461, 494–5
  manner 459, 472
  mode 459, 472, 493
  news 463–8
  normal non-fluency features 462, 481, 487
  prosodic features 461, 468, 476, 482, 486–7
  spoken *vs* written 457–8, 463, 482, 499
  status 459
  structure 460, 463, 466–7, 473, 480–1, 494
  topics 459–60, 468, 481, 485, 493

Canterbury Tales 131, 139
Cardiff accent 168–70
'caretaker speech' 184
cataphoric references 46
centring diphthongs 60
characterisation
  narratives 329–34
  poetry 357–9
child language 181–209
  behaviourist approach 182
  cognitive approach 182
  conversation skills 188–9, 191, 192, 199–200, 201–2, 203–4
  dialogue 199–204
  grammar 188, 190–1, 192, 195, 198–9
  interactive approach 183–4
  monologue 187, 193–9
  nativist approach 183
  pronunciation 188, 189, 191, 194–5, 197–8, 201–2
  stages of acquisition 185–92

vocabulary 187, 188, 189, 191, 194, 196–7
chronological texts 557, 558, 561, 567, 571
Church language *see* religious language
clauses 32–6, 90–1
  adverbial 39
  comparative 39
  elements 33–5
  non-finite 32, 39
  noun 38–9
  relative 39
  structure 35–6
  verbless 39, 303
clear *l* 55
clichés 246, 287
closed-class words 4, 16–21
close vowels 57
closing diphthongs 60
Cockney accent 166–8
cohesion 43–6, 91–2
collective nouns 5
collocations 43, 245, 337, 374, 388
comic strips 511, 528, 573–4, 575–6
commands 42
comment clauses 105, 228, 533, 552
common nouns 4
comparatives 7, 15
complements 34, 73
complex sentences 38–40, 72–3
compound–complex sentences 40, 73
compound sentences 37–8
compound vowels 60
concrete nouns 5
conjunctions 20–1, 46, 174
  co-ordinating 20, 37
  subordinating 38
consonance 82
consonants 56, 158, 161, 164, 167, 169
contact languages 117
continuants 55
convergence 155, 170

cooing 185
co-ordinating conjunctions 20, 37
copula verbs 7
Corpus project 213
correctness 98–9
countability 5
coursework 579–84
  adaptive writing 584
  analytical studies 583
  evaluating writing 580–1
  investigation 581–3
  original writing 579–80
courtroom language 384–90
creoles 118–19

dark *l* 55
declaratives 42
decreolisation 119
definite articles 18
deictic expressions 17, 105, 220
delayed subject 74
demonstrative pronouns 17
dentals 52
descriptive approach 98, 108, 109
determiners 18–19
diachronic approach 110, 111, 130
diacritics 48, 159
dialects 110, 171–7, 462
  grammar 173–6
  in literature 342–5, 367
  lexis 172
  regional 171
  social 172
diaries 569–70
dimeter 354
diphthongs 60–1, 155, 161, 165, 167, 170
direct speech 273, 280–1, 287, 328
direct *vs* indirect objects 34
divergence 156, 171
drama 475–87, 572–3
dummy subject 74
dynamic verbs 8

Early Modern English 130, 140–3
 grammar 141–2
 phonology 143
 spelling 141
 typographical features 143
 vocabulary 140–1, 142
electronic English 126–9
elision 65, 68, 155
ellipsis 37, 45
email 426–31
end focus 74
English
 future of 110, 123–6
 in France 125–6
 see also American English;
  Australian English;
  Black English; Received
  Pronunciation
English as a world language 123–6
Estuary English 98, 178
euphemisms 419
exaggeration 80
examination questions 584–602
 attitudes and opinions 590–3
 data-based 584–5
 original writing 586–7
 theme-based 593–7
 topic-based 585–6, 588–90
 variety-based 597–602
existential *there* 74, 77
exophoric references 46
extension 187

falling–rising tones 67
falling tones 67
farce 520–5
feet *see* foot, metrical
fiction *see* narratives
field 102, 104
figurative language 78
finite verbs 12
first words 187
foot, metrical 354–5
foregrounding 73, 76

free indirect speech 328
free indirect thought 331, 342
free variants 63
free verse 353
French, borrowing from 137, 139, 141
fricatives 54
frictionless continuants 55
fronting (grammatical) 73
function *vs* form 25–6
future time 10

Gawain and the Green Knight 131, 139
gender 111–16, 152
gestures 214
glides 60
glottals 53
glottal stops 54, 158
grammar
 child 188, 190–1, 192
 creoles 118
 Early Modern English 142
 in advertising 303
 in commentary 246–50, 251–2
 in dialect 173–6
 in humour 515
 in legal language 376–7
 in newspapers 271–2
 in politics 423–5
 in religion 397–9
 in speech 220–1
 Middle English 139
 Modern English 146
 Old English 134
 regional 173–6
 spoken *vs* written 105
grammatical words 4
graphology 135, 139

half-close vowels 57
half-open vowels 57
Hansard 421–2, 424–6, 446–53
headlines 263–8, 275–7, 282, 287–8
heptameter 354
hesitation 71

hexameter 354
historic present 175
holophrastic phase 187
homonyms 80
homophones 80, 520
hospitality tokens 217
house style 264
humour 501–56
 accents and dialects 506–7, 520
 context 504–8
 lexis 510–13
 manner 504, 523, 530
 mode 504, 523, 530
 phonology 519
 prosodics 510
 structure 509–10
 topics 508–9
 word play 512–13, 518
hyperbole 80
hypercorrection 156, 162, 429
hypercreolisation 119
hyponyms 43, 44, 187

iambic pentameter 355
identity 154
ideology 262, 277, 420
imperatives 42
indefinite articles 14
indefinite pronouns 17
Indian English 125
indirect objects 34
indirect speech 273, 328
 free 328
indirect thought 331, 342
infinitives 9, 29, 39
 split 100
inflection 133–4, 137–8, 139, 141, 142
information texts 561–6
 lectures 565–6
 publicity leaflets 564–5
 textbooks 562–4
inkhorn terms 142
innuendo 513
instruction texts 557–61
 manuals 559–61
 recipes 558–9

International Phonetic
    Alphabet 48, 49, 62
interrogatives 42
interviews 232–8
    vs telephone conversations
    238–9
intonation 67–8, 218
intransitive verbs 8
irony 79, 533
irregular verbs 9
isogloss 157, 171

Japanese English 125
jargon 186
Jewish English 124–5,
    507–8
jokes 507–8, 509, 516–20

labiodentals 52
language
    attitudes 98, 153–4
    change 98, 109–29, 152–4
    contact 117, 170–1, 177–8
Late Modern English 130
laterals 55
Latin, borrowing from 134,
    141
law, language of *see* legal
    language
lectures 565–6
legal language 372–93
    contracts 380–1
    grammar 376–7, 379–80,
    383–4, 389–90, 390–1
    language of the courts
    384–90
    lexis 374–6, 380–1,
    382–3, 388–9, 390
    manner 373
    spoken *vs* written 390–1
    statutes 377–80
    typography and layout
    373–4, 379, 382, 387–8,
    390
    wills 381–4
levelling 177
level tone 67
lexis
    lexical change 150

lexical choice 78–9, 87–8,
    113, 587
lexical diffusion 150
    see also advertising;
    broadcasting language;
    dialects; humour; legal
    language; narratives;
    newspapers; poetry;
    political language;
    religious language;
    spoken language
liaison 65, 68, 155, 158
lingua franca 118, 544
lip rounding 57
listing 84–5
literary devices 77–8,
    79–83, 88
    see also advertising;
    narratives; political
    language; religious
    language
litotes 81, 320
liturgy 395, 405–6
    see also religious language

main clauses 32, 36, 37
major sentences 40
malapropisms 347, 524
manner 102, 104
manner of articulation 53–6
marked themes 73, 76
metalinguistics 373, 388
metaphors 79
metonymy 79
metre 354–5
Middle English 130, 135–9
    dialects 139
    grammar 137–8, 139
    graphology 139
    phonology 139
    poetry 139
    spelling 137–8
    vocabulary 136–7, 138–9
minimal pairs 62–3
minor sentences 33, 40, 247
mismatches 187
modal verbs 9
mode 102, 104
Modern English 130, 143–6
    grammar 145–6

graphology 146
phonology 146
vocabulary 144–5, 146
modification 7–8, 26, 27–8,
    29, 31
monometer 354
mood 42–3
morphemes 21–2
morphology 3, 21–5
'motherese' 183

naming of participants
    269–70, 278–9, 286, 288,
    423, 451, 485, 531
narratives
    characterisation 329–34
    evoking an atmosphere
    339–42
    experimenting with
    language 342–8
    first person 326
    grammar 328
    interior monologues 327,
    330
    lexis 327
    literary devices 329, 333
    manner 326
    point of view 326–7
    rhetorical devices 329,
    330–1, 334, 341
    setting the scene 334–9
    speech 328, 330
    stream of consciousness
    327, 331
    style 328–9
    third person 326, 332–3
narrative texts 571–4
nasals 54–5
National Curriculum 153–4
negatives 175–6, 188, 191
    multiple 100, 120, 142,
    175–6, 177, 192
neologisms 302
neutral (lips) 57
news 256, 459, 460, 461,
    463–8
newspapers 256–92
    action stories 274–81
    broadsheets *vs* tabloids
    257–60
    compacts 257, 260–1

grammar 271–2
ideology 262
lexis 268–71
reports 268–74
running stories 281–90
sources 273
statement and opinion
stories 281
style 272–3
see also headlines
news values 256
non-chronological texts
557, 561, 567
non-count nouns 5
non-finite verbs 12
non-rhotic accents 56
non-sexist language 111–16
non-standard English 97,
342–3
Norfolk accent 163–5
normal non-fluency features
71, 192, 222–3, 237, 250,
462, 481, 487, 516, 539,
549, 553
nouns 4–6
abstract vs concrete 5
collective 5
count vs non-count 5
plural 5, 173
possessive 5–6
proper vs common 4
nucleus (of syllable) 69
numbers 19, 27

objects (grammatical)
clauses 34, 73
direct vs indirect 34
octameter 354
Old English 130, 131–5
closed-class words 133
grammar 134
graphology 135
inflections 134
open-class words 133
phonology 134–5
poetry 131
word order 133
Old Norse 134
onomatopoeia 82
open-class words 4–16
open vowels 57

over-extension 187
overcompensation 156
overstatement 80
oxymorons 80, 337

pace 70, 219
palatals 53
palato-alveolars 53
paradox 80
paralinguistic features 66,
214
parallelism 85
parental speech style 183–4,
185–6, 189–90
parent–child dialogue
199–204
parody 80, 525–33
parliamentary language
420–2, 424–5, 446–53
participants, naming of see
naming of participants
particles 20
passive voice 11–12, 75,
76–7, 280, 286–7, 376
Paston Letters 135–8, 140–2
past participles 9, 11, 12,
25, 39
past perfect 11
past tense 10, 25
patterning 85–6
pauses 70, 219–20, 222,
224–5, 245
pentameter 354–5
perfect aspect 11
personal pronouns 16
personal texts 566–70
diaries and journals
569–70
letters 135–8, 140–2,
567–9
phatic communication 213,
214
playscripts 521–5, 572–3,
598–9
personification 80
phonemic transcription 62,
93
phonetics 47–61, 92

phonetic transcription 62,
92–3
phonology 47, 61–71, 92
non-segmental 66–71
segmental 62–6
see also Early Modern
English; humour; Middle
English; Modern English;
Old English
phrasal verbs 31
phrases 26–32, 90
adjective 28–9
adverb 32
noun 26–8, 44, 45
prepositional 31–2
verb 30–1, 44, 45
pidgin languages 117–18
see also contact languages
pitch 68, 219
place of articulation 52–3
Plain English 372
pleonasms 347
plosives 54
plurals 5
poetry 351–71
characterising 357–9
evoking atmosphere
363–7
experimenting with
language and structure
367–9
form and structure 352–3
grammar 356
layout 357
lexis 355–6
metre 354–5
Middle English 131
Old English 131
poetic devices 353–5
setting the scene 359–63
style 356–7
point of view 326–7
political correctness 112,
115, 502
political language 419–55
grammar 423–5, 429–30,
435–6, 441–4, 452–3
Houses of Parliament
446–53
informality 421–2
lexis 422–3, 428–9,
433–5, 441, 450–2

literary devices 425–6, 430

manifestos and campaign statements 426–37

manner 420–1

pre-scripted speeches 438–46

rhetorical devices 430, 436, 444–5

sentence organisation 430–1, 436, 444

spoken features 445–6, 448

'Politics and the English Language' (George Orwell) 419

possessive pronouns 16–17

post-alveolars 52

post-creole continuum 119

post-modification 27–8, 29

post-vocalic /r/ 158

pragmatics 185, 204, 420

prayers 395, 399, 405–6

predeterminers 27

predicative adjectives 7

predicators 33, 35

prefixes 22–3

pre-modification 26–7, 29

prepositional verbs 31

prepositions 19–20, 173–4
at end of sentence 101

prescriptive approach to language 98, 99, 109, 146

present participle 9, 11, 12, 39

present perfect aspect 11

present tense 10

primary verbs 9

printing 137, 143

progressive aspect 11

pronouns 16–18, 114–15, 174
compound 18
demonstrative 17
indefinite 17–18
interrogative 17
personal 16
possessive 16
reflexive 17
relative 17

proper nouns 4

prosodics 66–71, 218–20, 226, 236–7, 244–5, 468, 486–7, 545–6

publicity leaflets 564–5

puns 80–1

qualifiers 26, 27

quality vs tabloid press 257–60

Queen's English 97

questions 9, 42
intonation 42, 67
political 424–5, 448–53
words 17, 188, 190, 192

quoted vs quoting clause 273

radio see broadcasting language

Received Pronunciation (RP) 98, 153, 457
modified 156

recipes 558–9

reduction 66, 155

reduplication 118, 186

referencing 45–6

reflexive pronouns 17

regional variation 157–71, 171–6

register 101–4, 514–15

relative clauses 28, 39

relative pronouns 17

religious language 394–418
grammar 397–9, 403–4, 410–11, 414–15
lexis 396–7, 402–3, 409–10, 413–14
literary devices 399–400, 404, 411, 415
liturgies 395, 405–6
manner 396, 408, 413
rhetorical devices 400, 404, 411–12, 415
rituals 404
sacred texts 394–5, 401–4
sentence organisation 400, 411, 415
sermons 395, 406–12
spiritual reflection 412–16

typographical features 400–1

repertoire 99, 154, 180

repetition 43, 85

reported clauses 273

rhetoric 78

rhetorical devices 83–6, 88–9, 94, 304, 329, 357, 400

rhotic accent 56

rhyme 82–3, 352

rhythm 68–71, 355

rising–falling tones 67

rising tones 67

rounding see lip rounding

RP see Received Pronunciation

runes 133, 135

satire 533–9

schwa 65

scientific language 562–4

selective perception 268, 271, 292

semi-vowels 52, 56

sentences 36–41
analysing a sentence 40–1
complex 38–40, 72–3
compound 37–8
compound–complex 40
major vs minor 40
organisation 72–5
simple 36–7, 72

sermons 406–12

sexist language 111–16

similes 81

situation comedies 546–7

sketch shows 539–46

slogans 299, 300

social tokens 467

social variation 110, 111–15, 152–4, 171

sound patterning 82–3, 88

speech 104–6, 215–25

spelling
American vs British 122, 124
Early Modern English 141, 142

Middle English 137, 138
Modern English 146
non-standard 302, 342–8
reform 142
split infinitives 100
Spoken Corpus project 213
spoken language 213–55
  grammar 220–1
  lexis 220
  manner 215
  prosodic features 218–20
  repairs 223–5
  structure 216–18
  topics 215–16, 459–60
  vocal effects 220
  see also broadcasting
    language; legal language;
    normal non-fluency
    features; political
    language
spoken narrative 225–8
spontaneity markers 438,
  448
sports commentary 239–52
Standard English (SE) 97,
  153–4
stand-up comedy 547–53
stative verbs 8
statutes 377–80
stereotypes 112, 294–5,
  299, 506, 539, 543–6
stress 69–70, 219
style 72–89, 94, 105–6,
  265–6, 304, 328–9,
  356–7
subjects (grammatical) 33,
  35–6
  delayed 74
  dummy 74
subordinate clauses 32,
  38–40
subordinating conjunctions
  38
substitution 37, 44

suffixes 22, 23
superlatives 7, 15
superordinates 43, 44
symbolism 81
synchronic approach 110,
  130
syndetic lists 84–5
synecdoche 81

tag questions 113, 183–4,
  235
telegraphic style 189, 194,
  266
telephone conversations
  228–32
  vs interviews 238–9
television see broadcasting
  language
tenses 10, 175
tetrameter 354
textbooks 562–4
texting 127–9
themes, marked 73, 76
tone units 69–70, 219
topic loops 223
topic shifts 216
transitive verbs 8
trimeter 354
tripling 85
trochee 354
turn-taking 217, 230,
  235–6, 243–4, 460, 473,
  485–6, 510, 537, 546
typography 143, 257, 304,
  357, 373–4, 400–1

under-extension 187
understatement 81
unparliamentary language
  421–2

unscripted commentary
  239–52

variants, free 63
velars 53
verbless clauses 32
verb phrases 30–1
verbs 8–12, 175
  as clause elements 33,
    35–6
  auxiliary vs lexical 9
  finite vs non–finite 12
  modal 9
  phrasal 31
  prepositional 31
  regular vs irregular 9
  stative vs dynamic 8
  transitive vs intransitive 8
  see also aspect; future time;
    passive voice; tenses
verse, blank 353, 361
vocatives 43
voice see passive voice
voicing 50–3
volume 68, 219
vowels 56–61, 158–9
  compound 60–1
  pure 56–9

wh- questions 17, 188, 190,
  192, 425
wills 381–4
word class 4–21
writing vs speech 104–6,
  214

yes/no questions 425, 451
Yorkshire accent 159–62
youth language 345, 537–8,
  544

0015837